STANHOPE

JAMES, EARL STANHOPE

From a portrait by Denner at Chevening

STANHOPE

A STUDY IN
EIGHTEENTH-CENTURY
WAR AND DIPLOMACY

BY

BASIL WILLIAMS

GREENWOOD PRESS, PUBLISHERS
WESTPORT, CONNECTICUT

Library of Congress Cataloging in Publication Data

Williams, Basil, 1867-1950.
    Stanhope : a study in eighteenth-century war and
diplomacy.

    Reprint of the ed. published by Clarendon Press,
Oxford, Eng.
    Bibliography: p.
    Includes index.
    1. Stanhope, James Stanhope, 1st Earl, 1673-1721.
2. Great Britain--Foreign relations--18th century.
3. Statesmen--Great Britain--Biography. I. Title.
DA497.S8W5   1979   941.06'8'0924   78-26687
ISBN 0-313-20918-9

IACOBI
PRIMI COMITIS STANHOPE
HEREDI PIISSIMO
IACOBO
COMITI SEPTIMO

PREFACE

WHEN my old University invited me to deliver the Ford Lectures in 1921, I determined to make them the foundation of a volume that should at least betoken my gratitude. This book, the fruit of ten years' intermittent labour in the intervals of lectures to Canadian and Scottish students, attempts to throw light on a somewhat dim period of our History, the early years of the Hanoverian era, and also on the life of a great Englishman who played one of the chief parts in those years. I make no apology for combining history and biography, since I believe that to view the scene of history through the eyes of some great actor in its events is as sound a way as any to make history a living thing.

A man staunch to his principles if ever there was one, courageous in war and peace, and one of the greatest of our foreign ministers, Stanhope has been strangely neglected by historians of his own race. But perhaps it was fitting that the memory of the Englishman who was unique in his day for knowledge of continental affairs and sympathetic understanding of other nations should have first been brought into prominence by a French and a German historian, Monsieur Louis Wiesener and Professor Wolfgang Michael. Their work has opened the way, and to them I am deeply indebted.

One of the joys of historical writing comes from the freemasonry of brother historians. Of this joy I have had ample measure. To Sir Charles Firth, in his retirement as prodigal of wise counsel and pregnant hints as he ever was when Regius Professor, and to George Trevelyan, a pattern among scholars for his sympathetic interest in the work of others engaged in cognate fields, who has twice sent me the first-fruits of valuable material unearthed for his own great history, I owe much. The kindness of my colleague, Dr. D. B. Horn, in reading through the whole manuscript, and of Professor G. N. Clark, Professor Norman Sykes and Mr. J. F. Chance, in making suggestions on certain chapters, has prevented many mistakes. My old student, Gilbert Yates, has helped me with copies of documents at the Quai d'Orsay; another colleague, Dr. Rothwell, has read all the proofs; the Deputy-

Keeper and Mr. Hilary Jenkinson have, as usual, given valuable assistance at the Record Office. To the Duke of Buccleuch, the Earl of Stair and the Hon. Hew Dalrymple, the Dean of Christ Church, Mr. Brian Tunstall and Don Modesto Bargallo of Guadalajara I am indebted for documents and maps they have allowed me to use.

Above all I am grateful to my wife for penetrating criticism, and to the Earl and Countess Stanhope for their abounding kindness in putting at my disposal the rich material at Chevening.

BASIL WILLIAMS.

EDINBURGH,
13 *February* 1932.

TABLE OF CONTENTS

LIST OF ILLUSTRATIONS

MAPS

BIBLIOGRAPHICAL GUIDE

NOTE.—To save undue expansion of the notes, most of the authorities used are here given for reference under the short titles quoted in the notes. A few authorities, sparsely used, are not given in this list, but are referred to by their full titles in the notes.

MS. AUTHORITIES

Add. MSS. = *Additional MSS.* in the British Museum.

A.E., *Angleterre* = MSS. relating to England in the Ministère des Affaires Étrangères, Paris.

Chevening MSS. = MSS. of James, 1st Earl Stanhope, and his relations in the *Old Library* at Chevening.

Oxenfoord MSS. = MSS. belonging to the Earl of Stair at Oxenfoord Castle.

R.O. = MSS. in the Public Record Office. References are given according to the latest system adopted by the Record Office. It may be hoped that this system is final and definitive, as changes in the system of reference create difficulties for students.

Stowe MSS. = *Stowe MSS.* in the British Museum.

Wake MSS. = MSS. in Archbishop Wake's collection at Christ Church, Oxford.

PRINTED BOOKS

Alberoni, *Lettres Intimes* = J. M. Alberoni, *Lettres Intimes au Comte de Rocca* (E. Bourgeois, ed.). Lyon, 1892.

Arneth = A. v. Arneth, *Prinz Eugen v. Savoyen.* 3 B. Wien, 1864.

Aubertin = C. Aubertin, *L'Esprit Publique au 18e Siècle.* Paris, 1873.

Baraudon = A. Baraudon, *La Maison de Savoie et la Triple Alliance.* Paris, 1896.

Baudrillart = A. Baudrillart, *Philippe V et la Cour de France.* 5 t. Paris, 1890, &c.

Bothmer, *Memoiren* = *Memoiren des Grafen v. Bothmer, 1718* (R. Doebner, ed.), *Forschungen zur deutsche Geschichte.* B. 26. Göttingen, 1886.

Bourgeois, *Dubois* = E. Bourgeois, *Le Secret de Dubois, 1718-23* ⎫
Bourgeois, *Farnèse* = E. Bourgeois, *Le Secret des Farnèse* ⎬ Paris n.d.
Bourgeois, *Régent* = E. Bourgeois, *Le Secret du Régent* ⎭

Boyer = A. Boyer, *Political State of Great Britain.* 60 vols. 1719-40.

Burnet = G. Burnet, *History of His Own Time* (with Dartmouth's notes). 6 vols. 1833.

Butler, *Catholics* = C. Butler, *Historical Memoirs respecting English, Irish and Scottish Catholics.* 4 vols. 1821.

Chance = J. F. Chance, *George I and Northern War.* 1909.

Carutti = D. Carutti, *Storia di Vittorio Amedeo II*. Torino, 1856.

Castagnoli = P. Castagnoli, *Il Cardinale Giulio Alberoni*. t. 1. Piacenza, 1929.

Colonial Calendar, 1714–15 = Calendar of State Papers, Colonial Series, *1714–15*. 1928.

Colonial Calendar, 1716–17 = Calendar of State Papers, Colonial Series, *1716–17*. 1930.

Coxe, *Austria* = W. Coxe, *History of House of Austria, 1218–1792*. 3 vols. 1847.

Coxe, *Bourbons* = W. Coxe, *Memoirs of Kings of Spain of House of Bourbon*. 5 vols. 1815.

Coxe, *Marlborough* = W. Coxe, *Memoirs of Marlborough with Original Correspondence*. 3 vols. 1818–19.

Coxe, *Walpole* = W. Coxe, *Memoirs of Life, &c., of Sir R. Walpole*. 3 vols. 1798.

Cunningham = A. Cunningham, *History of Great Britain, 1688 to Accession of George I* (trans. from Latin by W. Thomson). 2 vols. 1787.

Dickson = W. K. Dickson, *The Jacobite Attempt of 1719* (Scottish History Society). 1895.

Droysen = J. G. Droysen, *Geschichte d. preuss. Politik*. 5 B. (in 10 parts). 1868–86.

E.H.R. = *English Historical Review*.

Geikie and Montgomery = R. Geikie and I. A. Montgomery, *The Dutch Barrier, 1705–19*. Cambridge, 1930.

Hardwicke = *Miscellaneous State Papers, 1501–1726* (ed. by Earl of Hardwicke). 2 vols. 1778.

H. MSS., Portland, Townshend, &c. = Publications of Historical MSS. Commission, indicating the collection calendared.

History of Cardinal Alberoni (from the Italian)—pamphlet. London, 1719.

Instructions, France = British Diplomatic Instructions, France, *1689–1721* (L. G. Wickham Legg, ed.) R.H.S., 1925.

Instructions, Sweden = British Diplomatic Instructions, Sweden, *1689–1727* (J. F. Chance, ed.). R.H.S., 1922.

Kemble = J. M. Kemble, *State Papers and Correspondence*. 1857.

Klopp = Onno Klopp, *Fall des Hauses Stuart u. Succession d. Hauses Hannover*. 14 B. Wien, 1875–88.

Lady Cowper = Mary Countess Cowper, *Diary, 1714–20*. 1864.

Lamberty = G. de Lamberty, *Mémoires pour servir à l'Histoire du 18ᵉ Siècle*. 14 vols. Amsterdam, 1733–40.

Landau = M. Landau, *Geschichte Karls VI als König v. Spanien*. Stuttgart, 1889.

Leadam = I. S. Leadam, *History of England, 1702–60*. 1909.

Leake's Life = *Life of Sir John Leake* (Navy Records Society LII and LIII. G. Callender, ed.). 2 vols. 1890.

Lémontey = P. E. Lémontey, *Histoire de la Régence, &c.* 2 t. Paris, 1832.

Lockhart = George Lockhart, *The Lockhart Papers.* 1714.

Luttrell = N. Luttrell, *Brief Historical Narration, 1678–1714.* 6 vols. 1857.

Macky = J. Macky, *Memoirs of Secret Services.* 1733.

Macpherson = James Macpherson, *Original Papers.* 2 vols. 1775.

Mahon,[1] *Anne* = Lord Mahon, *History of England . . . reign of Anne until Peace of Utrecht, 1701–13.* 2 vols. 1889.

Mahon, *History* = Lord Mahon, *History of England from Peace of Utrecht, 1713–83.* 7 vols. 1858.

Mahon, *Spain* = Lord Mahon, *Spain under Charles II—Extracts from Correspondence of Hon. A. Stanhope . . . 1690–9* (privately printed, 2nd ed.). 1844.

Mahon, *Succession* = Lord Mahon, *History of War of Succession in Spain* (with Appendix of Letters). 1836.

Malortie = C. C. v. Malortie, *Beiträge zur Geschichte des braunschweig-lüneburgischen Hauses u. Hofes.* Heft 1. Hannover, 1860.

Marchmont, *Diary* = *A Selection from the Papers of the Earls of Marchmont . . . 1685–1750.* 3 vols. 1831.

Marlborough = *Letters and Despatches of the Duke of Marlborough* (Sir G. Murray, ed.). 5 vols. 1845.

Martens = F. de Martens, *Recueil des Traités, X Russie-Angleterre, 1710–1801.* St. Petersburg, 1892.

Michael = W. Michael, *Englische Geschichte im 18ten Jahrhundert,* 2 B. Hamburg, &c. 1896, 1920.

Oldmixon = J. Oldmixon, *History of England during William and Mary, Anne, George I.* 1735.

P.H. = *Parliamentary History of England to 1803* (ed. W. Cobbett). 1806–20.

Parnell = A. Parnell, *War of Succession in Spain, 1702–11.* 1888.

Pauli, *Actenstücke* = R. Pauli, *Actenstücke zur Thronbesteigung des Welfenhauses in England* (Hist. Verein für Niedersachsen). Hannover, 1883.

Pribram = A. F. Pribram, *Oesterreichische Staatsverträge, England.* 2 B. Wien, 1907.

Recueil, *Autriche, Savoie, &c.* = *Recueil des Instructions . . . aux Ambassadeurs . . . de France [1648–1789], Autriche, Savoie,* &c., &c. Paris, v.d.

Russell = F. S. Russell, *Earl of Peterborough.* 2 vols. 1887.

Salomon = F. Salomon, *Geschichte des letzten Ministerium Königin Annas.* Gotha, 1894.

St. Simon = *Mémoires de St. Simon* (Chéruel et Regnier, edd.). 19 t. Paris, 1873.

Sbornik = *Imperatorskoe Russkoe Istoricheskoe Obshchestvo-Sbornik.* Vols. 61 and 66. [Copies of dispatches between England and envoys in Russia, 1711–19.] St. Petersburg, v.d.

---

[1] To avoid confusion all the works of the 5th Earl Stanhope are quoted under Mahon, the title he had when most were written.

Sévelinges = C. L. de Sévelinges, *Mémoires secrets . . . du Cardinal Dubois.* 2 t. Paris, 1815.

Somerville = Th. Somerville, *History of Great Britain during reign of Anne.* 1798.

Stair Annals = J. M. Graham, *Annals . . . of the Viscount and 1st and 2nd Earls of Stair.* 2 vols. 1875.

Stanhope, *Answer* = Mr. *Stanhope's Answer to Report of Comm^rs sent into Spain* (pamphlet), 1714.

Stanhope, *Memoir* = *Memoirs of the Life and Action of the Rt. Hon. James, Earl Stanhope* (pamphlet) [by Hugh Stanhope, see ch. xv, p. 442, note 4]. 1721.

State Trials = *State Trials* (W. Cobbett and T. J. Howell, edd.). 34 vols. 1809–28.

Stebbing = W. Stebbing, *Peterborough.* 1890.

Stoerk = F. Stoerk, *Das Greifswald Bündnis . . . von 28/17 October 1715* (Pommersche Jahrbücher II). Greifswald, 1901.

Swift = Jonathan Swift, *Works.* 19 vols. 1883–4.

Sykes = N. Sykes, *Edmund Gibson, Bishop of London.* 1926.

Targe = J. B. Targe, *Hist. de l'Avènement de la Maison de Bourbon au trône d'Espagne.* 6 t. 1772.

Tindal = N. Tindal, *Continuation of Rapin's History of England* (vols. iii–v). 1757–63.

Torrens = W. M. Torrens, *History of Cabinets.* 2 vols. 1894.

Treasury Papers, 1708–14 = *Calendar of Treasury Papers.* Vol. 4. 1879.

Treasury Papers, 1714–20 = *Calendar of Treasury Papers.* Vol. 5. 1883.

Weber = O. Weber, *Die Quadrupel Allianz von 1718.* Wien, 1887.

Wentworth Papers = *Wentworth Papers, 1705–39* (J. J. Cartwright, ed.). 1883.

Wiesener = L. Wiesener, *Le Régent, l'Abbé Dubois et les Anglais.* 3 t. Paris, 1891–9.

Williams, *Chatham* = Basil Williams, *William Pitt, Earl of Chatham.* 2 vols. 1913.

GENEALOGICAL TABLE SHOWING STANHOPE CONNEXIONS

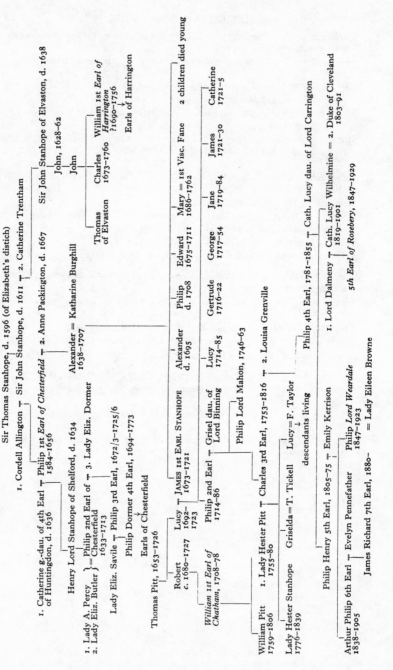

CHAPTER I

A COSMOPOLITAN TRAINING

§ 1

TOWARDS the end of April in the year 1691 a swarthy English youth of eighteen was on the quay at Alicante inquiring for the galley of Marquis Clerici, bound for Italy. James, for such was the youth's name, was the son of Alexander Stanhope, King William's envoy extraordinary to Spain. He had already had a taste of the world, for, after acquiring a lasting love of the classics at Eton and during a couple of years at Trinity College, Oxford, he had served his apprenticeship in diplomacy for the last twelvemonth under his father's eye at Madrid. He was now to seek his fortune in arms on the battle-fields of Savoy. His first voyage across the Mediterranean, of which he was destined to accomplish several more, proved a test of his powers of endurance. The Marquis's galley, he tells his father, was 'a stinking galley', while the marquis himself 'was as civil to me as I can expect from a wretch who grudges himself meat, much more me'. The voyage was broken for a few days at Palma in Majorca, where accommodation was almost unobtainable owing to the concourse of people come to witness the genial *fiesta* of three successive *auto-da-fés*, one of the few amusements pleasing to their decrepit and impotent King Charles II—'an execrable act' the indignant young Protestant called it. After this interlude the galley took him on to Genoa, whence he reached the allied head-quarters at Turin in the middle of June. There he found a motley host of Italians, Germans, Spaniards and 'religionaries' quarrelling among themselves and cowering under the walls of the city; and, learning that the Duke of Schomberg, to whose care his father had committed him, had not yet arrived, he decided to spend another month on a solitary tour to Milan and Pavia, precociously self-reliant.

James Stanhope is a portent in English history as a man of sound English stock with uncompromising English qualities and beliefs, yet less notable for his insight into the domestic problems of his countrymen than for his mastery of their foreign relations. In that sphere he has perhaps never been surpassed for his intimate knowledge of European politics and his influence not only on his own country's foreign policy but

on that of the principal states with which England had dealings. During his comparatively brief tenure of political
power, for the last seven years of his life, it is hardly an exaggeration to call him the diplomatic master of Europe. This
mastery is partly to be accounted for by the peculiar circumstances of his birth and early upbringing and by the general
tenor of his activities until he was nearly forty.

Born in 1673 in Paris, where his father was on a mission, he
was thereby technically an alien. He could not, indeed, enjoy
the full rights of citizenship or stand for Parliament until in
1696, at a cost of £50, he obtained a private act of naturaliza-
tion.[1] He never had a fixed home in England until he was
past forty; for his father was almost always abroad on some
diplomatic service, while with brief intervals he himself was
either fighting or travelling on the Continent during the
twenty-two years after he left Oxford. Small wonder then
that a lad of parts and observation such as he should have
picked up a remarkable knowledge of foreign courts and
statesmen and an appreciation of foreigners' points of view
altogether exceptional. It is more remarkable in these circumstances that he should have retained a sturdy English
judgement on foreign affairs and an unwavering devotion to
certain fundamental principles in English political life, characteristics in their turn to be accounted for partly by his
ancestry, partly by his father's influence.

The Stanhopes, a family long established in the Midlands,
were deemed worthy to be noted for their sturdy loyalty by
Queen Elizabeth in her famous distich about her Notting-
hamshire servants:

> Gervase the gentle, Stanhope the stout,
> Markham the lion and Sutton the lout.

One of the Stanhopes of her day, Sir Thomas, she chose as
Treasurer of her Chamber and Constable of Colchester
Castle. His grandson, Philip, was created Earl of Chesterfield by Charles I and with his kin proved his loyalty to the
King's cause in the Civil War. Chesterfield's fifth son, Colonel
Philip, lost his life defending the family seat Shelford against
the rebels, while his men would not budge from the church
steeple, where they had taken shelter, till they were smoked
out by Colonel Hutchinson's men—a piece of family history
remembered sixty-five years later by James, when he was

---

[1] Huguenot Society, xviii. 239, and *Chevening MSS.*

ferreting out fugitives from Philip V's army in Spain. The first Earl of Chesterfield was married twice; he lost all the sons by his first wife during his lifetime and was succeeded in the title by his grandson; his second wife, a daughter of Sir John Packington of Worcestershire, bore him only one child, Alexander, the father of James, who, though forty years younger, was thus first cousin to the second Earl of Chesterfield. This second Earl married in succession three great ladies, daughters of the Earl of Northumberland, the Duke of Ormonde and the Earl of Carnarvon, and figured as one of the handsomest gallants of the Restoration court. Though he did not think it incompatible with the family loyalty temporarily to supplant his royal master in Lady Castlemaine's light affections, he remained to the end of his long life of eighty years a sturdy Tory, refusing to accept any favour from William III or to take the oath of abjuration under Anne. But, in spite of the equally pronounced Whig proclivities of his uncle and cousin, not unmindful of family claims, he showed some countenance to James on his first somewhat friendless appearance in London.

From his father Alexander James Stanhope inherited his sturdy Whig principles. One of Alexander's first letters preserved at Chevening announces to his wife that, 'the rogue Chancellour Jeffreys is this day taken at Wapping. . . . We expect the Prince of Orange in town to-morrow, which will quiet all our disorders. . . . I just come from the tavern drinking the princes health, and so goodnight.' But he had little opportunity of displaying his zeal for the Revolution in domestic politics, for in the following year William III sent him as envoy to Spain. There he remained watching and reporting to William the manœuvres and intrigues of French, Austrian and Bavarian diplomats and of the corresponding Spanish parties over the prolonged agony of the imbecile king until, on news of the negotiations for the second Partition Treaty to divide the Spanish dominions, the Spanish court, with a last flicker of national pride, handed him his passport. Thereafter, until within a year of his death in 1707, he was at the Hague embassy helping William to bring about the Grand Alliance and later Marlborough to keep the Dutch up to the mark. His wife Katharine Burghill, also from the Midlands, gave him five sons and two daughters. One daughter, Mary, famous in her day as maid of honour to Queen Anne, and later as the wife of Viscount Fane, survived till 1762. All the rest died comparatively young, Alexander of fever aboard the fleet in 1695, Philip, also a sailor, killed at Port Mahon under his brother's command in 1708, and Edward, killed at the head of his regiment at the relief of Cardona three years later; William, the youngest son, and Catherine, the other daughter, both died as children. James, the eldest son, alone of the brothers reached the age of forty, and even he died before he was fifty.

Alexander does not appear to have been a great ambassador. In Spain he was not called upon for much more than to hold a watching brief, for the affairs of Spain were then largely determined upon by more vigorous rulers elsewhere; at the more exciting post at The Hague he hardly seems to have been of the calibre needed, for even his friend the Duke of Marlborough could not say more for him than that 'he has served long and is a very honest gentleman, his fault being want of judgement'. But, whatever his shortcomings as an ambassador, he was a wise and devoted father, especially to his favourite son James. In an age when literary accomplishments and a taste for good books were no longer rare in men of fashion and good birth, James Stanhope was noted for his learning and his knowledge of polite literature. In his speech in the Sacheverell trial he showed something more than a superficial knowledge of the works of Fortescue, Hooker and Locke; his friend Dubois described him to the Regent as 'un philosophe', and Speaker Onslow spoke of him as 'the best scholar perhaps of any gentleman of his time'.[1] Such acquirements, it is evident from the correspondence of father and son, were largely due to the father's encouragement. He frequently calls on his son to send him parcels of the latest books to Madrid, Dampier's *Voyages* and Locke's works among others, and they exchange confidences on their contents, especially on those of the great Whig writers such as Locke's *Essay on the Human Understanding*, while even the nonjuror Jeremy Collier's recently published *Short View* gives occasion for gloomy reflections on the immorality and profaneness of the English stage. Again, James's passionate conviction, as he expressed it in later life, that the Revolution was 'the greatest blessing we ever had' is a reflection of his father's devotion to the Great Deliverer and all he stood for. When James as a young man in London was thrown into the

[1] Macky; *The British Hero*, 1715; *State Anatomy of Great Britain*, 1717; *H. MSS. Onslow*, 511.

company of the young bloods, St. John and such like, whose
views were very different, Alexander took good care that he
should also meet his own Revolution friends, the great Marquis of Halifax, Montague, and Burnet of Salisbury, who, he
tells his son, 'notwithstanding the malice of some wanton
scribblers, has approved himself a very great man, and no
clergyman of all has contributed more for our present settlement both in Church and State'; and he even brought him
to the notice of the King himself, inserting in an important
dispatch a discreet commendation of his capacity. His, too,
was a brilliant inspiration to take away James at the impressionable age of seventeen from the sleepy Oxford of those
days and under his own experienced guidance to let him gain
an insight into the main objects of European statecraft, even
as illustrated by the sordid intrigues being woven round the
living corpse that was Charles II. It is good to think that the
loving father lived just long enough to see his foresight rewarded even more directly than he could have expected. For
before he died he saw James not only commander of the
English contingent but also holding his own post as representative of Queen Anne in Spain.

But the Stanhopes, father and son, had something more in
common than their tastes in literature, politics and diplomacy; something deeper in their relations than those of
teacher and taught. A rare and refreshing comradeship,
boyish almost in its spontaneity and strength, is apparent in
the letters of some fifteen years that passed between them. A
genuine comradeship between father and son is rare at all
times; in those days of stiffer family intercourse it was rarer
still. Fathers are apt to look back on their own youth through
a haze of glory and to expect from their sons much the same
aims, much the same capacity, as those of their own early
days; sons naturally have a different outlook on a world that
has advanced since those days, and tend to be impatient at a
want of ready sympathy with the new aspirations stirring
themselves and their contemporaries, and so often to reject the
riper judgement which might help them even in their new
circumstances. But when such comradeship comes, when the
son can communicate once more to the older man some of
the joys of new experience and the hopes of an ever-youthful
world, and, loving his father for help ungrudgingly given in
the past, can help him in his turn; when the father, remembering that he was young and callow once, can smile

indulgently at his son's mistakes and gently guide him with his wider knowledge: such rare comradeship appears to be one of the most delightful and most fruitful of all forms of human friendship. Such no doubt was the understanding between Chatham and his second son William, 'eager Mr William . . . the hope and comfort of my life'. Such, within living memory, was the beautiful devotion to one another of Sir William Harcourt and his elder son, and, if one may speak of the living, between Joseph Chamberlain and his first-born. But in all these cases the devotion was especially marked in the son to the commanding personality of a famous father. With the Stanhopes the comradeship was more equal, perhaps more fundamental, though with them, too, the son never forgets due respect and deference, or the father such loving counsel as he alone can give. James writes naturally, as if to one of his own age, of his journeys and adventures in foreign parts and of his experiences as a soldier, with the frankest of commentaries on the failings of his commanding officers, or of his difficulties in securing a footing in London. He gets into scrapes, as his father no doubt expected from an impetuous son, who, at least in early days, showed signs of the paternal 'want of judgement'; but he earns ready indulgence by his frank confession of 'a piece of indiscretion of my own which . . . I should have carefully concealed from any father but you, who have ever been more indulgent in forgiving and prudent in preventing the consequences of a fault than severe in resenting it'. Alexander in his own turn pours out his woes to James—the dullness of Madrid, the absurdities of the grandees, who fight like 'cat and dog, Turk and Moor'—relieved by a story of his own diplomatic ingenuity in staving off an unwanted visit from the Elector of Mainz's envoy. He calls upon his son to find him 'an ingenuous young man' as chaplain at £40 a year, all found. Two letters are devoted to the qualifications needed for the more important position of embassy cook at £20, who must be a man, for 'I am convinced by woeful experience women will not do in this country'; the dismissed cook, Mary, though looking after his linen well enough, was 'a dishonour to the nation in this sober country', being 'capable of nothing else, least of all for a kitchen, where the fire increases, or at least gives a pretence to, her constant thirst'; later, however, he compromises on a woman if she is 'past gallantry and the vanities of youth'. The deeper side of the father's affection emerges in such a

letter as that written to James on his arrival in Flanders for
the Namur campaign:

'I beseech Almighty God to bless and preserve you in all the
dangers you are like to encounter; since it has pleased him to
take away your poor brother [Alexander], you are now all the
comfort I have left. . . . . I have had condolences from the
Admiral . . . with the greatest commendation I have heard of
any young man except yourself; and indeed by the late knowledge I had of him the little time he was with me I believe he
deserved them all. . . . This I know is no proper subject for a
letter, but the tender affection of a father may excuse it who
desires your happiness equally with his own.'

Still more notable is this letter written by Alexander to his wife
in December 1695 on James's return from this Namur campaign. It reflects the deep and religious thought given by the
father to his son's proper sphere in the service of his country;
it also foreshadows something of that son's achievement by
the end of his career.

'James has behaved himself so well all this campagne that . . .
the King has promis'd him the first Company vacant in his
Guards which is six or seven hundred pds a year, and in honour
equall to the degree of a Colonel, an advancement few have
attained at his years, and purely by his own merit. I knowe and
consider with great uneasiness the hazards he must still run,
and that he is qualified for any civill employ but the onely way
of attaining to them in due time for a young man under such a
prince is by arms in his youth nor is his Ma^{ty} himselfe, who has
the most of any man to loose, lesse expos'd every year in his
own person than any comon man in the army. Yet God has
protected him, and I trust also still will, as also our son. There
is certainly a providence that overrules human affaires, which
will preserve the instruments it designs for such and such purposes, till they have accomplished them. I will believe my son
is to be one of them under his Matie for the freedome of our
world from french and popish tiranny, and at the worst I am
sure he failes in the pursuit of a just and honourable and religious cause. In a year or two more there must be peace and
then he may fairely pretend a preference to most others in pretensions to any civill posts. Consider beside that the exercise
of Arms is the original of all honour and nobility, by which our
ancestors distinguished us from the croud, and that the surest
way of maintaining these prerogatives is that by which they
were at first acquir'd. Let all this settle y^r mind as to him and
chearfully relie upon God whom we all depend on every
moment as well as in time of battle.'

§ 2

In the summer of 1691, when James Stanhope landed in Italy, the war of the League of Augsburg had run two years of its course. Of the several fields of operation open to the young beginner, Flanders, the Rhine and north Italy, his father had chosen the last, partly for its proximity, but chiefly because his friend Charles, Duke of Schomberg,[1] a son of the hero of the Boyne, was expected there with reinforcements and, he hoped, would instruct the young man in the art of war. In the previous year Victor Amedeus II, Duke of Savoy, had at last revolted against the oppressive and insulting tutelage of Louis XIV and joined William III's Grand Alliance. His relief at the change was reflected in his ambassador's words to William: 'That my master can now venture to express feelings which have long been concealed in the recesses of his heart is part of the debt which he owes to Your Majesty. You have inspired him with the hope of freedom after so many years of bondage.' But in spite of these brave words Victor Amedeus's cause seemed almost hopeless. Since Richelieu's time a French garrison was holding Pinerolo, commanding the Italian exit of the Mt. Genèvre Pass from Dauphiné into Piedmont and, for the last ten years, Casale on the Po; and between them these two fortresses to the south-west and east of Turin held Victor Amedeus's capital as in a vice. In 1690 Catinat, by his victory at Staffarda, had cleared the Mt. Cenis route to Susa due west of Turin, and in the spring of 1691 had captured Nice, and was besieging Coni where the road from the south across the Maritime Alps debouches into Piedmont. A sudden raid by one of his detachments had laid the ducal palace outside Turin in ruins.

But on Stanhope's return from his tour to Milan and Pavia the prospects seemed brighter. Schomberg had arrived and also the Elector of Bavaria, both with reinforcements that brought up Victor Amedeus's army to 48,000; better still, Prince Eugene, who, though only ten years older than Stanhope, was already renowned for his exploits against the

---

[1] Charles, though the fourth son of Marshal Schomberg, was at his father's death the only one naturalized as an Englishman, and so inherited his father's English honours. The eldest son, Meinhard, however, was naturalized in 1691, and was thus able to take the English title after Charles's death in 1693. In 1692 he had been created Duke of Leinster. Stanhope served under both brothers, under Charles in Italy, and under Meinhard in Portugal in 1704.

Turks, had come to direct and inspire the allies. Young Stanhope was at first too shy to present his letter of introduction to Schomberg, especially when he found that he could not afford the grand equipage expected of young men of his rank who followed a general's train. But in August, on a reiterated order from his father, he plucked up courage to present his letter and was at once received by Schomberg almost as a son. He was made welcome at his table, taken on as an aide-de-camp and introduced to the Duke of Savoy, and even allowed to accompany his chief on reconnoitring expeditions with Prince Eugene. But these were the least of the benefits he received from his father's friend. Schomberg was a great disciplinarian, having no hesitation in cashiering officers guilty of irregularities in his five Protestant regiments, chiefly composed of French Huguenot refugees, which thus became a model for the disorderly Germans and Spaniards; nor did he allow his young charge to idle his time solely in the ornamental duties of an aide-de-camp, but saw that he got the most drastic military training.

> 'I am at present cadet in the Marquis de Mombrun's regiment,' wrote Stanhope in the winter of 1691, 'and have for the last ten days performed all the duties of Sentinell, for at my entrance the Duke [Schomberg] told me he could at one dash make me an officer, but that his design was to make me a good officer, which he could not do better than making me pass gradatim through all the military degrees . . . [and so] understand perfectly what is the duty of each soldier and each inferior officer, having myself exercised all these functions.'

By the following February he had done well enough to be advanced to the rank of sergeant and was given hopes of becoming a 'leader of men' at the end of the next campaign.[1] The Duke also made him learn 'to dance, fence, ride and goe sometimes to court. . . and does me the honour to examine sometimes my progress in fortifications'. He was fortunate, too, in being allowed to live on the Duke's establishment, for in those days young gentlemen of good family were expected to pay heavily for the privilege of being shot at by the enemy. Stanhope was apparently allowed little or no pay, and the grand equipages expected of him in the field alone made a serious inroad on the allowance given him by his father. Nor

[1] Stanhope's commission as captain in Mombrun's regiment, preserved in the Chevening papers, is dated 1 May 1693.

was he allowed entirely to neglect polite studies, for Schomberg sent him off the first winter to read Italian and Latin with Mr. Poley, the English envoy at Turin; and in his second winter allowed him to go for a tour in Italy with his Oxford friend, Lord Warwick, and Prince Nassau. They visited Pavia, Piacenza, Venice, Loreto, Rome and Naples. Of all these places Venice alone disappointed him: no women were visible, he wrote, and there were no balls, 'so that the libertie which the Venetians bragg of in Carnaval time is a libertie which none but schoolboys in England would bragg of'; and he viewed with disfavour 'the arrogance of the nobles who spit on the Pit and throw down what they don't need'. The other cities pleased him well, but his somewhat trite remarks about them and his schoolboyish zest in airing his knowledge of classical allusions it would be tedious here to relate.

Of actual fighting Stanhope had his full share. Augmented by the reinforcements brought by Schomberg and the Elector, the Duke of Savoy's army felt able to take the offensive. By October 1691 it had cleared the outskirts of Turin, relieved Coni and driven the French over the Po. But this success was short-lived. Contrary to the understanding generally accepted in those days of leisurely warfare, that the troops, once settled in winter quarters, should have an off-time from fighting, in December Vauban himself was sent down to besiege Monmélian, the mountain fortress defending the frontiers of Savoy on the side of Dauphiné. Schomberg, accompanied by his young aide-de-camp, went off post-haste to Aosta to raise a relief force from the Protestant Vaudois of the mountain valleys. But the Imperialist general Caraffa would have no dealings with these heretics; so, for want of effective support, Monmélian fell. Nor was this all. In mid-January, 'a season so improper for action', writes Stanhope, his chief and the Duke of Savoy had to leave 'the diversions of the Carnival' to inspect the fortifications of Coni, once more threatened by the French. Later in 1692, however, Catinat's army was reduced to 16,000 men by the withdrawal of regiments to Flanders and the Rhine. Accordingly the allies felt strong enough to divert him from his activities in Piedmont by an invasion of Dauphiné. But this expedition effected little beyond the capture of Embrun and some aimless pillaging, carried out, according to Stanhope, even more brutally by the German troops than that of the Palatinate by the French; and, when Victor Amedeus fell ill of smallpox, the invading army, torn by jealousies between the other allied commanders, drifted off in confusion.

Next year a determined effort was made to capture Pinerolo and Casale, the standing menaces to Turin and the frontiers of Piedmont, while Catinat was kept waiting at Fenestrelle near Susa for reinforcements from Dauphiné. Leaving a force to mask Casale, Victor Amedeus attacked St. Bridget's, the outlying bastion of Pinerolo. The attack, in which Stanhope took part as a volunteer, was successful: but the allies had no time to profit from it before the French were upon them with a threat to their communications with Turin. Catinat, who was only too eager to celebrate his recent promotion to the rank of marshal by another victory, had obtained reinforcements in September and forthwith marched towards Victor Amedeus's capital. Fearing to be cut off, the allies withdrew from Pinerolo and went to meet Catinat as he debouched into the plain from the mountain passes. The two armies met near Marsaglia, between Pinerolo and Turin, on 4 October, Catinat's 40,000, the allies' only 25,000 strong. In the ensuing battle Victor Amedeus on the right held his own, but Catinat rolled up Eugene's left wing and threw his cavalry against the allied centre. Here Schomberg was holding his ground well when orders came to him to retreat. This he refused to do without an express command from the Duke of Savoy and expressed his resolve to go on fighting with his men till they died: nor would he leave till he was carried off the ground mortally wounded, to die a fortnight later. Stanhope admits that he himself saved his own life only by fleeing on foot from a cavalry charge. This need hardly be taken as a reflection on his own courage, for, as his mother once wrote to him, his chief temptation would be to run 'into danger upon a mistaken point of honour', a view confirmed by another account of his conduct in this battle, which says that 'he showed a Presence of Mind and gallant intrepidity that was admired by all about him'.[1]

This encounter at Marsaglia was the last serious engagement on the Savoy front. Louis XIV very soon realized the mistake he had made in antagonizing Victor Amedeus, 'un

[1] *Add. MSS.* 23709. On the other hand, Cunningham, i. 144, asserted that 'his speed in flight [on this occasion], as well as his talkativeness in England, served to raise his fortunes'. But Cunningham's evidence may be discounted, as he invariably took a jaundiced view of Stanhope's performances. See below p. 19, note 2. A good account of the battle is to be found in D. Carutti, *Storia di Vittorio Amedeo II* (Torino, 1856).

des adversaires de S. M. les plus coûteux et les plus redoutables', as his ambassadors told him.[1] Since the fall
of Monmélian he had been making advances to him, and
the Duke was quite willing to come to terms if they were
favourable enough to himself, all the more as the English fleet had been withdrawn from the Mediterranean.
So for the next two campaigns the war in Savoy lan-
guished, while behind the scenes Louis became more pressing and the Duke more exorbitant in his demands. Finally
in June 1696, by the Treaty of Turin, Victor Amedeus once
more changed sides, thus ridding Louis of a troublesome
diversion on his flank and obtaining in return not only all the
territory won by Catinat but the key fortresses of Pinerolo
and Casale to boot.

Marsaglia also brought to an abrupt end Stanhope's first
schooling in war, for with the death of his mentor there was
nothing to keep him in Italy. Schomberg indeed had promised to take him to England that winter and obtain for him
a commission in the Guards: now his whole prospect seemed
black. 'All my hopes', he wrote to his father, 'are cut off pre-
cisely in the time when I expected to reap some benefit from
the campaigns I have served here and the money I have
spent you.' So he obtained leave and funds from his father
to travel to London, there to seek his fortune for himself. With
the novelty of the journey, on which he was anxious to see
'what is most curious on the passage', his spirits soon revived.
Starting in November 1693 he crossed the St. Bernard, much
impressed by its 'vast precipices' and the warm welcome given
him by the monks at the Hospice, 'which the most rigid Presbyterian will own to be very well situated, for they give re-
freshment to all strangers who generally have great need of
them when they get thither'. Thence he passed through
Switzerland, whose inhabitants he dismissed with the verdict
that 'of all beasts none is liker a man than a Switzer', and
Germany, where he seems to have been chiefly struck with
the high charges and 'stinking' accommodation of its inn-
keepers. And so, without further adventure, to London,
which he reached in January 1694.

His two years' military training under Schomberg proved
eminently to his advantage. By his service in all ranks of the
army he acquired an appreciation, rare in those days, of the
common soldiers' needs, and, when he had men of his own

[1] *Recueil, Savoie*, &c., i, Introduction.

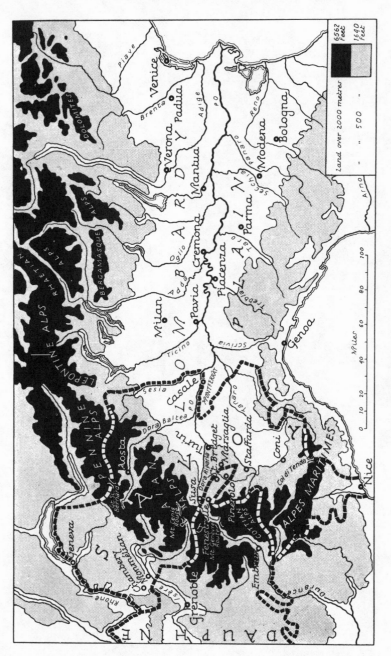

CAMPAIGNS IN SAVOY, 1691–3

to command in the Peninsula, was enabled, partly by his sympathetic care for their health and comfort, to get the best out of them. From Schomberg himself he learned all that the best type of God-fearing, gallant and strict commanding officer could teach him. From his humble association with Eugene he retained a lasting admiration for the great commander, second only to Marlborough in his time for strategic insight, personal bravery and noble courtesy, and in later life did his utmost to obtain the chance of serving under him again. Nor did he take lessons only from the allied commanders. Catinat, the great French marshal opposed to him, forms the subject of one of his most enthusiastic outbursts to his father. For here, he said, was a man of low birth, bred by the Jesuits, who had risen solely by making himself necessary to every commander under whom he served. When he attained independent command as governor of Casale he at once set himself to study all the details of the surrounding country and to perfect himself in siege warfare; for, he notes, 'he never was a man of pleasure but wholly applied himself to those arts which might contribute to his advancement'. This eulogy is singularly confirmed by that of St. Simon, who knew Catinat well, on his 'vertu, sagesse, modestie, désintéressement, la supériorité de ses sentimens, ses grandes parties de capitaine'. Apart from the soldiers, too, this shrewd young man had a valuable opportunity of gauging the character of the foxy Victor Amedeus, with whom he had several subsequent dealings, both as commander in Spain and as foreign minister at the time of the Quadruple Alliance; while his meetings with Caraffa and other Imperialists gave him a foretaste of the imperial courts' obstinacy and wooden diplomacy that he proved more successful in surmounting than any of his contemporaries.

§ 3

Barely twenty-one when he arrived in London early in 1694, Stanhope soon found it necessary to shoulder the full responsibilities of a man. He had not only to seek his own fortune, but, in the absence of his father, to act in his place as head of the family. His mother, after the birth of her last child in 1691, had left Spain for the sake of her health, and though her husband Alexander urged her to return a year later, bringing 'my girle with you—it will be diversion to me',

on her pleading continued illness, resigned himself to a solitary existence at Madrid. She was an affectionate mother,
very proud of James, and fond of airing to him her knowledge
of Roman history. In urging him to keep a journal of his
campaigns she assures him that 'it is not below a General
since Julius Ceasar allwais did it, and it will bee time beter
spent then either drinking or playing'. But she seems to have
been an unpractical woman, too much taken up with her
colds, vapours and intermittent fevers to be trusted to look
after the family concerns. At any rate the absent father came
more and more to rely on James in business matters. In one
of his letters he tells his wife that James has helped him much
in his affairs, and, 'no easy matter has got me some money',
probably by dunning the Treasury for arrears of salary and
allowances. The education of Molly, 'my girle', who grew
up to be a very lively young lady, was the subject of several
letters between the father and the precocious son. The father
recalls with approval a saying of the old gallant, his nephew
Lord Chesterfield, that 'he desired his wife and daughters, to
make good wives to whom they should marry, might have
Presbyterian education', and gloomily questions whether 'at
the rate of obscenity and profaneness of our English plays
there are . . . any fit for a young woman to see, who is designed to be bred virtuously and modestly. I need not tell
you that I mean this for your sister, and . . . I cannot suspect
that from my saying this you will believe me grown morose
because I am grown old, since you very well know the contrary.' In his turn James, then just twenty-five, solemnly lays
down the need for 'a good gait and gentle demeanour' for
Molly and discusses the merits and demerits of 'public
schools' for such as she: and he gladdens his father's heart by
reporting 'wonders of Phill [and that] everybody is charm'd
with Molly'. 'We ought', the happy father writes to his wife,
'to be very happy in our children.'

But first James had to secure for himself some opening in
his chosen profession, the army. With his patron Schomberg
dead, his father at the other end of Europe, and himself, after
four years' absence from England, almost forgotten by most
of his relations and boyish friends, it was uphill work. At
any rate he showed commendable persistence in knocking at
every possible door which might open an avenue to employment. 'At great expense for coach-hire', he tells his father,
he called on his Stanhope cousin, Lord Chesterfield, relic of

the Restoration, from whom he gets 'much civility but no kindness', and his son, Lord Stanhope, married to a daughter of the great Marquis of Halifax, who at least gave him a dinner. His father's friend, the gallant General Talmash, destined a few months later to fall a victim to Marlborough's treachery in the ill-fated Brest expedition, 'made offers of service signifying little'; from Lord Sidney, the King's friend and Master-General of the Ordnance, from Blathwayt, the Secretary at War, and from others he obtained nothing more than 'a put-off or at best a compliment'. Lord Halifax, however, proved very solicitous for him, and better still, the King himself was reported to have 'often promised he would take care of me'. And so it proved; for William III had a tender spot for the Stanhopes. As a boy he had known Lord Chesterfield in Holland and thought none the worse of him for his crusty Jacobitism, and he had always favoured James's father as one of the first who rallied to him in 1688. Accordingly, after less than a month the son was admitted to kiss the King's hand and before the end of March 1694 received his first commission as a captain in Gibbons's Foot.

Further expense for his father in a new equipage, which included two horses for himself, two for his servant and one, if not two, for his baggage, and an unfortunate experience for himself in a rascally Welsh lieutenant, sent to the Midlands to recruit for his company, who got no recruits and disappeared with all the levy money for which Stanhope was responsible;[1] and then by August he was over in Flanders. Here the form of warfare was very different from the irregular and disorderly proceedings he had witnessed in Savoy. Everything was conducted according to the strictest military etiquette. Once the troops were in winter quarters there were no such rude alarms as an unexpected siege. For during the winter months, when military operations were irksome, William and his leading English officers had to return to meet Parliament and perform the other state duties incumbent upon them, while the French marshals and nobles, Luxembourg, Boufflers and the rest, had to renew their vigour by basking once more in the life-giving rays of the sun of Versailles. William himself was not one to be bound by stupid formalities, when the great cause he had at heart was at stake—he had shown that once for all in 1672—but even

---

[1] The amount involved was £200, £160 of which was waived by the Treasury six years later (*Chevening MSS.*).

he was hampered to some extent by his civil duties and his troublesome Parliament. It is hardly surprising that this gentlemanly form of warfare should have been largely dominated by the ideas of the great military engineers, Vauban and Cohorn, with their elaborate science of fortification which necessitated leisurely operations. It needed the genius of Marlborough to break away from this tradition and on occasion to march across Europe to force a decisive issue.

In Flanders, therefore, Stanhope saw little of the rough and tumble of war such as he had experienced in Italy, much to his advantage when he came to fight in Spain. But in 1694 he was involved in a duel—'necessary and honourable on his part', says his father—killed his man and was wounded himself; and then was stripped to the shirt by Walloons. Otherwise his chief hardship was stringency of resources wherewith to meet the heavy expenses of equipage, servant and style of living expected from one in his position. Pay was doled out in such niggardly fashion that in one year the army pay was over four months in arrear, and to prevent a mutiny the officers had to advance money to the men out of their private means; and two days after he had reached camp in 1695 he was robbed of the gold watch his mother gave him, £120 in money, and a trunk full of clothes. The only serious fighting in which he took part was in the siege of Namur of that year. On 28 July he was on the counterscarp near St. Nicholas Gate where Captain Shandy got his famous wound; he also volunteered for the final assault on the castle, whereby William obtained his one great success of the war, and he was himself also wounded in the leg. His gallantry on this occasion earned him the King's favourable notice and a company in the Footguards carrying with it the rank of colonel in the army and pay, when obtainable, of some £600 or £700 a year.[1] In the following year he became brigade-major in the Guards, his first introduction to the rudimentary problems of staff work.

But though his three years in Flanders did not give him much variety in military operations, he was brought into touch with those who could either give him useful hints for his profession or help him in his career. He was befriended by the Prince de Vaudémont, the commander of the Dutch contingent who so skilfully headed off Villeroy from William when he was besieging Namur. The magnificent Duke of Ormonde, uncertain of purpose but a gallant soldier and as

[1] In fact he was getting only 10s. a week pay in 1697, so he tells his father.

a friend highly regarded by William, took favourable notice of him and within a few years gave him his first opportunity in Spain. Above all, he was admitted, as far as any one so young could be, to the intimacy of William, who, he tells his father with pardonable pride, 'several times asked me to eat with him'; and no one could be in close touch with William without learning something of that great soldier-statesman's sureness of vision and calm certainty of his ultimate aim in war and statecraft.

William's favour no doubt also gave him an opening he was quick to seize into the outskirts of diplomacy, for which he later proved more fitted than for war. By 1697 all the combatants were eager for peace. Louis XIV was anxious to reshuffle his cards in preparation for the fast-approaching demise of Charles II; the allies were equally tired of the war and dreaded the arrival of Catinat and his army released from Italy by the Treaty of Turin. Negotiations had begun at Ryswick in May 1697, but they were dragging; so the two principal adversaries, William and Louis, took a short cut to peace in a series of secret interviews between Portland and Boufflers, four of them in July in an orchard near Hal, and the last on 2 August on the outskirts of Brussels. To this final meeting Portland took Stanhope in his select staff of twenty officers, and, while the principals were conferring alone for upwards of two hours, Stanhope and his nineteen companions had to make what head they could with the brilliant cortège of 500 courtiers that Boufflers had brought in his train. Stanhope admits that he knew nothing of what had resulted from his chief's colloquy, but at any rate he began his acquaintance, afterwards so useful to him, with the leaders of the French social and political world. To such good purpose had he progressed that at the end of the two hours, 'I am engaged', he wrote, 'when the peace is made, to about 20 dukes, lieutenant-generals etc. to see them in their houses in Paris.' As a result of these secret negotiations the separate treaties of Ryswick between Louis and the Dutch, England, and Spain were signed on 20 September and that with the Emperor on 30 October.

Stanhope's acquaintances were, however, not confined to staid members of King William's court, French dukes and lieutenant-generals, or God-fearing seniors such as his first mentor Schomberg, nor were his tastes restricted to unremitting labour in his profession. As a young and brilliant

Guards officer he naturally fell among the young bloods of his own age who had more money than he had to waste, and for a time he entered with zest into their extravagant forms of dissipation. During the idle months that succeeded the signing of the peace, before the armies were disbanded, there was little for the officers to do except to enjoy themselves, and Stanhope threw himself unreservedly into the fashionable amusements of the time. He has to acknowledge to his father that at the Prince de Vaudémont's house, 'I unluckily . . . was engaged in play . . . I runn it up to £400, one of which [sc. £100] I got money of my arrears to pay. The remaining three are still due and must be paid some time or other; the gentleman to whom I owe it has been so civil as not to press me much.' His father paid up, and James, touched by his 'continued kindness and tenderness', declared that 'since the folly you paid so dear for, I have not once handled cards or dice', and promised 'to make the future course of my life express it, and in some measure atone for my past extravagance'. He did not entirely keep to these good resolutions, for two years later he is reported as travelling in a coach costing £100 and sending in the bill to Lord Tavistock, from whom he had won that amount at cards.[1] He also during the years of enforced leisure after the peace acquired an unenviable notoriety for wild debauches of hard-drinking, in which he found congenial boon-companions in Harry St. John and the young Lords Nairn and Widdrington, with whom as Secretary of State some twenty years later he was to have grimmer dealings.[2] One of these debauches in Brussels was, as described by one of his fellow-topers, merely a disgusting exhibition;[3] others, notably some in which Stanhope and St. John let themselves go in wild talk, may at any rate have been more amusing.

---

[1] *H. MSS., Bath,* iii. 384.
[2] See ch. vii, p. 195, below.
[3] The curious in such matters may be interested in Widdrington's account of this orgy written in November 1697 from Brussels to his friend Coke. After describing the fashionable society of the place and a meeting he and Stanhope had with Coke's 'charming mistress', to whom they both made a compliment from her lover; 'last night', he continues, 'Sir Francis Tempest, Stanhope, a Scotch gentleman, and myself, having drunk till 4 o'clock in the morning, went and roused the people of the Chocolat House, and drank 3 bottles of Pericco apiece, except Sir Francis, who after the 2nd could no more . . . Stanhope in the middle of a harangue fell dead off his chair as if he had been shot; there he lay till 5 o'clock in the afternoon, before he could possibly be wakened. . . . The Scotch gentleman . . . the next morning came and made me a visit being yet drunk' (*H. MSS., Cowper,* ii. 370).

The friendship sealed at this time over the bottle between Stanhope and St. John, in spite of a complete divergence of their political paths in after life, persisted till the end of Stanhope's life. Even then, in spite of doubts inspired by his dissolute habits and his wild escapades in London, St. John's personal charm and the prodigious attainments of his mind seemed to promise for him a future more brilliant than for all his contemporaries. Though as yet he had not even entered Parliament, the character written of him twenty years later by a hostile pamphleteer might already have been accepted.

'Nature', writes this pamphleteer in 1717, 'had not only shown him to be her Masterpiece in the Fabrick and Structure of his Body, but in the Beauties and Operations of his Soul. He was form'd by the one to please and Command the Eyes of all Beholders; and by the other, whenever he was heard to speak, to engross the Attention of all judges of Wit and Sound Reasoning. He was no less happy in the Brightness and Vivacity of his Expressions than in the Conclusiveness of his Periods and wheresoever he distinguished himself by his readiness of Thought, there also he was remarkably eminent for the Fluency and Poignancy of his Diction. . . . But as a counterpoise to all these virtues, he was so sunk into, and swallow'd up by Libidinous Courses; so lost to Shame and Repentance, by an intemperate Pursuit of the most odious and infamous Practices . . . that it will be conducive to the Honour of the Gods, as well as the Edification of our Readers, to cast a Veil over his Perfections and Imperfections, lest their Admiration of the Beauties of the First, should take off from their just Abhorrence of the Last; and the bewitching Allurements of the one, sh^d make them look with the eyes of Approbation on the other.'[1]

Stanhope, less brilliant if more stable, was captivated by St. John's convivial habits and had no qualms about engaging in the Alcibiadean discussions he provoked. One such discussion in 1700 became notorious for the scandal it created in high places.

St. John had just arrived in Paris after a tour in Italy with one Edward Hopkins and celebrated his return at a convivial meeting with Abraham Stanyan, Prior's successor as secretary to the embassy, Lord Sidney and Stanhope. The account of this affair given by Cunningham, who is never entirely to be trusted when Stanhope is in question,[2] is as follows:

'Mr Stanhope's [Alexander's] son, a youth of a very licentious

[1] *The History of the Rise and Fall of Count Hotspur* . . . (London, 1717), 12, 13.
[2] See Cunningham, i. 180. Alexander Cunningham was a Scot of some note

disposition, being at Paris to meet his father, associated himself with other young men, and in his cups was guilty of the most extravagant profanation of the Christian religion. This gave offence both to the embassy and the Church and also brought the secretary of the embassy into trouble. For the archbishop of Canterbury complained of it very heavily to the king, being afraid lest this fresh scandal, coming on the top of others already mentioned, should raise up a flame against the Whigs, who were charged at this time with everything reproachful. The secretary was recalled from the embassy. Mr Stanhope was sent ambassador to the Hague; but his son having much disgusted the king by his writing a book for disbanding the army and other things, was on the point of being disgraced, had not his father's entreaties and good services prevailed with the king to pardon him. For he was a young man that did not mind anything divine or human, when it came in competition with his own humour.'

It will be noted that in this account Stanhope has to bear all the brunt of the offence; but it can hardly be doubted that, if Stanhope was wild and profane, St. John was not behindhand in profanity or wild behaviour.

It may be admitted, once for all, that hard drinking, even by the standard of those bibulous days, was a failing to which Stanhope was particularly prone. In the early days of the war in Spain, Peterborough, then on terms of almost gushing affection with Stanhope, paid particular attention to supplying his friend's cellar; in later years Dubois, in close relation with him, could think of no more delicate attention to pay him than to send him several pipes of the strongest French vintages, and on one occasion boasted that he had surprised his secrets after a long sitting with hard-drinking Germans. Even his fatal seizure in the House of Lords was absurdly enough attributed by his enemies, not to his impetuous anger at an unjust charge against his honour, but to a drinking

in his day (1654–1737), who took a useful part in forwarding the Union. He was a strong Whig, but also a friend of Harley. During Stanhope's ministry he was under him as Resident at Venice. Here he wrote a *History of Great Britain, 1688–1714*, veiling it in the Latin tongue and never publishing it. It was discovered by Dr. W. Thomson, who translated and published it in 1787. In some respects Cunningham is singularly well informed, but his predilections (e.g. for Argyll) and his violent prejudices against others (e.g. Burnet) make his judgements most untrustworthy. He had, too, prolonged quarrels with both his predecessor and his successor at Venice. His animus against Stanhope is very marked, to the extent of attributing motives to him of which he could not possibly have had knowledge. The reason for this animus is unknown. Possibly Stanhope was not gentle to him at Venice. See also *E.H.R.* xxxiv. 394, for Edward Hopkins's statement.

debauch at Newcastle House on the previous day.[1] But at least the habit of hard drinking, acquired in youth, may well have become almost a necessity in later life to a man of his untiring energy and exuberant vitality. Carteret and the younger Pitt, equally remarkable for vigour, had the same failing, perhaps for the same reason; and similar instances are not unknown in later times. Also, as in the case of his grand-nephew Pitt, this extraordinary energy and the stimulant thought to be required for it may account for his premature death at an age when most men have barely passed the meridian of their powers.

Fortunately for Stanhope, he was soon drawn away from his life of dissipation in Brussels by a flattering invitation from Portland to continue their connexion by joining his household at the embassy in Paris. He felt obliged owing to his mother's illness to refuse the invitation when it was given in December 1697; but early in the following year he was established in the embassy, noting the discontent of the French nobility at the peace which deprived them of employment and many of them of livelihood. He had ample opportunity for gauging public opinion; for Portland, during his brief tenure of what Macaulay described as the most magnificent embassy ever sent to a foreign court, kept open house for all that was most distinguished in Paris. But short as Portland's tenure was of the embassy—for he returned to London to be Secretary of State in May—Stanhope's stay there was hardly longer. His impetuosity and want of restraint may not have accommodated themselves with Portland's austerity, but at any rate there was some misunderstanding with his superiors; and early in August Stanhope went off in a huff, not even troubling, as his friend Lord Raby complained, to take leave of 'our very civil court'. Matthew Prior, the Tory secretary of the embassy, may have had something to do with the quarrel, to judge from his letters to Stanhope's father and Portland. Writing to Alexander Stanhope in Madrid, after admitting that he 'would· never desire a better second for the pen' with the embassy correspondence than James, he adds:

'You will doubtless have heard from other hands . . . of a

---

[1] Lord Harley, writing to his father shortly after Stanhope's death, says that 'the great debauch which killed Stanhope and Craggs was at the Duke of Newcastle's. They drank excessively of new Tokay, Champagne, Visney, and Barba Water, thirteen hours it is said' (*H. MSS., Portland*, v. 616).

misunderstanding which happened between my Lord Ambas·
sador and him. I am sorry he resented anything ill after having
been treated with all kindness from my Lord. But he is of age, let
him answer for himself, and I have business enough of my own
not to meddle with anybody's else, though I have a friendship
for Mr. Stanhope which makes me wish that whole matter had
been otherwise.'

In spite of his protestations Prior went on meddling, for next
month he sent Portland an admittedly third-hand report
about a man who was 'in company with Colonel Stanhope
and [reported] that Stanhope had said he would be revenged
of my Lord Portland for the usage he had given him at Paris;
and desired this man to enter into measures with him in order
to form something that might prejudice your reputation.'
Portland drily replied : 'Il n'est pas imaginable qu'un homme
soit capable de cela', and evidently thought no more about it.
Prior himself in his last letter on this topic had to admit that
he had discovered a mare's nest.[1]

Even during this first short sojourn in Paris Stanhope had
already begun to form relationships with the French political
world which were to prove of the greatest value to himself
and still more to his country. Here at the house of Lady
Sandwich, who formed a link between English and French
society, he had first met the Duc de Chartres's tutor, the abbé
Dubois, and soon struck up a close friendship with him; as
St. Simon says in his expressive phrase, 'il le connut, comme
on dit, entre la poire et le fromage'. This friendship ripened
in London, where Stanhope met him again in Marshal
Tallard's ambassadorial train, and both were charmed with
one another not only as genial boon-companions but for a
literary taste and cultivated turn of mind each found in the
other. Dubois's stay in London was short, for his insinuating
manners and his mysterious proceedings aroused a suspicion
that he was intriguing with the Jacobites; so Louis, then
anxious not to antagonize King William, thought it wiser to
recall him. But Stanhope paid several more visits to Paris
before the end of the reign and saw much of Dubois and of
his pupil, later the Regent Orleans, who admitted him to his
little parties, more famous for the wit and effrontery of the
talk and behaviour than for their decorum. Nevertheless
Stanhope's more solid qualities appear to have made a permanent impression on his host who, twenty years later, wrote

[1] *H. MSS., Bath,* iii. 205 seq.

to him: 'Depuis que je vous ai connu, Monsieur, dans le temps
que milord Portland estoit icy, j'ai toujours conservé une
estime particulière pour votre mérite et grand désir d'entretenir votre amitié'.[1]

He was also privileged towards the end of the reign to
obtain a standing at The Hague, the great centre of European
diplomacy, and so to find himself in the thick of the negotiations that succeeded the proclamation of Louis's grandson
Philip as King of Spain. When his father was dismissed from
Madrid at the end of 1699, James went to Bordeaux to meet
him after nearly ten years' absence, and was taken on by him
to his new post in Holland to act as his secretary. Here he
had further opportunities of meeting William, frequently
over from England to consult with Heinsius and the envoys
of other Powers on the formation of his new Grand Alliance.
For already Louis XIV was attempting to exploit his grandson's newly acquired monarchy by appropriating the Spanish
Low Countries. William indeed at one time thought of sending James Stanhope to Sweden in connexion with these
negotiations; but that plan fell through.[2] To The Hague
William brought with him two men, of very different calibre,
with both of whom Stanhope was destined to have closer relations. One was Marlborough, who already began to mark
out the young man for future service, the other was Jean de
Robethon, the King's Huguenot secretary, even now showing
signs of the prying and meddlesome nature that made him so
unpopular as George I's secretary. In the fateful September
of 1701, when all the world was agog with rumours of plots
and sudden war, James writes to Robethon by his father's
courier to inform him of the suspicious escape from the
Bastille of the Italian Bottelli, said to be engaged in a plot to
assassinate William: 'Vous avez toujours été pour la guerre':
he concludes, 'vous n'aurez pas changé de sentiment à cette
heure que la France lâche ses assassins.'[3] In the same month
he was actually at Loo when the news came that Louis XIV
had acknowledged James III as King of England, the last
insulting act of imprudence which roused England to a fever
of enthusiasm for the inevitable war.

[1] St. Simon, iii. 23, 88; xii. 455; and Wiesener, ii. 59.
[2] Macky. This author's statements are not always to be trusted, but that
William designed Stanhope for this mission seems confirmed by the proposal
to send him there in 1702 (see below, ch. ii, p. 32 and note).
[3] *Stowe MSS.* 222, f. 99.

At home, too, his position in society was very different from what it had been a few years before, when, an almost unknown and shy youth, he had been received 'with more civility than kindness' even by his nearest relations. In the summer of 1699 he went a round of visits to the great houses in the Dukeries, Chatsworth, Mansfield and Welbeck. By the Duke of Newcastle,[1] his host at Welbeck, he was entrusted with the very special commission of procuring through Robethon a herd of German stags 'et des plus gros qui se trouvent en Allemagne, car M. le Duc en a déja bon nombre d'aussi grands qu'il y en ait en Angleterre, si bien que si ceux qui lui pourroient venir d'Allemagne ne l'étoient pas plus, vous voyez bien que ce seroit se donner et aux autres une peine inutile.'[2] He was 'under the protection', says Cunningham, of the 'proud' Duke of Somerset, a man of no great intellectual attainments but a stalwart Whig, who on two occasions at least, in James II's reign and at Anne's last council, had the courage of his opinions. He thought well enough of young Stanhope to correspond with him freely, signing himself, 'your most affectionate, humble Servant', and to recommend him for election in his own borough of Cockermouth for Anne's first Parliament. In the previous Parliament, on the day before King William's death, Stanhope had, at a bye-election, become M.P. for Newport, I.W., in place of 'Salamander' Cutts. A month previously he had been gazetted to the vacant colonelcy of the 11th Foot (N. Devons) and ordered to recruit it up to war strength.

Thus at the beginning of the new reign, at the age of twenty-nine, Stanhope seemed to have the ball at his feet. He had a training in diplomacy, he was already a marked man in the army, and if he chose politics he already had a seat in Parliament and was assured of another. He had his defects—a tendency to self-indulgence and extravagance and an impetuosity which sometimes drove him to passionate outbursts of temper. But at least these were the faults of a not ungenerous nature, and the older he grew the more controlled were they by his ambition to serve the public and the high principles of duty implanted in him by his father and developed by his own self-training and experience. He had,

[1] Thomas Holles, first Duke of Newcastle-on-Tyne of the second creation (1662–1711), not to be confused with his nephew the well-known politician, Thomas Pelham-Holles, Duke of Newcastle-upon-Tyne and Newcastle-under-Lyme (1693–1768), also a friend of Stanhope.
[2] *Stowe MSS.* 222, f. 99.

too, the gift of making friends and, once made, of not parting from them lightly. St. John, the brilliant, irresponsible booncompanion of his youth, to him was always 'Harry', even the Harry whom he saw last as a Jacobite and an exile. Above all, in a world so disturbed and uncertain that some of the greatest in England thought it wise to keep a footing in both camps, Stanhope had already made it plain that nothing would budge him from his Revolution creed.

What like was the Colonel Stanhope of this period? Macky in his *Memoirs of Secret Services*, written a few years later for the edification of the Electoral court, describes him as 'one of the finest young gentlemen we have; he is very learned with a great deal of wit. King William meant to send him to Sweden, and he would have negotiated well. . . . (He is) a handsome black man.' Swift has a malicious note to this, in which he substitutes 'ugly' for 'handsome', but, to judge from the portrait by Kneller in the National Portrait Gallery, Macky's epithet is to be preferred. In this picture he is represented as swarthy, with a high intellectual forehead, piercing eyes, a masterful nose, and a sensitive mouth suggesting not only eloquence but also a robust appreciation of this world's good things: obviously a man of vigour, impetuous and impatient of opposition, determined to have his own way. But the look of determination, even of sternness, is tempered by that of sympathy and humour which seems to lurk in the corners of his sensitive mouth and eyes. Here is obviously one who, besides the harder qualities needed for success, had the faculty of good comradeship and the qualities of tact and consideration for those under him unusual in one of his temperament and time, and so well illustrated during his command in Spain and still more when he was chief minister of the Crown.[1]

[1] The quotations from letters of the Stanhope family in this chapter are taken either from Mahon's *Spain under Charles II* or directly from the MSS. at Chevening.

CHAPTER II
STANHOPE AND PETERBOROUGH

§ 1

IN May 1702, on the eve of England's declaration of war against France and Spain, when the Emperor's troops were already fighting in Italy, Stanhope found himself marooned in Dublin. All his hopes of active service seemed vanishing, while most of his friends were already at the front or on the point of starting. Eugene had made his famous entry through a disused aqueduct into Cremona and carried off a marshal of France; Ormonde, 'very much his friend' since the Namur campaign, was making ready for some secret blow at Spain; Marlborough, with most of his younger friends, was about to leave for the fields of Flanders. Promises indeed had been made to Stanhope of active employment, but there he was, still in Dublin, left to the uncongenial task of collecting raw recruits and licking them into shape for his regiment. In desperation he writes early in May to the viceroy Rochester, the Queen's uncle, imploring him to 'make some amends for the disappointment by allowing me to waite on the Duke of Ormonde as a volunteer . . . to express in the best manner I can the zeal I have for her Majesty's service': as for his regiment, he could well be spared from it for it was in such good order that 'whoever reviews it two months hence shall be satisfied. I doe humbly entreat your Excellency that I may not have the mortification of staying idle here, after the hopes that have been given me that I should be better employed.'[1] By July he had his wish and was sailing to Spain on Ormonde's staff.

This expedition was all of a piece with William's far-seeing plans for loosening the intolerable stranglehold Louis was obtaining over Europe. For, fatal as 'the little gentleman in velvet' had been to William himself, his projects were all matured; and Marlborough, his political heir, and at least his equal in executive ability, adopted them as his own. The problem before him was formidable. The Dutch garrisons had been unceremoniously turned out of the fortresses they were holding in the Low Countries and replaced by French troops, ready to pounce on the exposed frontiers of

[1] *Add. MSS.* 15895, f. 213. Dublin, 28 Apr. 1702 (o.s.).

Holland. Spain, described by Fénélon as 'un corps mort qui ne se défend pas', had been taken in hand by a select band of French officials, who were attempting to revive the corpse and exploit the country's resources chiefly for the benefit of France. Spain's neighbour Portugal had made a treaty of alliance with France in 1701; in the previous year Victor Amedeus, the slippery guardian of the Alpine passes, had opened them by treaty to the French. On the Rhine the Elector of Cologne was with Louis, and farther south the Elector of Bavaria, having changed sides since the last war, was available as a spear-head against the Habsburg dominions. Opposed to Louis was the Grand Alliance, strong enough in appearance with its main constituents, England, the Dutch, the Emperor, Denmark and most of the North German princes: but Denmark and the German princes were distracted by apprehension of what might befall in Charles XII's northern war with Peter of Russia and Augustus of Poland and Saxony; while the Emperor, though freed from the Turkish menace by his recent Treaty of Carlowitz, was weakened by Rakoczy's insurrection in Hungary.

William had seen—and here Marlborough was his brilliant disciple—that the main points of danger for England were the Low Countries and the Mediterranean. The Low Countries, from time immemorial regarded by England as vital for her continental trade and even her national security, by the Dutch as the bulwark of their integrity, must in the first place be rescued from Louis's encroachment. Here then was to be the chief centre of the land operations, to be conducted by Marlborough himself. But almost equally important for English interests was the fate of the Mediterranean. Since Charles II's treaty of 1667 with Spain, England had enjoyed special advantages for her trade and had even been allowed to carry on flourishing industries in that country. With the success of Louis's policy of making Spain dependent on France such privileges were bound to disappear; thus it became a cardinal point in the policy of England to prevent this success. Thirteen years later Stanhope succinctly restated William's and Marlborough's policy in his instruction to Methuen at Madrid, that 'the preservation of the commerce between the kingdoms of Great Britain and Spain was one of the chief motives for entering into the long late and expensive war and one of the principal benefits expected by our people from the conclusion of a peace . . . and of the greatest importance to the interests of our subjects and the riches of our dominions.'[1] Nor was it merely the trade with Spain that turned Marlborough's eyes to the Mediterranean. Since Cromwell's day that sea had ceased to be almost a closed lake to our traders. The Levant Company was already gaining on its French rival in the Sultan's dominions, and English ships more than held their own in Italian as well as Spanish ports. To protect this Mediterranean trade Cromwell had already envisaged the idea of seizing Gibraltar; Charles II had held Tangier for the same purpose until induced by domestic considerations to abandon it. Now with France in command of all the ports on the eastern littoral of the Atlantic,[2] with no opponent to hinder the junction of her principal fleets at Brest and Toulon and with no friendly base nearer than England from which English fleets could operate, all our Mediterranean trade with Spain, Italy or the Levant would be at the mercy of the French. Thus an essential element in Marlborough's policy throughout the war, which Stanhope soon learned to forward with characteristic enthusiasm, was to rescue Spain from the domination of France and secure a base to protect our Mediterranean trade.[3]

The expedition on which Stanhope sailed in July 1702 was the firstfruits of this policy. Rooke, the admiral in command of a fleet of fifty English and Dutch ships, had instructions, first, to prevent an anticipated junction of the Brest and Toulon fleets; secondly, to intercept and capture a treasure fleet expected from the West Indies; and, thirdly, to seize some port on the coast of Spain, Cadiz for choice, as a base for the English fleets. For this last objective 14,000 English and Dutch troops under the Duke of Ormonde accompanied the fleet. The commanders were ill chosen for the purpose. Rooke was half-hearted about the Cadiz portion of his instructions and not the man to take risks for such an object: Ormonde, though a keen and gallant soldier, had not the strength of mind to stand up to the seamen, inclined to magnify the difficulties. When the fleet arrived before Cadiz in the last days of August, the Spanish garrison was neither numerous nor well provided, but was under the command

[1] R.O., *S.P.* 104/135. 15 Jan. 1714/15.
[2] By France's alliance with Portugal at the beginning of the war even Lisbon may be included.
[3] For a good exposition of the Mediterranean policy, see J. Corbett, *England in the Mediterranean*, 2 vols., 1904.

of the gallant old Marquis de Villadarias, Spain's best soldier. Cadiz itself stands on the islet of Leon at the entrance to the bay, connected with the mainland only by a narrow strip of sand. The soldiers' plan was to make a direct attack on the city under cover of the fleet, but Rooke rejected it on the ground that the covering ships could find no shelter and would be exposed to fire from the land forts. So it was decided to land in the Bay of Bulls farthest from Cadiz itself and attack some of the outlying forts on the mainland. Even in the Bay of Bulls, where this landing was effected, 'though the weather appeared moderate', wrote Stanhope to his father, 'there was such a violent surge on the strand that about 20 boats were sunk, and not a man got on shore who was not wet up to the neck. I must confess I never was so much afraid of drowning, and yet we lost not 20 men; for to do the sailors justice I never saw fellows bolder than they were to rescue our men in distress.' This landing was almost the only serious danger incurred by the troops. The small outlying forts, sparsely manned and equipped, had no means of resistance; and in dealing with them for terms of surrender Stanhope's knowledge of Spanish came in useful. At the fort of St. Mary's, when 300 Spaniards seemed inclined to resist, 'As I happened to be there', he wrote, 'I rid up to them, advised them to surrender, and offered them good quarter, which they gladly accepted.' The governor of St. Catherine's, in answer to Ormonde's letter, written by Stanhope demanding his submission, met the young staff-officer next day and surrendered at discretion. But after four weeks ashore on such petty business the allies were no nearer capturing Cadiz itself; and to another letter from Stanhope addressed on Ormonde's behalf to Villadarias himself, the fine old Spaniard returned the proud answer : 'Nos Españoles no mudamos Religión ni Rey'—'We Spaniards change not our Religion or our King.' On 9 September (N.S.) the fleet, having re-embarked the landing force, set sail for England.

The failure to gain any tangible success was the least evil resulting from this ill-managed enterprise. Already negotiations were afoot to set up the Emperor Leopold's second son, the Archduke Charles, as a rival candidate to Philip V for the Spanish throne. To ensure the success of such a project at least two conditions were essential, to draw Portugal away from her alliance with France and obtain Lisbon as a base for our fleet, and secondly to secure the goodwill of the Spanish people. Portugal was not likely to risk the enmity of France, with her command of Spain, without some more tangible evidence that the English fleet would be strong enough to protect her against the wrath of Louis XIV. Fortunately an almost accidental success for Rooke, immediately after the reverse at Cadiz, gave Portugal the required assurance. But on this their first appearance on Spanish soil, the English, destined to be the Archduke's chief supporters, gratuitously threw away the opportunity of posing as friends of the Spanish people. Not only was Cadiz itself, after its capture was recognized as impracticable, uselessly bombarded by the fleet, but the soldiers by their disorderly conduct in the outlying villages and by their wanton pillaging and desecration of churches permanently alienated Andalusia and most of the other provinces. Nor was this conduct simply the result of the men getting out of hand. Among the worst offenders in the wholesale robbery were two of their generals, Sir Henry Bellasis and Sir Charles O'Hara. Their conduct must have been specially outrageous, for, though a certain amount of plundering in war was then considered venial, on a complaint from the Emperor himself an inquiry was held on the two generals' conduct and Bellasis was cashiered. At the inquiry Stanhope refused to give evidence against Bellasis on the ground that he had served with him on Ormonde's staff, a questionable preference of personal loyalty to the country's interests. Nobody suffered more than Stanhope himself from the bad name that thereafter clung to the English troops as robbers and desecrators of churches, as he found in his subsequent efforts to induce Castile to accept Charles as King. Personally he was disgusted at the conduct of the troops and sent a scathing criticism to his father of the whole conduct of the expedition. Not only, he writes, were sea and land forces at variance, but also 'land against land and sea against sea', and while apportioning blame to the sailors as 'all along very resty', admits that this disgraceful plundering 'in spite of our solemn declaration' turned the scales against the soldiers. 'And so', he concludes, 'with a great deal of plundering and infamy, we shall, I believe, be sailing homewards in three weeks.'[1]

As Rooke and Ormonde were sailing home crestfallen,

---

[1] Mahon, *Spain*, 206. Even in Rooke's official journal (*Navy Records*, ix) the bad management, quarrelling and plundering are fairly evident.

a stroke of luck retrieved the expedition from absolute failure. Of the treasure fleet that Rooke had been instructed to intercept nothing had so far been seen, when one of his captains left behind to water at Lagos heard casually that it had not only arrived under French convoy but was safely ensconced in Vigo Bay. Pressing on all sail he caught up his admiral, who at once decided to turn about and secure the prize: before this the news had reached England, and Sir Clowdisley Shovell was also racing for the same point. When Rooke reached Vigo the gold and silver of the galleons had already been unloaded and preparations made to save the rest of the cargo in the magnificent land-locked harbour. Booms protected the ships anchored at the head of the bay; the Redondilla, a fort overlooking them, had been mounted with guns; and troops occupied points of vantage along the shore. But these precautions were of no avail. Rooke's ships bore through the booms, while Ormonde with a landing party silenced the shore guns and captured the Redondilla. Fourteen of the French and Spanish ships were taken, the rest sunk or run ashore, and merchandise to the value of £1,000,000 fell to the victors. Stanhope was specially mentioned in the *Gazette* for gallantry in the attack on the Redondilla: even more important for his own future and that of the allied cause, the King of Portugal's confidence in the British navy was restored.

With the return of Ormonde's expedition Stanhope's connexion with Spain, where he was to make his name as a soldier, seemed at first to be definitely closed. During the winter months of 1702-3, while military operations, according to the tacit convention, were in suspense, he had his first real taste of the House of Commons. Duly elected, during his absence on service, for Anne's first Parliament, as member for the Duke of Somerset's borough of Cockermouth, he took the first opportunity to proclaim his Whig convictions by voting against the Tory Occasional Conformity Bill and in favour of the Act of Abjuration of the Pretender's claims. In the spring he returned to regimental duties in Ireland, and in May brought over his 11th Foot to the English camp at Maestricht, too late to take part in the capture of Bonn, Marlborough's solitary success of the year. The operations of the next two months were inconclusive, chiefly owing to the refusal of the Dutch to follow Marlborough's directions and take any risks. But this brief term of service under the

great Duke had one advantage for Stanhope in confirming
Marlborough's good opinion of him. This appeared when
Stanhope, wearied perhaps by the futility of these operations,
or from a conviction that regimental duties were not his
special bent, renewed his application for the diplomatic
mission to Sweden originally designed for him by King
William. In the previous year Marlborough had told his
father Alexander that he was 'the properest person that can
be chosen' for this purpose, and in August gave him leave to
go to England, ostensibly to make regimental arrangements,
but partly, no doubt, to enable him to push his claims at
home; for he wrote privately to the Lord Treasurer Godolphin that though 'very loth to lose him in the service, . . .
having a personal friendship and kindness to him', he wished
to endorse his application.[1] But in spite of Marlborough's
influence, the Rev. John Robinson, afterwards Bishop of
Bristol and negotiator at Utrecht, was not displaced by
Stanhope as envoy to Charles XII. It is a pity, for Stanhope
was a greater diplomat than he was a soldier. Over Charles
XII he might well have exercised a good influence. Like
Charles, frank and direct in his methods, Stanhope was more
level headed and might have saved him from some of the
rashness that was his undoing, or at least persuaded him not
to estrange England, his best friend in a time of need, by
harassing her Baltic commerce.

But by the end of 1703 the way had been cleared for
Marlborough's Mediterranean policy, to forward which
Stanhope was to devote the rest of his military service.
Pedro II of Portugal, nervous at the proximity of his too
powerful Bourbon neighbour, had only been waiting for an
excuse to break his recent treaty with France. In urging him
to this course the English ambassador Methuen was warmly
seconded by Dom Pedro's cousin Prince George of Hesse-
Darmstadt, 'the idol of the Catalans', as Alexander Stanhope
described him to his son after his gallant defence of Barcelona
against a French army in 1697. Turned out of his governor-
ship of Catalonia by the Bourbons, he had convinced the
English government and also his Portuguese cousin that a
large party in that province would take up arms against
Philip V for the Archduke Charles. Impressed by the recent
victory of the English fleet at Vigo and by the prospect

[1] *Marlborough*, i. 141, 158, 190; Alexander Stanhope to his wife, 16/27 June
1702 in *Chevening MSS*.

offered by Prince George of a successful war in Spain, in May 1703 Dom Pedro concluded a treaty with Methuen recognizing the Archduke as Charles III of Spain and engaging to support him with an army of 28,000, provided he entered Spain through Portugal and that England and Holland also contributed 12,000 land-forces and a fleet. In the following December the trading interests of England were safeguarded by the famous Methuen treaty of commerce which gave reciprocal advantages to port wine in England and English woollens in Portugal.

In the same year the solid block of French interests in Italy was broken. Victor Amedeus, personally offended by his son-in-law Philip V and never loth to seek the highest bidder for Savoy's support, had proved so lukewarm an ally to France that Louis XIV had taken the extreme step of disarming the Duke's troops. Thereupon, in November, Savoy made a treaty with the Emperor and joined the allies on promise of a considerable increase of territory. Thus Marlborough had the prospect of shattering the French dream of the Mediterranean as a French lake. With the help of Savoy, our ally the Emperor might turn the Bourbons out of Milan and the Two Sicilies, and Toulon itself might be captured; by supporting Charles III we could hope to secure our Spanish trade and even obtain a naval base in the Mediterranean.

In accordance with the Portuguese treaty the new claimant to the Spanish throne, Charles III, came over to England, where he was received with royal honours, and thence sent off to Portugal escorted by a fleet, again under Rooke. Accompanying the fleet were transports to convey the stipulated quota of English and Dutch troops, including Stanhope's 11th Foot. The start was inauspicious for the flotilla. Driven back into Plymouth in January 1704 by contrary winds, the flotilla did not reach the Tagus till March. Nor was the opening campaign more promising. There was still a strong French party at court led by the Duc de Cadaval, while the corruption and incompetence at head-quarters was so great, declares Stanhope, that 'if the King of France had had an Intendant here to make a disposition of military matters, it could not have been more to his advantage'. The commander of the English contingent, Meinhard Duke of Schomberg, eldest brother of Stanhope's first instructor in the military art,[1] had none of his brother's, still less of his

---

[1] See ch. i, p. 8, note.

father's, military capacity. Instead of looking after his troops, distributed over the countryside in wretched quarters without adequate provisions, he made himself comfortable at Lisbon and quarrelled with his Dutch colleague Fagel. So far from Charles making his triumphal entry into Spain from Portugal, Philip V and his French commander, the Duc de Berwick, Marlborough's nephew, advanced into Portugal with an army of 28,000. The only attempt made by the Portuguese and allied commanders to stay their onset was to distribute their available forces by small detachments in isolated fortresses. These naturally fell an easy prey to the invaders. Among the captured detachments was Stanhope's 11th Foot, stationed near the frontier at Portalegre with two Portuguese battalions under a Portuguese commander. When attacked by the chevalier d'Asfeld, the panic-stricken population insisted that the governor should capitulate without a blow and deliver up the troops as prisoners of war. Fortunately for himself Stanhope was not present at this disgraceful affair. On reaching Portalegre he had been stricken with a bad attack of fever brought on by the hardships of the journey and the vileness of the Portuguese quarters. 'I made use there', he writes to his father from Lisbon, 'of a Portuguese doctor, who, by bleeding and dieting me, had almost done my business, so that, despairing of recovering there, and by easy days' journeys was transported hither.' By August Stanhope was back in London with the duty of reforming his regiment, most of the prisoners captured at Portalegre being exchanged and returning to England early in 1705. This was the last duty he performed for the 11th Foot, for on becoming a brigadier-general in April, he was succeeded in the colonelcy by Jack Hill, Mrs. Masham's brother, whose pretensions to a colonelcy of Dragoons almost caused the Duke of Marlborough's resignation in 1709.[1]

But in spite of these miserable operations in Portugal the outlook for the campaign of 1705 was promising. Blenheim

---

[1] The 11th Foot, originally raised in 1685 against Monmouth, was dogged by misfortune during this war. Returning to Spain in 1707 it was badly cut up at Almanza under Hill and had again to surrender. Re-formed in 1708, it was present in the two following years at some of Marlborough's victories in Flanders. In 1711 it was taken by Hill on his unfortunate expedition to Quebec. During Stanhope's ministry it fought at Sheriffmuir, where it suffered somewhat severely, and at Glenshiel in 1719. *Historical Record of the Eleventh or N. Devon Regiment of Foot* (1845).

had been won; and France was on the defensive for the rest
of the war. In the Cevennes the Camisards were becoming
so troublesome that a marshal of France had to be withdrawn
from the front to deal with them. Even in the Peninsula
Rooke had retrieved his failure at Cadiz by the capture of
Gibraltar and by sending the Toulon fleet battered to its
home port from Malaga; from October till the following
May Prince George of Hesse with a tiny garrison frustrated
the attempts of Villadarias and Marshal Tessé to recover
Gibraltar with a vastly superior force. The first stage of the
Mediterranean policy had thus proved its value. But much
yet remained to be done. Gibraltar, though occasionally
useful as a harbour of refuge, as Rooke and Leake had found,
was windswept and unsafe as a shelter for the fleet at certain
seasons, and the space available for its garrison was cramped
and needed much expense in fortification. Another safer
port either in the Mediterranean itself or else Cadiz, a lure
to English mariners since Elizabeth's day, was desirable.
Above all, a more determined attempt was required to put
Charles in possession of Spanish soil. Accordingly a more
ambitious scheme of operations was contemplated for
1705.

In Portugal the incompetent Schomberg was replaced by
the Huguenot refugee Ruvigny, who had entered William
III's service and been created Earl of Galway, with orders
to attack Spain from the west. In addition an imposing
fleet to be made up to sixty-six sail of the line after picking
up Leake's squadron, that had wintered in the Tagus, was
sent out in June, under the joint command of Lord Peterborough and Sir Clowdisley Shovell. By their instructions
Peterborough and Shovell were allowed a wide discretion
as to the nature and even the locality of the operations they
were to undertake. They might attack Cadiz or else seize
Barcelona and attempt to establish Charles III in Catalonia
as Prince George wished; they could even transfer the bulk
of their force to Italy and assist Victor Amedeus, then hard
pressed by Vendôme, and thence stretch out a helping hand
to the Camisards or attack Toulon. Stanhope, now promoted
to the rank of brigadier, was sent out on Peterborough's staff.

§ 2

Assuredly the man chosen to command the expedition sent
to the Peninsula in May 1705 was not one to quail before
any scheme, however ambitious. Charles Mordaunt, Earl of
Peterborough and Monmouth, Viscount Mordaunt of Avalon,
Baron Beauchamp and Mordaunt, to give him the romantic
grace of his full style, though still well under fifty years of age,
had already had adventures enough to satisfy most men's
appetite for knight-errantry. He had fought Algerine pirates
at sixteen, had defended Tangier against the infidel, had
been the friend and follower of Shaftesbury, Sidney and
Russell; at twenty-seven he had made the most effective
speech in the House of Lords against James's illegalities; he
had been one of the first to urge William to come over, had
accompanied him to Torbay and then had been sent ahead
with a regiment raised by himself, to prepare the way to
London; he had been First Lord of the Treasury, had been
one of William's companions in his famous landing in
Holland in an open boat through the fog and ice-floes of a
winter sea; he had then turned against William, as he did
on principle against most monarchs, and had never satis-
factorily explained some shady transactions in connexion
with Sir John Fenwick's trial, for which he was cast into the
Tower and lost most of the offices and wealth showered upon
him in the days of his favour. But, ever buoyant and unabashed, he was soon as full as ever of some new great
scheme, more intent on its conception than its execution, but
always ready to boast about it to all he met at Wills's or in
any other public place. As his best biographer writes, 'he
had only to be trusted with any business, for it to grow into
overwhelming importance'. As might be expected from one
of such mercurial nature, though he never lost the heart of
his first fair countess or of his second, the singer Anastasia
Robinson, to the end of his long life he was always having
tender passages with duchesses, countesses, fair ladies of high
or low degree in England, at Venice, in Spain, or wherever
he chanced to be, beauties who fell at once to the charm of
this romantic figure, most like, said Voltaire, to one of those
heroes so dear to Spanish story-tellers. But with all his boast-
ing talk he could be secret and dissimulating in action, if
he meditated a sudden stroke; with all his caprice and his

constant changes of friends, he was most happy in his twenty
acres of fruit garden at Parsons Green, most at his ease in
such company as that of Dryden, Swift, Locke, Newton,
Pope. Small wonder that it is from the poets that he obtained
the most affectionate tributes to his charm. To Swift he was
'the ramblingest lying rogue on earth', and, as Mordanto,
he who

> Knows every prince in Europe's face,
> Flies like a squib from place to place,
> And travels not but runs a race.
> . . . .
> A skeleton in outward figure,
> His meagre corps, though full of vigour,
> Would halt behind him, were it bigger.

Pope, at his request, not only wrote off some charming lines
for one of Peterborough's favourite singers, Durastanti, to
recite at her farewell performance, but in his first Satire
fondly gives a picture of the man as he knew him best:

> And he, whose lightning pierced the Iberian lines,
> Now forms my quincunx, and now ranks my vines,
> Or tames the genius of the stubborn plain
> Almost as quickly as he conquered Spain.[1]

Voltaire also succumbed to his genial ways during his sojourn
in England and spread his fame over the Continent not only
in his *Siècle de Louis XIV* but also in his novel, *Histoire de Jenni*,
which is much taken up with eulogies of Peterborough and
his confidant Dr. Freind.

Such was the man chosen, largely through the great
Duchess who ruled Marlborough, to lead the new expedition
to Spain in 1705. Mindful of the dissensions between sea and
land in the Rooke-Ormonde expedition, the ministry tried
to obviate the repetition of this difficulty by a curious
arrangement whereby Peterborough, who had never yet
held high command on land or sea, should not only be
commander-in-chief in Spain but also carry a commission
as admiral jointly with Shovell. He was also accredited as
envoy to the new King Charles III. Conyngham was his
second-in-command on land, but Stanhope at the outset
seems to have enjoyed all his confidence. Mercurial in his

---

[1] The best biography of Peterborough is that by William Stebbing (1890);
Parnell's *War of Succession in Spain*, admirably documented and excellent in
most respects, is marred by an extravagant prejudice against Peterborough.

likes and dislikes, as might be expected of him, he began by treating Stanhope as his most intimate friend and thought nothing too good for him. Before they had left England he suggests that his servant whom he is sending to Holland for tea, chocolate, rum, claret, Rhenish burgundy, sturgeon and other delicacies for his private commissariat, should execute similar commissions for Stanhope. For over a year he always signs himself to him 'your most affectionate friend'; sends him his most private letters to King Charles III to read, 'for to you everything is open, and particularly my heart'; informs him that 'it is no little satisfaction to me to find you are of the same mind; I wish we may always run the same fortune with the same opinion'; and even ventures on one of the supreme tests of intimacy, in criticizing his wines: 'your Hermitage is good, the rest indifferent'. But as was often the case with Peterborough's impetuous friendships, this one did not prove lasting. The two men became estranged, largely because Stanhope ventured to tell him the truth; and Peterborough for his part never quite forgave him.

In June a council of war was held in Lisbon to decide which of the two objectives offered to Peterborough and Shovell by their instructions should be chosen. In view of the division of Philip's scanty forces between Barcelona, where an attack was evidently expected, and on the western frontier against Galway, Peterborough strongly urged an attack on Valencia, where the inhabitants were said to be friendly and which was unguarded, as the best means of 'seating the Archduke on the throne and, as it were, surprising the whole Spanish nation into acquiescence and approbation of the change', for only fifty leagues and one fortified town, Requeña, separated Valencia from Madrid. It might be rash, but Peterborough urged that in a civil contest it was especially important to be prompt and vigorous.[1] Against this view Prince George urged an immediate attack on Barcelona with the assurance that the Catalans would join Charles III with enthusiasm and support him with their famous bands of Miquelets, the name given to the lightly armed levies of Catalonian peasants, reputed to be the best irregular troops in Europe.[2] The

[1] Quoted by Ballard, *The Great Earl of Peterborough*, 137, from a report of Stanhope.
[2] Mahon, *Succession*, 140-1.

council, won over by his arguments, decided unanimously to adopt his view. Accordingly the fleet set sail from the Tagus with Charles as Peterborough's guest on his flagship. The land force carried on the transports was raised to some 7,000–8,000 men, partly by exchanges with Galway, partly by three Guards' regiments taken up at Gibraltar. Peterborough also, perhaps with a premonition of the turmoil and controversies likely to arise as to his proceedings in Spain, took with him a Dr. Freind, a physician to the troops with a literary turn, to whom, on his recall two years later, he turned over all his papers and memoranda to make out the best case he could in his patron's favour.

At first all seemed to smile on the new King's progress. No French fleet appeared to oppose the expedition. At Denia and Altea in Valencia, where the fleet put in, the population welcomed Charles III as submissive subjects. But when the ships entered Barcelona roads on 16 August the capture of the capital of Catalonia appeared much less easy than Prince George had promised. The defences had been repaired and were in good case, and the garrison was not much inferior in numbers to the attacking force. The inhabitants, however much they may have sympathized with King Charles, were well under the control of the capable governor, Don Francisco Velasco. Even the promised rising of the country and the assistance of partisan bands of Miquelets were not at first in evidence. Peterborough, supported by Stanhope and most of the other military officers, was for abandoning the enterprise and taking fleet and army off to Italy to help the Duke of Savoy. But they had reckoned without the King. Charles III was barely twenty and still much swayed by his Viennese advisers, especially his old tutor Prince Lichtenstein and Major-General Count Uhlfeldt. He had all the obstinate pride and dilatoriness of his family and was very much a slave to the elaborate forms and etiquette of the court in which he had been brought up. But he was conscientious and fully alive to the royal duties he had assumed and, though sometimes excessively cautious under the influence of punctilious advisers, brave on occasions when he thought his honour involved. This was one of them. Backed by Prince George, he insisted on making the attempt on Barcelona, and Peterborough had reluctantly to agree to make a trial for eighteen days; but as time passed with no sign of success, he again

proposed to re-embark the troops and sail off to Italy.[1]
Charles and Prince George in despair turned to Shovell to
get Peterborough to make one more attempt. Peterborough
yielded, but characteristically maintained a profound
secrecy, even from Stanhope, about the cunning plan he
evolved.

Monjuich, an isolated fort held by the garrison of Barcelona
on a commanding eminence some 1,200 yards south of the
city walls, was chosen by Peterborough as his objective.
Whether Colonel Richards, the chief gunner, Prince George,
or Peterborough himself originated the idea of attacking at
this point has been a subject of controversy both in Peterborough's lifetime and ever since. But the point is comparatively immaterial, since Peterborough avowedly adopted the
idea, made all the arrangements for the enterprise and
preserved its secrecy, so deserves the full credit.[2] Two parties,
one of 1,000 infantry under brigadier Lord Charlemont,
the second of 1,000 more foot, 300 dragoons, and some guns
under Stanhope, were detailed for the attack. The first
party was to start at 6 p.m. on Sunday, 13 September, the
second under Stanhope six hours later and to march from
the camp to the west of Barcelona along the road towards
Tarragona and the south, in order to confirm the garrison
in the belief already spread abroad that the beleaguering
force intended to abandon the siege and make off to Valencia:
when on a level with Monjuich they were to make a sharp
turn to the left and advance to the attack. By 8 o'clock
next morning Charlemont was before Monjuich; Stanhope's
reserve was ordered to halt a mile in rear. The attack was a
complete surprise and the English were already on the east
and west bastions of the fort when a stray bullet struck down
Prince George, an irreparable loss both for his skill and
gallantry in the field and still more for his knowledge of the
Catalans. Thereupon ensued a panic among the main
attacking party in the outworks, which Charlemont either
shared or was unable to stem: Peterborough coming up

---

[1] Lamberty, xiv. 264 sqq., gives the decisions of the various councils of war.
[2] Parnell, p. 128, attributes all the arrangements for the attacking parties
and for the orders issued to them to Prince George, apparently on the sole
authority of a widow, who in her claim for a pension stated that her husband
had been picked out by Prince George for the attack on Monjuich. He may
have done so in this instance, but the Prince could not have issued general
orders to the English troops over whom he had no command; his being a
Roman Catholic was then an insuperable bar to army rank in England.

'in the horriblest rage that ever man was seen in', seized Charlemont's half-pike and rallied the men, 'with a resolution', says Richards, afterwards no indulgent critic of his lordship, 'becoming so great a man'.

But the first effects of the surprise attack had now worn off, and though Stanhope and his reserve were called up, the defenders in the main fort still held out and were reinforced by a detachment from the city. So Peterborough had to send for more guns from the fleet and settle down to a siege in form, during which the garrison guns did some damage to his men, Stanhope himself having the gruesome experience of seeing the head of one of his mess-companions blown off by a cannon-ball as they were sitting at dinner. Finally, after three days' siege, but not before a magazine in the fort had blown up and killed the commandant and fifty men, Monjuich was captured. After this success Peterborough set himself in grim earnest to gain Barcelona itself. The land force being without heavy artillery the fleet provided guns and gunners to man them and a large reinforcement to the attacking force in addition. On 9 October, when the walls had been breached in three places, Don Velasco agreed to evacuate the city on 14 October, Stanhope and a Spanish brigadier being exchanged as hostages for the observance of the terms. But hardly had the capitulation been signed before the population, hitherto held down by Don Velasco, began breaking all bounds, pillaging and rioting and inviting the irregular Miquelets outside to join them: at last the governor in despair had to beseech Peterborough to come in before the appointed day to keep order. Peterborough accordingly entered the city and with Stanhope rode about the streets quelling the tumult and saving their enemies from rapine and carnage. Stanhope afterwards confided to Burnet that he had never been in greater danger than he then was 'from the shooting and fire that was flying about in disorder'. Peterborough was characteristically fortunate in rescuing a beautiful lady, who turned out to be the Duchess of Popoli, as she fled with dishevelled hair from an infuriated mob of Miquelets; and he had to set a guard on a convent to which he sent her and other fair ladies in distress.

Immediately after Charles III's solemn entry into Barcelona amidst the enthusiastic plaudits of the Catalans, Stanhope was sent by Peterborough to England with dispatches glorifying his own part in the victory. Stanhope was also given sundry other commissions, some of a public nature, some relating to Peterborough's private concerns. Money for the expenses of the campaign was above all needed: Peterborough had been forced to borrow £100,000 from a Portuguese Jew in Lisbon; he had also, so he wrote to Godolphin, got 20,000 dollars from Genoa merchants, seized powder from ships going to Italy, contracted mortgages on his own estates, and advanced his own pay; but at least £60,000 more was urgently required to save his troops from starvation. Reinforcements also he must have. Then there was his own position. 'The first thing I desire you to press with my wife', he wrote to Stanhope, 'is the despatch of my commission as Vice-Admiral of England, or my leave to come home'; for, not content with the supreme command of the troops and his joint commission as admiral, he would be satisfied with nothing less than undivided control over the sea also. Further, Stanhope was charged with several private commissions such as that of clearing the title to his estate of Dauntsey in Wiltshire: 'I hope before this comes', he wrote to Stanhope, less than a month after he had sailed, 'you will have fought a parliamentary battle for me in relation to the confirmation of Dauncey by Act of Parliament.' And all these miscellaneous injunctions were interspersed with complaints, usual with Peterborough, about the misdeeds of those he had to work with. 'Our seamen' and 'sea politics' come in for some abuse; his second-in-command, Conyngham, 'is such an infernal screech-owl, and growing more and more disagreeable; if possible get him removed to some other service more suitable to his humour'; Charlemont also was to be got rid of; but the vials of his wrath are specially directed against Charles's German court, 'Litestein, Wolfeld [Lichtenstein, Uhlfeldt] and the whole Vienna crew. . . . Never Prince was accompanied by such wretches for Ministers; for they spend their whole time in selling places; they have neither money, sense, nor honour'; Cifuentes, the dashing leader of the Miquelets, who had just captured Lerida, was 'a Spanish bully, . . . the maddest of Spaniards'. Stanhope's friendship, patience and tact must have been put to a rude proof by all these exacting commissions: but at any rate in regard to the private concerns he gave complete satisfaction. 'My wife', writes Peterborough to Stanhope, 'repeats in every letter the sense she has of your sincere concern for my interests in England.' Nor is the devotion of his amiable countess less commendable. But while she was slaving away at his interests, he was exercising his fascinations over a 'little Marqueza' de la Casta, and doubtless many others, and writing to the Duchess of Marlborough that in Spain 'the only tolerable thing is your sex, and that attended with the greatest dangers'.[1]

'I was never so surprised as the night I writ my last', writes pretty Molly, now a toast of the Kit-Kat Club and Maid of Honour to the Queen, in December 1705, 'for about half an hour after I had sent my letter the Brigadier came to make me a visit with his face all over dirt just arrived from riding post. . . . Captain Edward [also serving in Spain] is very well and indeed I think mightily improved but he cannot be reconciled to the English ladies tho' he has seen the blossoms of our Court . . . and complains he has not seen one handsome woman here. Brother Philip [the sailor] is very well. I think I can never remember to have seen all my brothers together before.'

Two days after this joyful little family-meeting Stanhope was summoned to attend the Cabinet Council, presided over by the Queen herself, to lay before it the letters from Barcelona. Ministers knew their Peterborough and were not inclined to take all his vapourings too seriously. It was resolved to communicate to Parliament Peterborough's dispatch, all but the first paragraph, 'because he had, by way of valuing his Success, mentioned the great Danger of his Undertaking, in that he served a Kingdom where nothing was justified but by Success; which was thought might possibly give Occasion of Discourse to the Parliament: and for that he had, in the same Paragraph, insinuated as if the Advice to take Barcelona had come from himself originally; whereas Secretary Harley said, before the Council sat, that the Queen knew the same was not true.' Stanhope was then asked his own opinion on 'what was immediately necessary to be done to support their success'. In the first place, he replied, pay and clothing were needed for the troops, also money to encourage deserters from the other side, whom he put as high as 7,000, and to tempt others to follow their example, 'for which there was a general Disposition if those who had come in were well treated'. Above all, he added, in language which must have been pleasing to Marlborough, Port Mahon must be captured to serve as a Mediterranean base: if it were

[1] Peterborough's letters to Stanhope are at Chevening, most of them privately printed by the historian Stanhope.

taken, 'the general Opinion was of the French and Spaniards, that Languedoc would again revolt, the Insurrection [of the Camisards] not being put out'.

Except that no immediate decision on Port Mahon was taken, the resolutions of the Cabinet were all that Stanhope could desire. £250,000 was obtained from Parliament for expenses in Spain; ten more ships and five more regiments were ordered out; money and arms were dispatched to Catalonia; and Galway's proposal was approved of to advance into Spain from Portugal in order to draw off the French forces from Barcelona. But these brave resolutions, complained the Lord Keeper Cowper, were not followed up with 'so much Earnestness for a Dispatch as requisite; . . . a month or so sooner or later was heard [by the Cabinet] without any apparent concern'; and it was not till the middle of February 1706 that the relief squadron sailed for Lisbon. This dilatoriness was partly due to dissensions in the Cabinet itself between the Tories Harley and St. John, the Whigs Halifax and Cowper, and the two leaders Marlborough and Godolphin, originally Tories, but mainly concerned in carrying on the Queen's business and especially the war without party bias. Cowper himself draws a suggestive picture of this disunion in his account of a dinner intended to be reconciliatory at Harley's in January, attended by Marlborough, Godolphin, Boyle, St. John, Halifax and himself. When Harley drank 'love and friendship' in a bumper of Tokay, which was 'good but thick', Cowper remarked, alluding to Harley's shifty methods, that 'white Lisbon was best to drink it in, being very clear'; and most of the company took the point.[1]

Stanhope himself, who, even Cunningham admits, 'would seldom do any of the courtiers' dirty work', disgusted with these unpatriotic bickerings, 'pressed to have a clear account of the public money, the succession of the Crown as by law established and the liberties of the people maintained and everything to be openly and fairly transacted'. He even, on the eve of his return to Spain, 'made a long speech in parliament, to put his fellow-subjects in mind of their duty and at the same time warned them of their imminent danger, not so much from the enemy as from the parliament itself, and courageously turned the edge of his speech against men who

[1] The accounts of the Cabinet meeting and of this dinner are in *Lord Cowper's Diary* (Roxburgh Club, 1833).

pretended to the name of Whigs, but were staunch courtiers'. 'It grieves me', he concluded, 'that we should now desire to be such men as our ancestors would not have endured'.[1] Already Stanhope was a marked man. He had recently been left an annuity of £200 by the will of Lord Huntingdon 'to defend the liberty and laws of his country and the rights of the people', an anticipation of the legacy left for a similar purpose by the old Duchess of Marlborough to his nephew Pitt.[2] Marlborough was clearly impressed by his able reports on Spain and his vigorous support of his own and Godolphin's war policy in Parliament; for from this time dates his confidential correspondence with Stanhope, of whom he wrote a few months later, 'nobody can have a greater value and friendship for him than myself'.[3] In spite of his reluctance to besiege Barcelona, even more decided than Peterborough's, Charles III had written to Queen Anne praising his 'great zeal, vigilance and very wise conduct, of which he has given proofs on all occasions', and had indicated that he would be welcome to his court as the Queen's representative. Accordingly, while still retaining his military command, he was appointed, jointly with Peterborough, envoy to Charles, and kissed the Queen's hand on this appointment a week before he sailed. As secretary he took out Horatio Walpole, brother of the more famous Secretary at War, as Robert. Walpole soon became. His formal instructions turned principally on the commercial advantages in Spain to be extracted from Charles as a return for the military aid afforded him. Thus he was to obtain a promise that Gibraltar, not yet ceded to England, should be a free port, and that trade concessions should be granted, 'such as', is the cynical explanation, 'perhaps at another time cannot so well be insisted upon'.[4]

§ 3

When Stanhope arrived at Lisbon with his reinforcements in March 1706, he was able to send Marlborough an encour-

---

[1] Cunningham, i. 461. While evidently approving of this speech, Cunningham even here cannot resist sneering insinuations at Stanhope's motives, such as that he was out 'to serve the common cause and himself at the same time' and that he spoke 'to acquire to himself the reputation of a great patriot'.

[2] Ib. (Cunningham must needs add that Huntingdon 'was much deceived in Mr. Stanhope'); H. MSS., Portland, iv. 168.

[3] Marlborough, ii. 269.

[4] Instructions of 5 Jan. and 7 Feb. 1705/6 in R.O., S.P. 94/76. Charles's letter about Stanhope is quoted in Freind's Account of the E. of Peterborough.

aging report. After the capture of Barcelona Philip V had retreated across the border to Roussillon, thus leaving Charles for a time the only King of Spain on Spanish soil. Catalonia, long uneasy at the centralizing policy of the Habsburg kings and the loss of their historic rights and privileges and convinced that no relief was to be expected from the Bourbon Philip, looked on Charles as her saviour. For he had solemnly confirmed their ancient *fueros*, a pledge strengthened by Peterborough's declaration on behalf of the Queen that England bound herself to see those rights observed. The Catalan fortresses, Gerona, the northern 'barrier and key of the Country' as Stanhope called it, Urgel just south of the Pyrenees, Tortosa, Tarragona and Lerida had been easily captured by Cifuentes, the great leader of the Miquelets, and other partisan leaders. The whole province was thus in Charles's hands. Aragon, the neighbouring province to the west, also resentful at the loss of ancient liberties, was disposed to accept Charles, who had already gained two of its fortresses: Valencia to the south was rapidly succumbing to Peterborough's victorious energy. On the Portuguese border Galway was already assembling an army and hoped to start in a few days towards Madrid without, says Stanhope, waiting 'to amuse himself at any place that may cost time'. To spur on the Portuguese contingent to be ready in time Stanhope gave Dom Pedro the Queen's letters in support of the ambassador's efforts and told everybody what Marlborough had said to him about quickening things.[1] He was also anxious to rejoin Peterborough as soon as possible with the reinforcements he had brought, but unfortunately Leake, who was to command the fleet, was away on the look-out for galleons. Owing to this cause Stanhope and the fleet were not able to start on the voyage round Spain for another month.

This delay was the more unfortunate, since affairs in Catalonia had suddenly taken a turn for the worse. Philip had returned to Aragon by March with a Franco-Spanish army under Marshal Tessé; and early in April the Toulon fleet of twenty-eight men-of-war under the Comte de Toulouse had arrived at Barcelona, which on 4 April was closely invested by Tessé's army on the land side also. Meanwhile Peterborough was still in Valencia, having largely denuded of troops not only Barcelona but the other

[1] *Chevening MSS.*

two chief Catalan fortresses, Lerida and Tortosa. Thus Barcelona was left with only 300 English and 1,000 Spanish regulars and 1,500 irregulars to withstand Tessé's army of 20,000 supported by the blockading fleet.

Peterborough's Valencian adventure gave full scope to his resourceful cunning and his swaggering bravado. At the end of 1705 Charles and his German advisers were all for the safe policy of keeping their troops in Catalonia to hold the fortresses and the ground won, Peterborough all for breaking fresh ground by a dash into Valencia, already well disposed to Charles. Peterborough carried on his side of the controversy with his usual vehemence and in the end got his way. But hardly had he started early in January when Lichtenstein ordered him to return a Catalan regiment assigned to him. Peterborough, all aflame once more, threatened to replace it by the English garrison from Lerida, and so was naturally allowed to keep it. When he arrived in Valencia he found some of the coast towns already occupied by two of Charles's partisan leaders, but also a strong force under Las Torres, superior to anything Peterborough could muster, on the way to recover them. Nevertheless by the rapidity of his marches, his reckless courage and his magnificent bluff he outwitted it at every point. A certain Captain Jones with a few Miquelets was holding a town against 7,000 Spaniards; Peterborough arranged that a letter conveying false information to Jones should be intercepted by the Spaniards and in a genuine message told Jones to expect him, 'to answer with an English halloo' when he saw him, and then take to the hills—'it is no matter what becomes of the town; leave it to your mistresses'—and join forces with him—a scheme whereby Las Torres was put to precipitate flight. On another occasion he boldly rode up alone to the gates of an enemy town and obtained its surrender by threatening to bombard it with guns he did not possess. His knowledge of the enemy movements seemed almost miraculous to those who did not know that he obtained it chiefly from the frail beauties he courted so unblushingly and from the monks whom he had the art to conciliate. He was helped also, more than he was inclined to admit, by the bands of Charles's irregular supporters whom he had already found in the province and whose numbers increased with success. Within a few months the city of Valencia, most of the coast towns and many inland had submitted and were only too pleased to be governed by the jovial winner of hearts that was Peterborough. He had not, however, finished his work of establishing garrisons in the main strongholds before he was rudely interrupted by the danger to Barcelona.

Peterborough, of course, had an ingenious scheme for dealing with the difficulty. Charles was to abandon Barcelona while there was yet time, for it would never do for him to be captured, take ship at Denia for Portugal and there join Galway in what was to be the victorious march to Madrid. Meanwhile Peterborough himself was to be left in command of Catalonia and Valencia and occupy the enemy so as to prevent their interfering with Galway's progress. But Charles's good subjects in Barcelona would not hear of his leaving the city; and he threw himself gallantly into the work of organizing the defences. An auxiliary force of 5,000 citizens was raised, the ramparts were strengthened, and Cifuentes with his Miquelets took up a position outside the city and in the rear of Tessé's army, to cut off the French stragglers and make it impossible for them to draw supplies from the country. At the same time Charles and Lichtenstein sent urgent appeals to Leake to make all haste to relieve the threatened city. For Tessé, with the fleet as his base, was independent of extraneous supplies, and by the end of April had recovered Monjuich and made several breaches in the city walls. Even Peterborough could not entirely ignore the danger and had to tear himself away from Valencia and bring reinforcements to Cifuentes. All the same he kept on sending orders to Leake and Stanhope, contradictory to Charles's, to delay bringing forward the fleet to Barcelona until they had landed the troops from England in Valencia, and, lest Leake should ignore his orders and come straight on to Barcelona, instructed Stanhope to warn him of the fleet's approach by a blank piece of paper cut to a special pattern. But more than a month passed and May had begun without a sign of the fleet; and the state of Barcelona seemed desperate. Charles wrote to Stanhope that with the breaches in the walls an assault might at any moment prove fatal and to Leake urging him not to wait to disembark troops in Valencia, 'as some other persons may pretend to direct you', lest the fleet should arrive only to find his city of Barcelona captured and himself a prisoner.

Difficulties in collecting stray units of his fleet and then persistent east winds had kept Leake at Gibraltar till 24 April,

when he sailed for Barcelona with Stanhope and his reinforcements, rightly regarding Charles's summons as more
urgent than Peterborough's. Even so he hove to for a couple
of days off Altea to await further reinforcements. Reports
had magnified Toulouse's fleet of twenty-seven to forty ships
of the line and with his own greatly inferior force he dared
not risk an engagement, failure in which would not only
ensure the fall of Barcelona but leave the French complete
masters of the Mediterranean. However, when Byng arrived
with a squadron of thirteen ships from England and a convoy
of six more bringing more troops from Ireland, all haste was
made for Barcelona. Meanwhile Peterborough had received
Stanhope's blank paper cut to pattern, whereupon, slipping
away from Cifuentes's camp with some 2,000 men, he went
off to Sitges, a fishing village five leagues west of Barcelona,
to lie in wait for the fleet. For two successive nights he rowed
about the open sea in a tiny felucca, and on sighting it
got aboard Leake's flagship, the *Prince George*, displayed his
commission as admiral and hoisted his flag at the main,
though leaving Leake's flag also flying. But, after ordering
the embarkation of his 2,000 men from open boats, he left
Leake to conduct operations. He was disappointed, however,
in his hope of sending Toulouse's fleet to the bottom by
a fleet flying his flag, for on the day before he and Leake
appeared, on May 8, Toulouse had hurriedly left for Toulon.
Four days later Tessé, thus bereft of his source of supplies,
broke up his camp, left his sick to Peterborough's care and
marched away, harassed in his retreat by the Miquelets.
To add an element of terror to his precipitate flight, 'this
morning a little after nine', writes Stanhope, 'when their
rearguard was about a random Cannon shott distant from
ye Town there happened a very great Eclipse of ye sun which
our side were extremely pleased with, and have taken it as
a happy Omen threatening ruin to him who takes ye Sun
for his Device'.[1]

It was not merely 'the superstitious' at Barcelona, as
Stanhope's secretary Horatio Walpole wrote, who 'portended
the eternal setting of the Bourbon sun' during this year.
Ten days after Tessé's retreat Ramillies was fought and won,

---

[1] To Hedges, 12 May 1706, *Chevening MSS*. H. Walpole's letter in the next
paragraph is in *H. MSS., Hare*, 211. For Peterborough and Leake, see *Leake's
Life*. Stebbing and Parnell correct Mahon's account, too favourable to Peterborough. The dates given in the text are N.S.

Brabant was at Marlborough's feet, and the road, had the Dutch been only willing, might have been taken to Paris itself. By the end of the year Eugene had relieved Turin and driven the French out of Italy. Leake, by the hasty flight of the Toulon fleet, was left master of the Mediterranean and by the end of September had captured Iviza and Majorca besides Alicante and Cartagena, whereby Charles became master of the whole eastern coast-line of Spain; and he had opened communications with Italy. Philip V, instead of capturing his rival, as he had hoped, had to retire once more to France; and Louis XIV, reduced by all these disasters to sue for peace, wrote to his grandson in November deploring that it might be necessary for him to agree to a partition of the Spanish dominions.[1]

In Spain, unfortunately, these fair prospects were soon clouded, largely owing to Peterborough's unaccommodating methods and to hesitations at Charles III's court. At a council of war held a week after the relief of Barcelona it was resolved that Charles should as soon as possible go to his capital Madrid by way of Valencia. Galway with an English, Dutch and Portuguese army of some 20,000 was already approaching it from the Portuguese border; Peterborough was sent back to Valencia to prepare the way for Charles's march on Madrid from the east, nothing loth to quit Charles's court, nor unmindful of the amiable distractions awaiting him in the south. For, as he sent word to Halifax by another hand, being

'so stung with Musquitoes that I am not able to writte with my own, . . . there cannot be worse company than a beggarly German and a proud Spaniard . . . and were it not for the revenge we seek in the disagreeable men with the agreeable ladies, our condition were intollerable, black eyes and wit in the wives being what alone can make us endure the husbands; the Fair sex especially never failing to put in practise the making use of all opportunities in pleasures, the reverse of what our statesmen practise in business.'[2]

Meanwhile Stanhope, as envoy, was left at head-quarters to uphold English, and especially Peterborough's, interests. Still high in Charles's favour, he was offered the rank of major-general in the Spanish army, but wisely refused it and shortly afterwards was given the same

[1] Quoted in Vast, *Les Grands Traités de Louis XIV*, iii. 34.
[2] Kemble, 445.

brevet-rank in his own army.[1] While waiting for the word from Peterborough, Charles gave himself more elbow-room by again clearing the enemy out of Catalonia and invading the neighbouring province of Aragon. Noyelles, a naturalized Dutchman who had been sent for to command Charles's Spanish troops and had recently come out with Stanhope, even captured Saragossa the capital of Aragon, while Stanhope himself was sent to secure Gerona, that 'barrier and key of the country'. By June Charles was ready to start, according to plan, by Valencia, when Peterborough began to make difficulties, declaring that he had not enough money for the journey and that Charles must wait till he had distributed his troops in garrisons. Meanwhile Noyelles suggested an alternative but longer route to Madrid through Saragossa, whose citizens were said to be most anxious to welcome the King. Charles, no doubt only too glad of an excuse to be quit of the egotistical and impracticable Peterborough, decided for Noyelles's plan at a council of war, in which Stanhope found himself in a minority against Lichtenstein, Uhlfeldt and Cifuentes. Stanhope indeed, wrote young Methuen from Barcelona to his father in Lisbon, 'is extremely uneasy between the Court and my Lord Peterborough, and will have difficulty enough to manage it so as not to disoblige both'.[2] But in this instance he loyally supported the views of his chief in opposition to the Austrians and Noyelles, all the more since he had conceived a strong prejudice against them, and even ventured on uncourtly remonstrances to Charles himself. Provoked by the punctilios and ceremonies that delayed Charles's advance first from Barcelona and then from Saragossa, when 'nothing was wanting to the entire possession of Spain but that the King should get into his coach and drive to the capital, . . . the King said it was not for his Catholic honour to go without his retinue', he tartly rejoined that 'King William went post in a hackney coach with a few dragoons to London, or else he had lost the Crown'. 'However', concludes the account, 'folly prevailed.'[3]

Galway arrived in Madrid at the end of June, his army much diminished in strength by the long march, and soon

[1] R.O., S.P. 94/76. Stanhope to Hedges, 9 May 1706.
[2] 26 May 1706, Russell, ii. 306.
[3] H. MSS., Blenheim, 18. This story is questioned by Leadam, p. 90, note; but it is told in slightly different language by several independent authorities, e.g. Coxe, Memoirs of Lord Walpole, i. 9; Cunningham, ii. 6.

found himself in difficulties. Berwick was in the neighbour-hood with a reconstituted army as strong as Galway's, the population of Castile favoured Philip, and Peterborough, the nearest allied commander, made no move to support him. Finding Madrid untenable he moved to a stronger position at Guadalajara about fifty miles north-east, where Charles coming from Saragossa met him early in August. Then too at last Peterborough appeared, having ridden through Valencia with only 400 dragoons. Had he, instead of writing innumerable letters to Stanhope with shrill complaints of Charles's 'most fatal resolution' against the Valencia route, stretched a hand to Galway, which he might have done in June as easily as he could in August, Galway would not have had to abandon the capital. Nor were the troubles over when the three forces at last met at Guadalajara: for, as Stanhope had foretold to Godolphin, four generals there met, each with claim to command the allied army, das Minas, Galway's Portuguese colleague, Noyelles at the head of Charles's Spanish troops, Galway and Peterborough. Galway, though senior, and far the ablest, to save dispute, at once offered to serve under Peterborough; but the latter was by this time tired of Spain and suddenly proposed that he should go off to Italy, under some vague authority given him by the Secretary of State, and there raise some money for Charles. This proposal was welcomed with enthusiasm by the council of war, for by his egotism, his querulousness and his inability to work with others Peterborough had made himself impossible. 'It was', wrote Stanhope in his report to the ministry, 'judged by everybody to be for the service that his Lordship should leave the army, and, according to the orders his Lordship said he had, go on board the fleet and endeavour to secure for it a port . . . to winter in, and get money from Italy'.[1] He was back in January 1707 with nothing to show for his journey but some money obtained at exorbitant rates on the credit of the English Treasury, which he was not authorized to give. But he had enjoyed a delightful holiday, to which, as usual, the fair sex had contributed its part. 'I intend', he writes to Stanhope, 'to mortify you with the account of our happy days in Italy,—of the nights we will say nothing.'

He also came back with an entirely changed view as to the operations in Spain. During his absence Galway and

[1] H. MSS., Blenheim, 16.

Charles III, though not seriously molested by Berwick, had been obliged to take up winter quarters in Valencia: and two councils of war were held in January and February to decide on plans for the next campaign, whether to make a new attempt on Castile or simply to remain on the defensive in Valencia and Catalonia. Peterborough, hitherto the fiery advocate of widespread operations and an immediate advance on the capital, was now all for caution. In Italy he had apparently heard talk of the projected attack on Toulon by sea and land, and urged that as all the troops that could be spared would have to go on that service, the allied forces in Spain would be too weak to hold Catalonia and Valencia and also to occupy Castile. On the other hand, Galway was already expecting further reinforcements from England under Lord Rivers and was all for a forward policy. His strongest supporter was Stanhope, who argued that such a pusillanimous policy as Peterborough's would damp the ardour of all Charles's supporters in Aragon and the coast provinces, and admitted to the Secretary of State that he had 'perhaps been guilty of a fault in supporting my opinion, which is the same with my Lord Galway's, too warmly, . . . having said that her majesty did not spend such vast sums and did not send such a number of forces, to garrison towns in Catalonia and Valencia, but to make King Charles master of the Spanish monarchy.' This view was endorsed by the majority of the council and was subsequently approved by Sunderland. But, as events proved, this paradoxical instance of caution in Peterborough was more justified than Stanhope's rasher plan, which took too little account of the blight with which the jealousies and divided counsels at Charles's head-quarters seemed to infect every adventurous scheme of the allies.[1]

This was Peterborough's last contribution to the war in Spain, the ministry at home having already decided on his recall. Though at first his presumed part in the relief of Barcelona had been exalted almost to the level of Marlborough's victory at Ramillies, soon rumours, then more definite information, began to convince Marlborough and Godolphin that he was serving no good purpose to the allies in Spain. He had quarrelled not only with Charles and his German advisers but with Spaniards like the gallant Cifuentes, with Galway and most of his own staff, with Leake and

---

[1] Peterborough's arguments are set forth in Lamberty, iv. 572, Stanhope's in his letters to Hedges quoted in Mahon, *Succession*, Appendix.

the sailors whom he had insulted by the flag incident; and he ran down the Catalans, Charles's keenest supporters in Spain, just to raise his own credit and that of his beloved Valencians. Some of his ideas may have been good, but he flitted about from one to the other so capriciously that he never pursued one to the end.[1] Stanhope's secretary, Horatio Walpole, sent to England with dispatches in October, had taken with him a letter from Charles to Queen Anne making serious complaints about Peterborough, and Stanhope himself had felt bound, as the Queen's envoy, to report on the misunderstanding between his military chief and the King. At first, to save his face, hints, progressively broader, were given to him that he would do well to return to England of his own accord. Finally, as these proved ineffective, he was formally recalled at the end of February.

Unabashed by his disgrace, he attributed it entirely to the jealousy of those he had served, a view wittily expressed by his friend Voltaire:

'Milord Peterborough fut perdu dans l'esprit de la reine Anne et dans celui de l'archiduc, pour leur avoir donné Barcelone. Les courtisans lui reprochèrent d'avoir pris cette ville contre toutes les règles, avec une armée moins forte que la garnison. L'archiduc en fut d'abord très-piqué, et l'ami Freind fut obligé d'imprimer l'apologie du général.'[2]

Besides commissioning Freind to blow his trumpet, he himself made his return journey a triumphal progress through Italy, Germany and Holland, visiting the crowned heads and chief ministers in every country he passed through and giving himself an importance not everywhere accorded to him. Among others he forced himself on Charles XII at Altranstadt, and reported to Stanhope that 'the King of Sweden gives more fears by his silence than any other monarch gave by his threats . . . all we know is he has 50,000 men mad enough to obey with pleasure all he can command'. Marlborough does not appear to have found Charles XII so silent at the same place; and the Duke's own unfailing courtesy was put to a rude test by long visits to his headquarters from Peterborough in his most talkative mood. To Stanhope the Earl's breezy letters still for a short time continued, but though their paths crossed more than once

---

[1] See letter of P. Methuen to his father quoted in Russell, ii. 306.
[2] Voltaire, *Histoire de Jenni*. Freind's *Account* was prepared to meet charges brought later against Peterborough in the House of Lords.

afterwards, Peterborough never quite forgave him for his criticisms and his opposition during his last days in Spain. Horatio Walpole, writing to his brother Robert shortly after Peterborough's departure, says that 'though his lordship seems to have a tolerable good understanding with Mr. Stanhope, I find he is not very much pleased with him'.[1] Peterborough himself told Marlborough, after the news of Galway's defeat at Almanza, that 'Mr. Stanhope's politics have proved very fatal, having produced our misfortunes and prevented the greatest successes'; and three years later, according to Swift, he had the satisfaction of predicting at Harley's house that Stanhope would lose Spain before Christmas. All the same, few people, except perhaps the poets, who did not clash with Peterborough, could have boasted that they remained so long on good terms with him as Stanhope. While it lasted, the association, so full of surprises, must have been stimulating to one who had enough vehemence and impetuosity of his own to pardon an excess of these qualities in the vivacious knight-errant.[2]

[1] *Chevening MSS.*
[2] For this chapter Mahon's *Succession* and the *Chevening MSS.* are still useful. Other specific references are given in previous footnotes.

CHAPTER III

MINORCA

§ 1

IN 1707, the year of Peterborough's departure, the allies' cause in Spain was brought almost to its lowest ebb; so Stanhope had need of all his tact and patience to uphold his country's interests. His position was not easy. Left now as the sole representative of Queen Anne at the court of Charles III, his comparatively junior rank in the army gave him little power of influencing military policy, without which the best diplomacy was of small avail. One of his tasks was to compose the differences between the various sections of the allied forces, Imperialists, English, Dutch, Portuguese and native Spaniards, a motley crew almost as disunited as the host of Italians, Germans, Spaniards and 'religionaries' that he found at Turin in 1691; another was to persuade Charles III and his camarilla to adopt vigorous measures. But the forces against him were too strong, partly because England, on whom Marlborough claimed the first call for troops in Flanders, had not yet put her back into the Spanish struggle. The English levies for Spain, small as they were, were never even up to the strength sanctioned by Parliament and, owing to Peterborough's lax methods, were ill disciplined. Thus in 1706 it was reported that 'the generals were so indulgent to the colonels, captains, and other military men as to dispense with their absence from service; for no other reason that I know of, but only to keep them out of harm's way, and to give them the opportunity to show themselves more frequently in taverns and playhouses at London.'[1]

The haphazard methods of dealing with the peninsular war at this stage are illustrated by the incident of Lord Rivers. In the autumn of 1706 the English ministry dispatched some 45,000 troops under Rivers to support a rising in the Charente, but, as the expedition started too late to serve any good purpose, sent them on to Lisbon with instructions to make another attempt on Cadiz. This scheme also fell through, so Rivers was then ordered to Valencia to reinforce Galway. On arriving, Rivers discovered that he was the senior general in Spain and claimed to take over

[1] Cunningham, ii. 5.

Galway's command. The dispute between the two generals had been going on for some time when Stanhope came in as peacemaker, persuading Rivers to abandon his claims and return to England, a happy solution owing as much, says his secretary, H. Walpole, to Stanhope's 'mediation as to the discretion and prudence of both these lords'. So tactful indeed had Stanhope been that Rivers wrote afterwards assuring him of his 'singular esteem . . . and particular confidence'.[1]

In his dealings with Charles and his camarilla Stanhope was less successful. Charles himself, though capable, as at Barcelona, of acts of courage and decision, was normally a slave to deadening forms and punctilios and easily swayed by his favourite counsellors. Lichtenstein, who had given much trouble to Peterborough, in 1707 gave place to Sinzendorf, described by Stanhope as having 'just sense enough to have been able to supplant Lichtenstein'; but Noyelles, appointed by Charles to command his Spanish levies and treated as 'his sole minister', gave most trouble. He carried caution to excess and was chiefly preoccupied with the desire to have a separate command for himself. His main conception of strategy was, reports Stanhope, 'to disperse the poor remainders [of troops] we have left up and down in holes, where they must be lost as soon as the enemy think fit to show themselves'. Immediately after the councils held at Valencia at which, against Peterborough's advice, another advance on Madrid was decided upon, Noyelles, far from concentrating all available troops under Galway, persuaded Charles to drain Galway's army of some of its best units and go off with them to Catalonia, instead of taking his place at the head of the army that was to march to his capital. Having established themselves in safety, these advisers of Charles, if Peterborough is to be trusted, 'lost an Empire to their Prince by carrying him up and downe, selling offices and picking up little summs of money in exchange for Peru and Mexico'.[2] Stanhope himself, bound as envoy to attend Charles, however remote he might be from active operations, complained that 'the lethargy and hopelessness of his court is beyond expression, they have not in three weeks' time made one step to help themselves', and

---

[1] *H. MSS., Bath*, i. 114, 118, 123, 132, 164–7; and *Chevening MSS.*, H. Walpole to Spencer, Valencia, 19 Mar. 1707 (N.S.).
[2] To Wassenaer, 25 Aug. 1706 (N.S.) in Kemble, 452.

implored Marlborough and Godolphin to recall him from a post 'where I have the mortification to see a sure game thrown away without doing any good', a request which he repeated, 'as very much to the Queen's service, specially if Count Noyelles is to continue here, for though it has not been my good fortune to agree with him, yet I must be of opinion that if he is to stay here it is absolutely necessary that both her Majesty's general and ministers be such as may live well with him, which I despair of doing'.[1]

This last letter was written three months after the decisive battle of Almanza, lost to the allies chiefly owing to the mistaken policy deplored by Stanhope. Had it not been for Charles's hesitating attitude and the dispersal of troops advised by Noyelles, Galway would have had little difficulty in reaching Madrid from Valencia and of establishing himself there early in the spring. For Rivers's reinforcements had arrived, and Berwick, almost the only one of Philip's commanders in the field, was in inferior force. But by April, when Galway was at last able to advance across the border of Valencia, the positions were reversed. Galway could muster only 15,000 troops, half of them indifferent Portuguese regiments, while Berwick was ready for him in a prepared position at Almanza with 25,000 good troops. On Easter Sunday, 24 April 1707, it was sung of Galway's troops,

> Full twenty miles we marched that day,
> Without one drop of water,
> Till we poor souls were almost spent
> Before the bloody slaughter.[2]

On the Easter Monday Galway rashly launched his exhausted troops against Berwick, and, in spite of gallant fighting against odds by English and Dutch regiments, sustained a crushing defeat and the loss of half his army. In his report to Marlborough Stanhope estimated that in the English contingent alone only 500 men out of 43 battalions and 3,500 horse out of 51 squadrons engaged escaped death or capture.[3]

On the day following this defeat the Duke of Orleans, Stanhope's former acquaintance in Paris, took over the command of Berwick's army and for the rest of the year pursued the advantage with unrelenting energy. In May the province

---

[1] Letters to Marlborough in *Marlborough*, iii, and *Chevening MSS.*
[2] From *The Battle of Almanza*—a ballad printed in *A Pedlar's Pack* (W. H. Logan), 1869.
[3] 3 May 1707 (*Chevening MSS.*).

of Valencia, except for the ports of Denia and Alicante, was recovered for Philip V. Then advancing north the French captured Saragossa and drove Charles's garrisons out of the rest of Aragon, while Orleans himself invaded Catalonia. Stanhope obtained a long-coveted release from attendance at court on appointment to the command of the English troops covering Tortosa and Tarragona, strong fortresses to the south of the province; but in October Orleans captured Lerida, on the Segre near the western border of the province, a city which had once successfully resisted capture by the great Condé himself. According to Stanhope this loss was mainly due to the incompetence of Noyelles, who 'is turning all wee doe into Ridicule att Barcelona and hindred the King for above a fortnight from consenting to have either Troops or Miquelets assembled, affirming that Lerida would not be besieged till the verry day the news came that the trenches were opened.'[1] By the end of the year Charles and his army were once more driven almost up to the walls of Barcelona, and Orleans might have regained the whole province had Louis not been obliged to recall some of his troops to resist the advance on Toulon.

Almanza, followed as it was by Orleans's speedy recovery of Valencia and Aragon and his renewed invasion of Catalonia, was really the decisive battle of this peninsular war. It is true that in the negotiations of 1709 and 1710 Louis XIV, reduced to extremity by Marlborough's victories in Flanders, was willing to abandon his grandson's claims to the entire Spanish monarchy; but by that time Spain herself was not willing to give up Philip. This was not the case before Almanza. Philip had not then made himself popular in Spain, where the dominating influence of the French ideas and ministers he introduced was widely resented. Had Charles gained possession of the capital, until Almanza well within his grasp, and had he followed this up by a reasonably conciliatory system of government, the balance might well have turned in his favour. But Almanza secured Philip's position at the most favourable moment for himself. Much to the joy of his supporters, an heir had just been born to him on Spanish soil; he had already shown his determination on no consideration to abandon his Spanish subjects, and was beginning to wean himself from French tutelage. Thenceforward the great majority of the Spanish population made

[1] To Marlborough, 24 Oct. 1707 (*Chevening MSS.*).

it evident that, whatever the French King or the allied Powers might determine, they had no intention of letting Philip go. Three years later, it is true, the allies once more were victorious and once more occupied Castile and Madrid; but it was then too late. The population of that central province, which contained the real core of the Spanish nation, was by that time almost to a man against them. To succeed the allies would then have had to conquer the country not only from the French but from the Spaniards themselves.

But though Charles's prospects in Spain were overclouded, Marlborough's Mediterranean policy for England had not materially suffered. The attack on Toulon in the summer of 1707 had, it is true, miscarried; but the French fleet had not been able to leave Toulon and the English were masters of the sea, while even the abortive attack on that port had obliged Louis to withdraw troops from Spain. Moreover, Stanhope, however impotent on the military side, had obtained a most favourable commercial treaty for his country. His Instructions of January and February 1706 to obtain such advantageous terms from Charles as 'perhaps at another time cannot so well be insisted upon' had been supplemented in the following November by an order if possible to secure the lucrative Assiento or contract to supply slaves to the Spanish West Indies.[1] Charles was no more anxious than previous Spanish kings or his present rival to injure Spain, as was held by contemporary economists, by large concessions to English traders; but, especially after Almanza, found it difficult to refuse them to a nation on whose gold and troops he was more than ever dependent. Even so Stanhope found it difficult to exact such terms as he was instructed to demand, and might have failed had he not had recourse to such *douceurs* to influential courtiers as were common at the time but are reprobated in modern usage. His chief instruments were the Count and Countess Oropeza, especially the latter, 'a Lady of great wit, whose husband was one of the chief grandees of Spain, but who having abandonned all his great employments and vast estate, to follow King Charles's fortune, was reduced to extreme indigence; and therefore was the more liable to be managed by a Lady, for whom Mr. Stanhope had obtained a considerable present from the Queen'.[2] The main provisions of this treaty signed July 1707

[1] R.O., *S.P.* 94/76.
[2] Tindal, iv. 12. Stanhope gave a perfectly straightforward account of

not only renewed the favourable treaty of commerce of 1667
between the two nations, but gave English traders customs
and import privileges hardly inferior to those of the Spaniards
themselves, and, by a secret clause, allowed them to send ten
ships annually to trade with the hitherto closed West Indies
until an Anglo-Spanish trading company could be formed
after the war; it was also stipulated that the French were to
be permanently excluded from such privileges.

According to Stanhope, in his account to Marlborough,
the treaty was not quite so one-sided as might appear, since
Charles was anxious to secure the protection of the English
fleet for his own traders against France by enlisting the self-
interest of the English traders; in fact, Stanhope judged that
at the final peace Charles would insist on France being
entirely excluded from the West Indian trade.[1] Nevertheless,
the King had qualms about ratifying it, for fear of its effect
on Spanish opinion, and delayed doing so for six months.
The English ministry were naturally jubilant, for the cynical
reason given by Sunderland to Stanhope that 'it is very
fortunate to have this matter concluded whilst they are still
in adversity, for I am afraid their gratitude would hardly
effect it'. Our Dutch allies, however, were far from pleased
when they heard of it through the good offices of the French,
who captured a copy of the treaty sent over in a felucca to
Genoa and at once published it. It was justly regarded by
them as a breach of the Grand Alliance, which stipulated
that no ally should attempt to secure for itself special advantages; it also touched them in their tenderest spot, trade
interest. Later, with the Treaty of Utrecht and the recognition of Philip as King of Spain, the treaty naturally fell to
the ground. Being more favourable, however, to England
than the commercial treaty afterwards negotiated by the
Tory ministry, its parent, Stanhope, thought it worth publishing in March 1714 as a Whig tract to show up by comparison the delinquencies of the other side. But it is hardly
a transaction of which either Stanhope himself, or still less
the ministry who instructed him, have any reason to be proud.[2]

this transaction in his *Answer to the Report of the Commissioners into Spain*, 1714,
quoting orders from Godolphin and Sunderland to pay £1,000 to the Countess
and 500 pistoles to the Count for their help in forwarding the treaty (see
below, ch. v, p. 135).

[1] *Marlborough*, iii. 354, Stanhope to Marlborough, 6 June 1707.

[2] The treaty is printed in Lamberty, iv. 592. See also Klopp, v. 59; Landau,
445–7; Mahon, *Anne*, ii. 55, &c. Boyer, ix. 456, records its appearance as a
political tract in 1714.

One diplomatic service of a more private nature Stanhope
had also been able to render to his friend and patron Marlborough. After Ramillies, which made the allies masters of
Brabant and Flanders, the government of these two provinces
came up for decision. The Dutch were anxious to keep control of them to ensure that the Barrier of fortresses deemed
necessary for their security should be delivered to them; for
the same reason the Emperor and Charles III were against
Dutch control. Accordingly in June 1706 the Emperor issued
a patent appointing Marlborough governor of the Low
Countries, a patent which required confirmation by his
brother Charles III, in whose name they had been conquered. Stanhope, as soon as the news of Ramillies came,
not doubting that Charles 'would readily, when putt in mind
of it, have made the small compliment of offering to your
Grace the government of What your Arms have already putt
in y^r power', hinted to him that in his 'private opinion such
a thing would probably be acceptable to her My^{ty} and the
States Generall and would greatly conduce to the publick
service while the War lasted'. At first Charles 'seemed much
to relish' what appears to have been Stanhope's spontaneous
suggestion; but later Zinzerling began to raise difficulties
about religion. 'I have been upon Thorns', Stanhope concludes his letter to the Duke, 'in giving your Grace this
account but since I have playd the fool, and been so much
mistaken as to think these people capable of making a
reasonable step I think the best thing I can doe is to confess
my fault to yr Grace presuming upon yr goodness to forgive
it.' Charles indeed was no more anxious for Marlborough
than for the Dutch to have the government, wishing to keep
the control in his own hands, but nevertheless in October
grudgingly sent him the nomination accompanied by a broad
hint that he should not accept it. Marlborough, though
naturally not averse to holding a post reputed to be worth
£60,000 a year, on becoming aware that the Dutch would
strongly resent his accepting it, refused; 'for', said he to
Godolphin, 'the advantage and honour I might have by this
Commission is very insignificant, in comparison to the fatal
consequences that might be, if it should cause a jealousy
between the two nations'. To Stanhope he wrote in December that 'the unreasonable jealousies in Holland will not
permit me to exert that authority with which His Majesty
[Charles III] is pleased to invest me, till the business of the

Barrier is settled, in which I find no less difficulty'. None the less he expressed warm thanks to Stanhope for his zealous service on his behalf.[1]

In December 1707 Stanhope went home to report on the position in Spain and to make plans for the future. He himself was one of the few on the allied side who had not hitherto injured his reputation in Spain. Peterborough, for all his flashy success in Valencia, had made himself impossible by his impracticable and quarrelsome nature; Galway, though a gallant soldier, had Almanza to his discredit; Noyelles and the Portuguese das Minas had proved themselves contemptible as soldiers. Stanhope had not indeed yet been tested in high command, but he had performed his unpleasant duties as envoy with credit and, above all, in spite of frequent opposition to the views of Charles and his court, without arousing undue animosity.

> 'I may venture to say to *you*', he wrote with pardonable pride to his father in December 1706, 'that I can do more with this King than I believe any stranger will in haste. When he writ against my Lord Peterborough, he would have asked the command of his troops for me, if I had not prevented it. My having maintained an interest with him is the more extraordinary, because it has always been my duty to oppose what he has been inclined to . . . and if any measures of decent management have been kept, I may say it is, in a great measure, owing to me.'[2]

The events of the disastrous year 1707 and his constant clashes with Charles's favourite Noyelles had not impaired this confidence. On the contrary, he took with him to London an ambitious plan concerted with Charles for the final reduction of Spain in the following year.

But one of Stanhope's first duties on arriving in London was to settle the affairs of his family. For in the previous September the father, to whom, more than to any one else throughout his life, he revealed his secret thoughts and aspirations, and on whose loving counsel he had so long depended, had died, worn out by long service to the public. To James, as the eldest son, fell the duty of distributing the

---

[1] The letters to and from Stanhope are quoted from the *Chevening MSS.*, that to Godolphin from Coxe, *Marlborough*, i. 439. In 1708 and 1709 Marlborough refused renewed offers of the post, for the same patriotic reason, as 'inconsistent with the service of the public'; in 1710, when his position at home was becoming shaky, he asked for it, but Charles III told him it was then too late. An excellent account of this incident is given by Geikie and Montgomery, part i, chs. 1 and 2, and Appendix A.

[2] Mahon, *Succession*, Appendix.

small estate left by Alexander and providing for his mother.
After deducting the dowry of his sister Mary, lately married to
Charles Fane,[1] the amount available for his mother, the two
surviving brothers, Philip and Edward, and himself was little
over £10,000, and of this amount some £6,000 had still
to be recovered from the Treasury for back-pay owing to
Alexander. To his two brothers James assigned the certain
£4,000, for himself he took over the prospect of obtaining
payment of the £6,875 13s. 10d. owing by the Treasury, with
the obligation of providing an annuity of £200 for his
mother, a not ungenerous distribution in an age when an
eldest son usually obtained a much larger share of his father's
fortune.[2]

After his father's death unfortunately all intimate letters
from James come to an abrupt end. Any such to his brothers
and sister and later to his wife, if they ever existed, have
disappeared. Even from early days he had acquired the
reputation of being a bad correspondent. His cousin, Lord
Stanhope of Shelford, father of the letter-writer, writes to
him in 1700 that 'writing is so uneasy to you, that I am very
unwilling to put upon you an exercise that is so disagreeable
to you . . . I know no man so lazy in writing and so active in
Everything else for a friend as yourself'; and two years later
admits that 'considering what a supine and lasey temper you
are of, and how averse to writing (except when you launch
out upon Politicks) I ought not to take it ill or be surprised
that I have not yet heard [from you].'[3] With his mother he
certainly was a bad correspondent, for more than once in
the next two years she complains in some such strain as of
'hearing so seldom from a son who has deserved so well
of his country which consequently must make you valued by
all your friends, but most particularly by your affectionate
Mother'. Certainly this silence on his part does not mean that
he was not loved and loving. He was obviously beloved by
his brothers and his sister Molly; and the family tradition is
that he was lovable at home. But from this date, for the rest
of his life, he was so taken up by public responsibilities that
he may well have grown out of the habit of confiding by
letters even in those nearest to him. Few public men dare,

[1] Created Viscount in 1718.
[2] James's letter to Philip of 2 Mar. 1707/8 explaining this arrangement, and
the deed of the executors, of whom he was not one, dated six days later, assigning
the father's back pay to him are both in *Chevening MSS*.
[3] *Chevening MSS*.

like Disraeli, to be self-revealing, except perhaps at the fireside; and even with Disraeli how much of his self-revelation was a pose?

§ 2

In public affairs Stanhope found the party dissensions against which he had protested two years before as violent as ever. In the ministry itself the alliance between Whigs and moderate Tories was at breaking-point. Marlborough and Godolphin had come round to the view of the Whig Junto that the ministry should shed its Tory members, and as a first step had already brought in Sunderland, Marlborough's vehement son-in-law, as Secretary of State; Harley and St. John, on the other hand, were intriguing for the removal of Godolphin. By February 1708 the Tory malcontents were forced to resign, and with the admission of Somers and his friends the ministry became entirely Whig. Robert Walpole, a friend of Stanhope's, supplanted another friend, St. John, as Secretary at War. But the growing dissatisfaction of the public at the course of the war was not pacified by such changes. During the past year Marlborough had had no such successes as Blenheim and Ramillies; the Imperialists had been defeated by Villars at Stolhofen on the Rhine and Germany was once more invaded; the ambitious expedition for the capture of Toulon, whereby the allies were to obtain complete control of the Mediterranean, had been a failure; Hungary was in the hands of insurgents against the Emperor, and Starhemberg, his general, had only just been able to keep them out of the Austrian provinces; the only gleam of success had been the easy capture of Naples by the Imperialists, but even that was at the cost of proper support for the Toulon expedition and the Spanish campaign, the fact being that the Viennese court was quite willing to sacrifice Spain, one of the main objects of the other allies, as long as Spain's Italian provinces could be secured for the Emperor. Forbin even had ventured, while Parliament was sitting, to bring the Pretender with him on his expedition to Scotland in the hope of rousing the Scottish clans; an insult which aroused support for a Bill brought in by Stanhope to abrogate the allegiance of clans to disloyal chiefs.[1]

[1] Tindal, iv. 58; Mahon, *Anne*, ii. 61. This Bill was dropped when the danger passed. It was left to Hardwicke after the '45 to pass the Heritable Jurisdictions Act with the same object.

But the chief criticism brought against the ministry was on their conduct of the war in Spain, now again almost entirely under the sway of the Bourbon Philip. Peterborough, that stormy petrel, had returned from his tour round the courts of Europe, and finding his achievements insufficiently appreciated, threw in another apple of discord by bringing up the subject of his own merits. He handed over his notes and papers to his medical attendant, Dr. Freind, who produced *An Account of the Earl of Peterborough's Conduct in Spain* praising his patron to the top of his bent; and he himself brought up the question of the thanks due to him in the House of Lords. This led to a parliamentary inquiry into his actions, conducted entirely on political lines, the Tories generally favouring the Whig Peterborough, as he had been dismissed by Godolphin and Sunderland, the Whig majority refusing him a vote of thanks.

At any rate it could not be denied that after, if not because of, his recall things had gone worse in Spain. Another point fastened on by the Opposition was that whereas expenditure was lavished on Marlborough's own campaigns in Flanders, an undue parsimony was shown in providing troops for the Peninsula. This reproach Marlborough determined should no longer be justified. But the expense of sending and maintaining a large force of English troops to Spain had by experience proved to be wasteful, almost prohibitive;[1] and it was thought better to rely chiefly on foreign levies raised at English expense with a stiffening of English regiments. Accordingly Parliament agreed to pay half the cost of the Spanish troops raised by Charles, and in April the first of a series of conventions was made with the Emperor for levying, transporting, and paying 4,000 of his troops from Italy at the Queen's expense.[2] Thus, apart from English troops, Parliament made itself responsible in 1708 for 3,000 Imperialist, 1,200 Italian, 1,300 Palatine and 6,000 of Charles's 12,000 Spanish troops in Spain.[3] Then came up the question of unity of command to prevent the constant quarrels of incompetent generals such as Noyelles. The plan elaborated

---

[1] Lord Portmore, Galway's successor as commander in Portugal, complained that each English recruit levied for the Peninsula cost £8 9s., and that barely one-third of those embarked joined their regiment (*Treas. Papers, 1708–14*, 187).

[2] Pribram, i. 246. Similar conventions were made in January 1709, April, October, December 1710, and May 1711 for further levies amounting in all to 7,367 more Imperial troops for Spain (ib. 249–51).

[3] These are the figures quoted in Stanhope's *Answer*.

by Charles and Stanhope and submitted to Marlborough was no less than that the combination of himself and Eugene, that had proved so gloriously successful at Blenheim, should be repeated in Spain. This plan was briefly indicated to Marlborough in a letter from Charles of 8 January 1708: 'Le projet secret de Stanhope consiste en ce que vous (si cela se pourroit) veniez en Espagne avec 25 ou 20 mille hommes, avec lequel vous, entrant d'un côté, et le Prince Eugène et moi de l'autre, vous acheviez d'un coup glorieux cette longue et si sanglante guerre';[1] the main idea being that Eugene and Charles should occupy the centre of Spain while Marlborough landed in the north to stop the advance of any reinforcements coming from France. In the previous year Stanhope had written to Marlborough longing that he were in Spain 'to advise the King not to act against his own interests', and urging him to advance from Italy through Provence and Languedoc into Spain, a march such as was 'possible for him who marched from Holland to ye Danube to save the empire'.[2] But Marlborough was needed in Flanders and within reach of England, and it was hardly expected that he himself would be able to come. But at least Prince Eugene of Savoy was hopefully counted upon. Stanhope, who had recognized his great qualities when serving under him in his prentice days, had long been pressing for his appointment, failing Marlborough's, to the supreme command in Spain; and not only Marlborough but also Queen Anne and the Pensionary of Holland had been urging the Emperor to give his consent. Marlborough had gone so far as to write to Vienna, 'la dernière ressource du Roi [sc. Charles] est dans la présence de M. le Prince de Savoie pour commander l'armée l'année prochaine'.[3] But the Emperor would not hear of it, for political reasons and from fear of a Turkish war. As a substitute he offered Count Guido Starhemberg, a cool, experienced, and gallant commander, but without a spark of Eugene's genius and, like most of the Austrian school of generals, better at defensive than bold offensive warfare. Tindal in fact notes as his chief title to fame that he was 'the best general of the age for the defensive', not exactly the qualification then chiefly needed in Spain.[4] Marlborough was disappointed, but with his

---

[1] Arneth, ii. 460.
[2] *Chevening MSS.*, 22 Feb. and 3 May 1707 (N.S.).
[3] Arneth, ii. 2 sqq.   [4] Tindal, iv. 97.

usual serenity decided to accept the inevitable and to make things as easy as possible for Starhemberg.

Then came the question of who was to command the main English contingent in Catalonia. Galway was obviously too old, so he was left as minister to Portugal[1] and in command of the English detachment there. Stanhope may have been thought too young; he was still barely thirty-five, and he had long been asking for his recall from a post where he thought himself useless. At any rate up to the middle of March Marlborough's intention was to send Rivers, who had claimed to supersede Galway before Almanza, as commander in the field and Worsley as envoy to Charles in place of Stanhope. This did not imply any distrust of Stanhope, for Marlborough was still planning to take him to The Hague to discuss the plan of campaign with Eugene. Then suddenly he changed his mind. At the end of March it was decided that Stanhope should not only resume his post as envoy but also take command of the English troops in the Peninsula. We do not know the exact reasons for this change of plan; but obviously Stanhope had the advantage of being thoroughly conversant with the conditions in Spain. Moreover, he showed the Marlborough spirit in the determination he expressed 'to get out of Catalonia and enlarge our bounds' and was quite as enthusiastic as his chief on the cherished scheme of obtaining a permanent base for the fleet in the Mediterranean.[2] In his new post he no longer had as secretary Robert Walpole's well-informed, albeit prosy, brother Horatio, but took with him as commissary as well as secretary, James Craggs the younger, a cheery, capable, and acute man of affairs, who for the rest of their joint lives was closely connected with Stanhope's political fortunes.[3]

On 28 March 1708 (o.s.) Stanhope received his Instructions as Commander-in-Chief and Envoy Extraordinary to Spain, and on 9 April sailed from Margate with Marlborough for Holland. At The Hague the two English generals conferred with Heinsius and Eugene on the plans for the ensuing campaigns on all fields, the main scheme against France

[1] His credentials as minister are dated November 1707.
[2] See *Marlborough*, iii. 685 sqq.; Luttrell, ii. 251, 283; Mahon, *Succession*, 245 sqq.; Stanhope, *Answer*.
[3] Craggs received the rank of Resident at Charles III's court in September 1708, as a reward for his services as secretary to Stanhope and also as secretary of legation. H. Walpole seems to have been merely private secretary to Stanhope.

being a combined offensive from the Rhine, the Moselle and Flanders, while in Spain Stanhope was to 'enlarge the bounds' and co-operate with the fleet for Marlborough's project of a Mediterranean base. In the course of these conferences Eugene took aside his young English friend to give him hints on how to govern himself in relation to his new chief Starhemberg. He told Stanhope that Starhemberg knew as much about war as he did himself, and that if he were left alone and got what he wanted he would do the business. Above all, Starhemberg should not be worried with councils, which prevented the secrecy so necessary in war. 'J'ai aussi eu des troupes auxiliares sous moi en Italie', Eugene continued, 'et jamais personne s'avisa de me demander ce que je ferai, et la dernière campagne que l'on marcha à Turin, je les fis marcher un jour après l'autre sans qu'elles sussent ce qu'on allait faire, et lorsque cela vint au dernier jour on les fit combattre sans que peut-être elles s'y attendissent.' Stanhope thereupon raised the 'ridiculous objection', as it seemed to Count Gallas, who reported this interview to Starhemberg, 'que les sujets de ces deux puissances [English and Dutch] se ressentent partout de leur liberté'; to which Eugene retorted, 'Voila qui va bien, mais je vous dis encore que ce n'est pas la manière de pouvoir faire quelque chose de bon, et espérer les moindres progrès.'[1] But this was not the English way. Stanhope thought more of his national 'liberté' than of even Eugene's advice, and certainly never consented to follow Starhemberg blindly.

After these Hague conferences Stanhope travelled post-haste by Düsseldorf and Innsbruck to Milan, the Imperial head-quarters in Italy, visited Victor Amedeus and Chetwynd, the English envoy at Turin, and then went to Genoa, to raise money to pay levies for the Imperial troops and hasten their departure for Spain. By dint of urgent letters to Marlborough and Eugene and with the help of Victor Amedeus and Chetwynd, he stirred up the sluggish Imperialists, beat down the exorbitant claims of Italian money-lenders and, by his own fiery energy, hastened arrangements for embarking the troops. Then, chartering 'two clean Frigots' to carry himself and the 26,000 pistoles he took for immediate necessities, he sailed to Spain, full of confidence at the prospect of a new Parliament likely to be more zealous for vigorous campaigns, and at the

[1] This conversation was reported by Count Gallas to Starhemberg in a letter of 13 September 1709 (Arneth, ii. 470).

reports he heard of Starhemberg, who 'has given such proofs of his Ability that we may reasonably expect matters will be managed to the best advantage.'[1] But the news that pleased him best was of the timely death of Noyelles a few days before Starhemberg reached Spain, for that removed the most serious obstacle to the harmonious working of the new system.

On arriving at Barcelona Stanhope made it his first business to improve the discipline and conditions of the little force of 2,000 English troops he commanded. He sternly repressed the habit of plundering which had produced so ill an effect during the Cadiz expedition and even forbade foraging, as a fruitful cause of disorder and injustice to the inhabitants, compelling all ranks to buy their supplies from the army stores. Finding that this salutary rule would press hardly on the underpaid private soldiers, he empowered each company officer to keep fourteen vacancies in his company and claim the pay as a fund from which to make good the extra expense to the men. With equal strictness he discountenanced the absentee habits of favoured officers[2] and in filling up vacancies preferred those on the spot rather than the coffee-house loungers in London, it being 'very just that some distinction should be made between those that served well and those that do not serve at all'. Many of his letters to Marlborough and Walpole, the new Secretary at War, contain requests for the benefit of his men or to improve their efficiency in the field. Thus he insisted on all ranks being provided with proper clothing, he obtained more suitable arms for his horse and dragoon regiments and supplied them with breast-plates; and he asked Walpole to send him 200 recruits for his infantry regiments from the north of Ireland, 'where recruits are best made'. Under such a commander the morale of the men improved and Stanhope very soon expressed his pride and confidence in them, especially in his 'very pretty body of English horse and dragoons, [who] deserve to be taken care of', and he singled out Harvey's regiment of horse as 'the best in Europe'; while of another of his cavalry colonels he wrote that he had 'by his disinterestedness putt such an emulation in the Whole Army, that each is vying to outdo one another, and greater alterations in Troops than I have found in these I never saw'. To command his cavalry he begged Marlborough to send his friend Carpenter

---

[1] Stanhope to Manchester in Cole, *Historical and Political Memoirs*, 533.
[2] See above, ch. iii, p. 56.

with the rank of major-general, the senior officer, Pepper, though 'a very gallant man and a good colonel of dragoons' not having the qualities requisite for higher command, while he himself, he modestly adds, never having served with horse, needed the expert help of Carpenter in that arm of the service.[1] Officers under him were loud in praise of the improvements he was introducing, especially in the care of the men, while the cavalry, said one of them, was 'in better order than had ever been known in this country', and he congratulated himself on serving under such a general.[2]

Though Starhemberg, on his side, also did all that was possible to put fresh vigour into the rest of Charles's army, the two generals still found themselves powerless to enlarge their bounds, and on land were reduced to the defensive. Against Orleans's more homogeneous army of 22,000 they could at first muster a force of no more than 12,000 Germans, Spaniards, Dutch, Portuguese and English troops, and even by July, when they got 5,000 more Imperialists from Italy, they were still inferior by 5,000. In that month they lost Tortosa on the Ebro, one of their few remaining fortresses in Catalonia, and except for outposts at Cervera and Ampurdan near the borders of Aragon and Roussillon respectively, were almost confined to the surroundings of Barcelona. Had not many of Orleans's regiments been recalled after Oudenarde they might even have lost those outposts.

But at sea it was different. The French fleet since 1706 had entirely lost command of the Mediterranean, at any rate during the summer months, when Leake's fleet was supreme. Leake captured Sardinia without the slightest difficulty in August 1708, escorted the transports with troops from Italy and saw that supplies for the army in Catalonia were landed in safety. This supremacy in the Mediterranean was chiefly due to our possession of Gibraltar, the great safeguard against the junction of the Brest and Toulon fleets so much dreaded in

[1] Carpenter was given the rank asked for and came out in September to command Stanhope's cavalry.
[2] These and other details are found in Stanhope's correspondence with Marlborough and Walpole in *Chevening MSS*. It is interesting to note that Stanhope calculated the cavalry man's pay at 14*d*. p.d. against which the daily cost of forage was 7⅛*d*., bread 2⅝*d*., barley 7⅜*d*.—roughly 17*d*.; and that the pay of the fourteen vacancies would amount to 16*s*. 4*d*. p.d. The enthusiastic comments of officers, Col. St. Pierre and J. Cope, were written to Lord Raby, the absentee colonel of their regiment, the Royal Dragoons: *Add. MSS*. 22231, ff. 74, 76. J. Cope was the future commander-in-chief in Scotland during the '45.

1704. For the Toulon fleet by itself could not, as was apparent at Barcelona in 1706, hold out against England's summer fleet. But this security applied only to the summer months. When the autumn storms began most of the fleet had to return to England, and even the small squadron that could be left behind had to winter at Lisbon, for there was no safe harbour with adequate naval stores and dockyard accommodation in our control within the Mediterranean. Thus until the following spring an army in Catalonia had to depend entirely on its own resources for military supplies and even food. The only way of securing these essential services of the fleet throughout the year was to obtain a port near enough, where the fleet could take shelter and refit in the winter months.

There was such a port answering all these needs, the port referred to in the saying of the navy: 'June, July and Port Mahon are the only three first-class harbours in the Mediterranean.'[1] Marlborough's clear vision had from the outset been fixed on the need of commanding the Mediterranean in winter no less than in summer. He had thought in 1707 to secure this by capturing Toulon with the double object of depriving the French of their only Mediterranean port and annexing it for our own fleet. After the failure there he reverted to the idea of capturing Port Mahon with its excellent harbourage. 'I am so entirely convinced', he wrote to Stanhope in July, 'that nothing can be done effectually without the Fleet, that I conjure you if possible to take Port Mahon, or to let me have your reasons for any other Port, so that I may continue to press them in England.' Stanhope himself had long been of the same opinion; had expressed it indeed to the Cabinet in 1705,[2] and again in May 1708 when on his way to Genoa he wrote to Walpole: 'I do all in my letters to the ministry to represent the necessity of having a squadron winter in the Mediterranean, without which it will be impossible to support Catalonia in the winter', and to Marlborough, before the Duke's letter reached him, that 'unless we have shipps in these seas during the winter', it would be almost impossible to feed their horses or even their men.[3] The naval men were not

---

[1] Another version of this saying, attributed to Andrea Doria in the sixteenth century, is, 'Valencia, July and August, &c.' Port Mahon is not only almost landlocked but has harbourage deep enough for ships of the largest draught; it is, however, somewhat narrow, so that ships of the length built to-day cannot swing free at anchor. But in the eighteenth century this objection did not apply.
[2] See above, ch. ii, p. 43.
[3] Letters to or from Marlborough and Walpole in *Chevening MSS.*

backward and agreed at a council of war held at Barcelona at the end of May to make an attempt, if possible, on Port Mahon.

Unfortunately the co-ordination of plans by various members of the ministry was not then as perfect as it might have been, especially as Marlborough and Godolphin had a way of keeping their most important plans to their two selves— an excellent precaution in the famous instance of the Blenheim march, but not always so felicitous. Again, relations between army and navy, as Stanhope had noted at Cadiz, were often lacking in that cordiality needed for combined operations. These two defects were within an ace of wrecking the design on Port Mahon. Early in August, when, according to orders, Charles III's bride had been solemnly escorted to Barcelona, and Sardinia had been captured, Leake was uncertain how to employ his time, for he had received no explicit orders from home about Minorca. His latest instruction from the Secretary of State, Sunderland, who must have been unaware of his father-in-law's intentions, was to make a demonstration against the Pope for having 'in the most public and insolent manner' offered prayers for the success of the Pretender's expedition to Scotland, and at the cannon's mouth to demand 400,000 crowns from His Holiness for the insult. At a council of war the admirals decided that for want of other orders this was the most urgent business and between them concocted a suitable letter to the Pope. In the last week of August the fleet was just on the point of leaving Pula roadstead in Sardinia for Cività Vecchia, when a dispatch boat appeared with letters from Charles and Stanhope, and an extract from a dispatch of Godolphin to Stanhope, which put an entirely different complexion on the ministry's intentions.

Charles III's letter called on Leake to capture Minorca and Port Mahon, 'that the fleet may be secure in those seas and better security of my royal person; and likewise to guard the transports for the subsistence of the army, which this country cannot afford to do'; Stanhope enclosed Godolphin's orders to himself to make the attempt on Port Mahon and, if it were successful, to keep a squadron to winter in the harbour; and both Charles and Stanhope told Leake of preparations already made at Barcelona for the expedition. Leake and his council of war thereupon wisely decided to ignore Sunderland's orders, to let the Pope bide, and to do their

utmost to assist in the capture of Minorca, 'as judging it to
be more for the common benefit of the allies than any other
service that could be attempted'. Leake left Pula on 29
August and was off Minorca by 5 September. He at once
set to work reconnoitring the island and taking sound-
ings of the harbour of Port Mahon and sent off a couple
of ships to Majorca to meet Stanhope and help him to
embark troops that were to be drafted from the garrison.
On the 13th Stanhope arrived with his land troops for the
attack.

Stanhope on his side had wasted no time as soon as he
received Godolphin's dispatch dated 22 June. He was then
in camp at Cervera, twelve miles from Orleans's head-
quarters at Agramunt on the Segre, and at once obtained
leave from Starhemberg to detach for the expedition 500
Spanish, 600 Portuguese and 600 English troops, with a
battering train of 10 guns besides mortars and bombs, 15,000
cannon shot and 1,000 barrels of powder. Within five days
he had got the whole force embarked on transports at Barcelona, and with so much secrecy that even one of his staff
who was ordered to wait on him at the port writes that he 'is
going to imbarque on some Expedition, whither as yet is not
publicly known'. Here, however, the first hitch occurred,
one that gave Stanhope a pronounced bias against the navy.
To convey his transports he needed an escort of men-of-war,
of which there were four English and two Dutch lying in
Barcelona roads. But these were under the admiral's orders
and, for want of definite instructions from him, some of the
captains were for refusing to accompany him to Minorca.
Fortunately one of these captains was Stanhope's brother
Philip, H.M.S. *Milford*, who with Captain Travanyan,
H.M.S. *York*, persuaded the rest in council to allow them at
any rate to yield to Stanhope's request. Accordingly on
3 September Stanhope was able to sail on the *Milford* with
his transports and reached Majorca on the 6th, where he was
'very handsomely entertained' by Charles's Spanish governor while war-stores and 300 more men from the garrison
were being embarked. Two days later he was off again to
his tryst with Leake off Minorca. On 14 September, the day
after his arrival, Leake declared his decision, already arrived at in concert with his flag officers, to leave at once
on his return to England with fifteen of his ships in view of
the great danger in risking the whole fleet on the long voyage

when the season of gales was approaching; nor would he consent to any of the ships wintering at Port Mahon, in case of its capture, on the ground that there would be no naval stores there for refitting. He agreed, however, to leave Whittaker with the seventeen remaining ships of the fleet to assist Stanhope in the siege and afterwards convoy troops from Italy and, if necessary, overawe the Pope: he also handed back to Stanhope 600 marines previously drafted into the fleet and gave him all the bread and cannon shot he could spare.

The island of Minorca is about thirty miles long from east to west and some twelve miles across its widest part. It contains two harbours, one on the north defended by Fort Fornells, and Port Mahon on the south-east, protected by Fort St. Philip. Fort Fornells was soon reduced by Whittaker's squadron, and within a few days of Stanhope's appearance the rest of the island, including the capital Cuidadela on the west and the town of Mahon on the north-east, had not only surrendered but contributed some 500 volunteers to the allied forces. The one object, however, of the expedition was to secure Port Mahon as a naval base throughout the year for the English fleets. For the defence of Port Mahon the French and Spanish had concentrated most of their forces in a well-chosen position. The entrance to the harbour was guarded on one side by Fort St. Philip, a strong work on a promontory to the south-east of the town of Mahon, and on the other by a smaller Fort Philipet on a spit of land further east. Fort Philip, the main defence on which the security of the harbour depended, was itself protected on the sea-front by the outlying Fort Charles and on the land side by a wall half a mile to the north crowned by four old towers, each containing four guns. Within the space between this wall and the sea, besides the two Forts St. Philip and Charles, was room for a little town or village, cantonments for the troops and four batteries with 47 guns in all. The garrison was composed of 500 French and 500 Spanish soldiers, well armed and well provisioned, under a French commandant La Jonquière: so strong was the position and so adequate the garrison that Louis XIV expected it to withstand a long siege.

To secure the prompt reduction of Fort St. Philip Stanhope allowed his men no rest and took none himself. On the evening of 14 September he landed with 100 grenadiers within a mile to the south-west of the Fort and marched some three miles inland to make a personal reconnaissance of the enemy's position. Within the next three days, under cover of H.M.SS. *Dunkirk, York,* and *Centurion,* he landed the heavy guns and the rest of his force, amounting with the marines to 2,500, at a spot within half cannon-shot of the Fort, where he established his first camp. He at once set his men to work making a road for the guns over the rocky ground towards his second camp farther inland, from which a frontal attack could be made against the outer wall covering the garrison and the main fort. Every day he himself went on reconnoitring expeditions towards the fort, which, says one of his staff, 'the more was reconnoitred, the stronger was found'. To save bloodshed he conceived the ingenious idea, since the Spanish half of the garrison were reputed to favour King Charles, of shooting arrows into the fort with papers offering them good terms 'if they did not put him to the trouble of raising batteries'; but with no result.[1] By 23 September the guns had been brought up and gun emplacements were begun, Stanhope himself supervising the work 'every night till twelve o'clock, which forwarded it so much that the 28th we began to fire 6 cannon a Front, and 3 on the Tour which flanked us most'. When, after barely five hours' cannonade, eight of St. Philip's guns had been put out of action and the parapet of the protecting wall damaged, a general advance was ordered. Brigadier Wade led the attack against the enemy's lines on the left and, according to a staff-officer's account,

'General Stanhope sword in hand those on ye right, in which attack we had ye misfortune to loose Captain Stanhope the Gen[ll's] brother, which has damped all ye satisfaction this glorious Success would otherways have given us, notwithstanding this accident the Gen[ll] led ye men on to a towr under ye castle,[2] being all this time on horseback, exposed to ye enemys Cannon, small shot and Bombs, which they gave us as fast as possibly they could discharge a Load, we lost some men tho not so many as might be expected in ye gaining so good a post, we lodged our men in ye Town as much under cover of the houses as we could, and at night the Gen[ll] retired to his own Camp.'

That evening a boy of twelve from the garrison was caught spying in the camp; Stanhope, still hopeful of avoiding

[1] Tindal, iv. 94. Possibly this story is only another version of that given below of the boy sent into Fort St. Philip with invitations to the garrison to desert.

[2] i.e. the south-westerly tower on the wall, on the enemy's extreme left.

further bloodshed, instead of punishing him, had him loaded 'with a great quantity of papers to be sent to this purpose that all those who would desert should have two Pistoles each; half he writ in Spanish and ye rest in French and sowed them all round this said Boy, tyed his hands behind him and sent him back to ye Castle.' Next day, sure enough, the governor sent to ask Stanhope's terms for surrender. On 30 September Stanhope, his terms being accepted, marched into Fort St. Philip, thereby obtaining control of his long-coveted harbour.[1]

In his dispatch to Sunderland Stanhope writes that the English losses in killed and wounded were less than fifty. 'I only', he adds, 'have had the misfortune to lose my brother, who had been very instrumental in engaging the seamen in this enterprise, and unfortunately would have too great a share in the execution of it; but since he died in doing service to her Majesty and his country, I shall think his life well bestowed, as I would my own:' noble words that recall the father's words about James himself: 'at the worst . . . he failes in the pursuit of a just and honourable and religious cause'.[2] The success was cheaply won, as the English judged when they saw the strength of the defences and the ample supplies left in the fort: Louis XIV thought so too, and had La Jonquière, on his return to France, tried and sent to prison. An incidental result of the success was that the Pope thought it better to cease praying for the Pretender, and also to drop a scheme of alliance against the Emperor he had been promoting among the Italian princes. So Whittaker was saved the trouble of presenting the admirals' letter and bombarding Cività Vecchia.

It is unfortunate that this brilliant and rapid success should have been marred by friction between Stanhope and the naval men. The navy certainly contributed a good share to the preparatory work. Leake showed sound sense in deferring to the appeal for help from Charles and Stanhope, although no direct orders had been sent to himself, and, having engaged in the enterprise, gave prompt and most useful help to the land forces in reconnoitring the ground before Stanhope arrived. He also provided transports for the

---

[1] Many of the details given above come from letters of Stanhope's aide-de-camp, J. Cope, in the Raby Papers, *Add. MSS.* 22231, ff. 78 sqq. Details of the movements of the ships and of the landing of the troops are to be found in *Leake's Life.*

[2] See above, ch. i, p. 7. The dispatch is given in Mahon, *Succession*, Appendix.

force from Majorca, and supplied Stanhope's deficiencies in
men, ammunition, and stores. Friction between two services,
however, often arises rather from faults of manner than of
action. Leake was undoubtedly a first-rate sailor, but inclined, as in the relief of Barcelona, to err on the side of over-
caution, never a favourite virtue with Stanhope; also he was
apt to be brusque in manner. His decision to return home
himself, before Minorca had been subdued, though it was
palliated by his agreeing to leave Whittaker, may well have
seemed to Stanhope hazardous for the success of the enterprise at the time. But Stanhope's main grievance against the
navy was the difficulty made by the captains at Barcelona
about escorting his transports. Until then he had been on
excellent terms with the sailors and had written to Marlborough that 'the admirals have in everything comply'd with
what could reasonably be desired of them'. But this difficulty
at Barcelona infuriated him so much that after the capture
of Port Mahon he wrote to Sunderland that without his
brother and Travanyan 'this business would never have been
begun nor followed, for now that my poor brother is dead,
he is the only seaman I could persuade to hearken to it, and
their two ships were the only two I could engage to take the
resolution of coming hither till Sir John Leake came with the
fleet from Sardinia; and if . . . we had waited for the result
of a council of War at sea, I leave to your lordship to judge
what would have been the issue'; and he concludes with the
sweeping and certainly exaggerated statement: 'I may with
confidence tell your lordship that I have in all this affair met
with ten times more difficulty in dealing with the sea than
with the enemy.'[1] But however little justified may have been
such a verdict on the navy's share in the capture of Minorca,
Stanhope's was clearly the moving spirit in the enterprise.
Both for his unceasing energy and vigilance in preparation
and his impetuosity and brilliant leadership in the actual
attack on Fort St. Philip he could justly claim the lion's share
in the victory, which secured the permanent naval base in the
Mediterranean so long desired by Marlborough and Stanhope himself.

[1] Mahon, *Succession*, Appendix. Stanhope's historian-descendant both in
this book and in his *Anne* almost ignores the part played by the navy in the
capture of Minorca. This omission is to some extent corrected by Parnell,
252 sqq., and more fully by Professor Callender in his edition of *Leake's Life*.
He, however, in his anxiety to glorify Leake, is in turn inclined to depreciate
Stanhope's part.

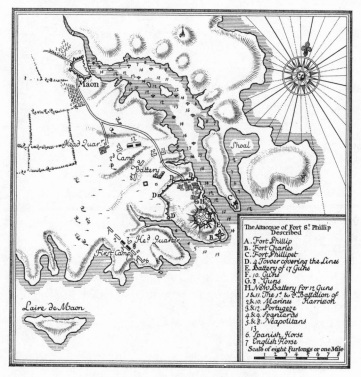

The Attacque of Fort St. Phillip
Described

A. . Fort Phillip
B. . Fort Charles
C. . Fort Phillipet
D. . 4 Tower covering the Lines
E. . Battery of 17 Guns
F. 10. Guns
G. 3 . Guns
H. New Battery for 12 Guns
1 & 11. The 1st & 2d Battalion of
2 & 10. Marines   Harrisson
3. & 12. Portugeze
4. & 9. Spaniards
5. & 8. Neapolitans
                    13
6. Spanish Horse
7 English Horse
Scale of eight Furlongs or one Mile
1 2 3 4 5 6 7 8

ATTACK ON PORT MAHON

From a map at Broughton House drawn by Delahaye. Reproduced by
kind permission of His Grace the Duke of Buccleuch and Queensberry

§ 3

Minorca had been conquered from the Bourbons in the name of Charles III as King of Spain: but from the first Stanhope had made up his mind that Port Mahon at any rate should be retained as an English possession. At the council of war held on the eve of Leake's departure he had arranged with the admiral that English troops alone should be admitted into Fort St. Philip. Accordingly, after the surrender, though he appointed a Spanish governor of the island, he made his chief engineer, Colonel Petit, governor of the fort, with a garrison of English marines and infantry, and instructed him to allow no interference by the governor of the island. In his dispatch to Sunderland announcing the capture he gave it 'as his humble opinion that England ought never to part with this island, which will give the law to the Mediterranean both in time of war and peace';[1] and for weeks he kept impressing this point on both Sunderland and Marlborough. 'Let who will be King of Spain', he wrote in another letter '. . . we should not temporise in the matter but have it absolutely yielded to us.'[2] He was indeed only preaching to the converted. The news of the victory came to London on 9 October (o.s.), 'at the same time', wrote Sunderland, 'as the news of the taking of Lisle, yet was not at all lessened by it: everybody looking upon our being in possession of Port Mahon as of the last consequence to the carrying on the war in Spain; besides the other advantages, which, if we are wise, we may reap from it both in War and Peace'.[3] Accordingly, in December formal instructions were sent by Sunderland confirming Petit as governor of Port Mahon, where he was not to admit the troops of any other power but garrison it 'by our own Troops only and none else', and ordering Stanhope to obtain from Charles III its cession to England, it being 'highly just, as reasonable that we should keep the said town of Port Mahon as some sort of security' for all our expenses in the Peninsula.[4]

As far as Charles III was concerned Stanhope's task of obtaining the cession of Minorca was comparatively easy. It is true the King had an even more rooted objection to

---

[1] Mahon, *Anne*, ii. 84. [2] Mahon, *Succession*, Appendix.
[3] Stanhope, *Answer*, 9.
[4] R.O., *S.P.* 94/77, Instruction of 9 Dec. 1708.

parting with any portion of the Spanish monarchy he claimed
than to making the commercial concessions he had already
agreed to by the treaty of 1707. He had in fact taken an
oath, on coming to Spain as King, not to diminish the possessions of Spain. But England, as the main supporter of his
cause in Spain by the troops she sent or paid for, had the
whip hand of him: and Stanhope was quite prepared to use
this advantage ruthlessly. Marlborough warned him, however, in January 1709 that it would be 'a ticklish business',
owing to the outcry that would be raised by the Dutch at the
advantage the possession of Port Mahon would give England
against them in the Mediterranean and Levant trade.[1] This
warning was all the more needed, since, while Stanhope was
treating about Minorca in Spain, delicate negotiations were
also proceeding in Holland between the English, Dutch
and other allies and France. For the combined effects of
Oudenarde, Lille and Port Mahon in 1708 had driven
Louis XIV in the following year to make desperate efforts
for peace, while the Dutch were determined to make a preliminary arrangement with England about the Barrier of
fortresses to be conceded to them in the Low Countries before
any settlement of territories was made with France. The
Dutch were asking far more than England was disposed to
concede for their Barrier, while England was demanding
concessions from Spain extremely repugnant to the Dutch,
both at the expense of the unfortunate Charles III. Godolphin, and to a less extent Marlborough, believed that it was
more important to reduce the Dutch claims in the Barrier
Treaty than to obtain Port Mahon from Spain, especially as
both the Emperor and his brother Charles dreaded the Dutch
predominance in the Low Countries which their proposals
for the Barrier would entail, and so was anxious not to make
the Dutch more obstinate in their view by another threat
to their Mediterranean interests.[2]

But Stanhope had received his instructions from Sunderland and was determined not to miss his opportunity. As to
the Dutch he was of opinion that they were, as usual, giving
too little and asking too much, and might need a lesson.
'I hope the Dutch will always be our friends', he wrote to
Sunderland, 'but if they should ever be otherwise, they will
never be able to carry on their trade to the Levant without
our leave, if we remain masters of the place [Port Mahon]'.

[1] *Marlborough*, iv. 408.   [2] Klopp, xiii. 281.

He did not even wait for the completion of the treaty to make arrangements for its defence on a visit he paid the island in March. These arrangements he detailed to Marlborough in a letter,[1] written apparently in answer to the Duke's warning about the 'ticklish business', extolling the advantages to be derived from its possession:

'. . . As to what yr Grace is pleased to mention concerning this island I will manage it with as much secrecy as the thing is capable of, but give me leave to observe on this occasion that what we demand is so natural that I believe all the world expects we should keep it and will be surprised at our modesty if we desire nothing more, and as for the Dutch they will have very ill grace to oppose us in that matter if they pretend as they doe that we should be assisting to them in obtaining a barrier. I have been very busy here in getting exact plans made of the situation of this fort and Harbour and of new works which will be necessary to make it answer the ends we propose, which I will in a very little time send to yr Grace by Mr Craggs, together with an estimate of the charge, and I may venture before hand to say thus much to yr Grace, that with about Sixty thousand pounds and I believe rather with less this place will be impregnable, if any place in the world may be reckoned so. the onely situation which ever I saw that could compare with it is that of Gibraltar but I think this will in many respects be preferable, for at Gibraltar there is one side attackable, and I verily think there cannot be any attack carried on here when our plan shall be executed, and I doe further believe that no superiour force at Sea can so block it up as to prevent small vessels going in and out. It is not above a days sail from Africa, Spain, France and Sardinia, to Majorca it is almost contiguous, and from Italy not above two days voyage at most with a tolerable wind. all our seamen agree that it is in all respects the most convenient harbour in Europe. I hope by Mr Craggs to send home either an absolute grant of it from this King to the Queen, or some instrument which shall be in effect equivalent to an absolute cession. As for the court of Madrid experience has taught us that nothing but fear can influence them, and I shall always think ourselves incomparably more secure of the performance of our treaty of commerce when we can awe them into a complyance than whilst we shall hold it precariously and depend onely upon gratitude. and that this port which is at the door of Spain, can intercept all communication with Italy will be as formidable to them as an army of twenty thousand men in Roussillon is passed all dispute. What influence it will have on all the States of Italy is as apparent, and it is worth

[1] Port Mahon, 29 Mar. 1709 (*Chevening MSS.*).

considering that from the Cevennes and the frontiers of Languedoc is but a days sail, and whenever we shall have another warr
with France this neighbourhood may procure us a very useful
diversion. yr Grace will pardon me for being so tedious on this
subject, but I think there cannot be too much said upon it.'

So enthusiastic did he become about the merits of the island
that in a later letter to Sunderland he wrote:

'I cannot give a greater demonstration of the opinion I have
how considerable an acquisition I judge this will be to England,
than by offering to stay and live there three or four years, to
put it in order. The fate of such kind of settlements generally
depends upon their being well-constituted at first; and though
I have not the vanity to think I have more ability to settle
matters well there than fifty other people, yet this I may say, I
should be more industrious and, perhaps, less interested.'[1]

Stanhope's efforts to wring the cession of Minorca from
Charles III were to some extent, no doubt, helped by Marlborough's diplomacy in resisting the exorbitant demands
made on Charles by the Dutch in respect to the Low Countries: for in May 1709 Marlborough sent him, for Charles's
information, these Dutch proposals as well as his own more
favourable counter-project requiring the Dutch, *inter alia*,
to guarantee to Charles the whole Spanish monarchy, and
in other respects safeguarding his interests. But Stanhope
depended chiefly on what can only be qualified as bullying methods. He not only made the most of the facts that
the acquisition of the island was entirely owing to English
initiative and leadership and that an English garrison was
already in possession, but chiefly laid stress on Charles's
almost entire dependence on English support, then more than
ever necessary for his continued existence in Spain.[2] Far
from attempting to gain his point by conciliatory methods he
haughtily advised Charles 'de prévenir par sa sagesse les
suites fâcheuses qui en [i.e. from a refusal] pourraient naître';
and when Charles attempted to put him off with evasive
replies left him at no loss as to his meaning by ordering
an English regiment sent to reinforce Starhemberg to re-
embark for Port Mahon. In April, while Stanhope himself
was away with the fleet at Minorca and elsewhere, his sec-

[1] Barcelona, 15 June 1709 (Mahon, *Succession*, Appendix).
[2] See Sinzendorf's despairing picture of the straits to which Charles was
reduced and his urgent appeal for more money in his letter to Marlborough of
30 Jan. 1709 (*Marlborough*, iv. 446).

retary Craggs, going one better than his master, obtained from one of Charles's ministers a promise to agree that the island should be handed over as a mortgage for the expense of the new fortifications and then suggested to the English ministers that this expense should be put at so high a figure as 'to put it out of possibility of being redeemed'. On his return in May Stanhope presented a memorial to Charles demanding not only the cession of Minorca till all the English subsidies had been repaid, but also a public expression of his 'sincere gratitude to the Queen' for all she had done for him. Finally, on 15 June Charles, hoping by a concession on Minorca to obtain England's support against the Dutch claims in the Low Countries, sent a letter to the Queen agreeing to a provisional cession, but saving his right of redemption and subject to the Emperor's consent. On the same day Stanhope, dissatisfied with these qualifications, wrote to Marlborough: 'the behaviour of these people in relation to Minorca has made me lose my temper with them. . . . This Court does not deserve from England nor from Your Grace the least part of the management you have for them, and . . . they would be rightly served if we complied with the demands of the Dutch, how exorbitant so ever.'

This is exactly what the English were driven to do, and without any advantage to themselves. The Dutch, whose trade was ever their prime object, had the greatest objection to England acquiring Minorca, so well adapted for controlling the Mediterranean trade. So when, in the spring of 1709, rumours came to them of Stanhope's high-handed dealings about the island, they were not in the best of humours. Townshend, then in charge of the negotiations at Gertruydenberg, was instructed to deny the truth of the rumours: but they had had their effect. At least Townshend gave them as his excuse for the poor bargain he struck with his first Barrier Treaty of October 1709, whereby the Dutch obtained practically all their original demands and evaded giving guarantees to secure either the whole Spanish monarchy for Charles or the demolition of Dunkirk required by England.

Nor even was Stanhope compensated by obtaining his Minorca by treaty with Charles. It is true that, in spite of Townshend's disavowal of any designs on the island, in August the draft treaty had been returned from London to Barcelona with strict orders to Stanhope to insist on Charles signing it, with or without the consent of his brother the

Emperor. Accordingly Stanhope kept on pressing the point.
But his correspondence relating to his Spanish treaties was
certainly dogged with ill luck; for, as in the case of the commercial treaty, the letters fell into the wrong hands. In
November 1709 letters from Moles, at Charles's court, to the
Emperor and Marlborough criticizing Stanhope's diplomatic
methods were captured by the French. Torcy kept them to
produce at an opportune moment when they would create
the maximum of ill feeling between England and the Dutch,
and did so with dramatic effect in January 1710 when he
was proposing new terms of peace likely to be more acceptable to the Dutch than to the English. Moles, in his
letter to Marlborough, had complained that Stanhope was
still insisting, 'avec une vivacité assez verte', on Charles
agreeing to the treaty at a time when the Dutch were under
the impression that the treaty had been dropped; he also
accused him of blurting out the secret negotiation in order
to obtain credit for himself in England. The Dutch were
naturally indignant, and Townshend was ordered to assure
the States formally, and, this time finally, in the Queen's
name that Stanhope's further negotiations had been carried
on without her knowledge and would not be pursued. This
disingenuous assurance entirely dissipated the ill humour of
the States and also put an end to the treaty.[1]

It is quite possible, as Lamberty suggests, that Stanhope, by
inadvertence, never received these orders countermanding
his instructions of August; for he was certainly not the man
to carry on negotiations he had been explicitly ordered to
stop. But he had not yet attained the suavity and conciliatory
methods later characteristic of his diplomacy, and still acted
too much the Brennus with his sword in the scales. It would
certainly, too, have been more to our national honour had
the ministry been faithful to the country's obligation by the
Grand Alliance that none of its members should seek special
advantages for itself. Still, it hardly lay with the Dutch to
reproach us after securing a Barrier Treaty the sole profit of
which was to fall to them. In the circumstances, though
Stanhope's methods were bad, there is much to be said for
the policy he advocated with so much vehemence. Charles
would hardly have remained a day longer in Spain had it

---

[1] Lamberty, vi. 7, 8, gives an account of the intercepted letters from Moles
and of their reception by the Dutch. The orders from London to Stanhope of
August 1709 are in *Marlborough*, vi. 569.

not been for English support, for which the only return he could make was by commercial or territorial concessions. Besides, Minorca, valuable only for its first-rate harbour, would have been useless in his hands, for neither he nor his brother the Emperor had a navy to protect it or use it, whereas in English hands, as Marlborough wrote to Vienna, it would entail on England an obligation to protect Charles's possession of Spain.[1] Stanhope indeed merely recognized facts in claiming that we should own what we alone could hold. In the end he obtained all that he aimed at without any treaty from Charles. The English garrison and the English fleet kept Port Mahon so secure that when all our troops left Spain before the peace, in Minorca most of them took refuge. Finally at Utrecht, by means of the Tories, the island was secured to us by a far more valid treaty than would have been one with the phantom King Charles.[2]

His own share in the conquest of Minorca was always a source of just pride to Stanhope. In the following year he was gazetted a Lieutenant-General in recognition of this achievement. On his elevation to the House of Lords eight years later he chose Mahon as his second title; and in his patent of peerage particular mention is made of the attack he made on the island of Minorca in the Balearics; and coupled with the account of its siege and speedy reduction is a touching allusion to the loss of his gallant sailor-brother.[3] Later, when it was a question of securing peace with Spain by the return of one of her lost possessions, he was prepared to cede Gibraltar, but neither he, nor in truth any one in England, so much as suggested parting with Port Mahon, one 'of the only three first-class harbours in the Mediterranean'.

[1] *Marlborough*, vi. 604: to Wratislaw, 26 Sept. 1709.

[2] Unfavourable views of Stanhope's attitude to Charles III are to be found in Landau, 537–42, and Klopp, xiii. 278 sqq. An admirable account of the relations between Stanhope's negotiation about Minorca and that on the Barrier Treaty is in Geikie and Montgomery, part i, chs. iv and v.

[3] The text of this passage in the patent runs: 'In Balearicam Insulam Minorcam Impetu facto, non sine Fratris egregie militantis Interitu, obsessor ad subitam Deditionem coegit.'

CHAPTER IV
BRIHUEGA

§ 1

STANHOPE needed all the comfort he derived from the conquest of Minorca, for otherwise the Spanish campaigns of 1708 and 1709 were barren of success. Denia was recaptured for Philip at the end of 1708; in April 1709 the citadel of Alicante, the last stronghold left in Valencia, fell to the chevalier d'Asfeld after a gallant resistance of five months. A noteworthy incident of the siege was the death of the commandant Richards with three of his staff on 3 March. Three times had the French, when their mining operations were completed, vainly offered honourable terms of surrender; Richards himself, on the very day of the explosion, would not allow any of the garrison but himself and his staff on the parade ground, which he suspected to be within the danger zone. So he and his brave companions were engulfed. Still his next in command carried on, hoping to be relieved by Byng and Stanhope with a squadron and reinforcements from Port Mahon. There was some delay in obtaining the troops needed from Italy, but at last on 15 April the fleet stood off Alicante; and Stanhope could see once more the quay from which he had sailed on his first adventure on Marquis Clerici's 'stinking galley'. D'Asfeld's batteries were cannonaded by the fleet without much effect; but next day a violent east wind forced the ships out for sea-room, and the French employed the time in fortifying the shore wherever there was any possible landing-place. So on 18 April Byng and Stanhope decided that a landing was impracticable and arranged that the garrison should surrender the citadel with the honours of war. Stanhope has been criticized for sanctioning this surrender, but without justice, for d'Asfeld had captured the town on the shore below the citadel in December, commanded all the landing-places, and had 14,000 men to pit against Stanhope's force which, even with the garrison, then reduced to 600, was greatly inferior. Stanhope also rightly thought that the garrison, whose services he retained by the terms of the capitulation, would be more useful to him elsewhere. So his aide-de-camp was probably not far wrong in concluding

JAMES, EARL STANHOPE
From a portrait by Sir Godfrey Kneller in the National Portrait Gallery

that, in the circumstances, 'the expedition has been very well ended'.[1]

Every available man indeed was needed by Charles to maintain himself in the little strip of territory still left to him near Barcelona. For though the Duke of Orleans himself had returned to France at the end of 1708, the French under Marshal Bezons remained in a commanding position on the Segre till the autumn of 1709, d'Asfeld was in force farther south, and in the spring the Spanish general Bay had once more defeated the unfortunate Galway on the borders of Portugal. A spirited attempt made by Starhemberg and Stanhope to recover Tortosa with a small body of English and German troops all but succeeded in December 1708, but in the end, wrote the English general, 'it proved a Cremona business. We got into the old town, killed the governor and about 200 men, brought off 9 officers and 50 men prisoners, but by an unlucky accident missed our aim'.[2] Though in the following July Balaguer on the Segre was recovered, Uhlfeldt lost several posts in the district of Ampurdan, essential for keeping away French reinforcements from Roussillon. In August, too, Stanhope told Godolphin that the enemy had 'double the number of forces in Valencia, Aragon, and Roussillon that we have here, [but that even so], the greatest enemy we have to fear is famine'. Faced with this fear for his men he sent off his capable secretary Craggs to buy corn in Barbary, and his quick brain devised the plan of hiring out government transports to Genoese merchants under contract to supply Charles's army with corn from the Levant.[3] But even these measures were only palliative.

The failure in Spain, when in other fields the allies were uniformly successful, was due partly to their numerical inferiority, partly to Charles III's unpopularity outside Catalonia, but also to the English ministry's ignorance of Spanish conditions and their tendency, when Marlborough was away, spasmodically to adopt crude schemes without consulting the men on the spot. The capture of Cadiz had become almost an obsession in England; and two expeditions

---

[1] *Add. MSS.* 31135, f. 90. Parnell, pp. 260 sqq., gives a good description of the siege and concludes with an unfavourable criticism of Stanhope's action; A few details are in Collins, *Peerage*, iv. 173.

[2] Mahon, *Succession*, 275. For the allusion to Cremona see above, ch. ii, p. 26.

[3] Mahon, *Succession*, Appendix; *Treas. Papers, 1708–14*, 307.

there had already proved abortive. In 1709, however, when every available man was wanted in Catalonia, they must needs send out a third, on Galway's suggestion, but against the opinion of Charles III and Marlborough. Stanhope also had disapproved and proposed the more promising alternative of attacking Roussillon—the gathering-ground for French reinforcements—as a means of diverting the French in Spain to the defence of their own country.[1] In the summer of 1709, not only were a fleet under Baker and 5,000 troops under Wills sent from England, but Byng's squadron and Stanhope with two regiments and a train of artillery were diverted from Catalonia for this renewed attack on Cadiz. Byng and Stanhope arrived at the rendezvous, Gibraltar, at the end of August, but were kept waiting till the first week in October before Baker and Wills, delayed by contrary winds, arrived. Before that the garrison of Cadiz had received timely notice of the scheme and made adequate preparations for defence; besides, the season was already too late, so Baker and Wills were ordered to drop the enterprise and sail with Stanhope back to Catalonia. Stanhope's enforced delay at Gibraltar was not entirely wasted, for he set himself to make a careful survey of the defences and the system of provisioning the garrison, both which he reported to the Secretary of State to be very defective. As a result, works planned by Stanhope to remedy these defects were set in hand the following year.[2]

But hard as conditions were for the allies in Spain during the first two years of Stanhope's command, there were indications here as elsewhere that France was near the breaking-point, and that, even if Philip V was determined to hold on, he would not be able to count much longer on his grandfather's support. The first indication of the collapse of France came to Stanhope as a diversion to his preoccupation about Minorca. It came too with all the melodramatic accompaniments of mysterious emissaries that could be disavowed, cryptic codes and secret interviews, so appropriate to an age in which the poisoning activities of a Mme de Brinvilliers or the lingering detention of the Man in the Iron

[1] *Marlborough*, iv. 582; Mahon, *Succession*, 280–4. See also Klopp, xiii. 278, where Stanhope is, no doubt correctly, represented as pressing the scheme on Charles III, in accordance with instructions from London. There was also a scheme proposed by Marlborough at this time for the capture of Sicily; but this came to nothing (ib. 279).

[2] *Treas. Papers, 1708–14*, 187; Mahon, *Succession*, Appendix.

Mask were affairs of state. Early in August 1708, when
Orleans seemed to have the allies in Catalonia almost at his
mercy, Philip Stanhope, just arrived at Barcelona on H.M.S.
Milford, came to his brother's head-quarters to report the
capture from a Leghorn felucca of a suspicious Sicilian
passenger named Doria, who gave himself out to be in the
Duke of Orleans's service and hinted that he was the bearer
of important proposals to Stanhope. On being brought up
before Stanhope, Doria delivered his message to the effect
that Orleans himself, as more remote from the succession
to the French crown and so less likely to unite France and
Spain under one head, might be substituted for Philip
as the Bourbon claimant to Spain; and that if Queen Anne
would agree to this proposal Orleans would hand over to
her Alicante, Cales, and other Spanish ports and grant her
subjects free trade with the Peninsula. As a proof of his good
faith he offered, if Stanhope would send him over to the
French camp, within eight days to bring a letter confirming
his statement from Orleans himself. Stanhope, with an eye
to the advantage of keeping Orleans quiet in camp during
a negotiation, agreed; and within the appointed time had
an answer from Orleans inquiring how he liked his 'present
of snuff' and suggesting a meeting at which its virtues could
be discussed. Accordingly Stanhope, with an escort of 100
horse, went to meet the Duke's envoy, who confirmed
Doria, and he duly reported the proposal to Charles III
and Sunderland.

There, for the time being, the matter rested, for Stanhope
became otherwise engaged in conquering Minorca; but it
was not the end of it. In the following November some
controversy arose as to the treatment accorded by their
captors to a French regiment taken at Port Mahon and to
an English regiment taken at Valencia. With the ostensible
object of settling this dispute Orleans, in the course of a
correspondence conducted between the two generals on
terms of high courtesy, invited Stanhope to meet Flotte, one
of his confidential servants. Orleans reminded Stanhope of
their previous meetings in Paris, Stanhope in return expresses
his humblest thanks for 'L'honneur que V.A.R. me fait de se
souvenir que je Luy ai fait ma révérence à Paris et les expressions obligeantes dont Elle accompagne ce souvenir.' Meanwhile Stanhope had discussed Orleans's proposal with his
own minister Sunderland and with Charles III, neither

of whom, naturally, was disposed to give up Charles's claim
to the Spanish monarchy. But it was agreed to try the effect
on Orleans of an offer suggested by Stanhope that a kingdom
should be carved out for him from Navarre and a part of
southern France. In recommending this proposal to Sunderland Stanhope's argument was that Orleans was worth con-
ciliating, 'since it is certainly in his power to put an end to
the war in Spain in a few months; . . . and when a man has
a crown on his head, it is no hard matter to engage him;
and considering the dispositions of the people of Languedoc,
we might very easily from Navarre extend ourselves as far
as the Rhône; and if the Duke has any party in the army he
commands (which one must suppose) by putting a trusty
garrison into Pamplona, he makes himself master of Navarre
in a week, and cuts off all communication from France to
Spain.' Whether this actual proposal was made by Stanhope
at the meeting of his emissary with Flotte is not known, but
at any rate Stanhope went so far as to arrange that Flotte
should go to the allied head-quarters in Holland to discuss
his master's proposal and promised if possible to meet him
there himself.[1]

Nothing actually came of this negotiation, for the principals were at cross purposes. The English ministry had no
intention of giving up Charles and substituting one French
prince for another in Spain. Orleans's overtures, which
Marlborough rightly suspected to have been in a certain
measure sanctioned by Louis XIV,[2] were merely an indication that France, hard hit by her defeats in Flanders, was
beginning to give up hope of retaining the whole Spanish
monarchy for Philip, and was anxious, in case Philip had to
leave Spain, to secure, as a *pis aller*, recognition of his cousin
Orleans's rights. To carve a separate kingdom for himself
out of his native land was the last thing in Orleans's thoughts
and was indignantly repudiated by him when he first heard

[1] In the *Chevening MSS.* are still to be seen copies of Stanhope's letters to
Flotte, forwarding his passport, and to Orleans, asking for one through France
to Holland for himself. There is even the passport, signed by Louis XIV and
dated 14 Dec. 1708, empowering Stanhope to pass to England from Catalonia
via Perpignan, Lyons, and Holland, and to return by the same route. There is
also at Chevening the draft of a letter of 24 Nov. 1708 addressed by Stanhope to
the man entrusted with the duty of conferring with Flotte. He enjoins on him
the need of an exact report that he can send to the ministry at home and
expresses regret that he cannot leave Spain to pursue the negotiation personally
in England or Holland.

[2] *Marlborough*, iv. 408, Brussels, 26 Jan. 1709.

of the idea on his return to France. Stanhope himself never
expected much result from this negotiation except, as actually
happened, that it 'very much abated', as he wrote to Sunderland, 'the edge of the Duke of Orleans this last campaign,
who might certainly have made better use of his superiority'.
Nevertheless some of the after-effects of the negotiations
were unfortunate. Philip, who had always been jealous of
his cousin, suspected that Orleans's designs were more self-
interested than they really were and were directed against
his throne. The Duke himself could not be attacked; but the
unfortunate Flotte and another agent of Orleans, Regnault,
were arrested and kept in prison on no definite charge for
over five years. Nor did Philip ever trust or forgive Orleans
thereafter, with unfortunate results in later years for Spain,
and indeed for Europe, when Orleans was Regent of France
and Stanhope chief minister in England.[1]

An even more significant indication of France's weariness of the struggle was the gradual withdrawal of French
troops from Spain. Already by July 1709 Bezons had been
warned by Louis XIV not to risk any general engagement;
and by the end of the year he and all his troops had been
recalled, leaving Philip to depend entirely on his inferior
Spanish commanders and troops. At the same time Louis
was preparing his last great campaign for peace with the
Dutch and the English Whigs, that resulted in the abortive
negotiations of Gertruydenberg from May to July 1710.
Stanhope, constantly kept in touch with the varying phases
of diplomatic activity by Marlborough, realized that the
one thing needed to secure a complete diplomatic victory
over Louis was the final expulsion of Philip from Spain.
This seemed at last made possible by the departure of French
troops, if only the allied forces were sufficiently strengthened.
To urge this need, he returned to England at the close of
1709.

[1] The above account is based mainly on Mahon, *Succession*, *Chevening MSS.*,
R.O., *S.P.* 94/77, *Add. MSS.* 35838, f. 342 (a full account of the negotiation).
St. Simon quotes a long account of Flotte's and Regnault's unhappy fate,
apparently from the Regent Orleans. See also Baudrillart, ii. 67–103; Noailles,
Mémoires, iv. 72; Sismondi, xxvii. 67. Landau, 477, quotes from Charles's secret
journal for 23 Aug. 1708: 'Stanhope redt wegen Orleans geheim' (Stanhope has
a secret talk about Orleans), showing Charles's early knowledge of the
negotiations.

§ 2

During the first three months of 1710 that he stayed in
England Stanhope saw enough to realize that the days in
which it might be possible for the Whigs to make peace on
their own terms were already numbered. Complaints about
the losses and expense of such victories as Malplaquet, the
ineffective campaigns in Spain and the rejection of the almost abject terms offered by Louis in the previous year were
beginning to make themselves heard. The Sacheverell trial,
in which he himself was chosen as a manager for the
Commons and made a much applauded speech,[1] would have
convinced a much less acute observer that popular feeling
had changed; even to a man of Marlborough's serenity the
political situation was becoming troublesome. Fearing that
by the revulsion of popular feeling all that he and Marlborough had been fighting for might be lost, Stanhope would
willingly have stayed at home, where he felt the danger to
be greatest; he felt, too, that his own political abilities were
beginning to be appreciated by his party and might be useful. So it was with a heavy heart that, near the end of March,
he started to resume his command in Spain.

But, once again launched on the Spanish adventure, he
was characteristically eager for one last vigorous effort against
France. His Instructions, no doubt drawn up by himself, were
to take full advantage of the departure of the French troops.
First Charles was to be urged to promise a generous amnesty
to all Philip's adherents who came over to his side when they
found themselves deserted by the French, and secondly he
himself was to press for an energetic offensive once the allies
obtained the initiative.[2] On his way through the Hague he
discussed with Marlborough and Eugene various schemes
for diverting attention from the main operations. One was
a plan proposed by a French traitor for seizing Calais,
another for an attempt to raise a rebellion in Languedoc
with the help of Norris's fleet in the Mediterranean, suggested
by Seissan, a shady adventurer of many nationalities, with
whom Stanhope was again to have dealings.[3] Above all,

---

[1] See below, ch. v, pp. 123–5.
[2] Instructions dated 25 Feb. 1709/10 in R.O., *S.P.* 94/77. Six months later,
after Almenara, Stanhope complains that the amnesty had only just been
drafted and then 'not as full as I could wish' (his Almenara dispatch of
31 July 1710).
[3] *H. MSS.*, *Hodgkin*, 86; Arneth, ii. 121. See below, ch. xii, p. 333.

he pressed, with some success, for more troops from the Emperor and more money from England for his own Spanish campaign.[1] Thereupon, accompanied by his faithful secretary and commissary Craggs, he started on another of his lightning journeys through Europe. The pace was too hot for Craggs, who at Frankfort writes that 'Mr. Stanhope and I arrived the 19th inst. [April]; he went away the same day by way of Swisserland; I was obliged to stay for my chaise which I had left to be mended six posts of . . . I hope to meet my master at Venice.' At Genoa Stanhope took specie for his bills of exchange and tried to hasten the embarkation of 3,000 Germans and other reinforcements. But, finding that haste, as he understood it, was not within the Imperialist vocabulary, and hearing that the campaign was on the point of opening in Catalonia, he left most of the Germans to follow at leisure and went off by himself on 16 May with £80,000 in specie and the 1,000 recruits he had been able to collect.[2]

His vigorous personality was sorely needed at the allies' head-quarters. There he found Charles and Starhemberg, that 'best general of the age for the defensive', still quite content to remain watching their opponents and, in spite of their own improved prospects, to leave them the initiative. For Philip, bereft of his French allies and refused by Louis even the help of Vendôme to command his troops, could muster only 22,000 Spanish troops under Villadarias, still gallant but rather elderly. Starhemberg's numbers were now almost equal and his material better, especially in Stanhope's little command of 4,200, consisting of eight English battalions under Wills, and Carpenter's 'very pretty body of English horse and dragoons', including Harvey's, 'the best in Europe'. Philip's head-quarters were at Lerida, the strong fortress just below the confluence of the Noguera and the Segre, the two rivers that formed the main defensive lines into Aragon. From Lerida Philip commanded the whole line of the Noguera, but his control of the Segre had been weakened by the recapture by Starhemberg in the previous year of Balaguer, some miles higher up that river. Little was done by Starhemberg in June and July to force his way across these rivers; in June, however, shortly after

[1] In the course of 1710 the Emperor agreed to send over 4,000 more troops to Spain (Pribram, i. 249 sqq.).
[2] H. MSS., Townshend, 64, 336.

Stanhope's arrival, Villadarias made a determined attempt
to regain the whole line of the Segre by an attack on Balaguer.
The allies retained this important position largely owing to
a cavalry charge led by Stanhope, who had two horses shot
under him.

By July, when Norris's Mediterranean fleet had brought
over reinforcements which gave Starhemberg a decided
superiority over Villadarias,[1] Stanhope lost all patience with
these weak defensive measures. 'Being thoroughly instructed
in the Queen's intentions', says Cunningham, ' . . . he
thought nothing could be more dangerous than delay . . .
especially when matters were in so great confusion in
England. He . . . being very eager to fight, said; they ought
to use their utmost endeavours to bring the enemy to an
engagement while the French were yet on the frontiers.'[2] In
June there had seemed some chance of his being allowed
to recover Valencia in co-operation with Norris's fleet; but
this came to nothing when Norris was called off to help
Seissan's invasion of Languedoc.[3] Now Stanhope demanded
that at least an effort should be made to 'enlarge their
bounds' by an advance into Aragon; and, though at the
council of war it was decided not to go beyond the Noguera
on the Catalonian frontier, he was quite content to leave
further progress to his own initiative. He himself, as was
his due, was put in command of the advance English detachment of cavalry and 1,000 grenadiers, with the task of crossing
the Segre at Balaguer and pushing on some twelve miles
to the bridge over the Noguera at Alfaraz. Once across the
Noguera the allies would have turned Philip's position at
Lerida and be able to cut off his retreat thence either north
or west.

Thus this first trial of strength resolved itself into a race
between Villadarias and Stanhope as to who should reach
Alfaraz first. Stanhope won, though his opponent was
marching on interior lines. When he had secured the
passage of the Noguera for Starhemberg's whole army on
27 July, Villadarias's army was just arriving at Almenara,
some two miles farther south. At noon Stanhope proposed

---

[1] For the composition of the opposing forces—Philip's 22,000, the allies'
24,500—see Parnell, 273 sqq.

[2] Cunningham, ii. 325.

[3] H. MSS., Hodgkin, 86; Parnell, 274. The rising in Languedoc failed, but
the expedition had some use in diverting Noailles's French troops from the
Spanish border.

making a cavalry attack on the enemy while they were still
in disorder from the march, but was stopped by the Marshal,
'who', says Stanhope, 'still seemed determined not to hazard
anything'. And so the afternoon wore on, Stanhope and
his cavalry idly watching their opponents forming up at
leisure on a hill opposite, until about six o'clock, to continue
Stanhope's account, 'the enemies having gott up all their
horses marched several squadrons down a little hill which
was between us, upon which we all cried out 'Shame,' and
I did earnestly press the King that we might have leave to
dislodge them', his chaplain adding the further quite credible
detail that Stanhope said aloud that if Charles and Starhemberg let slip so fair an opportunity he and his Dutch colleague, Belcastel, had orders to withdraw their troops, orders
which he would instantly obey and leave the country. At last,
near sunset, 'when the army were at such a shilly shally', a
messenger from Charles came to Stanhope with the order to
advance. With final instructions to his men: 'Keep close and
do not break yourselves—the only danger—for I am sure that
you will be as firm as rocks, and that all the enemy's squadrons will not be able to break you', he charged up the hill
with his left wing of twenty-six squadrons, followed later by
some cavalry sent by Starhemberg, against the enemy's forty-
two squadrons supported by a brigade and a half of infantry.
'The ennemies were so good as to give us the time we wanted'
after the charge up hill; then 'by the blessing of God we
broke their two lines' and drove them, and with them the
whole of Philip's army, in headlong flight to Lerida. An
incident in the fight not mentioned in Stanhope's dispatch,
but commemorated on a gold medal presented to him by
the Queen and still preserved at Chevening, is a hand-to-
hand combat, in the ancient style of knights in armour, he
had with the Spanish cavalry commander, hewing him to
the ground. In their precipitate flight Philip's army lost
a good part of their baggage and some of their guns, and
Philip himself and some of his horse are said to have fallen
into a canal. 'If we had had two hours daylight more',
concludes Stanhope, '. . . not one footsoldier of their army
would have escaped.' As it was, he complained in his letter
to Walpole:

'We can scarce expect to have such another occasion of ending
the war as has been missed twice in three days; the first time in
not marching to cut them off at Lerida, and the second time, in

not suffering us to attack some hours sooner as we had pressed
to do, and should have succeeded with less hazard, the Enemies
being much stronger when we attacked them than they had
been when we first proposed it.'[1]

This victory put an end to the idea of halting on the
Noguera, Stanhope always 'hectoring' the King and Starhemberg, as Carpenter says, to further successes. To avoid
being surrounded at Lerida Philip started for Saragossa on
12 August by the direct line along the Ebro and three days
later replaced Villadarias by Bay, the victor in Galway's
last engagement, who had been hastily summoned from
Estremadura. The allies made a sweep farther north, cutting
off stray detachments of Philip's army and besieging Monzon
and other strongholds in Aragon. Stanhope was in the
forefront of the march with his cavalry, who now showed
that their general's care for them and pride in their discipline
were well repaid. The going was hard, food and even water
were scarce in the burnt-up country; but animated by
Stanhope's contagious enthusiasm his men forgot to grumble.
At Sariñena, where an enemy detachment had taken refuge
in the church steeple, Stanhope, calling to mind how the
Parliamentarians had driven his grandfather's men out of
Shelford church steeple, smoked out the Spaniards in the
same way. From Sariñena the allies, Stanhope still leading,
turned southwards on 18 August and reached Osera on the
Ebro some twenty miles down-river from Saragossa, which
Philip had reached on the same day. Starhemberg was still
unwilling to venture on a decisive battle with Philip's army,
strongly posted as it was under the walls of the city, and
had intended to encamp on the left bank. But once more
Stanhope showed him the way to victory. The Spaniards
at Saragossa were on the right bank, so to that bank Stanhope at once crossed over, fording the river with Carpenter's
cavalry, 'and marched so near the enemy', writes Carpenter,
'that the Marshal could not avoid bringing up the army to
him, which was absolutely the occasion of the battle, though
his march so near them [the enemy] was contrary to orders'.

---

[1] The medal has the legend *Pugna Equestris Hispanis ad Almenaram Victis.
Julii Mensis MDCCX.* The name of the Spanish cavalry leader is given in
some books as Amezaga, but he was present at the later battle of Saragossa;
it may have been the Duke of Sarno. The details of this battle are taken mainly
from Stanhope's own dispatch in *Chevening MSS.*, and from his letter of the same
date (31 July) to Walpole in Somerville, 636; other touches come from Tindal,
iv. 176 sqq.; Mahon, *Succession*; *Add. MSS.* 31135, f. 231.

By the next evening the allied army of 23,500 was facing
Bay's army of 20,000 under the walls of Saragossa, separated
from it by the *Barranque de los Muertos*, a deep ravine so named
after Ferdinand of Aragon's victory there over the Moors.[1]

Next day the allies had to fight 'with empty bellies', as
one present reports, since the bread-convoy had not arrived,
but fought none the worse for that. Starhemberg was commanding their centre, Stanhope the left, and a Portuguese,
Atalaya, the right. Stanhope was faced by Philip's best
Spanish and Walloon troops, some of whom succeeded in
penetrating his line, pursuing some Portuguese cavalry for
over a league, and even cutting up one of Starhemberg's
batteries on their return. But Stanhope, calling on his
reserves, in his turn threw back the whole Spanish right.
Atalaya meanwhile had repulsed an attack on his position.
Starhemberg, hearing of the loss of his battery, is reported to
have said: 'That is no great matter; if Stanhope has beat the
right we are sure of a complete victory'; and, descending
into the ravine, put to flight the Spanish centre. Thus after
only three hours' fighting the whole of Philip's army was
driven off in disorder along the Ebro, not stopping to reform
till it reached Tudela, fifteen miles away. Even then only
8,000 answered the roll, some 12,000 having been killed,
captured, or dispersed. So, as Stanhope had hoped, was
Almanza retrieved. The King and Starhemberg themselves
owned that 'the Queen's troops got the day by the resolution
and conduct of Mr. Stanhope'.[2] Stanhope indeed had rough
methods of dealing with hesitating kings and generals, and
he was a fiery and a joyous fighter. He had, however,
another side, and this comes out in his instruction on the
battlefield, that every care be given to the wounded of either
side, for, said he, 'among the wounded there are never any
enemies'; a sentiment characteristic, so we are fain to believe,
of the good fighting Englishman, who, after the fight, bears
no malice to the former foe—one almost worthy to be ranked
with Wellington's cry of pity on the field of Waterloo:
'There is only one thing sadder than a battle won, and that is
the battle lost.'

[1] Carpenter to Walpole, 20 Aug. 1710, in Somerville, 638. The figures
quoted for the respective forces are those given by Parnell. Carpenter and other
contemporaries reverse the proportions.

[2] From Carpenter's letter (ib.). Stanhope's directions as to the wounded
are in Mahon, *Succession*, 312.

§ 3

This was the turning of the ways. After Saragossa there were two possible courses open to the allies: either to advance rapidly and secure the capital while the enemy was on the run, or to hold the country already gained and starve Philip of reinforcements by blocking up the exits from France. The choice between these two policies was vehemently debated at a council held at Saragossa on 27 August. The second more cautious policy was strongly advocated by Starhemberg: 'conquests', in his view, 'should be made step by step, and not by springs and bounds'. In detail his plan was that Charles's head-quarters should remain at Saragossa; that the eastern and western exits from France should be guarded by strong garrisons at Gerona and Pampeluna, on the borders of Roussillon and in Navarre respectively; that Lerida and Tortosa, Philip's two strong-holds in Catalonia, should be blockaded; and that the province of Valencia should be reoccupied to secure support from the Mediterranean fleet. By this scheme the whole of the northern and eastern block of Spain, Navarre, Catalonia, Aragon and Valencia would be secured for Charles, while Philip, cut off from France and with hardly an army of his own in being, would soon be reduced to extremities if not to submission. But this slow, unadventurous policy was not at all to Stanhope's liking. His natural bent was all for the daring, even risky, course in preference to the humdrum path of safety: he had shown it in the council before Almanza, when he had chided even the fiery Peterborough for excessive caution; he had shown it in his impetuous dash to Minorca, when, with his brother, he had bent the hesitating captains to his will; and throughout this year's campaign he had made no secret of his intention to make Starhemberg, that 'best general of the age for the defensive', and the formal, cautious Charles reach out, by a vigorous offensive, for the supreme prize—to win all or lose all. High political considerations also moved him to advocate the direct advance on Madrid. The conference at Gertruydenberg had just been broken off, leaving Louis no longer committed to his pledge to disown Philip; the war ministry in England was in a parlous condition and could only be galvanized into life by some striking success, while the Tories, if they came in, might, in their anxiety for peace, be willing to sacrifice even Spain, unless it were already in our hands. For his bold advice he had the direct authority of Marlborough, who, writing to Godolphin in the previous August, had urged that 'the reduction of Spain will never in my opinion be effected until the army in Catalonia and that in Portugal be in such a condition as that they may both march to Madrid; for if we shall think of forming projects for the reducing of the provinces of Spain, the war is likely to last much longer than I shall live.'[1] This conviction he had assuredly made known to Stanhope when they were together at the beginning of the year.

Stanhope's plan, therefore, was for Charles's army from Saragossa and Galway's from Portugal to converge by rapid marches on Madrid: at the same time he went so far with Starhemberg as to approve of strong garrisons being left in Catalonia and of the occupation of Pampeluna, and he appreciated the importance of keeping in touch with Norris's Mediterranean fleet and maintaining communication with a sea-base. Charles himself was inclined to support Starhemberg, partly on the ground that Castile was against them and would provide no supplies. But when he found the large majority of the council carried away by Stanhope's impetuous advocacy, he gave in, though with misgivings, for, as he wrote to his bride at Barcelona, 'if this plan of the English should succeed, all the glory will be theirs: if it fail, all the loss will be mine'. And so the die was cast. On the very day after this fateful decision Vendôme, whom Louis, at last yielding to his grandson's importunity, was sending to command in Spain, was on his way to Bayonne. Unfortunately, too, when a week later, at a council held at Calatayud, Stanhope reminded his colleagues of his own and Starhemberg's proposal to occupy Pampeluna, most of them, lured by the prospect of loot and glory at Madrid, paid no attention to his demand for a detachment to be sent there. Stanhope's old chief Peterborough, when he heard in London of Stanhope's proceedings, told Swift and others supping at Mr. Harley's that they might count on Stanhope losing Spain before Christmas and 'that he would venture his head upon it'.[2]

[1] Quoted in Geikie and Montgomery, 138, from the *Coxe Papers*, B.M.
[2] *Journal to Stella*, ii. 122. The various opinions expressed at the decisive council are given in Parnell, 282 sqq., but he does not mention the first council of 27 August at Saragossa and places all the proceedings at Calatayud on 4 September. This is almost certainly wrong, as the whole army would not

The march to Madrid presented no difficulty, for Philip's army had been scattered to the winds after Saragossa, nor was there any opposition to the entry into the city. Philip had fled there only to leave it on 9 September, taking with him the government officials, the grandees, and a large part of the population to Valladolid.[1] Twelve days later Stanhope with the advance guard of the army entered the city. But it was soon evident that little had been gained thereby. He set up a military government, assisted by the few Spaniards who could be persuaded to serve, commandeered provisions for the troops and sent to the basilica of Our Lady of Atocha to recover the allied standards lost at Almanza. On the 28th Charles arrived from Alcala. He first paid his devotions and made rich offerings at the shrine of Our Lady of Atocha, but 'the saint remained neuter; both kings had been her adorers', Cunningham drily remarks: then he made his solemn state-entry into his capital. There could be no doubt as to the sentiments of the inhabitants. Save for the feeble cries of a few children bribed with copper coins, Charles was received in stony silence, none but his own soldiers appeared in the streets and all the houses were closely shuttered. This was his last appearance in Madrid: refusing to stay at the royal palace in a city that seemed like one of the dead, he first took refuge in a country house in the neighbourhood and then at his camp at El Pardo six miles away. But this cold reception at Madrid was not the worst blow for the allied commanders. Though even on the east their communications were unduly long, yet on that side they could still count on keeping in touch with Catalonia and above all with the seaports open to Norris's ships. But on the west they were exposed to attack by any force Philip might be able to reconstitute. For the army from the Portuguese frontier which should have been there to protect their western flank and communications with Lisbon had not only failed to appear but was still on the Portuguese border. When the summons for a convergent march on Madrid

have advanced to Calatayud, on the way to Madrid, had the decision to go to the capital not already been taken. Tindal, iv. 179, clearly distinguishes the two councils. Interesting details are also found in Mahon, *Succession*, 312 sqq.; Cunningham, ii. 329; St. Simon, viii. 114 sqq. The importance attached by Stanhope to sea-communications is to be seen in his correspondence with Norris throughout the advance to Madrid in *Add. MSS.* 35838, ff. 356 sqq.

[1] No less than 30,000 of the population went with him according to a Spanish writer, C. P. Moreno, *Asalto de Brihuega* (Guadalajara, 1911).

arrived at the Anglo-Portuguese head-quarters, Galway had
already left for England, and his successor, Lord Portmore,
had not yet arrived: and without either of them the Portuguese commander could not be moved to cross into Estremadura, especially as French influence was again gaining
ground at the court of Lisbon.

If the inhabitants of Madrid were at first merely sullen, as
the weeks passed they began to appear dangerous. Their
feelings were inflamed by grievances, real or imaginary, but
all artfully exaggerated by rumour to enormous proportions.
Much indignation was expressed because Charles invited the
great ladies left in Madrid to come and kiss his hand when
his wife was not present: no King of Spain had made such
a request in the absence of his Queen. Other rumours were
more serious. It was, for example, widely believed that not
only the Protestant English but even the Catholic Starhemberg and his Germans had come to destroy their cherished
religion and forcibly convert them to Lutheranism. Queen
Anne, good, pious soul, had, it must be confessed, afforded
some basis to this belief by anticipating Borrow and exporting, with her soldiers, 14,000 copies of the Anglican catechism
for distribution among the deluded papists of Spain.[1] Nor
were the English ever able to live down the unsavoury
reputation they had justly earned in Spain after the first
Cadiz expedition of 1702 for desecrating and plundering
churches.[2] Stories were handed about of acts of sacrile-
gious rapine from the churches and monasteries. 'Throughout the length and breadth of Spain', it was reported, 'there
is no place big or small, wherein a saint has not been
deprived of arm or leg or an altar destroyed . . . for Queen
Anne's Bull grants plenary indulgence to all those who kill
Bishops, steal that which belongs to another, . . . in a word to
the followers of Luther.'[3] Stanhope, who had appointed as
magistrates a few Spaniards with a grievance against Philip's
rule, was credited in one of the Spanish fly-sheets with the
cynical advice of using the vengeance of these renegades
against their fellow citizens as a cloak for the Lutherans'
covetousness and plundering instincts and so 'to squeeze out
the juice of this lemon [sc. Madrid] . . . without breaking
its rind, and if the pips leap out under violence, we can

[1] Klopp, xiii. 282.
[2] See above, ch. ii, pp. 29, 30.
[3] *Dialogo entre un Afecto, y un Desafecto al General Estanop*, Madrid, 1710.

just throw them off the plate'.[1] Many of the rumours current during the allied occupation were, on Philip's return,
printed in broadsheets and squibs in verse or prose directed
against Guido Estaremberg and still more against Estanópe,
who was regarded as the chief villain and the most unscrupulous plunderer. These stories of plundering and worse were,
as was natural, greedily accepted in Paris; and St. Simon
tells a most unlikely and unconfirmed story of Stanhope's
carrying off two tapestries from the royal palace that he
perforce 'revomit' after Brihuega.[2] So little were these
stories of Estanópe himself true that, when he had been
taken prisoner, his second-in-command, Carpenter, wrote to
the Secretary of State that Stanhope when in command at
Madrid, allowed no plundering and 'suffer'd nothing to be
touched'.[3] But in time of war or popular excitement facts
have little chance against prejudice.

At any rate the allied generals soon had to admit that
Madrid, an unfortified city on an open plateau, was the
worst possible centre for an army of occupation. Not only
was a hostile population ever ready to kill isolated soldiers,
but supplies were almost impossible to procure from the
surrounding country owing to the activity of raiding bands
of guerillas under the partisan leaders Don Feliciano
Bracamonte, who lurked in the Guadarrama hills north
of Madrid, and Don José Vallejo, who was especially active
east of Madrid, cutting off stray parties who were guarding
the communications with Aragon and the coast. Vallejo
captured a Portuguese regiment at Ocaña, routed a Dutch
detachment on its way to Saragossa, defeated Stanhope
himself, who tried to capture him, near Alcala de Henares
on 1 October, and even penetrated to the suburbs of Madrid.[4]
It was therefore decided in October to move the government
and the main garrison for Castile fifty miles farther south to
Toledo, better suited for defence with its fortified hill encompassed on three sides by the Tagus. When the army left, the
wives of the grandees remaining in Madrid were also sent
to Toledo, where they could be better protected from insult
and mob violence, though naturally, in the excited state of
popular feeling, this banishment was attributed to sinister

---

[1] *Carta Para el Escarmiento*, Madrid, 1710. A great many of these broadsheets, &c., are collected in volumes called *Papeles Varios* (1302-3) in the
British Museum. There are copies also at Chevening.

[2] St. Simon, viii. 114 sqq.　　　　　　　　　[3] R.O., *S.P.* 94/77.

[4] Moreno, l.c. 15.

designs of Estaremberg and Estanópe on their virtue.
Although, as Stanhope had to confess to the Secretary of
State, Dartmouth, 'the country is our enemy; and we are
not masters, in Castile, of more ground than we encamp on',
yet the idea still was, as he had explained to Norris in
September, to winter in Castile and keep open the communications with Aragon and the coast-ports.[1] Above all,
it was hoped that even yet the western flank might be
protected by the army from Portugal. Five expresses urging
haste had Stanhope sent off before the middle of October
directed to Lord Portmore, whom he wrongly thought to
have arrived; 'few men', as he told Craggs, 'having taken
so much pains as I am doing to get a Viceroy over himself'
—for Portmore, as his senior, would have taken over the
command.[2] On 30 September, it is true, the Portuguese
commander, Villa Verde, had brought himself to venture
across the frontier, but had gone only thirty miles into Spain
when, hearing that the Spanish commander Bay was hovering about in the neighbourhood, he retired to Portugal on
the plea that his men were 'tired'. Meanwhile Stanhope had
gone down the Tagus to make connexion with him at the
bridge of Almaraz, but on arriving at Talavera, half-way,
in the middle of October, heard that Almaraz was already
occupied by Vendôme's troops; so he could do nothing but
return to Toledo. Vendôme indeed had seen at once that
the only chance left for the allies to maintain themselves
in Castile was to keep up communications with the Portuguese and that the bridge at Almaraz was the key position
for these communications. 'Your majesty has gained more,'
he said to Philip V, 'by the possession of the bridge at
Almaraz than the Archduke gained by the battle of Saragossa.'[3]

Vendôme, the son of one of Henri IV's bastards, had
much of his grandfather's military genius, especially in his
faculty of rapidly appreciating and meeting a serious emergency; but without such stimulus he was inordinately
sluggish and the slave of the most ignoble pleasures. On this
occasion he was on his mettle. In 1708 he had been sent
as mentor to Philip V's brother, the Duke of Burgundy,
who was nominal commander-in-chief in Flanders; but the

[1] Letters to Norris of 13 Sept. 1710. *Add. MSS.* 35838, f. 356: to Dartmouth
of 6 Nov. in *Chevening MSS.* quoted in Mahon, *Anne*, ii. 183.
[2] Mahon, *Anne*, ii. 280.   [3] Moreno, l.c. 17.

straight-laced Duke, owing to his loathing of Vendôme's
morals and, perhaps, some jealousy of his military genius,
had neglected to take advice from him which might have
prevented the disaster of Oudenarde and the loss of Lille.
Louis's grandson was naturally not the one to suffer for
these misfortunes, but Vendôme, who for two years was left
in the cold; and it was only with the utmost reluctance that
Louis consented to lend him to his other grandson Philip V
at the crisis of his fortunes. On parting with him Louis,
whose fault was never meanness in money matters, offered
him 50,000 crowns for his expenses, to which Vendôme, not
to be outdone in magnificence, replied, 'J'ai trouvé, Sire,
dans mes propres ressources de quoi faire ces campagnes,
j'espère même que je ne serai point à charge à l'Espagne.'[1]
The crisis was indeed great enough to make Vendôme
abandon his normal habits and display all his mastery in
war. At Bayonne he organized the French reinforcements for
service in Spain, then, reaching Valladolid on 17 September,
arranged his plan of campaign with Philip and Noailles,
called over to the conference from Roussillon. He found
his task lightened by the outburst of national feeling that
rallied to Philip in his distress; not only the grandees but
the whole population were eager to give their services in
the field and contributions in money or in kind to support
what since 1706 had become the national cause. And now
once more the undisciplined zeal of the Spanish levies was to
be directed by a master and controlled by the admixture of
some of the best French regiments. Vendôme's idea was to
hem in the invaders of Castile and cut off all their communications. He sent a detachment to Aranda on the Douro,
north of Madrid, to head them off from Aragon and Catalonia; Noailles was to enter Catalonia from Perpignan and
set siege to Gerona, 'the barrier and key' to the northern
passes; Bay was ordered to take command of the western
army of Estremadura with the easy task of keeping the un-
enterprising Portuguese within their own borders; Vendôme,
for his part, went by rapid marches through Salamanca, and
thence over the Sierras to Plasencia in Estremadura, meaning
to come to close quarters with Charles's army. On 17 October
he had sent his advance guard to hold the bridge at Almaraz
and by 8 November had arrived at Talavera, lately vacated

[1] Targe, v. 439. In the following pages are to be found details of Vendôme's
dispositions in Spain.

by Stanhope, and only about forty miles from Toledo. By this time, apart from the other detachments he had sent off to complete the circle, he had with him an army of 25,000 French and Spanish troops against Starhemberg's army, already reduced to 17,000.

Even then Stanhope was still clinging to the hope that it would be possible to winter in Castile on a line extending from Toledo to the mountains of Aragon, clinging to this scheme on the ground he had always maintained that it was 'of consequence to us in the opinion of the world to know that we are masters of Madrid and Toledo and continue in the heart of Castile'. When a few days later the last soldiers of the allies left Madrid amid the joy-bells of the churches, and all troops were concentrated either at Toledo or in the two camps formed farther east between the Tagus and Madrid, even when, on 18 November, Charles, anxious to see his wife at Barcelona, and on the plea that the defences of Gerona must be strengthened against Noailles, took off 2,000 of the cavalry that could ill be spared as an escort on his journey to Catalonia, this hope still lingered. But Stanhope finally had to bow to facts and the almost unanimous opinion of the council of war for retreat. At the end of November the garrison of Toledo was called in, unfortunately not before the Alcazar, the noble citadel that crowns Toledo's heights, had been damaged by fire;[1] and all detachments were concentrated at the camp of Chinchon some thirty miles south-east of Madrid. Thence on 2 December Stanhope wrote to Norris that next day they were to start on their 150-mile march back to Aragon under the worst possible conditions, without supplies or even money to buy food and 'with the country about us all up in arms'. Nor were the prospects too good in the country to which they were going, as French troops were said to be on the borders of Aragon and Noailles on the way to attack Gerona: all hope of safety depended on Norris's ability to bring succours by sea to Catalonia.[2]

So the retreat began on 3 December. To give greater

[1] A proposal was made by the Portuguese general Atalaya to burn Toledo to the ground before leaving it, but happily rejected by the allied commanders; unfortunately, however, they accidentally set fire to the Alcazar, the citadel that crowns its heights, in getting rid of surplus stores they could not take away and were unwilling to leave for Philip's troops.

[2] *Add. MSS.* 35838, ff. 360, 368, to Norris, 18 Nov. and 2 Dec. 1710; Mahon, *Succession*, 329, to Dartmouth, 18 Nov. 1710.

facilities for foraging, Starhemberg and Stanhope divided the army into three divisions, marching parallel with one another, the right under Atalaya with his Spanish and Portuguese levies, Starhemberg in the centre with the German troops and Stanhope with most of his English in the position of greatest danger on the left flank, exposed to the attacks of Vallejo and his irregulars. The last quarter, however, from which danger was anticipated was from Vendôme's army, last heard of at Talavera, some seventy miles from Chinchon.

But Vendôme was still in the mood to perform miracles. Entering Madrid with Philip on the very day the allies left Chinchon, he hardly allowed the King time to present oblations in his turn to Our Lady of Atocha and enjoy the enthusiastic welcome of his good people of Madrid before rushing him off with the main army to catch up an advance party of picked troops under Valdecañas already sent ahead to pursue the retreating allies. On 6 December Philip and Vendôme slept at Alcala de Henares; on the following day Vendôme, finding the Henares in flood at Guadalajara, sent the infantry over the bridge and himself plunged across the raging torrent at the head of the cavalry. At Guadalajara Vendôme heard that Stanhope with his left wing was already invested at Brihuega by Valdecañas, reinforced by Vallejo's and Bracamonte's irregulars. By midday on 8 December the King and Vendôme had brought up the artillery and the main army within sight of Brihuega.

By the evening of Saturday, 6 December, the three divisions of the allied army had marched some fifty to sixty miles in the four days since leaving Chinchon. Starhemberg's head-quarters were at Cifuentes, Atalaya farther east, and Stanhope's left wing at Brihuega on the river Tajuña, a good five-hours' march by bad and hilly roads from Cifuentes. A detachment of cavalry served as connecting link between Starhemberg and Stanhope. At that time two of the English infantry battalions and a squadron of dragoons under Brigadier Lepel were still with Starhemberg,[1] waiting to escort Du Bourgay's train of artillery to Stanhope, whose whole force at Brihuega, one Portuguese and seven English battalions and eight squadrons of English horse, was about

[1] With Lepel were a squadron of dragoons, Du Bourgay's and Richards's Foot, and the men of the artillery train. For Lepel's orders from Starhemberg see the chaplain's account in Tindal, iv. 179.

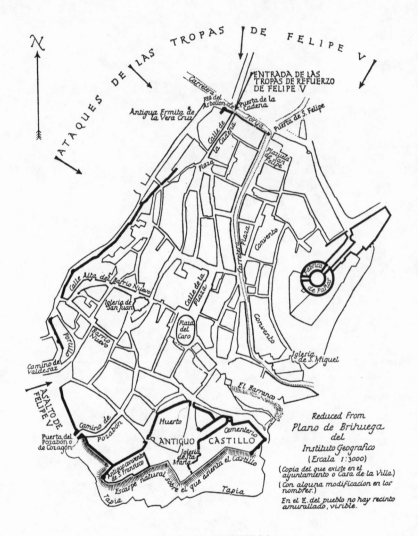

PLAN OF BRIHUEGA

4,500 men.[1] During his march the only hostile body observed by Stanhope were small detachments, taken to be Vallejo's irregulars with whom he had had a skirmish on the previous day at Horche; and thinking himself secure at Brihuega he sent a message to Starhemberg that he would remain there on the following day to bake bread for the troops. But on that very evening Valdecañas, who had reached Torija, only nine miles farther west, was told of Stanhope's proximity by a peasant and at once started off with his troops to join Vallejo and Bracamonte round Brihuega. Accordingly, on the Sunday morning, when Stanhope sent a small detachment to take possession of the bridge and ford over the Tajuña about 600 yards south of the town, he found them already held by Spanish troops. Even then Stanhope thought he had no other enemy near him than Vallejo's band of 1,200, easily brushed aside when he was on the march; so he went on levying corn and barley from the townspeople and baking bread for his men, and sent another message to Starhemberg describing his position. In fact Valdecañas was holding the bridge and had sent off Vallejo and Bracamonte to cut off Stanhope's communications with Starhemberg, which they accomplished by capturing the cavalry force acting as connecting link between them. Not till the morning of Monday the 8th, the Feast of the Immaculate Conception of the B.V.M., did Stanhope realize his mistake. Large bodies of horse, thickening as the day advanced, then appeared on the neighbouring heights, and four batteries could be seen taking position on the north and west of the town.

Stanhope cannot justly be blamed for not having thoroughly scouted the surrounding country on his march, since reconnaissance parties in adequate strength could not be spared from his small division; and it is not surprising that all attempts to get information from the country-people were

[1] With Stanhope were the R. Dragoons and Harvey's, Pepper' and Stanhope's Horse, and the following battalions of Foot Guards: Harrison's, Wade's, Dormer's, Bowles's, Marden's, Gore's and Dalzell's (Portuguese). His exact numbers are difficult to arrive at. Parnell, 288 sqq., put them at 2,536, Mahon, *Succession*, 333, at 5,500, Spanish authorities at 6,000 or more. Mr. C. T. Atkinson has kindly drawn my attention to various official lists to be found at the Record Office in *S.P.* 94/77 and /78, and in *Dom.* 110, pp. 363–70. Some of these give the rank and file only with Stanhope, 'at first cantonment' on the way to Brihuega; others give the number of prisoners—officers, N.C.O.'s and drummers as well as rank and file—captured at Brihuega. From a comparison of these lists I arrive at the approximate figure of Stanhope's force at Brihuega, 4,500. But statistics of armies on active service are notoriously untrustworthy.

useless, since they were all devoted adherents of Philip. As he tells Lord Dartmouth in his dispatch, until he was established in Brihuega he was convinced that he had no more formidable body against him than Vallejo's 1,200 irregular horsemen and had no inkling of Vendôme's proximity, believing him to be no nearer than Talavera, '45 long leagues distant'. But Major-General Pepper brought another charge against him, that he omitted to place outposts on the hills outside Brihuega, and Pepper even went so far as to tell Marlborough that, when he himself was about to post pickets on the hills, he was stopped from so doing by Lieut.-General Carpenter, apparently on orders from Stanhope.[1] Pepper, the man previously described by Stanhope as a good colonel of dragoons but not fit for higher command,[2] always bore him a grudge and cannot be regarded as a trustworthy witness against him: and this incident may refer to the time when Stanhope saw so many enemy horsemen already on the hills that the small reconnaissance party he could spare would be useless.[3] Nevertheless Stanhope can hardly be acquitted of remissness in not taking the elementary military precaution, immediately on his arrival at Brihuega, of placing outposts where they could give him timely warning of an approaching enemy.

Brihuega is an old Moorish town situated on a small plateau about 3,000 feet above sea-level at the confluence of two valleys sloping towards the Tajuña, a river rising in the Sierra de Guadarrama range and flowing southwards into the Tagus. On all sides it is commanded by low hills of limestone formation some 400 feet higher than the plateau on which it stands, the most prominent being Horca and the Cerro San José to the north. South and south-east of the town the ground dips steeply to the narrow gorge of the Tajuña and thence rises as steeply to the hills towards Cifuentes. The town, nearly a mile and a quarter in circumference, is encompassed by a Moorish wall, over two yards wide, of limestone and mud mixed with gravel, and is defended on the south by a Moorish citadel with a steep escarpment towards the river. In addition to the Puerta San Miguel at the south-east corner whence the road crossing

[1] Coxe, *Marlborough*, iii. 160. Tindal, iv. 180, says that Carpenter advised a guard on the high ground.
[2] See above, ch. iii, p. 71.
[3] See Stanhope's account to Dartmouth quoted in Mahon, *Succession*, 334.

the Tajuña issues, the main exits are the Puertas de San
Felipe and de la Cadena on the north and de Cozagón on
the west. With his small force Stanhope could not spare
enough men to dispute the possession of the surrounding
hills, nor was he strong enough to force his way through
to Starhemberg. Brihuega itself, owing to its large perimeter,
was not easy to defend, for he had no artillery and the
Moorish walls, though massive, had no projecting works
from which to take an attacking force in flank. But on
realizing his danger he took the best measures possible.
He sent his aide-de-camp Captain Cosby with five other
men to make their way through to Starhemberg and warn
him that it would not be possible to hold out in Brihuega
beyond the following day: since the bridge and ford were
held by the enemy, these brave men swam across the flooded
river and, eluding the Spanish cavalry guarding the hills
to the east, delivered their message to Starhemberg. Then
he set to work to improve the defences as best he could in
the time.

> 'With extraordinary speed and with the special capacity of the
> Anglo-Saxon race for mechanical work', says a Spanish account,
> 'in one day the besieged raised defence-works which would
> usually have taken a week to complete. They protected the four
> principal gates with strong parapets, crowned the walls with
> battlements, repaired the ruined turrets of the citadel, fortified
> houses, churches and sanctuaries, dug trenches and pits in the
> streets, and at vulnerable points collected stocks of combustible
> material, fully resolved to hold their own against the whole
> Spanish army until the Austrian general arrived.'[1]

Besides manning the walls, as far as his resources allowed
him, with four battalions under Carpenter and Wills to
protect the two northern gates and four more on the western
side, Stanhope sent a detachment to hold an outlying
hermitage de la Vera Cruz at the north-west angle and
kept his cavalry and dragoons, dismounted, in three of
the central squares as a reserve for emergencies.

By midday on the Monday Philip and Vendôme had
arrived with the main force of their army, which amounted
to some 10,000 men. Batteries were placed on the hills
Horca and San José to the north of the town and began firing
on the San Felipe and Cadena gates, a third at a spring
called Quiñoneros, a little south of San José and within range

[1] Moreno, l.c. 27.

of the hermitage and the Puerta Cadena, and a fourth in the roadway skirting La Atalaya hill to the west, to fire against the Puerta de Cozagón and the western ramparts. A nun of one of the convents in Brihuega relates that by the evening of that day 1,100 shots were fired at the town,[1] but, though the bombs and grape-shot fired inside caused some damage to the defenders, the round-shot aimed at the walls was ineffective, as the guns were only field-pieces and their elevation only enabled them to batter the tops of the ramparts. So far the besiegers' only success was in destroying the outlying hermitage de la Vera Cruz and driving its garrison into the town. In the afternoon a summons to surrender was sent to Stanhope, 'to which', he says, 'we made such an answer as became us'.

On Tuesday the 9th the guns were brought down below the crests of the hills and so were able to fire more advantageously at the walls; the two northern gates, San Felipe and Cadena, were shattered; and a mine was dug against the north-western salient near the Puerta de la Cadena. A few more belated Spanish regiments arrived early in the morning, whereupon Vendôme was urged by the soldiers to order a general assault on the town. This at first he refused to sanction as involving too great a risk before a practicable breach had been made. But he changed his mind on receiving a message from Bracamonte about 2 o'clock that Starhemberg was on the march and would arrive early next morning at Brihuega, for he was resolved at all costs to capture Stanhope's force before Starhemberg could rescue him and so present a united front to Philip's army. More cavalry was sent across the Tajuña to check Starhemberg's advance from Cifuentes, another summons to surrender was sent to Stanhope, who answered as before, and about 3 p.m. the attack was launched. The main attack under the Marqués de Toy was directed against the northern side, where part of the wall had been destroyed by the mine and the two gates shattered, while a second force under the Conde de Las Torres was sent to make a feint attack on the Barrio Nuevo and the Cozagón gate on the west; a third force under the Conde de San Esteban was held in reserve. To prevent the flight of the garrison, mounted troops were disposed along the heights and some battalions guarded the exit to the bridge over the Tajuña.

[1] Serrada, *La Razón de un Centenario*, 84, 126.

The fight that ensued is described by the Spanish historians
as the most hotly contested of all the battles in Spain during
this war, one in which prodigies of valour were performed
on both sides. The most determined assaults were those
made at the Puerta San Felipe, where Wills was in command,
and at an angle near the Puerta de la Cadena, where
Carpenter held the breach. The gaps in the wall made by the
cannon were high, in one place so high that they could only
be reached by cavalrymen standing on their horses' backs,
and so narrow that the assailants could only squeeze through
in single file. Carpenter, fighting with his men in the front
line, was wounded in the face and escaped death only by
a miracle. San Estebán, commanding the reserve, got
permission to lead his men into a breach, which he entered
first and stood helping them up the wall, and, when
he was remonstrated with for his rashness, called out
that his father the Marqués de Villena was a prisoner in
Italy and that he was determined to capture an English
general to exchange for him. Finally, as the early winter
evening was closing in, the Spaniards burst through by the
northern and western gates, climbed into the houses near
the wall and began firing at the English below. Even then
the fighting went on with unabated vigour. Contesting
every step in the narrow streets, the Englishmen fired at
the oncoming Spaniards from the fortified houses, engulfed
them in the trenches dug across the road and held them up
with heavy barricades hastily constructed. Stanhope himself animated his men and is credibly reported to have taken
a hand in the actual fighting. Darkness added horrors to the
scene of bloodshed, darkness occasionally lit up by the flares of
tow and damp wood set on fire by Stanhope's orders to choke
the enemy with the smoke and flames. Not till the Spaniards
had dragged guns into the town and begun clearing the
streets with grape-shot did Stanhope withdraw his men to
the citadel and offer to cease fighting on condition he and
his men were allowed to go free. But Vendôme was not
disposed to make a present of such valiant fighters to Starhemberg and curtly told Stanhope that, unless within an
hour they surrendered at discretion, they could expect no
mercy. By 7 o'clock of that winter evening barely 700 more
rounds of ammunition were left, over 2,000 of the enemy
were in the town, which in many parts was in flames, no
sign of relief had come from Starhemberg and, to quote

Stanhope's own dispatch, 'I thought myself in conscience
obliged to try and save so many brave men who had done
good service to the Queen and will, I hope, live to do so
again.' So he beat the chamade and agreed to a capitulation
whereby, on fairly favourable terms, he and his contingent
became prisoners of war. The loss on the English side
in killed and wounded was about 600, but Vendôme's
casualties were double that number. Most of the prisoners
were hurried off that very night by forced marches to prevent
their falling into Starhemberg's hands. It was noted by
devout Spaniards that 9 December, the day of their victory,
was the feast-day of Santa Leocadia the patron-saint of
Toledo, who thus avenged the outrage done to the Alcazar
of her chosen city.[1]

Some controversy, as might be expected, arose as to
Stanhope's generalship in this affair. It was asserted that
he went to Brihuega, too far to the left of Cifuentes, contrary to Starhemberg's orders, but of this there is no evidence.
On the contrary, Starhemberg, as commander-in-chief, is to
blame, if anybody, for leaving so wide a gap between himself and his left wing or at any rate for not seeing that his
communications with Stanhope were more secure. On the
other hand, Stanhope's omission to place outposts when
he arrived was, as we have seen, certainly an error of
judgement. It was also contended that before the encircle-
ment had been completed he might have broken out to
join Starhemberg, but the success of such a move, after he
had become fully aware of his danger, is more than doubtful. Pepper again brings the more serious charge against
him that there was no necessity to surrender so soon and
that both he and Carpenter were against it, since it was
still possible to hold out in the citadel. This criticism,

---

[1] From the English side the accounts of this battle are somewhat meagre.
The best is in Mahon, *Succession*, who prints Stanhope's dispatch to Dartmouth
in his Appendix, and in his text gives further details from the Stanhope MSS.
at Chevening; Parnell, 288 sqq., also has a good account. For the Spanish
side see San Felipe, *Comentarios . . . hasta 1725*, ii, and Targe, v. 464, largely
based on San Felipe. Two local accounts, brought out to celebrate the second
centenary of Brihuega and Villaviciosa, A. P. Serrada, *La Razón de un Centenario*, and C. P. Moreno, *Asalto de Brihuega y Batalla de Villaviciosa*, both
published at Guadalajara in 1911, have much valuable information and the
former has some useful documents. For a map of the country, a tracing of an
old plan of Brihuega in the Ayuntiamento and some interesting photographs
of the town and surroundings I am deeply indebted to Don Modesto Bargallo
of Guadalajara and to Mr. Robert Aitken who introduced me to Señor
Bargallo.

which is also levelled against him by St. Simon, is undoubtedly wrong; with his ammunition almost spent and with no word of Starhemberg Stanhope was right in refusing to sacrifice his men's lives uselessly against overwhelming odds.[1]

Starhemberg had marched from Cifuentes to relieve Stanhope, but did not reach the neighbourhood of Brihuega till after nightfall. He fired some guns as a signal, but hearing no guns in answer, concluded that Stanhope had not been able to hold out. He had received Stanhope's message late at night on the 8th, and had at once given orders for the march next morning. But there was delay in the arrival of Du Bourgay's train, and he would not allow even a strong detachment to go forward until his whole force was assembled about midday. Had he arrived a few hours earlier he would almost certainly have rescued Stanhope and probably won a decisive victory over Vendôme, whose army, already engaged with Stanhope, he would have been attacking from the rear. Even on the following day when he met Vendôme, flushed with victory, at Villaviciosa, he was able to beat him off the field and pursue his own march to Catalonia unmolested.[2]

This campaign proved to be the last of importance in the Peninsula during this war. Vendôme, having triumphantly restored Philip to his capital and driven the invaders back to the coast, during the next campaign returned to his more normal habit of sloth. The Tories were in power in England, and by an irony of fate had actually decided, on the eve of Brihuega, to replace Stanhope as commander of the English contingent by Argyll,[3] who in fact succeeded

[1] This criticism of Pepper's is in his letter to Marlborough already quoted and in another to Ormonde in *H. MSS., Ormonde*, viii. 324. See also St. Simon, viii. 114 sqq. *H. MSS., Portland*, v. 219, contains the charge that Stanhope went to Brihuega against Starhemberg's orders, but obviously only as a camp rumour from Barcelona likely to be pleasing to a Tory patron. The historian Stanhope has sufficiently exposed the absurdity of a story that Stanhope was betrayed to Vendôme by a French mistress he was taking with him through Spain. The whole story appears to be based on some *Mémoires de Mme de Muci*, purporting to have been written by her 'femme de Chambre Mlle D. . . .' (Amsterdam, 1731). The story appeared in the *Monthly Magazine* of September 1832 and Lord Stanhope's convincing refutation of it the month following. According to the tale, Stanhope, disguised as a woman, was accompanying Mme de Muci from Paris to Pampeluna at the very time when he was posting through Germany to Genoa with Craggs.

[2] Tindal, iv. 179 sqq. gives the best account of Starhemberg's movements, based on the narrative of an army chaplain with Lepel. Starhemberg's signal guns were heard by Vendôme but not by Stanhope; Klopp, xiii. 544.

[3] The rumour of this supersession is mentioned in Boyer, iii. 64, and in

him. But they were not inclined to delay their long-desired peace by taking vigorous measures even to secure for the faithful Catalans their local privileges assured to them in the Queen's name by both Peterborough and Stanhope. Charles, by the death of his brother Joseph, succeeded to the other Habsburg dominions and also became Emperor, and in the summer of 1711 left Spain never to return. A year after Brihuega the last English troops left in Spain or Portugal were taken off to Mahon and Gibraltar, the only permanent reminders, but those no mean ones, of England's achievements in this peninsular war. One of the concluding incidents in the war was the relief of Cardona by Starhemberg, when Stanhope's last remaining brother Edward, who, like Philip, had served under him, was killed in action. Charles, already Emperor, on hearing of this loss 'not only lamented the death of this gallant youth, but the unhappy state of the whole Stanhope family during this whole war'.[1]

§ 4

Brihuega was the end of Stanhope's military career. His dispatch to Dartmouth, written three weeks after the defeat, concludes with the words: 'I cannot express to your Lordship how much this blow has broken my spirits, which I shall never recover'; and to a friend he wrote: 'Fortune hath crushed me, and I know no remedy but patience. I am sensible how I shall be arraigned in England; but I assure you that thought is not half so mortifying to me as the consequences to the public.'[2] One need not of course take such words too literally, penned as they were under the immediate impression of the staggering blow that had dashed all his high hopes for this campaign; and, had the

a letter of R. Molesworth of 13 November 1710, 'the design being to lay Stanhope aside for beating the French king of Spain as soon as they can send a worse general in his room' (*H. MSS., Clements*, 248). The rumour is confirmed by a letter from Stanhope to Ormonde of 14 December 1710 in which he writes: 'My Enemys will alledge and report of me, that there being another general to come over in my Post, I was neglectful and did not value which side got the better; But I do assure your Grace, that I am not so great an Enemy of my country, having always acted in my Command with great sincerity, and according to the best of my Judgment.' This letter was published in a broadsheet, of which there is a copy in Sir Charles Firth's collection.

[1] Cunningham, ii. 373. For the close and long connexion of the Stanhope family with Spain see Appendix A, p. 447.
[2] Mahon, *Succession*, 340.

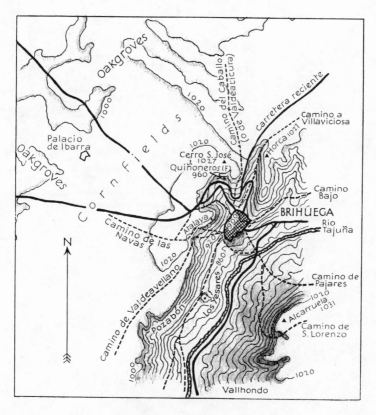

BRIHUEGA AND DISTRICT

chance been given him, he would assuredly have returned
to a military career with the same vigour and impetuosity as
ever. But he got no such chance, for he was kept a prisoner
of war for over a year and a half; and then the fighting was
over. Much of his time in captivity was taken up in disputes
about the non-observance of the terms of capitulation that
he and Vendôme had signed at Brihuega. Contrary to
Cunningham's characteristic jibe that Stanhope only stipulated 'for the safety of his own baggage and linen' and that
his men 'laying down their arms at Stanhope's command,
were stripped and sent like slaves into several parts of Spain',[1]
he had obtained permission for all ranks to keep their
personal baggage, for officers and men of the same regiment
to march together with adequate food and protection to
some seaport town to await exchange, and that due care
should be taken of the sick and the wounded.[2] But Cunningham's statement is true of the prisoners' actual condition.
Stanhope, writing in February 1711 to Vendôme, says
that 'depuis que j'ay eu l'honneur d'adresser a V.A. des
plaintes sur ce sujet on continue à disperser nos soldats sans
officiers; dans quelques villages on les enchaîne comme des
forçats et on leur fait payer l'eau qu'ils boivent'.[3] He himself was paying for the upkeep of the prisoners of war at
a monthly cost of nearly £9,000 until he obtained a credit
from the Treasury for that purpose; and it was not till May
1711 that he was able to negotiate a treaty of exchange
with Vendôme.[4] But this proved of no benefit to Stanhope.
To the great indignation of Marlborough and his other
friends an exchange was always being put off, even after the
Preliminaries of London had been signed on 8 October
1711, on the plea that there was no prisoner held by the
allies of equal rank with himself.[5] Starhemberg, with
whom the negotiations for exchange mainly rested, does not
seem to have pressed the matter very energetically, the
Tory ministry at home were in no hurry to have so ardent
a critic of their proceedings back in the House of Commons,[6]

[1] Cunningham, ii. 333.   [2] Mahon, *Succession*, 337.
[3] 11 Feb. 1711, *Chevening MSS.*
[4] *Treas. Papers, 1708–14*, 242, 258; R.O., *S.P.* 94/78, letter of 23 Feb. 1711.
[5] *Marlborough*, v. 264, 323, 464, 550.
[6] See *State Anatomy of Great Britain*, 1716: 'This new way of excluding ministers
they practised also against Gen¹ Stanhope, whom, after falling under the chance
of war, they left a prisoner as long as it suited their convenience; though he
made that valuable acquisition of Port Mahon, and though he serv'd it with
no less gallantry than disinterestedness, his hands being acknowledged no less

and Philip V is said to have been still obstructing his exchange in January 1712 'least he being a Whig should oppose the peace that France has agreed to with that nation'. Finally, after the armistice of June with France Stanhope was exchanged for the Duke of Escalona, arriving back in England in August 1712.

During his captivity in Spain he was at first sent to Valladolid, later to Saragossa and to Noguiera and finally to Pau. At first he was kept very strictly and found that even his letters were stopped, as he complains to Dartmouth. To his friend Sir John Cropley he writes, 'If I continue long a prisoner, which is not unlikely, I shall grow a philosopher, having no other comfort but books, yet even these are not to be found here', and he relates that when he asked the Jesuits for a Demosthenes they sent him a book with Demosthenes on the back in gilt letters: 'I opened it and found it to be a Tully; it might have been the Alcoran for aught they knew.' However, he had some alleviations. He was able, after a time, to exchange letters with his friends in England and had books sent him. Among these was the recently published *Characteristics* of his friend Lord Shaftesbury, who was so pleased with the commendation of this book sent him by Stanhope that he made him one of his executors.[1] At Valladolid he met Alberoni, then a comparatively unknown priest in Vendôme's train, who gained the favour of his patrons partly by his culinary art in preparing succulent Italian dishes, partly by his witty, not to say broad, stories and sayings. The two men occasionally dined together, and seem to have gained a respect for one another's abilities.[2] At any rate these meetings enabled Stanhope to add one more to his collection of European statesmen such as Orleans, Dubois, the Emperor Charles, Starhemberg, Victor Amedeus of Savoy and Prince Eugene, with whom he was on more or less close terms of intimacy; and he found the advantage of these early encounters when, in later life, he had to deal with them as a statesman. He could also use his enforced

clean by all sides, than his heart is honourable and brave, as his polite literature and capacity are unquestionable.'

[1] J. Micklethwait, Stanhope's man of business, saw that he was supplied with books and pamphlets and looked after his interests generally. In a letter of 1/12 July 1712 he tells Stanhope how delighted Shaftesbury was with his commendation. This and a letter from Shaftesbury to Cropley hoping that Stanhope would accept the executorship are in *Chevening MSS*.

[2] Alberoni, *Lettres Intimes*, 6 and 20 May 1711 and 26 Oct. 1712.

leisure in studying, under the new régime of the Bourbons, the springs of government in Spain; and he seems to have formed a shrewd judgement of Philip's character as well as of Alberoni's. No doubt, too, he had an opportunity of reading some of the numerous pasquinades and pamphlets which flowed from the presses of Madrid, Seville and Toledo to celebrate his defeat at Brihuega and the end of 'Lutheran' rule in Castile. Even if their abuse of Estanópe is somewhat crude and far fetched, at least the number and virulence of those devoted to attacking him, considerably in excess of those directed against Charles and Starhemberg, were a flattering tribute to the impression made on the Spaniards by his personality.

Clearly Stanhope was not one of the great soldiers of the world. It would be absurd to compare him in this aspect with his two great contemporaries: Marlborough with his unerring eye for the tactics of a battle, for the conduct of a campaign and for the strategy of a European war; Eugene whose eminence was dimmed only by his proximity to Marlborough. Even Peterborough, as compared with Stanhope, had a touch of genius for war, instances of which are his capture of Monjuich and his lightning campaign in Valencia, and, in spite of his caprice and personal vanity, had an element of sure judgement to temper his native impetuosity. It must indeed be admitted that Stanhope had great disadvantages to overcome. Most of his three years of command in Spain were those in which the allies had been driven into a corner after Almanza and were hopelessly outnumbered by Philip and his French auxiliaries. He had in addition to contend against the apathy and intrigues of an ill-assorted court presided over by a youthful archduke, who had his full share of the obstinacy and formality of his race. It is not surprising that in such surroundings a man of Stanhope's impetuous nature should always have been for bold action, even if it involved an undue element of risk, as against the everlasting caution, resulting in nothing, preconized by the 'timid warblers in the grove', as his nephew would have called his colleagues. He boiled with indignation that his own country should be at the chief expense for their futile proceedings, and was determined that at the least chance something should be attempted. But for bold action in a prolonged campaign you must be certain of those with whom you have to work. Stanhope's advice before Almanza would have

been good, had he been able to count on Charles and
Noyelles not withdrawing a large portion of the troops
on which Galway depended for victory. The advance on
Madrid in 1710 might conceivably not have been the fiasco
it became, had he been assured of the co-operation of the
Portuguese troops. But in neither case was the condition
so certain that the risk would have been taken by a wise
commander. Certainly in August 1710 Starhemberg's proposal to hold the frontier and starve Philip of succours from
France, besides being the safest course, was that most likely
to ensure the defeat of the Bourbons.

It was not perhaps Stanhope's business, as a soldier sent
to fight in Spain, to consider whether the task assigned to
him was feasible or not, especially when the task had been
assigned to him by a Marlborough. But at any rate he does
not appear to have realized till too late that the 'country
was the enemy' and that success for the allies would have
meant not only conquering Philip but subduing the great
majority of the Spanish people. In the end indeed, as his
faithful friend Craggs owned to Bolingbroke, he came to
the conviction that 'armies of 20 or 30,000 men might walk
about the country till doomsday without effect; that wherever
they came the people would submit to Charles III out of
terror and as soon as they were gone proclaim Philip V
again, out of affection'; and he himself, when he came back
to England a wiser man in 1712, told the Queen, speaking
very modestly of his own ability, that 'religion and liberty
being out of the case and the Duke of Anjou's having children turned the bias of his side with the Spanish people. . .
Upon the whole he could give little encouragement to
expect any great success in that part of the world, unless
there were other means than were known to him'.[1]

On the other hand, the stately tribute paid to his military
qualities in the preamble to his patent of peerage is fully
justified: ''Tis doubtful whether he most signaliz'd himself
by his Courage, which terrify'd the Hearts of the Enemy,
or by his Affability and Good-Nature, which gained him
those of his own Men, or by the Firmness of his mind, which
buoy'd up those of the Confederates.' Few could excel him
in carrying out a definite piece of military work. He had
a directness and a gift of common sense that brought him
straight to the point, and imagination withal to see the

[1] Bolingbroke, *Works*, viii. 208; Burnet, ii. 556, note by Lord Dartmouth.

difficulties of his own side as well as those of the enemy.
In his organization of the commissariat under most difficult
conditions, in the change he wrought in the discipline and
contentment of his men within a few months, these qualities
shone forth. His expedition to Minorca was admirably
planned and carried through with just the dash and spirit
needed for such a *coup de main*. Again, when it had once
been decided to advance towards Madrid, his 'hectoring'
of Charles and Starhemberg into rapid and resolute action
at Almenara, in the pursuit of Philip and at Saragossa,
was the only effective way of carrying out the policy. He
had indeed all the characteristics of the brave but un-
scientific soldier—great courage, immense tenacity, practical
sense and organizing power—that we so frequently find in
our annals. Kitchener, of whom it was said that at Paarde-
berg he shoved the men up into the battle as if it were
into a football squash, though he had far more military
science than Stanhope, was in many ways akin to him as
a soldier. Stanhope had also a quality equally useful to
him as a statesman and as a soldier, that of being able to
retain the respect and even the affection of those whom he
opposed most vigorously and impetuously. This was not
the case with Peterborough, though he could hardly have
been sharper in his criticisms or more ruthless in enforcing
his opinions than Stanhope. The difference was that Peterborough always gave the impression that his chief object
was to focus the limelight on himself, Stanhope that he was
fighting in the public interest. It would certainly never
have occurred to Stanhope to travel about Europe to adver-
tise his own importance or get his doctor to write up his
exploits in a pamphlet. The Archduke Charles, who could
not abide Peterborough, though often sore at Stanhope's
hardly less dictatorial ways with him, welcomed his successes
in his last campaign, sincerely deplored his misfortunes, and
when he was Emperor received him with real affection.
By his best officers he was loved; and his men, especially in
those long, hungry and thirsty marches through Aragon and
Castile in the summer of 1710, were ready to go through the
worst hardships under his leadership. One can understand
this when one reads these words in his last sad dispatch.
After giving merited praise to his chief officers he adds:

'I cannot again help repeating to your Lordship in general,
that if after this misfortune I should ever be entrusted with

troops, I never desire to serve with better men than all showed themselves to be, and whatever other things I may have failed in through ignorance, I am truly conscious to myself that, in the condition we were reduced to I could not do a better service to the Queen than to endeavour to preserve them by the only way which was left.'

CHAPTER V

THE FIGHT FOR REVOLUTION PRINCIPLES

§ 1

WHEN in August 1712 Stanhope returned from his captivity of nearly two years in Spain, it was almost as if
he were coming to a new world. Passing through Paris, the
arch-enemy's capital, he found his old friend Harry St. John,
just created Viscount Bolingbroke, thoroughly at home there
and on the best of terms with Louis XIV. Bolingbroke even
offered to present him to the King, but Stanhope, staunch
to the memory of William III, refused to have any personal
dealings with that hero's implacable adversary, though he
went so far as to see Louis go a-hunting in his chaise, 'with a
bright retinue of ladies of the first quality, like Amazons on
horseback',[1] and accompanied Bolingbroke to a magnificent
entertainment given by Noailles, his own former opponent
on the Roussillon frontier. On arriving in England, though
he was graciously received by the Queen, when he went to
report to her, and presented with the gold medal struck
to record his prowess at Almenara,[2] he was given the cold
shoulder by the new Lord Treasurer, the Earl of Oxford,
with whom as Harley and Secretary of State he had had relations in years gone by. To Stanhope's sarcastic expression of
surprise that he had at last remembered him in his captivity
and secured his exchange, Oxford curtly replied 'that he
might assure himself that he should never forget either him
or Brihuega'. Many of his friends in the army had been
cashiered, Robert Walpole had been released barely a month
from the Tower and had been expelled from the House of
Commons, Marlborough had been dismissed from all his
employments and, for fear of worse to follow, was on the eve
of retiring to Holland, with the cold approval of the Queen,
who said 'he did wisely'.[3] Stanhope himself had in his absence
been reflected upon in an inquiry held by the House of Lords,
at the instigation of the indefatigable Peterborough, into
the events preceding Almanza. This time Peterborough had
received the thanks sought by him since 1707, while Galway
with Stanhope and other supporters of the forward policy

[1] Boyer, iv. 118.   [2] Ib. 128.
[3] Lord Cowper, *Diary*, 54.

had been implicitly censured for acting on Sunderland's instructions and advocating a forward policy at the councils of war of January and February 1707.[1] Above all, instead of the Whig ministry Stanhope had left in England in 1710, there was a purely Tory administration, far more ruthless in their political proscriptions than the Whigs had ever been, with a Tory majority, flushed with the insolence of power, in the Commons, and a Tory majority in the Lords manufactured by an unheard-of use of the prerogative in the creation of twelve peers at one stroke. By a stringent Property Qualification Act they had attempted to secure for the landed interest, mainly Tory, the monopoly of representation in the Commons; and by the Occasional Conformity Act had weakened the power of the Dissenters, trusty allies of the Whigs and among the strongest supporters of the Revolution settlement. Peace had not yet actually been signed with France, but its sacrifice of much for which the Whigs had fought was made clear by the Preliminaries already submitted to Parliament; and the ignominious desertion of the allies was already proclaimed to the world by Ormonde's defection and the French victory at Denain. As for England, even the Protestant Succession seemed ill assured.

Stanhope, a joyous fighter on the battlefield, was now only too eager to join in the political fray and uphold his Revolution principles. Even before his defeat, when on active service in Spain, the critical state of affairs in England had made him impatient to quit his command and return home, 'for many reasons', he wrote to Marlborough, 'but especially that I may have an opportunity of making good what I have promised, to be faithful to your Grace in all events'; and to Craggs he had written, 'I am impatient to hear from you from England, where I think everybody is run mad, if half what I hear be true. But be it as it will, I pray you to get me home.'[2] Nor was his help in the political world to be despised, for, though most of his service had hitherto been on the battlefield, he had already shown that he was a force to be reckoned with in Parliament, especially in the great Sacheverell trial of 1710

---

[1] See above, ch. ii, p. 53; Luttrell, vi. 676-8; Russell, ii. 191 sqq.; *The Rise and Fall of Count Hotspur* (London, 1717), 70: 'The conduct of the libidinous, rash, luxurious, and profuse Mordanna [Peterborough] was honour'd with their Thanks . . . and the gallant, young, successful Stansidio [Stanhope] fell under the Reproaches of the Plebeians, instead of being rewarded with Statues of Brass, for his Victorious exploits.'

[2] Mahon, *Anne*, ii. 180-1.

and, vicariously, in the Westminster election that shortly followed it.

Dr. Sacheverell, a noisy, empty-headed fellow, was certainly not worthy of the solemn trial before the peers in Westminster Hall, decked with scaffolding for the occasion by the great Sir Christopher himself and graced by the presence of the Queen. But, although the Whigs' ardour in the pursuit of such small game recoiled immediately on themselves and was one of the principal causes for their subsequent rout at the polls, the proceedings at the trial served them well in two respects. Their opponents, the high-flying Tories, forced to come out into the open, revealed the weakness of their case by the shuffling explanations they gave of their doctrine of non-resistance and their want of courage in proclaiming their real opinions on the Revolution and the Pretender's claims; while they themselves found Westminster Hall an admirable platform from which boldly to restate the principles of the Revolution and their conception of the Constitution. In this exposition Stanhope, one of the managers of the impeachment for the Commons, was especially effective. The first and most important article against Sacheverell charged him with maintaining (1) that the necessary means used to bring about the happy Revolution were odious and unjustifiable; (2) that William III in his Declaration had disclaimed the least imputation of Resistance; and (3) 'that to impute Resistance to the said Revolution was to cast black and odious colours upon his late majesty and the said Revolution', statements that may appear to us unmeaning trivialities not worth disputing but which, to men of that time who feared the return of a Roman Catholic and prerogative king, seemed rife with danger to the existing happy establishment. Eight of the managers, including the law-officers, Walpole, Jekyll, and Stanhope himself, spoke to this article.

Speaking last, Stanhope addressed himself chiefly to the fundamentals of the Whig political theory. Nurtured as he had been on Locke, he grounded his exposition on the *Treatise on Civil Government*, aptly reinforced by appropriate quotations from Fortescue, Hooker and Grotius. All civil government he based upon a compact, the very nature of which implies a right of resistance by the party to the compact who feels himself justly aggrieved. 'I believe', he said, 'that there is not at this day subsisting any nation or government in the world, whose first original did not receive its foundation either from Resistance or compact; and as to our purpose, it is equal, if the latter be admitted. For wherever compact is admitted there must be admitted likewise a right to defend the rights accruing by such compact.' His defence of this doctrine of Resistance was all the more telling in that many of those present had themselves 'resisted' twenty years before at the Revolution. Thus, quoting from a sermon recently preached at the Tory university of Oxford by Atterbury, then Dean of Carlisle, who was present as one of Sacheverell's chief supporters, to the effect that it was justifiable to resist orders contrary to *jus divinum*,

> 'I apply this, my lords', he said, turning to the peers, 'to our present argument, I appeal to the memory of your lordships, whether King James did not command things contrary to the laws of God? . . . in short, whether the whole course of his reign was not a series of illegal commands, calculated to destroy our holy religion, and to violate all our religious and civil rights? Your lordships thought so; the Commons thought so; and in consequence of this doctrine, preached by St Peter, they chose to obey God before men. . . . Many of your lordships were actors in that Resistance. The greatest part of the nation did either actually resist, or countenance, abet, and support those who set them the glorious example. . . . My lords, if this doctrine of Non-Resistance be true . . . it doth involve the greatest part of this nation in the guilt of rebellion and treason.'

Yet where, he continued, could one find religion so much honoured as in England, with its Church looked on as 'the Mother of all the Reformed Churches of Europe'? Where such good administration of the laws, where such financial stability, in spite of the great sums willingly paid to carry on a just war? Where such glory in arms, 'which justly entitles our nation at present to hold the first rank'? Yet here was a man trying to persuade Englishmen that their exertions in this war were all to defend an unjust and wrongful government, a man belonging to that little sect of Non-Jurors, 'these undefiled pure Churchmen', who, though tolerated and allowed to 'have their conventicles and get money from a few deluded women', must at least be stopped when they dare to preach treason in St. Paul's. 'This man', he concluded, 'is an inconsiderable tool of a party, no ways worthy the trouble we have given your lordships', but you must scotch his doctrines and give him such punishment 'as may deter others from the like insolence'.[1]

[1] *State Trials*, xv. 126–34.

Stanhope's home thrusts seem to have told. Abigail Harley, lamenting the pother made about Sacheverell's sermon, 'the nonsensical harangue from a pragmatical insignificant man', wrote to her brother Edward, 'I hear the Dean of Carlisle was present to hear himself severely reflected on the other day by General Stanhope. In my opinion those clergymen were most prudent that kept out of the way of it.' Sacheverell himself 'who appeared unconcerned while the other . . . managers were speaking, turn'd pale and was disorder'd when he found himself treated with scorn and contempt by General Stanhope'.[1] For the moment the other side seems to have found no better retort than some doggerel verses, such as:

> Stanhope impatient no longer could bear
>   To see his own troops disappointed,
> But storms and discharges, and rattles in th'air
>   Against Kings and all that's anointed;[2]

but they marked down Stanhope as a formidable adversary. Swift talks of him as one of the leading managers and in the *Publick Spirit of the Whigs* coupled him with the dangerous Mr. Hoadly, an active pamphleteer, famous thereafter for starting the Bangorian controversy. When the news of Brihuega came to England, 'the misfortune which happened to General Stanhope', says Oldmixon, 'was some relief to high-church; . . . and they did not stick to rejoice at it'; and Swift, in the *Examiner*, bluntly writes that 'we have already got one comfortable loss in Spain, though by a G . . . l of our own'. Swift's correspondent Archbishop King, however, when told of the report that Stanhope's obstinacy was the cause of the disaster, demurred to the truth of this charge, 'till satisfied how far the kindness to him, as a manager, influences the report'.[3]

His own party, on the other hand, had been so much elated by this speech and the news of his first Spanish successes that at the general election of September 1710 they put him up as candidate for Westminster, conspicuous then, as in Fox's famous election of 1784, for the violence of the party feeling displayed. Stanhope, being absent in Spain, had to be represented by a proxy, General Davenport; but his absence did nothing to quench the ardour of his friends or

---

[1] *H. MSS., Portland*, iv. 533; Oldmixon, 434.
[2] From *The Westminster Combat* in Wilkins, *Political Ballads*, ii. 90.
[3] Swift, xv. 389, 396; Oldmixon, 452.

mitigate the virulence of his opponents. The Tories and High Churchmen concentrated all their forces against him, accused him of nameless vices and 'with having profanely defiled the altars', and on the very day the news came of his victory at Saragossa were engaged in pelting his proxy and knocking down his friends.[1] His supporters, inferior in brawn as in numbers, had the best of it in the quality and quantity of their literary output. Their hero was a more likely subject for eulogy in the form of ballads such as the *Glorious Warriour* or speeches by *General Alcibiades*, than his opponents, 'an eminent Brewer' and his colleague who 'regulated Quart Pots and Measures'. What more natural than that 'General Alcibiades' should contrast the Brewer 'tapping his liquors and gathering Hopps' with himself, who 'have been spilling my Blood and reaping Laurels. . . . Behold these Scars, behold this wound which still bleeds in your service. . . . Has he any other Wound about him except the accidental scaldings of his Wort, or Bruises from the Tub or Barrel?' The *Glorious Warriour* is an artless ballad 'to the tune of Fair Rosamund', in twenty-five stanzas, such as:

> The brave Stanhope was he she sent
>   To Spain with full command
> And bid him fall upon the French
>   And beat them out of hand
>
>   .   .   .   .   .   .
>
> You then who live near River Thames,
>   Near Abbey or Millbank,
> St. James, St. Anne, the Park, the Strand,
>   Of mean or highest rank,
>
> Don't be ingrate, to one who for
>   His country takes much Pains,
> In places far and wide, but last
>   In Saragossa's plains.

Swift himself even thought it worth his while to parody both the *Speech of Alcibiades* and, with Swiftian scurrility, the *Glorious Warriour*. The idea for the second parody, *An Excellent New Ballad being the Second Part of the Glorious Warriour*, Swift told Stella, came to him when he was riding in a coach, and, finding himself surrounded by supporters of Stanhope and the other Whig candidate, Sir Henry Dutton Colt, was 'always on their side' for fear that his windows might be smashed by dead cats. He adds that though the ballad took

[1] Oldmixon, 452.

him only half an hour to write and was good for nothing it was in great demand. But Swift need not have troubled. For Stanhope, like so many Whigs, was hopelessly beaten at this seat with a semblance of popular election and had to resort again to his friend the Duke of Somerset's haven at Cockermouth.[1] But it was a glorious election, that served only to enhance Stanhope's importance with his own party.[2]

So, if his opponents had begun to dread him, his friends had become no less anxious to have him back for the new Parliament. Walpole, on the eve of quitting office, had written, 'I believe your presence will be more necessary when there is a new secretary at war than it would be were I to continue', and later that his return is 'the only good effect I hoped from our celebrated peace'. Marlborough, Halifax, Sunderland, Somerset, Mohun had all been hoping for his return; Carpenter, Wade, Dormer and Lepel, his companions in arms released before him, echoed the wish.[3] He was sought after by political associates for aid in debate; and, as they and the Whig officers feared, even his sword might be needed once more to defend the constitution and succession as established by law.

But before he threw himself into the political fray Stanhope had, almost for the only time in his life, found occasion to take thought for his own private and domestic happiness. He does not appear hitherto to have been exactly an anchorite in the courts of love; and the fascination his good looks and vivid personality exercised on women is alluded to in one of the ballads relating to the Sacheverell trial:

> Stanhope soft as a dove,
> Form'd for arms and for love,
> With sweetest persuasion the ladies did move.[4]

[1] Even here he was put to the expense of contesting an election petition, the bill for which was for £641 10s. 8d.; *Chevening MSS.*

[2] The specimens of election literature quoted in the text are from rare broadsheets in Sir Charles Firth's collection. Swift's parody of the *Speech of Alcibiades* is in the *Examiner* of 30 November 1710. Elrington Ball, *Swift's Verse*, 108–11, identifies his parody of the *Glorious Warriour* mentioned in the Journal to Stella of 5 October 1710 with *A Ballad Writt by an eminent soldier at home* to be found in *The Whimsical Medley*, a three-volume MS. collection of contemporary verse in the library of Trinity College, Dublin (MS., No. 879, i. 5. 1–3). This MS. ballad is indeed sad doggerel, besides being a particularly offensive attack on Stanhope's sexual morality, the sort of attack commonly made by the baser writers of the time on the morality of other public men. Mr. Harold Williams, an eminent authority on Swift's writings and versification, has kindly examined this poem and tells me that it almost certainly is not Swift's work.

[3] Letters in *Chevening MSS.*

[4] *Salisbury Steeple Reversed*, in Wilkins, *Political Ballads*, ii. 96.

But at any rate he had not before found time or inclination in his busy career to form any lasting attachment. Now within six months of his return he had wooed and won as his bride Lucy, the younger daughter of the famous Governor Pitt, eighteen years younger than himself, then just forty. The marriage was celebrated on 24 February 1713. Stanhope proved as impetuous in the begetting of offspring as in his other activities; and although he did not marry till middle age, his wife bore him in their eight years of married life no fewer than seven children, including two sets of twins.[1] The family tradition speaks of the marriage as a very happy one —he quick at repartee, and a delightful companion, she of a singularly gentle nature, a trait which she most assuredly did not inherit from the rough hectoring old Governor. In one of the few letters of hers preserved at Chevening the depth of this simple love for her turbulent man is clearly revealed:

'18 August 1713.
'My dear Mr Stanhopes letter was very welcome to me, but I am very sorry you are like to be absent so much longer [than] I hoped you would, for I shall think every day an age and count the minutes till I see you. . . . I have no satisfaction at anything while you are away. . . . I am my dearest love your most affect. Loveing wife L. Stanhope.'

Two more of her letters written towards the end of their brief marriage show the same tender affection; and one may conclude that for her at least it was a happy union. Stanhope himself, after he came into office in 1714, overwhelmed by state business for the remainder of his life and liable to be called at a moment's notice to travel to The Hague, Vienna, Paris, Madrid or to sojourn for months with his master in Hanover, can have had little time for the more intimate happiness of married life. Nor did he make up for this by such letters as illuminate the brief absences from one another of his nephew Chatham and his beloved Lady Hester. After his father's death Stanhope wrote very few domestic letters. For this remissness during his first official journey to the Hague and Vienna Lucy sent him this mock-serious reproof by the hand of his cousin Charles:[2]

[1] The last twins were posthumous, being born six months after Stanhope's death.
[2] The brothers Charles and William Stanhope were but distant cousins of James, who, however, held their capacity in high esteem. Charles was his secretary and later on the Treasury board, William was sent as ambassador to Spain and subsequently became Lord Harrington.

LUCY, COUNTESS STANHOPE
From a portrait at Chevening

'Whitehall Nov. 2 1714.

'Sir,
   'I am commanded by your Lady to acquaint you she is scarce in charity with you for omitting to write to her from The Hague; and that you must not expect to hear from her, till you have made her reparation by a letter. however I have her leave to write word that she and the children are very well; and that she shall be glad to be friends with you as soon as may be. . . .'

Gentle as she was, Lucy Stanhope seems at least to have inherited some of her formidable father's business capacity, to judge from her admirable management of the Chevening property bought by her husband four years later at a time when he was far too busy with state affairs to see to all the building and ordering of the estate then put in hand.

With his father-in-law Stanhope at first found himself in complete sympathy politically. It is related that when Thomas Pitt on his return from India reached Holland in 1710, preceded by tales of his great diamond and fabulous wealth, an agent of Harley's plied him with good Dutch liquor and wrote to his patron saying that he was worth cultivating. But there was nothing of the Tory in the dour old man, whose 'gratitude as an Englishman', as he once expressed it, 'obliges me to pay all Defference to the Blessed Memory of King William', and who roundly abused his eldest son for his 'hellish acquaintance' with Tories and for 'contriving amongst you to put a French kickshaw upon the throne againe. . . . If I find or hear of any child of mine that herds with any to oppose her present Majesty's interest, I will renounce him for ever.' Such sentiments, not perhaps so ferociously expressed, were exactly Stanhope's, and from 1713 to 1716, the most critical years for the Hanover establishment, the father and son-in-law were entirely at one. In the latter year Stanhope as Secretary of State chose Pitt as Governor of Jamaica, where an unruly assembly seemed in need of a rough hand; but shortly afterwards the old man, acquiring a new fortune by the sale of his diamond to the Regent, decided to stay in England. In later years, when the Whig party was divided, the Governor opposed the powerful minister, expressing his dislike for the Peerage Bill in characteristically forcible language. But, though he quarrelled with most of his family, he always seems to have kept a tender spot in his heart for his daughter Lucy; and during the two years of her widowhood she lived with him either in Pall Mall or at

Swallowfield. His wife's brothers and sisters had little in common with Stanhope. One nephew, however, William Pitt, attracted his notice by his spirit and keen interest in military matters, and, though not thirteen when Stanhope died, had already earned from him the title of 'the young marshal', prophetic of the great war-minister's achievements.[1]

§ 2

When Stanhope took his place in the House of Commons in 1713, for the last session of the 1710 Parliament, although it looked as if the Tories had the ball at their feet, they, like the Whig minority, had their difficulties. Chief of these was the complete divergence of purpose between the two leading men of their side, Oxford and Bolingbroke. Oxford's idea of government had always been the same as that of William III and of Queen Anne, not to let any one party monopolize all offices and inspire all measures, but to have a judicious admixture of both under the supreme direction of the sovereign holding the balance more or less even. He had been quite willing to serve with Whigs in the early part of the reign and had only left the ministry in 1708, when there seemed a determination in the Whig Junto to enforce Whig conformity. When he returned in 1710 he had the same idea, and was only gradually driven by Bolingbroke and others to get rid of all the remaining Whig elements in the ministry. Bolingbroke, on the other hand, who in later days, finding no place in politics at all, took up with enthusiasm the idea of a patriot-king abolishing all party and governing through ministers of all complexions in accordance with Oxford's notions, was at that time determined to consolidate the government in the hands of a strong and undiluted Tory majority. He gained his point, but only at the cost of ruining himself and his party for more than a generation. Nor even on the question of a Jacobite revival were the Tories united. Oxford and Bolingbroke certainly corresponded with the Pretender while they were in office and gave him hopes of returning as king; but Oxford was mainly influenced by the idea of obtaining the support of James's Jacobite supporters in the House of Commons to enable him to carry the peace proposals; and when that had been achieved became distinctly colder in his response to advances from James III. Bolingbroke for his part was more genuinely

[1] See Williams, *Chatham*, i, ch. i, and p. 32.

alarmed at the prospect to himself and his party of a Hanoverian dynasty already alienated by the peace of Utrecht, and
was therefore more anxious for the success of the Pretender,
and believed that it was possible.[1] But here Bolingbroke mis-
calculated his own influence over his party. Many living
Tories had had as much part in the Revolution as the Whigs;
the Act of Settlement itself had been passed by a Tory Parliament, and a large section among the Tories still dreaded an
increase in French influence that would be the sure result of
a return of the Stuarts.

That this section of the Tories had to be reckoned with was
seen on the first move against the ministry made by the Whigs
after Stanhope's return and largely under his leadership. The
Treaty of Utrecht had been signed on 11 April 1713 and
ratified by the Queen seven days later. In the eyes of the
Whigs this treaty gave up nearly all that England had been
fighting for in the long war, Spain to a Bourbon and terms
to France of which she could hardly have dreamed in Marlborough's time. In the fury of party passion and at the end
of a triumphant, if exhausting war, it is not surprising that
they did not recognize, what is clear to us to-day, that in all
essential points, the command of the sea, the strengthening
and increase of our colonial empire, greater facilities for our
commerce, England by this treaty had virtually obtained
recognition of her pre-eminence as a world-power. As to the
underhand means by which it was obtained, involving the
desertion of the Emperor and the German princes, the Dutch
and the Catalans to whom we were pledged in honour,
the Whigs' criticisms have been justified by posterity. But the
question was now disposed of: nobody could then gainsay the
sovereign's right to accept any treaty she chose. So, as Stanhope wisely said, 'peace being now made, it is preposterous
to say anything for or against it'. There was, however, a subsidiary commercial treaty with France which in one particular did require the sanction of Parliament to become valid:
and on this point Stanhope and the Whigs gained a notable
success with the help of some of the Tories.

Sections 8 and 9 of this commercial treaty provided that
France and England should give one another the most
favoured nation treatment in trade, in other words, that
neither should levy a higher duty on goods from the other

---

[1] For the dealings of Oxford and Bolingbroke with the Pretender see Salomon,
passim.

than the lowest duty paid by any other nation; and that all prohibitive laws passed since 1664 by either nation against the other's products should be repealed. Since these provisions affected the customs duties levied solely on the authority of Parliament, they required parliamentary sanction. Such a measure of free trade, entirely alien to the generally accepted mercantile theories of the time, aroused an outcry from the greater part of the mercantile and industrial community, afraid that French products would ruin similar native industries. Another, really more important, difficulty was that these provisions would contravene the profitable Methuen Treaty of 1703 with Portugal, which stipulated that the tax on Portuguese wines should never exceed two-thirds of the tax on French wines. Lastly, the bitterness aroused by nearly a quarter of a century's war caused distrust even in the Tory ranks of Oxford's, and still more emphatically Bolingbroke's, desire, to draw closer politically as well as commercially to France. Here then was a magnificent chance of attacking the ministry with success, a chance of which Stanhope and his friends availed themselves to the full.

In the usual pamphlet-war stimulated by this controversy, Defoe, on behalf of Oxford and the ministry, was first in the field with his journal *Mercator or Commerce Retrieved*, in which he defended the treaty with arguments far too enlightened for his day. 'Trading nations, though Christian, ought to maintain commerce with all People they can get by', 'I let thee gain by me, that I may gain by thee', are among his most remarkable dicta; and he went so far as to argue that even in war-time trade should not cease with the enemy. As a counterblast to *Mercator* Stanhope, helped by Halifax, founder of the Bank of England, and Robert Walpole, together with some city merchants, brought out *The British Merchant or Commerce Preferred* in support of the orthodox view. This journal is said to have done much to educate Whig opinion in trade matters, and was so much regarded in this respect that it was republished in 1743 with a preface eulogizing Stanhope and Halifax for their part in its production.[1] As a result of the attention thus called to the treaty the 40,000 silk-weavers of Spitalfields and the woollen and linen trades protested against the danger of French competition, and petitions to the same effect were sent to the House of Commons

[1] *The British Merchant*, 1743. The preface of this republication gives an account of Stanhope's part in the debate that followed.

from Gloucestershire, Worcestershire, Oxfordshire, Devonshire, Somerset, Hampshire, from the eastern counties and
from Yorkshire.[1]

In April Stanhope demanded that the treaty should be
communicated to the House, and when, during May and June,
sections 8 and 9 came up for discussion, took a leading part
against them. He adopted Addison's argument of 1708, that
the introduction of French woollens into Spain would ruin
the English wool trade there, since 'the woollen manufacture
is the British strength, the staple commodity and proper
growth of our Country: if it fails us our Trade and Estates
must sink together, and all the Cash of the Nation be consumed on foreign Merchandize',[2] and argued that we should
ruin our woollen and other staple trades by admitting similar
French goods produced by cheaper labour to compete with
them. Then turning to the proposed introduction of French
wines at reduced rates, wines of which he spoke with unction
as known to be 'relishing liquor to English palates', he argued
that thereby our treaty with Portugal would be instantly
broken and we should lose our favourable market there for
English woollens, 'by which we should have lost above a
million sterling per annum and have reduced several 100,000
families to the Parish for subsistence'. In these debates Stanhope was in his most aggressive mood. Being corrected by
the Speaker on some point of fact on which he happened to be
right he 'animadverted with some vehemence on the Speaker's
blunder', and when one of the merchants who came to state
their case was interrupted, flamed up against the interrupter,
'hoping that no man should be reprimanded for standing up
for the trade of Great Britain'. There was little doubt from
the first as to the result of the agitation fostered by Stanhope
and his friends and of such appeals in the debate. In the
division a solid body of so-called Hanover Tories came over
to the Whigs and by a majority of 194 to 185 defeated Oxford's
and Bolingbroke's enlightened attempt to develop better relations and what might have proved a profitable trade with
France.

Again, on 1 July, Stanhope was instrumental in exposing
the unwillingness of James III's supporters in the House
of Commons to come out into the open. By the Treaty of

---

[1] For a good account of the agitation and issues involved see W. A. S.
Hewins, *English Trade and Finance in the 17th Century*, 1892, pp. 133–44.
[2] Addison's *State of the War and Necessity of an Augmentation*, 1708.

Utrecht Louis XIV had agreed that the Pretender should no longer find an asylum in France, but by a transparent evasion had allowed him to retire to Lorraine, then practically under his tutelage. Following the successful example in the House of Lords of the Earl of Wharton, whom he compared in his dying speech to Brutus, Stanhope moved for an address to the Queen asking her to require the Duke of Lorraine to expel James from his territory. As in the Lords, the Jacobites did not dare to oppose this motion, which was passed unanimously; and though Bolingbroke's representations to the courts of Versailles and Bar-le-duc were not very pressing and had no effect, the incident served to show the Jacobite party they could not rely on support even from a Tory Parliament.

Stanhope was clearly a formidable opponent. So the ministry decided to get him out of the way by much the same methods as they had used in excluding Walpole from the Commons. Not content with the condemnation expressed by the Lords on his conduct before Almanza, they appointed a commission presided over by the Tory Shippen to go into the accounts of the Spanish campaigns, in the hope of tripping him up on some financial irregularity. This was all the more inexcusable since in 1712 Harley himself told Stanhope's friend Micklethwait 'with strong Expressions of Esteem and great Friendship for you of y^r Wonderfull disinterestedness and no desire of obtaining Wealth, tho' you had not only just Pretences but an absolute right to ye full of what has all along been ordered to be payed you'.[1] In November 1713 the commissioners had completed their investigations and sent Stanhope a number of queries to answer, which in effect charged him with peculation. But the result was not what they had expected. Stanhope not only replied to all the charges with devastating effect, but exposed the animus of the commissioners and the ministry by publishing his *Answer to the Commissioners sent into Spain*.[2] Most of the expenses questioned were of the most trivial nature, such as an item of £20 paid to the master of a transport for the loss of an anchor in the Mahon operations; this Stanhope could not think misapplied, 'considering the success of the expedition'. To the commissioners' suggestion that Stanhope had paid for more mules than he had received, since the cost for mules was much greater in

---

[1] *Chevening MSS.* Th. Micklethwait to Stanhope, 11 Jan. 1711/12 (o.s.). Stanhope had previously written disclaiming part of his due emoluments.

[2] London (March), 1714.

1710 than in 1712, he replied by proving that in his last two years in Spain he had paid out of his own pocket over £500 more for mules than he had been allowed by the Treasury and commented on the 'most wonderful Discovery the Commissioners have made', that fewer mules were consumed by Starhemberg, when confined to a standing camp in 1712, than he himself had used up, when marching 1,000 miles in 1710. Why, then, it was asked, was Petit, governor of Port Mahon, allowed to accumulate the pay of no less than seven offices? For economy, replies Stanhope; he was the best man he could get and, for 'the several pompous offices here enumerated', his total pay was no more than £2 10s. p.d., while the whole cost of the establishment at Mahon amounted to only £6 0s. 2d. The main charges made by the commissioners related to his disposal of £5,000 granted to him for contingencies, for which he had rendered no account. For the omission to render accounts for this £5,000 he quoted specific instructions from the Lord Treasurer and Sunderland, an explanation which also covered the payments to Count Oropeza and his wife at the signature of the commercial treaty.[1] The commissioners also drew attention to the excessive amount of pay he himself drew as commander-in-chief, to which Stanhope had the conclusive answer that he had not only given up in 1708 the £10 p.d., to which he was entitled, to Galway, but also in the following year had purchased out of his own pay a diamond-hilted sword, costing £1,342 10s., that he had been instructed to present to Starhemberg. He did admit one error of £60 overcharged for fireworks at Tarragona on the Queen's birthday, but expressed himself pleased to find that in such very great sums 'this error of about £60 seems to be the only one that hath been discovered'. So the Tories got little by questioning Stanhope's honesty; on the contrary, he put in a claim for the pay owing to him, since, as he said in words of dignified reproach, 'it is evident by what hath been said, that the said sum falls short considerably of answering the just demands I could make, and which I would have made long ago, if I had not very much disregarded my own private Interest'. When he next met Shippen, the chairman of the commission, he warmly thanked him for the opportunity he had given him for claiming his just dues.

Stanhope was obviously not a man easily to be put in the

[1] See above, ch. iii, p. 60.

shade. When, at the general election in the autumn of 1713, he failed to keep his seat at Cockermouth, much to the indignation of the Duke of Somerset, patron of the borough, he was overwhelmed with offers of seats. The Duke of Bolton offered to put him up for Andover, professing that he would do anything for 'so good and useful a man at this criticall time'; a Scottish member wrote to Walpole, 'Had I but thought England so degenrate as not to reguard so much virtue and honour as Mr. Stanop has I would serve my country by haveing him represent the Burrour Im Elected for, yet Im not a little pleased that there still is a possibility to have our Northern Climat honored by Mr. Stanop's serving you in parliament'; and he suggested a seat in Sutherlandshire. Another admirer offered him Derby; but eventually Stanhope found refuge at Wendover.[1] In the first and only session of Anne's last Parliament he and Walpole were the undoubted leaders of the Whigs in the House of Commons. One of them stood on each side of Steele when he defended himself against the attack made on him for his pamphlet, *The Crisis*—but though both spoke for him, Walpole with great effect, they could not save him from expulsion. Stanhope also spoke in favour of the motion that the Protestant Succession was in danger under the existing government; he attacked the commercial treaty recently made with Spain, pointing out with justice that it gave far less advantage to our merchants than the treaty he himself had secured in 1707, or even than Charles II's treaty of 1667, which had ever since been regarded as the standard for our commercial relations with that country.

The only measure of real importance that came before this parliament was the Schism Act, which forbade, under severe penalties, anybody refusing to conform to the Church of England or to receive her Sacraments to take part in the education of the young. This was especially Bolingbroke's measure, whereby he hoped to unite the whole Tory and High Church party, and was a shrewd blow aimed at the Dissenting allies of the Whigs, whose main source of recruitment, in the young, was thereby endangered. This reactionary measure was fiercely resisted by Walpole, Lechmere, Jekyll, Stanhope, among others, who declared 'it looked more like a decree of Julian the apostate, than a law enacted by a Protestant parliament, since it tended to raise as great a

---

[1] The letters quoted are in *Chevening MSS*.

persecution against our Protestant brethren, as either the primitive Christians ever suffered from the heathen emperors, or the Protestants from Popery and the inquisition'. Stanhope, however, went farther. Much as he hated the methods and tenets of Roman Catholics, he had a sense of toleration that could embrace even them. Recalling similar oppressive laws against the Roman Catholics, which forbade them to educate their children in their own tenets at home, he pointed out that as a result of these laws such children were sent to Papist seminaries abroad, which not only 'drained the kingdom of great sums of money', as he said, but also 'filled the tender minds of young men with prejudices against their own country'; the same result, he inferred, would follow this legislation against the Protestant Dissenters. Then, with a courage remarkable for his age, when real tolerance was hardly known in Europe, and certainly no party in England had a word to say for removing Roman Catholic disabilities, he declared that 'instead of making new laws to encourage foreign education, he could wish those already in force against the Papists were mitigated, and that they should be allowed a certain number of schools'.[1] The united strength of the Tory party was naturally impervious to such enlightened arguments; and the Bill passed by a majority of over 100. But Stanhope was not content with giving expression to these tolerant views in opposition; later, when he was in power and secured the repeal of this and the Occasional Conformity Act, he attempted, again vainly against predominant prejudices, to introduce into his measures some relief for Roman Catholics.[2]

§ 3

The real battle-ground, however, during this last eventful year of the Stuart dynasty, was not so much in Parliament as throughout the country. The issue was of supreme importance for the future of the nation, whether the Protestant and Hanoverian succession, as laid down by the Act of Settlement, should be quietly accepted or whether confusion should be allowed to continue by the constant menace of the Pretender's claim. It was a period rarely equalled in English annals for the bitterness of party strife and for the ardour with

---

[1] *Debates and Speeches on Schism Act*, 1715 (pamphlet).
[2] See below, ch. xiv, pp. 395 sqq.

which men of all ranks and professions threw themselves into the fray. The political, social and literary worlds were for the first time so intermingled in the little society that then counted in England that few could stand aside from the exciting hurly-burly of controversy and invective. The Tories found a rallying-place in their October Club, where the pure milk of Jacobite doctrine was mingled with strong draughts of pure October ale; the Whigs were said to be responsible for the tumults and outrages of the bands of drunken Mohocks that infested the City. The talk in the coffee-houses was all of politics, and nearly every day brought forth rumours of some new plot. News of the Queen's serious illness and the report that she was dying at the beginning of 1714 caused a flutter in both camps, as neither was prepared for immediate action. Ministers were reported to be hedged in by Jacobite agents, and alarming news came from Holland of armed preparations by the Hanoverians. Lord Islay was said to have offered to raise 20,000 Highlanders for the Elector and to have answered for the loyalty of Edinburgh. On the other hand, Lockhart of Carnwath brought a 'high monarchical' address from the same city, which he presented to the Queen and exchanged with her depreciatory comments on the House of Hanover. He then spent his time in London gathering indications of Jacobite feeling and gloating maliciously over any sign of discomfiture of the Whigs.

Amid all these goings and comings the clergy on both sides were not the least zealous in the fray. Not counting the empty-pated Dr. Sacheverell, once more a hero when his three years' inhibition from preaching and preferment was removed, Atterbury, now Bishop of Rochester, and above all Swift, Dean of St. Patrick's in 1713, were prominent on the Tory side and easily outweighed Bishop Burnet of Salisbury and Hoadly, the two most prominent Whig clerics. Swift, of course, was the greatest of the Tory pamphleteers with his periodical *The Examiner*, his *Conduct of the Allies*, his *Reflections on the Barrier Treaty*, which more perhaps than anything had turned public opinion in favour of the peace, and his *Publick Spirit of the Whigs*, a crushing answer to Steele's indifferent performance in *The Crisis*; he showed no mealy-mouthed consideration for his adversaries, especially when dealing with a fellow cleric such as Burnet, as when he says of Steele that he is merely reproducing the 'Spittle of the Bishop of Sarum, which our author licks up, and swallows, and then

coughs out again, with an addition of his own Phlegm.' Of
the lay pamphleteers the Tories could not put up such a
brave show, having to rely on the hired pen of Defoe,
masterly though he was, against the unbought convictions of
Steele and Addison, the one with his *Englishman* the other
with *The Whig Examiner*, in which, says Johnson, 'is exhibited
all the force of gay malevolence and humorous satire'. In
April 1713 the time had come, adds Johnson, 'when those
who affected to think liberty in danger, affected likewise to
think that a stage-play might preserve it: and Addison was
importuned, in the name of the tutelary deities of Britain, to
shew his courage and his zeal' by producing his tragedy of
Cato, the noble Roman who died for liberty. The result was
better than could have been expected: a Jacobite spy declared
that 'a tragedy called *Cato*, made by the Whigs', was regarded
by that party as no less useful to them than Sacheverell's
sermons had been to the Tories. The play had an unprecedented run, the Whigs 'applauding every line in which
Liberty was mentioned as a satire on the Tories; and the
Tories echoing every clap, to shew that the satire was un-
felt'.[1]

In this hard-fought contest the Whigs had two initial advantages: first in standing for the law of the land as expressed
by the Act of Settlement of 1700 and the Succession to the
Crown Act of 1707; second in being a united party perfectly
certain of their aim, which was to secure an untroubled
succession for the Hanoverians on the Queen's death. The
cleavage in the Tory party had, on the other hand, become
even more pronounced as the end of the Queen's reign drew
near. The Hanover or 'Whimsical' Tories, a not inconsiderable section, led by the Speaker, Sir Thomas Hanmer,
would not have the Pretender at any price; another section,
probably the smallest and chiefly composed of Roman Catholics, would have welcomed the old dynasty without condition
of any kind; the majority would doubtless have preferred the
Stuarts to the Hanoverians, but with reservations, the most
important of which was that James should renounce Catholicism and adopt the Anglican Creed. This very heterogeneity
of the Tory party was one of the difficulties of the situation.

[1] Macpherson, ii. 406. In England it requires acute political controversy
to arouse such excitement in a theatre. In France the caesura in an unusual
place was enough to stimulate a riot at the representation of Victor Hugo's
Hernani.

It was so uncertain of itself and so doubtful of the backing
which any of its sections had in the country, that it never
dared to give a clear utterance on the succession question or
to make any effective opposition to the measures proposed
by the Whigs against the Pretender; nor did the Tory leaders
ever feel able to commit the party to a definite policy. But
that did not prevent them from forming secret plans and
intrigues of their own. Oxford, as we have seen, was quite
willing, for his own purposes, to lure the Pretender with
promises, Bolingbroke, his rival, was more genuinely convinced that his own plans would best be served by having
James on the throne, and at the beginning of 1714 sent him,
through the French envoy, a reasoned plan of operations. In
the first place James must become an Anglican, but he should
not be too sudden in announcing his conversion, as that would
give ground for suspicion; nor should he appear in arms
either in Scotland or in England, even on the Queen's death,
for civil war was above all things not to be contemplated.
But he should just bide his time and then England, duly prepared by a wise minister, himself to wit, would within a year
fall like ripe fruit into his hands. For Bolingbroke was convinced that the Hanoverians could never maintain themselves
in England without a foreign army, the bugbear of the nation,
and that then the whole country would turn to James as their
saviour and the restorer of their liberties. It was a pretty
scheme, worthy of Bolingbroke's subtle intellect, illuminated,
too, with some of those flashes of robust common sense that
frequently relieve his otherwise shallow political philosophy:
such as his determination not to have another civil war if he
could help it, and his remark dismissing the whole scheme,
when he heard that James would not abandon Catholicism,
that 'England would just as soon have a Turk as a Roman
Catholic for king'.[1]

Though such schemes split on the rock of the Pretender's
impracticability, or came to naught through disunion in the
Tory ranks, they were none the less dangerous in creating a
feeling of unrest and suspicion in public life and in raising the
hopes of the Jacobites. It was even reported that the Queen
herself would have preferred her brother to any of her Ger-

[1] See Salomon, 248-55, for Iberville's report on this scheme of Bolingbroke's.
Bolingbroke in his *Letter to Sir William Wyndham* gives a good account of the
Tory party's internal difficulties. He admits that in 1713 there was 'no formed
design in the party, whatever views some particular men might have, against
his majesty's [George I's] accession to the throne'.

man relations to succeed her; and stories were told of a secret
will, to be revealed at her death, declaring him her heir. So
the Whigs felt themselves abundantly justified in adopting
effective measures to preserve the succession as laid down
by law. But they, like the Tories, had difficulties with their
candidate for the throne. In the first instance they naturally
turned to the Elector George for assistance in maintaining
his mother's rights as well as his own. But George, like Sophia
herself, had hitherto shown wisdom in refusing to identify
himself exclusively with either of the two opposing parties.
The choice of Sophia and her heirs had originally been just
as much that of the Tories as of the Whigs; it would much
impair this national position if the Elector came to the throne
simply as the choice of one party, and thus fettered in the
selection of his ministers. George's anger at the betrayal by
the Tories of the common cause, as he regarded their peace
negotiations, had no doubt to some extent modified this view:
but even so he was determined not to do anything displeasing
to the Queen. This unfortunately was just what the Whigs
proposed, when they urged him either to come himself or
send his son to England to take up the position of an heir to
the throne. For Anne was determined not to have the concluding years of her reign disturbed by the presence in England of either of the rival claimants to her succession, whether
a member of the electoral family or even her own brother
James. This became very evident when, during the session of
1714 the electoral envoy Schütz, on the advice of the Whig
Junto, went to the Chancellor to demand a writ of summons
to the Lords for the Electoral Prince as Duke of Cambridge.
The Queen was furious, especially as the ministry agreed that
the writ could not legally be refused; but Schütz was recalled
even before the Queen demanded his dismissal and George
took good care that his son should make no use of the writ.
For the same reason the Elector was not prepared to spend
money on any of the schemes, fantastic or otherwise, proposed to him by the Whigs to advance his interests. One such
scheme was that he should buy seats in Parliament for his
Whig supporters, another that he should finance Steele's
Crisis. Cadogan coolly proposed that the necessities of im-
poverished peers holding Hanoverian sentiments should be
relieved at a cost of £20,000. Stanhope suggested that the
more modest sum of £2,000 should be expended on securing a favourable Common Council, arguing, according to

Schütz's report, that 'however far he is from proposing the
smallest expense to the Elector, he finds this so essential and
so seasonable, that he cannot avoid to conjure me to procure
it, as they are all sure that, being masters of the council,
London will present to Parliament any address they choose,
which will be an example to the rest of the kingdom and cannot fail to have great and good effect'.[1]

But though George would neither allow a member of his
family to reside in England nor spend money meddling in
the country's internal affairs, he so far realized the danger to
his succession from the Jacobite element in the Tory party as
to allow his envoys, Schütz, and, after his dismissal, the far
abler Bothmer, to take counsel with the leading Whigs as to
other precautions. Stanhope does not at first appear to have
been a member of this inner ring of Whigs, who had the
chief voice on policy. None but peers, Devonshire, Somerset, Nottingham, Argyll, Orford, Somers, Cowper, Halifax,
Wharton and Townshend, are mentioned as those who, in
April 1714, advised Schütz to apply for the writ. But some
impatience began to be expressed at the poor results visible
from their policy; and before that, certainly by the beginning
of 1714, Stanhope had been given charge, as supreme executive officer, of the military measures then being contemplated
to secure the undisturbed advent of the Hanoverian heir.[2]

Stanhope, never a man for compromise, had from the time
of the passing of the Schism Act been convinced, and with
cause, that the danger to the Succession was great and that
more active measures on their side were essential. Though
the Tories might not have agreed upon a settled policy of
their own, at any rate the ministry had decided to leave itself
a free hand for any emergency by filling 'the employments
of the kingdom down to the meanest with Tories',[3] and above
all by securing the docility of the army. Officers high and
low, known to be of Whig principles, were put on a black list
or cashiered and replaced by notorious Tories. Argyll, Stair,
Stanhope's proxy Davenport and Marlborough's favourite
Cadogan, besides many other brave men of lesser note, had
been 'turned out of the army', wrote Marlborough in May
1714, 'after having fought so long in the glorious cause of

<hr />

[1] Macpherson, ii. 519.
[2] The Elector George did not himself become the immediate heir to the
throne till his mother Sophia's death, 8 June 1714.
[3] *Letter to Sir William Wyndham.*

liberty, some for talking, some for thinking, and wretches put into their place that never served'.[1] Sir Richard Temple, afterwards Lord Cobham, and Colonel Coote were deprived of their regiments. Admiral Byng, who had stopped the Pretender from reaching Scotland in 1708, was turned out of the Admiralty;[2] Jacobite Highland chieftains had been financed; and there was said to be a plan to lay aside seventy-two officers and nine battalions on the Irish establishment, 'thought to be improper for the design in hand', and raise fifty new battalions 'that would be sure to obey all commands'.[3] Speaking to Schütz as early as August 1713 on the Elector's refusal to let his son come to England, Stanhope had declared that unless something were done the Elector would never obtain the throne, even if he came over with an army; what the Whigs needed, he declared, was a leader on the spot and ready to take action if the Pretender was brought over in the Queen's lifetime.[4] For want of such a leader from Hanover, he himself assumed the responsibility. At the end of 1713 Cadogan was sent over from Holland by Marlborough to consult with him as to the transport of Dutch troops to England, if need be, and on a scheme to secure Dunkirk under Armstrong, a faithful officer of Marlborough's.[5] When early in the following year the Queen seemed to be on the point of death, alarming reports were brought over as to the movements of French troops to ports on the Flemish coast. Stanhope at once sent over some officers to investigate the truth of these reports on the spot, where they were openly told by some of the French officers that they 'had orders to be ready to march upon a minute's warning'.[6]

By March Stanhope had made his preparations to support the law, if necessary by armed force. He sought out the French refugees, of whom there had been a considerable colony in England since William's time and who had provided some notable officers for the army such as Schomberg and Ruvigny. They were well disposed towards him, having, in spite of pressing appeals from the government, voted for him at Westminster in 1710, and responded in large numbers to his call to arms. A *Whig Association* had been formed and

[1] Kemble, 500.
[2] Byng was dismissed in Jan. 1713/14, Aislabie, the other Whig on the Board, in April (Admiralty Lists).
[3] See Stair's memorial to Marlborough in Hardwicke, ii. 522, and Michael, i. 359–60, who quotes *An Inquiry into Miscarriages of the last four Years*, 1714.
[4] Salomon, 231.   [5] Coxe, *Marlborough*, iii. 350.   [6] Macpherson, ii. 567.

large sums of money contributed for the purchase of arms and ammunition by the heads of the party and rich City merchants. Many Whig officers of those discharged, 'some for talking, some for thinking', declared themselves ready to obey Stanhope's orders. Preparations had even gone so far, according to Lockhart, that 'severall thousand figures of a small fusie about two inches long in brass, and some few in silver and gold, were dispersed amongst the chiefs and more zealous of the partie as a signall in the day of tryall'. A definite plan of operations had been drawn up for this army under Stanhope's command to be used at the first sign of Jacobite aggression; all the half-pay officers who had signed the *Association* were to hold their arms in readiness in their bedchambers and be prepared at a minute's warning to repair with them to the rendezvous behind Montagu House, while Cadogan with a picked band was immediately to seize the Tower.[1] This plan was never betrayed by any one of the thousands admitted to the secret; and Bolingbroke himself, who had his spies everywhere, had never heard of it until, many years later, it was revealed to him by Stanhope's cousin Chesterfield.[2]

But in spite of all his careful preparations even Stanhope had his moods of depression. On 9 July, after the Queen had prorogued her last session of Parliament with a petulant little speech, reputed to have been drawn up by Bolingbroke, in which the Whigs were rated for their opposition to her government, the Scottish Tory Lockhart came upon Stanhope

'walking all alone and very humdrum in Westminster Hall. I askt him what the matter was with him, for he seemed out of humour when everybody was glad to get into the country? He answered that he thought all true Brittains had reason to be out of humour. I reply'd, that I thought myself a Brittain true

[1] Lockhart, i. 462–3, who mentions that he got hold of one of these fusies and sent it to the Queen, and that he also jokes about it with Sir R. Pollock, 'a true Staunch Whig', in the House of Commons; Mahon, *History*, i. 91.

[2] Chesterfield, *Memoirs*, i. 15–16. Some doubt has been cast on this story owing to the difficulty of believing that a secret committed to so many did not leak out at the time. But Professor Browning of Glasgow University reminds me of the parallel case in 1688, when the government of James II was equally ignorant of the even more extensive preparations made for the support of William of Orange. For the story in the text there is confirmatory evidence from two sources, Lockhart and Chesterfield. It is, of course, also possible that at the time Bolingbroke had some inkling of the project but dismissed it from his mind as unworthy of serious attention, and when reminded of it by Chesterfield many years later had entirely forgotten it. For further illustration of the organized measures for securing the Hanoverian succession see App. F, p. 464.

enough, and yet was in a very good humour. Why, returned he, then it seems you have not consider'd the Queen's speech. Yes, said I, I have and was pleased with it, for I think she spoke like herself. That's true, answered he, for from what she said I look upon our liberties as gone. I wish with all my soul it were so, said I. Why, returned he, do ye declare openly for the Pretender? The Pretender, said I, I was not so much as thinking of him; but as you Englishmen have made slaves of us Scotsmen, I would be glad to see you reduced to the same state, and then we shou'd be both on an equal footing. . . . Well; well, said he, 'tis no jest, you'll get your Pretender, and you'll repent it, I dare answer for it, e'er long; and with that he went off in a prodigious fury.'

He adds in his diary that Stanhope was not the only person in a fury, 'for all the Whigs and Tories thought the Queen had decided to restore James III'.[1]

But the case of the Tories was really far worse; and after this the tide turned all in favour of the Whigs. At the end of July Oxford was dismissed and Bolingbroke for a brief moment held the reins, only to find that with no fixed policy, with the Whigs well prepared under his old friend Stanhope, and a considerable section of his own party against him, his prospects of real power were bleak. On the very day of his triumph over Oxford he bethought himself of the need of allies, and 'either smelling a falling house', as his enemies surmised, 'or foreseeing a storm, which he despaired to be able to weather, designed to reconcile himself with the Whigs'.[2] This was not the first approach made by one of the sections of the Tory party to the Whigs. Hanmer's group of Hanover Tories were indeed as anxious for the Protestant succession as their opponents and had already on several occasions voted with them. In May Oxford, alarmed at Bolingbroke's intrigues, had also made advances to some of the Whigs and been told that their alliance depended on his support of the Hanoverian succession. Bolingbroke's approach took the form of a dinner. 'Would not the world have roared against the dragon [Oxford] for such a thing?' writes Erasmus Lewis to Swift, 'Mercurialis [Bolingbroke] entertained Stanhope, Craggs, Pulteney and Walpole. What if the dragon had done so?' At this dinner-party Bolingbroke suggested an alliance and offered a few places in the government

---

[1] Lockhart, i. 479. See also Klopp, xiv. 620, who quotes Bothmer's and Hoffman's (envoy from Vienna) reports on the effect of the Queen's speech.

[2] Boyer, ii. 4.

to Whigs. Before discussing such a proposal Stanhope required him to show his hand and demanded, as an earnest of his fine words, that he should offer Marlborough the army and Orford the Admiralty. Bolingbroke would not, or could not, agree, knowing that the Queen would never again admit Marlborough into favour; and the party broke up with these words from Stanhope: 'Harry! you have only two ways of escaping the gallows. The first is to join the honest party of the Whigs, the other to give yourself up entirely to the French king and seek his help for the Pretender. If you do not choose the first course, we can only imagine that you have decided for the second.'[1]

The well-known events of the next few days may best be summarized here by the letter written by Stanhope, two days before the Queen's death, to the Emperor, his companion-in-arms in Spain.

30 July / 10 Aug. 1714.
'Sire,
    'I may, I believe, announce to your Imperial and Catholic Majesty that at this moment the Queen is lying in her death agony. After feeling unwell for two days, this morning she had an apoplectic stroke which for two hours left her unconscious. About eleven o'clock she recovered slightly, and the Council, already assembled, took advantage of this lucid interval to obtain her approval for the nomination of the Duke of Shrewsbury as Lord Treasurer, in place of the five Commissioners of the Treasury who had been suggested and who would have been subordinate to Lord Bolingbroke as chief minister. The Council remains in continuous session and gives all necessary orders for preserving the peace of the Realm and securing the Elector's accession. This afternoon about 3 o'clock the four physicians informed the Council that the remedies they had employed, two most potent emetics, were producing no effect and that according to the rules of their craft the Queen had no more than twelve hours to live.
    'This sudden and unforeseen occurrence comes as a thunderclap to the Jacobite party, who have not yet taken the measures necessary for carrying out their designs with the necessary despatch. Therefore I can assure your Imperial Majesty that, if the physicians' opinion proves true, the Elector will be proclaimed King and will take possession of his Kingdom as peacefully as any of his predecessors. If however, the Queen's illness were to be prolonged, even for a few weeks, we should indeed

---

[1] Salomon, 312 sqq.; Michael, i. 358; both these authors give reasons for thinking that Walpole was not present at this dinner (Swift, xvi. 166).

be greatly embarrassed; but all those who have seen the Queen and spoken with the physicians, agree that the end cannot be later than tomorrow.

'I have felt it my duty to inform your Imperial Majesty of all I have been able to find out in so delicate a turn of affairs. I hope, too, that I am saying nothing new in giving the assurance that all right-thinking people here are as indignant at the perfidious conduct of the last Ministry against your Imperial Majesty, as could be any Austrian or Spaniard, and that, as soon as the opportunity occurs, they will exert all their energies to repair this disgrace to our Nation; I also flatter myself that I have not erred in assuring these right-thinking people on every occasion, that Your Majesty will always find your own interest to consist in supporting English liberty, and the rights of the House of Brunswick, and in defending us, if need be, against the common enemy. God grant that the good understanding that has brought about such glorious results, may be once more knit into an everlasting friendship. Meanwhile I most humbly beg your Imperial and Catholic Majesty to believe that I am and shall always be your Majesty's most obedient, humble servant.'[1]

[1] Klopp, xiv. 633-4, gives a German translation of the French original which he found in the Vienna archives. He sent a copy of this original to the historian Lord Stanhope in March 1873; this copy is at Chevening. My translation is from the Chevening copy, since on inquiry of the keeper of the Archives at Vienna I learned that the original could not at present be found.

CHAPTER VI

GEORGE I'S ACCESSION AND
STANHOPE'S MISSION TO VIENNA

§ 1

THE death of Anne occurred on 1/12 August 1714, but more than six weeks passed before the new King George, Elector of Hanover, came over to take up his English heritage. Just such an interregnum had been above all dreaded by the most ardent Whigs; to the Jacobites it had appeared likely to present their great opportunity. In the event the hopes and fears of either party proved equally baseless. The general feeling at the news of the Queen's death was one of relief from the strain and uncertainty of the last four years. George was proclaimed King by the heralds in the chief cities of the kingdom amidst almost universal acclamations. Stanhope's carefully laid plans for seizing the Tower and securing the lawful succession by his own and Marlborough's Whig veterans were quite uncalled for. The triumphant appearance of the Pretender at the critical moment was ignominiously stopped by Louis XIV's order that he should not leave Lorraine; in England hardly a voice was openly raised in his favour. This easy acceptance of the Hanoverian is the more remarkable inasmuch as, though both candidates for the throne were personally unknown in England, what little was known of George was dim and unattractive, whereas the Pretender had all the glamour of a prince exiled from his native country, debarred from his natural inheritance, and, in contrast to George, eager to come and reign over his own people. Moreover, the Whigs, the only organized party in the state supporting the Hanover Succession as part of their policy, had in the last two Parliaments been in a minority, and of that minority some at least had had surreptitious dealings with the Pretender; the Tories, on the other hand, in power since 1710, though divided in their allegiance, had by their policy and their distribution of favours increased the influence and aroused the hopes of the Jacobites.

How then is the signal triumph of the Whigs to be accounted for? Undoubtedly the refusal of the Pretender to abjure Roman Catholicism was, as Bolingbroke saw, one of the main reasons, for even the Tory High Churchmen had not forgotten that their loyalty had been no protection to their religion under the last Roman Catholic king. Another reason is to be found in Bolingbroke. Consumed with jealousy of any superior, he had jockeyed out the cautious and prudent leader of his party, Oxford, only to find himself obliged at the moment of his triumph to accept—even to propose—Shrewsbury, a convinced Hanoverian, for the Treasurer's staff and his own return to a secondary place. And the critical moment found him aimless and still in search of a policy. He would have liked James as king, for James would have to depend on the Tory party, which he himself hoped to mould and lead; but he was afraid of the risk, for he was not the man to risk his head for a visionary project, and refused, at Atterbury's entreaty, to proclaim James III at Charing Cross. And with Bolingbroke floating in uncertainty there was no Jacobite left of the influence and personality to lead a revolution. It is true the Whigs themselves had no outstanding leader; but they had in their ranks an array of men experienced in statecraft and passionately determined to maintain the succession established by law, as the only means of safeguarding the liberties of the people, its established religion and the foreign policy of the country laid down by the Great Deliverer. Their strength lay not so much in flashes of genius but rather in a stolid English common sense that would stand no playing with the law of the land they were determined to see observed. Such were Somers the wise counsellor of the Union, Halifax, William's great financial reformer, Townshend and his brother-in-law Robert Walpole, the astute party manager, and Stanhope, still thought of as in the second line of statesmen but second to none in fiery devotion to the cause. He had none of the doubts that many even of his fellow Whigs had felt in the past, but was absolutely single-minded and uncompromising in his Revolution sentiments. Moreover, when he found that, wisely perhaps, the Elector would take no active steps to secure his rights during the Queen's lifetime, he had seen to it in his straightforward way that England should be prepared, if necessary, to support her own choice with her own arms. Without Stanhope and others, like him direct and determined, the Pretender, though not likely ever to have been accepted in England, might have caused years of confusion and civil disturbance.

George himself, too, though absent, had contributed not a little to his own quiet succession. Elector of Hanover since 1705, he had shown courage and some ability as a commander in the field, both in the imperial war against the Turks and as a staunch ally of Marlborough in the War of the Spanish Succession. He had protested against what seemed to him a betrayal of the allied cause by the Tories, and had refused any longer to stand with the English troops when Ormonde left Eugene in the lurch before Denain. As a prince of the Empire he had taken a prominent part in the politics of northern Germany, showing undeviating loyalty to the Emperor and asserting with considerable success the rights of his little electorate against the overgrown power of Sweden and the increasing ambitions of his neighbour and son-in-law Frederick William, who since 1713 ruled over the new kingdom of Prussia. Devoted to his electorate, he had never shown the same pride as his mother Sophia at the prospect of leaving it for England, and was only reconciled after 1710 to his new heritage by his hatred of France, and his fear that England would be irretrievably dragged into the vortex of French anti-imperial policy, if he were supplanted by his rival the Pretender. His determination not to identify himself with either of the English parties until Tory intrigues had almost forced him to draw closer to the Whigs, and his refusal even then to allow his son to take his seat in the House of Lords, had given a favourable impression of his fair-minded attitude on English politics. On the other hand, he had always kept himself well informed about the state of affairs in England, not only through the letters of his Whig friends, but also through his electoral agents. After Schütz's dismissal for his tactless demand for the writ, Bothmer, a much abler diplomatist, took his place and was in England on the Queen's death. But his most useful informant on English affairs was Jean de Robethon, one of the numerous French Huguenots who fled from France in 1685. Patronized by Mary of Orange, he had become secretary first to Portland and then, as we have seen, to William III. After William's death he had attached himself to Bernstorff, who in 1705 became George's chief minister in Hanover, and was soon reputed to be the master-mind of the two. Few men of this time had a more intimate knowledge of the state secrets of Holland, England, Hanover and the Empire, or even of France, few a closer acquaintance with most of the leading European statesmen. He corresponded as an equal with men like Marlborough and Prince Eugene; the leading English Whigs gave him their confidence and accepted his advice. Already in 1701, it will be remembered, Stanhope was writing to him on familiar terms.[1] Shortly after the Queen's death Robethon writes to Stanhope from Hanover that the King was designing to offer him a high post in the government, and Stanhope replies thanking him for his good offices, to which he attributed the King's favourable notice of him.[2]

Primed with such good information on the state of parties and of affairs in England, George was left in no doubt as to whom he could depend upon. The first evidence of this was in his choice of names for the Council of Regency, contained in his letter opened by the Privy Council on the day of the Queen's death. Of the eighteen appointed only four were Tories, and they men noted for their loyalty to the Hanoverian Succession, the rest being all Whigs; and not the least indication of his acumen was that among the names those of Marlborough, who had only recently been corresponding with Berwick, and his son-in-law Sunderland were not to be found; the only surprising omission was that of Somers, possibly owing to his bad health. Shortly afterwards, on further orders from Hanover, Bolingbroke was summarily dismissed and his papers put under seal.

Not until the middle of September, when the Regency had made all ready for his reception, and a loyal, if not enthusiastic welcome was assured him from his new subjects, did George set forth on his journey from Hanover. Besides these prudential considerations an unwillingness to tear himself away from his dear Electorate may have partly accounted for the delay. When the deputation from England had come to announce to him the Queen's death, they had found him in his orangery engaged in plucking blossoms from his orange trees. No doubt the thought that such simple joys would no more be his when he was once committed to the turbulent people whose language and politics he did not understand, prompted the parting words he addressed to his beloved home at Herrenhausen: 'Adieu, dear spot, where I have spent so many happy and peaceful hours. I leave thee, but not for ever, for I hope at times to behold thee again.' At any rate he took with him a long train of Hanoverian friends and servants to remind him of his past happiness, beings with whom he might enjoy conversation not translated into French or Latin. Among his attendants were Bernstorff and Goertz, the two rival ministers. Bernstorff was by origin a Mecklenburger and still had large estates and interests in that duchy; he had first served George's uncle the Duke of Celle and on his death transferred himself to Hanover. A hard-working and conscientious minister with a real grasp of German politics, Bernstorff had great influence with his master, especially in encouraging his anti-Prussian and anti-Swedish inclinations. He also tried to influence his English policy, a habit which finally brought him into conflict with Stanhope and other English ministers. Goertz, his rival personally and politically, was of less account and did not trouble himself about England. Robethon naturally came with Bernstorff and from the very indefiniteness of his official position and from the trust reposed in him by the King, who employed him as confidential secretary, was able to exercise a more lasting influence than any of the other Germans on English foreign policy. This influence was all the greater from the fact that in his vast correspondence with English ministers and English ambassadors he was apt to leave it uncertain whether he was writing to them on behalf of the Elector or the King of England. George also brought one of his mistresses, Mme Kielmansegge, her senior coadjutor Mme Schulenberg remaining behind till it was more certain how the land lay in England, as well as Mme von Platen, the youngest and most pleasing. Not the least attractive of George's suite in the eyes of his new subjects were the two silent and ferocious-looking Turks, Mehemet and Mustapha, captured by him in his Turkish campaign. With him also came his son George, shortly to be created Prince of Wales; but his wife, the engaging Princess Caroline of Anspach, did not arrive till a month later with her daughters. Their son Prince Frederick was left at Hanover to receive a purely German education and remained there during the whole of his grandfather's reign.[1]

On Saturday 18/29 September George landed at Greenwich and next day held a court in the Palace to receive the humble duty of courtiers and place-hunters of both parties who crowded the rooms in the hope of basking in the new

[1] Malortie, 57 sqq.; Chance, 52–6.

ruler's smile. There was Marlborough, already restored to his old office of Captain-General; but, though he was graciously received for an hour by his old comrade-in-arms, he was soon made to feel that his influence was extinct and that his loyalty was justly suspected. Oxford also came to kiss hands, but after that ceremony the King ostentatiously turned his back upon him. Stanhope, already named among the thirty-eight appointed to the new Privy Council, made his obeisance.[1] Ormonde and Bolingbroke wisely did not appear. The King indeed had already determined to give his confidence only to those he had good reason to trust from their previous conduct, as appeared from the list of the new ministry announced a few days later.

The ministry had been composed partly on Robethon's suggestions, but mainly on the advice of Bothmer. He, while ruling out the old ministers, after consultation not only with the Whig leaders but also with the Hanover Tory Nottingham, had counselled a choice as comprehensive as possible of both Tories and Whigs, provided they had shown loyalty to Hanover.[2] In those days there was no ostensible Prime Minister, such as we understand him, though the holder of the Lord High Treasurer's staff was generally looked upon as the leading servant of the Crown.[3] Viscount Halifax, conscious of his services to the Whig cause and of his financial ability, aspired to that prize. But both Bothmer and Robethon had advised against any subject being raised to such an eminence; and from that date this historic office has remained in abeyance. Halifax was merely appointed First Lord of the Treasury Board, and consoled, inadequately in his own estimation, by an earldom and the Garter. Nor was he even regarded unofficially as the leading minister. That distinction was attributed by the memoir writers of the time to Viscount Townshend, appointed Secretary of State for the Northern Department, a staunch Whig who had come into prominence as the chief English representative at the abortive negotiations of Gertruydenberg and as responsible for the one-sided Barrier Treaty of 1709. Transparently honest, but obstinate and limited in his views, he soon showed that he had not the capacity for leadership attributed to him. He carried with him into the ministry his brother-in-law Robert Walpole, who obtained the lucrative post of Paymaster.

[1] Pauli, *Actenstücke*.   [2] Pauli, ib.
[3] For a discussion on the office of Prime Minister see below, ch. x, pp. 255 sqq.

Shrewsbury and the High Church Tory, Nottingham, were
given offices of minor importance. There was even some
thought of sending Ormonde back to his old post in Ireland,
but Bothmer very soon dismissed the idea of employing a
man so distasteful to his master. The provision of offices for
two men, whose claims could not, it was felt, be overlooked,
proved a difficult problem, but for very different reasons.
Sunderland, a vehement and impetuous Whig, who shared
in the distrust with which his father-in-law Marlborough was
regarded, was ambitious and anxious to be a Secretary of
State; and one of Bothmer's ideas was to substitute him
for Townshend. Later he suggested that he should take
Shrewsbury's former post as Viceroy of Ireland; and so it was
decided, though both Marlborough and Sunderland himself
regarded it as a device for shelving him. There remained
Stanhope.

Hitherto Stanhope had generally been looked upon as
marked out for a military career; and accordingly both
Bothmer and Robethon first proposed that he should be sent
as commander-in-chief to Ireland. Then Bothmer discovered
that many thought 'he will be more useful in the English
parliament', this view being very strongly urged by his old
friends Robert and Horatio Walpole and by Townshend.
Horatio Walpole indeed, never apt to underrate his own
importance, claimed credit for having proposed Stanhope to
Townshend as his brother-secretary, 'knowing that he had
a fruitfull and luxuriant genius in foreign affairs, which
I hoped he would have suffered to be check'd or pruned by
Lord Townshend's prudence'.[1] Accordingly he was offered
the second most important post in the ministry, that of
Secretary for the Southern Department, where he would be
in close collaboration with Townshend and have the leading
position in the House of Commons. The offer seems to have
come as a surprise to some of the Whigs as well as to Stanhope
himself. 'We Whigs', wrote one of the party, 'are already
divided among ourselves and as an instance, Mr. Stanhope
is not the man some of us would have desired for Secretary,
Mr. Boil was there man.'[2] When Walpole came to announce
the offer to Stanhope, so the story goes, his first impulse was

---

[1] Coxe, *Walpole*, ii. 48.
[2] *Wentworth Papers*, 427. 'Mr. Boil' is meant for the Hon. Henry Boyle,
Chancellor of the Exchequer and then Secretary of State in the Whig administration from 1702 to 1710.

to refuse, touching his sword to indicate how he thought he could render the best service to the King; but on being assured that he was thought indispensable for that great office he accepted it, fortunately for himself and the country.[1]

During most of the eighteenth century the two Secretaries of State were the sole channels whereby the King's commands were signified for the whole internal administration of the country as well as for the conduct of foreign policy. In purely domestic concerns there appears to have been no discrimination of duties between the two Secretaries; each in turn may be found dealing with the same matter, as suited the convenience of the moment; there is an instance of Stanhope adding a postscript to a letter already signed by Townshend, and another when both jointly sign a letter on a question of peculiar importance. Colonial affairs were confined to the department of the Southern Secretary. But for foreign affairs Europe was marked out by a rough geographical division into a sphere comprising Turkey and the Latin countries, assigned to the Southern Secretary, relations with the rest of Europe falling to his Northern colleague. Such a system required for harmonious working either an extraordinary affinity between the views of the two Secretaries or else a willingness of one to subordinate his views almost entirely to those of the other. At first Townshend, owing to his greater experience, seems to have set the tone in their common business, but Stanhope very soon proved himself at least his equal in ability and decision and his superior in knowledge of continental conditions; fortunately during the first and most critical period of their union as colleagues they agreed so closely and worked so harmoniously together that no question arose as to who should take the leading part.[2]

The King himself took comparatively little interest in the details of domestic politics and left his ministers a fairly free hand in dealing with such details. But it is a mistake to represent him as uninterested in the main issues even

[1] For Bothmer's and Robethon's share in forming the ministry, besides authorities already quoted, see Macpherson, ii. 640–1; Lady Mary Wortley Montagu, *Letters*, &c., i. 120–41; Coxe, *Walpole*, i. 96. Stanhope was sworn in as Secretary of State and to the Privy Council on 27 September 1714; R.O., *S.P. Dom. Geo. I*, i.

[2] Good illustrations of dovetailing work between the two Secretaries may be seen in correspondence given in *H. MSS.*, *Townshend*, 173–86, during the 1715 rebellion. For a fuller description of the spheres of the Northern and Southern Departments see Williams, *Chatham*, i. 325–7.

of domestic administration. It is true that he very soon abandoned his predecessors' custom of presiding at Cabinet meetings for the decision of policy;[1] but that was simply because he could not follow discussions in English; and he kept himself well informed through reports from his ministers who addressed him in French or, as in the case of Walpole, in Latin. Whether in England or in Hanover, he always kept a sharp eye on appointments to important offices and on the general trend of government in England, and made the Peerage Bill, for example, quite as much part of his personal policy as it was of his ministers. In foreign policy he was unquestionably master. He never allowed any minister, German or English, or however trusted, to act without his knowledge and sanction and required to be kept exactly informed of what was happening in foreign courts. When Stanhope was on a mission to Paris Craggs wrote to him that the King was complaining of the infrequency of his dispatches and 'always expresses a good deal of dislike when a post arrives without any letters'.[2] On another occasion Stanhope took it upon himself to give directions on an urgent matter to St. Saphorin at Vienna without having had an opportunity of consulting the King; a week later he cancelled these directions, having since spoken to his royal master and finding that he 'had quite different views on the proposals made to you . . . from those I first conceived on reading your despatch'.[3] All dispatches on foreign affairs, both outgoing and incoming, had to be written in or translated into French for submission to the King; and the same rule applied even to important domestic letters.[4] It was natural and advantageous to the country that George I should have taken this personal interest in foreign affairs. He knew far more about German politics and those of the northern powers than any of his English ministers; and, though his view in this sphere was to a certain extent distorted by his Hanoverian prejudices, he did useful work in introducing English statesmen to. a broader outlook on foreign policy. Hitherto England had confined her attention mainly to southern and western Europe. George's Hanoverian interests now compelled her

---

[1] Michael, i. 439, quotes at least two instances of George I attending Cabinet meetings early in his reign.

[2] R.O., S.P. 104/29, Craggs to Stanhope and Stair 11 and 16 September 1718.

[3] R.O., S.P. 104/42, to St. Saphorin, 13 and 20 May 1720. This particular matter concerned Hanoverian more closely than English interests.

[4] An instance of this occurs in H. MSS., Townshend, 176.

to recognize the importance of the new eastern and northern questions which for the first time were assuming European importance.

§ 2

When Stanhope, in the last week of September 1714, took over his duties of Secretary of State he found his office in confusion and the outlook for England on the Continent anything but promising. Bolingbroke, Secretary for the Southern Department since August 1713, during his last month of office after the Queen's death had taken the opportunity of carrying off or destroying compromising letters, so that it was sometimes difficult for the new ministers to pick up the threads of previous negotiations. In October Stanhope has to write to the English agent in Madrid to ask him for copies of all letters he had received from Bolingbroke and others, since, as he puts it euphemistically, 'by the exchange of offices and the necessary removal of papers from one office to another, things have been in such a confusion that it has not been possible to have these matters before us in a true light'.[1] Nor was the foreign policy of the last four years, as far as it could be ascertained, at all to the liking of the new Whig ministry or to the interests of their new master.

Although the Whigs still regarded the Anglo-French Treaty of Utrecht as an inadequate return for the country's achievements and expenditure and were unwilling to cover it with their formal sanction, they felt bound to accept it as irrevocable.[2] None the less they were soon brought to realize that, chiefly owing to the cynical disregard for the allies displayed by the Tories in the preliminary negotiations, it had left England with hardly a friend in Europe. Our former allies, Savoy and the Dutch, the Emperor and the Princes of the Empire, including the Elector of Hanover himself, were all justly aggrieved at the way in which its terms had been settled behind their backs. The desertion of the Catalans and French Huguenots, in spite of solemn engagements, had cast a slur on our good name. Moreover, in regard to the rest of Europe, the general settlement attempted by the other treaties of Utrecht and of Rastadt and Baden had by no means decided the issues of the war or established a stable peace in Europe. The Emperor Charles VI, in his separate

[1] R.O., *S.P.* 104/135.　　　　　[2] See above, ch. v, p. 131.

Treaty of Rastadt with France, had not acknowledged the rights of the Duke of Savoy to territory he had previously promised him. In respect of German territory restored by France to the Empire he had neglected to repair the breach made in the defences of German Protestantism by the Treaty of Ryswick. That treaty had ignored the famous principle consecrated in 1648, *cujus regio ejus religio*, that made each German ruler the arbiter of the religious creed to be observed in his state, by the stipulation that in territory returned by Louis, even to Protestant princes, Roman Catholicism should still remain the established religion.[1] This covert attack on Protestantism and still more the Emperor's omission at Rastadt and Baden even to guarantee the Protestant succession in England caused serious uneasiness to George and the English Whigs. Hitherto also the Emperor had refused to make any arrangement with the Dutch about the Barrier fortresses they were to hold as a condition for his taking over the Low Countries.[2] Above all he had made no treaty with Philip V; he maintained his claims to the entire Spanish monarchy and, with true Habsburg obstinacy, refused to give his rival any other title than that of Duke of Anjou. Philip in his turn still spoke of Charles VI merely as the Archduke and in his own long list of titles included those of *Archidux Austriae, Dux Burgundiae, Brabantiae et Mediolani, Comes Habsburgi, Flandriae, Tyrolis*, as if he were back in the days of Charles V. In fact there was still a state of war between Spain and the Emperor. The Emperor still held Majorca; while Barcelona, besieged for the fourth time within twenty years, had been heroically defended till September by his Catalan supporters against Philip.

Commerce too, a special interest of the Whigs, had not been too flourishing since the end of the war. It is true that a favourable treaty of commerce had been signed at Utrecht with Spain, and the Assiento, or right of importing slaves to

[1] By Clause 4 of Louis XIV's treaty with the Emperor at Ryswick (1697) the German territory restored to the Empire was to retain the Catholic religion established by Louis. By Clause 21 of the Anglo-French treaty of Utrecht Louis had promised to restore the conditions of the Westphalian Settlement but in Clauses 3, 25, and 27 of the treaties of Rastadt (with Emperor) and Baden (with Empire) had confirmed anew the objectionable Clause 4 of Ryswick. On the religious question Charles VI saw eye to eye with Louis and was no doubt pleased enough to estrange the Protestant princes of the Empire from France.

[2] § vii of Franco-Dutch Treaty of Utrecht; H. Vast, *Les Grands Traités de Louis XIV*, iii. 142.

the Spanish colonies, assigned to us. But the value of these concessions had been whittled away by explanatory notes attached to the ratification of the treaty, allowed, it was whispered, for corrupt motives by Bolingbroke; and our merchants in Spain were still molested by arbitrary and vexatious dues and regulations. No wonder Stanhope contrasted the Tory arrangement with his own favourable treaty of 1707 with Charles III.[1] Again, our import of naval stores from the Baltic had come almost to a standstill. So indispensable was this source of supply for the upkeep of the navy that on its temporary failure in 1716 Townshend declared it would be impossible to fit out ships for the following year and so 'the whole navy would become perfectly useless'.[2] The difficulty had arisen from Charles XII's declaration that any ship trading with his Baltic provinces seized by the Tsar, whence came most of these supplies, would be treated as a pirate; and, since his fleet still commanded the Baltic, he could put his threats into effect. Against these threats Bolingbroke, who was Northern Secretary during the first years of the Tory administration, frankly confessed his impotence: 'Every measure that occurs to one's thoughts', he wrote, 'is immediately attended by a crowd of objections; and yet the necessity of resolving on something presses us hard.' His resolution merely took the form of a 'trimming, dilatory game', and only resulted in a reply from Charles which 'proved as disagreeable and contained as flat a denial' as the Swedish chancellor had given our minister-resident Jefferyes to expect. So urgent had become the difficulties that even before the King's arrival from Hanover the Council of Regency had instructed Bolingbroke's Tory colleague Bromley 'to represent to your Majesty the unfortunate condition of your subjects of Great Britain trading to the Balticke Sea, whose ships and effects are daily seized by the Suedish men of war and privateers'.[3]

Bolingbroke's remedy for our isolation and for most of these difficulties had been to draw England ever closer to our traditional enemy France. One reason for his 'trimming, dilatory game' with Sweden was that he was considering an alliance with Louis XIV and Prussia to protect Charles XII from his numerous enemies, a scheme which fell through

[1] See above, ch. iii, pp. 60-1.   [2] Coxe, *Walpole*, ii. 88.
[3] *Instructions, Sweden*, i. 50 sqq.; R.O., *S.P.* 95/131 (*Memorandum of Affairs with Sweden, 1711–19*).

because Prussia had designs of her own on Charles's possession of Stettin.[1] He was also meditating another treaty with
France to include Savoy and possibly Spain, directed mainly
against the Emperor and his Italian ambitions. So nearly
consummated was this last project that before he left office
he had already sent to Prior in Paris full powers to sign the
treaty. But though Louis was quite willing to draw England
once more into the orbit of his client states, he showed his
contempt for her friendless position by evasions of the recent
Treaty of Utrecht. The Pretender, in spite of Parliament's
protests and Bolingbroke's tepid remonstrances, had been
allowed to remain in the close proximity of Lorraine, whence
he issued treasonable proclamations to the English nobility
and was easily accessible to Jacobite conspirators. Then
there were 'the cursed sluices of Dunkirk', as Bolingbroke
called them. This port had been a terror to English traders
during the war from the safe harbourage it afforded to
privateers, ready, at a moment's notice, to pounce out upon
our shipping. It was only rendered accessible to these
privateers by an elaborate system of canals and sluices constructed to maintain the right depth of water; and one of the
clauses of the Treaty of Utrecht stipulated that these sluices
should be destroyed and the canals filled up. There was
considerable delay by the French in fulfilling this condition,
and even when these 'cursed sluices' were at last put out of
action, by a transparent evasion of the treaty work was immediately started on making sluices and deepening channels
in the neighbouring port of Mardyk, which would have made
it as dangerous as Dunkirk. Against these proceedings
Bolingbroke and his emissary Prior had made no effective
protest.[2]

George's accession soon put an end to Bolingbroke's
'dapplings' with France. Two days after the Queen's death,
the Regency ordered Prior at once to suspend negotiations
for the defensive alliance with France, Savoy and Spain and
to await the King's further instructions before proceeding
in the matter.[3] The further instructions never came. Bolingbroke's scheme of an intimate alliance with France in opposition to the Emperor was entirely alien not only to the

[1] Michael, i. 713.
[2] *Instructions, France*, 54 sqq. For a full and well-documented account of
the Dunkirk question see A. de St. Léger, *La Flandre Maritime et Dunkerque sous
la Domination française, 1659-1789* (Paris, 1900).
[3] *Instructions, France*, i. 75.

views of George I, always staunch to the ruler to whom his house owed the Electoral dignity, but also to the traditional policy of his English Whig ministry. In fact the difficulties Louis was making about Dunkirk and the development of the neighbouring port of Mardyk and his scarcely veiled sympathy with the Pretender caused them to envisage as highly probable a renewal of war with him. This made it all the more necessary to bring back the States and the Emperor to the old footing of close alliance.

Unfortunately both these powers were sore with England for her desertion of them at Utrecht and were by no means eager to undertake engagements that might lead to another war. The Emperor also had doubts as to the stability of the Hanoverian dynasty and was disinclined to commit himself too far in its support. But the principal difficulty in a joint alliance with the two powers was that they needed first to be reconciled to each other on the Barrier question, without a settlement of which the Emperor could not enter into possession of the Spanish Low Countries. The struggle for existence of the Dutch against France, almost continuous since 1672, had impressed them painfully with their vulnerability to attack through the Low Countries. Spain had proved far too weak to defend them, and, though Spain was now to be superseded by the Emperor's more effective power, the Dutch had never swerved from their cardinal principle of securing themselves by a line of Barrier fortresses, garrisoned by their own troops, across this buffer territory. They also required to be repaid the cost of these garrisons by commercial concessions and a share in the Low Countries' customs duties. The Emperor naturally objected to this invasion of his sovereign rights; England also, as the trade rival of the Dutch, was suspicious of the commercial grip they would thereby obtain over the rich trade of the Low Countries. Two attempts had already been made by England to bring about a preliminary arrangement with the Dutch. Negotiations conducted by Marlborough in 1706 had proved abortive. By Townshend's treaty of 1709, as we have seen,[1] English interests had been almost entirely sacrificed to the Dutch demands. This treaty had been repudiated by Bolingbroke, who in January 1713 had imposed a new treaty on the Dutch, whereby the fortresses assigned to them were severely cut down, and England regained her full share of

[1] See above, ch. iii, p. 83.

economic advantages. But neither of these treaties had been accepted by the Emperor; so the whole matter still rested in suspense. Until that was settled it was seen to be impossible to restore the old triple alliance of the Emperor and the Maritime Powers, the first object of the new government's foreign policy. Accordingly even before the coronation on 20 October it was decided to send an ambassador who should first ascertain the Dutch proposals at The Hague and then proceed to Vienna to act as a go-between on the Barrier question and sound the Emperor as to a renewal of the alliance. To mark the importance attached to this embassy a Secretary of State was chosen for the mission.

Of the two Secretaries it would have seemed more natural to send Townshend, for not only were relations with both The Hague and Vienna within his province, but he was also well posted in the Barrier problems and had already negotiated one treaty in the attempt to solve them. Possibly, however, this last circumstance may have been a reason why he was not sent, since by this time the treaty of 1709 was regarded, even by the Whigs and Townshend himself, as too favourable to the Dutch. In his stead the choice fell upon Stanhope.

Stanhope certainly had qualifications for this important mission. His service as secretary to his father at The Hague and his visits there in Marlborough's company to confer with Heinsius and Prince Eugene had already made him familiar with the idiosyncrasies of Dutch statesmen. In Vienna also he would find many associates of his Spanish days, such as Sinzendorf, the man who had 'just sense enough to supplant Lichtenstein', Eugene again and the Emperor Charles himself, in respect of whom the King, so ran Stanhope's instructions, doubted not 'but the favour and distinction which his Imperial Majesty formerly showed you during your attendance on him in Spain will contribute to render your instances the more effectual'.[1] Much indeed was hoped from this mission, which, says Boyer, 'opened a new Scene of Speculation, and set all Europe at a gaze'.[2] No more striking demonstration could have been given of the new ministry's resolve to break away from Bolingbroke's pro-French policy and return to the Old System, as it was affectionately called; and the choice of Stanhope made it all

---

[1] R.O., *F.O.* 90/3. Instructions of 18 October 1714.
[2] Boyer, viii. 362.

the more striking. Only a few days before starting he had
used language to the French envoy, Iberville, which amounted
almost to a threat of war if the Dunkirk clauses of Utrecht
were not promptly executed; and although Stanhope's vehement language had been partially explained away, the uneasiness in France was reflected in the disparaging references
to him and the advances made to the Emperor by Louis in
his instructions to du Luc, his first ambassador to Vienna.[1]
Hardly waiting for the conclusion of the coronation festivities,
on 21 October Stanhope set forth, accompanied by Lord
Cobham, the new envoy to Vienna, on the first of the many
diplomatic journeys he undertook during the remaining
seven years of his life.

Four points are insisted upon in his Instructions.[2] He was
to protest to the Emperor, as he had already done specifically
to Louis XIV,[3] against the clauses of the treaties of Ryswick
and Baden that ignored the principle of *cujus regio ejus religio*.
He was also to enlist the Emperor's support in bringing
pressure on Louis effectively to demolish the Dunkirk and
Mardyk forts and sluices. But his chief business was to settle
the questions about the Low Countries and the Barrier. This
was all the more necessary, since the English government had
got wind of a project of the Emperor to hand over the Low
Countries to the Elector of Bavaria in exchange for Bavaria.
Such a transaction had much to recommend it in Vienna;
the Emperor would thereby be quit of provinces somewhat
remote from his hereditary dominions and saddled with the
exigencies of the Dutch, and obtain instead a neighbouring
territory that had hitherto served the French as a convenient
jumping-off ground to his own capital. To this idea, however, England was uncompromising in her opposition: 'We
look upon the Spanish Low Countries', so ran Stanhope's
Instructions, 'to be by their situation the truest and surest
pledge of a firm and perpetual Friendship between Us, the
Emperor and the States General; and consequently the
strongest bulwark against the encroaching Power of France.
. . . The greatest struggle of all the wars during the last
Century has been to secure and invade these Countries.' To
allow the Elector of Bavaria, with a strong bias for France

---

[1] Michael, i. 634–5; *Recueil, Autriche*, 163.
[2] R.O., *F.O.* 90/3. These instructions of 18 October 1714 are addressed to
Stanhope and Cobham jointly.
[3] *Instructions, France*, i. 76–7; see above, p. 158.

and too weak to defend the Low Countries, to hold such a key position was therefore judged to be entirely against the interests of the Maritime Powers. These were the main points specified to Stanhope, but it was also understood that he should sound the Emperor on the renewal of the triple alliance with Holland and England in the not unlikely event of another war against France.[1]

On his way to Vienna Stanhope broke his journey at The Hague to ascertain the views of the Dutch on the Barrier. He found them in a far more chastened mood than when he was there early in 1710. They had lost all the arrogance they had displayed at Gertruydenberg and the self-satisfaction engendered by the Townshend Barrier Treaty and had only two ideas, first to avoid another war, second to make sure of that Barrier which was their only gain at Utrecht. They had already found that the Emperor was not prepared to go nearly as far to meet them as they hoped; and negotiations were at a deadlock when Stanhope arrived. He explained to them that England was anxious to renew the old alliance for no bellicose purpose and offered to take their proposals for the Barrier for discussion at Vienna, for, as he wrote to Townshend, 'si on ne les aide pas à faire leurs propres affaires, ils ne les feront jamais, car il n'y a personne parmi eux qui ose rien prendre sur soi'. This unwillingness of the Dutch to take a bold decision, the natural result of exhaustion after nearly a century and a half of struggles against Spain and France, became almost a settled policy with them, not only during Stanhope's ministry but throughout the forthcoming century. But at any rate, as he also discovered, they retained a remarkable gift of obstinacy in resisting proposals which seemed to involve any risk to their commercial interests.

Personally Stanhope had nothing to complain of in his reception at the Imperial court. On the day of his arrival, 11/22 November, he was granted a private interview by the Emperor, who embraced him and welcomed him as an old friend, and on his departure towards the end of December presented him with his portrait set in diamonds.[2] But as regards the immediate objects of his visit he found the greatest difficulties. At the best of times negotiation was peculiarly

[1] For Stanhope's Instructions, *vide u.s.* For Stanhope's dispatches during his mission see Mahon, *History*, ii, App.; R.O., *S.P.* 80/32.

[2] It is characteristic of Stanhope that he did not regard these diamonds as a personal present, but sold them and accounted for the proceeds as a set off to his expenses. See ch. x, p. 269, note.

difficult with the *Augustissima Casa*, as Bolingbroke in a moment of pique described the Imperial court, owing to its dilatory methods and its arrogant attitude to mere Republics or even Kings; and it had never been so difficult as at this time. Any question for decision might be brought before six different councils in turn, each of which generally contributed some obstacle to the conclusion of any business. There were normally the Councils of War and Finance, the Aulic and State Councils, the last composed of some hundred members, and the Conference, a small cabinet presided over by Eugene; to these had recently been added a Council of Spain, of which a leading member was formerly a Neapolitan muleteer, to keep Charles constantly in mind that he still claimed the Spanish monarchy and that in most transactions Spanish interests had to be considered.[1] Then again, as far as the Imperial court was concerned, the Treaties of Utrecht might well have been non-existent, for, besides the extreme Spanish party, a more moderate party among the Emperor's counsellors specially resented the failure to obtain Sicily as well as Naples and refused to acknowledge Victor Amedeus's royal title. On the Barrier question some were for ignoring most of the Dutch claims, others for getting rid of the Low Countries altogether. The sudden eruption of that unaccountable genius Charles XII from Bender, and his refusal to visit the Emperor in the course of his wild ride past Vienna to Stralsund, caused a great turmoil and apprehension of renewed war in the north. In the south, too, the Turks, unwontedly tranquil throughout the late war, were once more threatening an attack on the Emperor's ally Venice.

It is hardly surprising, therefore, that at first Stanhope found it almost impossible to extract definite answers from anybody on the Barrier or any other question. Eugene seemed anxious to be rid of the Low Countries altogether, and to be opposed to a renewal of the alliance. Sinzendorf and the Emperor seemed more forthcoming, the Emperor going so far as to admit that George I was bound to support the Dutch as they alone had guaranteed his throne in 1713; but even they showed little inclination for serious discussions. However, Stanhope did accomplish something by the extreme step of announcing his immediate return to England and actually taking leave of the Emperor on 16 December. This threat at last brought the Viennese court to business. The Emperor

[1] Baraudon, ch. v, has a good account of all these councils.

waived his objection to George receiving an ambassador from the King of Sicily, which George had hitherto avoided in deference to the Emperor's susceptibilities. More important were the concessions made about the Low Countries. The Emperor gave a definite promise that the idea of exchanging them for Bavaria would no longer be entertained, and agreed to a scheme for the Barrier which went some, if not the whole, way towards meeting the Dutch demands. But on the question of renewing the alliance with England Stanhope obtained no satisfaction. In spite of threats from the Turks, anxiety about the north and unsatisfied ambitions regarding the Spanish monarchy, 'cependant', he drily observes, 'je ne remarque aucun empressement dans le ministère d'ici à se faire des amis'. The fact was that, though both the Emperor and Stanhope's master were in need of allies, they wanted them for different purposes. The Emperor was chiefly concerned about retaining Majorca, gaining Sicily and preventing Spain from once more acquiring a foothold in Italy, and for those purposes would have been only too glad to have an English squadron to help him in the Mediterranean; but he was not anxious to embark on another war against France. Stanhope was particularly anxious to remain on good terms with Spain in order to obtain further commercial concessions, and had been instructed on no account to agree to an English squadron being kept in the Mediterranean as being most likely to lead to open war;[1] on the other hand he pressed for a guarantee from the Emperor for George's throne and also for assistance in the not unlikely event of another war with France. The utmost, however, that the Emperor would offer was a project for a treaty with the Maritime Powers all to his own advantage, whereby they should support him not only in retaining Majorca but also in acquiring as much more of the Spanish monarchy as he could and in ensuring that on the imminent failure of the Medici line in Tuscany, that Grand Duchy should not go to a Bourbon.[2] So convinced was Stanhope that such a one-sided project had not a chance of acceptance

[1] This was not at first Stanhope's view, for in the *Chevening MSS.* are two letters, one from him to Townshend dated from Harwich on 22 October, the very day after he left London, urging that the promise of such a squadron would be the best means of inducing the Emperor to agree to a Barrier, the other Townshend's reply of 26 October instructing Stanhope as stated in the text.

[2] Pribram, i. 329 sqq. See, too, Weber, 3.

in England that he does not seem to have troubled even to show it to his English colleagues. But with that and the Barrier proposals he had to be content when he finally left Vienna two days before Christmas.

Nor, when he brought his sheaves back to the Dutch, were they satisfied. Another visit to Vienna by Cadogan and nearly a year more of haggling was needed before Dutch, English, and Imperial plenipotentiaries signed the final Barrier Treaty of November 1715. Even then further differences arose between Emperor and Dutch, so that the ratifications were not exchanged till May 1719. By this settlement the Emperor entered into possession of his Low Countries, the Dutch obtained as their Barrier Namur at the junction of the Sambre and Meuse, six other fortresses stretching from Tournay on the Scheldt to the sea-coast and the right of providing half the garrison of Dendermonde between Ghent and Antwerp, besides a subsidy of 500,000 crowns for the cost of these garrisons; English and Dutch also retained valuable privileges for trade with the Low Countries. But those squabbles had been prolonged chiefly by the Dutch to avoid the renewal of the Old System of alliance, the very object of Stanhope and the ministry in promoting a settlement, and they succeeded so well that by May 1719 it was too late for them to play an effective part in Stanhope's Quadruple Alliance. In the end the Barrier itself, the grand object of the Dutch, proved an entirely illusory defence. The first time they might have been useful, in 1745 when Maurice de Saxe overran the Low Countries, the Barrier fortresses were the first to fall. Finally Joseph II, finding them a burden and expense rather than a help to the defence of his possessions, turned the Dutch ignominiously out of the whole line.[1]

Late in the evening of New Year's Day (o.s.), 1715, Stanhope arrived in London with Strafford, one of the negotiators of Utrecht. Next day he was graciously received by the King and Prince and Princess of Wales, the last receiving him with a 'polite easie Wit Affability and Graciousness' admired by all, and Stanhope answering all the pertinent questions with which he was plied by King and Prince about the Imperial court and government 'with great solidity of judgment'. The town, however, was disappointed that no news was vouchsafed of progress towards a Barrier treaty.[2] But, though

[1] For the Barrier Treaty see Geikie and Montgomery, 334–70, 395–415.
[2] Boyer, ix. 2.

barren of any immediate fruit, Stanhope's first mission was
not without value. It gave him an indispensable insight into
the objects of Dutch and Imperial policy and into the personalities at The Hague and Vienna he would have to cope
with during the next six years. If it did not at once bring
round the Emperor to the Old System it certainly helped to
that result in 1716 by restoring his confidence in English
diplomacy. Further, by the alarm it created in France, and
by the indications it gave that England was no longer entirely
friendless in Europe, this mission no doubt helped to determine
the Regent to abstain from effective support to the Pretender
in the critical months at the end of 1715. The mission is
also notable as inaugurating what became with Stanhope
a settled habit, the habit of making himself personally ac-
quainted on the spot with the problems presented to him and
still more with the chief personalities responsible for their
solution. He thus introduced a personal touch hitherto rare
in the cumbersome methods of diplomacy and far more
effective than reams of reports and correspondence. His
frank ways and social charm invited confidence and inspired
trust, and his clear statement of his own aims gave him a
ready ascendancy over most of the foreign statesmen with
whom he had to deal; he himself attributed his success chiefly
to the fact that 'during his ministry he always imposed on
foreign ministers by telling them the naked truth'.[1] Unfortunately his habit of being his own ambassador almost
entirely died out with himself, only to be revived in our own
age by the beneficent custom, almost forced on the statesmen
of the world by the needs of the League of Nations, of making
personal contact with one another at least once a year.

[1] Lady M. Wortley Montagu, *Letters*, &c., ii. 230.

CHAPTER VII

STANHOPE AND THE REBELLION

§ 1

FOR over a year after his return to England in January 1715 Stanhope's energies were almost entirely absorbed in the task of consolidating the dynasty at home. On 15 January a royal proclamation was issued, at Walpole's suggestion it was said, calling on the electors to choose for the new Parliament only 'such as shewed a firmness to the Protestant succession, when it was in danger', or in other words to vote only for the Whigs. This injunction was generally followed; in fact, as Stanhope wrote jubilantly to Stair, 'so many Whiggs have never been returned since the revolution',[1] and they were assured of a majority of 150 in the House of Commons. This sudden change from two Tory majorities within the last four years was certainly not caused by any affection for the new King, whose aloofness and inability to converse with his subjects were not such as to induce popularity. No doubt the ministry in power had means of influencing votes, and those anxious for state favours would naturally be disposed to support the dispensers of patronage; but majorities cannot entirely be accounted for, even in the eighteenth century, by motives of self-interest. A craving for settled order at home and abroad had much to do with these results. In 1710 and 1713 the people, weary of the glory and expense of nearly twenty years of warfare and of nearly a century of civil strife, voted for the Tories mainly because they promised peace abroad. In 1715 they voted for the Whigs, who promised to save them from the Pretender and the civil strife he would be bound to stir up at home.

Having obtained their majority the Whigs set to work ruthlessly to crush their opponents and to prevent, so far as was humanly possible, a repetition of the Tory policy of 1710–14. And among the most ruthless in these proceedings was Stanhope. To us to-day, with our ordered constitution and complete control by a fully representative Parliament over all the actions of government, many of the measures taken against the Tories during Stanhope's administration appear to have been a vindictive abuse of temporary power.

[1] *Oxenfoord MSS.* ii, 21 Feb. 1714/5.

But Stanhope and his friends had this excuse, that even at the beginning of the eighteenth century they were barely emerging from an era of rebellion and revolution, in which the normal method of government for the party temporarily in power was to safeguard its position by a display of force. In those days, and till at least the middle of the eighteenth century, English statesmen professed to be in fear of their lives if they decided on an unpopular course of action. With Newcastle the dread of losing his head in an outburst of popular indignation was a constant obsession and one secret of his vacillating policy: even the elder Pitt may have been half serious in 1761 when he declared to the House of Commons, 'Some are for keeping Canada, some Guadaloupe; who will tell me which I shall be hanged for not keeping?' During their recent four years of office the Tories had used the most questionable methods to entrench themselves in power, sending their opponents to the Tower or driving them into exile, cashiering officers loyal to the Protestant Succession and replacing them by Jacobites, packing the House of Lords and persecuting the Whigs' Nonconformist allies, reversing the country's established foreign policy and plotting, as was strongly suspected, the return of the exiled Roman Catholic dynasty. It is hardly surprising that men like Stanhope, who regarded the Revolution settlement as sacrosanct, should have thought extreme measures justified to protect it from further attacks. A step had already been taken, by the use of the royal prerogative of peace and war, to return to the Whig foreign policy. The authority of Parliament was required for such further measures as were necessary to restore the rights of Protestant Nonconformists, to limit the right to create peers wholesale for a party purpose, and above all to make an example for the future of the chief Tory culprits.

In preparation for a parliamentary inquiry into the peace negotiations Stanhope in January ordered Lord Stair, the new ambassador to France, to obtain from his predecessor Prior all his papers relating to the negotiations. Stair reported that Prior 'had a good deal of pain to let go' these papers, but finally surrendered them. Townshend made a similar demand on Lord Strafford, one of the plenipotentiaries at Utrecht, who also complied under protest. Bolingbroke's papers had been put under seal at the end of August and were examined by Stanhope himself, as appears from a

letter written to him by a very humble Bolingbroke, in which
he expresses satisfaction at the choice of his old friend for
that duty, and adds that 'it will be of use that I have the
opportunity of speaking to you. I am now ready and will
wait upon you wherever you command; and I shall not take
two minutes of your time'.[1] In the debate on the Address
of 23 March the ministry announced their intention of
setting up a committee of inquiry on the strength of these
documents. The Tories tried to make out that such an inquiry
was a veiled attack on the sacred memory of the late Queen,
a charge repudiated by Stanhope, who declared that any
censure would be confined to the late ministers: it was true,
he added, that they had taken away papers from offices,
to cover the traces of their mismanagement, but enough had
been found to convict them of being 'the most corrupt that
ever sat at the helm', and that it would appear that 'a certain
English general had acted in concert with, if not received
orders from, Marshal Villars'. About a fortnight later Stanhope moved for a committee of secrecy to examine these
papers and if necessary found charges upon them. A committee of twenty-one was accordingly appointed; but it had
no pretension to be called impartial, consisting as it did
entirely of Whigs, and with Walpole as chairman and Stanhope as vice-chairman.

The mere intimation of the inquiry had been enough to
drive Bolingbroke to a furtive evasion to France. But, though
the committee sat for two months examining papers and
witnesses, they could find no very conclusive evidence on
which to establish proofs of treason. This may have been
partly due to gaps in the papers. They had no inkling, for
example, of what would have proved a damning piece of
evidence against Bolingbroke, that the original peace proposals came not from Louis but from the English ministry.[2]
Thus the committee's work resolved itself chiefly into a
fishing inquiry, conducted in a haphazard and disorderly
fashion, if we may believe Prior's account of his own examination.[3] When he came into the room he found Walpole in
the chair and Stanhope sitting next to him with the books

[1] *Stowe MSS.* 242, f. 179, 15 Mar. 1715. Stanhope was advised, very
properly, not to see him in the circumstances (Torrens, i. 92).
[2] Michael, i. 477.
[3] In *P.H.* vii, Appendix, ccxxi sqq. This examination took place after the
inquiry preliminary to the formal impeachments had been concluded and when
the Articles were being prepared.

and papers of the Secretary's office before him. No attempt at a reasoned examination of the witness seems to have been made; members simply asked him questions, without any method or connexion, about his funds and his banker at Paris, his acquaintance with the French emissaries to London, Mesnager and Gaultier, and his correspondence with Oxford, shouting together and hardly waiting to hear his answers. At the height of the clamour Prior noticed 'Stanhope and Walpole frowning and nodding at each other and extremely ashamed at this vile stuff'. On his own showing, however, Prior was a most unwilling witness, especially with regard to his correspondence with Oxford, which Stanhope was anxious to elucidate; and he accounted for the disappearance of important letters of his own by the lame explanation that he probably destroyed them. Upon this, amid a loud hubbub, occurred this interlude with Stanhope:

> 'Stanhope [speaking] yet louder than he, swore that he could produce every individual scrap of paper that had been written to him by any man alive, or that he had written to any man during his being a minister abroad. *Prior*—Mr. Stanhope, I am sorry I cannot do the like. If it be so, you are the most careful minister that ever yet was sent abroad.'

But nothing more explicit could be obtained from Prior, who was removed in the custody of the messenger, leaving 'Walpole and Stanhope . . . mightily perplexed, one in a sullen, the other in an unbounded passion'. After two months of such unsatisfactory work, by June the clamour from both sides of the House for some definite action became so great that the ministry felt bound to impeach the four men considered the principal culprits, Oxford, Bolingbroke, Ormonde and Strafford, the first three for high treason, Strafford for high crimes and misdemeanours. Walpole proposed the impeachment of Bolingbroke and was effectively supported by Stanhope, who enlarged on Bolingbroke's crimes, especially in making the Queen utter falsehoods 'to the contempt of her subjects', on the perniciousness of the Preliminaries 'which put us under the thumb of France', and on the ruin of our trade with Spain and Portugal as a result of the treaty—'and all this with a warmth which raised a great spirit in the house'.[1] It also fell to Stanhope to propose the articles against Ormonde, charged with

---

[1] R.O., *S.P. Dom. Geo. I*, 3; *Account of proceedings on Secret Report*, 10 June 1715.

treason for acting in concert with Villars and against the interests of the allies before peace had been concluded.[1] For personal reasons he did so unwillingly, since he had himself fought under Ormonde, at one time 'very much his friend', wishing, as he said, 'he were not obliged to break silence on that occasion, but, as a member of the Secret Committee and of that great assembly that ought to do the nation justice', he felt compelled to take action. But though Walpole and Stanhope believed in the guilt of these men they were obviously uneasy at the want of definite proofs that could be produced. Bolingbroke, the guiltiest and probably the easiest to convict, had saved them trouble by escaping to France: they would have been only too glad if all the rest had followed his example. In Ormonde's case Stanhope went so far as to send his brother-in-law Robert Pitt to advise him to leave the country and to assure him, with the King's approval, that on his return after six months' absence he would be well received at court. But on his way to the Duke's house at Richmond Pitt heard that he had already fled, thus making himself, in Bolingbroke's contemptuous phrase, 'the bubble of his own popularity'.[2] Had he gone to the west? was Stanhope's first question to his emissary, for the Jacobites were known to have planned a rising there and were hoping for Ormonde to lead them. 'No', replied Pitt, 'but far enough from your pursuit'. 'Then all is well', exclaimed Stanhope, snapping his fingers.[3]

Thus Bolingbroke and Ormonde were easily disposed of. Their evasion and still more their public adherence to the Pretender's cause were naturally regarded as a confession of guilt. So, 'after diligent search and inquiry had been made after them and they were not to be found', they were declared traitors by Acts of Attainder. But Oxford and Strafford were not so accommodating as to leave the country. Strafford was too insignificant to be worth troubling about, so the case against him was simply dropped after 1715. Oxford could hardly be dismissed with the same ease. Sent to the Tower

[1] Perhaps the most damning evidence discovered by the Committee was the correspondence about the so-called 'Restraining Orders' affecting both Ormonde and Bolingbroke. In his formal Instructions signed by the Queen, Ormonde had been told to act with the allies; nevertheless he made the secret arrangement with Villars before Denain on a mere letter from Bolingbroke, who had no authority to supersede the formal Instructions. See *P.H.* vii, Appendix xxx.

[2] *Letter to Sir William Wyndham.*

[3] *H. MSS., Egmont,* i. 400–1.

in 1715 on notice of his impeachment, he was confined
there for two years before the Commons made any attempt
to make good their charges. Finally in May 1717, on
receiving a petition from Oxford for an early trial, the
Peers called on the Commons to prefer Articles of Impeachment. But by that time Walpole, the chief mover of his
impeachment, had quarrelled with Stanhope and was in
opposition, and his zeal against Oxford had evaporated.
Previously the most emphatic in his assurance to the House
that Oxford's treason could be proved to the hilt, he now
even refused to attend the committee for drawing up the
articles and had to be superseded as chairman; and, when
twitted in the House with his change of front, made the lamest
of apologies. When the Articles were produced in June it
appeared that the Commons, doubtful of their ability to
prove treason, also accused him on the lesser count of high
crimes and misdemeanours and hoped by combining the two
indictments to make out some case against him.[1] This the
Lords would not allow, deciding that the Commons must
first prove the graver charge before dealing with the lesser:
whereupon the Commons, foiled in their manœuvre, refused
to put in an appearance before the Lords. Oxford was
accordingly, on 1 July 1717, acquitted by the unanimous
vote of his peers. On the same day a proposal was made in
the Commons to pass an Act of Attainder against him, a
proposal said to have been supported by Stanhope, 'who in
a warm discourse laid open the whole series of infamy the
Earle of Oxford and his Ministry were guilty of in bringing
about the peace':[2] two days later better counsels prevailed,
for nobody seconded the introduction of the measure. Nevertheless Oxford, on Stanhope's motion, was shortly afterwards
excluded from the Act of Grace, promulgated by the King,
so as not to exclude further charges being made against him,
and he was forbidden the Court.[3] The only excuse for such
vindictiveness—futile as it proved, since Oxford was not
debarred from the House of Lords—was Stanhope's deep
conviction of Oxford's guilt. Whether actual treason could
be proved or not, nothing could shake him in his belief that

[1] As early as November 1716, when Stanhope was in Hanover, Townshend
told him that at a council meeting it was decided that there was no evidence
warranting more than a charge of misdemeanour against Oxford (Coxe,
Walpole, ii. 123).
[2] *H. MSS., Polwarth*, i. 288.
[3] Michael, ii. 49, quoting a report of the Prussian agent.

the methods of the Oxford ministry in bringing about the Peace of Utrecht, the desertion of allies, and the repudiation of solemn obligations were not only unconstitutional but a disgrace to the country. But a desire for retribution pushed to extreme limits is a poor counsellor in politics or in any walk of life.[1]

Fortunately these are the last instances in our annals of impeachment on purely political grounds. Even at this date impeachment for such a reason had become a musty survival of the time when the Commons had no other means of asserting themselves against the King's ministers. With Parliament's greater control over ministers since the Revolution, political impeachments served simply to cover a bad case. The few remaining impeachments of the next century were aimed at definite crimes and misdemeanours, either to mark the gravity of the offences, such as those of the rebel lords in 1715, of Lovat in 1745 and of Macclesfield and Melville, accused of corruption in high office; or else because the law of the land did not extend to India, as in the case of Warren Hastings.

§ 2

On 20 July 1715 a dispatch reached Stanhope from Stair in Paris announcing a scheme projected by the Pretender for a descent on the English coast. This in itself was a sufficient excuse for postponing the proceedings on Oxford's impeachment, for the danger seemed so serious that Stanhope and his colleagues had then no leisure for raking up grievances of the past. Bolingbroke early in 1714 had prophesied to the Pretender that within a year of the Hanoverian's accession the people would be so tired of him that they would gladly turn to James for relief: and he appeared to many observers to have been a true prophet, among others to the Prussian envoy Bonet, who asserted that eight months of George's rule had done more to help the Jacobites than four years of a Tory ministry. His view was confirmed by that of the Imperial envoy Hoffmann, who reported in August that two-thirds of the nation were opposed to the Hanoverian dynasty.[2]

[1] The proceedings against Bolingbroke, Ormonde, Strafford and Oxford are in *State Trials*, xv. 994-1195. The Commons' proceedings are in *P.H.* vi. 57 sqq., and vii. 475 sqq.
[2] See above, ch. v, p. 140, and Michael, i. 486, 488.

Undoubtedly there was much discontent in the country. The German King with his German courtiers jarred on the flamboyant patriotism of the true-born Englishman; his inaccessibility to his subjects, whose language he could not talk, stories of the harsh punishment of his unfaithful wife Sophia Dorothea and her lover, and his notorious jealousy of his heir increased his unpopularity. Even his Lutheran tenets gave an excuse for raising the old cry of 'the Church in danger'; and an ardent Churchman went so far as to declare publicly that King George had no right to the throne, that his council was a pack of rascals, and his son and his issue were fools.[1] Outbreaks of mob violence especially directed against Dissenters became so formidable that a Riot Act had to be passed in July. In Parliament the Whig majority had not saved the King from pointed criticism; and Stanhope had been hard put to it to justify the £200,000 increase on Anne's civil list proposed by the ministry; while the royal proclamation about the elections had been attacked in such disloyal language by the Tory Sir William Wyndham that he only escaped the Tower by a judicious adjournment. The general discontent had been further accentuated by a serious outbreak of cattle-plague that caused widespread distress, attributed with as little reason as usual to the party in power. Above all, the government had then no effective means of coping either with internal risings or external invasion. For so great was the dread of a standing army in peace-time that the army of 87,320 in 1711 had by the beginning of 1715 been reduced to less than 16,000 for all home and foreign garrisons, of which barely half was available for the defence of Great Britain itself.[2]

On the other hand, glowing accounts of the Pretender's chances were sent by his agents in Great Britain to the little court at Commercy in Lorraine. Ormonde, until his flight to France in August the chief representative of the Jacobites in England, enjoyed immense popularity not confined to his own party. When his impeachment was moved by Stanhope, he found defenders even among the Whigs, for everybody liked this 'good-natured, profuse, innocent man', as Sir John Clerk described him,[3] and even Addison wrote to the under-

[1] In R.O., *S.P.* 44/117, is a letter of 8 December 1715 from Stanhope to the Attorney-General gravely requiring an opinion whether a bishop could legally refuse to institute a curate who had used such language.

[2] R.O., *W.O.* 25/3029.

[3] *Memoirs of Sir J. Clerk* (Roxburgh Club, 1895), 80.

secretary Delafaye to explain that he could not vote for his impeachment owing to the services Ormonde had rendered him at Cambridge and in Ireland:[1] in fact the motion passed by a majority of only forty-seven. Lavish and magnificent in the use of his wealth, in striking contrast to Marlborough, whose rival he affected to be in the military sphere, he held great state and open house in his palace at Richmond, and by his generosity and winning ways had won many adherents to the Pretender. As Lord-Lieutenant of Somersetshire he used his great influence to encourage a rising in the west. Mar too from Scotland reported widespread loyalty to the Stuarts. Abroad James's prospects seemed bright. Throughout Europe the Hanoverians could count on no allies except the weary Dutchmen. According to Bolingbroke Charles XII of Sweden was mainly deterred from lending aid to the Jacobites by the want of suitable troops.[2] Louis XIV, though unwilling too flagrantly to repudiate his engagements at Utrecht, gave the Pretender secret facilities and procured for him a loan from Philip of Spain. Ormonde's sword, for what it was worth, as well as his wealth, was now publicly put at the Pretender's disposal. Above all, Bolingbroke, who on his flight to Paris in April had at first sent professions of loyalty to Stanhope, 'which might take off any imputation of neglect of the government',[2] in July had taken the plunge and offered his services to the Pretender, thus bringing some talent for statesmanship and a knowledge of English conditions sorely needed in Jacobite circles abroad.

But the signs of weakness and dissatisfaction in England, so cheering to the Jacobites, were deceptive. Englishmen might refuse to forgo their inherent right to grumble at constituted authorities, but had no intention of putting a 'French kickshaw'—the description was that of Stanhope's father-in-law—on the throne instead of George. On the very morning that Stair's warning reached Stanhope a council was summoned to decide on measures, and in the afternoon the King went in person to the House of Lords to call on Parliament to meet the danger. Both Houses forthwith voted loyal addresses to the King without a dissentient voice and agreed to any increases of the forces that might be deemed necessary by him and his advisers. On the same

[1] R.O., *S.P. Dom. Geo. I*, 3, Addison to Delafaye, 18 June 1715.
[2] *Letter to Sir William Wyndham.*

evening Stanhope replied to Stair in a proper English spirit. He was not to make formal complaint of the unfriendly attitude of the French court:

'Whatever encouragement or assistance that court has thought fit to give for promoting the design which now seems to be on foot in his [the Pretender's] favour, his Majesty judges that the surest way to defeat it is to show spirit and vigour here, and which I hope has been done today both by his Majesty and the two Houses of parliament, of which your lordship will be able to judge by his Majesty's speech, and the address of the House of Commons . . . herewith transmitted to you.'

Four days later he tells him that the House has sanctioned the raising of twenty-one new regiments and an additional half-battalion of the Guards, and that the executive has been strengthened by the suspension for six months of the Habeas Corpus Act.[1] The loyally minded gentry, of whom Governor Pitt and his second son were among the foremost,[2] showed so much zeal in raising and equipping the new regiments sanctioned by Parliament, that at first it was not thought necessary to call up the 6,000 Dutch troops available for such an emergency by the Barrier Treaty of 1713. The Dissenters also especially distinguished themselves in rallying to the Crown: Wood, one of their ministers, even raised a corps of 400 volunteers, many of them men of independent means, the rest maintained at Wood's own expense.[3] Two days after the receipt of Stair's dispatch Admiral Byng, restored to the active list from which he had been excluded by the Tories, had a squadron in the Channel and was receiving instructions from Stanhope to 'procure by all possible means exact intelligence of what passes in the several Ports of France and . . . to search such ships as you may suspect have Arms and Ammunition on board them'.[4] For additional precaution Stanhope gave strict orders to the customs officers to examine closely all passengers landing in the country; and Privy seals

---

[1] *Stair Annals*, i. 269, to Stair 20 July 1715; R.O., *F.O.* 90/14, to Stair 24 July 1715. Orders for raising these new regiments were actually issued by Stanhope on 22 July and for their arms and equipment on 26 July; R.O., *S.P.* 44/176 and 177 (under those dates).

[2] Williams, *Chatham*, i. 23-4.

[3] Torrens, i. 112.

[4] From letters of 22, 26 July and 3 September 1715 from Stanhope to Byng in a collection belonging to Lord Strafford. Professor Callender has had the use of the collection for publication by the Navy Records Society and has kindly allowed me to quote these letters. To him and to Mr. Brian Tunstall I am grateful for their generous gift of copies from this collection.

were issued recalling certain subjects of the King from France. He also sent troops to Bath to arrest Papists and to visit Oxford, where a store of sword-blades for the rebels had been discovered at Vincent the cutler's, but they found little to do beyond silencing some rowdy scholars who shouted treasonable sentiments in Cat Street and arresting some Wadham men for attempting to corrupt the soldiers with money. More to the purpose were the garrisons told off to secure Bristol, Southampton and Plymouth, the west being notoriously disaffected and these being ports where a landing might be expected. The Londoners, too, were delighted to have the Guards encamped in Hyde Park, for they served not only as a protection against invasion, but also against the footpads and highwaymen who used to infest the road from London to the fashionable village of Kensington, where Lady Cowper said she intended to stay as long as the camp remained, since 'one might come from London any time of the Night without Danger'.[1]

The Jacobites had certainly not taken sufficiently into account the strength of a determined ministry. To three men in this ministry the country and the Hanoverians mainly owed their deliverance from the Jacobite danger of 1715. Robert Walpole, after holding a subordinate post for a year, was promoted shortly after the death of Halifax to the offices of First Lord of the Treasury and Chancellor of the Exchequer, a just tribute to his financial ability and his skill and readiness in parliamentary debate. His management of the House of Commons and his sound sense gave invaluable support to the two Secretaries of State, Townshend and Stanhope, on whom fell the entire burden of administration during the anxious months of the Rebellion. These two worked together almost as one mind. Townshend was at his best when he had a clear-cut issue before him and was convinced of the merits of his cause, for his main qualities were obstinacy and courage, a signal instance of which was his conduct in insisting upon the arrest of the Duke of Somerset's son-in-law Sir William Wyndham on a charge of treason.[2] Stanhope, 'dear Don' as he is addressed in private letters from his fellow Secretary, no less devoted to his cause, or convinced of its justice, and with equal courage, had more imagination. This

[1] *Treas. Papers, 1714–20*, 124; R.O., *S.P.* 44/117; *H. MSS., Townshend*, 166–7; Lady Cowper, 49.
[2] See below, p. 186.

precious gift, coupled with his sanguine temperament, his robust common sense, and a sturdy belief in the soundness of his countrymen, enabled him to take risks cheerfully and to pass off awkward situations with a jest. It also helped him to pretty accurate estimates of friends and opponents such as Ormonde and Bolingbroke, and a sympathetic understanding of his own people and of the characteristics of other nations. At this crisis his experience in the field stood him in good stead: still more the judgements he had been able to form during his ten years of campaigning on most of those now available for command on sea or land, men such as Byng, with whom he had fought at Valencia, Norris, the rough admiral who as a captain had taken him home to England after the capture of Barcelona, Carpenter, Wade, Wills, Pepper, his own officers in the Peninsula, and Cadogan, Marlborough's favourite pupil in the Low Countries. Rash impetuosity was his besetting fault, but there was Walpole at hand with his wise prudence to temper it and, maybe, the recollection of his own disaster at Brihuega. Above all he was absolutely frank and direct, and nobody ever whispered a word against his personal honour.

The concentration of all executive power in the hands of two Secretaries of State, as compared with the excessive subdivision of administrative authority among our six Secretaries and other heads of departments of to-day, was all to the advantage of a clear-cut policy followed by swift action, especially when those two Secretaries were as capable and harmonious as Townshend and Stanhope were at this time. But the strain on them must have been tremendous. They corresponded with the Lords-Lieutenant and Justices of the Peace about risings or suspicious movements in their counties and instructed them how to meet the danger. They kept a strict watch on all letters coming from abroad, and in case of doubt examined them personally for evidence of treason: they also had before them and personally cross-questioned people whose loyalty was suspect. They received innumerable reports from spies sent in by Stair and other ambassadors and from agents in England, or themselves corresponded with the most prominent among them, among whom was included the notorious Lord Lovat. Among other agents they employed was Daniel Defoe, with whom Townshend made an arrangement that he should go on writing for the Tory papers, as he had done in Harley's time, but in such a way as to make their fulminations innocuous, and at the same time give information to the government of any treasonable papers to be issued by the opposition press. This arrangement was continued after the Rebellion by Sunderland and afterwards by Stanhope, to whom Defoe expressed gratitude 'that his Lordship is satisfied to go upon the Foot of former capitulations'. Defoe naturally found this 'bowing in the House of Rimmon' a hazardous business, so added, 'I must humbly recommend myself to his lordship's protection, or I may be undone the sooner by how much the more faithfully I execute the commands I am under'.[1] The Secretaries were also in constant communication with the commanders in the field and the admirals watching the French coasts, gave them their orders, either directly or through the Admiralty in the case of the seamen, while in the case of the generals Townshend and Stanhope together told Argyll to adopt his subordinate Cadogan's plan without further question; Stanhope during the Preston campaign of November sent detailed orders almost daily to Wills and Carpenter by 'flying pacquet', as to where they were to concentrate and when to advance. They even recalled them if necessary, as in the case of Argyll. When prisoners were taken, one of the Secretaries decided whether they were to be tried and where, and if not how they were to be disposed of.[2] In addition to all these duties there were frequent Councils to attend; and the King's pleasure had to be obtained on all important decisions, after the relevant documents had been translated into French. And, as if all this were not enough, early in August the Duke of Montrose vacated his post in Scotland; and during the whole period of the Rebellion Stanhope and Townshend, in addition to all their other duties, had to perform his duties of Secretary for Scotland.[3]

An unexpected sidelight is cast on the harassing nature of

---

[1] R.O., *S.P. Dom. Geo. I*, 11 (124), Defoe to . . . 26 April 1718 (quoted in Lee's *Daniel Defoe* (1869), i. ix; other letters of Defoe on this business are in *S.P. Dom. Geo. I*, 12. Among the Tory papers to which he contributed on this understanding were *Mercurius Politicus* and the notorious Mist's *Weekly Journal*. He also was the means of suppressing certain libels on the King.

[2] Examples of these activities may be studied in detail in R.O., *S.P.* 44/117, 176, 177, and in *H. MSS.*, *Townshend*, 173–86.

[3] R.O., *S.P.* 44/117, 6 Aug. 1715. Montrose, as a member of the *Squadrone* opposed to Argyll, was probably got rid of to avoid friction between the Secretary of State and the commander-in-chief in Scotland during the Rebellion. In December 1716, when the danger was passed, the Duke of Roxburgh was appointed Scottish Secretary.

these multifarious preoccupations by a passage in the proceedings against one Francia for high treason. Under a warrant of Townshend's this man was summoned in September 1715 to be examined by the two Secretaries in person. During his formal trial, which did not take place till two years later, it appeared that the record of his examination by them on two consecutive days was defective inasmuch as Stanhope's signature did not appear with Townshend's for the first, but only for the second day. Nevertheless Stanhope in evidence stated he was present at the examination on both days and had heard both records read over to the prisoner, and he gave this illuminating account of his omission to sign the record for the first day:

> 'I believe at twice we spent about two hours in the examination of the prisoner, and these examinations were taken from his own mouth; and I can be positive there is not a passage in them, that he did not repeat more than once or twice. The reason why my name is to one and not to the other, may be, because the room where he was examined was next to the room where the council used to meet; and I believe I might be going in and out between the two rooms, and might not think it proper to set my name to what I did not see signed. But . . . I read the first examination more than once or twice to him, and did examine him to all the particulars of it.'[1]

So absorbed were the two Secretaries by internal affairs during 1715, first with the impeachments and then with the Rebellion, that the Imperial and Prussian envoys complained that they could get no attention from them on foreign business, and that they had to conduct all their negotiations with Bernstorff and other German ministers.[2] This may have been true of Townshend, with whom these envoys had to deal, but it was certainly not the case with Stanhope, who was never more taken up with the correspondence with France than during the Rebellion. France was the headquarters of the rebels: thither Bolingbroke, Ormonde and other leading Jacobites had gone for refuge and had found no difficulty in carrying on thence their plots with the Pretender in Lorraine. This duchy, enclosed on almost every side by French territory, might just as well have been a part of France for all the difference it made to the Pretender's movements. If he wanted to send arms to England or Scotland he simply shipped them from French ports, and when

---

[1] *State Trials*, xv. 926.   [2] Michael, i. 499, 514.

he embarked from Dunkirk nobody interfered with him. Fortunately Stanhope could also depend on obtaining the best intelligence of the Jacobite plans and movements from France. Stair, at Paris since the beginning of 1715, was a haughty Scots peer, very punctilious about the deference due to himself and the country he represented, an idiosyncrasy which had already provoked so serious a quarrel with the French minister Torcy that he was not on speaking terms with him. But he was extraordinarily successful in obtaining information about the Jacobites by an elaborate system of spies, who reported to him almost every word and gesture of the Pretender, Bolingbroke, Ormonde, and the lesser fry.[1] Not only had Stanhope received from Stair towards the end of July the first definite information that a serious plot was brewing, but, as long as the danger lasted, very little of importance that was happening across the Channel escaped Stair's observation.

§ 3

It was fortunate that Stanhope and Townshend had over a month's breathing space after the warning from Stair before any overt act of rebellion occurred, and that they had no serious danger to meet for yet another month. For in spite of their ceaseless energy it naturally took some time for the reinforcements cheerfully voted by Parliament to be embodied. Not content with the new regiments authorized in July, in September they increased the Guards' companies from 40 to 70 and the establishment of the line regiments from 10 companies of 40 to 12 of 50 men.[2] By the end of the year they had increased the embodied troops in Great Britain alone from 8,000 to nearly 33,000,[3] amply sufficient, with

---

[1] In the second half of a volume labelled *Bolingbroke Papers* among the *Oxenfoord MSS.* is a large collection of letters to Stair from the spies employed by him during his embassy. One of them, Stephen Lynch, declares that he sailed with the Pretender from Dunkirk and then surrendered to Argyll and gave information about the Pretender's plans. Another, J. Rampson, offers to give up papers found in the closet of James II's widow, but does not wish his name divulged, because 'I am a young Villain tho' no young man and I would perish a hundred times rather than have any mortal on earth know what I have done'. The expense of this spy-system must have been considerable, to judge from the demands of an anonymous gentleman writing from The Hague who offered to spy on the Pretender at Rome: 'The least a gentleman can spend on such a business, and manage well too, will be a hundred pounds per quarter, and travelling charges bore', besides a sum of £1,200 due to him for similar services from the late government.

[2] R.O., *S.P.* 44/117, 19 Sept. 1715.   [3] R.O., *W.O.* 25/3029.

the 6,000 Dutch troops brought over in November, to meet any emergency. But in August and September, before these preparations were completed, it must have been anxious work for the two Secretaries, since the few troops then available might be required at many different points simultaneously. There was danger of an armed rising in the west of England and also in the north, in which parts most of the English Jacobite and Roman Catholic families were concentrated; Scotland, especially the Highlands, was also a certain centre of disturbance. Then an invasion by the Pretender from France had to be guarded against, the most likely quarter to be chosen, according to information sent by the vigilant Stair and Byng, who was hovering round the French Channel ports, being somewhere on the west coast of England.

Actually Mar was the first to raise the standard of revolt on 6 September at Perth, but he obtained recruits slowly and by the end of the month had hardly more than 1,000 followers; and an attempt made by the Jacobites in Edinburgh on 9 September to seize the Castle was frustrated. The hesitation of the Pretender's Scottish supporters in coming forward during these early days, when the government was not fully prepared, may have been partly due to Stanhope's Act for the Encouragement of Loyalty in Scotland. This Act, introduced on 24 July, empowered the government to take security from all Scottish owners of property whose loyalty was suspected and to give the freehold of their tenements to all loyal lessees of rebel lairds. Even if it did not produce loyalty, this Act at any rate helped the government to find out who were their enemies. To concert military measures Argyll, the commander-in-chief for Scotland, had already on 1 September been sent to command the royal troops at Stirling; while the Earl of Sutherland and Lord Lovat were sent to Sutherland and Inverness to gather their clansmen for the King in the rear of Mar's head-quarters. The choice of Argyll and Sutherland, Scotsmen to fight Scotsmen, was wise; for when Sutherland with his northern clansmen, and the chief of the Campbells in the west, were fighting for the Hanoverians, there could be no talk of a purely national rising for the Stuarts. How far Lovat was as useful and loyal on this occasion as his own letters to Stanhope and his statement at his trial made out is less certain; at any rate, though amply rewarded, four years later he supported the Spanish raid on behalf of the Pretender.[1] Unfortunately few troops could be spared for Argyll, no more than 1,300 at first to hold the gate of the Highlands, besides the garrisons at Fort William and Edinburgh. Argyll allowed himself to 'fly out prodigiously' at this parsimonious treatment, which his friends attributed to the jealousy of Townshend, Walpole, Sunderland and Bernstorff and their desire 'to lessen his reputation'; and Lord Cowper went so far as to represent to the King that 'if any disgrace befall Your Majesty's troops in Scotland, Insurrections will immediately follow in England'.[2] Stanhope and Townshend convinced the King that England was the chief seat of danger, and was most in need of defence. Insurrections, as Stanhope patiently explained to Argyll on 26 September, were being planned, according to their information, in the west, the north, and the midlands of England in support of the Scots; nothing, he added, 'in my poor opinion . . . will so dishearten the rebels in Scotland as to find themselves disappointed of the hopes which had been given them from hence . . . [by our keeping] this nation in some posture of defence'. But Argyll was not to be placated and sent a violently worded protest to the Secretaries. This protest was translated into French for submission to the King, who ordered Stanhope and Townshend to send a joint letter informing the haughty Duke that

'His Majesty hath had and has good reasons for all the resolutions he has taken, which a very little time may possibly demonstrate, and however your Grace may please to treat his Ministers, certainly some respect is due to the resolutions of the King.'[3]

Their judgement had already been justified. In September a report sent by Stair, on information from a Scottish Jacobite, was so explicit about an intended rising in the west in co-operation with an invasion under Ormonde, that immediate action could be taken against the leaders in England. Lords Dupplin and Lansdowne and other conspirators were arrested and sent to the Tower, and a message was brought by Stanhope to the House of Commons,

[1] As to Lord Lovat's activities for the King see what he says at his trial in 1746, *State Trials*, xviii. 829–31; in his letter to Stanhope in Mahon, *History*, ii, Appendix, p. lii; and one in *A.E. Angleterre*, 290, f. 377, where he calls Inverness 'the key of Scotland'. Stanhope's letters to him promising a reward for his services are in *H. MSS., Stuart*, ii. 36, 103.

[2] Lady Cowper, 58–9, 180.

[3] *H. MSS., Townshend*, 173–86. The joint letter is dated 2 November.

demanding the arrest of Sir William Wyndham and five other
members. After first trying to evade arrest Wyndham took
refuge with Lord Hertford, who wrote to inform Stanhope.
A council was thereupon called, attended amongst others
by Wyndham's father-in-law Somerset, Master of the Horse,
to decide on what action should be taken. Somerset, the
proudest duke in England at a time when every English duke
was a very high and puissant personage, offered to stand
surety for Wyndham's good behaviour. At first Townshend
alone had the courage to declare that in such a national
danger the personal feelings of even the greatest in the
land must not be considered and gave his sentence for
Wyndham's arrest. But this utterance was followed by the
silence, unbroken for ten minutes, of the other counsellors.
At last the spell was broken and the rest pronounced for
Townshend's proposal. The King, grasping Townshend's
hand, thanked him for the service he had done him that day.[1]
The care of the royal horses was withdrawn from Somerset,
who thereafter cherished an implacable grudge against the
ministry. He ostentatiously joined the disaffected clique of
Argyll and his brother Islay and specially singled out for
his disapprobation his former protégé Stanhope, who, most
likely, was the first to adopt Townshend's view. Whereas
in the past he had zealously supported Stanhope's electoral
interests and used to sign himself as his 'most affectionate,
humble Servant'—and a recollection of these old ties may
have been the reason why Stanhope did not adopt Townshend's view forthwith—after this incident the Duke came to
write of him as a man who 'hath noe interest in the nation'
and as one 'exposed to the contempt of the House of Commons'.[2] Stanhope and Townshend could well remain indifferent to such abuse, for their stern measures against the
western ringleaders were effective. When Ormonde, 'that
great general', as Stanhope called him to Stair, arrived next
month off Torbay to rouse the country for the Pretender, the
wind that brought him over produced no such success as the
Protestant breeze he had welcomed when it brought another
invader to the same coast. He saw no sign of Jacobite supporters to rise in answer to his call and had tamely to submit
to the orders of a few customs officers who refused him a
landing.

More serious was the rising in the north of England, which,

[1] Coxe, *Walpole*, i. 71.   [2] Ib., ii. 148.

long expected, took place in October. This proved at first the more dangerous as the leaders were able to make communication with parties of the rebels from over the border. The rebellion first broke out in Northumberland under Lords Derwentwater and Widdrington, both Roman Catholics, and the Protestant squire Thomas Forster. Though Forster, as his cousin Lady Cowper remarked, 'had never seen an army in his life', and was described by another acquaintance as 'an idle, drunken, senseless man and not good enough to head a company of militia',[1] nevertheless, as a Protestant, he was put in command of the rebels. After failing in an attempt to seize Newcastle, Forster joined forces with some Lowlanders raised by Lords Kenmure, Carnwath and Wintoun and appealed for support to Mar. In response to this appeal Mar detached one of his bravest chieftains, McIntosh, or old Borlum as he was called in the Highlands, whom Stanhope had ordered Argyll to arrest early in September. First Borlum crossed the Forth with his men almost within sight of the King's ships, seized an old Cromwellian castle near Leith and proved so troublesome a neighbour to Edinburgh that Argyll had to go himself with 600 men from his small force to protect the capital. Thereupon McIntosh slipped away to Kelso to meet Forster's band and the Lowlanders. The united force, amounting to some 2,000 after many of the Highlanders had drifted back, decided to cross the border towards the notoriously Jacobite county of Lancashire. Picking up some recruits on their way through Cumberland, they reached Preston on 9 November.

Two of Stanhope's generals of Spanish days, Wills and Carpenter, were on the look-out for them. On 14 October Carpenter, who was on the east coast with a small force of dragoons and infantry, was ordered by Stanhope to pursue the rebels in Northumberland and arrest all suspects. He had successfully harassed Forster during the early part of their march westward from Kelso, but by a ruse of the enemy had been diverted back to Newcastle. Now, on hearing the true state of affairs, he was marching in all haste westwards to meet the rebels. Wills with a somewhat larger force of six dragoon and two infantry regiments had been instructed by Stanhope on 29 October to make Chester his headquarters, whence, on news of Forster's approach, he had advanced to Wigan. On 12 November he seized the bridge

[1] Lady Cowper, 57; *Memoirs of Sir J. Clerk* (Roxburgh Club, 1895), p. 91.

over the Ribble, an admirable position for defence neglected by Forster, but had to fall back for the night before the superior force of the enemy defending Preston. Next day Carpenter arrived, whereupon Forster, though still superior in numbers, offered to treat, much to the indignation of his men. The only concession Wills would grant was that if the rebels laid down their arms they should be saved from the fury of the soldiers and left to the discretion of the government, terms which were accepted by Forster. Many of the rebels, not distinguished by any uniform, no doubt easily escaped in the confusion, for out of a force estimated at from four to five thousand only 1,600 surrendered as prisoners.[1]

On the very day of the victory at Preston Argyll and Mar at last met at Sheriffmuir. Argyll's force even by that time, he complained, was still no more than 3,300 to guard the approach to Stirling. Mar, on the other hand, had now about 10,000 men and was emboldened to send forward a detachment to occupy Dunblane, commanding Stirling from the north, closely following it with the rest of his force. But Argyll had been too quick for him. Mar found Dunblane already in possession of the King's troops and Argyll ready for him on Sheriffmuir, the plateau above Dunblane well adapted to his superior cavalry. In the ensuing battle Argyll routed the Jacobites' left wing, but, pursuing too ardently, lost sight of his own left wing, which in turn was overwhelmed by Mar's right and driven three miles beyond Dunblane. But though the actual fighting was indecisive, the fruits of victory remained with Argyll, who finally recalled his left wing and encamped on the battlefield: Mar had entirely failed in his object and retreated towards Perth.

These two battles, though not the conclusion of the

[1] Stanhope's instructions to Wills and Carpenter are in R.O., *S.P.* 44/177. The account of the events at Preston in Michael, i. 550–4, useful for the details given by the envoys Bonet and Hoffmann, should be compared with that in Mahon, *History*, i. 168–72. Michael questions the relative numbers given by Mahon of the two forces, because of the comparatively small numbers of prisoners taken: this, however, may be accounted for by the reason given above. At the trial of the rebel lords it was suggested that at Preston a promise of the King's mercy was given to those who submitted. But the evidence given by both Wills and Carpenter and their subordinates at Lord Wintoun's trial gives no ground for this suggestion. Though there seems to have been some confusion between the negotiators sent by Wills and those sent independently by Carpenter to the rebels, both sets strenuously denied that they promised mercy. In this trial and in writing to the Secretary of State Carpenter showed some resentment at his junior Wills presuming to claim equality with himself. See *State Trials*, xv. 852–9; *H. MSS., Townshend*, 170. The map of Preston with the rebels' positions marked, sent to Stanhope, is still to be seen at Chevening.

Rebellion, virtually decided its result. So far James III and VIII, for whom Englishmen and Scots were fruitlessly incurring the pains of high treason or of exile, had not shown himself in the realms he claimed. This was not due to any want of courage on his part, but to his dependence on the attitude of France. Louis XIV, though unwilling openly to break the Treaty of Utrecht, at any rate until he saw his way clear to a successful issue, was not averse to giving him all the secret support he could. But on 1 September the old King had died. Bolingbroke, writing to Mar three weeks later, described the depression this event caused in the Jacobite camp and the reason for the change of attitude at Versailles:

> 'If the French King had lived we should have obtained some assistance directly, much more indirectly, and a great many facilities by connivance. . . . But the case is altered; he is dead, the Regent is in quite other dispositions. The prospect of opposition to his regency made him enter into engagements with Hanover, and the prospect of opposition to his seizing the Crown, in case of the young King's death, makes him adhere to those engagements.'[1]

Even before Louis's death Stair had held secret meetings, in woods or elsewhere, with the Duke of Orleans and his confidants. Convinced that his personal interests made some understanding with George I advisable, Orleans had even proposed that on attaining the Regency he should enter into a treaty with George for the mutual guarantee of their respective rights. Stanhope showed himself quite willing to consider this proposal, the details of which must be left to the next chapter. Had the Regent, on attaining power, seriously persisted in this proposal, the Jacobite cause would have been even more hopeless than it proved. But politically the Regent was timid. The gathering of an army, small though it was, by Mar, and the occupation of Perth in the heart of Scotland, had given a false impression of Jacobite strength. Louis XIV's old ministers, still in power at Versailles, represented not only the traditional policy of France but also the general sympathy of the French people for the Pretender, influences against which the Regent did not feel strong enough to enforce his will. He began to drag out the negotiations for the treaty, constantly starting new

[1] Mahon, *History*, i, Appendix.

questions and new difficulties. Finally Stanhope on 20 October, before any success had attended the King's arms, bluntly instructed Stair that 'the King will not suffer himself to be amused by a tedious negotiation', while the Regent was waiting to see the result of the Rebellion. He himself, he added, was confident that 'a few months will effectually crush them [the rebels], and his Majesty will then be in such a condition that I believe every power in Europe will court his friendship. The Duke of Orleans hath now an opportunity of securing it for ever.' Ten days later he informed Stair that the King took the attitude of the French court 'as he ought, and it will be of some use to his Majesty to have learnt how much he can rely upon the Regent, . . . who can be diverted by the frenzy of these madmen from pursuing his true interest.' Stair was further instructed to ask no more favours of the Regent in his present mood or even to appear much at court: the best answer to his hesitations would be our success.[1]

The consequence of the Regent's balancing policy was that, though unwilling to declare himself openly for the Pretender, he reverted to his uncle's old method, described by Bolingbroke as 'indirect assistance and facilities by connivance'. Nevertheless the Jacobites in France could not execute their plans with too much publicity. In September Byng found a ship-load of arms for the rebels at Havre, and the Regent, though he did not confiscate them, ordered them to be kept in a depot on shore.[2] Ormonde, on the other hand, had no obstacles put in his way when he started on his expedition to Devonshire from a French port or when he made another attempt, more futile still, in December. One 'Sunday 10 at night'—in the hurry no further clue to the date, actually the last day of October, is added—Stanhope warns Lord Orford at the Admiralty of an advice just received from Stair that the Pretender had slept last night at Chateau Thierry on his way to a coast port: four days later Townshend is able to tell Argyll that on Stair's representations the Regent had ordered him back to Lorraine. But at the end of November, when he made another attempt to reach the coast, it was merely intimated to him that he must not start from a port in Normandy or Picardy, but that other districts would not

[1] R.O., *S.P.* 78/160, ff. 131, 160, 20 and 31 Oct. 1715. Part of the first dispatch is in *Instructions, France*, i. 101. See also R.O., *S.P.* 90/14.
[2] Mahon, *History*, i. 142.

be too closely watched. In fact he had no difficulty in sailing from Dunkirk.[1]

The Pretender arrived too late to infuse vigour into an already dying cause. His original intention had been to appear in the west of England, but the arrest of Wyndham and his friends and the defeat of the rebels at Preston had destroyed all hope of a further rising in that quarter. Mar, though defeated, still held Perth and much of the Highlands; so at the end of December the Pretender landed at Peterhead to join him. But Stanhope had been no bad prophet when he wrote to Stair on receiving the first news of the Pretender's embarkation: 'I think it would be by no means a misfortune that he should land in Scotland'.[2] His melancholy appearance and unattractive manners were far from inspiring renewed confidence in an army already apprehensive of an advance against them by Argyll with large reinforcements.

Since Sheriffmuir Stanhope and Townshend had been able to satisfy Argyll's insistent demands for more troops. Their decision to be certain of England's security from the rebels before sending more of the few troops available to Scotland was undoubtedly sound. For the rebellion in the Highlands, though serious enough, could be localized and showed no likelihood of spreading to the Lowlands, whereas there were many danger-points in England and any success of the rebels there would have been more vital. It had been necessary, owing to the disturbed state of the west and north of England, to send in October for the 6,000 Dutch troops and some Swiss auxiliaries, though even then Stanhope refused the offer of Hanoverian troops to be shipped from Bremen, so intense was the national dislike of allowing the Electorate to have any part in English concerns.[3] When the Dutch troops landed in the Humber, he first directed them to go to Lancashire, but as soon as he had news of Preston sent them off to Scotland.[4] When these troops arrived, Argyll's army, already reinforced by three regiments from Ireland, was superior to Mar's, which was by now beginning to dwindle away. But Argyll still made difficulties about advancing: he wanted to negotiate with the rebels, he complained that the snow on the roads made progress too difficult, he several times asked

---

[1] The letter to Orford is in the *Strafford Papers* referred to above, p. 178, note 4, that to Argyll in *H. MSS., Townshend*, 173–86.
[2] *S.P.* 90/14, Jan. 1715/16.   [3] Michael, i. 731.
[4] R.O., *S.P.* 44/117 (15 and 20 Nov.).

for leave to come up to London. But Stanhope was anxious that there should be no more delay in finishing with the Scottish rebellion, for he feared that if Mar's army was still in existence in the spring the Regent would no longer refrain from active intervention.[1] Cadogan was sent to stir Argyll to more energetic action and even to propose a definite plan of operations. When Argyll complained to the Secretaries of Cadogan's interference, he was sharply ordered to set about the plan whosesoever it was, and at last in February, after long forbearance from himself and Stanhope at his shrill complaints and reiterated requests for leave, Townshend curtly informed him that he not only had leave but explicit orders to return at once and report to the King. Four months later Stanhope wrote intimating 'his Majesty's pleasure to resume the several employments and pensions which he had conferred upon him'.[2] Argyll's ill humour and unwillingness to take active measures against the Jacobites may have arisen partly from a pardonable reluctance to be too severe on his own countrymen, partly too from pique at the pressure put upon him by Cadogan. But it was largely due to his veiled opposition to the government. He was Groom of the Stole to the Prince of Wales and with the Chancellor Cowper and others espoused the Prince's side in the growing quarrel between father and son and was not averse to creating difficulties for the King's ministers. At the outset the Duke may have had some reason to complain of his inadequate force, but Stanhope and Townshend had to consider the needs of the country as a whole, and at last were well rid of the touchy and self-opinionated Duke. In times of national danger busy men in charge of affairs have no time to waste on the punctilios and reproaches of unwilling or unruly subordinates, however eminent.[3]

On 4 February 1716, a fortnight before Argyll's recall, the Pretender, after abandoning Perth, had furtively re-embarked with Mar for France. Again no want of personal courage drove him to this step, but simply the conviction that his cause was lost and that his followers might get better terms without him. At any rate they, deserted now by King and commander-in-chief, had to shift for themselves, as best they could. Some escaped overseas, the rest were ruthlessly

---

[1] Michael, i. 578.   [2] R.O., *S.P.* 44/117.
[3] For the relations of Argyll with Stanhope, Townshend and Cadogan, see Coxe, *Marlborough*, vi; *H. MSS.*, *Townshend*, 173-86; Lady Cowper.

hunted down by Cadogan, who succeeded Argyll in the Scottish command. By April the rising had been entirely suppressed both in England and in Scotland.

Already in January Parliament had given further testimony of its loyalty to the throne. In spite of opposition from Shippen, most respected of the Tories, Stanhope, after showing that the ministry had made no wanton use of the extraordinary powers granted them, obtained a renewed suspension of the Habeas Corpus Act. In fact Stanhope's main difficulty was to moderate the excessive zeal of the House of Commons. As in the last year of William III, loyal feeling was aroused almost to fever-heat by the suspicion that France had been interfering in our domestic concerns. Sixteen more new battalions were sanctioned for England in addition to others for Ireland; and Stanhope, writing to Stair, declared that the King's servants had much ado to moderate the warmth against France:

'had they encouraged the temper which appeared, I do verily believe a warr would have been voted before the rising of the House. . . . The Regent has told your Lordship that the bent and inclination of the people of France are strong for the Pretender. I must tell Your Lordship with as much truth that the bent and disposition of the British Parliament is to resent the Injurys of any who shall assist him. The King, thank God, can govern his Parliament, and we are willing to hope the Regent may govern the subjects of France.'[1]

§ 4

Considering the more ferocious habits of the times and the fact that every rebel had incurred the death penalty, no specially vindictive spirit was displayed against the prisoners captured at Preston and in Scotland. Owing to the difficulty of obtaining convictions from Scottish juries, about a hundred Scottish prisoners, under power given by a recent Act, were sent for trial to Carlisle. Of the 1,600 prisoners taken at Preston 200 were men of property, the rest of the meaner sort. Stanhope instructed Carpenter to provide subsistence for the prisoners at a groat a day, to have all deserters from the King's army court-martialled on the spot, and to send all the chief men in irons to London, where they were taken through the streets on horses led by soldiers, as an example

[1] R.O. 90/14 (partly printed in *Instructions, France*, i. 102).

to the public. A large number of the prisoners managed to escape, including Forster. Only comparatively few were brought to trial; most of those condemned were reprieved; and it is stated that no more than twenty-six were hanged.[1]

As to the meaner sort, both English and Scottish, those who signed an acknowledgement of their guilt were, by Stanhope's orders, excused a trial but transported to the West Indies on seven years' indenture of service. Those who refused to enter voluntarily into indentures Stanhope ordered the West Indian governors to:

> 'dispose of in the same manner as those that have, only the Governor is to give proper Certificates to those who purchase them, that it is his Majesty's pleasure that they shall continue Servants to them and their Assigns for the Term of Seven Years, which Certificates the Governor is to cause to be recorded for the satisfaction of those who purchase them, least they should at any time attempt to make their Escape, not being bound.'

There is a list of some 700 shipped overseas on these terms; but not all of them reached their destination. A letter of the following September came to Mar informing him that the party to which the writer belonged had overpowered the master of their ship and were awaiting King James III's orders at St. Martin's.[2]

There still remained the rebel Lords Derwentwater, Widdrington, Nithsdale, Wintoun, Carnwath, Kenmure and Nairn, whose high position seemed to call for a more solemn form of trial and more condign punishment. In January Lechmere, an old Whig ally of Stanhope's, proposed their impeachment. In his survey of events leading up to the Rebellion he dwelt on the guilt of the late government in preparing the way for it:

> 'Every man', he declared, 'who favoured the Hanoverian succession was to be worried, and all open and scandalous assertors of contrary principles were treated with all the care and tenderness of friends.'

and after adverting to the persecutions inflicted on Marlborough and Townshend he turned to

> 'two honourable gentlemen [Walpole and Stanhope], now sitting near me, [who] felt the severity of those times; they had

---

[1] For estimates of numbers see Leadam, 265; Michael, i. 553; see also Lady Cowper, 113.

[2] *Colonial Calendar, 1716–17*, §§ 128, 144, 309–14; *H. MSS., Stuart*, iv. 87.

distinguished themselves by their zeal and firmness to the true interest of the country, and were too considerable to escape the malice of those who had other views.'

The House at once agreed to the impeachment and the seven peers were forthwith brought to trial before the House of Lords. Lord Cowper, acting as Lord Steward, presided with a dignity and good feeling commended, says his wife, by everybody. The trials were soon over, for all except Lord Wintoun pleaded guilty. All were sentenced to death.

But only two of the condemned peers were executed. The King himself seems to have been the least inclined to mercy, and he was supported by the arguments of those who maintained that as some of the rank and file had suffered the extreme penalty it was only right that those who had led them to treason should also suffer. But powerful influences were at work for leniency. Nottingham, the only Tory left in the Cabinet, was for pardon, and many, including Stanhope and Sunderland, agreed with him that so wholesale an execution would not increase the popularity of the dynasty. Most, too, of the rebel lords were closely connected with those in power, Widdrington, for example, being a cousin of Lady Cowper and once a boon companion of Stanhope. In the event only the two most prominent, Lords Derwentwater and Kenmure, were beheaded on Tower Hill. For the rest reprieves were obtained, even for Lord Nithsdale before it was known that his courageous wife had saved him. Nairn, so the story goes, owed his pardon to Stanhope, who had been a boy with him at Eton, and who threatened to resign if he did not obtain a reprieve for his old friend.[1] Widdrington also expressed warm thanks to Stanhope for his 'goodness and generous friendship' during his imprisonment in the Tower.[2] To this time also belongs another story of Stanhope and a rebel. In this instance the rebel was a schoolboy, Lord Erskine, Mar's eldest son, then one of the most brilliant

[1] Mahon, *History*, i. 194; *State Trials*, xv. 769, where allusion is made to the similar story, told in *Spectator*, No. 373, of a Westminster boy saved during the Protectorate by his old schoolfellow, one of Cromwell's judges; Torrens, i. 116–17. Recently some doubt has been cast on this story on the ground that Nairn is not recorded to have been at Eton and that even if he was he could not have been a contemporary there of Stanhope's. See *Etoniana*, No. 40 (2 Aug. 1926), pp. 631–2. But at any rate Nairn is known to have been an early friend of Stanhope's, so that the well-attested story about Stanhope saving Nairn may be true even if they were not at Eton together.

[2] See Widdrington's letter of 24 Jan. 1716 (o.s.), evidently addressed to Stanhope, who had just returned from Hanover, in *Sundon Memoirs*, i. 160.

boys at Westminster: and in the encounter the schoolboy certainly did not come off second best. 'On a public occasion', writes P. Guthrie to the boy's exiled father,

'the General went to Westminster School and discovering something extraordinary in Lord Erskine's aspect asked whose son that glorious child was, and being told he was Lord Mar's son, he went up and asked him if he learned well. My lord replied he learned indifferently well. Pray, said the General, mind your book, and learn not to be a rebel like your father. My lord put his hands in his sides, and with a stern countenance told the General that that matter was not yet decided, who were the rebels.'[1]

Some indication may be found of the opinion held about Stanhope's part in suppressing the Rebellion in the contemporary pamphlet *The British Hero*. It was a pamphlet written to encourage loyalty to King George at this crisis and was dedicated to Stanhope, because of his

'generous stand upon all occasions . . . in the Senate and in the Field in defence of the Revolution and the Protestant Succession. . . . Unutterable returns these Kingdoms owe you for the Dangers and Sufferings you have willingly embraced and shared, in contending for and maintaining our religious and civil rights. . . . Conduct and Valour, Learning and Eloquence, Generosity, Sincerity and Humanity are the Distinguishing parts of your Character.'[2]

Although the Rebellion had been scotched, it could not be said that the dynasty was yet entirely out of danger. There was still unrest in the country and enemies on the watch to make mischief; as late as July 1716 Stanhope warns the governors of Hull, Portsmouth and Sheerness of plots to surprise them.[3] The prospect of a general election, due under the Triennial Act at latest in December 1717, was therefore a cause of anxiety to the government, as likely to provide countless opportunities of stirring up strife and arousing passions. Even in normal times triennial parliaments had not proved satisfactory. The first session, as Steele argued, was apt to be taken up in clearing away the mess caused by the past election and the third in preparing for the next: the second session alone could be devoted to serious business.

---

[1] H. MSS., *Stuart*, iii. 143. Another version of the same story is given in a letter from Fanny Oglethorpe to Mar.
[2] *The British Hero* (R. Tookey, 1715).
[3] R.O., S.P. 44/117.

Mainly for the first reason, partly also using Steele's plea, the ministry brought in a Bill to extend the duration of parliaments, including that sitting at the time, to seven years. Against this proposal the opposition objected with considerable force that a House of Commons elected for three years only had no right to prolong its own existence. This, as Dicey points out, is a strong argument, not against the power of Parliament to make such a change, but as stating a clear breach of the understanding on which members had been elected. But on the principle, *rei publicae salus suprema lex*, the Septennial Bill was passed without any difficulty in the House of Lords, as well as in the Commons, where, in Walpole's absence, Stanhope had charge of it.

In his speech recommending the Bill Stanhope gave an alarming picture of the support the Pretender was obtaining in France. He was appearing in public 'with great numbers of his pretended subjects', and his cousin the Duke of Berwick had just been made governor of Guienne. The Regent had been calling up an army of 30,000, and 'it was very visible another invasion was hourly expected and that the Regent was in the Pretender's interest'. But his chief argument was that it was high time to look for security by foreign alliances, but 'unless this Bill passed, no foreign power would enter into alliance with us lest the next Parliament should annul what this had done'. In conclusion he expressed the hope that 'when the evil spirit was cast out', the Bill would be repealed.[1] During the subsequent debate he wisely resisted a wrecking amendment moved by Lechmere, who was already gaining the character of 'always damning everything that does not originally come from himself', to exclude pensioners during pleasure from both Houses. While approving of the principle of reducing the royal influence in Parliament by terminable pensions and other means, Stanhope knew that the Peers would never agree to such a clause applicable to themselves and that it might endanger the whole measure. But he met Lechmere by passing a separate Act to the same effect, applicable only to the House of Commons. Apart from its tranquillizing effect on domestic politics at a critical period, the Septennial Act was fully justified by the impression of stability in the country it gave to foreign nations and was one of the factors that enabled Stanhope to raise England's

[1] *H. MSS.*, *Stuart*, ii. 140, 144, letters of 26 & 30 April 1716; Torrens, i. 123.

influence in Europe to the height it attained within the next few years.

Feeling now secure in England by the suppression of the rebellion and the assurance of a Whig majority in Parliament for another five years, George once more began to turn his thoughts to his orangery and the other delights of his beloved Hanover. To the strong objections against his absence from England at such a time urged in a cabinet minute drafted by Townshend[1] he would not pay the slightest attention. But there was an obstacle that had to be overcome in section 3 of the Act of Settlement, which forbade the King to leave the country without express parliamentary sanction. To overcome this humiliating condition he had a Bill brought in by the ministry to repeal this section, a Bill which was passed without opposition: by the Whigs because they did not like to oppose the King's wishes at such a time, by the Tories because they were glad to have him absent. A third difficulty was the Regency. The choice of Regent during the King's absence would naturally fall on the Prince of Wales; and the King felt that he could not entirely pass him over. But from jealousy of his greater popularity with the people and fear of what he might do to counteract his own policy, for the second time he rejected the cabinet's advice, strictly limited his son's power of making civil and military appointments and, instead of Regent, gave him the inferior title of Guardian and Lieutenant of the Realm. He also made him dismiss Argyll, suspected of being a focus of discontent, from his office of Groom of the Stole to the Prince, at the same time as he put him out of all his state offices. Having thus made things as difficult as he could for his son and representative, on 9 July 1716 he started on the first of his numerous and most unpopular journeys to Hanover.

During the King's absence all state business had formally to be conducted by the ministers left in England on behalf of the Guardian of the Realm. But in fact George was resolved to conduct the most important business himself. Accordingly, besides Bernstorff, he took with him Stanhope, the Secretary in whom he already seems to have reposed the most confidence, while Methuen was appointed to act for Stanhope at home. The long sojourns in Hanover, five of which occurred during George I's reign, twelve in the reign of his successor, were a fruitful cause of discontent at home and of

[1] Coxe, *Walpole*, ii. 51.

difficulty to the government. Business was confused and delayed. Matters of moment were referred backwards and forwards between Hanover and England. Envoys abroad were often in doubt whether to take their instructions from the Secretary at home or his colleague at Hanover. Cabals and intrigues were encouraged. One Secretary had every opportunity of supplanting his colleague in the royal favour, the other of strengthening his political position in England. On one occasion the two Secretaries were so afraid of one another's intrigues that both accompanied their master to Hanover; on another, a vice-secretary was appointed for Hanover, while both remained at home. Then it was always suspected, with some reason, that at Hanover the King was more than ever inclined to neglect English for Hanoverian interests and to inoculate the Secretary in attendance with the same perverted view. These disadvantages were constantly represented to George I and his son by men of all parties, not to speak of anti-dynastic pamphlets, but all unavailingly.

'How business can be carried on in a practical manner', complained Horatio Walpole, 'between the distance of the King at Hanover and his council in England, especially if there should be different opinions, is inconceivable, but should they always agree the tediousness of it would be intolerable.'[1]

Stanhope was too ardent and sagacious an Englishman to be hypnotized out of his English principles by the air of Hanover and its German court; but even he could not avoid a serious difference with his colleague Townshend and the still more formidable Robert Walpole, a quarrel which would almost certainly not have occurred, had the three men been able at the outset to discuss their differences round a table.

[1] Coxe, *Walpole*, iii. 250.

CHAPTER VIII
THE TRIPLE ALLIANCE

§ I

STANHOPE'S journey to Hanover with George I in July 1716 marks the period from which he became, for the rest of his life, almost solely responsible for England's foreign policy. The two years he had already been in office show a remarkable development in his character and a constantly broadening view of his national duty. When first appointed Secretary of State he had very little experience of foreign politics except the rough diplomacy of the battle-field, or of domestic politics except in a time of acute, almost violent, controversy. Small wonder that with his impetuous and bellicose nature he at first seemed to have scarcely any other aim than to re-establish the Whig policy both at home and abroad and was quite prepared for a renewal of hostilities with France. Hardly more than a month in office, he had threatened Iberville with war if our demands about Dunkirk were not promptly fulfilled, and had envisaged an offensive alliance with the Emperor as one of the main objects of his mission to Vienna. Even after his return, during the first half of 1715, several of his utterances seemed to imply that he was only waiting for the death of Louis XIV to attack both France and Savoy.[1] So convinced was Louis XIV of his bellicose aims that, referring to Stanhope's visit to Vienna in instructions to his ambassador at that court, he speaks of the English ministry's design 'd'attaquer et de perdre les ministres de la feue reine . . . et pour cet effet d'engager toute la nation dans une nouvelle guerre'.[2] But, whether as a result of the Rebellion or, more probably, because with growing experience he gained a wider view of general European conditions and of his own country's true interests, he gradually abandoned this warlike attitude and devoted himself to maintaining the peace of the world. He would still flare up and take a haughty tone when he thought his country's honour or interests involved; his dispatches and interviews with foreign envoys lose none of

[1] Michael, i. 498, 656–8 for utterances to that effect reported to Vienna by Hoffman.
[2] *Recueil, Autriche*, 185.

their vigour and frankness; but in his general policy he becomes mellower, more tolerant and more statesmanlike. The most marked sign of this change is seen in his dealings with France during his sojourn abroad in the latter half of 1716.

To a proud and patriotic man like Stanhope this change came all the easier from the more assured condition of England since August 1714. The Jacobites had made their bid for power and had failed; since then the Pretender himself had been forbidden to re-enter Lorraine and had taken refuge at Avignon, the Papal enclave in French territory, and had contumeliously dismissed Bolingbroke, almost the only man of intelligence among his adherents. Moreover the nation, isolated and friendless in 1714, had been able to renew her old alliances and was even being courted by her adversary France. Commerce, next to security her main interest abroad, had also revived under the ministry's prudent and vigorous measures.

For trade as well as defence England's chief need was a plentiful supply of hemp, tar, pitch and timber for the upkeep of her ships. This island, unable to produce them in sufficient quantities, looked to the almost inexhaustible supplies of the Baltic provinces and, more recently, with hope to the still undeveloped sources in her own American plantations. In both directions the new government had taken energetic measures. In place of Bolingbroke's 'trimming, dilatory game', and his plaintive and futile reproaches to Charles XII for interfering with our Baltic trade,[1] Admiral Norris was sent in May 1715 with a fleet to protect our merchants, and instructions to take action against all Swedish men-of-war and privateers that interfered with them; he was also to call on Charles to withdraw his edict against freedom of trade and to make reparations for losses in past years.[2] By the end of July Norris had convoyed the traders to their Baltic ports and by the end of October brought them back safe and sound to England. In the following year he was sent again on the same errand. The further activities of the fleets sent to the Baltic in these years, activities not solely concerned with the protection of our trade, will call for comment later; but at any rate in the primary object of trade-protection this new and vigorous policy was entirely successful.

[1] See above, ch. vi, p. 159.   [2] *Instructions, Sweden*, i. 74.

Stanhope himself was especially responsible for renewed efforts to encourage the development of a trade in naval stores from the Plantations. Ever since James I's time attempts to do so had been made spasmodically, the last being an Act of Godolphin's ministry for 'Encouraging the Importation of Naval Stores from H.M.'s Plantations in America';[1] hitherto with poor results. Recognizing the precarious dependence to be placed on Baltic supplies in time of war, Stanhope in his earliest instructions to the Governors of New York and Virginia directs them to promote the trade in ' pines fit for pitch and tar and some fit for masts for our first-rate ships of war and oaks and timber trees fit for beams, knees, planks &c. for our Navy . . . it being highly for Our Service and ye Advantage of this Kingdom that all sorts of Naval Stores be as much as possible produced in Our Plantations in America and thence imported'. These instructions were followed by the reappointment of one J. Bridger to the Office of 'Surveyor of Woods on the Continent of America', from which he had been dismissed by the Tory government. To him Stanhope sends orders to mark all trees fit for masts in the royal reserves of 'Massachusetts, New Hampshire, Maine, Rhode Island, Providence, Narranganset Country, Connecticut, New York, and New Jersey, as well as in the newly acquired province of Nova Scotia'; and 'whereas We are desirous that these Our Dominions be furnished with Pitch, Tar, Hemp and other Naval Stores from Our Plantations rather than from Foreign Parts', he directs him to instruct merchants in America how best to prepare pitch and tar for the English markets by removing dirt and dross and putting them up in uniform casks clearly marked with the traders' names, as the best means of competing with similar goods 'imported from the East Countries and other Foreign Parts'. The trusty and capable Bridger certainly had no sinecure as 'Surveyor of Woods on the Continent of America', for which he touched £250 as salary, 'he being obliged to lye out in the Woods Exposed to the Rigour of the Seasons and the Eastern Indians in War with us'; but he showed good returns for it. Already by 1715 Stanhope was able to sign a contract for the supply of masts, bowsprits and yards from the New England forests, to be delivered at Portsmouth and Plymouth during the next six years; two years later the agents for

[1] 3 and 4 Anne, cap. 9.

Carolina and Pennsylvania reported that they could already supply pitch and tar at a considerably lower price than the Swedish importers.[1] Even when Stanhope had become Northern Secretary and so had no direct concern with colonial affairs, he had not lost his interest in this matter; for in October 1719 he writes to his colleague Craggs to recommend Captain Coram's scheme of taking up land on the borders of New England on which to develop the production of naval stores.[2] The whole incident is characteristic of Stanhope's thoroughness in the public service. First he chooses his man with wisdom, a man who had already proved his capacity. He then gives him practical directions to attain the objects aimed at; and, even when some success has justified his policy and he himself has other duties, does not allow his successor to lose sight of the public interests involved.

The grievances of our merchants engaged in the Spanish trade have already been referred to; they also had been taken up with warmth by Stanhope. One of his first acts on his return from Vienna in January 1715 had been to call the attention of our minister at Madrid, Methuen, to the benefits expected from this trade on the conclusion of peace and to the poor results hitherto obtained.[3] In the succeeding months he had constantly to remind him and—when Methuen retired, worn out by his fruitless representations to the Spanish Court—his successor Bubb,[4] of the merchants' grievances, such as the enormous import duty of 24 per cent. *ad valorem*, the special favours granted to the French wool-trade to our disadvantage, the extortions of fraudulent customs officers, seizures of British ships for the Spanish service, and intolerable obstacles to the Assiento trade. But far from attempting to gain his point by a system of retaliation he showed our goodwill by sternly repressing the activities of English privateers. Thus he severely reprimanded

---

[1] J. Bridger had first been made Surveyor of Woods in 1696, but his tenure of the office had not been continuous, depending, as it probably did, on the interest of the Secretary of State for the time being in the production of naval stores from the Plantations. For his reappointment by Stanhope see *Colonial Calendar, 1714-15*, §§ 336, 561, 597. The Instructions to him are in R.O., *C.O.* 5/190, f. 309; those to the governors, ib., f. 283; the reports of the agents in March 1716/17 in R.O., *C.O.* 5/1293. See also *Acts of Privy Council (Colonial)*, ii, § 908 for Bridger's account of his hard life. An interesting report on the trade in naval stores from America is in *Colonial Calendar, 1716-17*, § 515.

[2] R.O., *S.P.* 104/220, 12 Oct. 1719.

[3] See above, ch. ii, p. 27.

[4] Better known by his later name, Bubb Dodington.

governors and other officials who had neglected to make
an example of a pirate guilty of robbing a governor of the
Spanish West Indies and insisted on the stolen money, plate
and jewels being restored, 'to the preservation of the honour
of the nation and to the visible interest of all the King's
subjects who trade in those parts'.[1] Finding complaints and
acts of courtesy equally useless, in October 1715 he wrote
directly to Cardinal del Giudice, Philip's chief minister,
warning him that if they obtained no redress the English
would be obliged to give up trading with Spain, much
to their own regret since 'le commerce doit assurément
être considéré comme le plus fort pour cimenter la bonne
intelligence et la sincère amitié que le Roi mon Maître
souhaitte passionément de voir rétablis entre les deux
couronnes'.[2] But already the Spanish court was preparing,
through another agent than del Giudice, for a complete
volte-face in commercial relations with England.

Alberoni, the stout, jovial little Italian priest, then in
Vendôme's train, whom Stanhope had met at dinner when
he was a prisoner in Spain,[3] had gone far during the last
five years. The son of a gardener at Piacenza, he owed his
success to his peasant's shrewdness and joviality, racy of the
soil, his gift for intrigue, his carefully veiled ambition, and
not least to the opportunity given by the Roman Church
even to the humblest of her votaries to show their capacity.
He had won the favour of Vendôme in Italy by the tact
and skill he showed in negotiating with him in 1703 on
behalf of his master the Duke of Parma and had thereafter
followed Vendôme's fortunes. After the Marshal's death in
1712 he had remained in Spain as envoy for the Duke of
Parma, weaving subtle plans for his master's and his own
advantage. On the death, in February 1714, of Philip's
first wife, Marie Louise of Savoy, he set about providing
him with another, for, as Alberoni remarked, Philip's nature

---

[1] Colonial Calendar, 1714–15, §§ 665–7; 1716–17, §§ 41, 208.
[2] R.O., S.P. 104/135, 136.
[3] See above, ch. iv, p. 116. He is described in The History of Cardinal Alberoni
(London, 1719), as 'a little man inclining to be fat, having no beauty in the
lineaments of his face, which is too broad and his head too big: but the eyes, the
windows of the soul, discover at first view the greatness of Alberoni, by a lustre
accompanied with an uncommon sweetness mixed with majesty, and he knows
how to give his voice such an insinuating turn, as renders his conversation always
agreeable and charming.' This pamphlet, a translation of one in Italian published at Genoa in the same year, contains much material which was evidently
given to the writer by Alberoni himself.

was such that he could be ruled only by a confessor or a wife, preferably the latter;[1] and he cast his eyes on the twenty-year-old niece of his own Duke, Elizabeth Farnese. But he had to go warily, for in his widower-hood Philip was more than ever ruled by his grandfather's agent the all-powerful Princesse des Ursins, whose mission it was to keep Spain tied to French leading strings. He accordingly insinuated Elizabeth's name so cunningly to the Princess that she believed it to be her own suggestion; and represented to her that one so young and from so obscure a court as Parma could attribute her elevation to the throne of Spain entirely to the Princess and would be correspondingly subservient to her. Elizabeth's portrait was procured, the King was attracted by her face and figure; and the match was concluded. Alberoni obtained for himself the mission of meeting the timid young Queen, as he represented her, on her entry into Spain at Pampeluna. So well did he indoctrinate her with his notions during the twelve days they travelled together before meeting the Princess at Jadraque, that Queen and Princess had hardly been half an hour together on the night of 23 December 1714 before Elizabeth flung open the door and ordered the captain of the guard to take fifty men and without a moment's delay to escort that madwoman, *pazza*, over the frontier.[2]

From this moment Alberoni was on the way to become the most powerful man in Spain. Having by his bold advice secured the gratitude and favour of the new Queen, he was secure also of the King, who at first sight of Elizabeth became more uxorious than ever. Alberoni's primary object was to clear away the old incapable office-bearers who impeded the country's development and to make Spain once more a formidable power; the ultimate object to which all his plans tended was, by means of a rejuvenated Spain, to free his beloved Italy from the Habsburgs and other foreign invaders and substitute for them princes of the Farnese stock to be expected from Elizabeth's fruitful womb. The double task he thus undertook would have taxed the powers of a greater statesman than Alberoni. In spite of the exertions of Louis's French officials, Spain itself, Fénélon's 'corps

[1] Or, as Alberoni crudely expressed it after his disgrace, 'c'est un roi à qui il ne fallait qu'un prie-Dieu et les cuisses d'une femme'.
[2] For a good description of the scene see Alberoni's latest biographer Castagnoli, 175 sqq.

mort qui ne se défend pas', had hardly recovered from its state of semi-inanition under the last Habsburg rulers. Of Italy Alberoni himself wrote in 1713 to his friend Rocca at Parma,

'L'Italie souffre d'un mal qui ne pourra se guérir que par le fer et le feu. C'est un corps politique dont les os ont été disloqués par la guerre et la paix, et doivent être remis en place avant qu'il ne s'y soit formé des calus et des exostoses.'[1]

For the Spanish part of his programme Alberoni had to feel his way, for old-established Spanish grandees were no more easily moved than privileged incapables usually are. For long he worked quietly behind the scenes as the Queen's intimate and unofficial adviser, making himself necessary to her in the dull, formal surroundings of the Spanish court by the savoury Italian dishes he cooked to perfection and the hardly less savoury audacity of his conversation.[2]

Alberoni found his opportunity for a change in Spanish policy after the death of Louis XIV. Philip V, in spite of his solemn renunciation of all claims to the French throne at Utrecht, none the less cherished the hope that his claim might still be asserted in the event of the infant Louis XV's death; he had even thought seriously of claiming the Regency while he was still alive. To both claims the Regent Orleans, already suspect to Philip since his command in Spain and his negotiations with Stanhope,[3] was a bar; and in his dissatisfaction with the Regent's government Philip was quite ready to reconstitute the barrier of the Pyrenees and seek for other friends elsewhere in Europe. For Alberoni, in pursuance of this policy, to turn to England at the end of 1715 showed considerable foresight and cunning. The Pretender's forces were still active in England and Scotland when his first approaches were made; he had probably been shrewd enough to guess that the Pretender had no staying-power and that a friendly advance would be all the more welcome, when the issue was not yet sure and the Regent seemed to be repenting of his early overtures for an alliance.

---

[1] Bourgeois, *Farnèse*, 200.
[2] As instances of his racy talk with the Queen may be quoted his conversation with her on the birth of one of her children: 'Si les choses vont de ce train', he observed, 'nous aurons bientôt des princes à peupler l'univers'; and later, 'Quand on fait si bien et si facilement ce métier-la, il faut le faire souvent, dis-je à la reine, qui me repond qu'elle voudrait que je le fasse une fois pour voir.' (Alberoni, *Lettres Intimes*, 435, 457.)
[3] See above, ch. iv, pp. 88–91.

Alberoni and Stanhope had liked one another at their former meetings, and Alberoni no doubt thought the Englishman's friendship worth securing. Lastly, for any ultimate designs on Italy it would be wiser to have the English fleet on his side than against him. At any rate he determined to clear away misunderstandings by generous concessions on the commerce so dear to Englishmen.

Alberoni opened the negotiation in characteristically melodramatic style. Bubb was sitting in his house in Madrid one evening late in September 1715 when he received a visit from Ripperda, the Dutch envoy, an adventurer of much the same type as Alberoni, though of considerably less ability.[1] Ripperda came to Bubb with a secret message from the favourite to say that he was prepared to make a clean sweep of all England's commercial grievances and draw up a new and entirely satisfactory treaty. Bubb wrote off that very night to Stanhope to announce the welcome change of front. Stanhope, nothing loth, in his reply gave Bubb a list of all the demands to be made while dispositions were so accommodating in Spain. Nearly all these were accepted, and within less than three months the treaty was concluded and signed. The commercial treaty of 14 December 1715 conceded to England that the customs should be no higher than as arranged by the favourable treaty of 1667, that her traders should be put on the same footing as Spanish traders, that the officials' irregular exactions should be abolished, and, above all, that the most-favoured-nation clause should be extended even to wool, which, as Bubb complacently remarked, 'must be a stroke to the French trade here and particularly their wool-trade'. Stanhope in his letter of thanks to Alberoni of 30 December 1715, recalls their former friendship in Vendôme's times and gracefully alludes to the fulfilment of his own predictions that merit so distinguished could not fail of advancement. 'England knows how to be a friend', he adds,

'She has expended 200 million crowns with the sole view of having a King of Spain her friend. The present King has just given solid proof of his amicable intentions. Judge then what we should do for him, should it happen that he has occasion for us.'

But Stanhope combined business with compliment and took

[1] Later Ripperda also hypnotized Philip and Elizabeth by his grandiose schemes and for a brief spell became the ruling spirit in Spain. But that was some time after Alberoni's fall.

the occasion to press for the further boon of a revision of the
Assiento Treaty.

> 'This stumbling block once removed, I see nothing to affect the
> union between the two powers, which we in England think
> absolutely necessary for the tranquillity of all Europe. I wish
> with all my heart that you may have the honour to strengthen this
> salutary union more and more, by your advice and good offices.'

By 26 May 1716 a new Assiento Treaty was also signed, and
it looked as if all disputes between the two countries had
been cleared away. This unfortunately did not prove to be
the case. The Spaniards still had a grievance in the refusal
of the English government to countenance their fishing off
Newfoundland in spite of a vague assertion in the Treaty
of Utrecht that any claims to do so that they could substan-
tiate would be admitted. Stanhope himself was so anxious to
remove difficulties with Spain that as late as July 1717 he
professed a willingness to accept their claim. But soon after
that relations between the two countries became too much
strained for any satisfactory settlement to be attained; and
the question remained a sore point between the two countries
for the next sixty years, notably in 1761.[1] Moreover, the
treaties of December 1715 and May 1716 from the first
proved unsatisfactory; for the Spanish officials continued to
administer the new regulations so vexatiously that Alberoni
himself was suspected of merely wishing to throw dust in
Stanhope's eyes. If so, he overreached himself, for Stanhope's
confidence was gradually changed into deep mistrust. For
the time being, however, the treaties were useful to England,
at a critical period for the dynasty, by increasing her prestige in Europe and demonstrating to both France and the
Emperor that her friendship was still sought after. They
also illustrate the trend of our policy, constantly followed for
a quarter of a century by Walpole no less than Stanhope,
to prefer the commercial advantages resulting from a good
understanding with Spain to any other foreign connexions.
For even when Spain proved most intractable during this
period, the earliest occasion for recovering these advantages
was always seized with alacrity.[2]

---

[1] A good discussion of the Newfoundland fishery dispute during the eighteenth century is to be found in a paper by Miss Vera Lee Brown in the *Annual
Report* of the Canadian Historical Association for 1925.
[2] For these negotiations see R.O., *S.P.* 104/135, 136; Coxe, *Bourbons*, ii. 233;
Michael, i; Baudrillart, ii. 218 sqq.; Bourgeois, *Farnèse*.

The treaty with Spain of December 1715 was followed in February by another triumph for English diplomacy in the renewal of the treaty of guarantee and alliance with the Dutch. These treaties began to alarm both the Regent and the Emperor, on whom it was beginning to dawn that, whereas hardly more than a year ago England had been the friendless power, they were now likely to play that role. Ever since Stanhope's journey to Vienna in 1714 the Emperor had been turning over with increasing approbation the suggestion for renewing the alliance with England, to which events were now driving him. The Turks had declared war against Venice at the end of 1714 and in the following year had overrun the Morea and attacked Dalmatia. The Emperor was not only bound by the Treaty of Carlowitz to come to the aid of Venice, but feared also for his own possessions. Eugene was all for war, which was actually declared in the middle of 1716. With his eyes turned southwards, there was grave danger that the Emperor's western interests might be jeopardized. To hold a strong position in Italy had always been the policy of Vienna, but, with Spain ever anxious to recover the lost portions of the monarchy and Victor Amedeus always on the look-out for more leaves of the artichoke, the Emperor's position there was none too secure. England alone, because of her fleet, could help him to protect his existing possessions in Italy, perhaps even to secure for him Victor Amedeus's coveted Kingdom of Sicily. So, on the eve of the Turkish war, negotiations with England were eagerly resumed.

In the course of the negotiations two difficulties arose. The first was as to the inclusion of the Dutch in the proposed alliance. England already had her treaty with the Dutch but was anxious to include them in a triple alliance with the Emperor and so revive the old system of the late war in its integrity; the Emperor objected, partly because there were still some unsettled questions about the Barrier, partly because he wished to conclude the treaty without the delay inevitable whenever the Dutch were concerned. Finally our ministers gave way on this point, since they also wished to conclude before the King sailed for Hanover and found the Dutch keener on a proposed triple alliance with England and France. The second difficulty was more serious. The Emperor wished to obtain England's guarantee not only for his existing possessions but also for those to which he laid claims, a stipulation which might embrace not only Sicily but all the Spanish monarchy and, as Townshend said, might involve us in an interminable war: on the other hand, he did not propose to guarantee any of George I's possessions. In April 1716 a letter came to Volkra and Hoffman, the two Imperial plenipotentiaries in London, in the most august style of the *Augustissima Casa*. A draft treaty was enclosed stipulating that not only the actual possessions but the 'honour, dignity and rights' claimed by either of the parties must be supported by the other, a clause clearly pointing to the defence of the Emperor's claims on Italy and Spain; the draft also laid down that in case of war the Emperor need contribute only 12,000 troops as against 10,000 troops and 20 men-of-war from George I: in the instruction the plenipotentiaries were forbidden to allow the change of a 'single letter' in this draft.[1] The English ministers naturally would not accept so one-sided a treaty, which did not even include a specific guarantee for the Hanoverian Succession, one of their main objects. The Austrians were in a dilemma, for in spite of the instruction not to allow the change of a single letter they knew the Emperor, threatened by the Turks, was in dire need of allies. Accordingly they consented to a compromise on the two crucial points. The contribution of each side was fixed at 12,000 men, with the proviso that England might substitute ships at the same cost. The other question was more difficult to adjust since it involved Imperial *'dignitas et honor'*. The Emperor's two envoys sat with Bernstorff, Marlborough, Townshend and Stanhope, discussing the point for a whole afternoon and well into the night before coming to an agreement. Finally Stanhope found the solution. Taking up a pen he rapidly amended the clause making George responsible for defending any *Honor, Dignitas et Jura* to which the Emperor might lay claim, by the addition of the few words *eo quo sunt statu et quibus unusquisque actualiter gaudet et fruitur* (i.e. only those rights, &c., actually enjoyed at the time), which in fact limited George's obligations to existing rights and extended a similar obligation to the Emperor for the Hanoverian Succession. The exhausted ministers were only too glad to accept Stanhope's words; and, although the Emperor complained of the change, he

---

1 'Ingestalten ihr nicht einen Buchstaben weder davon noch darzu zu thuen.'

accepted the Treaty of Westminster concluded on this basis on 25 May/5 June 1716.[1]

Thus by the time George I and Stanhope sailed for Hanover England had a treaty of guarantee with Holland and had brought the Emperor and Dutch together on the Barrier question, she had a treaty of alliance with the Emperor and for the time being was on the best of terms with Spain. It soon appeared that a treaty of alliance with the Regent could be had almost for the asking.

§ 2

One of the first acts of the Duke of Orleans on becoming Regent, it will be remembered, had been to invite George I to enter into an alliance with him, mutually to reinsure one another's rights, as laid down in the Treaty of Utrecht, in England and France respectively.[2] Stanhope, with the Rebellion then looming over England, had welcomed the proposals and sent Stair full powers to conclude a treaty of guarantee pure and simple. So anxious indeed did he then appear to conclude the treaty that he made no special stipulations about the Dunkirk and Mardyk dispute. But even then, remembering Bolingbroke's treaty of commerce which in 1713 he had taken so large a part in rejecting, he refused to consider the Regent's further proposal of another commercial treaty, which, he wrote, 'can produce no other Effect than to create Disputes and Animosities which we do sincerely desire to avoid'. With the rise of the Pretender's prospects the Regent had cooled off and began starting 'things which if comply'd with wou'd necessarily spin out the Negotiation to a very great length'. Stanhope in his turn entirely dropped all allusion to the proposed treaty, believing that the Regent would soon return to a sense of his own interests if he thought England could do without him.[3] When, by March 1716, the Rebellion was crushed, the Regent, as Stanhope had anticipated, again brought up the question.

[1] For this treaty and the negotiations leading to it, see Pribram, i. 333 sqq.; Michael, i. 672–3; Weber, 19; Wiesener, i. 210. By a separate article added to the Treaty of Westminster in 1717 the Emperor agreed to expel the Jacobites from his dominions in return for the adjustment of some back claims for pay he made on England. The Emperor had objected that this expulsion would 'make him odious to other Catholic states', but Stanhope had insisted (Pribram, i. 338).

[2] Ch. vii, p. 189.   [3] *Instructions, France*, i. 99–102.

The new overture from the Regent came by the hand of the abbé Dubois, formerly Orleans's tutor and since then his constant companion and secretary. Though probably not the instigator and partner of his master's orgies, as malevolent tongues in Paris asserted, he had at any rate shown no inconvenient austerity in reproving them. He was chosen for this delicate approach as being fully in sympathy with his master's policy, whereas the Regent's official advisers, notably Huxelles and Torcy, being all of the old Louis XIV tradition, had no liking for an English alliance and were not so set on checkmating Philip V's aspirations to the French throne as Orleans naturally was. Dubois and Stanhope had met many years before in London and in Paris, when neither of them was indifferent to the delights of joyous living; hence a discreet allusion to this former friendship made a ready opening to Dubois. Beyond this Dubois's first letter of 12 March 1716 was confined to a somewhat audacious expression of the delight felt in France at the Pretender's defeat and an ardent wish that nothing should interfere with the closest relations between their respective masters. Stanhope's reply is a masterpiece of delicate irony.[1] He is overjoyed to learn on such good authority, in spite of alarming appearances to the contrary, of the French court's friendly disposition: he is quite ready to accept Dubois's word that the accounts of secret support for the Pretender from the French court were mere lies spread by the Jacobites to encourage their own side; nor can he believe that so enlightened a prince as the Regent can fail to see that he has a simple means of ensuring our confidence by not welcoming Jacobite traitors and not suffering the Pretender to continue hatching his plots against England at Avignon, to all intents and purposes within the French territory; and so, with the characteristic conclusion, 'Vous voyez que je vous tiens parole et vous parle franchement; je crois que c'est toujours le meilleur que de savoir à quoi s'en tenir', he takes leave of the wily abbé.

Little satisfaction could be extracted from this answer, so Dubois was set to make another attempt. In his letter of 10 April he reminds Stanhope of a remark he had once heard him make that no solid union was possible between princes unless each of them found his advantage in the arrangement and, enlarging on that, dilates in some-

[1] Stanhope's draft in his own hand can still be seen in R.O., *S.P.* 78/160.

what general language on the benefits George I and the
Regent would each derive from the proposed alliance; and
rounds off his argument with this not over-delicate piece
of flattery:

'Au surplus, Milord, outre l'intérêt de nos deux maîtres, je
déclare que je serais ravi que vous ne bussiez que du meilleur
vin de France, au lieu de vin de Portugal, et moi du cidre de
Goldpepin, au lieu de notre gros cidre de Normandie. J'y ajou-
terai un intérêt encore plus sensuel pour moi, qui est celui de
pouvoir, sans interruption, cultiver l'honneur de votre amitié.'

Stanhope was not to be taken in by this sort of blarney and
did not even vouchsafe a reply. But in an official dispatch
to Stair he expressed his deep distrust of the Regent's sincerity and announced that if the Regent wished to resume
negotiations for a treaty of guarantee he must first fulfil
three preliminary conditions. These were that the Pretender
should be expelled from Avignon and sent beyond the Alps,
that notorious Jacobites should not be allowed a right of
asylum in France, and that the provisions of Utrecht about
Dunkirk must be exactly observed; then, but not before,
would he talk about guarantees.[1]

Besides the Regent's attitude during the Rebellion Stanhope had another cause for suspecting his sincerity. These
surreptitious manœuvres by Dubois to gain Stanhope took
on a different complexion when it appeared that Huxelles,
ostensibly responsible for French foreign policy, had instructed Châteauneuf, the French ambassador at The Hague,
to enter into separate negotiations with the Dutch. Huxelles's
proposals also purported to have for their object a treaty of
guarantee embracing England and France as well as Holland.
But the emphasis with Huxelles was quite different from
Dubois's. Whereas Dubois's object appeared to be solely to
secure England's alliance for the Regent, Huxelles clearly designed to bring about a misunderstanding between England
and the Emperor at the very time when the Treaty of Westminster was still under discussion between them, and also
to bring the Dutch once more within the orbit of France.
Stanhope's suspicions were also aroused by the evident
intention of Huxelles to take all negotiations out of Stair's
hands and confine them to the dilatory Dutch. In fact,
it seemed a negotiation intended merely to gain time and

[1] Dubois's two letters are in Sévelinges, i. 165-8; Stanhope's letters to Stair of
31 May and 7 June 176 in *Instructions, France*, i. 105-8.

to isolate England. Stanhope and Townshend did not actually forbid Horatio Walpole, our ambassador at The Hague, to continue the conversations on these separate proposals, but instructed him to insist on Stanhope's three conditions as a preliminary to any treaty.[1] Stanhope for his part was confirmed in his disbelief that any good would result from France's dubious offers. Thus when he and the King were on the way to Hanover in July the negotiation for a treaty of guarantee with France was hanging fire. On the other hand, the Regent's personal anxiety for it was increasing; for, if the ailing young King died, he could only look to England for support against the claim Philip V would unquestionably assert to the French throne. So he decided once more to pass over the ordinary diplomatic channels and attempt to negotiate directly with Stanhope.

Accordingly on 5 July a mysterious traveller, calling himself Monsieur St. Albin, accompanied by a valet, arrived at The Hague. He found a lodging conveniently near the French embassy and to those who inquired his business gave out that he was a collector of books, pictures and objects of art, for which he seemed willing to give good prices; he specially enlarged on his desire to acquire Poussin's *Seven Sacraments*, bought by some Dutch connoisseur, and restore it to its French home. In this ambition he succeeded and also purchased other notable *bibelots* and rare books. It appeared, however, that he was not unacquainted with Châteauneuf, and it was even reported that they had had a secret interview in the embassy stables. In fact the mysterious Monsieur St. Albin was none other than the ingenious abbé Dubois, who had adopted this comic opera travesty in order to waylay Stanhope when he landed in Holland. As Stanhope stepped off the boat at Helvoetsluis on 20 July a note from Dubois was put in his hand. It is characteristic of Dubois's meticulous care for the smallest details that he made six drafts of this note, all preserved in the French archives, before arriving to his satisfaction at this final version:

'Je n'ai pû résister à la tentation de profiter de vôtre passage par la Hollande pour avoir l'honneur de vous embrasser. Je suis à la Haye à l'insu de tout le monde et entièrement inconnû, je vous en demande le secret, et je vous supplie de vouloir bien me faire savoir en quel endroit vous jugez à propos que je me rende,

[1] *Instructions, France*, i. 106–7, Stanhope to Stair, 7 June 1716.

et en quel tems, pour vous entretenir librement; j'espère que vous voudrez bien accorder cette grâce à l'ancienne amitié, dont vous m'avez honoré, et à l'intérêt sincère que je prends à tout ce qui vous regarde.'[1]

Stanhope replied that he would meet him next day at Horatio Walpole's house at The Hague.

Stanhope, as he himself afterwards admitted to Townshend,[2] was the minister least inclined at that time to make a separate treaty with France. In his instructions to Dubois the Regent had fully recognized this difficulty, warning his emissary to be circumspect in his dealings with one 'entièrement livré aux intérêts de la Cour de Vienne, [qui] n'a rien oublié jusqu'à présent pour traverser la proposition d'une alliance'.[3] But at any rate, even if Stanhope could not be brought to change his sentiments, it could do nothing but good to make known the Regent's offers to England. These were to guarantee the Hanoverian Succession and the Dutch Barrier and to concede Stanhope's three points about the Pretender, the Jacobites in France and the Dunkirk clause, with this one reservation, however, that these last should not be preliminary to but an integral part of the treaty; otherwise the Regent might find himself under onerous obligations but with no treaty. The Regent was even willing to go so far as to discuss a guarantee for George's German possessions, including Bremen and Verden, the provinces conquered by Denmark from Sweden and recently ceded to George as Elector of Hanover.[4] The Regent then discusses what possible reasons could induce the Whig ministers to reject these seductive offers and can only offer three suggestions, all of which show a singular inability to understand English politics. Perhaps they fear that an alliance with France would make George so powerful that he could dispense with the Whigs and commit himself entirely to the Tories with their more congenial respect for the royal prerogative; or a secure peace with France might oblige them to reduce the standing army, or even constrain them to give up their 'passion particulière' for abasing France. Of the advantages to himself in the proposed treaty the Regent is in no doubt: it would give him

'les moyens de faire valoir ses droits . . . et l'on assurera

---

[1] A. E., *Angleterre*, 277, ff. 128–33.   [2] Coxe, *Walpole*, ii. 85.
[3] A.E., *Angleterre*, 277, ff. 22–6.   [4] See next chapter.

en même tems l'exécution de tout ce qui a esté statué en faveur de S.A.R. par rapport à l'ordre de la succession à la couronne.'[1]

Stanhope and Dubois had hitherto only talked as friends in gallant company or over a glass of wine. Now they were to meet as two expert fencers in a duelling bout, watchful for any weak spot in the adversary's defence and ready with the quick riposte to the unguarded attack: the prize no mere personal triumph, but to one the satisfaction of his master's ambition, to the other the advantage of his country. Absolutely different in their methods, they were worthy of each other's steel. The Frenchman had untiring persistence, all the delicacy of touch of his race, and a cunning and resource in attack and defence which often gave him a momentary advantage. The Englishman, with less cunning, had a more direct method of approach: brushing aside his adversary's irrelevant feints he went direct to the point with a jovial, but by no means unreflecting, audacity that was apt to carry all before it. Stanhope had this further advantage, that, whereas Dubois felt that his master's whole future depended on his success, he for his part now had no such anxiety as to the result for England's safety.

The antagonists had two preliminary bouts at The Hague. In the first Dubois for some time kept up his pose as the wandering connoisseur chiefly interested in Poussin's *Seven Sacraments* and in the catalogue of William III's library shortly to be sold at Leyden. Then, taking as his cue some secret correspondence of William, he asked Stanhope why he had not answered his last private letter. And so the transition to business was made. His first move was perhaps not quite tactful, for he produced a letter the Regent had written him, saying that if, as he had heard, Stanhope was involved in Argyll's disgrace at court, he would gladly offer him any money, good offices or other help he might need. Stanhope, while expressing deep gratitude to the Regent, said he was not concerned in Argyll's troubles and politely waved aside the offer. Next Dubois tried to represent the Regent as a much misunderstood man, who had never ceased to proffer the hand of kindness to the King. How then was it, Stanhope drily asked, that the Regent's 'frank and early' offers of alliance had been so soon followed

[1] A.E., *Angleterre*, 277, ff. 20–38.

by the many notorious instances of his favour to the Pretender just at the time when England seemed to be in danger: such marks of favour could only be atoned for to the King by the immediate dispatch of the Pretender beyond the Alps; as to himself, he added, the Pretender's presence in France was a matter of supreme indifference, for if ever the French had any designs against England, the best way to assure their failure would be to put the Pretender in command of the enterprise. Then, turning to the proposal for a treaty of alliance between Regent and King, he warned Dubois not to expect them to guarantee the Treaty of Utrecht in its entirety, for the Emperor had never accepted that treaty, and they had no intention of alienating an old friend to please new and uncertain allies. This thrust went home, for thereupon Dubois rose to go, saying that he was sorry to have wasted so much of Stanhope's precious time. Not at all, replied Stanhope, it is always useful to know exactly where we stand; and he agreed without demur to another meeting for the same evening.

Stanhope, in his report to Townshend, expressed his belief that 'the man is really frighted', or, as Methuen put it more colloquially to Stair, the abbé 'was sent back with a flea in his ear and frighted out of his wits with the reception he had'. But the fright had this good result, that Dubois, after consultation with Châteauneuf, came to the conclusion that it was no use beating about the bush and that the only way of winning Stanhope was to make firm and explicit proposals. So at the evening meeting at his lodgings, where Stanhope discovered him surrounded by his precious purchases, he soon came to business. After he had been brought tacitly to admit that the Regent was in greater need of an understanding than George I, he and Stanhope found themselves in agreement on the use to which an alliance between the two rulers could be put in safeguarding the peace of Europe, a consideration evidently all-important to Stanhope. Thereafter many of the obstacles to such understanding proved easier to remove. Stanhope was brought to admit that the Regent could hardly be expected to expel the Pretender from Avignon before he had the certainty of a treaty; and he implied that some compromise on that point might be found; and, though he held out no hope that the King would guarantee the entire Treaty of Utrecht, he seemed to think that the King might consent to a treaty of alliance and a specific guarantee of the Regent's rights of succession to the French throne. For his part Dubois recognized that the Regent's proposals about the Dunkirk and Mardyk issue, 'que Stanhope a paru regarder comme le plus important et même comme décisif',[1] must be revised as quite inadequate. He also agreed that Châteauneuf's separate negotiation at The Hague, so offensive to the Emperor, might be suspended, while the details of a triple alliance between England, France, and the Dutch were being worked out between himself and Stanhope at Hanover. When they found themselves on this more satisfactory footing Dubois brought out of his pocket two autograph letters from the Regent to George I and Stanhope, which he had been too much 'frighted' to produce earlier. In his letter to Stanhope, the Regent reminded him of their former meetings and bade him count on his future friendship, in return for which he expected Stanhope to forward, by all means in his power, a close union between himself and George I.

There had been an interlude for supper during this business talk; and there can be no doubt that the supper was excellent, for Dubois believed as firmly as Alberoni in the emollient effect on political intercourse of well-chosen food and wine. Business was dropped, at any rate while the lackeys were in the room, and lighter topics were touched upon as in the old days in London or Paris. Each confessed his love of the classics, each expressed his contempt for the pretentious pedants who thought such love incompatible with a taste for modern favourites of theirs, Tasso, Corneille and Racine. Under the mellowing influences of the good cheer they even began to jest and sharpen their wits on one another. Dubois took leave to commiserate with Stanhope on the prodigious size of England's national debt—some £47,000,000:[2] Stanhope airily replied that great as it might be, and greater as it would some day assuredly become, it would never give a moment's anxiety to their government or to a people as resourceful as the English. I am charmed to hear it, retorted Dubois, but at any rate how much better off, how much more secure is the French nation than yours: you have to depend on subsidies doled out by a

---

[1] So it was stated in the *Mémoire* of 9 Aug. 1716 taken as his Instruction by Dubois to Hanover (A.E., *Angleterre*, 277, ff. 113–15).

[2] This was an under-estimate on Dubois's part. The total debt appears to have been £54,000,000. See below, ch. x, p. 261.

parsimonious Parliament, while our King, by his mere command, can draw on the entire resources and domains of his people. 'What, M. l'abbé!' cried Stanhope, 'you must have gone to Turkey for your knowledge of public law.' At this sally Dubois, as he himself relates, had a good laugh; and the two men parted the best of friends.[1]

After one more interview with Stanhope two days later, Dubois hastened back to Paris to report his success to the Regent. Thence he was sent off to continue the conversations at Hanover. The Regent was all the more anxious for the success of his mission, since his emissary Louville had signally failed in an attempt to arrive at an understanding with Philip V.[2] Huxelles also professed to favour Dubois's mission. He and the old guard probably hoped that Dubois, with his little experience of diplomacy, would fail so egregiously that he and his scheme of alliance would be heard of no more. In the memoir given to Dubois by the French minister Stanhope is still described as the main obstacle to any treaty and as likely, even if he did not ostensibly reject it, to 'chercher dans des voyes extraordinaires et détournées des moyens d'en empêcher la conclusion'.[3] On 10 August Dubois started for Hanover, with the same elaborate incognito as before, and awaited Stanhope's directions at the post-house at Osnabruck. Stanhope, no less anxious to keep the affair secret, sent for him to Hanover, where he lodged him surreptitiously in the house he was occupying, with a door of communication between their apartments.

The meetings at The Hague had been only in the nature of preliminary skirmishes: at Hanover the two statesmen settled down to the serious business of discussing the terms of a treaty. Stanhope's objects were clearly defined. He wanted the Utrecht conditions about Dunkirk loyally observed by France, the Pretender to be sent beyond the Alps and countenance withdrawn from the Jacobites, and a mutual guarantee by the Regent and George I for the succession in England and France as settled by the Utrecht treaty. To this last stipulation he was comparatively indifferent, for to the throne of England George already had guarantees from both the Dutch and the Emperor. Moreover, just before Dubois's

[1] Stanhope's dispatches to Townshend, Townshend's answers, and the Regent's letter to Stanhope are quoted from the R.O. documents by Wiesener, i. 469-78. For Dubois's account of the interviews see Sévelinges, i. 189 sqq.
[2] *Recueil, Espagne*, ii. 245 sqq.; Baudrillart, ii.
[3] A.E., *Angleterre*, 277, ff. 113-15.

arrival his hand was singularly strengthened by the news of Eugene's great victory of 5 August over the Turks at Peterwardein, which promised to relieve the Emperor of the Turkish menace and leave him free to carry out his obligations to England and attend to his Italian interests. Dubois's aim, on the other hand, was really confined to the one object of securing his master's succession to the throne against Philip V's pretensions. But, unfortunately for him, he could not lay his cards openly on the table, for he was instructed to ask for a guarantee of the whole Utrecht settlement[1] and not specifically of that one clause governing the French succession; otherwise

> 'les malintentionnés pourraient dire que Mgr. le Duc d'Orléans n'aura fait ce traité que pour son propre intérêt, et pour s'assurer la succession à la couronne de France après la mort du Roy, qu'il regarde comme prochaine.'[2]

To a general guarantee of the Utrecht settlement Stanhope was determined not to agree, since that would antagonize both our allies, the Dutch, who had not recognized Victor Amedeus as King of Sicily, and the Emperor, who was still nominally at war with Spain. In this resolution he had the whip hand of Dubois, since with the shrewd instinct of the able diplomat he had soon penetrated the motives of the French court and bluntly told Methuen that though

> 'the guaranty of the succession be the only true and real motive which induces the regent to seek his majesty's friendship, yet the abbé was instructed rather to have it brought in, as an accessory to the treaty, than to have an article so framed as should make it evident that was his only drift, and intent.'[3]

Above all, England could get along quite well without a treaty; to the Regent in his friendless state it was essential.

With these trump cards in his hand it says much for Stanhope's tactful diplomacy that when, after five days' discussion, a preliminary convention was agreed upon, Dubois wrote to the Regent that had he had such cards, 'by a show of greater dignity and *hauteur* we should have managed to obtain greater advantages' than Stanhope had secured. In fact Stanhope obtained all he wanted but forbore from

[1] It may be useful to recall that at Utrecht there were no less than eleven separate treaties, of which France signed seven; with England (two), with Portugal, with Prussia, with Savoy, with the Dutch (two), the rest being between Spain and England, Spain and Savoy, Spain and Holland, and Spain and Portugal.

[2] A.E., *Angleterre*, 277, ff. 226-7.   [3] Coxe, *Walpole*, ii. 69.

pressing his advantage against the Regent in non-essentials. Thus, to save the Regent's face among his people without abandoning his own principles, he agreed to a clause guaranteeing the provisions of Utrecht which affected English, Dutch and French interests without specifically mentioning the French succession: again, he agreed that the Regent should not be called upon to expel the Pretender before the treaty was signed but secured his object by stipulating that it should be done before ratification. But he took a firm stand against the inadequate French proposals about Dunkirk and Mardyk:

> 'Remember', he told Dubois, 'that when the French took Dunkirk in 1658, cardinal Mazarin gave it with all its fortifications standing, to Cromwell, just to secure his friendship. When your Regent needs us, permit me to tell you that he makes too much of a business of one wretched canal, which he assures us he intends to put to no bad use.'[1]

Dubois, by this time really frightened lest the whole treaty should fall to the ground, agreed that this clause should be left over for settlement to the satisfaction of the Admiralty by Iberville in London. On these terms, therefore, on 24 August a preliminary project was drafted by Stanhope and Dubois. Dubois was frankly overjoyed and described the agreement as 'almost a miracle'. But the business was not yet quite concluded. The Dunkirk clause had to be settled and the consent of the ministry in London obtained, and, if possible, the Dutch induced to come in as the third party to a triple alliance.

For the six more weeks consumed in these proceedings Dubois, though well enough lodged, as he admits, had to remain a close prisoner in Stanhope's house, 'every minute of that time counting as an hour does to a schoolboy kept in for some ungrateful task'. He is in constant agony lest his incognito or the object of his mission be disclosed, especially when an envoy from the Emperor appears on the scene, 'for the Emperor's star, or rather his comet—for it is a most alarming star—has a terrible influence on this court'; and it takes even more than Stanhope's assurance to convince him that this envoy knows nothing about him. Then comes another alarm: Sunderland is expected from England and he is 'the declared enemy of our alliance and of those concerned with it'; another mare's nest, since Sunderland

---

[1] Bourgeois, *Régent*, 117.

proved to be one of its most zealous supporters. There was more reason for his apprehension of delays in England, where, as Stanhope admits, there was no great enthusiasm for the treaty, and still more of intrigues and obstacles in Paris, where the Regent was finding it hard to stand up against the prejudices of the old court. So fearful was Dubois of his master's weakness that he spent most of his six weeks deluging him and his friends at court with impassioned appeals to get the business finished and make Iberville show a more conciliatory attitude about Mardyk: he even offered to go himself to London or to Paris to expedite matters. Then the poor man was seized with a serious illness, brought on no doubt by suspense and lack of exercise, and had to be attended by the King's physician. Almost his only relaxation consisted in talks with his genial host. Stanhope, as usual, was perfectly open with him. He admitted that he himself had distrusted the Regent at the outset, and that, even after his interviews at The Hague, he had found the King so set against the alliance that it had required three audiences before he could persuade him to allow Dubois to come to Hanover. He acknowledged that there was great regard for the Emperor's susceptibilities both in London and Hanover, and that they had been most careful not to insert anything in the treaty with France that could possibly prejudice the Emperor; if necessary he would himself go to Vienna once more to explain this. He frankly told Dubois that, though England needed peace, especially for the restoration of her finances, yet he would not be unduly disturbed even if the Regent played them false by rejecting the treaty at the last moment, for they would not want for allies, since other powers, and especially the Emperor, would always be glad of English help. Sometimes indeed Dubois had his little triumph. One day Stanhope announced with a sigh that he had to entertain at dinner sixteen heavy Hanoverians, who between them managed to get through seventy bottles of wine and six of brandy. After this orgy Stanhope passed through the communicating door for a more congenial chat with his French friend; but he also had helped to empty the bottles. So Dubois, always alert for business, was able to boast of having extracted from Stanhope, in his unguarded moment, confidences that might otherwise not have escaped him.[1]

[1] Dubois's alarms and talks with Stanhope are described in his letters of 28 and 31 Aug. in A.E., *Angleterre*, 277, ff. 274–88.

At last, after much vexatious haggling, Iberville, on peremptory orders from Paris, had proposed an expedient for making the Mardyk canal impassable for ships of war and privateers, to the complete satisfaction of the English sailors and engineers.[1] With this difficulty disposed of, the project of 24 August was redrafted in the form of a convention and signed by Stanhope and Dubois at Hanover on 9 October 1716. Dubois was at length brought out of his hiding-place and most graciously received at a public audience by George I. Five days later he was on his way to The Hague, armed with full powers to sign the treaty with the English and also, if possible, with the Dutch plenipotentiaries, and exuberant in his expressions of gratitude to the King and above all to Stanhope. He had indeed attempted to give a tangible form to this gratitude. At one of the most difficult stages in the negotiation, by order of the Regent he had offered him a *douceur* of £3,000 as a mark of friendship. Stanhope showed no indignation at the offer, merely remarking that it could cause no blush in any one to receive a mark of so great a prince's generosity, but that at least he must apply himself to render him some service. Seven or eight times Dubois renewed the offer and made a final attempt on the day of his departure. In those days it was considered no disgrace in most countries, after the conclusion of a successful negotiation, for a statesman to accept such a gift. Nevertheless Stanhope refused, but in such a way that his refusal appeared a compliment. Dubois, 'étonné d'un refus qu'il qualifie d'héroique et d'admirable', thus describes the incident to his master:

'Il me déclara que votre Altesse Royale était un grand prince qui pouvait dans mille occasions lui faire plaisir, qu'il me priait de lui faire mille remercîments des offres généreuses que je lui avais faites, qu'il avait estimé toute sa vie Votre Altesse Royale, et regardé comme le seul prince de l'Europe qui fût instruit, et que cette estime suffisait pour qu'il lui fût dévoué toute sa vie; qu'il ne m'avait pas dit sa pensée jusqu'à ce moment, de peur que cela ne me contraignît et ne me rendît moins hardi à lui proposer tout ce qui pouvait convenir à Votre Altesse Royale. Je n'oubliai rien pour l'ébranler, sans y réussir; toutes mes figures de rhétorique furent inutiles—Voilà le seul point de la négociation où j'ai totalement échoué.'

Still undefeated, Dubois hopes that at least the King and

[1] Coxe, *Walpole*, ii. 82–3, 11/22 Sept. 1716.

his minister will accept two parcels of wine, which he begs the Regent to procure and send forward: for the King '30 pièces de Champagne du plus fort . . . . et de bon vin de Sillery', for Stanhope '15 pièces de Champagne de la même qualité, 10 pièces de Bourgogne et du plus fort aussi, et cinq pièces de vin de Volnay'. It is to be hoped that these Gargantuan gifts were accepted; to Stanhope at any rate his would be welcome.[1]

But even after Dubois's arrival in Holland further difficulties arose. The Dutch were nervous of any new engagements and could always find an excuse for delay in the form of their constitution, whereby the refusal of even one of the seven provinces could hold up business indefinitely. The Emperor was afraid of the new alliance and was doing all he could to encourage opposition to it in Holland. Dubois and Stanhope, however, had arranged that, if the Dutch held back, England and France should sign it forthwith and let the Dutch come in afterwards. Dubois had always regarded the treaty as his own child and the only security for the rights of his pupil the Regent, and was afraid that delay would only strengthen the opposition of the old court party and of Philip's partisans or even affect the Regent's infirm purpose. A remarkable change had also come over the attitude of George I and Stanhope. Immediately after the collapse of the Rebellion they had been comparatively indifferent to the Regent's proposals and had only gradually been brought to see the value of a treaty which would clear away all differences between the two countries and might contribute to a stable settlement of Europe. As late as 8 September Stanhope wrote to London that the King would not mind if the treaty fell through, and his first intimation to Townshend that the King had become anxious for its immediate completion comes in a dispatch of 25 September (N.S.).[2]

This sudden change of attitude was due to none of the considerations which had hitherto weighed with George I and Stanhope in consenting, without great enthusiasm, to the treaty with France, but to ominous signs in the north of Europe. The Tsar Peter, hitherto in alliance with George as Elector by the Treaty of Greifswald of 1715, had suddenly

[1] Aubertin, 74 sqq.
[2] Coxe, *Walpole*, ii. 79, 84–5. These dates, as Michael, i. 762, points out, entirely rule out the suggestion of Wiesener, i. 301 sqq., that the small concessions made to Dubois by Stanhope in the first project of 24 Aug. were due to the King's anxiety at that time to conclude the treaty promptly.

shown a disposition to establish himself in Germany and had actually begun to quarter his troops in Mecklenburg, a neighbouring state in which Hanover had interests. This obviously affected only the Electorate, but on a wider view, to which Stanhope became converted, any disturbance of the Empire by the intrusion of an alien Power was bound to affect the general peace of Europe. More serious, however, from an English standpoint was a cooling off of the Tsar's antagonism to Charles XII of Sweden, just at the time when Charles appeared to be considering aggressive action against George. A report of 15 September (o.s.) indicated a revival of spirit in Jacobite circles at St. Germains and Avignon owing to expectations of an invasion of Scotland under Charles XII's auspices; and this report seemed to be shortly afterwards confirmed by letters of Gyllenborg, the Swedish envoy in London, that were intercepted by Townshend, indicating that he was in correspondence with the Jacobites both in England and France.[1] Serious and unexpected dangers from the north thus threatened both Hanover and Great Britain. To avert them the alliance with France suddenly seemed urgent to George and his counsellors at Hanover. For France by her ancient alliance with Sweden and her more recent relations with Russia, was the most influential of the western powers in the north: the treaty once made, this powerful influence would be on George's side, but, if the completion of the treaty were too long delayed, it might be cast in the scales of Sweden and Russia. Accordingly on 8 October (N.S.), the day before he signed the convention with Dubois at Hanover, Stanhope had sent the most urgent instructions to London to get the treaty completed, with or without the Dutch, at the earliest possible moment.[2]

The first difficulty came from Stanhope's former secretary Horatio Walpole, who was originally in charge of the negotiations for a triple alliance with Châteauneuf and the Dutch. These negotiations had been in abeyance while Stanhope and Dubois were discussing terms at Hanover; but Walpole had taken upon himself to assure the Dutch that no treaty would be concluded till they also were ready to sign; and he now refused to belie his word by signing without them.[3]

[1] *Instructions, Sweden*, i. 92; Coxe, *Walpole*, ii. 113–14, 120, 308–10.
[2] Coxe, *Walpole*, ii. 99, 100. For a fuller discussion of the northern troubles and of the ministerial crisis see below, ch. ix.
[3] H. Walpole says that he gave the assurance in the King's name (Coxe,

This difficulty might have been overcome by empowering Cadogan, also accredited to the States, to sign alone. But there were also difficulties in England. Townshend and Robert Walpole, with the rest of the Prince of Wales's advisers, had always insisted that the Dutch should be brought into the treaty at the same time as the French,[1] and were entirely unconvinced that England had any concern in these northern troubles or in the occupation of Mecklenburg by the Tsar. Townshend even sent word to Horatio Walpole that he and the Prince of Wales 'were entirely of your opinion as to the inconveniencys that may be apprehended from signing this treaty separately', and comforted him with the hope that contrary winds and other causes of delay might prevent his receiving his full powers for signing before the Dutch had agreed to come in. He also wrote to H. Walpole and Cadogan that the Prince of Wales thinks

> 'it would be in many ways the more preferable way to stay for the States, rather than to press the signing the Treaty with France without them. . . . However if the reasons His Majesty has for hastning this treaty should happen to overbalance them, we must submit to his Royal Pleasure.'[2]

Then a series of unfortunate mistakes in drawing up the full powers in London caused further delay. More than a fortnight elapsed before the first mistake had been rectified: nearly a month after that Cadogan's authority to sign was questioned as not being in proper form. These mistakes are not to be attributed to deliberate malice on Townshend's part, for, though he was self-willed and obstinate, he was not dishonest: but so many delays might not have occurred had he been whole-hearted in the business. Dubois himself also raised a difficulty at one stage about a sudden illness of the Pretender, which might make it impossible to remove him from Avignon before ratification: but this obstacle was surmounted by Stanhope's tact in assuring him that the King would not be unreasonable in the case of such an unforeseen accident. To the ministry in London Stanhope

---

Walpole, ii. 107); Stanhope tells Dubois that Walpole took it upon himself to do so (A.E., *Angleterre*, 277, f. 150); these two accounts are not necessarily contradictory. But it is to be noted that H. Walpole, writing to Robethon on 29 Aug. 1716, admits he told Buys that if the Dutch delayed too long England 'would make an allyance . . . with France without them' (*Stowe MSS*. 229, f. 62).

[1] R.O., *S.P.* 44/268, Townshend to Stanhope, 25 Aug. 1716.

[2] Coxe, *Walpole*, ii. 112–13; R.O., *S.P.* 104/81, 5 Oct. 1716.

pictured the dangers incurred by further procrastination, especially as Prussia had joined the Tsar and might drag in France. Finally the King, described by Stanhope to Dubois as now 'inébranlable', took a hand himself and wrote ordering Townshend to put an immediate end to all these difficulties.[1]

At last the treaty, in the form agreed upon by Dubois and Stanhope on 9 October, was signed at The Hague by Dubois and Cadogan as plenipotentiaries on 28 November 1716. The Dutch delayed coming in till they were brought to their senses by an ultimatum from Dubois and signed it on 4 January 1717, again with Dubois and Cadogan. Eleven days later Stanhope, coming from Hanover on his way back to England, met Dubois once more at The Hague, no longer, as had been the case six months before, as a suspect to be guarded against, but almost as an old crony, with their common task accomplished. They celebrated the occasion by burning their copies of the incomplete dual alliance of 28 November as no longer needed since the desired Triple Alliance of January 1717 had been brought into being.

'Votre voyage à la Haye, M. l'abbé, a sauvé bien du sang humain et il y aura bien des peuples qui vous auront obligation de leur tranquillité': in these words Stanhope complimented Dubois at the end of their labours. The compliment was not undeserved, but it applies to Stanhope even more than to Dubois. The idea of the alliance no doubt originated in the fertile brain of the little abbé, chiefly as a means of protecting his master's personal interests. Stanhope at first opposed it, but conquered his own original prejudices when he saw to what use it might be put for the general pacification of Europe. Having once adopted it, he carried it through, almost unaided by his own people, with the vehemence and enthusiasm he had sometimes devoted to worse causes. The alliance lasted nominally till the declaration of war between England and France in 1744: practically it was a potent factor in European politics till 1731. To England its advantage can hardly be exaggerated. It saved the country from any serious Jacobite danger during the crucial years when the Protestant dynasty was establishing itself in the habits, if not the affections, of the people; for, excluded from France, the

[1] R.O., *S.P.* 44/269; Coxe, *Walpole*, ii. 84–136; Wiesener, i. 489 sqq.

Jacobites were comparatively innocuous. The positive gain of French diplomatic assistance was apparent from the outset; for France had as yet lost little of the great prestige she had acquired under Louis XIV, her diplomatists were the most experienced and the ablest in Europe, and her influence with Germany and the northern Powers supplied that in which England was deficient. Barely six months after the signature of the treaty the Regent's offices, according to Dubois, had induced the Tsar to clear his troops out of Mecklenburg, a signal justification of Stanhope's and the King's eagerness to conclude promptly; and by the same means Charles XII was induced to disavow his intriguing envoys Goertz and Gyllenborg.[1] Until the advent to power of Fleury in 1726, and for some time after, England under Stanhope and Walpole set the tone of the two Powers' joint policy, for the Regent and Dubois depended on Stanhope even against some of their own people, and their successor Bourbon was not one to hold his own against Walpole and Townshend. Nor did English statesmen during the active period of the alliance allow themselves to be lulled by a false sense of security to neglect the navy or England's colonial and commercial interests. France also found her profit in the alliance. She was preserved thereby from the worst dangers of a disputed claim to the throne during Louis XV's minority, and the Regent's government was materially strengthened. Still more was France saved from the formidable coalition of Spain and the Emperor in 1725 by England's loyalty to the alliance, when she had many inducements to abandon it. Its value was not even confined to the chief signatories, England and France. During the uneasy years between 1716 and 1731 when Europe was trying to find her bearings after the War of the Spanish Succession and the catastrophic northern war, the union of the two chief western powers, though it did not entirely prevent disturbance, helped materially to limit its area and finally to evolve a pacific settlement. Above all, Italy, since the fall of Rome the prey of ravening conquerors, for the first time, largely through the interposition of England and France, was given the beginnings of a system not entirely alien to the wishes of Italians. The Triple Alliance has indeed some points in common with the Entente of 1904, also comprising England and France. In both cases the

[1] R.O., *S.P.* 104/219 B, Dubois to Stanhope, 14 June 1717.

avowed object was not only to appease ancient quarrels between two great nations, but to work for the preservation of European peace. Who shall say that Stanhope and Dubois were less successful than Lansdowne and Delcassé? This at least is clear, that the Triple Alliance of 1717 was Stanhope's greatest achievement in foreign policy.

CHAPTER IX

THE NORTHERN WAR AND THE BREAK-UP
OF THE MINISTRY

§ 1

WHEN Norris was sent to the Baltic in 1715 George I
and his Hanoverian advisers had a purpose of their
own distinct from the purely English object of trade protection. To realize Stanhope's difficulties between these two
policies one must cast one's eyes for a moment on northern
Europe. Here was that great Swedish empire, built up by
Gustavus Adolphus and his successors, ready to fall to pieces.
When that meteoric genius Charles XII had succeeded to
the throne in 1697 this empire had comprised not only
Sweden itself and Finland but all the territories on the other
side of the Baltic, and great possessions, notably Pomerania
and Bremen and Verden, in the north of Germany. After
a few brilliant campaigns resulting in further conquests
Charles XII had staked and lost almost all by the mad
incursion into Russia which ended in disaster at Poltava.
This proved the opportunity for the neighbouring Powers
who had all been watching for the moment to secure the
prize that suited each best. Denmark and the north German
princes of Hanover and Prussia hoped to expel the Swedes
from their possessions in the Empire and share the spoils
among themselves, while Russia and Poland looked to expel
them from their possessions on the Baltic. Already Russia,
that great new Power in the north, had captured Ingria and
most of the other provinces on her side of the Baltic. In
1712 Denmark had conquered the Swedish province of
Bremen, coterminous with Hanover and commanding the
mouth of the Elbe. Denmark was hardly strong enough
to retain this province, long an object of George's ambition,
as giving him access to the sea and providing him with a port
of his own as a connecting link with England. Accordingly
George had sent troops into Verden, the province next to
Bremen, also belonging to the Swedes, to save it from the
Danes, and made a series of treaties to secure both provinces
for the Electorate. In November 1714 he obtained Prussia's
consent, in July 1715 he induced the Danes to sell them to
him for £150,000, and in the following October, by the

Treaty of Greifswald, he engaged the Tsar Peter to guarantee to him their possession.[1] Naturally George did not obtain these treaties for mere motives of benevolence, but on condition that he in turn assisted them to obtain advantages from Sweden. Denmark wanted help in asserting disputed claims to the Holstein duchies, Prussia in conquering Swedish Pomerania, and the Tsar in securing his conquests from Charles XII. By all these treaties George was committed as Elector to hostilities with Sweden, but his allies did not reckon much on his assistance in that capacity, but chiefly on the naval support they hoped to get from him as King of England.

Here, then, were the elements of a pretty tangle. England was not only nominally at peace with Sweden but bound by a treaty of 1700 to aid Sweden against her enemies. It is true England had serious grievances against Charles XII for interference with her commerce, and was perfectly entitled to protect her traders and even to make reprisals on Sweden for her losses; for, according to the vague ideas of international law then current, such proceedings were quite compatible with the maintenance of the alliance and the defence of Sweden against aggressors, as contemplated by the treaty of 1700.[2] But to make an open attack on her possessions would be a breach of international faith: it would also run counter to England's established policy of maintaining the *status quo* in the Baltic. Above all, it might be held to conflict with the clause in the Act of Settlement forbidding any war in 'defence of any Dominions or Territories which do not belong to the Crown of England, without the consent of Parliament'. Thus George I found his engagements as King and as Elector hard to reconcile. So when asked by the King of Prussia in 1715 what part Norris's fleet would take against Sweden, he merely vouchsafed the following vague and unsatisfactory assurance:

'We promise the King of Prussia on Our royal faith and troth that the said squadron shall in every way second operations in

[1] For these treaties see Chance, 70–1.

[2] The classic instances in the eighteenth century of these loose conceptions of belligerency are in the War of the Austrian Succession, when the French, nominally at peace with Maria Theresa, were helping her adversaries with their armies, and when George I at Dettingen defeated a French army without any declaration of war and without incurring any reproach. Russia's action against England at the time of the first Armed Neutrality is another case in point. Even in our own century Italy, though at war with Austria from the spring of 1915, did not declare war against Germany until a year later.

Pomerania against Sweden, and hope his Prussian Majesty will believe Our word that there will be no want in the fulfilling of this promise. But we could not give a written engagement, since the providing of this squadron pertains to Us as King, and if We gave a written engagement We could not use Our German ministers, but We should have to give it by the hands of English ministers.'

This answer puts in a nutshell the difficulty George found in distinguishing between his electoral and royal functions, a difficulty peculiarly irritating to his English subjects. As he said to his electoral envoy in Berlin, 'it is to be hoped that We shall not be urged to have superfluous and unnecessary demonstrations of hostility made against Sweden... since this would only cause Us *embarras* here, and would do no good there'. Nevertheless, in October 1715 he declared war as Elector against Sweden, and Norris was given to understand that he was to make himself as unpleasant to the Swedes and as helpful to their adversaries as possible.[1]

Townshend's formal instructions to Norris of May 1715 and his later directions convey no hint that he was to exceed his duty of securing the trade and making reprisals for losses. But George had other means of communicating with Norris than through the Secretary of State. Robethon, Bernstorff's confidential man and George's secretary, was very convenient for such a purpose, since it was not always clear whether the orders he transmitted came from the King or the Elector. Bernstorff himself, with less excuse, also on occasion conveyed the King's wishes to those charged with English interests; and it was a bold man in those days who refused to obey royal orders even by such an irregular channel. It was Bernstorff, according to the Prussian envoy, who saw Norris privately after he had received his formal instructions from Townshend and told him what the King really wished him to do. So it was that in his first expedition in 1715, though Norris took no ostensible part in the operations against Stralsund, where Danes, Prussians, and Russians were besieging Charles XII, yet by his presence in the Baltic he materially helped the more aggressive action of Russians and Danes. Moreover, when he was on the point of returning with his convoy of traders, he received an order from Townshend

---

[1] Stoerk, who has an excellent account, based on Hanoverian state papers, of George's relations with Peter 1715–16. Chance, *passim*, is essential for all these dealings with Sweden.

to leave eight of his ships under Hopson to continue reprisals against the Swedes, this being the pretext given by George to Townshend for issuing this order. No Swedish prizes were taken, but this English reinforcement just enabled the Danes to continue their operations in security. For Hopson, being too weak to act alone, was instructed to join the Danish fleet, and by obligingly stringing out his ships round the island of Rügen effectually prevented the Swedes from throwing succours into the beleaguered city. Stralsund, after an heroic defence, fell in December: and George could point out with some truth to Prussia that, though as King he had not declared war, his English fleet had materially contributed to this result. In October he had already reaped his Electoral reward by obtaining delivery of Bremen and Verden from Denmark.[1]

In 1716 Norris was again sent to escort the merchantmen to the Baltic, but this time with more explicit directions from Townshend for vigorous action against Sweden. This seemed necessary to the English ministry, partly because of the increasing audacity of the Swedish privateers, one of whom actually captured an English ship off Yarmouth and took her off as prize to Gothenburg,[2] but chiefly owing to their fear of another Jacobite rising supported by Sweden. For Stair in Paris and other agents reported that the Pretender's people were counting on Charles XII's assistance, and especially on his projected attack on Norway, where they hoped to find a convenient base for a descent on England. Later, in July, when Norris's letter peremptorily demanding reparation for past injuries had been contemptuously ignored by Charles XII, the admiral was further instructed in the King's name that,

'Whereas We are informed that Our dear brother the king of Sweden has thought fit, instead of answering the memorial which you had transmitted to him by Our order, not to receive the same but to send back your packetts unopened',

he was to join the English fleet with that of 'Our dear brother the king of Denmark', actively to pursue reprisals and to drive the Swedish ships off the sea. By this time the English court had moved to Hanover and these northern affairs were

[1] Townshend's official Instructions to Norris are in *Instructions, Sweden,* i. 74 sqq. Michael, i. 716–33 gives useful information based on the German and Austrian archives. See also Chance, 90 sqq.

[2] *Stowe MSS.* 229, f. 149.

practically taken out of Townshend's hands. Decisions were taken by George I, mainly in consultation with Bernstorff, and the correspondence with Norris went through Stanhope's hands.

Already, however, the confederates who had planned to divide the Swedish lion's skin had begun to fall out among themselves. George I and the Tsar had for some time been exchanging somewhat acid epistles. After congratulating George on being the first to obtain his portion in Bremen and Verden the Tsar suggests that he should now come out openly against Sweden with his English fleet and also send troops to assist him and Prussia to reduce Wismar in Mecklenburg, and Stettin in Pomerania: George in reply depreciates the value of Bremen and Verden and reiterates that as King he cannot appear openly as Charles's enemy; but he shows considerable alarm at Peter's proposal to land troops in Germany, and urges that before such a step is taken, at any rate the Emperor should be consulted.[1] The idea was distasteful to George for two reasons. The presence of the Swede in Germany was bad enough, but that of the Tsar would be as obnoxious and far more dangerous. He also had a special objection to the Russians meddling in Mecklenburg on the borders of Hanover, for he himself was interested in the politics of that duchy and his minister Bernstorff and others of his court owned several of its villages.[2] Hardly less strained were now becoming the relations between George and his son-in-law and nephew Frederick William. The King of Prussia, it is true, had no great desire to see the Russians in Mecklenburg, for he himself had a reversionary interest in the succession to the duchy; but he had a wholesome fear of the Tsar's capacity to invade his outlying possession of Prussia, and even to cross his wholly unprotected eastern frontier of Brandenburg; he also had great need of Russian help to secure Stettin and other parts of Pomerania. Further, he had no love for George and great jealousy of the royal eminence he had attained. Accordingly when he had to make the choice between Tsar and Elector he chose the former. He refused an invitation to Hanover and arranged a meeting with Peter at Havelberg to settle the terms of closer co-opera-

[1] Peter's letter of 26 Mar. and George's answer of 1/12 May in Stoerk.

[2] Mecklenburg was distracted by a long-standing dispute between the Duke and his nobles. In Oct. 1717 George as Elector was given an Imperial commission to restore order and levy execution on the recalcitrant Duke. See Chance, 225 and below, ch. xiii, p. 361.

tion. Thus George as Elector found himself deserted by his two principal allies and left with only Denmark, a weak and bankrupt state, more of a burden than a help to her friends.[1]

Great then was the agitation in Hanover when, at the end of September, news came that the Tsar had given up the proposed expedition against Scania, the southern promontory of Sweden, and seemed disposed to keep his troops in winter quarters in Denmark and Mecklenburg.[2] In a letter to Townshend of 25 September Stanhope graphically describes the excitement. 'Mr. Bernsdorf', he writes, 'thinks it necessary to crush the czar immediately, to secure his ships, and even to seize his person to be kept till his troops shall have evacuated Denmark and Germany.' Stanhope himself was hardly less excited:

> 'I do verily believe', he continues, 'things will come to an eclat, perhaps before I can have an answer from you. I shall check my own nature upon this occasion, which was ever inclined to bold strokes, till I can hear from you.'

He wrote off to Norris and Polwarth, the English envoy at Copenhagen, to protest in the King's name against the violation of Danish territory, for though Mecklenburg might solely concern Hanover, England was bound by treaty to Denmark. He ended his letter to Townshend by adjuring him above all to get the French treaty concluded, since the French alone had influence in the north and could checkmate any Jacobite schemes to fish in those troubled waters;

> 'I am perhaps too easily alarmed, but I confess that I think it will be of fatal consequence, if the negociation should miscarry; which it certainly will do, if this eclat in the North breaks out before we have finished. . . . I was, you know, very averse at first to this treaty, but I think truly as things now stand we ought not to lose a minute in finishing it.'[3]

To Townshend and Walpole all this excitement seemed a storm in a tea-cup, and they refused to accept the view that

---

[1] For George's relations with Frederick William at this juncture see Droysen, iv. 181 sqq. and Chance, 174 sqq. The Tsar's meeting with Frederick William at Havelberg did not actually take place till the end of November, just before the signature of the Anglo-French treaty by Dubois and Cadogan.

[2] The rendezvous for the Russo-Danish expedition against Scania had been the Danish province of Zealand. When Peter refused to proceed with the expedition he kept some of his troops in Zealand and sent the rest over to Mecklenburg. All his troops had left Zealand by October. See Chance, 130, 144.

[3] Coxe, *Walpole*, ii. 84, to Townshend, 25 Sept.; R.O., *S.P.* 44/269, to Norris and Polwarth, 26 Sept.

Hanover's troubles with the Baltic powers were a reason for
such a desperate hurry about signing the English treaty with
France. Horatio Walpole, too, from the Hague wrote:

> 'I can't for my life see the connection between our immediate
> signing and that affair, or why the whole system of affairs in
> Europe, especially in relation to the interest of England, must
> be entirely subverted on account of Mecklenbourgh.'

Townshend, indeed, with more reason, saw that it would
never do for the Tsar to get complete control of the Baltic,
but he was not far wrong in complaining that 'this Northern
war has been managed so stupidly, that it will be our ruin'.
He even ventured to condemn George's mistakes in no
measured terms. As if it were not enough to have Sweden as
an enemy planning a Jacobite raid, he must needs antagonize the Tsar, Sweden's most powerful adversary, and also
Frederick William, 'by the jealousy that has long prevailed
between our court and that of Prussia'. The 'greatness of
the Czar' he attributed partly to this jealousy of Prussia,
partly to George's parsimony in 'not caring to be at the
expense of having a sufficient number of his own troops to
support the figure he ought to have made [by bringing up his
electoral army] to such number . . . as shall shew the czar,
that his majesty does intend to be master so near home.'
He added that while agreeing with Stanhope that 'England
as well as the rest of Europe, ever had and always must have
a great interest in the preservation of the ballance of the
north', yet, if Parliament were asked for assistance upon the
present footing of northern affairs, 'there would be great
danger from such a step of ruining his credit and influence
in both houses'.[1]

Such criticisms of the King's Baltic policy only served to
accentuate the differences due to other causes between London
and Hanover. Robert Walpole had already offended the
King by contradicting him on a question of fact as to payments due to some German troops raised by Munster and
Saxe Gotha but not employed in suppressing the Rebellion.[2]
More serious still was the impression subtly conveyed to
George that, in spite of all the care he had taken to limit his
son's powers as Guardian of the Realm, his Ministers were
in league with the Prince of Wales against him. During his

    [1] Coxe, *Walpole*, ii. 86 sqq.
    [2] Ib. 108–9, 115–17, 125, 135.

absence letters came at least twice a week from Bothmer, the Hanoverian envoy in London, to Robethon in Hanover with full details of all the Prince's and courtiers' proceedings; in addition a weekly 'feuillet', or news-sheet, prepared by Schrader, a Hanoverian secretary of legation, was sent to the King himself and eight of his principal German advisers.[1] These reports all emphasized the efforts, in marked contrast with the King's aloofness, of the Prince and his witty and capable Princess to court the affections of the people. During their sojourn at Hampton Court they kept open house and made disaffected Whigs like Argyll, and even Tories, as welcome as the regular court party; everybody seemed happy there except some of the ladies, 'qui se plaignent un peu de l'excés des promenades, et d'estre obligés de monter si haut pour venir à leurs chambres'. Rumours are quoted as current that the King meant to leave the government of England entirely to the Prince in order to 'vivre en repos à Hannover', and that Stanhope was to be superseded as Secretary by Methuen. Ample details are given of the Prince's progress to Portsmouth to review the troops and of his great reception at the houses of the nobility where he broke his journey. The Duke of Dorset provided dinner at five tables, holding twelve to fifteen people each, and at two more, each for fifty of 'les gens plus ordinaires'; while the Duke of Newcastle, to save the Prince fatigue in the evening, entertained only thirty guests at dinner, but made up for it next day by having 4,000 people to a *déjeuner*. So popular were these manifestations of the Prince's forthcoming disposition that loyal addresses began pouring in with hardly veiled comparisons of his affability with his father's coldness. The Prince, indeed, had the wisdom to send them back with the intimation that loyal addresses had better wait till the King's return: none the less the King became convinced that his son was trying to supplant him. The influence of Argyll, already in disgrace with the King, was represented to him as greater than ever, especially in Scotland, where 'une des premières cours du Royaume ose refuser de suivre les ordres du Roy, et mépriser la commission signée de sa main, parceque la personne n'est pas agréable au duc d'Argyll'. Care also was taken to emphasize the difference between London and Hanover about Sweden: 'je ne trouve rien de si vrai que ce que ce vous dîtes, Monsieur, sur les affaires du Nord', runs a

[1] *Stowe MSS.* 229, 230 (*Robethon Papers*).

report to Robethon, 'que nos Ministres ont tort d'avoir tant de ménagements avec la Suède'.[1]

Such reports, together with the complaints coming from Walpole and Townshend in their turn about the Hanoverian ministers, and their delays in forwarding effective full powers to Cadogan and Horatio Walpole, had a cumulative effect in antagonizing the King. But the most convincing proof to George I that his son and his ministers in London were in league against him came from a proposal of their own. For some time they had been urging the King to return before the end of the year to open Parliament, and finally, failing to obtain a satisfactory answer, suggested that if the King meant to stay much longer in Hanover the Prince should not only be empowered to open Parliament but have further discretionary powers granted him to deal with matters that might arise in debate.[2] Stanhope himself also began to share the King's views, especially when he found his own treaty with France delayed by what appeared to him the unnecessary punctilios of his colleagues.

The dual capacity of George as King and Elector certainly lent itself to more confusion and friction than would be the case to-day. The present theory of our constitution makes it much easier for a man with dual functions to keep them distinct and for us to understand such a possibility. For example, a Governor-General of South Africa is a purely constitutional figure-head incapable of taking any action except on the advice of his South African ministers: hitherto the same man has also been High Commissioner for South Africa with wide powers over native territories under the King's protectorate, and in this capacity has had to take decisions on his own responsibility. The distinction between the two functions has been fully understood, and there has been no confusion between them.[3] But although, since 1689, the evolution of the King from the status of personal ruler to that of figure-head and mouth-piece of his ministers had begun, it was far from complete and barely appreciated by political thinkers. The King was still regarded as having a personality and will of his own; and, in spite of attempts in the Act of Settlement, it was still hard to distinguish exactly

[1] 'Feuillet' of 13/24 Nov. 1716. This report may have finally decided the King to dismiss Townshend from the secretaryship; see below, p. 245.
[2] Coxe, *Walpole*, ii. 123.
[3] It has recently been decided to appoint a High Commissioner for South Africa distinct from the Governor-General: but this does not affect the argument.

between his functions as Elector and as King. This was especially the case with ministers who were in constant contact with him and looked on him, as in fact he was, as the chief source of their power. The first revolt against this confusion of the King's dual personalities naturally came from Walpole and Townshend during their six months in England away from the light of his countenance. Stanhope, less experienced in English administration, was then less troubled by the dangers of German interference, and from his facilities at Hanover for closer observation of conditions in north-eastern Europe, had become more impressed than his colleagues by England's real interests in these Baltic difficulties. Later he also began to appreciate some of the evil effects of Hanoverian influences on English policy and ultimately succeeded in throwing them off more effectively than Walpole and Townshend were able to do by their present querulous attitude.

Many of the English ministers' complaints about the Hanoverians were undoubtedly justified. It was intolerable that they should be spied on and reported on behind their backs by Hanoverian agents. Nor was this supervision the less galling from the greed of these foreigners, who incidentally took good care to feather their own nests and claim English perquisites as legitimate plunder for themselves. Schrader, for example, complains to Robethon that the 'Bord du Green Cloth' has refused his demand for 'bougies' on the ground that

'eux, les étrangers, avoient consumé beaucoup. J'ai cru que sans peine je pourrois me faire continuer ces petits profits', he represents to Robethon, '(et) comme cela m'a la mine que ces Messieurs voudroient ôter par envie ces petits profits aux étrangers, il seroit bon, tant pour votre intérêt que pour celui des autres étrangers que vous parlassiez la dessus à Mr Stanhope ou à Mr Boscawen.'[1]

Robethon probably did not attack Stanhope on this question, for Stanhope was certainly not the man to give away English 'bougies' to predatory Germans. But even in 1720, when the influence of the Hanoverians had been severely curtailed, Craggs complains to Stanhope that Bothmer had taken in a piece of St. James's Park, 'which gives great distaste, and one sees all the

---

[1] *Stowe MSS.* 229, f. 284. The Board of Green Cloth provided for the needs and perquisites of the royal household. The allowances of candles and such-like were no doubt greatly in excess of the recipients' needs and enabled them to dispose profitably of the surplus.

common people as they walk stop and complain of it'.[1] Walpole
was also fully justified in objecting to the immense if indeter-
minate powers as 'domestick secretary' of Robethon, whom
he once publicly qualified as 'a mean fellow (of what nation
I know not) who is anxious to dispose preferments'. Lady
Cowper, who curtly dismisses him as 'a knave' and quotes
the Princess's description of him as 'insupportable when he
pretends to be witty or pleasant', illustrates his rapacity by
stories of his selling the clerkship of the Parliaments to her
brother-in-law for £1,800 and of his being 'entirely gained'
to the Prince of Wales by a pension of £300. More serious
was his constant meddling with foreign affairs. The correspondence of Lord Polwarth, who was envoy to Denmark from
1716 to 1721, amply illustrates this habit of his. Although
there was also a Hanoverian envoy at Copenhagen, Robethon
writes to Polwarth by every mail, and is answered by
Polwarth in letters more frequent and fuller than those to
Stanhope. Robethon gains his correspondent's goodwill by
being the first to announce to him that he has been made
Lord Register of Scotland and by encouraging his ambition
to obtain the 'green ruban' of the Thistle, 'to give His
Majesty's minister an air'. Having thus secured his man, he
gives him secret orders sometimes directly contrary to the
Secretary of State's, and, as a precaution in such cases, with
the postscript, 'brûlez ceci'. Stanhope, for example, writing
on 3/14 November 1716, tells Polwarth that the squadron
left in the Baltic by Norris was to return home; on the very
same day Robethon bids him keep it, as 'the King expects
this and will be displeased if it is not done'. Sometimes,
however, Robethon came across men less complaisant than
Polwarth. One such was the bluff and illiterate Norris, who
writes to Polwarth in June 1718:

'I observe robetons to you ses he dus not dout our hindering the
Russians joyning the Swedes. Now I would ask you a question
. . . have I any orders to give them battell or make warr upon
them? I thinck not, and our frind in that ses more then becurns
him without getting the King's commands signified to me.'

Stanhope had obviously no very high opinion of Robethon,
but as certainly underrates his capacity for mischief when,
in answer to Townshend's complaints, he writes:

'As for Robethon you know he is naturally impertinent and

busying himself, but at present the man certainly does not mean ill, and tho' he did, I do not think it will be proper to complain to the king of him at this time. I will endeavour to give him some advice and shall, I believe, prevent his doing any hurt.'[1]

Thus all the elements of an explosion, or as Stanhope would have said an *éclat*, between Hanover and London were present. The man who applied the spark seems to have been Sunderland. With all the talent for intrigue of his father, James II's minister, he had none of his suavity, being noted for his rashness and overbearing disposition. Intensely ambitious and, as Marlborough's son-in-law, powerful politically in the last reign, he had been the first member of the Whig Junto to obtain office in 1706, and two years later had been mainly instrumental in the fall of Harley and St. John. He was one of the chief supporters of Sacheverell's ill-advised impeachment, so justifying Somers's 'constant fear of his bringing all things into confusion by his boldness and inexperience'. The first of the Whigs to be dismissed in 1710, he had shown his factiousness in opposition by supporting the Occasional Conformity Bill, directed against his former allies the Dissenters, and by advocating the repeal of the Union he had helped to draft. But with all his faults it may be put to his credit that he was not corrupt in money matters, and that though he had two expensive tastes, gambling and acquiring priceless *incunabula* for his incomparable library at Althorp. On his dismissal he refused a pension of £3,000, saying, 'if I cannot have the honour to serve my country I will not plunder her'. Nor did he ever swerve in his support of the Hanoverian Succession; in fact he had been one of the most forward in suggesting extreme measures to secure it. Great, then, had been his disillusion when he found himself omitted from George's council of Regency after the Queen's death and, instead of being Secretary of State, relegated to the comparative obscurity of Ireland. He never went to Ireland nor did he long retain the office, exchanging it in 1715 for that of Privy Seal. During the first month of the King's absence in Hanover he did his utmost to overcome the bad impression his erratic proceedings had created in the minds of Walpole and Townshend, in order to pave the way to a position of greater influence. His next step was to discover that his health

[1] Lady Cowper, 42, 87, 101; Coxe, *Walpole*, ii. 93, 109, 111; *H. MSS.*, *Polwarth*, i, ii, *passim*.

required him to take the waters of Aix, whence it would seem
only natural to go on to Hanover to pay his respects to the
King. Knowing that he was not looked on with favour by
either the King or Stanhope, he took care to obtain a letter
from Walpole to Stanhope urging that permission should
be given him for the journey, and consulted both Walpole
and Townshend as to his conduct at Hanover. Stanhope
in reply assured Walpole that there need be no fear that
Sunderland would be able to exercise undue influence at
court, since it was only with the greatest difficulty that the
King had been induced to give the required permission.
Lady Cowper, with truer insight, saw that this journey
portended a revolution in the ministry.[1]

Sunderland, fresh from England, seems to have confirmed
the King in his suspicions of plots being formed against him
by the Prince and his advisers, for in later years the Prince
spoke of him as 'that scoundrel and puppy and knave' who
had induced his father to disbelieve his word. Townshend
also declared he had seen a letter from Sunderland charging
himself, Walpole and the Chancellor with having entered
into engagements with the Prince and Argyll against the
King's authority.[2] Sunderland no doubt also insinuated to
Stanhope that the delays in signing the French treaty at
The Hague were not accidental but a deliberate attempt by
Townshend and the Walpoles to impede Stanhope's policy.
Even without such suggestions a man much less impetuous
and hot tempered than Stanhope might well have been
deeply hurt by the stream of criticism from his colleagues
ever since he announced to them that he had signed the
convention with Dubois and told them the reasons that
seemed good to himself and the King for haste. These
criticisms, coupled with the unaccountable delays in sending
proper full powers to The Hague, made him feel that they
were deliberately disclaiming responsibility for his actions.
So acutely did he feel this that early in November he put his
own resignation in the King's hands.

George I refused to accept Stanhope's resignation; on the
contrary he ordered him to write to Townshend demanding
an explanation of the blunders and delays about the full

[1] Coxe, *Walpole*, ii. 59, 79. These letters show that in his text, i. 96, Coxe is
wrong in suggesting that Walpole urged Stanhope to prevent Sunderland
coming to Hanover. Lady Cowper, 121–5.
[2] Coxe, *Walpole*, ii. 160.

powers. Not only that, but the King himself wrote a letter to Townshend in his own hand to the same effect, 'a thing he has not done to his ministers since he came to the throne', Stanhope informs Dubois.[1] Stanhope's dignified letter of 11 November, more sorrowful than reproachful, dwelt on the unaccountable hitches that had occurred in drawing up the full powers and on the marked silence with which the news of his signing the convention with Dubois had been received by Townshend:

'tout cela ensemble, my lord, je vous avoue, me fait imaginer que ce que j'ay fait icy est tellement désapprouvé, que l'on se tient sur ses gardes pour ne pas faire une démarche, qui puisse m'avouer.'

This letter could hardly have aroused Townshend's indignation to the pitch it did, had it not been accompanied by a hectoring and insolent letter from Sunderland, none of whose business it was. Townshend was as hot tempered as Stanhope and was not the man to brook being addressed thus by Sunderland:

'I must be so plain as to tell you, that I never saw the king resent anything so much, as this affair, in which he thinks not only Mr secretary Stanhope but himself not well used; and indeed I think it wants to be explained';

or being told, however just the criticism may have been, that his want of interest in the Northern troubles

'is nothing but the old Tory notion, that England can subsist by itself, whatever becomes of the rest of Europe, which has been so justly exploded ever since the revolution.'

Townshend replied by a long letter of explanation to the King, in which, while admitting some carelessness in the preparation of the full powers and pleading some ill luck, he disculpates himself of intentional disobedience. To Stanhope he merely enclosed a copy of his letter to the King with this sad note of reproach,

'my heart is so full with the thoughts of having received this usage from you, to whom I have always been a faithful friend, that you will excuse my not saying more at this time. I pray God forgive you; I do.'

Sunderland's letter he ignored.[2]

[1] A.E., *Angleterre*, 286, f. 187, 14 Nov. 1716.
[2] Coxe, *Walpole*, ii. 126 sqq.

On 22 November (N.s.) when Townshend was writing these letters of explanation and reproach to the King and Stanhope, Horatio Walpole arrived at Hanover with the unfortunate dispatch pressing for the opening of Parliament and suggesting the grant of extended powers to the Prince of Wales. The King would not hear of any such proposal and ordered Parliament to be prorogued till January, when he expected to be in England himself. But in his talks with Stanhope Horatio Walpole gathered that 'all past misunderstandings would be entirely forgotten, and a happy union and harmony be once more re-established between his majesty's faithfull and honest servants'; and on his return to England early in December he was charged with messages and letters of goodwill to Townshend and Robert Walpole. Delayed by various accidents on the way he did not reach London till 22 December (N.s.). He at once saw Walpole and Townshend and by the letters he brought and his reports of Stanhope's conversation felt he had succeeded in his mission of conciliation and that the old friendly relations between the two brothers[1] and Stanhope would be re-established. But that same evening all his hopes were dashed to the ground by a bomb-shell that widened the breach irreparably. A King's messenger sent from Hanover more than a week after Horatio's departure arrived with a curt letter from Stanhope to Townshend informing him that the King had dismissed him from his office of Secretary and appointed him Lord-Lieutenant of Ireland with a seat in the Cabinet. Another letter to Robert Walpole urged him to persuade Townshend to accept 'the greatest employment a King of England has to give'. In this letter Stanhope does not profess to understand fully the motives for this sudden change of front by the King but makes it clear that neither he nor Sunderland had any hand in the business:

> 'His Majesty', he writes, 'hath been more uneasy of late than I care to say; and I must own, I think he has reason, tho' I don't pretend to know so much of the matter as the king does; his majesty receiving many advices, which come neither through my hands nor my lord Sunderland's. But I cannot help observing to you, that he is jealous of certain intimacys with the two brothers',

evidently referring to Bothmer's reports on Argyll's influence

[1] Robert Walpole and Townshend, who had married Walpole's sister, are frequently referred to in the correspondence of the time as 'the two brothers'.

and especially, no doubt, to the most recent of them that criticized the ministry's attitude on Northern policy.[1] In a later letter he replies to Walpole's charge of breach of friendship by revealing that he was responsible for 'procuring the offer of Ireland, at a time when the King was determined he should not be Secretary'. Townshend, however, resolutely refused to accept Ireland, briefly informing Stanhope that he had been 'weak enough to think your partiality to me had given you a favourable opinion of my services', but that Stanhope's last letter made him dismiss 'this idle notion'. Walpole wrote some angry letters to Stanhope, who sent more and more conciliatory answers, till finally he had to tell Methuen, Secretary in Townshend's place, that if the brothers persisted in a sullen refusal of any accommodation,

'they may possibly unking their master, or (which I do before God think very possible) make him abdicate England; but they will certainly not force him to make my lord Townshend secretary.'

In London the news of Townshend's dismissal created great excitement and alarm. Many feared that it implied a complete victory of German over English influence in the administration. Brereton, the messenger who brought over Stanhope's letters, wrote in an exaggerated strain to Charles Stanhope at Hanover that

'the town is in greater confusion now than it was in any part, or at any alterations whatsoever made in the late Queen's reign, and all public credit will continue daily to sink till his majesty's arrival.'[2]

Philip Yorke, then a rising young barrister of the Middle Temple, wrote that, though Sunderland was believed to be chiefly to blame for the change, Stanhope 'does not stand clear of suspicion in this affair' and that the offer of Ireland was 'thought a grimace'; at the same time, with precocious shrewdness, he attributes Townshend's disgrace to his lukewarmness to the French treaty, his favour to Argyll, his objection to the repeal of the disabling clause in the Act of Settlement, and his opposition to a standing army.[3]

The strain was to some extent eased on the King's return at the end of January. On information they received in Holland not only Stanhope and Sunderland but the King himself saw

[1] See above, pp. 237–8. [2] Coxe, *Walpole*, ii. 139 sqq.
[3] *Add. MSS.* 35, 584, f. 163, 22 Dec. 1716.

reason to believe that they had been misled by the Germans as to any deliberate intention on Townshend's part to obstruct the French treaty; they were also impressed by the anxiety felt by some of the leading Dutchmen lest Whig dissensions should give an opening to the Tories.[1] As soon as he arrived in London the King received Townshend, admitted he might have made a mistake and persuaded him to accept Ireland. He even persuaded him and Walpole to go to dinner with Sunderland and make friends over a bottle. 'Then all will go merrily', writes Robethon, 'and the friends of these Lords in Parliament will concur unanimously to carry matters along all right.'[2] But the reconciliation was only superficial. Townshend was touchy and apt to brood over real or fancied slights. Besides, both his and Walpole's view of Northern policy was fundamentally opposed to Stanhope's. The next measure taken by Stanhope widened the breach irreparably.

Townshend himself had been the first to discover some correspondence implicating the Swedish ambassador Gyllenborg in Jacobite plots, but he had treated it chiefly as an argument against George's policy.[3] Stanhope now felt justified in persuading the Cabinet to have Gyllenborg arrested and his papers impounded. It appeared from these papers, which were in part published, that not only Gyllenborg but also Sparre, the Swedish ambassador at Paris, were both involved in the scheme of which Goertz at The Hague, who professed to have full powers from Charles XII, was the prime mover. Goertz was to obtain an advance of £60,000 from the Pretender and his supporters; with this money a force of 12,000 Swedes was to be levied for an invasion of Scotland in support of a Jacobite rising; Gyllenborg was to issue anonymous pamphlets against the government to which he was accredited and induce the English Jacobites to rise also; the Tsar, through the medium of his Scottish physician Erskine, was to be reconciled with Charles XII and assist the plot. Gyllenborg protested against this violation of diplomatic immunity but was supported only by the Spaniard Monteleone; the other foreign ministers at St. James's tacitly admitted that the revelations in this correspondence justified Stanhope's strong measure in arresting a foreign envoy. The Dutch in their turn, on Stanhope's appeal to them 'to bear their proper burden', arrested Goertz. The Regent and Dubois expressed pleasure at Gyllenborg's arrest, but were not so pleased at Stanhope's *gaucherie* in publishing a 'maudite lettre' which attributed to the Regent the sinister design of getting rid of the boy king in order to secure the crown for himself.[1] These revelations removed all Stanhope's remaining scruples about supporting George's electoral policy against Sweden and Russia. In March, two months earlier than in 1715 or 1716, the usual fleet was sent to the Baltic, this time under Byng, who was instructed to 'burn sink destroy or take all such ships belonging to Sueden as may come in your way', and to abstain from 'aiding or abetting the proceedings of the Muscovites, whilst they forcibly continue to take quarters for their troops in the Empire'.[2]

Here was a clear-cut issue between the two sections of the Whig party. Up to a point Townshend and Walpole were at one with Stanhope and Sunderland in seeing the necessity of vigorous measures to preserve our Baltic trade from interference, and the two brothers had actually agreed to the Cabinet decision of 29 January to arrest Gyllenborg;[3] but at that point their agreement stopped. Stanhope's practical sense very soon enabled him to see that mere commerce protection was not enough to stop Charles XII's attacks on our traders and that if he were to be taught a lesson it would be difficult to avoid co-operation with his avowed adversaries Denmark and Russia. Nor, after his opportunity of studying Northern politics on the spot at Hanover, was he so convinced as Townshend that the Elector's interests were incompatible with the King of England's. Clearly George's more forward policy against Sweden was dictated largely by his desire to secure Bremen and Verden for the Electorate; but might not this acquisition also be in England's interest? For, as he pointed out to Townshend, Cromwell, 'who understood very well the interest of England with respect to foreign powers', not only sent out fleets to secure freedom of trade in the Baltic but 'frequently offered considerable summs of money to the King of Sweden for Bremen'.[4] Again, he had a good defence for his own and the King's change of attitude towards Russia. Peter's incursion into Mecklenburg was not merely against

[1] Wiesener, ii. 3 sqq.; Chance, 167 sqq.; Tindal, xxvi. 372 sqq., has an abstract of the correspondence; see also *P.H.* vii.
[2] *Instructions, Sweden,* 97.
[3] R.O., *S.P. Dom. Geo. I,* 8, 19, Cabinet minute in Stanhope's hand.
[4] Coxe, *Walpole,* ii. 109, 16 Oct. 1716. Cromwell in 1657 had asked for the cession of Bremen in return for help in ships and money required by Charles X of Sweden; Firth, *Last Years of Protectorate,* ii. 319.

Hanoverian interests but was disturbing to the Empire; and, as he pointed out, it was a moot point whether we were not bound by the recent Treaty of Westminster to support the Emperor's interests in that quarter. He was also becoming seriously alarmed at the danger to English interests from Russia's growing power in the Baltic, which bid fair entirely to drive out Sweden's and to convert that sea into a Russian lake, and also at Peter's evident intention to promote the trade of his own country to the destruction of English traders in Russia. So impressed was he with this danger that in September he had forwarded an elaborate report to London on Peter's measures to extend Russian trade at our expense.[1] Townshend and Walpole on the other hand, to judge from the expositions of their views they gave in October,[2] while appreciating some of the difficulties of this very complicated Baltic situation, had no very clear policy to put forward except even more vigorous measures against the Tsar and a peace with Sweden, which was quite hopeless in Charles XII's present mood. There was indeed some justification for Sunderland's brutal retort to Townshend that he had not cast off the old Tory notion that 'England can subsist by itself, whatever becomes of other nations'. But Townshend certainly made a strong point in criticizing George's failure to keep on good terms with Prussia, Hanover's most natural ally in the Empire. Bernstorff's influence, preoccupied as he was with his Mecklenburg villages at the mercy of Russian soldiers, was all cast in the scale against Russia's ally Prussia. As yet this influence was too powerful to be resisted; but in due course Stanhope found himself strong enough to renew relations with Prussia in the very teeth of Bernstorff.

The issue between the two policies was now transferred to Parliament when in April Stanhope asked for supplies to enable the King to form alliances and take measures of defence against Sweden. During the debates Walpole and his friends still in the ministry were either silent or lukewarm, so Stanhope had to bear the brunt of criticism not only from Tories but from dissatisfied Whigs such as the Speaker himself. Their main lines of attack were, first, that Sweden would never have been antagonized had not George taken Bremen and Verden, and, secondly, that the vaunted Triple Alliance was not much good if it had to be supplemented so soon by

[1] This report, in R.O., *S.P.* 44/269 is analysed by Chance, 185–6.
[2] Coxe, *Walpole*, ii. 87–92.

further alliances. As usual Stanhope showed more pugnacity than tact in his replies. In answer to Shippen's insolent attack on the King for his 'little acquaintance with the usage and forms of parliamentary proceedings, as with the language of our country', he gave offence, according to the parliamentary report, by retorting that none would vote against the motion except those who 'were not the King's friends or distrusted the honesty of ministers'. Nor was his argument for the need of further security than that provided by the Triple Alliance likely to please French susceptibilities:

'that the said Treaty had met with so great opposition at the French court, that had not the Regent stickled strenuously for it, it would have infallibly miscarried; and though hitherto we had all the reason imaginable to commend the honesty and candour of that prince; yet in good policy we ought not to depend on the treaty any longer than it shall be the interest of France to observe it';

an utterance which provoked from Huxelles the comment: 'Mr. Stanhope s'est laissé entraîner à sa vivacité en cette occasion.'[1]

In closing the debate on a grant of £250,000 for defensive preparations, however, Stanhope made an effective defence of his Baltic policy. We had, it is true, incurred the Tsar's enmity, but this was due partly to the King's refusal to guarantee his conquests, which it was hardly in England's interests to do, partly because the King objected to the invasion of the Empire, which as the Emperor's ally England was bound to resist. As for Charles XII, his obstinate refusal to make the smallest concession likely to extricate him from his difficulties was the chief reason why the King had failed in his earnest endeavours to restore peace to the North. Turning to the main argument of the opposition, that Hanover's acquisition of Bremen and Verden had dragged England into war with Sweden and involved her in the danger of another Jacobite raid, Stanhope ventured to believe that

'if gentlemen would give themselves the trouble to cast their eyes upon the map, to see where Bremen and Verden lie, they would not be indifferent as to the possession of these two duchies, but would agree with him that their being in the King's hands suited far better with the interests of Great Britain, than if they

---

[1] *Chevening MSS.*, Huxelles to Iberville, 3 May 1717 (in cypher).

were in the hands either of the Czar, who gives already too much jealousy to the Empire, or of the King of Sweden, who endeavoured to raise a rebellion in Great Britain, and harbours our fugitive rebels.'

This speech made a good impression. In a recent division on Swedish measures the ministry had a majority of only four votes; but after Stanhope's speech the supply asked for was obtained without much difficulty, even Walpole, by this time in open opposition, feeling compelled to vote for it.[1]

On 9/20 April, three days before this vote on supply, Stanhope and Townshend came to the final breach. Never really reconciled to his dismissal from the Secretaryship, Townshend had encouraged Walpole and his friends in their sullen attitude in the Commons; in the Lords he had himself voted against the Mutiny Bill and even signed a protest against it in company with the red-hot Jacobite, Atterbury. So marked was this disaffection that, immediately after the government majority had fallen to four, Stanhope sent Townshend a curt note stating that the King had dismissed him from his Irish post. In itself the loss of Townshend was by this time not very serious, for he had become impracticable and was fast being superseded as leader of his section of the Whigs by his abler brother-in-law. Unfortunately he took with him this brother-in-law, whose financial genius, sound political sense and growing mastery of the House of Commons could ill be spared, especially at a time when he was just elaborating a scheme for the reconstruction of the national finances. On the day following Townshend's dismissal Walpole went to the King to return his seals of office. Nine times, it was said, did George, with the words *rogo te*, in the only language they could both understand, return the seals into Walpole's hat as he knelt in the royal presence, and nine times did Walpole lay them back on the table. Both men were moved to tears. The two brothers also took with them from George's first ministry Methuen, Orford, Devonshire and Pulteney. So complete seemed the division of the Whigs that the Tory Erasmus Lewis said to Swift with a chuckle:

[1] For these debates see *P.H.* vii. 437 sqq.; Tindal, xxvii. 2 sqq.; and for additional details *H. MSS., Polwarth*, i. 211. Chance, 183, takes the view that the publication of the Gyllenborg correspondence was quite unnecessary for the security of the country and that it was done only for the purpose of supporting the King's northern policy, which was undoubtedly unpopular. Even so it appears to me that the publication was quite justified.

'Morally speaking, nothing but another rebellion can ever unite them.'[1]

Fortunately this division did not have the fatal effects expected. Stanhope, now unquestionably the chief man in the ministry, carried on the King's government with success for over three years; and this in spite of the determined and often virulent opposition of the Walpole-Townshend section of Whigs, who sometimes did not hesitate to find allies even among the Tories. This was mainly due to the importance during these three years of foreign affairs, in which Stanhope's genius shone forth without a rival. When domestic politics, and especially finance, again assumed supreme importance, Stanhope was obliged to have recourse to Walpole's great abilities. But, apart from the value of Stanhope's diplomatic achievements and of some of his domestic measures during these three years, his administration was of service to the dynasty and to England in demonstrating that the Whig theory of government was strong enough to establish itself even when the Whig party itself was divided, and that in such circumstances it was not necessary to have recourse to a party not whole-heartedly in favour of the Revolution settlement.

The question remains how far Stanhope himself was really responsible for the breach with colleagues who had had some part in placing him in his present position. Stanhope certainly took very much amiss the coldness shown by Townshend and Walpole to his success in the negotiations with Dubois and their unwillingness to accept his and the King's view of the urgency for concluding the treaty. Nor can it be doubted from Townshend's correspondence with Horatio Walpole[2] that, without actual disobedience to the King's orders, the brothers did not press forward the business as they might have. But for Townshend's supersession as

---

[1] For an unfavourable view of Walpole's and Townshend's actions at this time see *The Rise and Fall of Count Hotspur* [*Townshend*], *with that of his Brother-in-Law Colonel Headstrong* [*Walpole*] (London, 1717). In this pamphlet the two brothers, whose conduct before 1714 is praised, are accused of attempting later to monopolize all power, even the King's. Thus Walpole is said to have 'Elbow'd himself into the supreme ministry by his advancement to Montacutio's [Halifax] post.' The breach in the ministry produced a cloud of pamphlets on either side. On Stanhope's side appeared, besides *Count Hotspur*, *The Defection Considered* (1717), *The Detection Considered* (1718), *The Detection further Considered* (1718); on Walpole's and Townshend's side *The Detection Detected* (1718), *Some Persons Vindicated against the Author of the Detection* (1718), *The Resigners Vindicated*, Parts I and II (1718).

[2] Ch. viii, pp. 225-6.

Secretary Stanhope was clearly not responsible. The Germans and, to some extent, Sunderland seem to have convinced the King that Townshend was disloyal; and thereafter the decision was entirely the King's own. Nor is there any reason to doubt Stanhope's sincerity in asserting that he alone persuaded the King to lighten his fall by the offer of Ireland. When Townshend subsequently voted against the ministry's measures and allowed his friends to do so, his final dismissal was inevitable.

The personal question, however, as usually occurs in political disputes, was inextricably interwoven with a difference of view on public policy. The brothers at this time, as was the case with so many English politicians between 1714 and 1760, had the Hanoverian danger on the brain and had almost come to believe the interests of Hanover to be necessarily antagonistic to those of England. Stanhope, with further experience, also recognized that the Hanoverian clique, with its petty jealousy of Prussia, might impede the common interests, and when he realized it took effective steps to remove the danger. But he had a sure instinct in taking the wider view that the peace of Europe, and the interests of England not least, required serious attention to the rise of the new Russian power and the conflicting forces in the Baltic. Even with regard to Hanover herself, however inexpedient it might be to allow England to be dragged into her quarrels, it was obviously impossible, with the junction of the Crowns, to allow the King's Hanoverian possessions to be jeopardized. Stanhope indeed was broad minded enough to understand that there was much to be learned for his country from the hated 'meridian of Hanover', and from the experience its rulers had gained of eastern and mid-European politics, hitherto very much of a closed book to Englishmen. During this his first sojourn at Hanover, he may have been somewhat over-influenced by the strong prejudices of his obstinate master and the intrigues of his court: but at least that sojourn helped to broaden his conception of European politics. For he was not only the first English statesman but one of the first statesmen in Europe who saw and attempted to grapple with the new problems arising from the emergence of Russia, 'that great cloud of power in the North'.[1]

[1] His nephew Chatham's phrase.

CHAPTER X
STANHOPE'S MINISTRY—CHEVENING

§ 1

STANHOPE was a very great foreign minister. But it was a cruel fate that drove him after Walpole's resignation to assume his rival's offices of First Lord and Chancellor of the Exchequer and to become leader of the House of Commons. In the sudden emergency of 1715, when vigorous and decisive action was required, he had indeed shown himself at his best at home. But he had little knowledge of finance and still less experience of the arts required to bend a popular assembly to his will. He was too hot tempered, too authoritative to turn away opposition by tactful concessions and conciliatory methods; and, in spite of the respect in which his public spirit and transparent honesty were held, he never gained the ear of the House of Commons or even fully that of the House of Lords. It was all the harder for him that his chief adversary was Robert Walpole, the most consummate manager of the House of Commons there has ever been. For support he had at first mainly to rely upon Sunderland, who with age had shed none of the rashness and over-ingenuity of his youth, nor gained the confidence of his contemporaries. In December 1716, when Townshend was dismissed from his secretary-ship, Stanhope took over the Northern province, abandoning the Southern to Methuen, but in the following April, when Walpole, Townshend and Methuen left the ministry, Stanhope took over Walpole's duties, while Sunderland and his protégé Addison became secretaries for the North and South respectively. Sunderland faithfully carried out Stanhope's policy, but poor Addison, already declining in health, proved himself unequal either to taking his part in debate or performing the duties of his office, and within a year was obliged to admit his own incompetence and resign. Fortunately, even under this arrangement, Stanhope took as much part as before in the direction of foreign affairs, and in the following year exchanged offices with Sunderland. For the rest of his life he was ostensibly, as well as really, responsible for the country's foreign business, the department most suited to his genius.

While that point is clear, it is not at first sight so evident in that age of constitutional transition what were the main governing forces in English politics during the years 1717 to 1719. Swift's correspondent Erasmus Lewis writes on the eve of George I's return from Hanover: 'Sunderland, Stanhope, and Cadogan are of one side; Townshend, Walpole, Orford, Devonshire, and the Chancellor (Cowper) on the other . . . They are both making court to the Tories, who I hope will be a body by themselves, and not serve as recruits to either of the other two.'[1] Dr. Michael, in his great work on English history in the eighteenth century, describes the government of England during these years as virtually in the hands of a triumvirate composed of Stanhope, Sunderland and Cadogan, with Cadogan, who was made an earl at the same time as Stanhope, playing the part of Antony, and with the whole triumvirate dependent mainly on the favour of Bernstorff and tied to his foreign policy.[2] One of Dr. Michael's great services to the history of this period is the light he has thrown on English politics, both foreign and domestic, from the reports of foreign envoys and other state papers to be found in the Hanover, Vienna, Berlin and other foreign archives, not hitherto much used by English historians. But there is a danger of overrating these sources, an error into which the author rarely falls, though he appears to do so in this instance; for in making this statement he seems to rely almost exclusively on the reports of the Prussian envoy Bonet, who probably took most of his information from the Hanoverians themselves, and was known as a mischief-maker.[3]

In the first place it seems to be a mistake to put Cadogan on anything like a par with Stanhope and Sunderland in the political world. He was a capable diplomat and a good soldier, trained and highly thought of by Marlborough, who regarded him as his possible successor. His ambitions seem to have been entirely military, and it was purely as a soldier that he could in any way be regarded as Stanhope's rival. Stanhope, it is true, in spite of his great achievements in diplomacy, long retained a hankering for a military career. He had made a special merit of his advocacy of the alliance in his conversations with Dubois at Hanover, since, as he told him, in case of war he had been promised a high command by the King;[4] two months later Dubois, on a

[1] Swift, *Correspondence*, ii. 360–1 (12 Jan. 1716/17).
[2] Michael, ii. 37, 556 sqq.   [3] See below, ch. xiii, p. 374.
[4] A.E., *Angleterre*, 277, ff. 274 sqq., Dubois to Huxelles, 28 Aug. 1716.

rumour that Marlborough was dying and that Stanhope was
to succeed him, wrote imploring him to abandon his military
ambitions and stick to diplomacy.[1] Many allusions also
occur in the Stuart Papers to his rivalry with Cadogan in
this respect and a prophecy that on Marlborough's death
'there will be a bonnet off between Stanhope and Cadogan,
pares aquilas'.[2] But there seems no evidence that Cadogan
had any influence on decisions either in domestic or foreign
affairs, even though he was a greater favourite with Bernstorff. In fact, directly he began to give trouble in the Closet
by childish opposition to recommendations of Stanhope,
Sunderland and Craggs, he was packed off as ambassador
to Holland.[3]

Again, it is by no means clear that Stanhope and Sunderland were entirely dependent on Bernstorff's favour. They
were no doubt preferred by the King to Walpole and Townshend as more in sympathy with his own and Bernstorff's
northern policy. It is true also that Bernstorff, owing to his
close acquaintance with German and north European politics,
was often consulted by Stanhope as to the details and even
the general conception of English foreign policy; and that
he, with the busybody Robethon, took more interest in
internal affairs than was entirely approved in England,
notably when personal decisions were referred to the King.
But because Stanhope in foreign affairs and Sunderland to a
less extent in domestic questions were sometimes willing to
seek light from Bernstorff and even to modify their views
according to his, that is no proof that they were subservient
to him. In fact, as will appear hereafter, when Stanhope
found that his foreign policy was being impeded by Bernstorff and that the Hanoverian ministers were interfering
too much in English concerns, he was so little dependent on
Bernstorff's favour that he not only rebelled against his
attempts at dictation, but obtained an order from the King
forbidding him for the future to interfere in English affairs.

It would not, however, be correct to speak of the ministry
of that time as Stanhope's in the same sense as we speak of
Mr. Baldwin's or Mr. Ramsay Macdonald's ministries to-day;

[1] R.O., *S.P.* 44/269, quoted by Wiesener i. 500.
[2] *H. MSS., Stuart*, iii. 251 (see also 477, 488).
[3] *Stair Annals*, ii. 103–6. See also *H. MSS.* ii, Appendix, 189; an unknown
writer to Stair from the Cockpit, 10 Mar. 1719, says Cadogan 'has certainly
blown the coals; he has a notion of being premier ministre, which I believe you
will with me think a very Irish one'.

still less to give Stanhope the formal title of Prime Minister.[1] In those days there was no recognized Prime Minister, for the simple reason that each minister was in theory, and to a large extent in practice, directly responsible to the King for the duties of his office, and would have resented any one of his colleagues assuming control over his activities. The expression Prime Minister was not indeed entirely unknown in political terminology: thus we find Marlborough and Godolphin spoken of together as 'Prime Ministers' of Anne, in the sense of the two most important ministers; more pertinent at first sight seems the application of the term 'Prime Minister' to both Godolphin and Oxford in turn,[2] but the expression in these cases was probably due only to the fact that each in succession held the office of Lord Treasurer, an ancient office which gave definite precedence to its holders, without necessarily carrying any right of interference with their colleagues. This office was, however, left unfilled by George I with the deliberate purpose of giving no one minister this pre-eminence, quite in accordance with the Whig doctrine that no too powerful subject should be officially raised above his fellow ministers. During most of the eighteenth century, though a few instances may be quoted from Newcastle's private correspondence in which he talks of his brother Pelham as 'premier' or 'prime minister', the term Prime Minister was chiefly used in an invidious sense of a statesman such as Walpole who seemed to his opponents to take too much upon himself the air of being solely responsible for the whole government.[3] It does not appear that the term was generally recognized as denoting the head of the government until the younger Pitt's time. As an official title carrying with it due precedence in rank, it was not adopted till the present century, when Campbell Bannerman, under an Order in Council proposed by his predecessor Balfour, was officially recognized as Prime Minister.[4]

But though never spoken of as Prime Minister, Stanhope, from Townshend's fall till his own death four years later,

---

[1] See above, ch. vi, p. 153.

[2] See *Memoirs of Sir J. Clerk* (Roxburghe Club 1895), 53, 72.

[3] See Torrens, i. 164: 'Prime Minister was a phrase of compliment occasionally bestowed in conversation or private correspondence, but for which there was no official warrant or continuing usage.'

[4] For a discussion of this point see review on *The Austrian Succession* in *The Times Literary Supplement* of 27 Feb. 1930 and the correspondence ibidem of the following 6, 13 and 20 Mar.

was the leading figure and the moving spirit in the government. His only possible rival was Sunderland, who had the advantages of longer experience in office, wealth and family connexions, as well as a higher position in the peerage. Later Sunderland was the more active in domestic matters, the ill-fated Peerage Bill being mainly his idea and the South Sea Scheme originally due to his fertile brain; and it was he who kept members in a good temper by a public table kept up at vast expense, and by other less avowable means: and it is perhaps for this reason that Hervey speaks of 'Lord Sunderland's administration'. But, except for the country's purely financial business, Stanhope never lost his grasp of domestic affairs and assumed full responsibility for the Peerage Bill. Thus on the eve of the Session in 1718 it was not to Sunderland's house but to 'Earl Stanhope's Great Room in the Cockpit' that peers supporting the ministry were summoned to discuss the government programme. Again when, in the same year, Cowper was thinking of resigning the Great Seal, it was Stanhope, not Sunderland, who wrote to dissuade him in the tone a modern Prime Minister would adopt to one of his colleagues.[1] In foreign affairs, even when not nominally responsible, Stanhope was admittedly supreme. Above all he had the ear of the King, then essential for ministerial predominance. He and Sunderland worked well together and were the only ministers who counted until the younger Craggs superseded Addison in 1718. But Stanhope could have carried on without Sunderland, for, as Onslow said, 'Stanhope contributed more than any in reconciling the party to the loss of Walpole and Townshend',[2] whereas the converse was never true, as Walpole recognized in making Stanhope the chief target of his attacks.

Stanhope's task was, indeed, no easy one when he undertook the chief responsibility for the government on the disruption of the Whig party. The full support of the Crown was doubtless of immense importance in those days, but even so an adverse vote in Parliament might have been fatal not only to the ministry but even to the security of the dynasty. This was all the more to be feared owing to Walpole's attitude. On resigning he had declared that he would indulge in no factious opposition: but he very soon belied his words

[1] R.O., *S.P. Dom. Geo. I*, 13 (Monday, 10 Nov. 1718). The letter to Cowper of 15 Apr. 1718 is in *Chevening MSS.*
[2] *H. MSS.*, Onslow, 511-12.

and was quite ready to join forces with Tories or even Jacobites in the attempt to overthrow Stanhope's administration. Only the unwillingness of the Jacobites to play his game of substituting Robert Walpole's section of the Whigs for Stanhope's prevented the complete success of his manœuvres. As it was, he seized every opportunity, with a cynical disregard of his previously expressed opinions, to make difficulties for the government. On his side, Stanhope, though always uncompromising with the Jacobite element among the Tories, after the collapse of the Rebellion and still more after the secession of Walpole and his Whig followers, was not indisposed to seek further support for the dynasty in the loyal section of the Tory party.[1] This now seemed feasible owing to his long-standing relations with the chief leader of the Tories, and this leader's complete conversion to the Hanoverian dynasty in 1716.

Bolingbroke, after his ignominious dismissal by the Pretender, entirely repudiated his allegiance to him and began taking active steps to wean the Tories from all taint of Jacobitism. He confided in Stair, an old friend, saw much of him in Paris, and through him tried to obtain the King's pardon and permission to return to England. He even sent a letter to Wyndham, the leader of the Tories, in September 1716, to urge him not to engage in any new enterprise of the Jacobites, giving it to the younger Craggs in Paris to forward to his father the Postmaster-General, so that the government might see its contents.[2] In February of the following year he wrote a long letter to Stair defining his position: in this letter he admits his error in joining the Pretender and declares that nothing would ever induce him to serve him again; for the future, though he will never betray the confidences of those who trusted him while he was minister to the Pretender—'these I will rather starve to death than ever disclose', he says in another letter—he is ready to give the King information of the highest value for his security. But his chief object in asking for pardon and permission to return is in order to 'ramener les esprits des Tories' to the throne by his personal influence on the members of his party:

[1] The Tories themselves, even those not of the extreme Jacobite section, were not anxious to join either section of the Whigs. Erasmus Lewis, for example, hopes the Tories 'will be a body by themselves, and not serve as recruits to either of the other two [Whig sections]' (Swift, *Correspondence*, ii. 360–1).

[2] Coxe, *Walpole*, ii. 308, referring to the *Letter to Sir William Wyndham*.

'ce n'est pas que je m'imagine qu'il soit possible d'ébranler le throne de sa Maj^{té}, mais il me semble qu'on doit désirer de rendre le gouvernement tranquil, tant pour le repos du Roy, que pour le bien de la Patrie, bonheur qui ne sera jamais parfait tant qu'il restera de ce levain jacobite dans la masse de la nation.'

And he returns to this object over and over again in his letters to Stair:

'Partys are like flocks of sheep'; he reminds him, 'they will stand sullen and be run over till they hear the bell-weather, and then they follow without knowing very well where . . . [but if I am allowed to return I hope] to break ye opposition to ye King and to increase ye number of those who write in an affectionate submission to his government.'[1]

The desire here expressed by Bolingbroke to lead the old Tory party out of the wilderness of Jacobitism and make of it a party ready to support the throne and take a part in the national politics seems to have been perfectly genuine. Indeed, he spent the rest of his life trying to educate the Tory party to become dutiful servants of a Patriot King of the Hanover dynasty. This desire was certainly accepted as genuine by Stanhope and Sunderland. Stair was encouraged to keep in touch with him through Saladin, a Genoese; his agent Brinsden was allowed to come to England; Stanhope's father-in-law, Governor Pitt, was apparently empowered to negotiate with him in Paris; and the Regent was informed that he was 'under his Majesty's protection, to prevent any insults that may be offered him, on account of the inclination he has shown to serve his Majesty and reconcile himself to his royal favour'.[2] He had many friends in England who for personal as well as political reasons would have been well pleased to see him back, notably the younger Craggs and his old friend Stanhope. Had it rested solely with Stanhope he would certainly have been allowed to return; but the general feeling of the Whigs was against it. Walpole, who in 1723 himself procured Bolingbroke's pardon, in 1719 flared up at the mere hint of his 'villany' being condoned by the reversal of his attainder; the supporters of the ministry were almost as much against it. So Bolingbroke had to recognize that ministers would be forced 'to act timorously with a precarious majority . . . and [in spite of] the friendship

[1] *Oxenfoord MSS.*, *Bolingbroke Papers*, ff. 10–12, 20 Feb. 1717; f. 38, 19 Dec. 1717; f. 60, 10 Jan. 1719.
[2] *Stair Annals*, ii. 24, 2 Sept. 1717.

which the men in power at our court have express'd . . . I shall continue in exile'. To Stanhope he wrote, 'I will please myself with the thought that you desired to have it done'; to Stair he expressed regret that he was not allowed to contribute towards abating 'the phrenzy in England' among the Tories; 'you will see those malignant humours so blended in the mass of blood that there will not remain a possibility of rooting them out . . . [since] every delay renders me less capable of doing the King service'. But though Bolingbroke was not allowed to return before Stanhope's death, he continued to give the ministry, through Stair, some useful information and some criticisms of their policy, to which perhaps less attention was paid.[1] Stanhope himself when passing through Paris made a point of meeting Bolingbroke and discussing policy with him.[2] He never seems to have lost the affection he conceived in youth for his brilliant friend, but, wiser than most of the Whigs, was convinced that with all his brilliance he had no staying power and would never recover the ground once lost in a moment of panic, or again become a danger to the state. To Bolingbroke, as it has been said of another of our most brilliant statesmen, the line of Virgil is applicable:

Cui spes,
Cui sit conditio dulcis sine pulvere palmae.[3]

Stanhope then, on Walpole's resignation, was constrained to rely almost entirely on his own resources and from a sense of public duty to take up offices for which he was singularly ill fitted, those of First Lord and Chancellor of the Exchequer. That they were a misfit he himself seems to have felt, for in introducing his first financial measures, he 'ingenuously owned his incapacity for affairs of Treasury, which were so remote from his studies and inclination'; admitted that he would have preferred his old employment which was more 'pleasant and profitable', but thought it his duty to obey the King's commands, and 'would endeavour to make up by application, honesty and disinterestedness what he wanted in abilities and experience'. As Chancellor of the Exchequer it fell to him to carry through the House the comprehensive financial scheme partly introduced by his predecessor.

---

[1] Mahon, *History*, ii. 51; ib., Appendix (Bolingbroke to Stanhope, 9 Nov. 1717); *Oxenfoord MSS.* (*Bolingbroke Papers*, ff. 37, 47, 49).
[2] See below, ch. xi, p. 310.　　　　　　　[3] Horace, *Epistles*, i. 50–1.

On the accession of George I the national debt had stood
at fifty-four million pounds odd, an amount then deemed
dangerously excessive, while the interest paid on the various
stocks into which the debt was divided ranged from 7 to 9 per
cent., though the average market rate of interest was only 4 to
5 per cent. The Rebellion and uncertainty about the dynasty's
permanence accounted in the first two years of the reign for
creditors' unwillingness to accept a lower rate of interest;
but during the autumn of 1716 Walpole had begun to improve
the revenue returns and to form his plans for reducing interest
and paying off a portion of the debt.[1] Before his resignation
he had been able to carry resolutions in committee of the
House authorizing the main lines of his scheme. He proposed
to raise a new loan of £600,000 at 5 per cent., to induce as
many holders of the old stock as possible to exchange it for
the new stock, and to redeem, as occasion served, partly by
the proceeds of the new loan, partly by the income accruing
to a new Sinking Fund, the rest of the old stock, especially
annuities held by the Bank of England and the South Sea
Company. This Sinking Fund was to be formed of all savings
made by the reduction of interest or the redemption of old
debts and was to be used solely for the further extinction of
debt. On the day of his resignation Walpole consented to
introduce a Redemption Bill, the first of those founded on
these resolutions, but only, as he put it, as 'a country gentleman' without the authority of the government behind him,
and with the hope that 'it would not fare worse for having
two fathers and that his successor would bring it to perfection'.

Stanhope naturally required some time to make himself
familiar with the circumstances and did not bring in the
remaining bills necessary for the completion of the scheme
for another month. Unfortunately, during his brief tenure of
the Exchequer he had discovered methods practised at the
office less to the advantage of the public than to that of
office-holders, and thought it his duty to call attention to
such abuses in his usual direct language. He found

'it had been the common practice of those concerned in the
administration of the treasury, to make bargains for the public
with the governors and directors of companies, by which some
private advantage was generally made, but that in his opinion
such bargains ought to be made at the bar of the House by the
representatives of all the Commons of Great Britain; and that if

[1] Coxe, *Walpole*, ii. 95.

any advantages could be made, the public ought to have the benefit of them.'

Again, in a subsequent speech he took occasion to denounce another common abuse in the public life of the time, declaring that he

'would content himself with his salary and lawful perquisites of office; and though he had quitted a better place, he would not quarter himself on anybody to make it up: he had no brothers nor other relations to provide for: and that on first entering the Treasury he had made a standing order against the late practice of granting reversions of places.'

May we not believe that straight dealing with the public purse thus became a family tradition and bore fruit in the refusal of Stanhope's favourite nephew, the Great Commoner, in his turn to accept the usual perquisites of his office?[1] But at the time Walpole, taking Stanhope's words as a reflection on himself, jumped up to complain warmly of what he called a breach of friendship and a betrayal of private conversation. He admitted he had served his friends and relations, but only within reason and justice.

'As to the granting of reversions', he said, 'I am willing to acquaint the House with the meaning of the charge that is now urged against me. I have no objections to the German ministers whom the King brought with him from Hanover and who, as far as I have observed, have behaved themselves like men of honour, but there is a mean fellow [Robethon], of what nation I know not, who is eager to dispose of employments. This man having obtained the grant of a reversion, which he designed for his son, I thought it too good for him, and therefore reserved it for my own son. On this disappointment, the foreigner was so saucy as to demand £2,500, under pretence that he had been offered that sum for the reversion; but I was wiser than to comply with his demands. And I am bold to acknowledge, one of the chief reasons that made me resign was, because I could not connive at some things that were carrying on.'

Walpole's cynical avowal of his method of intercepting Robethon's 'petits profits' for the benefit of his own relations was hardly a convincing reply to Stanhope's criticism.[2] So Stanhope himself seems to have thought, and answered

---

[1] See Williams, *Chatham*, i. 152 sqq.
[2] Even Walpole's strongest defenders could put up only the lamest excuse for his methods of patronage. *The Detection Detected* (1718), a pro-Walpole pamphlet, says, 'I do not believe that he [R. Walpole] is the only person that had made advantages of the Disposal of Places for himself . . . Why then should that Practice be brought in as Criminal in him that is allowable in others?'

Walpole so hotly that Methuen and Boscawen, fearing that their angry rejoinders to one another might cause them to seek an issue with the sword, made a motion that the dispute should be carried no further.[1]

Walpole's antagonism was aroused not only by the criticism of his system of patronage but also by a modification made by Stanhope in his original plan. In the course of the debates the Bank of England and the South Sea Company, who held government stock of one and a quarter and ten millions sterling respectively at 6 per cent., offered to advance another four and a half millions between them and to accept interest at 5 per cent. on the old stock as well as on the new advance. Stanhope proposed to accept these offers in lieu of that part of Walpole's scheme which dealt with the Bank and South Sea Annuities, and with the new money advanced and the saving of interest on the former annuities to pay off other annuitants entitled to higher rates of interest. Walpole, fearing perhaps that this arrangement might give these two powerful corporations too strong a hold over the government, opposed it as detrimental to the public. It was nevertheless carried on 5 June 1717. On the same day Walpole's great scheme, as amended, was completed by the sanction given to his Sinking Fund, into which all savings of interest and capital were to be paid and used only for further redemption of debt. In its immediate object the scheme was highly successful. By the end of the reign, ten years later, six and a quarter millions of debt had been paid off and the interest on the rest reduced; even earlier, in 1721, Walpole's task of restoring confidence after the South Sea panic was lightened by the sound condition of the national finances. Its political effects were even more important. The additional subscribers to the Bank and South Sea stocks, who thereby participated in the government loan, were all so many more interested supporters of the dynasty, for on its permanence alone depended the security for the interest and capital of the government loans. Commerce also was helped· by the increased stability of the national finances, and the growing commercial community bound more firmly than ever to the existing system of government.[2]

The success of these measures was triumphantly demon-

[1] *P.H.*, vii. 449 sqq.
[2] N. A. Brisco, *Economic Policy of Walpole* (N.Y., 1907), has a good account of these financial transactions.

strated by Stanhope in the House of Lords in the following
year. In January 1718 an attack was made on the government for the scarcity of silver coin in the country, a scarcity
reported on by Sir Isaac Newton as Master of the Mint.
Oxford, a former Lord High Treasurer and now free to
speak in the House, took occasion to make 'some reflection' on
the government's recent financial policy and was answered
by Stanhope, who though recently elevated to the peerage,
was still First Lord of the Treasury and Chancellor of the
Exchequer, the last instance in our history of a Chancellor
of the Exchequer in the House of Lords. He 'returned very
smartly' according to the report, attributing the scarcity to
four causes, the growing luxury of the age shown in the
demand for silver-plate,[1] the East India Company's practice
of exporting silver to the East in the course of trade, the
exchange of silver for gold from Holland, and lastly, with a
sting in the tail, 'the malice of some persons who, by hoarding
up silver, thought to distress the government'. The dearth
of silver, he concluded, was not the fault of the Treasury,
'on the contrary it might to their praise be observed that the
public credit never ran so high in other hands, since the
government could now borrow great sums at $3\frac{1}{2}$ per cent.'[2]
Stanhope was fully justified in making this boast, for, though
admittedly no great financier nor even the originator of the
conversion scheme, he had been quick to seize its political
importance, especially in his own sphere of foreign politics. He
had already made good his proud boast, in answer to Dubois's
idle gibe, that England had not the slightest anxiety about
the size of her debt, and in assuming responsibility for his
predecessor's plan and putting it through Parliament deserves
a share in the credit to which Walpole, as its originator, is
mainly entitled.

The moderate opposition Stanhope had to encounter on
these financial measures hardly gave a foretaste of the bitter
attacks, especially from Walpole, to which his policy was
exposed during his last session in the House of Commons.
Even before the disruption of the party the opposition
of many Whigs to Stanhope's and the King's northern
policy had been evident: now it became more openly and
vehemently expressed. On Stanhope's motion of 12 April
for a grant of £250,000 to provide for the defence of the

[1] The vast wine-coolers, dishes &c., in silver of this period, still to be seen
in country houses, give point to this remark.　　　　[2] P.H. vii. 532 sq.

kingdom in view of the revelations in the Gyllenborg papers
of Swedish and Jacobite plots, Walpole only grudgingly gave
his vote for it, and he could do no less for, as he admitted,
when in office he had agreed to the proposal: but his supporter
Pulteney, who had also just resigned, actually opposed it.[1] He
sullenly refused to take any further part in the proceedings
against Oxford, though formerly the keenest to press them,
and left Stanhope to bear all the odium of their failure.[2] He
joined the Tories in an attack on Cadogan, who had stood
by the Stanhope and Sunderland group, charging him with
embezzlement of public moneys entrusted to him for bringing
over the Dutch troops in 1715. Such a charge, as Walpole
might have remembered from his own experience under a
Tory government, was little more than a convenient method
of besmirching a political opponent. He and his party,
together with the Tories, even went so far in their vendetta
against the King's government as to propose a vote of thanks
to Argyll, who had been removed from the Scottish command
in favour of Cadogan by Townshend himself. Such conduct
was the more unscrupulous because Walpole, when himself
in charge of the national finances, had never questioned
Cadogan's accounts, while the proposal to thank Argyll was
little short of a personal affront to the King. But in his
embittered mood Walpole cared nothing for his own con-
sistency or the King's feelings, and became so fierce in his
attack that after laying about him in a speech of two hours
he was seized with a violent bleeding of the nose and
had to retire from the House. As it was, in spite of evidence
given at the bar vindicating Cadogan, Stanhope defeated
the motion by only ten votes.[3]

Walpole lost ground by his factious opposition, often in
direct contradiction to his former opinions, during the only
session when he and Stanhope were actually pitted against
one another on the floor of the House of Commons. Stanhope, by his dogged persistence in carrying on the King's
government against opponents such as Walpole and Pulteney,
both much better debaters than himself, and by his evident
sincerity earned the respect that character always obtains
in politics as in every other walk of life; and the better he
was known the more he was trusted. For two years after his
resignation Walpole was comparatively impotent because he

---

[1] *P.H.* vii. 443 sqq.   [2] See above, ch. vii, p. 174.
              [3] *P.H.* vii. 466 sqq.

had not yet found, as he did in 1719, a cause to fight for better than his own injured feelings. By openly taking the side of the Prince of Wales when, at the end of 1717, the breach between George I and his son became definite and notorious, Walpole made even more patent his own impotence.

The innocent cause of this definite breach between the royal father and son was a young recruit to the ministry, the twenty-four-year-old Duke of Newcastle, just starting on his half-century of official life. By his marriage with Godolphin's daughter Newcastle had become a member of the powerful Marlborough clan and a nephew of Sunderland; he was also a brother-in-law of Townshend and connected with the Dukes of Devonshire, Portland and Montagu, with Walpole and with the Earl of Oxford. By these connexions, by the profuse hospitality an income of nearly £50,000 enabled him to display, by his precocious skill in managing his own boroughs and influencing other elections, and by his close attention to indications of popular feeling, he was already regarded as a valuable ally in the political world. As yet his timidity and want of judgement and his intense jealousy of colleagues likely to overshadow him by their ability were not in evidence, and for the next fourteen years he was quite content to attach himself to the ruling minister of the day, were he Stanhope or Walpole.[1] The office he had obtained in 1717 was that of Lord Chamberlain, whereby he un-wittingly came into conflict with the Prince of Wales. For many years there had been no love lost between King and Prince, as, until recent times, has been normally the case in our royal family. When another son was born to the Prince in December 1717, the father desired that the godparents, besides the King, should all be of royal lineage. But the new Lord Chamberlain discovered that he had a vested right to be a godfather in such a case, and was supported in his assertion of it by the King; so the Prince had no alternative but to submit. But after the christening, which took place in the Princess's chamber, the Prince went up to Newcastle and taking him by the arm shouted angrily, 'You rascal, I'll find you', which the timorous duke, misunderstanding the Prince's German pronunciation, took to be, 'You rascal, I'll fight you'. Newcastle, all of a twitter, at once went to consult Stanhope as to what was to be done and took him round to see Sunder-

[1] See article on 'Duke of Newcastle and Election of 1734' in *E.H.R.*, July 1897.

land, who was then celebrating his daughter's wedding and
was not best pleased to be disturbed, and lastly to Bernstorff,
who decided that the King must be told. George was furious
at the version of the Prince's words as reported to him by
Newcastle, and, after holding a Cabinet Council, ordered
three ministers to see the Prince and explain to him that
Newcastle had been acting as godfather on the King's express
commands. In reply the Prince curtly told the deputation
that he did not believe a word of it and that it was simply
Newcastle's officiousness—a piece of impertinence for which
the King put him under arrest in the Palace. Even then the
only form of submission vouchsafed by the Prince was a
letter to the King stating that he would show no further
resentment against Newcastle, whereupon he was ordered
to leave the Palace and the courtiers were forbidden to pay
their respects to him. For over two years the Prince remained
an exile from his father's court, and not unnaturally became
the focus of opposition to his policy. None but dissatisfied
politicians, such as Walpole and Townshend, were to be
seen at his levées; but, though the public breach between the
father and son gave plenty of occasion for scandal and tittle-
tattle, no great sympathy was shown for the Prince, who in
this instance was felt to have been in the wrong; and the few
who still frequented his house were made to feel as much left
out in the cold as he was himself.[1]

§ 2

Before this incident occurred Stanhope had left the House of
Commons on his elevation to the peerage as Baron Stanhope
of Elvaston in the County of Derby and Viscount Stanhope
of Mahon. The stately and sonorous Latin of his patent of
peerage recounts the chief incidents of his career that justified
the honour conferred on him.

'If such Persons', are the opening words, 'as have distinguished themselves in an extraordinary manner by the Arts
either of War or Peace, are fit to be advanced to the chief

---

[1] Horace Walpole, *Reminiscences*, ch. iii; Lord Hervey, *Memoirs* (1931 Edition),
29, 845–9; Michael, ii. 625–6 for the Prince's letters to the King. In R.O., *S.P.
Dom. Geo. I*, 10, are a letter and memorandum from Delafaye to Whitworth
giving the official account of the incident. The ferocious suggestion about the
Prince attributed by Hervey (l.c.) to Stanhope is most improbable: it depends
entirely on Queen Caroline's version of letters which had been destroyed.

Honours in the State, We have just reason to chuse into the Number of the Peers of Our Kingdom James Stanhope'.[1]

The passage about Minorca has been already quoted:[2] his measures for the reduction of interest and the establishment of a sinking fund are happily characterized as 'Laws . . . assuredly most welcome to My whole People, whom it was necessary to relieve of so great a Burden of Debt, and successful in the even harder task of satisfying the Creditors themselves.'[3]

His promotion to the House of Lords did not at first release him, as we have seen, from his inappropriate duties as head of the Treasury, though even then most of his attention was devoted to the delicate negotiations for the Quadruple Alliance, of which he took entire charge. But before the next session was over the absurdity of keeping the greatest foreign minister of the day engaged mainly in duties for which he had no special bent was recognized. At the end of March 1718 Stanhope handed over the Treasury to Sunderland and the Exchequer to Aislabie, a member of the House of Commons, and himself returned to the post of Secretary for the North. At the same time he was able to strengthen the government in the Lower House owing to the fortunate resignation of Addison, ineffective both as Secretary of State and as debater, and the substitution for him of his old henchman the younger Craggs, who worked well with Stanhope in the Southern Department and could hold his own even against Walpole and Pulteney as an exponent of the government policy. A couple of weeks later a further testimony of the King's favour was conferred on Stanhope by his elevation to an earldom.

To a man so fully occupied in delicate negotiations the comparative calm of the House of Lords was a welcome and almost necessary release from the anxiety of contested elections and the more strenuous debates of the House of Commons. A house in the country as a refuge from the turmoil of London and the press of business was also a need as much

---

[1] 'Si qui aut Belli aut Pacis Artibus eximii inclaruerunt ad summos Reipublicae Honores rite admovendi sint, non immerito egregium Virum utroque Nomine celebrandum Jacobum Stanhope . . . in Procerum Nostrorum Numerum cooptari voluimus.'
[2] See above, ch. iii, p. 85.
[3] 'Leges . . . universo Populo, cui tanto onere sublevare expedit, certe acceptissimae, et, quod difficillimum videtur, Foeneratoribus ipsis non ingratae.' The text of the patent with English translation is in Boyer, xiv. 76.

for statesmen of those days as of to-day, besides satisfying the wellnigh universal craving of rich and poor alike for a house and a bit of land of their own, in which to root a family and a lineage. A homeless wanderer for most of his life, Stanhope was none the less possessed by this craving, which was hardly satisfied with his house 'by the Cockpit, Whitehall', needed for his official duties. He also had a special reason for desiring a larger house, to display on its walls a magnificent set of four tapestries made in Berlin by Barraband, a Huguenot refugee from the Beauvais tapestry factory, and presented to him in 1708, no doubt after his victory at Minorca, by Frederic I of Prussia. These tapestries were so vast, each 28 feet in length, that for want of space on which to display them they had hitherto been rolled up in obscurity. On 15 June 1717 therefore, a month before he was made a Viscount, he acquired from the daughters of the Earl of Sussex, who died without male issue in 1715, the estate of Chevening near Sevenoaks in Kent, which seemed to meet all his desires. This estate of 3,466 acres, with a rent-roll of £1,176, he purchased for the sum of £28,000, most of which probably came out of his wife's jointure from her father 'Diamond' Pitt, since he himself had small means beyond his income of some £3,000 as Secretary of State,[1] and the purchase, as appears from the trust-deed, was made in

[1] See above, ch. iii, p. 64. The salary of Secretary of State came principally from fees and allowances, amounting in his nephew Pitt's time to some £5,680, out of which nearly half went in office expenses, leaving about £3,000 net (see Williams, *Chatham*, i. 327, note). Stanhope also got some extraordinary allowances: thus under date 20 Sept. 1718 in *Treasury Minute Books*, 'Earl Stanhope to have £5,000 in consideration of his eminent and faithful services and his charges and expenses to and from the courts of France and Spain.' But this grant fell far short of his actual expenses in foreign journeys, as appears from a statement preserved at Chevening:

Expenses		*Received to balance this*	
Journey to Vienna about	£800	a present of diamonds from the Emperor which I have sold for	£1060
1st „ „ Hanover about	£2000		
Difference between App^{ts} of S. of S. & Ch. of Exch. & 1st Comm^r of Treasury for one year	£2800	a bounty of £5000 from the King while deducting fees comes to about	£4740
2nd Journey to Hanover over & above £800 which has been paid me for expresses	£1800	Due to make me no loser	£5800 £3266
Journey to France & Spain	£1300		
2nd „ „ „	£366		
	£9066		£9066

the name of three trustees, Stanhope's old friend General Carpenter, his cousin and secretary Charles Stanhope, and his wife's distant cousin George Pitt of Stratfieldsea. The lord of the manor's house, built for the Dacres by Inigo Jones about 1630, stands in a noble park facing north to a wooded chalk ridge, along which runs the Pilgrim's Way; old Chevening Church, containing monuments of the Dacres as well as of the Stanhopes, and its tiny village nestle well into the landscape on the eastern edge of the park; south, the house looks over open ground towards the ridge above Sevenoaks, and on the west again is open country. But Stanhope, like his famous nephew, had grandiose ideas of the style of house and grounds suitable for himself and his family. He at once set to work enlarging the house and laying out the grounds on a scale so ambitious that the work had not been fully completed four years later when he died.[1] The sides of the old Inigo Jones house, originally a parallelogram in shape, were thrown out and connected by colonnaded corridors with large pavilions on each side of the gates of the fore-court. In these pavilions were the stables and offices, includ-ing a vast kitchen worthy of an Oxford college. Gates and balustrades curiously wrought in *clairvoyée* of Sussex iron were substituted for the original gates and stone balustrades. Within the house all the fittings, such as locks on doors and ramps for the service staircase, were fashioned by the best craftsmen. Inigo Jones's principal interior staircase of stone was removed and in its place a marvellous 'hanging staircase', two stories high, was constructed of Spanish oak. This staircase, which has no support except on the ground and by the insertion into the wall of three steps in each flight, though it sensibly sways as one ascends it and may not be used by more than twenty people at a time, still stands after over two centuries of wear. For the grounds designs were made, though not carried out, for the figure of a gladiator on a pedestal in the forecourt and for military trophies in the blank windows of the corridors leading to the pavilions. A maze in the Dutch fashion was planted to the west of the house and from the south front a Dutch garden, with its trim alleys of symmetrical trees, its quincunxes and neatly shorn box hedges, was made to extend on each side of a long piece of water as far as a classic pavilion. In the glades of the park north and west of the house could be seen herds of deer.

[1] The improvements were carried out at a cost of £12,000.

Stanhope, having once made the plans, could not devote much attention to the details of all these improvements or the management of the estate. But in his Countess Lucy, the capable daughter of a first-rate business man, he had an excellent substitute. She kept the rent-book, balanced the accounts, paid the church ringers and strewers on ceremonial occasions, kept an eye on the tenants, gave orders to the workmen and paid them when their work was completed, no less in her lord's lifetime than during her brief widowhood. Stanhope himself can have snatched only rare moments of rest and delight in his new domain, for he was too busy travelling to France, Spain or Germany, or on affairs of state in London, to afford much time for his own private business, nor did he live to enjoy a well-earned repose at Chevening. But the place still seems permeated by his spirit. The house and surroundings remain much as he had planned them, except that the third Earl spoilt the front by raising the wall so as to conceal Inigo Jones's sloping roof and covered it with a non-inflammable composition of his own invention,[1] and that the Dutch garden has given place to groves of fine trees on each side of the stretch of water. But on the walls still hang his portraits and those of his family and descendants, his medals and trophies and his tapestries still serve to remind us of his achievements and of the honour in which he was held. Even his books, most of which had been kept at his house by the Cockpit during his lifetime, were all brought to Chevening by the second Earl. In 1817 the fourth Earl piously catalogued and arranged them in the Old Library, still reserved exclusively for James's books and papers. James Stanhope's library consists of 1,600 volumes, mostly his own books with a few that belonged to his father, his brothers Philip and Edward, who died before him, and his Countess. As Macaulay observed when he saw the library in 1856, 'the collection has a unique interest as an example of what were the books of an English gentleman exactly as they stood a century and a half ago'. It is also remarkable for the evidence it affords of Stanhope's wide range of interests, containing as it does French, Italian, Spanish, Portuguese and classical books, works on history, philosophy, politics, divinity, gardening,

[1] The third Earl also appears to have sold, in order to pay for his building operations, 'the quantity of One Thousand & Fifteen Ounces and Fifteen Penny Weight of White Plate [given by the King in 1717] . . . in Consideracōn of the many good & acceptable Services Performed unto Us by the said James Viscount Stanhope' (*Country Life*, 1 May 1920).

the culinary art and English literature, besides some fine examples of good binding, some probably acquired by his father in Spain. Nor were these books bought simply to have a good appearance on his bookshelves, for his contemporaries unite in testifying to his scholarship and interest in literature, notable in a man with so little leisure.

Chevening is not merely a repository of past memories of its founder, but even to-day seems to bear the impress of a fine tradition of public service inaugurated by James and never lost sight of by its owners. Two of these owners have been men of marked scientific attainments, one was a notable historian who incidentally did much to increase the first Earl's reputation as a warrior and statesman: all have taken a worthy part in national or local affairs. Stanhope's nephew Chatham loved the place and not only stayed there for some months but contributed to its beauty and grandeur by cutting the finely graded road, still called Chatham's Ride, up the steep wooded side to the crest of the ridge north of the house. Rosebery, the one Prime Minister among his descendants, always looked on Chevening with affection and almost as a home. All who have lived at Chevening have cared for it, and maintained its beauty and traditions in their several ways. It is one of those homes, so characteristic of England, with a personality all its own, a personality fostered by generations of loving and public-spirited men and women.[1]

[1] I have derived many suggestions for this account of Chevening from the admirably illustrated articles on Chevening by Mr. Avray Tipping in *Country Life* (four articles, 17 April to 8 May 1920).

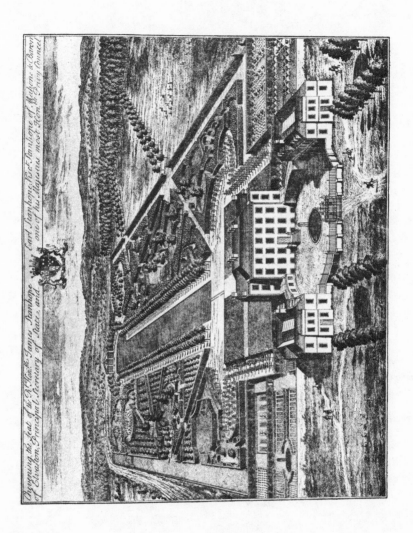

Displaying the Seat of the R.t Hon.ble James Stanhope Earl Stanhope, &c. Viscount of Mahone & Baron of Elvaston, Principal Secretary of State, and one of his Majesties most Hon.ble Privy Council

CHAPTER XI

THE QUADRUPLE ALLIANCE

§ 1

EVEN after the Treaty of Westminster of 1716 and the Triple Alliance of 1717 much still remained to be done before Europe or England could be assured of a stable peace. To attain this assurance Stanhope devoted most of his exuberant energy during the remaining years of his life, hardly less during the year that he was primarily responsible for the country's finances than after March 1718, when he again became Secretary of State. The problem before him was almost world-wide and might have proved insoluble, had it not been for the co-operation of France secured by the Triple Alliance. The northern war still raged with unabated vigour. The Treaty of Utrecht, which purported to bring peace to the whole of western Europe, had, like the two great treaties at the beginning of each of the following centuries, left almost as many obstacles to peace as it had removed. Leaving aside northern Europe for the time being, he first concentrated his attention on the chief danger-point in southern Europe.

The most glaring failure of the eleven treaties of Utrecht and of the treaties of Rastadt and Baden was that no peace had been made between the two nominal protagonists in the war. They left the Emperor Charles and Philip of Spain still unreconciled, still childishly claiming each other's titles. Apart from such puerilities the two monarchs found a definite grievance in the settlement of Italy. Until the eighteenth century the Spanish Habsburgs had been masters of the Milanese, Sardinia and the Two Sicilies, as Naples and the island of Sicily were then called: now Philip found himself without a foot of Italian soil. After the War of the Spanish Succession most of these possessions had gone to the Emperor, to whom had been allotted the Milanese, Sardinia and Naples; yet the Emperor in turn had a grievance of his own in that Sicily itself had been torn away from Naples and constituted a kingdom for Victor Amedeus of Savoy. So the Emperor would not rest till he had reunited the Two Sicilies under his own sway; Philip would not rest till he had regained the former Italian provinces, including the Two Sicilies, for

Spain. There was a further complication due to the approaching extinction of the male lines of the Medici in Tuscany and the Farnese in Parma and Piacenza. The Emperors had long claimed a feudal superiority over these duchies, and Charles VI thought this a favourable opportunity for insisting on this claim and even for taking over the direct rule of Tuscany as a set-off to French claims on Lorraine. Here again Spanish ambitions stood in his way. Philip's second wife Elizabeth was a Farnese and, in default of male heirs, claimed the succession to the duchy; she also, as a more distant connexion of the Medici, put forward a similar claim to Tuscany. Elizabeth was really less concerned with abstract rights than with apprehension about her own and her sons' future. For them there seemed little chance of succeeding to the Spanish crown, since Philip already had two sons by his first wife: for herself she dreaded the position of a Spanish king's widow, having seen the neglected state of Charles II's former wife. She could count on the support of her uxorious Philip, who could deny his wife nothing and was only too anxious to recover part of Italy for his stock; she could also count on that of Alberoni. This Parmesan priest, amid all the extravagant schemes concocted by his fertile brain, never lost sight of one great object—to expel the Germans from Italian soil and restore to his beloved peninsula something of her own individuality and independence. He had not indeed conceived the ideal of the next century, a united Italy mistress in her own house, but he was passionately anxious to confine her many rulers to those of Italian lineage and Latin sympathies. Princes of Elizabeth's Parmesan stock would answer this need well enough and would at any rate be more congenial to Italian aspirations than the hated Germans. Thus, though not entirely at one with Philip and his impetuous consort as to the time and method for bringing their schemes to fruition, he was ready to back them up in the ultimate objects of their Italian policy.

Another factor had to reckoned with in the Italian imbroglio: Victor Amedeus II of Savoy, now King of Sicily. Rulers of the Alpine passes that led into France and Germany, the Dukes of Savoy, whose ideal, according to Victor Amedeus, was 'vivre en repos avec nos moutons, nos femmes, nos mères, nos maîtresses et nos domestiques', had found their position between France and the Habsburgs incom-'

patible with such an idyllic existence. Since Richelieu's time they had been mere satellites of France till, after 1690, Victor Amedeus discovered that by playing off his two neighbours against one another he could not only shake off the yoke of France but gain advantages for himself. When Stanhope first met him in 1691 he had at last taken part against France: four years later by deserting his allies he had obtained valuable concessions from Louis.[1] When the War of the Spanish Succession began he was still on Louis's side, but soon came over to the allies on promise from the Emperor of territory in the Milanese; he was again on the point of deserting them before peace was made. No wonder French diplomatists began to acquire a wholesome respect for a prince whom they described as 'un des adversaires les plus coûteux et les plus redoutables de sa Majesté', able 'de tout temps s'attirer une considération fort audessus de celle qu'auroit pu lui procurer la médiocrité de sa puissance'.[2] At Utrecht he obtained full value for his craftiness, for besides Sicily and the royal title he obtained the reversion, on failure of the Anjou line, of the whole Spanish monarchy.

But he had already begun to find that his sudden elevation had its dangers. His changes of front and unscrupulous diplomacy had left him with few friends in Europe. The crown of Sicily, obtained by the favour of Louis XIV and the Tory ministry in England, was not without its thorns. The Sicilians had been quite content with the easy Spanish rule and the opportunities for advancement that a great monarchy gave them, but that a poor little north Italian state could not afford. They resented Victor Amedeus's refusal to make Palermo his capital and his attempts to turn their island to profitable uses; and they were not sorry to find the new king engaged in a damaging contest with the Pope on ecclesiastical rights.[3] Both the Emperor and Spain grudged him the possession of Sicily. Such indeed were his difficulties that Victor Amedeus soon realized it would be impossible for him to defend Sicily unless he were assured of support from the English fleet. The Tories had been willing to give him this support and had been on the point of signing the treaty with France to guarantee his

---

[1] See above, ch. i, pp. 8 sqq.
[2] *Recueil, Savoie, &c.*, i, Introduction and p. 311.
[3] See Baraudon and Carutti for accounts of these Sicilian difficulties.

possessions. But the Whigs had other views and soon put
an end to that project: in fact they were disposed to favour
the Emperor's desire to reunite the Two Sicilies in his own
hands.[1]

The behaviour of Charles VI and Philip V, playing with
one another's titles like a couple of naughty children and
refusing to call each other by their proper names, was not
only ludicrous but a menace to peace. Stanhope was determined to put a stop to it. But some solatium for their
offended dignity must be found; and where could it better
be found than in Italy, where each of the two sulky
monarchs was claiming substantial advantages? To modern
notions the idea of appeasing such rivalries by carving
compensations out of the fair land of Italy seems the height
of cynicism. But there was this excuse, that Italy, as a result
of centuries of invasion and oppression by alien conquerors,
had then no national feeling left, hardly any local feeling
except in the small cities. A few enlightened men, such as
Alberoni and later the Frenchman Argenson, conceived the
idea of freeing Italy from the strangers and keeping her
separate states under the rule of natives: but even such
notions were vague, were more in the interests of the rulers
than of the ruled, and found no response in the inert mass
of the population. It needed a catastrophic event like the
French Revolution, a tremendous personality like Napoleon's
to awaken the slumbering instincts for liberty and national
vigour in the inheritors of republican Rome. In those days,
if peace could be brought to Europe by satisfying the rival
claims of Habsburg and Bourbon through some adjustment
of territories in Italy, the statesman who seized that opportunity can hardly be condemned.

Even before the conclusion of the Triple Alliance Stanhope
had been exploring the ground and thinking out schemes
for reconciling the Emperor and Philip V. In September
1716, while still negotiating with Dubois at Hanover, he
wrote to Townshend: 'If we close with France, I think I have
a plan for Spain, which will not displease you, which I will
communicate to your Lordship in a short time'; and to
Horatio Walpole in October he recommended the agreement with Dubois mainly on the ground that France was
thereby committed to secure further advantages for the
Emperor in Italy, provided he gave up his absurd claim to

[1] See above, ch. vi, pp. 159, 160.

the Spanish monarchy.[1] What those advantages were may be gathered from an interview Stanhope had in the preceding February with Victor Amedeus's envoy in London. The King of Sicily was much troubled because the Emperor refused to acknowledge his royal title and had broken off relations with him, and he wished Stanhope to make his peace with Vienna; he even offered, so Stanhope informed Stair, to give up Sicily in exchange for Sardinia, though later he drew back from this offer unless he could at any rate obtain higher terms. At the time Stanhope had encouraged this proposal, for it afforded the very opening he desired for negotiating with the Emperor. He also knew what would satisfy Spain from the correspondence of Bubb who, shortly after the commercial treaty of 1716, had written that 'the absolute controul over Spain will belong to the highest bidder for the Queen's son. This is the grand and only maxim which has never changed since I have been here': in other words a duchy in Italy must be found for this son, Don Carlos.[2]

Thus primed, in December 1716 Stanhope made definite proposals to the Emperor and Spain. The Emperor was now more inclined to an accommodation. The war with Turkey, in spite of Eugene's great victory at Peterwardein, still left him dependent on England for the defence of his Italian interests; the death of his only son made him anxious for support for the Pragmatic Sanction he desired to promulgate in favour of his daughters; even his so-called 'Council of Spain' had lost hope of recovering that monarchy; and the recent alliance of England with France was disturbing. Accordingly he sent Pentenriedter, accompanied by St. Saphorin, the resident for England at Vienna, to Hanover to discuss Stanhope's proposals. Stanhope, after stating that the Emperor would be welcomed into the Triple Alliance, outlined his scheme for a settlement with Spain:

1. Charles VI was to give up his 'idées chimériques' on Spain and renounce that throne.
2. The Emperor's possessions in Flanders and Italy were to be

<hr />

[1] Coxe, *Walpole*, ii. 86, 99.
[2] R.O., *S.P.* 78/160, Stanhope to Stair 3 Feb. 1716; Coxe, *Walpole*, ii. 124, Stanhope to Townshend, 6 Nov. 1716; see also Baraudon, 124; and St. Simon, xiii. 21, who declares that the first suggestion for the exchange of Sicily came from Stanhope. This does not seem to be the case, though it is true that later, when Victor Amedeus hung back, Stanhope urged him strongly to make the exchange; Coxe, *Bourbons*, ii. 239.

guaranteed, and in return he was to guarantee the succession as established in England and France.

3. The Emperor was to obtain Sicily; also Tuscany, Parma and Piacenza as imperial fiefs; but in Parma and Piacenza he was to institute Don Carlos as reigning duke on the extinction of the direct male line of the Farnese.

Pentenriedter, true to the diplomatic traditions of his court, made a series of captious criticisms and exorbitant demands. The Emperor would admit Philip's *de facto* possession of Spain but would not explicitly abandon his own claims, 'Vienna being accustomed', as Bothmer drily remarked, 'to treat a claim to territory as almost equivalent to its possession'; and even for this concession he demanded Mexico and Peru; he would accept Sicily from Victor Amedeus in exchange for Sardinia but asked for Montferrat in addition. Finally losing patience, as St. Saphorin reported, at Pentenriedter's tiresome and procrastinating method of negotiating,

> 'qui n'aboutit qu'à perdre du temps et à rendre difficiles les choses les plus aisées, . . . Milord Stanhope, avec son esprit de précision et sa franchise ordinaire, sçut bientôt abréger tout cela.'

Whereas the craftier Sunderland, as a concession to the Emperor's susceptibilities, spoke of Philip V as the Duke of Anjou, Stanhope bluntly called him the King of Spain and told Pentenriedter that his demands on Spain were quite out of the question, as they would involve war with that country: in two days he could persuade Parliament to declare war on France, but it would cost him his head to propose hostilities against Spain. Nothing indeed was settled at this conference; but Stanhope's proposals were sent to Vienna to be solemnly and with imperial leisure discussed by the Secret Council.[1] Dubois warmly welcomed the scheme as a further guarantee of the Regent's position and a new proof of its author's capacity.[2]

At The Hague, on his way back to England, Stanhope sounded the Spanish ambassador Beretti-Landi as to the cession of Sicily to the Emperor in return for that of Parma to the Infant. He also wrote to the same effect to Alberoni with a warning not to rely too much on the mediation of the

---

[1] Bothmer, *Memoiren*; Weber, 28–30; Wiesener, ii. 41 sqq.; Baraudon, 180–1; Baudrillart, ii. 269 sq.

[2] A.E., *Angleterre*, 295, ff. 192 sqq.

Pope, who was rumoured to be urging Spain to make peace with the Emperor by his means. Alberoni in his answer denied having any dealings with the Pope and seemed favourable to Stanhope's plan.[1] Having thus thrown out his rough idea of a settlement, Stanhope left it to simmer in the minds of the statesmen most concerned, but for the first few months after his return to England was too much taken up with the Gyllenborg affair and the ministerial crisis to pursue the matter farther.

When, in the spring of 1717, Stanhope was able to resume negotiations, he found that his only chance of carrying through his plan was in the closest co-operation with France. For Alberoni, on further reflection, demanded the Emperor's evacuation of Mantua and the immediate establishment of a Spanish garrison in Parma as preliminaries to peace; otherwise, as he told Bubb, the Emperor might seize Parma and Tuscany before Spain and England could take any measures to prevent him.[2] The Emperor still maintained the impossible terms put forward by Pentenriedter and was even said by Stanhope's correspondent Bonneval, a renegade Frenchman in the Emperor's service, to be toying with the idea of supporting, with the Pope, another Jacobite rebellion.[3] On the other hand, the Regent was especially anxious to secure the mutual renunciations of the Emperor and Philip V; for in them he saw the best safeguard for his Regency and his claims to the French throne, which would always be disputed by Philip as long as his own hold on the Spanish throne was jeopardized by the Emperor's refusal to recognize his title. Dubois fully shared his master's view but had his own difficulties to contend with. Huxelles, in charge of foreign affairs, and all the old advisers of Louis XIV, such as Torcy and Villeroy, now the young King's governor, were wedded to their master's former policy of enmity to England and the Emperor and of close

[1] So Stanhope told Monteleone, the Spanish ambassador, in a letter of 26 May 1718, R.O., *S.P.* 104/219 B; see also Alberoni's letter of 8 Feb. 1717 to the Duke of Parma confirming this in Castagnoli 269; and Dubois's memoir of 20 June 1718 in A.E., *Angleterre*, 312, ff. 303–10.

[2] Bourgeois, *Farnèse*, 249; Coxe, *Bourbons*, ii. 264.

[3] A copy of Bonneval's letter of 13 Mar. 1717 is in A.E., *Angleterre*, 300, f. 15. Bonneval, a Frenchman of good family and remarkable ability, after a quarrel with his superiors in France, had taken service under the Emperor and distinguished himself highly. Another quarrel with the authorities in Vienna drove him on to Constantinople, where he entered the Turkish service, ending his days as a Pasha and a Musulman. He occasionally sent Stanhope information from Vienna.

relations with the Bourbon line in Spain. They had never
approved of the Triple Alliance and dreaded these new
proposals of Stanhope, which appeared to them unduly
favourable to the Emperor and such as Philip would never
accept without coercion. In this view they undoubtedly
represented popular opinion in France, which resented the
idea of suddenly turning against a French prince for whose
sake so much French blood and treasure had been poured
out. Nor could Dubois rely even upon the Regent. Though
convinced of his personal interest in holding fast to the
English alliance, in action he was weak and undecided and
mortally afraid of running counter to the views of the old
court and the country, or of appearing to think of his own
advantage:

> 'Vous n'ignorez pas', he once wrote to Dubois, 'les raisons que
> j'ai de désirer que l'on ne puisse jamais supposer que mes in-
> térêts ayent esté la règle de mes résolutions, lorsqu'en effet je ne
> suis occupé que de ceux du Roy et de l'État.'[1]

Dubois, almost alone in France, was undeviating in his
support of the English alliance and of Stanhope's policy of
pacification, and, though he was generally able to keep the
Regent on the same lines when he was on the spot, in his
absence the old court was constantly reasserting its influence.

Unfortunately it so happened that the French court was
in one of its cold fits towards England in the spring of
1717, partly owing to Stanhope's publication of Gyllenborg's 'maudite lettre' about the Regent,[2] partly owing to a
divergence of view about Prussia. Dubois was very anxious
that Prussia should be admitted into the Triple Alliance
on the ground that Prussia would prove a very useful make-
weight against the Emperor in the negotiations about Italy
and Spain. But Stanhope would not hear of Prussia's admission, partly owing to George I's natural indignation at
Frederick William's understanding with the Tsar at Havelberg,[3] but chiefly for the very reason for which Dubois
recommended it. Stanhope had no intention of antagonizing the Emperor, as he certainly would if he admitted
Prussia to an alliance to which the head of the Empire was
not a party, and was most anxious to obtain his willing
co-operation in the proposed arrangements with Spain. In

---

[1] A.E., *Angleterre*, 297, ff. 78 sq., 28 Dec. 1717.
[2] See above, ch. ix, p. 247.   [3] Ib., p. 234.

this affair, as usual in his dealings with Dubois, Stanhope had his way; and Frederick William was not admitted to the Triple Alliance. But on another point Stanhope made no difficulty in conceding a point to Dubois and the Regent. They proposed that the negotiations with the Emperor and Spain should be conducted in the first instance by England, ostensibly on the ground that her relations with both Vienna and Madrid were more friendly than those of France, but really because the Regent was afraid he would have to bear the brunt of Spain's indignation when that court found the terms to be offered to her fell so far below Spanish expectations. In return, Dubois offered to continue acting for England as well as France in dealing with the northern Powers. In fact, this division of labour exactly suited Stanhope, who tactfully announced that one of his chief aims was to secure, by guarantees from the chief European powers, the Regent's right of succession to the French throne, as well as to prevent a general war about Italy which might put the fate of Spain, of the Emperor, and even of France 'to the hazard of fortune again': and so it was arranged to the satisfaction of both courts.[1]

But before the negotiators could get to work Spain suddenly exploded a bombshell in their midst. In July 1716 Alberoni had obtained the dismissal of Cardinal del Giudice, Philip's chief minister, and had thus become the ostensible as well as the real master of Spanish policy. Among other posts vacated by Giudice was that of Grand Inquisitor of Spain, which was bestowed on Molinez, Philip's minister at the Papal court. Not till May 1717, however, was Molinez summoned to assume his functions in Spain. Molinez was then eighty years old and, fearing the sea voyage, imprudently came overland through the Milanese, where, in spite of a safe-conduct from Rome, he was arrested by the Imperial governor. Philip V, enraged at the insult and only too glad of an excuse to pursue his Italian aims while the Emperor's attention was distracted by the Turks, was all for immediate vengeance. Alberoni, though as keen as Philip on Italian conquests, was strongly against precipitate action and cursed Molinez as a pompous old fool—*solennissima bestia*—for getting them into the scrape. Not only were there clauses in the treaties of Utrecht and Baden

---

[1] A.E., *Angleterre*, 300, f. 10; and for a précis of this whole correspondence between Stanhope and Dubois, ib. 295, ff. 12–48.

declaring the neutrality of Italy, but at the Pope's instigation Spain among others had agreed specifically to respect that neutrality as long as the Emperor was waging a holy war against the Infidels: the breach of such an understanding would outrage the Pope and Catholic feeling throughout Europe. Alberoni also had a personal reason for delay in antagonizing the Pope, for he was moving heaven and earth to obtain a cardinal's hat and knew that an attack at such a time on the Emperor would at once destroy his chances at the Papal court. Nor did he feel that Spain was yet ready for the great effort involved in such an enterprise. Since he came into power he had already done wonders in restoring Spanish industries, in reforming abuses and lightening the burdens on the people, and in building, equipping and manning fleets, and reorganizing the army: but even so the work was no more than half done and might all be wasted by premature action. However, since Philip and Elizabeth were determined, he bowed to necessity and organized the expedition with his accustomed vigour; but he took care to keep its object secret till the last moment and even gave out that it was designed against the Infidel. On 25 July news came to Madrid that the Pope had declared Alberoni a cardinal: he was congratulated by the envoys of all the Powers, among others by Bubb, who, however, added significantly that King George could not believe that the fleet then arming could be designed to attack the Emperor, for, were it so, he would be obliged to help his ally. Four days later the fleet started from Barcelona with orders to seize Sardinia. On 22 August it arrived at Cagliari and found little difficulty in entirely subduing the island within a couple of months. Alberoni, when reminded of Spain's engagement to respect the neutrality of Italy, coolly replied that it was not customary for Kings to observe treaties any longer when circumstances that made them necessary had changed. In fact, nice treaties must curtsey to Kings of Spain.[1]

This success naturally made the Spanish court more intractable. So serious a view did Stanhope take of its attitude that he offered himself to pay a flying visit to

[1] See the accounts of this incident in Baudrillart, ii. 274–6; Castagnoli, 273 sqq.; Coxe, *Bourbons*, ii. 268 sqq. Baudrillart argues that, in spite of a strong letter from Alberoni to the Duke of Popoli against the expedition, Alberoni's only reason for delay was the doubt about the cardinalate: but his argument is not convincing. For Alberoni's remark about obsolete treaties see Bothmer, *Memoiren*.

Madrid, but, finding he could not be spared from home, sent out his cousin, William Stanhope, to represent his views.[1] The Emperor, on the other hand, became more pliable, especially when it was explained to him that he could expect no help from England in the Mediterranean unless he agreed to some such settlement as Stanhope had proposed. Stanhope and Dubois were anxious at all costs to prevent an extension of hostilities and agreed to settle terms at a conference in London. The Emperor and Philip, as the parties mainly interested, were invited to send representatives to this conference: Philip refused to have anything to do with it, but the Emperor sent Pentenriedter.

§ 2

Dubois arrived in England at the end of September 1717, but had to wait for the opening of the formal conferences till Pentenriedter arrived a month later. He employed his time well, however, in accommodating himself to his new surroundings and taking stock of the trend of opinion in England. He was curious to see Parliament; accordingly, 'having desired to be an ocular witness of the important debate [on the number of the land forces], he was admitted *incognito* into the House of Commons; a favour which that day was refused to several British Peers'.[2] On this occasion he had the good fortune to hear speeches from Walpole, Craggs, Lechmere and Shippen, and the motion for committing Shippen to the Tower for words reflecting on the King. But, practised diplomatist as he was, he was not content to meet only the politicians. He renewed his old friendships in English society and made many new ones. With the men he became popular for the French delicacies and rare French wines always to be found at his table, with the ladies he soon became a favourite for his courtly manners and insinuating address and for his complaisance in forwarding their commissions for exquisite French fabrics and knick-knacks to the best Paris dealers. Nor did he neglect his own personal appearance, sending most exact directions to his nephew as to the cut and fabric of his garments, which were always to be purple, as befitted an abbé. He was somewhat troubled by the English habits of deep drinking, being

[1] A.E., *Angleterre*, 295, ff. 111 sqq.; Dubois to Regent, 4 Oct. 1717.
[2] *Collection of Parliamentary Debates* (Dublin), vii. 46.

himself most abstemious, but bravely sacrificed his stomach in the good cause. This apparent trifling was not wasted; for, going everywhere and seeing everybody, he formed shrewd judgements on the men with whom he had to deal and the general current of opinion in the country.

He was, of course, warmly welcomed by Stanhope, who found room for him at Hampton Court Palace in his own apartments, which consisted of the 'two Rooms, two closetts and the garretts over them', usually assigned to the Chancellor of the Exchequer, and the 'three rooms and one closett' appropriated to the Lord Treasurer.[1] Stanhope also engaged for himself and Dubois a house next to the King's at Newmarket for the racing season.[2] In his reports to Paris Dubois notes with admiration the tranquillity of the country and the credit of Stanhope's ministry so few months after the disruption of the Whig party. He attributes this happy state of affairs partly to the ministry's lenient treatment of opponents, but chiefly to the conversion of the debt and lowering of interest and their financial and commercial policy generally. In his eyes Stanhope towers head and shoulders above his colleagues and even to the Prince of Wales, he notes, he is 'the least odious' of the ministers; above all, he is a true friend of France, 'the only man on whom we can count absolutely and who can hold the others in leash'; if he were to die, says Dubois on the occasion of a passing illness of Stanhope's, 'France could not suffer a greater loss in this country . . . . c'est un philosophe homme de bien qui aime sa patrie mais qui aime V.A.R. presque autant qu'elle'.[3]

At no time in his strenuous career had Stanhope to sustain so heavy a burden of work and responsibility as during the negotiations for the Quadruple Alliance. In the early stages, until March 1718, he was not even Secretary of State; but Sunderland, who was, conscious, as Bothmer says, that Stanhope 'excelled him in foreign affairs',[4] was content to leave him in charge of the discussions; and even after that he was nominally responsible only for the Northern

---

[1] *Chevening MSS.*, Warrant of 13 June 1717 signed by Newcastle as Lord Chamberlain.

[2] J. Coke's letter to Stanhope in *Chevening MSS.* The house-rent was wasted, as Stanhope was too ill to go to the races and Dubois would not go without him (A.E., *Angleterre*, 295, ff. 111 sqq.).

[3] For Dubois's reports and comments on England, see A.E., *Angleterre*, 295 and 296, *passim*; and Aubertin.

[4] Bothmer, *Memoiren.*

Department. But throughout he kept all the threads of the complicated negotiations in his own hands and, without any regard for narrow departmental limits, wrote most of the important dispatches. How he managed to cope with it all is a marvel, only to be explained by his absolute devotion to the public interest and his enormous capacity for work. For, though he had some devoted subordinates, the younger Craggs, Lukas Schaub and, later, the most brilliant of them all, the youthful Lord Carteret, he had not seemingly the faculty of some great men—such as his nephew Chatham—of picking out his agents with such unerring judgement that after a few general directions he could safely leave them to carry out a campaign or a policy: on the contrary he saw to almost every detail himself. One instance of his unresting energy we have seen when he dashed through Germany to Italy in 1710, leaving Craggs to follow him as best he could.[1] In his numerous journeys to the Continent as a minister he never seemed to know fatigue or care for danger. On one occasion his cousin Charles reports his arrival at Hanover after travelling four days and nights on end without going to bed, 'which I was very much surprised to find could be done without any fatigue'. A dangerous crossing of the Channel had no terrors for him when it was a case of promptly settling some difficulty with the Regent or Dubois. He cheerfully undertook a tiresome journey to Madrid to see Alberoni for a few days, and entirely ignored the danger he ran of being detained as a hostage for his pains. His constant vigilance during the Rebellion is only one illustration of a habit. Thus in a letter to Stair giving a full and lucid exposition of his views on the Quadruple Alliance, he incidentally mentions that in order to write the letter, 'I have withdrawn myself for a few minutes from a great meeting of Lords, who are now at my house, making their disposition [for a momentous debate in Parliament].' But even Stanhope's splendid constitution, taxed to the utmost not only by his incessant labours but also, it seems, by good living, sometimes showed signs of wear under the strain. For three weeks during the early part of Dubois's stay in London he appears to have been somewhat seriously ill. Again, a year later his absence in Bath gave rise to rumours that he and Sunderland had quarrelled and that he was about to resign. In fact his short absence was due chiefly to indisposition;

[1] See above, ch. iv, p. 93.

and, so far from having quarrelled with Sunderland, he was staying at his lodgings in Bath and playing chess with him of an evening, while as to the rumour of his resignation he assured Stair that

'never was lie set about with so little foundation; for if there has been any period of time since the King's coming to his Crown at which, more than at another, I have been intent to carry on his service, and at which his Majesty hath been good and gracious to me, it hath been since my return from France [a week or so previously].'

Stanhope, indeed, was one of those who felt he was doing good work and loved it; nor was he the man to give in while he had strength.[1]

When the Hampton Court Conference met in November 1717 the method of proceeding arranged by Stanhope and Dubois was as follows. The French and English negotiators, in consultation with the Emperor's representative only, since Spain refused to be represented, were to draw up terms of peace between Spain and the Emperor and for the adjustment of claims in Italy. These terms, when finally agreed upon by the King of England and the Regent, were to be sent to the Emperor for his consent: the States General were also to be invited to accede to what would then become a Quadruple Alliance for carrying out the agreed terms and enforcing them on Spain if she refused to accept them. At Hampton Court Pentenriedter at first, owing perhaps to some imperial punctilio, did not meet Dubois face to face, but had messages from the main conference brought to him by the English ministers. Stanhope's task was really that of mediator between Pentenriedter, with his exorbitant claims for the Emperor, and Dubois, who had been instructed to favour Spain as much as possible and to obtain Tuscany as well as Parma for the Infant, and the immediate admission of Spanish garrisons into the Duchies. Pentenriedter, who had hardly abated anything from his demands of the previous year, was the more difficult to deal with, since the King's German advisers were inclined to support the Emperor against France and Spain. But Dubois had great confidence in Stanhope for dealing with the long-winded Austrian, for he was 'un grand abréviateur qui

---

[1] Mahon, *History*, ii, Appendix, Stanhope to Stair, 17 Feb. 1718; *H. MSS., Polwarth*, i. 629; ib., *Portland*, v. 563; *Stair Annals*, ii. 64.

lui parlerait fortement et le clouerait'.[1] Stanhope's fiery temper certainly came in useful, when, in reply to Penten-riedter's cool proposal that Majorca should be obtained for the Emperor by means of the English fleet, he retorted that England would never fight Spain for such an object—speaking 'si fortement', says Dubois—that the other ministers present were scandalized: but no more was heard of the proposal. The fleet indeed, as always, was Stanhope's trump card with the Emperor, who was brought to realize that the help of the English navy in the Mediterranean was only for those who would fall in with English plans. Finally, at a meeting between Dubois and the English and German ministers held on 22 November at the Duke of Newcastle's house, the concessions required of the Emperor for a settlement were drafted: he was to renounce all claim to the Spanish monarchy and give up Parma and Piacenza to the Infant; but as a set-off against these concessions he was to receive Sicily from Victor Amedeus in exchange for Sardinia. The draft was then handed to Pentenriedter for consideration by the Emperor's advisers in Vienna. But this was by no means an end of the difficulties, even between England and France.[2]

For some time Dubois had been troubled by the news from France that the Regent had once more fallen under the influence of the pro-Spanish party and had been negotiating on his own account at Madrid. In September Philip V had been seriously ill and, thinking himself on the point of death, made a will naming his wife as regent for her young stepson, and Alberoni president of the council of regency. Such an accession to Alberoni's power alarmed the Duke of Orleans, while Alberoni became apprehensive for his own future during a minority when the Queen might not prove strong enough to support him against the opposition of grandees who hated him as an upstart and a foreigner. Both, therefore, were inclined to come to terms; and Alberoni took advantage of the Regent's forthcoming disposition to draw him away from England. He continued to treat the English envoy, William Stanhope, with marked discourtesy and even violence, and insinuated to his French colleague that the Emperor wished to wrest the Indies from Spain in order to hand them over to England for her support.

[1] Bourgeois, *Régent*, 252.
[2] Bothmer, *Memoiren*; Pribram, i. 353 sqq.; Wiesener, ii. 112 sqq.

So much alarmed was the Regent that in an instruction to Dubois he warned him of this danger and made it plain that he was veering towards Spain. Dubois in answer implored him not to continue these underhand negotiations and warned him that though, as Pentenriedter spitefully observed, he was now more popular in England than in France, if such proceedings were discovered he would never be able to regain the English ministers' confidence: at present they were anxious not to commit themselves too deeply to the Emperor; once convinced, however, that the Regent was playing them false, they would throw themselves entirely into his arms.[1] But these warnings had so little effect that at the end of November, after the completion of the draft plan, Dubois decided to go to Paris himself, to try the effect of his personal influence on his master.

Within a fortnight Dubois had won back the Regent to his policy and wrote to Stanhope that France would accept the plan if the Infant obtained Tuscany as well as Parma and the Emperor made an unequivocal renunciation of Spain. By Christmas he had returned to London and was able to resume negotiations with Stanhope. In February 1718 they had completed the treaty in a form for presentation to the governments concerned. This draft treaty differed little from the outline sent to Vienna in November except for modifications, introduced by the Regent's wish, in favour of Spain. The Emperor was definitely to renounce all claim to Spain but to recover Sardinia and then exchange it with Victor Amedeus for Sicily. Spain was to recognize the Emperor's rights and titles and in return to obtain Tuscany as well as Parma and Piacenza for the Infant. As a guarantee to the Emperor against the use of the four Tuscan ports—Presidii so called—for the transport of Spanish troops into Italy, two of them, Pisa and Leghorn, were to be erected into an independent republic; but Stanhope brushed aside the Hanoverians' demand that the other two should also be taken with the common-sense argument that 'it would be like giving a man a house, but refusing him the use of the doors'.[2] Holland was to be invited to join England and France as one of the original signatories. The draft treaty was thereupon handed to Lukas Schaub, a Swiss secretary employed by Stanhope and much trusted by him

---

[1] Bourgeois, *Régent*, 233; Wiesener, ii. 115; Baudrillart, ii. 283 sqq.
[2] Pribram, i. 356–7; Bothmer, *Memoiren*.

and Dubois, to take to the Regent for his approval with or without modification; then Schaub was to continue his journey to Vienna and submit the treaty with the Regent's amendments to the Emperor. Another copy was sent to the Spanish court. Lastly, Sunderland sent a copy to Holland with a request for the accession of the States General to the Quadruple Alliance.[1]

The English government's anxiety to secure the Dutch as parties to the Alliance was not due to any exaggerated hopes of their military aid against Spain or even of diplomatic pressure from them on the Emperor or Spain, but partly to the desire of keeping up the association with an old ally, partly to the fear that without such an engagement the Dutch, in case of England's rupture with Spain, would entirely oust our traders from their favourable position there. The attitude of Ripperda, the Dutch envoy at Madrid, gave ground for this apprehension. Not only had he illuminated his house in honour of Spain's conquest of Sardinia, but in November had declared that Holland, in the interests of her trade, would not oppose Spain's policy in Italy. In this Ripperda may have gone beyond his instructions: nevertheless the Dutch found plenty of excuses for not joining the new alliance. At one time it was an unsettled account for £200,000 due to them for expenses in the last war; at another a dispute about paying for a garrison in Parma; a very real grievance was the Emperor's delay in concluding an agreement needed to confirm and supplement the Barrier Treaty of 1715, but even when he had done so at the end of 1718 they found excuses for not ratifying it themselves till the following May.[2] When all other excuses failed they could always fall back on their clumsy, but often convenient, constitution, which, in addition to the assent of the States General to a treaty, also required that of each separate province. These evasions were enough to enrage a more patient man than Stanhope, who after listening to a series of such excuses burst out at the trembling Dutch delegate:

'You make many difficulties, but perhaps we can live without you: don't imagine that we shall allow you to enrich yourselves in the Spanish trade while we only pocket the loss.'

But even Stanhope was not able to 'boost' the Dutch, any

[1] Mahon, *History*, ii, Appendix, Stanhope to Stair, 23 Jan. 1717/18; R.O. S.P. 104/219 B, Sunderland to Whitworth, 28 Feb. 1717/18.
[2] Pribram, i. 385; Geikie and Montgomery, 364–8.

more than could Carteret twenty-five years later, once they had dug their toes well into the ground. Though always on the point of doing so, they never actually joined the famous Alliance which has gone down to history, but never really achieved the full aim of its projectors, as the Quadruple Alliance.[1]

Other incidental difficulties distracted Stanhope in his endeavours to adjust the divergent views of Emperor and Regent and accommodate them both with a recalcitrant Spain. One was the attitude of Victor Amedeus. At first, it will be remembered, he had not only agreed but proposed to give up Sicily to the Emperor for a suitable compensation: now he was playing his old game of intriguing concurrently with both sides in the hope of obtaining a larger reward. To Spain he professed himself willing to give up Sicily, if Philip would help him to gain a large slice of the Emperor's Milanese territory: to the Emperor he also offered Sicily in exchange for Tuscany, and besides asked for an Archduchess as a wife for his son. For months he carried on this double game, but he overreached himself. The other Powers, after long experience of his double dealings, were at least able to agree in giving him the cold shoulder; and almost for the first time in his long reign Victor Amedeus failed to make a profit for himself out of his neighbours' dissensions.[2]

Even at home Stanhope could by no means feel sure of his ground. In the King's speech at the opening of the session on 21 November 1717 it was announced that the army had been reduced by nearly one-half, to 16,000 men, but that vigilance in preserving the peace of Europe was still needed:

'The eyes of all Europe', the speech concluded, 'are upon you at this critical juncture. It is your interest, for which I think it mine, that my endeavours for procuring the peace and quiet of Christendom, should take effect. Nothing can so much contribute to this desirable end, as the unanimity, despatch and vigour of your resolutions for the support of my government'

—hopeful words, but sadly belied by the event. Stanhope's aim was peace, but before obtaining it he was resolved to take elementary precautions; and in the unsettled state of Europe, both in the north and the south, this small land

[1] See Appendix B, p. 449, on the Dutch attitude to the Quadruple Alliance.
[2] R.O., *S.P.* 104/219 B, Stanhope to William Stanhope, 11 Apr. 1718; *Stair Annals*, ii. 351; Baraudon, 245 sqq., 290 sqq.; Wiesener, ii. 137 sqq.; Weber, 68 sq.

force might have appeared the minimum needed. But Walpole and the Tories would have none of it. They thundered against standing armies in general as a menace to the liberties of the people and proposed to reduce the army still further to 12,000. It was in the course of these debates that Shippen deplored the King's ignorance of the language and feelings of his people and talked of a foreign policy calculated by 'the meridian of Germany', language which resulted in his committal to the Tower by a majority of nearly 100 votes. But on the main issue of the reduction of the army Walpole lost by only 50 votes, and even so the amount for the pay of the army was reduced. The next attack came in January on the Mutiny Bill legalizing courts martial. In the Commons the government carried the crucial clause by a majority of only 18, and the contest was resumed in the Lords. Stanhope started his defence badly by remarking that 'he was not like some persons that changed their opinions according as they were in or out of place', an insinuation which provoked an angry retort from Argyll. In the later stages of the debate Stanhope was more effective, pointing out that the changes in the Bill proposed by the opposition

'would render it ineffectual, banish all manner of discipline from the army, and consequently render it entirely useless . . . If', he continued, 'the government was now obliged to keep a greater number of forces than formerly, it was partly owing to the situation in which the affairs of Europe had been left by the late scandalous peace. . . . [In the present state of Europe] we must not imagine we could be out of the case, for though we might by mean, pitiful methods avoid a war for a few months, sooner or later we must have our share in it, and then the succession to the Crown of Britain might come to be disputed as well as that of Spain.'[1]

He carried his Bill by adequate majorities, but his anxiety about the result is shown in a letter to Stair urging the need of an early understanding with Spain, since

'it very much behoves us to be very cautious how we engage in any war, when I shall tell you the united strength of the Tories and discontented Whigs, headed and animated by one you may guess, are to give us battle tomorrow in the House of Lords, upon the Bill for punishing mutiny and desertion. . . . We think

[1] The debates on the land forces and on the Mutiny Bill are in *P.H.* vii. 505–23, 536–48; further details are given in Jacobite reports in *H. MSS., Stuart*, vi. 85, 352.

ourselves sure of carrying the question; but I am sorry to tell you that it will be by a slender majority.'[1]

During the first half of this century an attack on the standing army, however small, was always a sure card for an opposition to play, so lively still were the recollections of the Rebellion and the Revolution. Fortunately there was never the same objection to the navy; and when in March the King asked for an increase in the number of seamen to provide for fleets being sent to the Baltic and the Mediterranean, Walpole appears to have been the only speaker against the motion.[2] More serious was the discontent in the trading community as to the prohibition of commerce with Sweden and the fear of war with Spain. The grievances of the Baltic traders were discussed in the House of Commons in February, but no action was taken in the matter since in the previous year, after the Gyllenborg disclosures, Parliament itself had asked the King to prohibit commerce with Sweden.[3] In May the South Sea Company sent a deputation to Stanhope to protest against the dispatch of a fleet to the Mediterranean and to ask if it would be safe to send off their trading ship with its cargo valued at £80,000. It is evidence of Stanhope's continued optimism about bringing Spain into his scheme of pacification that even then he made light of the Company's fears and advised them to send their ship. He assured them that he had every hope that Spain would accept the good terms offered by the allies and that the fleet was being sent merely as a precautionary measure to prevent a war in Italy and, even if there were any trouble, was as likely as not to find itself on Spain's side.[4]

Lastly, there was an incident which, though no doubt disturbing at the time, afforded some comic relief. The hero of the incident was Stanhope's old acquaintance and companion-in-arms, Peterborough, still never happy unless he was in the limelight. After his recall from Spain by the Whigs he had made friends with the Tories and on their obtaining power had claimed employment. Knowing his volatile and unstable nature they had got rid of him on a mission in which he had no chance of doing much harm.

---

[1] Mahon, *History*, ii, Appendix, Stanhope to Stair, 17 Feb. 1718. 'One you may guess' was no doubt meant for Walpole.
[2] *P.H.* vii. 555–6; Michael, i. 806.
[3] *P.H.* vii. 548–50.
[4] *H. MSS.*, *Stuart*, vi. 442–3; Bourgeois, *Farnèse*, 308.

After the return of the Whigs with George I his craving for notoriety induced him to try and assume control of the negotiations for the Triple Alliance. He suddenly appeared 'tout botté', at Stair's house in 1716 to give directions on this subject. 'If I am mighty complaisant', writes Stair, giving the gist of his remarks, 'I may have the honour of making this treaty; if I happen to be rusty it will go into other hands.'[1] He also kept the Regent and Townshend up to the mark, thoughtfully writing his letter of advice to the latter in French to ensure its being shown to and understood by the King.[2]

After the completion of the Triple Alliance without his help he turned his attention to the Italian problem. He had few lasting ideas, but among these was a grudge against Charles VI, to whom mainly he attributed his recall from Spain and the loss of his famous conquests in Valencia. Accordingly he was against any concession to Charles in Italy and busied himself with a scheme for reconciling Philip V and the Regent and forming, with the aid of the Duke of Parma, a league of Italian princes with the two Bourbon Powers. In pursuit of this chimera in the autumn of 1717 'that old Don Quixote, the last of the knights errant', as Stanhope called him, started on a tour of visits to the Italian princes. But, on reaching the Pope's dominions after visiting Parma and Turin, he was suddenly arrested by the Papal *sbirri* and put into rigorous confinement at Bologna on the absurd charge of meditating the assassination of the Pretender. News of his arrest came to London just as Dubois arrived there, and he describes with malicious pleasure the derision with which the news was received at Hampton Court. Some asked who would claim him, others plausibly suspected him of inventing the whole story to see what its effect would be. But, however ridiculous Peterborough might be, the government felt they could not tamely submit to this outrage on an English peer. The Secretary of State asked the Imperial ambassador at Rome to demand his immediate release, and at the same time to require the Pope to cease offering public prayers for the success of the Pretender; unless he complied, the fleet would be ordered to Civita Vecchia to exact satisfaction. To show that this was no vain threat the Barbary fleet was reinforced with eight men-of-war and ordered to be in readiness to

[1] Hardwicke, ii, *Stair's Journal*, 2 Dec. 1715.
[2] A.E., *Angleterre*, 285, ff. 22-6 has a copy of this letter.

sail forthwith to the coast of Italy.[1] These orders, issued as
they were during the course of the Hampton Court negotiations, caused some alarm at the French court, since it
was feared that a reinforced English fleet in the Mediterranean might encourage the Emperor's bellicose tendencies to
Spain's disadvantage. Fortunately the Pope forestalled the
necessity of force by apologizing and setting Peterborough
free to pursue his vagaries.

Unfortunately his own imprisonment was the least of the
troubles arising from Peterborough's meddlesome proclivities. Dubois's abrupt return to France from the Hampton
Court Conference had been due partly to the impression
Peterborough's scheme had made on the Regent and the
consequent advances from France to Spain. Alberoni also
coquetted with the scheme, all the more as Peterborough
encouraged him to demand the retention of Sardinia. All
through the next year, too, Peterborough persisted with his
amateur diplomacy, cloaking his proceedings with an osten-
tatious mystery which naturally excited comment. Bolingbroke reported to Stair in March 1718 that Peterborough
had asked for an interview on some highly 'necessary and
important affair', but a month later writes,

'I have seen the Knight errant, and am willing to hope that our
meeting was the pure effects of friendship, for I profess I could
discover no business which we had to concert. We were together from six till twelve in conversation. The adventure at
Bologna you will imagine took up some hours in relating. He
seem'd to me very easy in giving his Holiness absolution. I am
not concerned att the £10000 Ster: which the imprisonment cost
him. He ask'd me if I had any measure to keep with Oxford,
talk'd of printing some what against that worthy person, whom
he accuses of having given occasion to the reports which were
spread in consequence whereof he was arrested. . . . We parted
without settling this. We forgot it in the heat of discourse, and
yet it seem'd to be the only thing we had to agree upon.'[2]

In the following September he was still harping on his
scheme in a long letter to the Regent, in which he offers
to go on a mission to Madrid, 'unofficially, as our ministers
would, I think, prefer', he has the grace to add.[3]

---

[1] R.O., *S.P.* 104/96, Addison's letters of 14 and 28 Oct. 1717.
[2] *Oxenfoord MSS.*, Bolingbroke Papers, f. 51, 13 Apr. 1718.
[3] A.E., *Angleterre*, 309, ff. 207–9, 6 Sept. 1718. For Peterborough's proceedings see Bourgeois, *Régent*, 233 sq., 254 sq., 314 sq.; id., *Farnèse*, 268, 320 sqq.;
Castagnoli, 301–2.

§ 3

Meanwhile Schaub had been cooling his heels in Vienna for nearly three months waiting for the decision of the Emperor and his councils on the draft treaty of February. In Paris on the way out he had found, in spite of a sheaf of objections from Huxelles and Torcy, little difficulty in adjusting matters with the Regent. For when Stanhope had agreed to waive his proposal for a separate republic of two Tuscan ports, Schaub, after an assurance from the Regent of his 'great respect for Lord Stanhope', was able to take away the treaty with no other material alterations. So protracted, however, were the discussions on every detail in Vienna, that once more Stanhope had to bring forward his great argument for forcing the Emperor to a prompt decision, his weakness in the Mediterranean without the help of the English fleet. To Pentenriedter in London he declared that 'England would not fire a shot against Spain';[1] to Schaub and St. Saphorin he sent a detailed statement to be submitted to the Emperor. Money for the fleet, he wrote, had been voted, the ships were ready for sea: but, until news came of the Emperor's signature, nobody in England knew where they were to be sent; for of one thing the Emperor might be assured, that without his signature not a ship would be sent to the Mediterranean. Even then Pentenriedter was afraid that England's ties with Spain would prevent her taking any action. Stanhope, however, soon set that right. Early in April he had been dining out of town with Pentenriedter and Cadogan and drove them back in his coach to London.

'During the drive', he told St. Saphorin, 'the question of the treaty was brought up . . . and we had a thorough discussion of the difficulties we should all have to face if the treaty were not signed without further delay.'

Pentenriedter was much impressed by Stanhope's arguments, especially when he declared that on the day after the treaty was signed not only would England execute all the other conditions, but would forthwith send the fleet with a due complement of land troops to the Mediterranean, carrying orders concerted with Pentenriedter himself. Next day Stanhope reported this conversation to the King, who

[1] Bothmer, *Memoiren*.

ordered Stanhope, Sunderland and Cadogan to repeat these
assurances in his own name, with the result that the ambassador sent off a courier at once to Vienna and expected
to get orders to sign by return.[1] Before Pentenriedter's
courier had reached Vienna the Emperor had at last, on
4 April (N.S.) agreed in principle to the treaty, and in
particular to an absolute renunciation of the Spanish
monarchy and to the concession of Tuscany, as well as
Parma, to the Infant.[2] Although there were still some
points to be adjusted in the draft, Stanhope, true to his
promise, on the very morning that he received the news
sent urgent orders to hasten the departure of the fleet, with
five regiments of infantry on board, to the Mediterranean.

Even then there was another long pause. So dilatory was
the Imperial chancery in its proceedings that two more
months passed before Schaub arrived back in Paris with the
draft as finally adjusted and translated into Latin. Most
of the changes from the Paris draft were small alterations of
form, but two modifications had been introduced to which
both Stanhope and the Regent objected. By the first the
Emperor proposed that the garrisons sent to secure the
duchies should not be Spanish, as the Regent claimed,
but Imperial: as a compromise Stair and Schaub, by Stanhope's orders, suggested that neutral troops, either Swiss
or English, should be employed. Secondly, the Emperor
required fresh renunciations of the Spanish throne by Louis
XV and the Regent: with this the Regent refused to comply, and Stanhope also objected on the ground that thereby
all the other provisions of the Treaty of Utrecht might
be called into question for want of explicit confirmation.
Stanhope also disagreed with two minor proposals of the
Emperor, that the feudal sovereignty of the duchies should
be attached to his line and not to the Empire and that,
failing the Anjou line, the House of Savoy should not, as
at Utrecht, be designated for the inheritance of the Spanish
monarchy. The Regent naturally agreed to Stanhope's
suggestions as presented to him by Stair and Schaub, and
when orders were given for the new draft to be made by
the French foreign office within three days all seemed to
be in a fair way for settlement. But the three days passed
and no draft appeared: in its place Stair and Schaub were

[1] R.O., S.P. 104/219 B, Stanhope to Schaub and St. Saphorin 28 Mar., 1 and
4 Apr. 1718.   [2] R.O., S.P. 78/160, Stanhope to Stair, 14 Apr. 1718.

handed by Huxelles a 'volume' of counter-remarks to the treaty and of new demands, and were told they represented France's ultimatum. Schaub, seeing that in Dubois's absence the old court party had once more obtained the upper hand, decided to return at once to London. When he went with Stair to take his leave of the Regent they were both ostentatiously neglected for two hours in the public rooms. Finally, when the Regent had gone into his private room to take his chocolate, he sent a message inquiring if they had nothing to say to him. When they complained of Huxelles's 'volume', he made some fumbling excuse and declared he had nothing with which to reproach himself: 'that may be so', they replied, 'but your ministers have'.

Schaub's hasty return from Paris and its cause seriously disturbed Dubois. He had already been troubled at reports of another change of attitude in Paris and had sent a masterly defence of the allied policy to the King's governor, Marshal Villeroy, one of the leaders of the old court party. Philip V, he had argued, had everything to gain by the proposed treaty, for not only would he for the first time have his title recognized by the Emperor but also obtain an appanage for his son Don Carlos. The only alternative to the allies' scheme was a general war, into which France might be dragged by Spain against both the Emperor and England, already bound by treaty to support the Emperor. Better than plunging Europe into another general war would it be, at the worst, for France to make a brief demonstration of force against Spain to induce her to accept the favourable terms offered. No response had come to this appeal; in fact, a note is still attached to the memoir stating that the Marshal 'avait dit qu'il répondroit à ce mémoire, mais il a ensuite changé de sentiment'.[1] In desperation the poor abbé could see no other means of stemming 'the torrent of opposition' in France but to persuade Stanhope himself to go over to Paris and deal personally with the Regent. The King consenting, Stanhope was quite willing to go. The delay in concluding the Quadruple Alliance, the Emperor's difficulties with the Turks, and the fear that the Regent might even now combine with Spain against us were causing alarm in England.[2] Stanhope realized that he alone perhaps

[1] A.E., *Angleterre*, 312, f. 303.
[2] See *A Letter . . . concerning the Danger of Europe . . . in case the Quadruple Alliance should not succeed* (E. Smith, 1718).

could fix the Regent's wavering purpose. Accordingly he wrote to Stair,

> 'taking the liberty to bespeak a bed at your house'; and told him that 'as open dealing in these affairs is the best policy, I have by order acquainted Mr. de Pentenriedter with the state of our project and with the doubts and difficultys that arise';

if, however, the Regent is willing to conclude before his arrival Stair is not to hesitate to do so, for

> 'a prince of the Regent's temper may be in the humour of concluding one day what it will cost great pains to bring him to if any opportunity be let slip.'[1]

The formal Instructions, dated 13 June 1718,[2] drawn up, presumably, by Stanhope and addressed to himself and Stair, deal with the following main points:

i. Spain, in spite of the Emperor's objections, should have reasonable security for the possession of the duchies; so it is proposed that 6,000 Swiss or alternatively 3,000 English and 3,000 Swiss troops should garrison them: England would even be prepared to send 6,000 at once till the Swiss quota was ready.

ii. As soon as the terms of the treaty have been finally settled between England and France, since Spain and the Emperor might still raise difficulties, which the Regent might make an excuse for shuffling out of his engagements, a secret convention should forthwith be drawn up and signed by England and France binding both parties to abide by the treaty as settled by themselves, to sign that treaty immediately on the Emperor's accession and mutually to defend each other against attack.

iii. Thereupon, if the Regent agrees, Stanhope may go to Madrid to induce Spain to accede to the treaty.

iv. Since the Regent's hesitations may be due to his own unpopularity and his trouble with his Parlements, an offer of English assistance is to be made to him.

Of these provisions by far the most important and the most difficult to secure was that requiring the Regent to sign a secret convention which would leave him no escape from his engagements.

On Sunday 15/26 June, after a final conference with Sunderland and the German ministers, Stanhope drove off with Schaub on his way to Dover, stopping only at Tonbridge to say goodbye to his wife, who had come over to see him

---

[1] R.O., *S.P.* 104/219 B, Stanhope to Stair, 10 June 1718.
[2] *Instructions, France*, i. 123.

from Chevening.[1] 'A Whig minister does not drone like a Tory one', was a Jacobite comment on Stanhope's characteristic haste, 'and so Lord Stanhope was despatched immediately with full instructions, and no doubt he'll try your Regent's mettle'.[2] At Calais Stanhope found a despairing letter from Stair, but had better news at the next stage; at Paris the Regent seemed overjoyed to see him. He was at once invited to a private interview, to which he only consented to go without Stair when Stair had assured him that he had no objection and that it was the Regent's way of doing business. In this interview the Regent made no difficulty of any sort either about the neutral garrisons or even the convention, which would bind him to England whatever happened. 'It is impossible', wrote Stanhope to Sunderland, 'to talk with more good sense and seeming frankness and sincerity than the Regent hath done to us.'[3] Mindful of his maxim about 'plain dealing', Stanhope also informed the Imperial ambassador of the agreement, and expected at any moment to be called upon to approve of the new draft to the Emperor and sign the convention with the Regent. Then suddenly Huxelles, who since Stanhope's arrival seemed to have dropped all opposition, announced that he would be no party to the convention, which seemed to be principally aimed at Philip V, a son of France. Since Huxelles refused, the Regent next directed Cheverny, another minister, to sign it: he also refused. Well then, said the Regent, Dubois shall have full powers to sign it in London. But Stanhope and Stair saw at once that this would mean the end of both treaty and convention, since they knew their Dubois and that he would never have the courage to sign what ministers under the Regent's eyes had refused to accept. They represented to the Regent into what a ridiculous position he would put himself and how fatal it would be to his power if he now drew back, for all Paris knew that orders for signing the convention had already been issued under the Great Seal, and the Imperial ambassador, who had kept his courier waiting ten days for the documents, would

[1] Bothmer, *Memoiren*, who states that during the conference Robethon and Schaub were whispering so loudly to one another that the rest could hardly hear themselves talk.

[2] *H. MSS., Stuart*, vi. 595; at Calais his arrival was carefully noted by John Ogilvie, a Jacobite correspondent of Mar. Both sides kept spies on one another, for Ogilvie asserts that Stanhope was accompanied by a staff of twelve English government spies. Ib. vii. 11.

[3] *Add. MSS.* 37368, f. 340, 30 June 1718.

want to know where the hitch was. The prospect of making himself ridiculous and of having to confess his own impotence to the ambassador was the one argument that told with the Regent. It gave him the courage to grasp the nettle and inform Huxelles that he must either sign or quit. Huxelles was not prepared to quit, so he fixed a day on which Stanhope and Stair should meet him for the signature. Even then his shifts were not exhausted. Relying on the fact, admitted by Stanhope himself, that 'the general disaffection to this Treaty throughout France is greater than can be expressed, and great variety of malicious reports are industriously spread to throw odium on the Regent', he began to find new reasons for delay and went about saying that the Regent could not coerce him to sign the secret convention. When therefore Stanhope and Stair came to the Palais Royal at the appointed time they found no Huxelles but only another 'volume' of objections he had left behind for them to read.

This was too much. They went off at once to the Regent to complain of the deception. At first, all the Regent could do was to bemoan his inability to find one of his ministers courageous enough to sign the convention: nobody indeed would take the responsibility for secret articles which might lead to war with Spain, for, however secret they might be, the Council of Regency would be sure to hear of them and feel it had been deceived. At this Stanhope had a happy inspiration, most in keeping with his own direct methods. 'Why not', he exclaimed, 'put everything boldly and frankly before the Council and see what they say?' The very boldness of the idea appealed to the Regent. He began to reckon up how many of the twenty members of the Council he could depend on and, having done so, decided to risk it. The Council was secretly summoned for the afternoon of Sunday, 17 July. On the morning of that day Stanhope and Stair saw the Regent and found him quite confident of the result; in the evening they had a message from him to say that all had gone well: the modifications of the treaty and the secret convention had been agreed to in Council with hardly a dissentient voice. At the meeting, so the messenger informed them, the Regent had spoken 'divinely', and, according to St. Simon, Huxelles, of all people, spoke so persuasively in favour of the proposals that the rest of the Council were won over 'par les lumières de M. le Maréchal'.

Next morning without further palaver Huxelles and Cheverny came to sign the secret convention with Stanhope and Stair.

The convention, as finally agreed upon, set forth that George I and Louis XV, moved by the desire to reconcile the Emperor, the King of Spain and the King of Sicily, bound themselves to propose to the Emperor for his acceptance as an ultimatum the treaty known as the Quadruple Alliance, and, as soon as the Emperor's envoy was authorized to sign it, to sign it themselves. They would also use their best endeavours to persuade Spain and Sicily and other powers to accede to the treaty. At the request of the French the clause originally proposed about mutual help in case of attack was dropped, and a stipulation accepted by the English that if the Emperor had not signed their main treaty within three months Louis XV would no longer be bound by the convention. Such was the convention that finally achieved the joint purpose of Stanhope and Dubois to bind George I and the Regent to one another even more closely than by the Triple Alliance. For now they were definitely committed to a common policy whereby they must stand or fall together.

Schaub, writing to Craggs, speaks of the almost incredible difficulties the English plenipotentiaries had in supporting the Regent against the enemies of the treaty, 'who became more violent and more outrageous, the nearer they saw to be the conclusion of our great business'. But, above all, to Stanhope's personal influence with the Regent and the respect his straight dealing won at the Regent's court he attributes the final success. The last scene indeed illustrates the value of Stanhope's maxim, 'to tell people the naked truth'.[1]

§ 4

The difficulties with France had now been settled, the Emperor had agreed in principle to the treaty: but there still remained Spain. Stanhope's whole object throughout the

---

[1] The twists and turns of this laborious negotiation before and during Stanhope's stay in Paris are fully described in Stanhope's and Schaub's letters to London and Vienna in R.O., S.P. 78/161 and R.O., S.P. 104/219 B; Wiesener, ii. 169 sqq., has a detailed account based mainly on the same material. See also Baudrillart, ii. 296 sqq.; Bourgeois, Régent, 336 sqq.; Weber, 75 sqq.; Michael, i. 798–803, who draws attention to the change made in the convention from the original draft.

negotiations had been to obtain a peaceful settlement between the Emperor and Philip V and, above all, to avoid a break with Philip. He well understood how strong was the feeling in France against a war with Louis XIV's grandson, and he appreciated more than any one the value of England's commercial interests in Spain, which in case of a rupture were bound to suffer. Indeed his commercial treaties of 1715 and 1716 with Spain were among the achievements of which he was most proud. He believed, too, that Alberoni himself was still of the friendly disposition he had shown when those treaties were made. He had never dropped his personal correspondence with him and, as recently as 9 April, had written him a long letter enlarging on the advantages to Spain of the proposed plan by which she would secure Parma and Tuscany for the Infant, and that their possession would be all the more secure since he had insisted that these duchies should be Imperial, not Habsburg, fiefs and so under the protection of the Empire.[1] Again six weeks later, when the Spanish ambassador Monteleone presented an angry protest from Alberoni on England's neglect of Spanish interests, Stanhope in his reply patiently recapitulated all the vain attempts made to obtain some inkling of Spain's wishes and stated that, had he known sooner of her strong wish to retain Sardinia, he would have attempted to satisfy her on that point. England was bound by treaty with the Emperor to protect his interests in Italy, hence the dispatch of Byng's fleet. Peace was the consideration beyond all others of the King and his ministers and indeed of the whole nation: 'mais avec la paix on préfèrera toujours l'amitié et les avantages du Roy Catholique à ceux de toute autre puissance'.[2]

On the Emperor's assent in April 1718 to the principles of the Quadruple Alliance, orders had immediately been given to Byng's fleet to prepare for the Mediterranean; and Byng actually sailed at the beginning of June. By the terms of the Treaty of Westminster with the Emperor the ministry could do no less than send out this force in view of the Spanish capture of Sardinia in 1717 and of the feverish preparations known to be going on in Spanish ports for another expedition. But it is clear that Stanhope hoped that Byng would not be obliged to take hostile measures against Spain. Had he expected it, he would not have been so ill advised as to tell

---

[1] R.O., *S.P.* 104/219 B, Stanhope to Alberoni, 9 Apr. 1718.
[2] Ib., Stanhope to Monteleone, 26 May 1718.

the South Sea Company that they could safely send out their valuable trading ship to Spain,[1] and his belief that Spain would not make hostilities necessary is obvious from his numerous conversations with Monteleone reported at length by St. Simon.[2] He certainly made it quite plain to the Spaniard, who ventured to threaten that if Byng sailed to the Mediterranean the opposition in Parliament would be stirred up by Philip to avenge him, that the King of England took no orders about his fleet from any foreign power, and also that if Byng found the Spanish fleet attacking the Emperor's possessions in Italy he was instructed to oppose their enterprise and, if necessary, to treat the Spanish ships as enemies. But, on the other hand, except in such an event Byng was instructed to be on good terms with Spain. Indeed, he hoped that instead of opposing Spain, Byng might best serve the interests of peace by facilitating the transfer of Parma and Tuscany to Spain in case the Emperor made any further difficulties, a point on which he often insisted. 'L'explication', as St. Simon admits, 'étoit claire et nette'. It was also an exact statement of Byng's formal Instructions of 26 May, that he was to use all efforts in his power to bring about a cessation of hostilities, should these have actually commenced:

> 'But in case the Spaniards do still insist with their ships of war and forces to attack the kingdom of Naples, or other territories of the Emperor in Italy, or to land in any part of Italy, which can only be with a design to invade the Emperor's dominions, against whom only they have declared war by invading Sardinia; or if they should endeavour to make themselves masters of the kingdom of Sicily, which must be with a design to invade the kingdom of Naples, in such case you are, with all your power, to hinder and obstruct the same'.

He was also instructed, if the Spaniards had already landed, to try and get them away amiably: if they would not go, he was to fight them.[3] It is further proof of Stanhope's belief that no action by Byng would be necessary, or that at any rate the mere statement of his orders would keep the Spaniards quiet, that Byng was told to show his instructions to the court of Spain on his voyage out to the Mediterranean. In a word, Stanhope's policy was to keep the peace with

[1] See above, p. 292.   [2] *St. Simon*, xiv. 449 sqq., xv. 1–200, *passim*.
[3] Byng's instructions are printed by T. C. [Thomas Corbett], *Account of the Expedition of the British Fleet to Sicily . . . under . . . Sir George Byng* (3rd edition), 1739, pp. 91–3; see also Michael, i. 807–8.

Spain at almost any cost and prevent the outbreak of another European war. The whole object of the Quadruple Alliance was to prevent that: the mere presence of Byng's fleet, he hoped, would be the final argument to Spain for coming into the Alliance. In reporting its dispatch to William Stanhope, he wrote, 'I heartily wish the Court of Spain may give the King an opportunity of employing it in his Catholic Majesty's service'.[1]

Stanhope, however, was wrong in believing that Alberoni was still anxious for peace. When William Stanhope came to see him he would treat him to outbursts of abuse on the allies' proposals, 'informes, indigestes et scandaleuses', and compare the English ministers to rogues, '*Birbanti*', who 'without rhyme or reason, if not for their own personal ends, cut up and pare states as if they were so many Dutch cheeses'. When Byng, as directed, wrote to inform the Spanish court of his Instructions, Alberoni curtly replied that, 'Sa Majesté Catholique m'a fait l'honneur de me dire que M. le Chevalier Byng peut exécuter les ordres du Roy son Maître.'[2] Sometimes, indeed, when Philip had had a fit of vomiting followed by ague, and Alberoni had apprehensions as to his own fate if the King died, he became less ferocious. Once, after displaying at a morning interview his 'usual vehemence against the partiality of the plan' to the Emperor, by 10 o'clock that evening he had changed his tone and expressed Philip's anxiety to prevent, on any honourable terms, 'the war that seemed at present to threaten the greatest part of Europe'. On another occasion Alberoni hinted that Spain might make use of the Pretender against England, but when the envoy retorted that the Emperor might prove at least as dangerous a claimant to Spain as the Pretender was to England, he said no more on that head.[3] In fact, however, Alberoni was already weaving a network of intrigues with Russia, Sweden, Savoy, Turkey and the Emperor's Hungarian subjects, and, having obtained his cardinal's hat, had even broken off relations with the Pope for protesting against his designs on Italy.

These designs were quite unsatisfied by the easy capture of Sardinia. For months Alberoni had been working night and day with all his immense energy, preparing such a fleet as Spain had never seen even in the days of the

[1] R.O., *S.P.* 104/219 B, Stanhope to W. Stanhope at Madrid, 26 May 1718.
[2] See Appendix C, p. 451.   [3] Michael, ii. 372; Weber, 67, 89.

Emperor Charles V or of Philip II. When it put to sea from
Barcelona on 18 June, three days after Byng sailed from
Spithead,[1] 'it covered a space of six leagues and was composed of 500 sail, May God prosper it!' as Alberoni wrote to
his correspondent in Parma. It sailed under sealed orders,
only to be opened at Cagliari in Sardinia, and known only
to the King and Queen and two others, Alberoni and his
faithful henchman Don Jose Patiño. Philip had originally
designed the fleet for a direct attack on the Emperor's dominions in Naples, but Alberoni had persuaded him to alter
the objective to Sicily, an ingenious move since England
was not bound by treaty to defend Victor Amedeus's possessions as she was the Emperor's, while the capture of Sicily
might take away one of the principal inducements to the
Emperor to come into the Quadruple Alliance. By 3 July
Palermo was captured by the Spanish fleet, and the army
under the Marquis de Lede was preparing to complete the
conquest of the island. News of the capture of Palermo came
to Stanhope while he was still wrestling with Huxelles's
never-ending scruples. It was for him to make the decision
as to Byng's action, since Byng had been instructed to take
his orders directly from Stanhope during Stanhope's absence
on the Continent. Stanhope for his part had no doubt that
Spain's action, though not ostensibly directed against the
Emperor, was an attack on the neutrality of Italy and indirectly on the Emperor's possessions, since he was to receive
Sicily by the Quadruple Alliance. Accordingly, in conjunction with Stair, he sent Byng orders on 21 July (N.S.) to
resist the capture of Sicily, by force of arms if necessary.
Craggs from London, more ferocious, wrote to Byng a few
days later that, if any orders came from Stanhope to attack
the Spanish fleet, 'you are not to amuse yourself by beginning
to take any single ships, but you are, the first blow you strike,
to endeavour to destroy their whole force'; and later so that
there should be no mistake about his meaning, he repeats,
'you should endeavour at once to destroy their whole Navy
the very first blow you strike, ... [since] our trade ... will be
as entirely lost, as it can be in time of war', if their naval
strength is allowed to increase. In fact Byng did not wait
for these orders before acting according to what was clearly
the spirit of his original instructions.[2]

[1] Byng sailed on 4 June (o.s.).
[2] *Stair Annals*, ii. 77, Stanhope and Stair to Byng, 21 July 1718 (N.S.);

But in spite of Spain's armada and its attack on Sicily Stanhope was so incurably optimistic as to believe that Alberoni himself was still amenable to reason. He accordingly decided, with the Regent's approval, to avail himself of the permission given him by his Instructions and try the effect of his personal representations at Madrid. Considering the orders already issued to Byng this was a questionable move on Stanhope's part, and, after the event as will be seen, not unnaturally aroused Alberoni's indignation. Possibly Stanhope hardly realized the delicacy of the position: at any rate with the Spaniards in full career of victory and with the possibility of a clash at any moment between the English and Spanish fleets, as dictated by his own orders, it says much for Stanhope's courage that he ventured into the Spanish stronghold, and also for his real determination at any risk to himself to prevent a serious war. Had news of a naval battle come to Spain during Stanhope's presence in Spain, or even had it been suspected that Byng was taking his orders directly from him, Stanhope might very possibly have been detained as a hostage. No wonder the King expressed 'great apprehension that your Excellency should be seized and detained at Madrid by the Cardinal', and that Craggs adds on his own behalf, 'considering this Eminency's rash temper, the thing appears to me very feasible. Your friends here are in no small pain about you and indeed I cannot express to you my own private uneasyness.'[1]

When after a journey of eight days from Bayonne, which even he confessed to have been fatiguing, Stanhope arrived at the Escorial, he was well enough received by the Cardinal, and entertained in a castle a mile from the palace, specially furnished for him. Alberoni was indeed in his most insinuating mood, lamenting his sovereigns' obstinacy in pursuing their Italian schemes, whereas he would have liked to continue peacefully developing the industries, finances and trade of Spain herself. This gave Stanhope an opening for a well-merited tribute to the forceful personality who had 'reanimated this Spanish corpse', as he had known it in the past; a compliment that pleased the Cardinal so well

Wiesener, ii. 229 says that this letter was held back by Stair; R.O., *S.P.* 104/96, Craggs to Byng 14 July 1718 (o.s.); R.O., *S.P.* 104/138, Craggs to Stanhope 17 July 1718 (o.s.). There appears to be no ground for Lord Hervey's statement, *Memoirs* 38 (1931 ed.), that Byng's action was due to clandestine orders from Bernstorff: but it no doubt represents a popular opinion at the time.

[1] R.O., *S.P.* 104/29, Craggs to Stanhope, 30 June 1718; R.O., *S.P.* 104/135, same to same, 26 July 1718.

that in one of his letters to Parma he spoke of Stanhope as 'my old acquaintance, now my admirer'; nor did he take it amiss when Stanhope, pointing to a map, suggested that Oran would be a more suitable field for Spanish enterprise than Italy. The King and Queen granted him two interviews and also treated him graciously; but neither they nor the Cardinal showed any inclination to discuss the Quadruple Alliance or to give up their Italian expedition; least of all would they consider ceding Sicily to the Emperor. On the contrary their terms were most uncompromising. Sicily and Sardinia were to remain for ever Spanish, the Emperor's troops in Italy were to be limited and Savoy was to be compensated for Sicily by a large slice of the Milanese, the Emperor was not to meddle with the succession to Parma and Tuscany, and the English fleet was to be at once recalled from the Mediterranean. They were strengthened in their determination by the news of the capture of Messina, which arrived when Stanhope was sitting at dessert with Alberoni and drew from him the dubious compliment that Spain had not done anything so praiseworthy since the discovery of the New World.[1] But its immediate effect was that Alberoni summarily rejected Stanhope's proposal of a three months' armistice that he had previously seemed not to dislike. Even Stanhope's offer to restore Gibraltar, the loss of which was deeply felt by Philip,[2] for the moment had no effect, while Alberoni darkly hinted at an alliance between Russia and Sweden with the object of coercing England. Thus Stanhope's fortnight in Madrid[3] seemed not to have advanced matters a whit, though he himself thought it might have paved the way for an accommodation in the future. He still believed in the Cardinal's conciliatory disposition, being perhaps misled by 'the tears he shed when I parted from him, and his promise to write to me, and to let slip no occasion that may offer of adjusting this business amicably'; and, according to the French ambassador, Nancré, he went away with 'une meilleure opinion de son adversaire et le regret de voir l'Espagne se refuser à une accession qu'il jugeait absolument nécessaire'.[4] He might not have taken so hopeful a view had he known what the Cardinal wrote shortly after-

[1] H. MSS., Stuart, vii. 190.
[2] For Stanhope's authority to offer Gibraltar, see Mahon, History, ii. Appendix, Craggs to Stanhope, 17 July 1718.
[3] He arrived in Madrid on 12 Aug. and left on 26 Aug. (N.S.).
[4] Recueil, Espagne, ii. 281.

wards to his friend at Parma—that if Stanhope could not produce better offers before the winter 'there will be a good war—*una buona guerra*—next spring'. But, however sanguine he might be, Stanhope was not to be caught napping:

> 'We should', he wrote to Stair, 'have a door open to negotiate with Spain—and that, I believe, they will at last come to;—at the same time, I say, I think it absolutely necessary to redouble our vigour, upon their hanging back, and to let them see that what shall not be complied by fair means will certainly be done by force.'[1]

Stanhope was well out of Spain by the beginning of September; for Byng, acting according to his Instructions and without waiting for further orders from Stanhope or England, after a warning to the Spaniards to cease hostilities, had attacked their fleet on 11 August at Cape Passaro. Within a few hours he had sunk or captured nearly the whole of the great armada that had sailed so proudly from Barcelona two months before, thus fulfilling the King's wish that by 'the gallantry and known Courage of English Seamen the first expedition of his Reign' might prove successful. As Byng had thereby destroyed all means of sea-communication between Sicily and Spain, news of the disaster did not reach Madrid till a month later, when Stanhope had been over the border for a week. On hearing of the destruction of all Philip's hopes of an empire in Italy and of his own to make Spain once more the leading naval power, Alberoni burst into one of his most violent storms of passion. The vials of his wrath were mainly expended on Stanhope, vicariously through his unfortunate relative, for having dared to come on a mission of peace when such orders had been given. William Stanhope made the best defence he could by reminding him that he had been shown Byng's Instructions; to which Alberoni retorted that 'notwithstanding what was told them, they could never believe he was to put those orders in execution, and particularly at the same time that Mylord Stanhope was come into this country to treat of peace'. Certainly Alberoni could not complain that he had not had fair warning, for Byng in forwarding his Instructions to Madrid, wherein Sicily was specifically mentioned,[2] had explicitly stated the King's orders to

[1] Alberoni, *Lettres Intimes* and the *History of Cardinal Alberoni* (London, 1719) give Alberoni's views of Stanhope's visit and the allied terms; Stanhope's accounts are in his letters in Mahon, *History*, ii, Appendix.
[2] See above, p. 303.

'use all the power of his Fleet and Forces with me to maintain
... the neutrality of Italy, and defend the Emperor's territories
therein, by opposing all force that shall endeavour to attack
him in his Dominions there.'[1]

At the same time Alberoni, however unjustifiable may have
been his attack on Victor Amedeus, with whom he was at
peace, and indirectly on the Emperor, had some justification
in assuming that, at any rate during Stanhope's pacific visit,
the hostile orders to Byng would remain in abeyance. This
adventure of Stanhope's is certainly more creditable to his
courage than to his appreciation of diplomatic decency and
almost justifies the stinging rebuke addressed to him by
Alberoni:

'Men were universally surprised at the arrival of the first minister of Great Britain at the court of the Catholic King, there to
make proposals of peace and of suspension of arms, at the same
time that the naval force of the Potentate who should have been
Mediator, was performing the actions of an open Rupture. ...
Tis nowhere to be found in history, nor is it compatible with
good faith, neither have the most barbarous people yet learnt
the maxim of sending a minister from one court to another with
the character of mediator, there to treat of peace, and of execut-
ing at the same time the utmost rigours of war.'[2]

§ 5

During Stanhope's absence in Spain the Emperor had given
his formal adherence to the Quadruple Alliance. Largely
through English mediation on 21 July he had concluded at
Passarowitz a most favourable treaty with the Turks, whereby
he not only gained a large accession of territory in the Balkans
but was enabled to transfer troops to Italy. But he was still
in great need of the English fleet and of French support for
the defence of Naples and Sicily. On 2 August, therefore,
Pentenriedter was empowered to sign the treaties in London with Dubois and the English plenipotentiaries. Victor
Amedeus, after being repulsed in nearly every western court

[1] See above, p. 304, and Appendix C, p. 451.
[2] This reproof, written in a letter from Alberoni to Monteleone, 10 Oct. 1718,
as well as the extract from Byng's letter are quoted from the *History of Cardinal
Alberoni*, on which see above, ch. viii, p. 204, note 3. There appears to be no
ground for the statement made by two of Mar's correspondents that Stanhope disapproved of Byng's action in attacking without his knowledge and
quarrelled with Sunderland on the subject. *H. MSS., Stuart*, vii. 406, 446, 456.

during his search for special advantages for himself, found it wise to embrace the offer still open to him from the allies of compensation for the loss of Sicily; he signed the treaty on 8 November. Holland, as we know, never signed; Spain only had yet to come in. After the signature on 2 August Dubois returned in triumph from Hampton Court to France, being escorted, by the King's order, by Craggs as far as Dartford.

The conditions of the so-called Quadruple Alliance were contained in the main treaty between England, France, the Emperor and Holland, had she been willing to come in, and two subsidiary treaties to be signed by the Emperor and Spain and the Emperor and Victor Amedeus respectively. In addition there were twelve secret articles attached to the main treaty. The effect of these treaties was to assign Sicily to the Emperor; Sardinia, Montferrat, and a part of the Milanese to Victor Amedeus; Parma and Tuscany as imperial fiefs to the Infant: the Emperor and Philip V were mutually to recognize one another's titles and possessions; the succession in England and France as established at Utrecht was to be guaranteed. In the secret articles provision was made for action by the three principal signatories in case of refusal by Spain (or Savoy) to accept these terms. After three month's delay France and England were to join forces with the Emperor in coercing Spain, whose contumacy might cause her to forfeit some of the advantages secured to her by the treaty.[1]

To Stanhope must be attributed whatever blame or merit attaches to this treaty, for it was his conception, and most of the details were elaborated by him. It was a difficult task that Stanhope had set himself, no less than to solve the problem found impossible at Utrecht, Rastadt and Baden, how to complete the pacification of western Europe by reconciling the nominal protagonists in the late war, the Emperor and Philip V. It was all the more difficult, since the only material compensation for the sacrifice of *amour-propre* by the two most touchy monarchs in Europe was to be found in Italy, where each had the same ambitions. One serious contemporary criticism of Stanhope's Italian compromise was made by Bolingbroke, who naturally objected to any tampering with his own handiwork at Utrecht. He and Stanhope, still, as ever, personal friends, met at supper when Stanhope was at Paris in that July, and during supper

---

[1] For a complete survey of the three treaties and the secret articles see Wiesener, ii. 205 sqq.

discussed Stanhope's treaty. Bolingbroke's main criticism was that Stanhope made a mistake, which he himself had carefully avoided at Utrecht, in allowing both the rival powers, Habsburg and Bourbon, to have a footing in Italy, where their proximity was bound to breed future wars, involving England on one side or the other. But you yourself, retorted Stanhope, lay yourself open to the same charge by the provision in the Treaty of Utrecht admitting Spain to the reversion of Sicily on failure of the Savoy line. Oh, I was not responsible for that clause, airily answered Bolingbroke: it must have slipped in as a result of one of Oxford's private negotiations. What you should have done, since you knew that Spain intended an attack on Italy, was to have delayed your Quadruple Alliance for six weeks and, when Spain had actually broken the neutrality of Italy, said to her, 'we must, in pursuance of our treaties, arm against you, as you have broken the treaties; we will no longer be bound by the strange article of the reversibility of Sicily, but will give it to the Emperor, and satisfy otherwise the Duke of Savoy'. In a letter of February 1736 to Sir William Wyndham Bolingbroke amplifies this argument:

> 'The great point for securing the publick peace, was to keep the Spaniard out, to hinder the two rivals from tredding on the same continent; and that point was given up when the principle of the Utrecht treaty was departed from, under pretence of consummating the peace, and of satisfying the unsatiable ambition of the queen of Spain.'

But the brief account given by Bolingbroke to Marchmont nearly thirty years after this supper party probably does not represent the whole of his argument. It may be suspected that his chief objection to his friend's policy was, not so much the settlement for Italy then arranged, as the obligation assumed by England for the future, to support Bolingbroke's *bête noire*, the Emperor. Anyhow, Stanhope laughingly ended the discussion with the remark, 'Harry, you was always an enemy to the House of Austria'.[1]

It was easy for Bolingbroke to be wise after the event, for no doubt his recollections of this conversation given to Marchmont were coloured by the occurrences of the succeeding years. In one respect Bolingbroke was justified in criticizing the settlement—that it proved by no means a final

[1] Marchmont, *Diary*, 9 Aug. 1744; Coxe, *Walpole*, ii. 341; *H. MSS., Stuart*, vii. 48. I have combined the gist of the first two accounts.

solution of the difficulties. Spain, once more established in Italy, was not satisfied till she had driven the Habsburgs from the Two Sicilies and established one Infant there as well as another in Parma. But would Bolingbroke's Utrecht settlement have been any more permanent? In the first place, as he admitted himself to Wyndham, Savoy would sooner or later have been obliged to give up Sicily to the Emperor. Then there was the question of the 'unsatiable queen', and not only of her but of her Spanish subjects, who felt bitterly the loss of all their Italian possessions. As Stanhope clearly saw, no peace with the Emperor imposed upon Spain could have been lasting had she been left with that rankling grievance; and so eager was he for peace that, not content with adjusting claims in Italy, he was actually willing to give up England's Gibraltar to secure it. Even, too, if Spain's ambitions could have been entirely brushed aside, France, so essential an element in Stanhope's pacification scheme, would never have allowed the Emperor to be aggrandized without adequate compensation to Spain. He might indeed have allowed Spain to recover Sicily, the chief object of her ambition in Italy: but to do this he would have had to break an understanding with our ally the Emperor. From the English point of view also, as Defoe pointed out in a defence of the treaty,[1] it mattered enormously for our trade that Sicily should be held by a sufficiently strong Power on whose friendship we could depend. Nor did Stanhope need to learn this from Defoe, for he had long since learned from his master Marlborough how essential a strong position and loyal allies in the Mediterranean were to our naval and commercial security. Spain under Alberoni was too little to be depended upon as an ally to be allowed to hold so important an outpost of the Levant trade as Sicily. The Emperor, bound to England by strong interests and dependent on her fleet for the protection of Sicily, was more likely to prove a friendly guardian of the island. Even in the interests of poor neglected Italy there was something to be said for the Quadruple Alliance settlement. The Duchies of Parma and Tuscany were not to be handed over to another alien Power and governed by viceroys sent from another country, as had for so long been the mode of government in the Spanish provinces of Italy. The Infant who was to succeed to them

---

[1] In an article in *Whitehall Evening Post* of Nov. 1718 epitomized in Michael, ii. 151.

was to be cut off from Spain and govern them in his own right, and therefore with some consideration for the welfare of the inhabitants. It was a step, if a small step, towards the creation of more really native Powers in Italy, a step which was imitated thereafter when Spain conquered the Two Sicilies for Don Carlos. From this beginning, due to Stanhope's treaty, by the middle of the century the Habsburg domination in the Milanese was the only truly alien domination left in Italy.

Stanhope's solution was not indeed perfect. It did not entirely prevent a short bout of restricted hostilities before Spain yielded to reason: nor did it prove a final solution. But it was an improvement on the treaty of Utrecht as a settlement and prevented the widespread war which might otherwise have arisen between Spain and France on the one side and England and the Emperor on the other, just at the very time when Europe was chiefly in need of peace and reconstruction.

CHAPTER XII
THE MINISTER OF PEACE—I. SPAIN

§ I

'His Britannic Majesty, moved by an object so great and so worthy of his care . . . as peace between the Emperor and the King of Spain and between the Emperor and the King of Sicily, . . . communicated his ideas for attaining it to the most Christian King and their High Mightinesses the States General,[1] who embraced with zeal so right a design. Since then the said three powers have been jointly endeavouring to obtain the interested parties' consent to the means necessary to that end. But when the Catholic King forcibly seized the island of Sardinia, then in the Emperor's possession, and the three powers aforesaid were unable by the most instant representations to prevent this enterprise or obtain reparation for the attack on the neutrality of Italy . . . they felt constrained to redouble their efforts to extinguish this fire in its early stages and to prevent, while there is yet time, the evils and calamities with which Europe is threatened. . . . In order therefore to bring a general and lasting peace to Europe, still suffering from the effects of prolonged and exhausting wars . . . they have . . . after mature deliberation . . . agreed that in the following articles would be found an equitable basis for perpetual peace between his Imperial Majesty and his Catholic Majesty and between his Imperial Majesty and the King of Sicily.'

So ran the original preamble to the Quadruple Alliance. Such a claim by three Powers to authority over the rest of Europe was not unnaturally resented, especially by the Emperor; and, in deference to his susceptibilities, in the final draft of the treaty this preamble was suppressed. Nevertheless it exactly represents Stanhope's conception of the treaty and his determination not to allow the quarrels about Italy of Spain, Savoy and the Emperor to remain an obstacle to European peace. His was the conception; and, after the Emperor in August and Victor Amedeus in November 1718 had acceded to the treaty, his the motive force that made the treaty effective as an instrument for peace.[2]

---

[1] This treaty was drafted on the assumption that the Dutch would be one of the mediating Powers, an assumption which, as we have seen, was never fulfilled.

[2] For this suppressed preamble see Michael, ii. 135 sqq. and 626, where it is printed in the original French from the copy in the Record Office.

The main problem still left was to persuade Spain to come in quietly, or, if this proved impossible, to coerce her. England could not hope to do this alone without the Emperor and the Regent; and in spite of the treaty it needed all Stanhope's skill to keep in hand that ill-matched pair. The Emperor had never concealed his dislike of the provision to enable Spain once more to obtain a footing in Italy, and was only too anxious that she should exceed her time-limit of three months for agreeing to the treaty and so provide him with an excuse for excluding her altogether. The shifts of the *Augustissima Casa* for evading a direct issue seemed almost inexhaustible. Even when the copies of the Emperor's ratification of the treaty arrived at Paris in October it was discovered that he had particularly avoided renouncing Spain 'in perpetuity', had excluded the French collateral branches from the succession in case the Anjou branch failed, and in one of the copies still gave himself the title King of Spain and referred to Philip as Duke of Anjou. Dubois in despair wrote pathetic appeals to Stanhope, Craggs and Stair, declaring that if such evasions were accepted he would not dare to show his face in France and imploring them to get him out of the scrape. Stanhope and the King took these silly tricks of the Viennese ministers almost as much amiss as Dubois and the Regent, and only after further tiresome correspondence obtained the renunciations in proper form.[1]

There were also difficulties with the Regent. Shifty and impressionable, of whom it was wittily said that 'la conversation était son triomphe', he could never be tied down to a policy for long. Even after he had agreed to the treaty and the convention he felt qualms about the strength of popular opinion in France against the coercion of Philip and was ready to catch at any straws rather than commit himself to drastic action; and the majority of his advisers were of the same mind. Stanhope had long come to the conclusion that the Regent could never be trusted to keep to the lines of the Alliance until a clean sweep had been made of these old advisers and in their place Dubois, the one firm supporter of the new policy at the Regent's court, raised to the position of responsible minister. The Regent himself was not blind to the disadvantages of entrusting men who thoroughly disapproved of his policy with the task of carrying it out. But

[1] Sévelinges, i. 246 sqq.; Wiesener, ii. 272 sqq.; Pribram, i. 400; Bourgeois, *Dubois*, 6 sqq.; Weber, 85.

he not unnaturally resented hints to that effect from Stair
and the Imperial ambassador, and tartly informed Stair that
if he did make a change it might be to replace Huxelles
by Torcy, who was not only as deeply committed to the
old policy but much abler. On his return from Spain in
September 1718 Stanhope found the Regent undecided as
ever. But what Stair could not do Stanhope, with his blunt
directness, brought about. At his first interview, without any
beating about the bush, he told the Regent outright that
he had better entrust foreign affairs to Dubois: a few weeks
later the Regent announced the abolition of Huxelles's
council of foreign affairs and the appointment of Dubois
to the sole charge of that department. At the same time
Villars, another obstructive marshal, was deprived of the
War Department and replaced by Le Blanc, one of Dubois's
cronies. It is true the Regent still, characteristically, kept a
foot in the other camp by retaining Torcy as master of posts,
an office which gave him access to the Regent and enabled
him to examine and take a copy of every letter that passed
through the kingdom. Nevertheless it was a great advance to
have Dubois in charge of foreign affairs. That the ruler of
a proud country like France should have changed his most
important minister at the instigation of a foreign statesman
is a tribute to Stanhope's influence such as perhaps never
before or since has been accorded to an English minister.
Dubois himself fully recognized to whom he owed his elevation. 'Je vous dois', he wrote effusively to Stanhope, 'jusqu'à
la place que j'occupe, dont je souhaite avec passion de faire
usage selon votre cœur, c'est à dire, pour le service de Sa
Majesté Britannique, dont les intérêts me seront toujours
sacrés.'[1]

By the end of the month Stanhope was able to return to
London, fairly confident that he could now rely on more
consistent support from Paris. The result of this journey to
Paris and Madrid inspired the poet Tickell with an ode
addressed to the minister returning with his sheaves. This
ode no doubt reflected the satisfaction of the court with
Stanhope's achievements and, with due allowance for its
turgid language, gives a fairly accurate statement of the
facts.

[1] Sévelinges, i. 247; for the whole incident Wiesener ii. 260 sqq.

I

Fair Daughter once of *Windsor's* Woods!
In Safety o'er the rowling Floods
Britannia's Boast and darling Care,
Big with the Fate of *Europe*, bear.
May Winds propitious on his Way
The Minister of Peace convey;
Nor Rebel Wave nor rising Storm
Great George's liquid Realms deform.

II

Our Vows are heard. Thy crowded Sails
Already swell with Western Gales;
Already *Albion's* Coast retires,
And *Calais* Multiplies her Spires:
At length has Royal *Orleans* prest
With open Arms, the well-known Guest;
Before in sacred Friendship join'd,
And now in Counsels of Mankind.

III

Whilst his clear Schemes our Patriot shows,
And planns the threaten'd World's Repose,
They fix each haughty Monarch's Doom,
And bless whole Ages yet to come.
Henceforth great BRUNSWICK shall decree
What flag must awe the *Tyrrhene* Sea;
For whom the *Tuscan* Grape shall glow;
And fruitful *Arethusa* flow.

IV

See in firm Leagues with *Thames* combine
The *Seine*, the *Maese*, and distant *Rhine!*
Nor, *Ebro*, let thy Single Rage
With half the warring World engage.
Oh! call to mind thy Thousands slain,
And *Almanara's* fatal Plain;
While yet the *Gallic* Terrours sleep,
Nor *Britain* Thunders from the Deep.[1]

Having once obtained the treaty laying down the conditions of an Italian settlement between Spain and the Emperor,

[1] *An Ode Occasioned by His Excellency the Earl Stanhope's Voyage to France*, By
Mr. *Tickell*. Idem Pacis eras mediusque belli. Printed for Jacob Tonson 1718;
preserved at Chevening. The first line is obviously Tickell's method of indicating the packet-boat, made of timber from the royal forest, that conveyed Stanhope across the Channel.

both the Regent and Stanhope were anxious to give Spain the fullest possible extension of time for acceding to the arrangement. Though they realized that some measure of coercion might be necessary to induce Spain to accept the treaty, both were equally determined not to leave the Emperor with all the advantages nor to sow the seeds of future wars by irrevocably excluding Spain from Italy. The procrastination of the Dutch about coming into the treaty gave a convenient excuse for extending the three months' term originally allowed to Spain. In November 1718, as soon as the first three months since the signing of the treaty had elapsed, the Emperor began making plans for the redivision of the Italian spoil whereby the Duke of Lorraine, his close ally, was to get Tuscany and the Duke of Modena Piacenza. But already in October Stanhope had suggested to the Dutch that they should stipulate, as a condition for coming in, that the term of three months should be counted as beginning only from the date of their accession, a proposal which the Dutch gladly accepted and to which the Emperor was constrained to agree.[1] The Dutch of course never did come in but were always on the point of doing so; hence, throughout the following year, even though England and France were engaged in hostilities with Spain, the excuse provided by Dutch hesitations served successively to renew the three months' term until finally 18 November 1719 was laid down as the definite *terminus a quo* the three months should run: after those three months the Spanish Infant was definitely to be excluded from the Duchies. And this, as will appear, proved sufficient.[2]

At first there seemed some prospect of Spain coming into the treaty of her own accord. By the end of August Alberoni himself was inclined for peace. The Emperor, he reflected, was free after Passarowitz to turn his undivided attention to Italy; the battle of Passaro had not only destroyed Spain's great fleet but cut off all communication with the army in Sicily; while the Tsar, with whom he had hoped to concert an attack on England, failing to make his peace with Sweden, was again making advances to France and England. There seemed little hope for Spain in prolonging the struggle against such formidable odds as the Quadruple Alliance without a friend in prospect. Nor indeed were the induce-

---

[1] R.O., *S.P.* 110/77 Stanhope to Stair, 14 Oct. 1718.
[2] Ib., Stanhope to Cadogan and Whitworth, 2 Nov. 1718; see also Pribram. i. 400 sqq.; Weber, 91; Wiesener, iii. 9, 106, 213–14.

ments offered to Spain to be despised, especially if Gibraltar, once offered by Stanhope, could still be obtained. Philip V, though weak, had his lucid moments and was disposed to agree with Alberoni; the only obstacle left was the Queen's *spretae injuria formae*. She was specially aggrieved that, though provision had been made for her family, no power, no means even for supporting her dignity in widowhood, had been devised for her by those who framed the treaty. Stanhope himself had an inkling of the gravity of this omission and regretted it too late. This grievance appears to have been her main motive for opposing Alberoni, with all the obstinacy of which she was mistress, in his effort to convince the not unwilling King to negotiate for terms. By 19 October Alberoni thought he had carried the day: but that night the Queen exercised all her arts on the King and next morning the confessor Daubenton, then an ally of Alberoni's, sorrowfully admitted 'que le prie-Dieu a dû céder à l'alcôve'. And so it was decided to break off relations with the allies. William Stanhope and Nancré left Madrid, Monteleone was recalled from London; and in spite of the treaty obligation to give English traders six months to settle their affairs even after a formal declaration of war, some of them were thrown into prison, their goods were seized, and privateers were armed to attack English commerce.[1]

From the moment that Philip and Elizabeth had made their decision, Alberoni adopted their warlike policy as his own. Once more he began hunting through Europe, in Sweden and Russia, in Italy, among the Jacobites and even in Vienna itself, for enemies to raise against England and France. In all the ship-building yards of Spain new ships were laid down and workmen were employed night and day in the effort to repair the fatal losses of Passaro. Whether from change of conviction or simply to retain the royal favour by the violence of his language and his feverish energy in forming schemes to set all Europe ablaze rather than yield a jot of Spain's pretensions, the cardinal seemed bent on identifying himself personally with the extreme war party. This truculent attitude of Alberoni served the Regent very well and was the worst possible policy for Spain. Thereby the Regent could avoid the odium he was bound to incur in his own country by an attack on Philip V personally and was able to represent the removal of a dangerous

[1] Bourgeois, *Farnèse*, 330 sqq.; Castagnoli, 339 sqq.

counsellor from Philip's court as the sole object of hostilities against Spain. When war was actually declared Dubois asserted its sole reason to be the outrageous conduct of the cardinal, 'qui a juré la perte du Roi de la Grande Bretagne et de son Altesse Royale, pour bien montrer qu'on ne le faisait pas au Roi Catholique et à la nation Espagnole, mais à ce ministre turbulent'. Stanhope himself, who up to 18 November was still persuaded of the cardinal's inclination to peace,[1] was so much incensed by his subsequent violence that he entirely changed his view of him. In common with the Regent and Dubois he began to talk of Alberoni as the 'firebrand of Europe' and to treat him as a dangerous animal, the sole obstacle to a general peace, the root-cause of all the mischief. 'Il faut le terrasser', he must be crushed, he wrote to Dubois in July 1719, and afterwards declared that any peace concluded with the cardinal would be as worthless as an indefinite armistice.[2]

It was evident by November that Alberoni would stick at no measures to injure England. Stanhope realized that it was essential not only to be prepared to meet attack but also to carry the people with him in any action that might be called for. In this respect he was more fortunate than the Regent, who, though conscious of court intrigues and of popular opinion against his policy, had no assembly, except his small council of Regency, in which he could argue his case with his opponents. Stanhope, on the other hand, could meet his critics in the open across the floor of Parliament and, having convinced them by public argument or beaten them by majorities, confidently proceed with his policy. Parliament met in the middle of November, but before that the ministers had the ground well prepared. Defoe and other lesser writers published pamphlets and articles expounding the government's policy for securing a permanent peace. The mercantile community, who in the previous year had expressed apprehension at the naval preparations,[3] were now thoroughly alarmed by Spain's arbitrary confiscation of English goods and attacks on English shipping, and sent in petitions to the government praying for protection; and these petitions were duly published. Stanhope himself drew up the King's Speech in words 'captivating of the people'. In it

---

[1] *Stair Annals*, ii. 85.
[2] Bourgeois, *Farnèse*, 337, 364; Coxe, *Bourbons*, ii. 365.
[3] See above, ch. xi, p. 292.

he set forth the various inducements offered to Spain to make
her accept even greater advantages than she had been offered
at Utrecht and her persistent refusal of any accommodation;
and stress was laid on the attacks she had made on English
trade and shipping: yet in spite of these attacks, so little
did the King contemplate an aggressive war, that on the conclusion of the Quadruple Alliance he had ordered the army
estimates to be reduced by one-half of what they were in 1716,
'nor could I better express, than by so doing, how little we
apprehend the attempts of our enemies to disturb the peace
of my kingdoms; even though Spain should continue some
time in war'. But the naval services of defence could not be
dispensed with, so, in conclusion, an eloquent appeal was
addressed to Parliament to make good the supplies needed
for that purpose.

> 'I have done my part. It remains with you to give the last
> finishing to this great work. Our friends and our enemies,
> both at home and abroad, are waiting the event of your
> resolutions; And I dare promise myself that the former have
> nothing to apprehend, nor the others to hope, from your con-
> duct in this important conjuncture, who have, during the
> whole course of my reign, given such lively proofs of your
> zeal and affection to my person, and of your love to your
> country.'[1]

The debate in the Lords on the Address moved by Lord
Carteret was the occasion for much criticism of Byng's
action at Passaro. Stanhope in reply justified Byng's Instructions by our engagements to the Emperor in the Treaty of
Westminster of 1716 and the Quadruple Alliance. He accused
Spain of having violated the Treaty of Utrecht, and of having
attacked the Emperor while he was engaged with the Turks
and rejected all offers of mediation; 'he thought it an honour
to have advised His Majesty in these measures because he
was persuaded they entirely agreed with the honour and
interest of his country; he doubted not but upon the strictest
examination these measures would be approved by all true
Englishmen, and was ready to answer for them with his
head'. This speech, adds the report, 'delivered with becoming
vehemence, made a great impression on the House'; and the

---

[1] *P.H.*, vii. 558 sqq.; Michael, ii. 150–5, who quotes reports of the Prussian
minister Bonet stating that among other ministerial precautions substantial
inducements were offered to members for favourable votes; but this may have
been merely hearsay.

Address was carried by a good majority. So also was the Address moved in the Commons, in spite of a virulent attack by Walpole on Stanhope's policy as 'contrary to the interests and rights of the nation', and a sneering allusion to the itch for continental journeys of this 'knight errant of English diplomacy'.[1]

But though England had plenty of reasons for declaring war at once on Spain, based on attacks on her commerce both in Europe and the West Indies, and unprovoked aggressions in Italy contrary to treaties, another month passed before the actual declaration, a month spent in the peaceful task of removing the Nonconformists' grievances. The Regent, as usual, was shivering on the brink of definite action against his cousin, Holland was still wobbling; Stanhope for his part was not inclined to pull the chestnuts out of the fire alone and allow Holland and France, by posing as more friendly to Spain, to filch away our trade. Without the Dutch he was anxious, without the French he was determined, not to fight. In spite of representations made to him by Stair and Craggs as well as Stanhope, Dubois kept putting off the decision as to a definite date when France would fulfil her obligations under the secret clauses of the Quadruple Alliance and declare war on Spain. In fact Dubois was waiting for his enemies to deliver themselves into his hands and so enable him to convince the most doubting Frenchmen of Spain's hostile intentions. For some time he had been aware that the Spanish ambassador Cellamare had been hatching a plot against the Regent in concert with the Duchesse du Maine, the ambitious wife of one of Louis XIV's legitimized sons. But he had no definite proof of the plot until, at the beginning of December, one of Cellamare's couriers was arrested with thoroughly compromising letters. Cellamare was at once put under guard and conducted across the frontier, and, as had been done with the Gyllenborg correspondence, a selection of the most incriminating letters was published. Stanhope at once drafted a personal letter from George I to the Regent, congratulating him on his escape from the dangerous conspiracy.[2] Dubois wrote to announce that France would declare war against Spain within a month at most after England's declaration: he also asked whether in the manifesto setting forth the French case

[1] *P.H.* vii. 561–6; Bourgeois, *Dubois*, 16, for points in Walpole's speech.
[2] The draft is in the *Chevening MSS*.

against Spain, which was being prepared by the eminent academician Fontenelle, it might be stated that the Regent had tried to obtain from King George the return of Gibraltar to Philip. Stanhope replied cautiously:

> 'Vous pouvez insérer dans votre manifeste que Monseigneur le Régent s'était fait fort de procurer au roi d'Espagne la cession de Gibraltar, pourvu que les termes soient ménagés de manière à ne pas exprimer un engagement positif de notre part.'

Unfortunately Dubois went beyond this very guarded statement, for in Fontenelle's manifesto the incident was referred to as 'la *promesse* que Sa Majesté lui procurerait la restitution de Gibraltar', a phrase destined to create considerable trouble in the following year.[1] Meanwhile on 16/28 December 1718 Stanhope announced to Parliament that on that day the King had declared war and 'he durst answer beforehand that upon the strictest examination it would be found that His Majesty and his ministers had done nothing against the faith of Treaties or the honour and interest of the nation'.[2] Twelve days later France's declaration also appeared. Having taken this momentous step, which was certainly not popular in France, the timorous Dubois more than ever sought comfort in his dependence on England and especially on Stanhope. In a letter of 16 January 1719 he explained to him that the war must be aimed at Alberoni, not at Philip, and that even so it would almost be in the nature of a civil war for both England and France, since many Frenchmen and many English Jacobites would be found to sympathize with Philip rather than with George and the Regent; he adds:

> 'je suis persuadé que nous devons préférer l'Angleterre à toute autre puissance et que l'Angleterre doit préférer la France à toute autre liaison. . . . Il ne faut pas vivre ensemble avec fidélité seulement pour les engagements pris et avec de simples égards les uns pour les autres, mais en intime liaison et en amitié de la même manière que si les deux états appartenaient au même maître. . . . Notre but . . . doit être de porter l'union jusqu'à une union nationale.'[3]

§ 2

Although England and France had taken the initiative in declaring war, Alberoni had forestalled them in actual

---

[1] Lemontey, ii. 395; Wiesener, ii. 320 sqq.   [2] *P.H.* vii. 583.
[3] Baudrillart, ii. 354–5.

hostilities. Writing to Stair in December 1718 Bolingbroke sums up his own alarmist view of the dangers to England:

> 'I hear that the Duke of Or[monde] is att Madrid and that the Ab. Brigault was preparing to go to England. . . . Good God, my Lord, what have we seen in this age? The Princes of the North, the Jacobites in Brittain, the faction of the old court in this country [France], the pope and some of the princes of Italy underhand, and the great Turk till he was beat out of these measures acting in concert together, and Alberoni att the head of the League.'[1]

In fact in August Alberoni had offered the Tsar a subsidy to join Spain against England and, when Peter turned down this proposal, sent Sir Patrick Lawless, a Jacobite in the Spanish service, to make similar offers to Charles XII of Sweden. For the plan he had in view was to promote Jacobite risings in England and Scotland with the support of Spanish and Swedish ships and men.[2] Accordingly, early in November, Ormonde, who was in Paris, received an invitation to come to Spain to concert measures with the cardinal. On 3 December he and Alberoni met at Madrid and within a fortnight had settled on a plan of campaign. On Ormonde's request for 7,000 to 8,000 men, and arms for 15,000, Alberoni said there might be some difficulty about the men, as most of the Spanish army was locked up in Sicily, but there would be none about the arms or a sufficient subsidy to enable Charles XII to provide a fleet in support, since the confiscated property of the English traders had brought funds into the royal treasury. The scheme agreed upon was that Ormonde himself should lead an expedition, fitted out in Spain, to the west of England, and the Earl Marischal, then a refugee in Paris, should create a diversion in Scotland with the help of Charles XII. Alberoni was able to give Ormonde full details of the recent proceedings in Parliament, and the two derived much satisfaction from the reduction of the land forces announced in the King's Speech. Later, on news of the proposals for repealing the measures against the Nonconformists,[3] Ormonde wrote gleefully to the cardinal that 'if anything could increase the discontent in England, it

---

[1] *Oxenford MSS.* (*Bolingbroke Papers*, f. 58).

[2] Chance, 287 sqq.; Castagnoli, 337–8; Michael, ii. 375 sqq. See also R.O., *S.P.* 104/96, Craggs to Byng, 29 Dec. 1718, which shows what accurate knowledge the English ministry had of Alberoni's plans.

[3] See below, ch. xiv.

would be the news which you send me of what has taken place in Parliament, at the instance of your friend Stanhope, about the Nonconformists . . ., which will not only enrage the Anglicans, but also displease the Moderates'. To remove the Pretender from his dangerous proximity to the Emperor's agents in Rome, and to animate by his presence the Jacobites now flocking to Spain to take part in the expedition, James III himself was invited to Madrid. In March 1719 he arrived and was received with royal honours.[1]

Before James's arrival, however, the keystone of Alberoni's plan had fallen out. On 11 December 1718 Charles XII ended his meteoric career through a stray shot fired from the walls of Frederikshald in Norway. He was succeeded by his sister Ulrica, and power was regained by the nobility of Sweden, whose privileges had been taken away by Charles and his predecessors and whose principal aim was peace. Goertz, the busy intriguer who had abetted Charles's ambitious schemes and had been the mainstay of the alliance with Spain, was arrested and executed on 3 March. Swedish support was now out of the question; but Alberoni had gone too far to draw back and by his supplies of men and arms to Ormonde proved even better than his word. Early in March five men-of-war and transports carrying 5,000 men and arms for 30,000 more were dispatched from Cadiz to the west of England under the command of Ormonde, and, even though no support was now to be had from Sweden, the Earl Marischal, Seaforth and Tullibardine were given a couple of frigates and 300 Spanish soldiers as a nucleus for a rising in the Highlands. Small as these forces were for the enterprise of expelling George I from his throne, Alberoni reckoned on the secrecy of his preparations and on the reduction of the land forces in England for success. He was also perhaps misled by the incurable optimism of the Jacobites, who were convinced of the English government's unpopularity and believed their supporters to be ready to rise *en masse* at the first indication of outside support.[2] Dubois, however, through his spies, knew of these plans from the first and at once passed on the intelligence to Stanhope and Craggs. The King

[1] For Ormonde's plans concerted with Alberoni see Dickson, 1–47; for an account of the Pretender's secret evasion from Rome, ib., 206 sqq.

[2] The reports from the west of England in R.O., *S.P. Dom. Geo. I*, 15, to the Secretaries of State show that there was not much Jacobite feeling except in Bristol, where, though the magistrates were loyal, two-thirds of the population might have risen for the Pretender.

immediately informed Parliament of the danger and was unanimously given a free hand to raise whatever additional land forces he might think necessary.[1] Four regiments were brought over from Ireland to Bristol, and some Dutch and Austrian regiments were, according to treaty, landed from the Netherlands for the defence of England.[2] Dubois, in his zeal, offered to move French regiments to the northern coast in readiness to cross the Channel if need arose, and even sent over French sailors to Portsmouth to help man the English fleet. Stanhope, not to be outdone in courtesy, offered in turn to assist in suppressing a rising expected in Brittany; while Craggs, on rumours of unrest among the French Protestants, wrote that the King,

> 'believing his credit among a set of people that are Protestants might be of some weight . . . [was sending] to them a person in his name to let them know how much he thinks it for their interest as well as their duty to behave themselves with decency and quietness.'

But Dubois's offers were politely refused. The French sailors were sent back to France with a month's pay in their pockets and a message that 'our navy pride themselves on doing their own service, without any obligation to foreign helps'.[3] In fact the fleet under Norris and Lord Berkeley, the first Lord of the Admiralty, that was ordered to cruise about the entrance to the Channel, was looked upon as the surest protection for the country from invasion.

These precautions were hardly needed. On 28 March the Spanish squadron under Ormonde, with the ill luck that persistently dogged that unfortunate duke's enterprises, was beset by so terrific a storm in the Bay of Biscay that all its ships were scattered to the winds and in maimed condition crept back as best they could to the nearest Spanish ports. The Earl Marischal's two frigates with the 300 Spaniards did indeed evade Norris and Berkeley and reached the island of Lewis off the west coast of Scotland at the end of March. Here they were joined by a small shipload of Jacobites from France under Tullibardine, and they decided to land on the mainland near Kintail, hoping that the neighbouring clans would rally to them. But the leaders quarrelled, the High-

landers came in slowly, most of their ammunition and
supplies were destroyed by an English squadron sent to cut
off their retreat by sea, and on 10 June General Wightman
came up with 1,000 royal troops from Inverness to attack
them on the land side. By that time the rebel force numbered
some 1,000 also, but was easily defeated by Wightman at
Glenshiel. The Spaniards surrendered, but the Highlanders
and their leaders saved the government the distasteful task
of dealing with them as rebels by dispersing to almost inaccessible fastnesses.[1] Even before this feeble conclusion to
all Alberoni's dreams of turning out George I Stanhope had
felt England safe enough for him to accompany the King on
another of his visits to Hanover. His adversary, after these
successive disasters, was forced to confess himself almost at
the end of his tether. On the news of the storm that overwhelmed Ormonde's squadron he wrote to his Parmesan
confidant in a strangely chastened mood:

> 'If only a single one of the plans I had formed had succeeded,
> that alone would have been enough to upset all the enemies'
> designs: God has brought them all to naught. All that is left to
> us is to adore His just judgments and to submit with complete
> resignation to His divine will.'

Even before sending forth that expedition he had admitted
that 'if it fails Spain will be forced to accept peace on any
conditions'.[2]

But it was now too late for the cardinal to think of peace.
His exacting sovereigns were not yet in the mood to accept
the Italian compromise, and the allies, threatened by risings
in Brittany, England and Scotland, and by Spanish attempts
to set all Europe aflame once more, were determined to get
rid of the 'fire-brand of Europe', whose presence seemed to
make any stable peace impossible. Stanhope as usual took
the lead in laying down the common policy. On 30 March
1719, in answer to reports from Dubois on Alberoni's schemes,
he sent him a long dispatch with his views on the plan of
campaign to be pursued and the objects to be attained
thereby.[3] The protection of the French and English coasts
could, he suggested, well be left to the English navy; but

---

[1] An admirable account of Glenshiel, illustrated by a contemporary sketch-
plan of the battle, is given in Dickson, xli–liv. 269 sqq.
[2] Bourgeois, *Farnèse*, 353.
[3] This dispatch is printed in full from a copy in the Hanover Archives in
Michael, ii. 627 sqq.; a short extract from it is in *Stair Annals*, ii. 387–8.

that would not be enough, 'nous ne devons pas nous arrêter à nous garantir seulement de leurs insultes si nous ne voulons pas y demeurer exposés continuellement, et il faut pousser le Cardinal Alberoni chez lui pour l'empêcher de porter ses vues au dehors'. This pressure on the cardinal must be the task of France by means of an army which was being made ready under Stanhope's old opponent Berwick and was to enter Spain from the Pyrenean frontier; for the operations of this army, Stanhope, reminding Dubois of his own long experience of Spanish conditions, laid down a detailed plan. The first objective should be the port of Passages, where all the shipping, either completed or on the stocks, with which Alberoni hoped to make good his losses at Passaro and elsewhere, should be destroyed. Next the French army should be divided into two, one division remaining in the northern province of Biscaya, the other proceeding to Catalonia. In both provinces proclamations were to be issued declaring that the Regent had no intention of conquering an inch of Spanish territory for himself but that his sole object was to free the country of an alien minister who was oppressing it and leading it to destruction: at the same time he should offer to those provinces under the guarantee of England and France the restoration of their cherished provincial liberties which they had nearly won in the last war but which had then been ruthlessly torn from them.[1] Incidentally this plan would be to the benefit of both England and France. France would be permanently relieved of danger on the frontier, for these provinces would have a sense of gratitude to the Regent for the recovery of their liberties, while the central government, unable to tax them to the same extent, would no longer be capable of launching out into such ambitious schemes as Alberoni's. The English traders also—though this was not a point on which Stanhope dwelt—would feel more secure after the destruction of Spanish shipping. As the English representative to give the King's guarantee for the Catalan and Biscayan liberties, and also to make certain that these suggestions should be followed, Stanhope sent his cousin, the late envoy at Madrid, as an observer on Berwick's staff. At the same time every care was taken to avoid hurting French susceptibilities; for William Stanhope was ordered, not only

[1] The Catalans have long memories for the rights they claimed, as recent events have shown.

to show his Instructions to the Regent, but even to ask him to amplify them if he thought fit.[1]

The military operations in Spain were carried out according to Stanhope's plan. Berwick with an army of 30,000 crossed the Spanish frontier at the end of April 1719 and captured Passages, where six half-completed ships and a vast amount of naval stores were destroyed. In June Fuentarabia was captured almost under the nose of Philip, who with Alberoni had joined his little army of 13,000. In the same month William Stanhope, with a party of French volunteers, destroyed some more shipping and naval stores at Santona. In August San Sebastian was taken by assault, the Basque country submitted, and the Biscayans were guaranteed their liberties. Then Berwick crossed back into France and after marching along the northern side of the Pyrenees descended on Catalonia in October. In the same month an expedition sent out by Stanhope under Lord Cobham captured Vigo and destroyed more Spanish shipping. But the campaign had yielded little satisfaction to the French. Berwick himself, though too good a soldier not to do his duty, was probably half-hearted in a war against Philip, whom he had helped to maintain on his throne; some of his officers and men, enticed by Philip's proclamations representing himself as the true upholder of French interests, went over to the Spanish camp or back to France. The destruction of Spanish shipping, almost the only definite result of the campaign, was chiefly for the benefit of England. Nevertheless this 'civil war' served its purpose to this extent, that it brought home to Alberoni on what a slender basis his own power rested, without a navy and with his main army locked up in Sicily.

In spite of a victory over the Austrians in June this Spanish army in Sicily had lost Messina in August and was ultimately bound to succumb, since Byng was master of their communications. The English government had seen to that. Strict instructions were sent to him to allow no supplies or reinforcements from Sardinia or Italian ports to reach the Spanish army in Sicily, and above all to prevent its return to Spain. As usual, the Emperor was expecting his allies to do all the fighting for him and had to be reminded by Stanhope that it was his business to send troops into Italy and Sicily to complete what Byng had so well begun. A

---

[1] William Stanhope's Instructions of 29 Apr. 1719 are in *Instructions, France*, i. 148–51.

prolongation of the war would, he said, have a bad effect
in Parliament, where already the English merchants were
complaining of their loss of trade, while as to the effect on
France, 'vous savez combien la France s'est révoltée contre
notre *Quadruple Alliance* et combien on s'y recrie encore sur
ce que l'on prétend que le traité rend l'Empereur tout
puissant en Italie'. It was suspected that the Emperor would
be only too pleased to save himself the trouble of beating the
Spaniards in Italy by giving them a free passage back to
Spain, where they might create formidable difficulties for
Berwick's enterprise. Accordingly Craggs sent explicit orders
to Byng to sink 'to the bottom of the sea' any ships, even the
Emperor's, attempting to transport them across the Mediterranean.[1] By June, if not before, Alberoni had realized
that the game was up.

Even then Alberoni tried to wriggle out of his difficulties
by dividing the allies and getting France to agree to a
fantastic scheme to the profit of Spain. If, as seemed not
unlikely, Louis XV died without issue, the scheme was that
Philip and one of his sons were to reign in Spain and France
respectively, the Regent to be compensated by a kingdom
carved out of the French, Burgundian and Austrian Low
Countries, and the Emperor by Alsace; the Pretender was to
have a kingdom erected for him of Scotland and Ireland
whence he would be able to keep in order George I, confined to the narrow bounds of England. Philip's letter recommending this remarkable proposal to the Regent urged that
it would be a more suitable redivision of Europe than
that proposed in the Quadruple Alliance, 'one that would
unite France, Spain and the Emperor in reducing the pride
of that King [George I], who acted as if he were the arbiter of
Europe, taking away and dividing monarchies as he fancied
and raising himself above the sovereigns of Germany, not
excepting the Emperor, by means of the power Great Britain
gave him'.[2] Such a scheme came ill from the man who
complained of Stanhope 'cutting up and paring states as if
they were so many Dutch cheeses';[3] and it was lucky for its
author that the Regent was not cruel enough to publish it,
as the knowledge of it could hardly have failed to destroy

[1] R.O., *S.P.* 104/96 Craggs to Byng, 17 Jan. 1718/19 and 29 June 1719;
R.O., *S.P.* 44/269, Stanhope to Pentenriedter, 19 Aug. 1719.
[2] Baudrillart, ii. 367–70; Wiesener, iii. 64–7.
[3] See above, ch. xi, p. 304.

what affection for Philip still lingered in France. But no
answer to this proposal was vouchsafed; so in August Alberoni
went off on another tack to attain the peace he now ardently
desired, a tack which finally led to his own destruction.

Throughout his triumphant career in Spain Alberoni had
always remained loyal to his own native state, Parma. He
was in constant correspondence with the Duke and members
of his court, especially his old friend the finance minister
Rocca.[1] In his Italian policy he often deferred to the Duke's
views even when they were not quite his own. At this
juncture of his affairs he committed his fortunes largely to
another fellow countryman. His latest idea was to obtain
peace through the mediation of the Dutch, who had never
joined the Alliance and were evidently anxious not to forgo
their Spanish trade. As a messenger to the Dutch he chose
the Marquis Scotti, recently sent as Parmesan envoy to
Madrid, who, as a neutral, would be able to travel through
France on his way to the Hague. Even then, when sending
Scotti on a mission of peace, he must needs also be planning
a revolt in Brittany and trying through Lawless to persuade
the Tsar to attack Hanover and Scotland.[2] On arriving in
Paris Scotti refused to reveal the proposals he was to make
to the Dutch, but it soon appeared from the indiscretions of
Beretti-Landi in Holland that though Philip now consented,
perforce, to give up Sicily, he asked for Sardinia, Gibraltar
and Port Mahon in return. At first the Regent and Dubois
were inclined to let Scotti proceed on his journey, but on
further reflection refused permission for fear the Dutch,
already getting profit from hostilities in which they took no
part, might secure further advantages as mediators. Stanhope also reminded them that nothing was said in these
proposals about Alberoni's disgrace, the allies' *sine qua non*
for peace.

'His unbounded ambition', he wrote to Dubois, 'has been the
sole cause of the war. . . . If he is compelled to accept peace, he
will only yield to necessity, with the resolution to seize the first
opportunity of vengeance. . . . When he is reduced, let us not
suffer him to recover. . . . Let us hold forth this example to
Europe, as a means of intimidating every turbulent minister
who breaks the most solemn treaties, and attacks the persons of
princes in the most scandalous manner. . . .'

---

[1] This correspondence is published by E. Bourgeois, *Lettres Intimes de J. M.
Alberoni*, 1892.   [2] Bourgeois, *Farnèse*, 363.

Stanhope had his way. Scotti was not allowed to continue his journey to the Hague with his dubious message of peace. But he did not leave Paris forthwith, for there were deeper schemes afoot, in which he was to play a very different part.[1]

Then once more, and for the last time, appears our friend Peterborough. Undeterred by his misadventure at Bologna and eager as ever to play a leading part on the European stage, like the rest of the allied world he had now decided that Alberoni must be got rid of and persuaded himself that the idea had come to him sooner than to any one else. On Scotti's arrival in Paris he had gone over there to keep an eye on the negotiations and, finding that Alberoni's fall was regarded as an essential for peace, went on to Italy under the assumed name of Antonio Gavassi to arrange the affair secretly with two confidants of the Duke of Parma. Writing to the Regent on 20 November 1719 from Novi he claimed the merit of having 'persuaded Lords Sunderland and Stanhope that this turbulent minister would never be brought under except by necessity, and that it was requisite to attack him with a vigour equal to his obstinacy'. On the same day he wrote to Stanhope that owing to his persuasion the Duke of Parma was only anxious for 'the opportunity of making that insolent Minister repent . . . all his mistaken measures' and would urge the King of Spain to dismiss him if he can obtain a letter from the Regent, 'to intimate that the Allies will no longer have patience, but are taking the resolution to enter into no negotiations of peace till the Cardinal be removed from the Ministry'. Even in this letter he could not forbear airing his old grievance against the Emperor and concluding with a eulogy of his own generosity to that ruler:

'My Lord, I shall add but one word. Pray consider all I have done and suffered for the interest of the present Emperor. The jealousies of the court of Vienna, upon my subject, are as pitiful as unjust. I am confident you will answer for me. I endeavour nothing but a peace, upon those terms which might satisfy, in my opinion, his Imperial Majesty. My Lord, I am persuaded you will tell some of their Ministers they are in the wrong.'

The Duke of Parma's sudden anxiety for the dismissal of Alberoni is more likely to have been due to the exactions of

---

[1] For Scotti's mission see Bourgeois, *Farnèse*, 364 sqq.; Castagnoli, 365–8; Stanhope's letter (translated) is in Coxe, *Bourbons*, ii. 365.

the Austrian troops in the proximity of Parma than to the arguments of Peterborough, whom he describes as 'possessed by the itch for perpetual motion'; nor are Stanhope or Dubois likely to have trusted him with any serious business. Craggs wrote explicitly to Stair to warn him that 'this lord had no directions from his Majesty or any of his ministers to concern himself in any negotiation of that kind; . . . and particularly his Majesty would have your Excellency assure the Regent and the Abbé Dubois that whatever negotiation my Lord Peterborough may be entered into, it is entirely voluntary and of his own head, without the least authority from hence for so doing'. Stanhope himself had also written to Dubois bidding him beware of Peterborough's indiscretions and of his habits of consorting with dubious characters and abusing his own government. But at any rate Peterborough seems to have obtained the desired letter from the Regent and a considerable sum of money with which to keep alive the Duke of Parma's animosity against Alberoni. Whether as a result of Peterborough's diplomacy or of direct negotiations with Paris, at the end of October the Duke ordered Scotti to return from Paris to Madrid and bring about the Cardinal's fall.[1]

The Duke of Parma, by his advice to Philip V and Elizabeth and his urgent representations to Alberoni himself, had been largely responsible for initiating the Italian policy, against which Alberoni had originally protested and which was the chief cause of the dead set made against him by the allies. Now the Duke had at least the grace, on Peterborough's suggestion, to offer Alberoni a bridge whereby he could escape ignominious dismissal; for he advised him to resign of his own accord on the ground of his earnest desire to bring about European peace and then throw himself on the Regent's mercy.[2] But Alberoni would have none of it: he still believed he had the confidence of the King and refused to abdicate voluntarily. He may perhaps have counted on the success of one last throw he had made for peace on conditions not too humiliating for himself and Spain. His intermediary was a certain colonel or general Seissan, a renegade Frenchman then in the service of Poland, 'qui après être

---

[1] For Peterborough's part in this affair see Castagnoli, 368–9, 381–4; Bourgeois, *Farnèse*, 366 sqq.; Wiesener, iii. 215 sqq.; Mahon, *History*, i. 350, ii, Appendix; *Stair Annals*, ii. 122, 403.

[2] Castagnoli, 381 sqq., Duke of Parma to Scotti, 13 Nov. 1719.

tombé ici pour quelque affaire qui le regarde', was returning to Holland by way of England.[1] Alberoni entrusted this casual personage with a letter to Stanhope recalling their last farewells at the Escorial and their mutual promises to confide to one another any means that might occur to them of reconciling their masters and 'promoting the mutual felicity of their two nations'; he also expressed his delight that to Stanhope was given the chance of claiming all the merit for the peace and so 'fortifying him in the good graces of the King his master and gaining him much reputation in his own country and abroad'. The letter concluded with Alberoni's proposals for peace, which went far beyond those he had made in June and July: the terms offered by Stanhope on his visit to the Escorial would be accepted on condition the Dukes of Parma and Tuscany should forthwith declare the Infant their heir and that on failure of direct issue Sardinia, the two Sicilies and the Milanese should revert to Spain. Verbally also Seissan was charged with seductive offers to England of free commerce with Mexico, and to the Emperor of a marriage between the Prince of Asturias and an archduchess. When Seissan appeared in Stanhope's presence Alberoni had already fallen and there was no need to consider his proposals in detail.[2]

Scotti arrived in Madrid at the end of October. After the Duke of Parma's failure to induce Alberoni to resign voluntarily the only course left was for Scotti to press the demand for his dismissal on Philip V. At first this task was none too easy. Alberoni had a shrewd suspicion of Scotti's real object and succeeded for nearly a month in excluding him from the royal presence, access to which he guarded with extraordinary vigilance. But one member of the royal household was not amenable to Alberoni's influence, the Queen's old nurse, Laura Pescatori, who had been brought over from Italy and came to reign almost supreme in her mistress's confidence. She had a grudge against Alberoni, who disliked her and feared her intriguing disposition. Through her, therefore, Scotti contrived to convey to Philip the Duke of Parma's advice to get rid of the cardinal as the only means of saving Spain, and to insinuate that in his private letters to Parma Alberoni attributed the war exclusively to Philip's personal self-seeking and obstinacy. The effect of the message

[1] See above, ch. iv, p. 92.
[2] *Stair Annals*, ii. 392–4, Alberoni to Stanhope, 15 Nov. 1719.

was sudden and dramatic. On the evening of 4 December Alberoni had his usual audience of the King for the transaction of current business: on the following morning Philip went off on a hunting expedition with the Queen, leaving a curt message to be delivered to Alberoni informing him that he was dismissed from all his employments and ordering him to leave Madrid within eight days and in three weeks to be outside Spanish territory. No letters from Alberoni could procure him an audience—the royal pair no doubt dreaded that his insinuating plausibility might weaken their resolution —and Alberoni had to flee like a hunted criminal from the capital where for years he had given the law to the proudest grandees of Spain and whence he had spun intrigues in all the courts of Europe. Nor was he spared the last indignity of being caught up at Lerida by the police, who ransacked his effects and carried off all his papers, that he was charged with having stolen from the royal archives. He had written to the Regent for permission to travel to Italy through France. This permission was willingly granted, and at the frontier he found M. de Marcieu, sent by the Regent to accompany him through France and extract from him all the confidences about the court of Spain that he might utter in the bitterness of his soul. Alberoni did not mince his words about the uxorious King and his Queen, 'qui avait le diable au corps et ne tarderait pas à faire du vacarme en Europe', but he gave Marcieu little information not already known at the French court.[1] When he first arrived in Italy he was hunted about from pillar to post, seeking refuge from Pope Clement XI, who wished to bring him before the Conclave to be tried as a malefactor for his misdeeds and deprived of the purple. Under later Popes, however, he found a limited scope for his energy and masterful nature as papal legate over the territories of the Church, and he did not bring his turbulent career to an end till 1752.

Dubois himself wrote to inform Stanhope of the cardinal's fall, adding to the news this just tribute to Stanhope's part in it:

'On ne peut pas apprendre ce dénouement sans faire réflexion, My lord, sur la justice qu'on doit à Votre Excellence d'avoir proposé de si grands projets et des mesures aussi justes pour les conduire à leur fin et pour épargner par des soins et des

[1] Marcieu's account is in *Recueil, Espagne*, ii. 383; see also Baudrillart, ii. 397–9.

dépenses médiocres et passagères les malheurs infinis qu'une guerre générale pouvait attirer.'

Destouches, the French envoy, had been told to deliver the note at once, wherever Stanhope might happen to be. The House of Lords was then sitting and Stanhope was fetched out into the lobby. On reading the letter he embraced Destouches and took him into the House, where he read out the glad tidings to the assembled peers. In the Commons, Craggs did the same. Walpole's comment was that George I should follow Philip V's good example and get rid of a bad minister, to which Craggs smartly retorted that this was exactly the course adopted by the King two years previously.[1]

Alberoni suffered unjustly in being held mainly responsible for the policy Spain had been pursuing. There is, indeed, no reason to doubt the truth of his assertion to Stanhope and Marcieu that the war in Italy was begun against his will and that he would have preferred peace for another five or six years to enable him to develop Spain's industries and give her a formidable army and navy. During that last hopeless campaign against Berwick, undertaken in spite of his entreaties to the King to make peace as the only means of saving Spain from defeat, the truth was wrung from him in the cry of anguish he addressed to his friend Rocca:

'The King is deeply offended at any contradiction, and whatever arguments are put before him he has always believed that his own personal interests should be preferred to all others and even to any consideration of the calamities that might be caused by war. With my rulers there is nothing to do but state my case and then obey their will. In speech and writing I tried to deter the King from his rupture with France: but when it has become a question of obeying orders, the fact that I opposed the war has not diminished by one iota the zeal and devotion to business which I owe to my Master and Benefactor.'[2]

But it suited the Regent and Dubois, anxious above all not to appear to have any animosity against a son of France, to find in Alberoni a scapegoat for Philip's policy. In England the commercial community, already suffering, in spite of treaties, from Spanish obstruction to their trade and the attacks of Spanish privateers, was certainly more alarmed at Alberoni's own plans for reviving the naval and military

[1] Bourgeois, *Farnèse*, 379; Baudrillart, ii. 399.
[2] Castagnoli, 362, Alberoni to Rocca, 8 June 1719.

strength of Spain than at Philip's quarrels with the Emperor: but Stanhope for long credited Alberoni with a genuine desire for peace and was only converted to the French view when he found Alberoni ready to ruin Europe for a Spanish punctilio. In fact Alberoni was not the originator of the Italian adventure; but he became all the more dangerous for his fatal facility in sinking his own convictions before the King's in order to keep his place. And, having once adopted Philip's schemes, no fear of consequences, no consideration of the interests of other nations, stood in the way of any enterprise, however outrageous, with which he hoped to force these schemes upon an unwilling world. Thus he had come to be regarded as the mad dog of Europe: to Stanhope and Dubois came the conviction that without his removal no peace was possible. At any rate with his removal the main obstacle to peace disappeared.

§ 3

Alberoni's disgrace did not indeed bring about immediate peace. Philip himself, it appeared, still claimed the right of dictating the terms as victor. In addition to those lately sent by Alberoni to Stanhope he required the immediate evacuation of the places occupied by the French in Spain, damages for his losses at Passaro and transport back to Spain for his troops marooned in Sicily.[1]

Apart, too, from Philip's exaggerated pretensions Stanhope had serious difficulties with his team of allies. The Emperor, though one of the chief beneficiaries from the Alliance, was always giving trouble. He had not only made little contribution to the efforts of England and France against Spain,[2] but on several matters was in acute conflict with the English government. The treatment of the Protestants in Germany was a standing cause of offence and provoked angry remonstrances to Vienna throughout the year 1720.[3] The Emperor's sanction, contrary to treaties, of an Ostend East India Company in competition with the English East India Company was another and almost led to war during Walpole's administration.[4] The Emperor's formal Investiture of George I with

---

[1] Baudrillart, ii. 300.
[2] See above, p. 329.
[3] This dispute is more amply dealt with in ch. xiv, pp. 388–9.
[4] R.O., *S.P.* 104/42 has Craggs's protests against this Company to St. Saphorin, 9 Sept. and 31 Oct. 1718.

Bremen and Verden was vexatiously delayed. Then in the latter part of 1718 considerable soreness had been engendered between the two courts by the Princess Sobieski incident, in which Stanhope and the English government did not play a very generous or dignified part. For some time the Pretender had been seeking a royal bride who should add prestige to his pretensions and had finally pitched upon the Princess Clementina Sobieski, grand-daughter of John Sobieski, a former King of Poland. It was understood that some form of marriage by proxy had been celebrated, but when the Princess was travelling through the Emperor's dominions on her way to join the bridegroom in Italy, she was arrested at the request of the English government and imprisoned at Innsbruck. But after her arrest the Emperor had religious qualms about this forcible separation of man and wife whose union was reported to have been blessed by Holy Church. Stanhope replied with some asperity and the lack of delicacy characteristic of his day that the marriage had not been consummated, and if a mere marriage by proxy were held binding, 'les archiduchesses ne seraient plus en sécurité dans le palais même de l'Empereur'; he also denied, as it turned out correctly, that there had been any marriage ceremony, even by proxy. In a series of angry dispatches to Vienna, he vehemently upbraided the Emperor for daring to think of letting her out. In one dispatch, after recounting all the services of George I to the Emperor, he concludes that 'une conscience maniée par le Clergé Catholique dégage de tous les liens d'amitié et d'alliance'; in another, on the news that the Emperor had consented not to release her, he suggests that she should be married to Prince Anthony of Parma so as to remove all chance of her marriage to the Pretender, and urges the Emperor to make it an affair of state with Clementina's father, since the priests were still making a point of the fictitious marriage ceremony. The princess, a child of sixteen, was, however, kept a prisoner through the winter and spring of 1718–19, but at last, through the daring of the Jacobite adventurer Charles Wogan, managed to escape to Italy, where she was duly married to the Pretender on his return from Madrid. No such serious results followed from the marriage as Stanhope had anticipated, but, even had they, this vendetta against an innocent child would not have been worthy of a great nation's dignity: it can only be partially excused by the very real alarm still felt in England at the prospect of a successful attempt on the throne by the Pretender.[1] As a result of all these disputes in August 1720 Craggs summed up the grievances against the Emperor in a long dispatch to Cadogan: the marriage of the Pretender, the oppression of Protestants, the Ostend traffic, differences about the Tsar and the settlement of the North, undue favour to Savoy and not enough regard for our useful ally the Duke of Parma; and he concludes that though we are always helping the Emperor with 'money ships or good offices, and I think in my conscience they envy Us in being able to do it, we have never anything to ask of them but not to doe Us and commonly themselves with Us a mischief, and if in ten such applications we succeed in two, they reproach Us with it as if they had overpaid all the Services they ever received.'[2]

But these difficulties with Spain and the Emperor would not have mattered so much, had it not been for a certain cooling off in our friendly relations with France. During the year 1719 both nations found grievances, grievances trivial in themselves, but in their sum disturbing to the harmony of close allies. Several of the French ambassadors, especially in Northern courts, out of sympathy with the Regent's policy, were working against English interests. 'The cursed sluices of Dunkirk' once more were a subject of controversy, not so much from any failure of the Regent's government in observing its treaty obligations to destroy the port, but from the determination of the inhabitants quietly to preserve its efficiency. There were also disputes about the limits of Nova Scotia, handed over to England by the Treaty of Utrecht, and about the rights of French fishermen in Newfoundland. The island of St. Lucia in the West Indies, declared neutral by the same treaty, was ceded by the Regent to a French noble, and, when after protest he was turned out, by George I to an English duke.[3] These small disputes were not minimized by Stair, never an easy man to deal with and apt

[1] A good account of the incident is in Dickson, xxiii, xxvii, lvi, lvii. Stanhope's dispatches of 17, 28 Oct., 4, 28 Nov., 12, 30 Dec. 1718 are in R.O., S.P. 110/77. Even after the marriage the English agents abroad show little generosity in their accounts of the unhappy pair. In R. O., S.P. 92/30 there is an account of the birth of the young Pretender in Jan. 1721 in the presence of all the Pope's relations, several cardinals, bishops and princesses, 'and to end ye farce ye peaceful guns of Castle St. Angelo were fired to welcome ye infant's appearance in ye world.'

[2] R.O., S.P. 104/42, Craggs to Cadogan, 24 Aug. 1720.

[3] Wiesener, iii. 158–70; Stair Annals, ii. 111, 140, 408.

on the smallest provocation to be suspicious of every French
politician in turn, from the Regent and Dubois downwards.
He had disputes with Dubois and was not on speaking terms
with John Law, the all-powerful Scottish financier, then at
the height of his success in re-establishing French credit.
On the occasion of his ceremonial entry into Paris as ambassador, which did not take place till February 1719, his excessive punctilio about questions of etiquette brought him into
conflict with a prince of the blood and provoked a long and
tiresome correspondence.[1] The most serious report, however,
from Stair was that the French court was once more veering
towards a separate agreement with Spain and an anti-
English policy, and that Dubois was losing favour and likely
to be superseded as chief minister by Law, who had often
expressed Jacobite sentiments. Once more, therefore, Stanhope decided to pay a flying visit to Paris, to straighten out
the tangle and especially to strengthen Dubois against internal
and external opposition.

Being neither of aristocratic origin nor in sympathy with
the political ideas of the powerful members of the old court,
Dubois had found immense difficulties, not only in climb-
ing to his present position as secretary of state, but also in
maintaining himself there. The one ally on whose unflinch-
ing support he could in all circumstances depend was the
Englishman Stanhope, who had materially helped him to
his present position and, in the interests of his own country,
was ready to do anything to keep him there. Dubois, casting
about for means of entrenching himself, had imagined that
if he obtained a cardinal's hat, like his great rival in Spain,
as a Prince of the Church he would be more than the equal
of all the aristocrats who despised him, and less subject to
the Regent's varying whims. Since 1718 he had been employing an agent at Rome to intrigue for this object, which soon
became so much of an obsession to him that, as Stair drily
remarked, 'le chapeau de cardinal a tourné la tête à notre
pauvre abbé'. Not content with his private agent, he set
strings working throughout Europe, especially by Stanhope's
means. Stanhope approved of St. Saphorin getting the
Emperor to support his candidature, and told Stair to induce
the Regent, not particularly inclined to raise his old tutor to
such an eminence, also to urge it at the Vatican. Owing
to his 'délicatesse' Dubois was not to be supposed to know

[1] *Stair Annals*, ii. 97 sqq.

of this approach to the Regent, but Stanhope adds as an afterthought it would perhaps be as well to show him the letter privately before it was given to the Regent. As long as Pope Clement XI lived Dubois failed to secure the coveted hat, in spite of his timely conversion from Jansenist leanings to the policy expressed in the papal Bull *Unigenitus*, which he forced on an unwilling Parlement. Meanwhile, as a consolation, early in 1720 he was elevated to the archbishopric of Cambrai, largely through Stanhope's influence with the Regent, a position which gave him some of the prestige of rank that he needed; not till six months after the death of his Protestant friend in England did he attain the purple through the negotiations previously carried on by Stanhope in several Catholic courts as well as by the support of such incongruous backers as the Emperor, the King of Spain and the Pretender.

An even more pressing reason for Stanhope's visit to France than the constant need for bolstering up Dubois was Stair's vendetta against Law, which threatened seriously to impair the good relations between France and England. Since Stanhope's last visit to Paris this remarkable man, then already active in French finance, had suddenly risen to his giddy pinnacle and gained almost undisputed power over the Regent and the government of France. Coming over to France at the beginning of the Regency, John Law had found the public finances in a state of chaos owing to the enormous burden of debt accumulated during Louis XIV's wars, to the faulty methods of assessing and collecting the revenue and to the progressive debasement of the coinage. Recognizing that the weakness of the Regent's administration was largely due to this impoverishment of the royal exchequer, which made him the sport of Parlements and exorbitant creditors, he gained the Regent's ear by bold proposals for a change of system. His first step in May 1716 was to obtain a charter for a private bank which issued notes promising repayment at their face value in gold, instead of in the debased coinage: thus these notes appreciated so much in value, as compared with the debased coinage, that a year later the collectors of taxes were ordered to make their remittances to the Treasury only in Law's notes. In December 1718 Law's bank was turned into a Royal Bank, and its notes made legal currency for all purposes, but, by an unfortunate modification of Law's original plan, the notes were no longer convertible into gold, but only represented the bad current coinage. Meanwhile Law, following the English analogy of interesting the public creditors in the stability of the government and allowing them to promote the commercial advantage of the community by using their interest as trading capital, had in 1717 established a Company of the West, the so-called Mississippi scheme. The funds subscribed by the members of this company were advanced to the government at a comparatively low rate of interest for the purpose of extinguishing a corresponding amount of public debt at higher interest, and the subscribers were given the monopoly of exploiting the vast Mississippi region west of the Alleghanies, originally opened up by La Salle. Gradually this Company of the West absorbed all the other trading and exploiting companies of France and obtained a monopoly of trade with India, China, Senegal, Guinea and the Barbary states: at the beginning of 1720 it was merged with Law's other enterprise, the Royal Bank. In the second half of 1719 Law had also acquired the tobacco monopoly, the right of coinage for nine years and a lease of all the taxes, and he offered to lend the King 1,200 million livres at 3 per cent. to pay off all debt charges issued at 4 per cent. Finally, after a convenient conversion to Catholicism under the tuition of the abbé Tencin, said to have been paid £10,000 for his pains, at the beginning of 1720 he was put in charge of the whole of the national finances as Controller-General. These all-embracing schemes gave great advantages to the nation. Many oppressive taxes of the past were reduced or abolished, while by better management the government obtained a better revenue: private profiteers were discouraged, money was advanced on easy terms to help manufacturers: useful public works were started, industry, especially that of the overtaxed peasants, was encouraged. But unfortunately, excellent as most of Law's schemes were and especially adapted to French conditions, they required a vast amount of ready money to finance them all; consequently shares for his various enterprises were issued at an enormous premium and even those high prices were enhanced by the wild speculation that ensued. Thus in 1719 shares of the nominal value of 500 livres and carrying interest at 12 per cent. were issued at 1,500 and were soon raised by speculation to 12,000, so that the purchasers could not hope to get more than ½ per cent. on their investments.

Law's ideas had, indeed, much to recommend them, and had he been content, as he himself afterwards admitted, to introduce his reforms more gradually, they would have proved of the greatest benefit to France.[1]

At the first indications of Law's success Stanhope himself had taken the part that might have been expected from so firm an ally of France. 'Je ne puis finir', he wrote to Dubois in October 1719, 'sans me réjouir avec Votre Excellence de l'heureux état ou se trouvent vos finances . . . Le rétablissement si prompt et si surprenant de vos finances fait l'admiration de toute l'Europe'; to which Dubois replied denying the reports that he was at odds with Law and insisting that the rehabilitation of French credit was of advantage to England as well as to France in contributing 'à leur deffense commune et au soutien de leurs intérêts qui sont inséparables'. But both statesmen were troubled at Stair's attitude. Law had no doubt, in the intoxication of his early success, let fall some injudicious expressions about England, which in Stair's fevered imagination became magnified into a 'daily discourse that he will raise France to a greater height than ever she was upon the ruin of England and Holland', and he may have had Jacobite leanings, which, without being very serious, gave great offence to the tetchy ambassador. To such an extreme had Stair carried his hostility that he would have no personal dealings with the man who, he himself said, must be looked upon 'as the first minister'. He also began anew his carping criticisms of Dubois, so that even his good friend Craggs expressed a mild wish that 'you would not so frequently engage yourself in personal hostilities with those employed by the Regent'. Stanhope himself took a sterner view.

'Rien', he wrote to Dubois, 'ne pouvait nous arriver de plus affligeant que la malheureuse animosité qui s'était élevée entre Milord Stair et M. Law; nous en sommes d'autant plus en peine que Milord Stair nous l'apprend lui-même, et s'en fait un mérite. Il attribue à M. Law beaucoup de mauvaise volonté contre nous. . . . Je vous avoue, Monsieur, que je ne saurais m'imaginer que ce soient là les sentimens de M. Law; je sais combien il s'est intéressé au traité qui devait affermir notre union, et qu'il a regardé l'union des deux Couronnes comme la base de ses projets.'

[1] A very clear account of Law's System is contained in J. Shield Nicholson's *Treatise on Money*, &c. ('Essay on John Law').

He even began to question the use of an ambassador on the worst possible terms with the two most influential men in France and went so far as to tell Dubois that he would be recalled if such was the desire of the French court.[1]

After a stormy passage to France, when both masts of his ship were carried away, Stanhope once more succeeded in straightening things out in Paris. He put up at Stair's house, and very sensibly, though greatly to the chagrin of his host, made his first call upon the fire-eater Law. Stair even went so far as to complain about Stanhope's action to Craggs, who naturally asked him what else he could have expected Stanhope to do:

> 'The King ordered Stanhope to talk with Law, and judge as well as he could what he designed. Your Lordship had put things upon that foot with this man, or he with you, that 'twas not possible for him to set foot within your house. Was Lord Stanhope, who was dispatched to see whether Hannibal was at the gates, to be disputing punctilios—either not to have gone to your house that he might receive the first visit from Mr. Law, or when he was there, pass that fortnight he stayed in a negotiation to meet with a man the King had absolutely directed him to talk with? I must confess I think he did well in going straight to him and asking him to explain himself on the necessary heads.'[2]

Stanhope came promptly to two conclusions: first, that Law had no such evil designs on England as Stair made out, and that, even if he had, to insist that the Regent should dismiss one of his ablest servants was not the best way of arriving at an understanding with him; and secondly that Stair himself had become impossible and must be superseded. After disposing of these personal matters Stanhope came to the more important business of the method to be adopted with Spain. If the Regent ever had any inclination to weaken on the terms of the Quadruple Alliance, it was soon swept away by Stanhope's breezy and determined attitude. He spoke quite frankly to the Regent about the various causes of grievance that the English had against France, especially the continued presence of notorious Jacobites in France, all which the Regent promised to remedy: in fact three weeks later, on the occasion of Dubois's consecration as Archbishop of Cambrai,

---

[1] Wiesener, iii. 245; Bourgeois, *Dubois*, 187; Mahon, *History*, ii, Appendix, Stanhope to Dubois, 18 Dec. 1719; see also *Stair Annals*, ii. 124–5, 411.

[2] *Stair Annals*, ii. 411.

an ordinance was published, 'au son de trompe', requiring all rebel foreigners to leave the country within eight days.[1] On the main issue of keeping the Regent to his obligations about Spain, Stanhope secured a joint declaration, signed by the representatives of England, France, the Emperor and Savoy, that Spain must be strictly kept to the terms laid down in the Quadruple Alliance. Finally, on the Regent's own proposal, Stanhope's faithful secretary Luke Schaub was chosen to take the terms to Madrid and obtain the assent of Philip; a choice, said Stanhope, which alone was ample reward for his journey to France.

So successful indeed had been Stanhope's brief sojourn of only eleven days—9 to 20 January—in Paris that not only were misunderstandings between the two allied governments entirely removed for the time being, but on 26 January Philip agreed to the terms brought by Schaub. On 17 February his representative at the Hague signed the Quadruple Alliance without any reservations.[2] Thus at last were Stanhope's long and intricate labours to this end, an end he believed essential to peace for England and Europe, brought to a close. Philip V and the Emperor were now formally at peace and formally recognized one another's titles. The Duke of Orleans's position as Regent was consolidated and his right to the throne, if Louis XV died childless, admitted even by his cousin. The restless Spanish Queen had her claim to Italian duchies for her son formally sanctioned by all the great powers. England explicitly gained only another formal guarantee of the Hanoverian succession, which had never been seriously endangered by Spain; but the chief profit she hoped to derive from the peace was further security for her lucrative Spanish trade.

One immediate result of Spain's accession to the Quadruple Alliance was that both England and France began to veer away from the Emperor and make approaches to Spain. In both cases this result was only natural. The traditional policy of antagonism to the Habsburgs died hard in France, and the Regent was only too delighted to return to the intimate relations with Philip most pleasing to the French people. In England the constant exigencies of the House of Austria were found by Stanhope as hard to stomach as they

---

[1] St. Simon, xvii. 1.
[2] For Stanhope's negotiations at Paris and their result see Boyer, xix. 68 sqq.; St. Simon, xvi. 101 and xvii. 1 sqq.; Baudrillart, ii. 401.

had been by Bolingbroke before him and were to be by his successor Townshend. No sooner had Spain made peace than the Emperor at once started the old Viennese game of putting interminable obstacles in the way of securing possession of the duchies to Don Carlos, a game which the English, with their eye to commercial advantages in Spain, were as determined to resist as the French. Unfortunately, far from cementing more closely the alliance between France and England, this common impulse to draw nearer to Spain had at first almost the effect of creating dissension between the allies. The Regent's main object now was to represent himself as Spain's only friend and thereby to obtain from her equal if not superior trading privileges to those obtained by England at Utrecht and by Bubb's treaty. Stanhope for his part was resolved to regain the ground lost by English traders during the years of suspicion and hostility and certainly not to admit France to a more privileged position in the Spanish markets.

In his new-found zeal for Spanish interests the Regent scored an initial point over Stanhope by resuscitating the offer of Gibraltar made in very different circumstances. It is true Stanhope, during his visit to Madrid in 1718, had offered to return Gibraltar to Spain as an inducement to prompt acceptance of the Quadruple Alliance, but the offer had then been contemptuously put aside by Philip and Alberoni. Six months later, by what appeared on the face of it a piece of sharp practice at the French court, the Regent in his declaration of war against Spain was made to refer to a 'promise' that Gibraltar would be restored.[1] Now that all his and Alberoni's ambitious schemes had failed Philip was bent on at least recovering Gibraltar, which he spoke of as 'the thorns in his feet'. He wrote to the Regent implying that his accession to the Quadruple Alliance was due to his belief that Gibraltar would be his reward, and instructed his envoy Lawless to obtain from the Regent the fulfilment of the so-called promise. The Regent, anxious to prove himself an effective friend to Spain, and perhaps genuinely convinced that Stanhope's original offer had not lapsed, made himself responsible to Philip for obtaining Gibraltar and called on England to honour his engagement.[2]

Stanhope himself had never attached great importance to

[1] See above, ch. xi, p. 307; ch. xii, p. 323.
[2] *Recueil, Espagne,* ii. 344 sqq.; Baudrillart, ii. 411.

the possession of Gibraltar. When he was there in 1709 he was chiefly impressed by the bad state of its defences and had proposed an extensive and somewhat costly scheme for securing it from attack; in 1716, when he was in office, he and his colleagues, according to the Prussian envoy Bonet, regarded its annual cost in upkeep of over £90,000 as excessive and were even then ready to give it back to Spain in exchange for commercial concessions. Stanhope himself with pardonable partiality believed that Port Mahon, a less costly possession, fully answered the purpose of a Mediterranean base; and he was not alone in thinking so. So, when Dubois in November 1717, 'raisonnant avec Mylord Stanhope sur le peu d'étoffe qu'il y avait pour contenter les parties intéressées au traité', had suggested its offer to Spain as a make-weight, Stanhope had acquiesced.[1] But while quite prepared to give up Gibraltar for value received, such as prompt accession to the treaty in 1718 or valuable commercial concessions, he had no intention, after all the expense and anxiety of the previous year's hostilities, of giving it up without a *quid pro quo*, still less to allow France to oust England from her trade with Spain by obtaining the entire credit for such a concession. He was also beginning to realize that the House of Commons and public opinion in England valued Gibraltar far more highly than he did himself. On a rumour that it was about to be surrendered the pamphleteers got busy with arguments for retaining it. The writer of *Considerations . . . upon . . . the approaching Peace and the importance of Gibraltar*, a pamphlet of 1720, places its value as holding the keys of the Mediterranean higher than that of Port Mahon, and ironically assumes that there can be no danger of the fortress being abandoned, since 'God has now sent us a Ministry who will mend all those faults they were the first to condemn: the Interest of the Public is their Interest'. On the ministers' mere suggestion 'to pass a Bill, for the purpose of leaving to the King the power of disposing of that fortress for the advantage of his subjects', an address against surrendering Gibraltar was talked of in Parliament and was dropped only on the 'assurance given by the ministry to members from man to man, that nothing of that kind should be done'.[2] At any rate Stanhope had given no

---

[1] See above, ch. iv, p. 88; Michael, ii. 632; Lemontey, ii. 395.
[2] Mahon, *History*, ii. 129, letter from Stanhope to Schaub of 20 March 1720; Coxe, *Walpole*, ii. 183; Coxe, *Bourbons*, iii. 10 sqq.

countenance to the Regent's present demand on behalf of
Philip. In his answer to Alberoni's last proposals brought
by Seissan[1] he had specifically stated that his offer of Gibraltar, made in the previous year at the Escorial, no longer held
good, and in his recent visit to Paris he gave the Regent no
hope that the cession would be considered; in fact the question was not even touched upon.[2]

But the Regent was very insistent: there seemed even a
danger that on this question a serious breach might occur
between the allies at the very moment when success had
crowned their joint efforts. Once more the old court party
in France began to raise their heads at the prospect of a
new honeymoon with Spain, reinforced this time by Law.
Rendered desperate by the gradual collapse of his financial
edifice and feverishly casting about for powerful supporters,
by the violence of his language against England the Scots-
man was now more than justifying Stair's former strictures
on him. Dubois himself was in disgrace with the Regent,
who blamed him for revealing Spain's accession to the
Quadruple Alliance in such a hurry to Stanhope, without
waiting for the letter conveying the demand for Gibraltar.
Again Dubois found no resource for himself or for the maintenance of the alliance but in desperate appeals to Stanhope,
first to persuade the King to yield to the Regent's representations, and, when those proved abortive, to come over to
Paris himself to retrieve the situation. Accordingly, less
than three months after his stormy voyage in January,
Stanhope started once more, on 22 March 1720, on what
was to be his last visit to the Regent's court.

> 'For some weeks', he told St. Saphorin, 'we have been within
> an ace of foundering. This court [the Regent's] has come to
> believe that it could dispose of Spain as it pleases. That being so,
> a cabal has been formed which a fortnight ago was the most
> powerful, and may become so a fortnight hence, and which did
> not hesitate to propose to the Duke of Orleans to make war
> against the Emperor and ourselves. The abbé Dubois thought
> himself ruined, and called for help and made me come here.'[3]

In his first interview with the Regent, however, Stanhope
found the usual gracious reception, the usual honeyed words;
indeed he had never been so well received: nor was the

---

[1] Above, p. 334.
[2] *Stair Annals*, ii. 413–16, Craggs to Stair, 18 Feb. 1720.
[3] Quoted by Wiesener, iii. 304 (in the original French) from the R.O. copy.

graciousness at all affected by Stanhope's frank expostula-
tions about the Regent's attempt to negotiate behind England's back with Spain and his readiness to listen to strange
counsellors instead of to the faithful Dubois. But even
Stanhope did not quite succeed in recovering the old spirit
of complete and intimate confidence that he was wont to
find at the Palais Royal directly he appeared. The utmost
that he could attain was a promise from the Regent not to
press the cession of Gibraltar immediately, but that a decision should be postponed until the meeting of a congress
shortly to be held at Cambrai to adjust certain details of
the treaty; at Cambrai France was to retain the liberty
of using her good offices on behalf of Spain in persuading
England to restore Gibraltar.

But that was not the end of the Gibraltar affair. Convinced
after this visit to Paris that the Regent was bent on coming
to a separate understanding with Spain, Stanhope on his
side saw that the friendship he was also anxious to renew
with Spain must be obtained independently. For this friendship he was willing to pay a fair price: Gibraltar, if need
be. But, to secure the full advantage of such a concession,
Gibraltar must be given, not at the dictation of France, for
then Philip would feel no gratitude to England, but spon-
taneously and in exchange for corresponding advantages
from Spain, say Florida or increased commercial favours.
When, in September 1720, Philip claimed the right of interfering with our commercial privileges till Gibraltar was
restored, Stanhope sharply told him that he must give up
such a claim without further ado if he wished for English
support at the Congress of Cambrai.[1] Nevertheless, in a letter
he wrote to Craggs from Hanover in the following month,[2]
he entered exhaustively into the question, pointing out the
heavy annual expense to England of the upkeep of Gibraltar
and the still heavier expense needed to make it safe from an
attack by Spain in the event of war, whereas Philip had its
recovery so much at heart that he would probably be willing
to make considerable concessions in trade or territory for it.

'However favourable', he concludes, 'may be the dispositions
of the Spaniards, we cannot flatter ourselves we shall gain their
confidence as long as we persist in retaining Gibraltar, which

[1] R.O., C.O 95/3 contains a MS. account of Gibraltar, 1704-25, with a copy
of Stanhope's letter (addressed to Sutton at Paris) of 8 Sept. 1720.
[2] Mahon, *History*, ii, Appendix, Stanhope to Craggs, 1 Oct. 1720.

serves as a permanent memorial to them of the calamities we have brought upon them and would always be the most powerful inducement in the hands of the priests for stirring up a proud and bigoted nation against us strangers and heretics.'

Accordingly he asked the Lords Justices to consider whether, in exchange for commercial advantages, it might not be worth giving up the fortress. The Lords Justices entirely agreed with Stanhope's view, subject to the proviso made by Townshend, who by that time had returned to the ministry, that the equivalent should be territorial, either Hispaniola or Florida.[1] In this form, accordingly, the proposal was mooted in Spain but fell to the ground owing to Philip's refusal to accept it except as a free gift without equivalent. So the matter was left at the death of Stanhope in the following February: but in June 1721 George I was induced to promise Philip the restitution of Gibraltar without equivalent on the 'first favourable opportunity to regulate this article with consent of my Parliament'. In 1729, after another short bout of hostilities, Spain, taking ground on this very conditional promise, again demanded Gibraltar and again without success. In effect the stipulation of Parliamentary consent as an essential condition for its cession was equivalent to relegating such a sacrifice to the Greek calends. From the outset Gibraltar has appealed to the popular imagination of Englishmen, who, unlike the statesmen, were far more attached to it than to Port Mahon. Once more a great statesman, Stanhope's nephew the elder Pitt, was prepared, in the early stages of the Seven Years' War, to give up Gibraltar, in exchange for the active co-operation of Spain against France: but once more, as in 1718, Spain did not take up the offer. That was her last opportunity of doing so. Heathfield's gallant defence of the Rock for nearly four years during the American war against the combined efforts of France and Spain so firmly established Gibraltar in the affections and national pride of Englishmen, that thereafter no statesman would have dared to propose its abandonment.[2]

---

[1] Craggs had also been pressing for the acquisition of Florida in addition to increased commercial privileges, with which Stanhope would have been content. Writing in Aug. 1720 he urged that 'somewhat in the W. Indies would have a much better appearance'; Florida would suit well and is not much good to Spain with the French 'pushing on their designs in those parts. . . . Whereas we can now defend that and ourselves too if we had it.' *Chevening MSS.*, Craggs to Stanhope, 2 Aug. 1720.

[2] Mahon, *History*, ii. 127 sqq., contains a fairly exhaustive account of the Gibraltar affair; see also Michael, ii. 256-60. Sandwich and Bedford were for

Stanhope himself did not live to see the Spanish Infant established in Italy. Ten more years were to elapse before the arrangements contemplated by his Quadruple Alliance were completed. Two congresses, at Cambrai and Soissons, failed to remove all the difficulties. The Emperor still hoped, by vexatious punctilios and the usual shifts of the Viennese chancery, to stave off the introduction of the Bourbons into Italy. Spain, at first loyally supported by England and France, growing impatient at these delays and finally outraged by the insulting return of the Infanta affianced to Louis XV, sought by a sudden *volte-face* to obtain her ends through a close alliance with the Emperor. The terms of this remarkable alliance threatened once more to embroil the whole of Europe in war, and mild hostilities were actually begun between England and Spain in 1727. Then came a series of inconclusive treaties and conventions until finally, in March 1731, England, breaking away from her close understanding with France, made the Treaty of Vienna with the Emperor whereby he at last agreed to the introduction of Spanish garrisons into the Italian duchies. In the following July Don Carlos and 6,000 Spanish troops were ceremoniously escorted to Italy by an English and a Spanish fleet; Don Carlos took formal possession of Parma, its last Farnese duke having died, and Spanish troops were put into Tuscany to await the death of the last Medici Grand Duke.[1]

Stanhope's solution of the South European problem was thus adopted, though after much greater delay than he had anticipated. Even so it proved no final solution of the Italian difficulty; for within a few years Don Carlos obtained the Two Sicilies in exchange for Parma and Tuscany, and in 1748 Don Philip, another Infant, recovered Parma for the Spanish Bourbons. To this extent, however, the course of events proved Stanhope to have been right as against Bolingbroke, in insisting on a portion in Italy for a son of Philip's Parmesan wife: Spain, entirely shut out of Italy, would never have remained quiet; and it is significant that, when the two half-Italian Infants had been established in north and south Italy, that arrangement lasted in spite of

giving up Gibraltar, instead of Louisburg, in 1748, but Newcastle scotched the proposal (H. Richmond, *Navy in War of 1739–48*, iii. 238–9).
[1] I have given an account of these events, between Stanhope's death and the Treaty of Vienna of Mar. 1731, in six articles on the 'Foreign Policy of Walpole' in vols. xv and xvi of the *E.H.R.* (Apr. 1900–July 1901).

two more European wars; indeed Italy was at peace from 1748 till the French Revolution upset everything. Stanhope, too, saw as clearly as anybody how weak was the Emperor's grasp on the Two Sicilies, unless supported by the English fleet; but he also saw that, so soon after Utrecht, any attempt to exclude the Emperor from the south of the peninsula would have made it impossible to secure Parma and Tuscany in the north, where the Emperor was strong, for the Infant.

On the larger issues of securing peace in the south of Europe and safeguarding English interests, Stanhope was clearly right in his close alliance with France, the one power which could otherwise have made all his plans impossible, and in making every effort to keep on good terms with Spain for the sake of English trade, as long as that was possible, and, though this had proved impossible during Alberoni's régime, in reverting to that policy as soon as the danger was removed. The renewal of England's commercial privileges in Spain did not indeed take place till six months after his death; but he had prepared the way for it. It is true Spain always proved an uneasy and unaccommodating ally, as even his successor Walpole found, who carried complaisance to Spain, so most of his contemporaries thought, beyond the limits of national honour. Nevertheless, Stanhope's policy of alliance with France and conciliatory measures with Spain, faithfully continued as it was by Walpole, enabled England within thirty years to recover entirely from the effects of Marlborough's wars and to consolidate her chosen dynasty. Within this period she had so much improved her trade and strengthened her navy that even under the weak and vacillating Pelham administration she held her own against a formidable European confederation and then was ready to make the supreme efforts required of her by the clarion voice of Stanhope's nephew.

CHAPTER XIII

THE MINISTER OF PEACE—II. THE NORTH

§ 1

'A strange planet rules in all the northern circle. Chimeras, romantick fancys and shadows are preferred to sound reason and solid advantages, and, what is still worse, experience does not undeceive them.'

SUCH is the picture of northern politics given by Whitworth,[1] the English diplomatist best qualified to judge of them in the early days of the eighteenth century. It is not an exaggerated picture and might well have proved the despair of a statesman anxious to bring order out of chaos. But to Stanhope peace in the North was clearly as important as the settlement of Spanish and Imperial disputes in the South. English interests were involved in the Baltic, nor was it possible to make sure of peace in the South as long as that turbid northern sea, with its cross-currents of conflicting and ever-changing interests, proved a lure to those anxious to fish in troubled waters. Those two freebooters, Alberoni and the Pretender, impeded by the union of England, France, the Emperor and Holland, pinned great hopes, as we have seen, on dragging Charles XII and the Tsar into their quarrels and so embroiling the whole of Europe. During all those four years from 1717 to 1720, when he was bearing almost the whole burden of the Quadruple Alliance in its object of averting the Spanish danger, Stanhope also took upon himself the task of restoring peace to the northern nations convulsed by more than twenty years of war. One of the difficulties of historical narrative is to present a clear statement of events and at the same time to give an impression of the manifold and almost simultaneous activities of such a statesman as Stanhope, who may be compared to a great organ-player with both hands and feet engaged in darting about the various pedals and keyboards of his instrument and in pulling out or replacing stops before he can produce the harmony he has in mind. While busy with the South Stanhope could hardly for an instant neglect the North, and in fact during these four busy years he had the

[1] *H.MSS. Polwarth*, ii. 212, Whitworth to Polwarth, 30 June/11 July 1719.

whole of Europe for his province. Only a man with so comprehensive a view of all the issues involved could have kept his object so clearly before him in the maze of conflicting interests and ambitions with which he had to deal.

Since the early months of 1717, when events in the North had been partly responsible for the break-up of the ministry,[1] the situation there had rapidly become even more involved. Of the five Powers chiefly concerned Charles XII was as uncompromising and as impervious to facts as ever: though he had lost all Sweden's Baltic and German provinces, he still refused all advice from those, such as England and France, who might have helped him; he would yield nothing and still spoke and acted as if he were master of the North. Peter of Russia, gorged with the spoils of Sweden, was now willing enough to make peace with Charles and seemed chiefly bent on securing a foothold in the Empire, a first step towards recognition by the western Powers as one of themselves in deciding on the affairs of Europe. Both Charles and Peter were giving heed to the blandishments of Alberoni, anxious to involve them in his schemes for supporting a Jacobite rising in England. Frederick William of Prussia had swung off from his alliance with Hanover towards the Tsar, of his two neighbours the one more to be feared for his army on Prussia's unprotected eastern frontier. George and his Hanoverian ministers, partly owing to their special interest in the affairs of Mecklenburg, partly from frontier disputes and jealousy of the Prussian royal family, partly too from loyalty to the Empire, had broken with their allies of 1715, Prussia and Russia, but were not reconciled with Sweden owing to the outstanding question of Bremen and Verden. Poland, once the great Power in eastern Europe, since Charles XII's campaigns had clearly declined from her high estate and, in spite of spasmodic efforts by her king, the Saxon Elector Augustus, was fast becoming a mere satellite of the masterful Tsar, who soothed her with delusive promises of restoring her ancient province of Livonia. Denmark alone of the northern kingdoms remained where she had always been, not to be diverted by any change of attitude of Russ, Pole or Prussian from her secular enmity with the hated Swede.

Three other Powers, more remote from the scene of hostilities, were especially interested in their issue, the

[1] See above, ch. ix.

Emperor, France and England. The Emperor was naturally interested in affairs relating to the Empire, where Sweden had possessions in dispute between the Powers concerned in the war; he dreaded an intrusion by Russia into Germany; and he had already in 1712 called a congress at Brunswick, attended by delegates of nominally neutral German states. To this congress were referred such questions as the Mecklenburg dispute, the Protestant grievances, the investitures of Bremen and Verden; but, as usual with Imperial Congresses, this one dragged on for many years with frequent prorogations, without coming to any important decisions. The court of Vienna had not much leisure to devote to Northern affairs between 1716 and 1718 owing to the Turkish war and Spanish aggression in Italy, but in the latter year, mainly through Stanhope's diplomacy, he was relieved of most of his anxiety in both those quarters, by the Quadruple Alliance and the Treaty of Passarowitz. At first the Emperor, elated by Prince Eugene's successful campaigns, had determined to carry on negotiations for peace with the Turks at his own time and without any mediation. But Stanhope, anxious for an early peace and distrusting the cumbrous machinery of Viennese diplomacy, persuaded the Emperor to entrust the negotiations to English mediation, which had been so successful in 1699 when Lord Paget had mediated the treaty of Carlowitz. Edward Wortley Montagu, Lady Mary's husband, the ambassador at Constantinople on whom the brunt of the negotiations would fall, was not a *persona grata* to Vienna; so he was recalled on a flimsy pretext,[1] and the mediation entrusted to his successor Stanyan, jointly with Sir Robert Sutton, who had helped to negotiate the Russo-Turkish treaty of 1712. In fact, barring the great figure of Eugene looming in the background, Sutton bore the principal part at Passarowitz. The treaty of July 1718, eminently favourable to the Emperor, greatly enhanced George I's prestige at Vienna and throughout Christendom. Although the negotiations actually fell within the province of the Southern Secretary, Stanhope kept a vigilant eye on the proceedings at Passarowitz, on which he counted to help his Spanish as well as his Northern policy. He had copies of all Sutton's dispatches sent to him direct, and thought so highly of his merits that in 1720 he appointed him to

[1] See Lady M. Wortley Montagu, *Letters*, &c. (1861), i. 359, for Addison's polite letter recalling Montagu.

succeed Stair in Paris.[1] But Vienna was rarely grateful for services rendered. Relieved, chiefly by England's exertions, of anxiety about the Turks in 1718 and about Spain in the following year, in spite of common interests in the Northern question, the Emperor presumed on his immunity from danger to create difficulties about religion in the Empire and otherwise to put obstacles in the way of Stanhope's policy.

France was chiefly interested in the North owing to her traditionally close ties with Sweden and Poland, as well as Turkey, allies useful to her as a counterpoise to the Austrian Habsburgs. As lately as April 1715 she had made a new treaty of guarantee with Charles XII, promising her good offices to get his German possessions restored to him and to grant him a subsidy of 600,000 crowns for three years. Ever since the Treaty of Westphalia France had attached special importance to these German possessions of Sweden's as giving her a voice in the Diet in the French interest. On the other hand, Peter was pressing the claims of Russia to take Sweden's place as France's most valuable ally in the east of Europe, but, whether it was loyalty to an old ally or blind adherence to a traditional policy, French statesmen had hitherto shown little inclination to meet Peter's advances.

Lastly England, as we have seen, had a long-standing alliance with Sweden. At the same time she had recently suffered much from the attacks of Swedish privateers on her commerce, she had been influenced, indirectly no doubt but to some effect, by the anti-Swedish policy of her Hanoverian king, and finally had been driven to avowedly hostile measures by the revelations of the Gyllenborg letters and the fear of support from Charles to the Pretender. So far this was a fairly simple issue, but then came in the complication of the Tsar's activities. Annoying and irksome as were many of the manifestations of Charles's ill humour, he was not regarded as permanently dangerous by English statesmen; in fact, Sweden in the past, as the chief guardian of the Baltic, had proved a good friend to English commerce: now this

---

[1] Michael, i. 819–31, has a good account of these negotiations based largely on Sutton's and Stanyan's letters to St. Saphorin in the Hanover archives; in the *Chevening MSS.* are letters from Sutton to Stanhope enclosing copies of his official dispatches to the other Secretary; R.O., *S.P.* 104/42 has Sunderland's letters to Stanyan about the mediation, July–Nov. 1717; R.O., *S.P.* 97/24 has some of the official dispatches from Passarowitz. Sutton did not prove equally successful at Paris.

semi-barbarian upstart from the wilds of Russia had deprived Sweden of all her Baltic provinces and bade fair to become in his turn the arbiter of that sea from the shores of which still came the bulk of England's naval stores. England would have been only too glad to assist Charles against the Tsar and even help him to recover some of his Baltic provinces, if only he would abstain from interrupting her commerce and plotting with her enemies. On the other hand, England had no interest in Sweden's retention of her German possessions, to which France attached so much importance, and would willingly have seen them go, if it were a choice between them and the Baltic provinces. Thus by the middle of 1717 England found herself, almost perforce, in antagonism to both the leading Baltic Powers and with objects hard to reconcile with those of her principal ally France; even the Emperor's support was not to be counted upon; Prussia was definitely hostile.

§ 2

The Instructions given to Byng in 1717, when he replaced Norris in command of the Baltic squadron, illustrate England's ambiguous position. They committed him to hostilities with Sweden owing to the revelations of the Gyllenborg correspondence and also to naval precautions against Sweden's chief adversary Russia on account of the invasion of Mecklenburg and the fear of Russian supremacy in the Baltic. Byng sailed to the Baltic in March, two months earlier than Norris in the two preceding years, with the special object of preventing the Swedish fleet from passing the Sound for a possible descent on Great Britain; in a letter amplifying his Instructions Stanhope ordered him, if he had occasion to attack the Swedes, 'to burn sink destroy or take all ships belonging to Sweden as may come in your way'.[1] At the same time he was not to help the Tsar, so long as the Russian troops remained in Mecklenburg, and he was actively to prevent the Tsar's suspected design of wresting Wismar, captured from Sweden in 1716, from its Danish garrison. But in the course of the year relations became more friendly with the Tsar. In answer to a memorial from Veselovsky, the Russian resident in London, protesting

---

[1] *Instructions, Sweden*, i. 98; Torrens, i. 154, quotes the cabinet minute authorizing this instruction, which is to be found in Stanhope's hand-writing in R.O., *S.P. Dom. Geo. I.*, 8.

against insinuations in the Gyllenborg correspondence that the Tsar was favouring the Jacobites, Stanhope and the Hanoverian ministers sent courteous replies to the effect that George I would have no quarrel with the Tsar if his troops were withdrawn from Mecklenburg and he made no separate peace with Sweden.[1] The Tsar himself spent several months of the year travelling in Europe, staying in Amsterdam and Paris, mainly with the object of forming alliances with the western Powers. He was especially anxious to obtain a treaty with France, and during the two months he spent in Paris under the amused observation of St. Simon endeavoured to secure Sweden's post as France's chief ally in the North and the reversion of Sweden's subsidy due to expire in the following year. But the sudden rise of Russia and Peter's barbaric methods did not inspire enough confidence in the Regent and his ministers for them to give up a well-tried ally for such an uncertain supporter. In exchange for the evacuation of Mecklenburg by the Russian troops, secured on behalf of George I, they merely agreed to a non-committal treaty, to which Prussia also was a party, containing little more than a promise of commercial relations and that the subsidy to Sweden should cease in 1718.[2] While he was in Paris Peter also made advances to England through Stair, whereupon Norris, an old acquaintance, and Whitworth were commissioned to hear his proposals at Amsterdam. Nothing came of these negotiations, because the English were most concerned in obtaining a commercial treaty with Russia, while the Tsar, bent only on help from the English fleet to secure and enlarge his Baltic conquests, refused meanwhile to discuss the commercial treaty.[3] Rebuffed by the western Powers, Peter on his return to Russia in the autumn of 1717 was disposed to listen to overtures made to him in December for direct negotiations with Charles XII.

The originator of these overtures was Charles's agent Goertz, the arch-plotter revealed in the Gyllenborg correspondence. Escaping from confinement in Holland he had at once resumed his intrigues on the Continent and finally, after evading the attentions of Byng's fleet, returned to Sweden in September 1717. Here he found one Fabrice, a Hanoverian

---

[1] The three memorials were published and can be seen in Boyer, xii. 248 sqq., 349 sqq.

[2] Chance, 222 sqq.; *Recueil, Russie*, 169 sqq.; Wiesener, ii. 19 sqq.

[3] R.O., *S.P.* 104/122. Sunderland to Norris and Whitworth, 2/13 Aug. 1717; *Instructions, Sweden*, i. 100; *Sbornik*, lxvi. 385–442.

counsellor of George's, engaged in a secret negotiation with
Charles. In December he proposed that Peter should be
invited in his turn to discuss terms of peace with Sweden.
Peter agreed; and for the first seven months of 1718 conferences between Swedish and Russian delegates were carried
on intermittently on Åland Island. For some time Goertz
also kept on the negotiations with Fabrice, playing off one set
of negotiations against the other. But his real aim was to
reconcile Peter and Charles and adopt Alberoni's proposal
that they should then both support the Pretender and turn
their arms against England.[1] Peter, on his side, as long as
the Åland Island conferences seemed to promise a successful
issue, dropped his dealings with Hanover and England; but
when, in August 1718, the conferences came to an end,
owing to Charles XII's refusal to give up his claim to recover
all his lost provinces both in Germany and the Baltic,[2] he
once more made approaches to England, and requested 'His
Majesty to take measures in concert, to force the King of
Sweden to a general peace'.

All this uncertainty about the diplomatic situation in 1718
was reflected in the various orders given to Norris, who was
once more in command of the Baltic fleet. In his original
Instructions of April he was ordered to combine with the
Danes and Dutch specially against Sweden. In August,
when the negotiations of Åland seemed likely to result in
an alliance between Sweden and Russia, Norris was told to
attack the Muscovite as well as the Swedish fleet if they tried
to pass the Sound together on 'projects such as will be prejudicial to Us & Our kingdome. . . . [But] as this is a point
of great nicety We do direct that you keep this instruction
private, so that in case there be no occasion to make use of
it the contents thereof may never be known but may be
buried in silence, as if it had not been given to you.'[3] This
secrecy was justified, for before the new orders could be
executed the diplomatic situation had again changed with
the renewed approaches from the Tsar. On his return to
Paris from Madrid in September Stanhope heard of the
Tsar's overture and was all for meeting it half-way. He was
the more eager to do so because Alberoni, in his recent

[1] Bourgeois, *Régent*, 347 sqq.
[2] For a full account of the Fabrice and Åland Island negotiations see Chance,
240–51, 277–82.
[3] *Instructions, Sweden*, i. 100–4.

interviews with him, had let drop a hint that he had hopes
of assistance from Charles XII and Peter, and that 'something considerable' might be expected from that quarter.
So optimistically did Stanhope view this new offer from the
Tsar that he concluded, 'we may still make almost our own
terms at least with respect to the Czar . . . & this other great
resource of the Cardinal, the affairs of the North, is as likely
to prove abortive as his other schemes'.[1] Once more Norris,
this time in conjunction with Jefferyes, was commissioned
to take stock of the new proposals, whether their object was
'to beget a real understanding between us, which is on this side
very sincerely and heartily desired, or, if the Czar means only
to amuse the King . . . plainly to discover these views & make
it notorious to the world, that it doth not lye at our door,
if there be not a good understanding between us.' Stanhope
also sent a long memorandum to Norris recapitulating the
grievances against the Tsar: such as his double-dealing with
Sweden and England; his threats to Poland and the Empire;
his favour to emissaries of the Pretender and Jacobites
resident in Russia; his attempts to prevent the Quadruple
Alliance; and his attacks on English ships.[2] Norris had no
stomach for another mission to the Tsar, likely, he thought,
to be as bootless as that of the preceding year in Amsterdam,
and took care to have left for Copenhagen with his fleet
when Jefferyes arrived with the full Instructions; so Jefferyes
went on alone to St. Petersburg. Meanwhile the Tsar had
protested his innocence of all the charges brought against
him by Stanhope, protestations not believed in England, and
rightly so, since Peter was at the time in active correspondence
with Alberoni's emissaries. Jefferyes found moreover that,
far from having any definite offers to make, the Russian
ministers expected him to make the first offer, and once more
flatly refused to consider a commercial treaty, England's
main object, before the conclusion of a vague defensive
treaty.[3]

Stanhope and his English colleagues appear to have been
quite straightforward in these negotiations with Peter,
but the same cannot be said of George I and his Hanoverians. At the very time that Jefferyes was on his mission
to St. Petersburg, St. Saphorin at Vienna, on instructions

---

[1] Quoted by Chance, 283–4.
[2] R.O., *S.P.* 104/122, Stanhope to Norris, 5 and 14 Nov. 1718.
[3] *Sbornik*, lxi. 459–72; Chance, 285–90.

from the Electoral court, was secretly negotiating a treaty
directed against the Tsar and his ally Frederick William of
Prussia, an incident which throws a high light on the danger
to England of George's dual capacity as King and Elector.
The four rulers most affected by the proximity of Russian
troops to Germany and Poland were Frederick William,
Augustus of Poland and Saxony, George as Elector and the
Emperor. Frederick William had thought it wiser to avert
the danger by his separate treaty with the Tsar at Havelberg.[1]
The Emperor, at first too preoccupied by the Turkish war to
pay much attention to north-eastern Europe, after Passarowitz
turned a readier ear to St. Saphorin's representations. Accordingly on 5 January 1719 a treaty was signed at Vienna
between the Emperor, Hanover and Saxony, with provision
for the adhesion of Poland, ostensibly of a purely defensive
character, but containing secret articles and declarations
of a more threatening nature. By these secret provisions the
allies bound themselves to mutual support against Russia
and Prussia if those powers attempted to interfere with the
execution of George's Imperial commission to restore order
in Mecklenburg[2] or to carry out their suspected intention
of seizing Polish territory: it was even implied that in case of
trouble with Prussia the allies might compensate themselves by
annexing portions of Prussian territory. So far George was
within his rights as Elector, but in two respects he exceeded
those rights and brought up in an acute form the question
of Anglo-Hanoverian relations. Although he had a regular
Hanoverian representative at Vienna he passed him over and
conducted the negotiations through the English representative St. Saphorin, on instructions from the Hanoverian
chancery. Even more serious was a secret declaration signed
by St. Saphorin that George would repel any attack on
the Polish ports of Danzig and Elbing with his English
fleet, a declaration signed without the consent or even the
knowledge of the English ministers. On ratification the
difficulty arose that such a declaration was valueless unless
countersigned by an English minister, and, in spite of
desperate attempts by the Hanoverians to overcome the
English objection, no English minister would consent to
countersign the engagement. As events turned out no need
arose for the provision or for the treaty itself. Either as a
result of its rumoured contents or on account of renewed

[1] See above, ch. ix, pp. 234-5.   [2] See above, ch. ix, p. 234, note 2.

hostilities with Sweden, Peter withdrew his troops menacing the borders of Poland and Mecklenburg; while Frederick William grew more disposed to come to terms with his father-in-law. But the incident had other important effects. It strengthened Stanhope in his growing conviction that the separate provinces of English and Hanoverian ministers must be clearly defined, and that the Hanoverians should no longer be permitted to interfere in English concerns. He also resolved to put an end to the vendetta against Prussia, into which, under Bernstorff's malign influence, England as well as Hanover had been drawn. For he rightly saw in Prussia England's most natural ally, both against Russia and for the settlement of the North.[1]

§ 3

That school of historians who regard individuals, even the greatest, as negligible factors in the stream of historical events, must be hard put to it to explain away the effect of the stray cannon-ball fired from Frederikshald, whereby Charles XII, still in the prime of his vigour, was laid low. Had he lived, he might even yet have given Peter a fall and recovered some of his Baltic provinces; peace at any rate could hardly have come without many more weary years of war. For Charles himself, 'the darling both of his Nobles and Commons', as Carteret once described him,[2] seemed impervious to defeats and disasters in his obstinate determination to recover all his lost provinces, and every one of his subjects was ready to sacrifice his life for any wild scheme he might devise. With his death, on 11 December 1718, the only real obstacle to the peace of the North was removed. He was succeeded by his younger sister Ulrica Eleanora, elected Queen in February after she had issued a proclamation resigning her brother's absolute powers and restoring the chief authority in the State to the Senate. Goertz, Charles's resourceful and intriguing adviser, was sent to prison, which he left only for the scaffold. In March 1720 the Queen's husband, Prince Frederick of Hesse Cassel, was elected King in her place and

---

[1] For this treaty of Vienna see Droysen, IV. ii. 247 sqq.; Michael, ii. 464 sqq.; Chance, 291–3; important discussions on the incidents of the treaty are also to be found in articles by Droysen in *Zeitschrift für preussische Geschichte*, v (Berlin, 1868), 635–52, and Michael in *Historische Zeitschrift*, lxxxviii (München u. Berlin, 1902), 56 sqq.

[2] *P.H.* viii. 1251.

with her consent, partly as a safeguard against the other
candidate to the throne, Charles XII's nephew the Duke
of Holstein, who, owing to his claims against Denmark for
Schleswig, represented the most bellicose party in Sweden.
The Swedish people, who for twenty years, fascinated by
their heroic king, had endured without a murmur a constant
state of war, and in the last years one of semi-starvation,
suddenly seemed to have awoken from a hideous night-
mare and were determined to have peace. Ulrica and her
husband sent 'very respectfull & obliging letters' to George I,
who replied that the growth of the Tsar's power 'began to
give just umbrage all over the north', and encouraged their
advances.[1] The Swedish Senate, restored to its ancient privileges and authority, were in doubt only as to the best means
of securing the peace all longed for.

Sweden's chief difficulty was that offers of peace came
from two quarters, so incompatible with one another that
the acceptance of one party's terms seemed bound to entail
a continuation of the war with the other. On the one side
came Peter with an offer to secure the restoration to Sweden
of some of her lost German provinces, if she would leave him
in undisturbed possession of all the Baltic provinces. On the
other side were England and Hanover, who proposed to help
Sweden to reconquer some of the Baltic provinces from Peter,
on condition that the German territories were abandoned. But
their methods were different. Peter's plan was to come with
an imposing fleet and a flaming sword to ravage the coast
of Sweden and so bring conviction that he was too strong to
be resisted. The method adopted by the other side was to
persuade Sweden by a less violent form of diplomacy that
they were her best protection against any such aggressor.

At the outset Stanhope realized that there were two
serious obstacles to his Swedish policy, the attitude of France
and that of Prussia. The Regent and Dubois were annoyed
when they heard of the secret Treaty of Vienna of January
1719, largely directed against Prussia, none the less since
they had themselves made a secret engagement with Prussia
and Russia in 1717 and had guaranteed to the former the
possession of Stettin in Swedish Pomerania.[2] For the Vienna
treaty Stanhope and the English ministers, as we have seen,
were in no way responsible, but they had to bear some of

[1] R.O., *S.P.* 95/131, *Mem. of Affairs with Sweden*, 1711–19.
[2] Wiesener, iii. 20 sqq.

the odium for it. More serious difficulties to overcome were France's comparative indifference to the fate of the Baltic provinces and her fixed policy, dating from the Peace of Westphalia, to retain for Sweden a footing in the Empire as a counterpoise to the Emperor's influence. In the early part of 1719 Stanhope and Dubois exchanged views on their respective policies. Dubois started the correspondence by pointing out that Charles XII's death offered a favourable opportunity for making an attempt at peace in the North, a peace, as he insinuated, especially necessary for England's commercial interests. While admitting that Hanover should be allowed to retain Bremen and Verden and that Prussia should also obtain some Swedish territory in Germany, he insisted that France could never allow her ancient ally to be robbed of all her German possessions, least of all of Stralsund and Rügen for the benefit of Denmark; lastly he urged that the Tsar should be included in the settlement, which would probably involve his retaining all his Baltic conquests from Sweden—Livonia, Esthonia, Ingria, Carelia and most of Finland. In reply Stanhope pressed for a general peace to include Denmark as well as Prussia and also safeguards for the integrity of Poland against the Tsar's designs of partition, which Stanhope was among the first of European statesmen to foresee as the eventual fate of that monarchy. In answer to Dubois's plea for Sweden's German provinces, he asserted that they had been merely a burden to her in the past, whereas Esthonia and Livonia were essential to her position as a Baltic power, and equally essential to the interests of England, as a protection against Russian dominance in the Baltic. For this reason he argued against any attempt to bring the Tsar into the negotiations, since he would not yield his conquests. In February Dubois announced that the Regent had been convinced by Stanhope's arguments and would adopt his policy.[1]

But, though the Regent and Dubois might formulate an official policy, it was by no means certain that their representatives abroad would loyally carry it out. One of the great difficulties, not only in the early stages, but throughout the course of the close alliance between France and England, was the unwillingness of most of the French envoys abroad, nurtured in the anti-English traditions of Louis XIV's

---

[1] Copies of Stanhope's correspondence with Dubois are in *Add. MSS.* 37373 (*Whitworth Papers*), ff. 32–41. See also Michael, ii. 479–85.

system, to adapt themselves to the new orientation of the Regent's court. Châteauneuf in Holland, La Marck in Sweden, Iberville in London, some of the ambassadors in Spain, and above all, perhaps, Bonac in Constantinople, seemed more intent on counteracting than on supporting the pro-English policy enjoined upon them. This was the more prejudicial to English interests since the diplomats trained under the old French court were the ablest of their calling in Europe. Dubois, it is true, as he gradually consolidated his own position, was able to replace several of the recalcitrant diplomats by creatures of his own more amenable to his policy; but the difficulty was never entirely surmounted.[1] Naturally at this conjuncture one of the most important diplomatic posts was at Stockholm. In 1717 the Comte de La Marck had been sent thither with instructions to persuade Charles XII to come to terms with England;[2] but when he came back to Paris in April 1719 to report on the prospects of peace, Stair found him entirely set on recovering some of the German provinces for Sweden, including even a part of George's Bremen and Verden. The ambassador's own views would not have mattered so much had not Stair found that with his arrival Dubois himself was beginning to waver and to hark back to the old French policy of entrenching Sweden in the Empire. Stanhope once more felt it incumbent upon him to take a hand personally with the French court, and, as a result of his interposition, La Marck was superseded and in June 1719 replaced by Campredon, who promised to work harmoniously with the English ambassador in Stockholm. On the way to his post Campredon was fortified in his good intentions by a talk with Stanhope at Hanover.[3]

The estrangement of the English and Hanoverian courts from Prussia was the other difficulty that Stanhope set himself to overcome. It was clear to him that Prussia was essential as an ally against Russia and that without Prussia's co-operation it would be difficult to persuade Sweden to prefer England's terms to those proposed with such a convincing display of force by Russia. To a large extent too Prussia's interests in the peace were identical with those of Hanover, since both aimed at securing some of Sweden's German

[1] See for later instances after Stanhope's death, *E.H.R.* xv. 681–2 (Oct. 1900).
[2] *Recueil, Suède*, 277 sqq.
[3] Wiesener, iii. 127–30; Michael, ii. 485–9; Chance, 343, note 2.

possessions, and neither was anxious to have Russia as the dominating power in the Baltic. Unfortunately the two monarchs had drifted apart a year after their treaty of 1715, partly from family jealousies, partly for political reasons. Frederick William thought that George, having obtained his share in Bremen and Verden, had not properly supported the other allies less fortunate than himself; George deeply resented his son-in-law's support of the Tsar in the Mecklenburg dispute and his suspected designs on Poland. But even these grievances, brooded over, as they were, by a couple of obstinate and irascible autocrats, might have been disposed of, had it not been for a personal grievance of the Hanoverian minister Bernstorff. He owned three villages as part of his estate of Gartow right on the borders of Brandenburg. Over these villages Frederick William also exercised some rights of feudal sovereignty with which he was loth to part, since by their position in an elbow of the Elbe these villages interrupted communication between two districts of his own dominions. However, by the treaty with Hanover of 1715 he had agreed to give up his feudal rights, but had never done so, chiefly owing to Bernstorff's own fault in setting about ostentatiously to fortify them. Thereafter these three wretched villages became a matter of European importance. For Bernstorff bore Frederick William an undying grudge for not fulfilling that clause of the treaty, and used all his great influence over George I not only to prevent a reconciliation with Frederick William but to add fuel to his resentment against him. The Hanoverian treaty of Vienna of January 1719, directed at least as much against Prussia as against Russia, was entirely Bernstorff's handiwork and entirely opposed to Stanhope's anxiety for a *rapprochement* with Prussia. 'I think never any scheme was framed so impracticable, so dishonourable, nor so pernicious', wrote Stanhope to Sunderland about this treaty, 'as what this old man has in his head. He proposes, besides part of the spoils of Prussia for his master, to get for himself certain baillages situate about Wismar',[1] no doubt in compensation for his precious villages.[2]

On this question, therefore, of fresh approaches to Prussia,

[1] Quoted in Droysen, iv. ii. 188 and confirmed by the Prussian envoy Wallenrodt's report from Hanover stating that Bernstorff's lukewarmness about the persecution of Roman Catholics in the Empire was due to his hope of obtaining these Wismar baillages from the Emperor, ib. 256–7.

[2] See Chance, 61, 72, 314, &c., for Bernstorff's 'three villages'.

when the death of Charles XII made a settlement of the North seem possible, Stanhope elected to have his first serious trial of strength with the German ministers, and to pay them back for stealing a march at Vienna on himself and his colleagues. He lent a willing ear to suggestions made by the Prussian envoy Bonet for a friendly talk on Anglo-Prussian relations, and in March 1719 had so far influenced the King that he was able to write to Dubois:

'Il n'y a qu'une chose sur laquelle le Roi ait pris son parti; c'est de chercher en premier lieu à s'unir avec le Roi de Prusse, suivant ce que vous n'avez cessé de nous inculquer. S.M. comprend parfaitement combien il est important au repos du nord de faire envisager à ce prince d'autres . . . ressources que celles qu'il croit trouver dans le Czar, et de le fixer à ses vrais intérêts par des liaisons plus voisines'; [1]

and in a later letter of July he emphasizes his belief that friendship with Prussia must be the pivotal point for the allies' Northern policy:

'ce seroit le moyen le plus efficace de rompre les liaisons bâties principalement sur un démembrement de la Pologne et . . . le concours de ce royaume seroit d'une nécessité absolue s'il s'agissoit d'arracher par la force des armes au Czar ses conquêtes.' [2]

The ground being thus cleared for negotiating a satisfactory peace for the North, Stanhope's next task was to choose capable representatives to treat of terms at the two most important centres, Berlin and Stockholm. For Berlin he had the ambassador clearly indicated in Charles Whitworth, who had more experience and grasp of Northern politics than any other English diplomatist. He had been on missions to St. Petersburg, to Ratisbon and The Hague, and at all those posts had acquitted himself well. Above all he had already been to Berlin in 1716–17, when he had made a favourable impression on Frederick William and had formed shrewd judgements on the ministers and courtiers who influenced that difficult monarch. For Stockholm, destined to be an even more important centre of negotiation, the choice was not so obvious. Since Robinson's mission at the beginning of the century it had not seemed worth while

[1] Michael, ii. 631. This passage occurs at the end of Stanhope's long dispatch to Dubois of 30 Mar. 1719 about plans against Spain; see above, ch. xii, pp. 327–8.
[2] Stanhope to Dubois, 2/13 July 1719, quoted by Wiesener, ii. 126 sqq.

to send a diplomatist of much importance to attend on so peripatetic a monarch as Charles XII, and for some time Robert Jackson had been holding little more than a watching brief as minister resident: but he was not of the calibre to negotiate a series of important treaties. Robethon suggested to Lord Polwarth at Copenhagen that he should offer to go,[1] but fortunately Stanhope, if he heard of it, did not accept the suggestion. Instead he chose Lord Carteret, a young man under thirty with no previous experience of diplomacy.

John Lord Carteret, descended on both sides from families of gallant fighters and staunch cavaliers, succeeded to his father's peerage in 1695, at the age of five. His mother, a notable woman and plain of speech like her friend Sarah of Marlborough, was created by George I a countess in her own right and survived to see her son twice Secretary of State and the leading member of a ministry. From Christchurch, according to Swift, Carteret, 'with a singularity scarce to be justified carried away more Greek, Latin and philosophy than properly became a person of his rank'. In 1711, directly he came of age, he took his seat on the Tory benches, as befitted his family connexions and his close friendship with Harley and St. John; but he very soon attached himself to the Hanover, or 'Whimsical', wing of the party devoted to the Protestant Succession. By the accession of George I he had become to all intents and purposes a Whig. From the outset interested in foreign affairs, he was specially fitted for their conduct by his gift for languages, including German, then a rare accomplishment in England, and by his careful study of the intricate system of the Empire. In after years, when the budding Sandwich presumed to lecture him on German politics, he retorted by referring to his own 'long acquaintance with the constitution of the Empire, which I understood before the noble lord, who has entertained you with a discourse upon it, was in being'.[2] Both this accomplishment and his knowledge of German gained him the special favour of George I and his son. Stanhope, to whose section of the Whigs Carteret attached himself at the time of the Whig split, soon recognized the ability of his speeches in debate, especially that on the Septennial Bill, and his grasp of foreign politics,

[1] *H.MSS.*, *Polwarth*, ii. 16.
[2] Speech of 1 Feb. 1743 in *P.H.* xii. 1085.

and marked him down as a youngster to be made use of.
The opportunity came when Queen Ulrica's 'respectfull and
obliging letters' at last gave an opening at Stockholm. For
this post Stanhope looked for a man of quick resource, able
to grasp his own wide view of national policy, and not afraid
to take risks; and in Carteret he found the qualities needed.
By 19 April 1719 he had drawn up Whitworth's Instructions
and by 6 May Carteret's:[1] and the two ambassadors were
promptly sent off to their posts, Whitworth somewhat in
advance, since Stanhope was anxious, if possible, to work
harmoniously with Prussia at Stockholm, though Carteret's
main negotiation was not on that account to be unduly
delayed.

§ 4

Whitworth's main object was to be to wean Frederick
William from his alliance with the Tsar and persuade him
to co-operate with his neighbours and fellow members of
the Empire in settling a comprehensive peace in the North,
one that should serve the interests of England, Hanover,
Prussia, Poland and Denmark, as well as of Sweden herself. He was specially to be invited to sign two treaties,
one with Hanover guaranteeing Stettin to Prussia and
Bremen and Verden to Hanover, and another with England.
This English treaty should confirm the Hanoverian treaty
and offer Sweden help in recovering some of her Baltic
provinces as a compensation for the loss of her German
possessions, and in order, as it is ingenuously expressed,
that there may be security of trade in the Baltic for England,
France and Holland. In other words Stanhope's idea was
to form so strong a league of North-German and Scandinavian Powers that Russia would be forced to abandon the
dangerous hegemony she had acquired in the Baltic.

Whitworth's negotiations were prolonged over three
months, from May to August 1719, and several times
seemed on the point of breaking down altogether. Once
indeed, at the end of June, Whitworth, despairing of success,
returned to Hanover to report to George I and Stanhope;
and had it not been for Stanhope's firmness both treaties
would have fallen to the ground. There were serious

---

[1] Whitworth's three sets of Instructions are in R.O., *S.P.* 110/78 and are
exhaustively analysed in Chance, 310 sqq. Carteret's are printed in *Instructions,
Sweden,* i. 106–12.

difficulties on both sides. Frederick William had a lively apprehension of the Tsar's resentment at his signing a treaty in which Russia was not included, and even when he seemed to have made up his mind to risk the danger, was constantly harking back to his old objections. He also objected to any advantage coming to the King of Poland, who had recently revived the Polish claim of suzerainty over East Prussia.[1] Lastly, there was his invincible objection to Bernstorff's fortification of his villages. No less serious were the criticisms of the Hanoverians arising from their persistent opposition to the whole project of an alliance with Prussia. It was fortunate, therefore, that Stanhope was on the spot to counteract their influence on the King and to find expedients to soothe the irritable and undecided Prussian monarch. One of Bernstorff's strongest arguments was that the Emperor might take amiss too close an alliance with the growing power of Prussia in the Empire; he also played on George's jealousy of his son-in-law and made the utmost of his grievance about his 'three villages'. Nearly two months after the beginning of the negotiations Craggs wrote despairingly to Schaub about the

'bad situation of affairs in the North. I should not regard it in that light, were we permitted to employ such means as may be found to extricate ourselves with honour. But as long as that mischievous old man [*sc.* Bernstorff] retains his influence, it will hardly be possible. So contracted are his views with regard to the public, and so confined his ideas to his own Mecklenburg and his three villages, that the credit and security of all Europe are not able to rouse him. . . . Such principles will never advance our affairs.'[2]

Stanhope, strongly supported by the French envoy at Hanover, made light of Bernstorff's objections. The Emperor's feelings need not, he pointed out, be too seriously considered, since he had recently aroused strong resentment in England by his connivance with the Roman Catholic campaign against the Protestants in the Empire,[3] and Bernstorff himself was suspected for purposes of his own to be lukewarm in this matter. Besides, the Emperor still needed England's support more than England needed his, since the Spanish difficulty was not yet settled and there were

[1] Poland had abandoned this claim in the treaty of Oliva, 1660.
[2] Mahon, *History*, ii, Appendix, Craggs to Schaub, 30 June 1719 (o.s.).
[3] See below, ch. xiv, p. 389.

serious apprehensions both at Vienna and in Paris that, if a
northern league of Prussia, Russia and Sweden were allowed
to dominate the North, England's chief attention and her
powerful influence might be diverted to the Baltic from the
critical situation in the Mediterranean. As to Bernstorff's
'three villages', he would have liked to see them at the
bottom of the sea;[1] nor did he believe that family jealousies
should be fostered as a permanent obstacle to peace.

Finally he had it out with the Hanoverians at a council
held in the King's presence, telling George plainly that he
should not be led astray by trifling questions of frontier or of
some tiny village, since the English nation would willingly
make good to His Majesty whatever he needed in money,
ships or troops to effect so great an object as this treaty.[2]
He proposed ways of meeting Frederick William's objections
by a compromise on the 'three villages' and by agreeing that
Poland should not be admitted as a party to the treaties
until the claim to suzerainty over East Prussia had been
withdrawn; he even suggested that a treaty with the Tsar
might be arranged by the mediation of Prussia, but with
his experience of former unsatisfactory dealings with Peter
insisted that the Prussian treaty should come first. He would
not, however, listen to an underhand expedient for saving
Frederick William's face with the Tsar proposed by the
Prussian minister Ilgen, that two treaties should be made,
one public, including the Tsar as a party, the other secret,
excluding him. His sense of fair dealing revolted against
such a trick. 'De signer dans le même jour deux traittez
contradictoires', he wrote to Dubois, 'je vous avoue que je
ne voudrais pas le faire pour tromper même les Moscovites.'[3]
It was a hard struggle to overcome the Hanoverian influence,
but in the end Stanhope carried the day. On 10 July he
wrote triumphantly to Sunderland:

'We have been in very great agitation here for some time, but
have, at last, got a complete victory over the old man. The
King has twice, in council, before all his German Ministers,
overruled him with an air of authority in relation to our negotiation with Prussia. One of these rebukes ought to be the more
sensible to him, as it concerned the three villages you have so
often heard of. The old gentleman affects to appear very supple

[1] Quoted from a letter of Stanhope's by Droysen, IV. ii. 269.
[2] Droysen, IV. ii. 264.
[3] 2/13 July 1719, quoted in Wiesener, iii. 133.

to me since, and the new instructions to M. Heusch [Hanoverian minister at Berlin] are preparing as I would have them.' [1]

When Whitworth returned to Berlin in July these concessions seemed to have removed Frederick William's scruples. On 22 July he wrote to Whitworth 'je signeray le dit traitté', and on the same day the French ambassador Rottembourg announced that France would renew her guarantee of Stettin to Prussia as well as of Bremen and Verden to Hanover. Stanhope sent his congratulations to Whitworth and pressed for an early signature to enable Carteret to support Prussia's claims at Stockholm, and he assured the Prussian envoy Wallenrodt of whole-hearted co-operation in all pending questions. But there was yet another alarm before the treaty was finally signed. Disquieting news from Vienna and Dresden once more made Frederick William distrust England's sincerity, and, though he finally on 12 August felt bound to allow his ministers to carry out his engagement, he took to his bed with an attack of dysentery, brought on by anxiety, and committed to the archives of his House one of the most humiliating records of his own vacillations and self-abasement ever left by a ruler as a warning to his successors.

'Would to God', he wrote, 'I had never promised to complete the treaty; an evil spirit inspired me to do so. . . . If only God would take me from this evil world before I must needs sign! . . . My interest is to have the Tsar ready at hand, for if I send him money, I can have as many troops as I wish; the Tsar is ready to make a treaty with me at once; with the English it is all a pack of lies, just as in 1715 they deceived me in knavish fashion. . . . I shall pray God to support me in playing a peculiar part, one that I play against my will, for it is not that of an honest man; I shall sign the treaty, but have no intention of observing it, and then, on throwing off the mask, I shall tell the whole world what designs these false friends have against me. . . . Let my successors learn to guard themselves against such friends and not to follow the evil and ungodly maxims I have adopted in this treaty, but to hold fast to the friends one has and cast off false friends. Therefore I enjoin on my descendants to keep up an even stronger army than I have. On these principles will I live and die.' [2]

The two treaties between Prussia and Hanover and England and Prussia were finally ratified on 15 September.

---

[1] Mahon, *History*, ii, Appendix.   [2] Droysen, IV. ii. 266–7.

By the former the two contracting parties agreed to bring about a peace in the North; Bremen and Verden were to be secured to Hanover and Stettin to Prussia, Sweden receiving a money compensation for these possessions; Prussia agreed not to disturb the King of Poland and to renew friendly relations with him when he had withdrawn his obnoxious claim, and never to support the Tsar in any designs against the Empire; the 'three villages' question was also finally disposed of. By the English treaty the two rulers agreed to co-operate in establishing peace in the North and to restore complete freedom of commerce in the Baltic. On Stanhope's suggestion the original signature to both treaties was ante-dated from 12 August to 4 August. The reason for this shady transaction was that news of a convention obtained by Carteret for the cession of Bremen and Verden to Hanover as a condition of naval support to Sweden against the Tsar reached Stanhope after 4 August, and he now wished to represent England and Hanover as already committed to Prussia's similar claim to Stettin as a means of forcing Sweden to grant that also before obtaining the promised support. Stanhope's only possible excuse for this piece of sharp practice, not easily to be reconciled with his usual straightforward and direct diplomatic methods, is that he may have regarded Frederick William's written promise of 22 July to sign the treaties as equally binding with the formal signature. None the less the incident is a blot on English diplomacy and on Stanhope's otherwise stainless reputation for honest dealing.[1]

Apart from this incident Stanhope's statesmanship stands out at its best in these transactions with Prussia. He, almost alone at first, recognized the importance for England, no less than for Hanover, of an understanding with that Power as an ally against the Tsar's designs on the Baltic and the Empire, in defence of Protestantism in the Empire and for a satisfactory peace in the North. For the rest of Stanhope's life and for some years later the renewed good feeling between George I and Frederick William was not impaired. Frederick William, in spite of his torturing anguish of apprehension up to the very eve of signing, when the deed was

---

[1] For full accounts of the negotiations and contents of these treaties see Chance, ch. xxiii, and Droysen, iv. ii. 260 sqq. Chance notes (p. 324) that Whitworth suggested the ante-dating on the ground that the signature of the treaty was delayed by the King of Prussia's illness; still, Stanhope connived.

once accomplished soon lost his fears and seemed to be as delighted at the reconciliation with his father-in-law as Stanhope himself. The good relations were still further improved by an informal visit, the first for five years, of Frederick William and his wife to Hanover in November 1719, followed by a journey of Stanhope to Berlin in July 1720, and by a second visit of the Prussian pair to George I in August. Of this last visit we obtain glimpses from the local gossips, one of whom tells of Stanhope entertaining the two Kings at dinner and waiting respectfully in the street to see their coaches come up and drive away; while the English court chaplain describes Frederick William as having 'a brisk enterprising look, wears a short waistcoat, narrow hat and broadsword and has his own hair tied back, and because his army is clothed in blue he generally wears the same colour himself'. More important were some of the political results of these visits. One was that Bonet, the Prussian envoy in London, an intriguing mischief-maker, was replaced by a more friendly representative: and during his visit to Berlin Stanhope was so successful in bringing Frederick William over to his own way of thinking about Russia, that he persuaded him to write a letter of his own dictation to the Tsar, offering Prussia's and England's joint mediation for peace with Sweden.[1]

Carteret meanwhile in Stockholm had been obliged to rely far more on his own native wit than Whitworth in Berlin. Travelling as speedily as he could, he took nearly a month on the journey from England to Stockholm, and it took nearly as long to obtain answers to his dispatches from Stanhope in Hanover; most of his news from the Continent came to him through Polwarth in Copenhagen, and as hostilities were proceeding between Danes and Swedes this channel was none too sure. Thus he was almost isolated for comparatively long periods and was often driven to take momentous decisions on his own responsibility. Fortunately—and that no doubt was the chief reason why Stanhope chose him for the post—he was not one to shrink from responsibility. 'I have a working brain & will be an adventurer with you', he wrote to Norris; and again, 'I am in a station where I

[1] For these visits see Malortie, 79, 85; Michael, ii. 527–8; Ellis, *Original Letters*, 2nd Ser. iv. 320; Chance, 399, note; R.O., *S.P.* 104/220 Stanhope to Delafaye, 1 Nov. 1719 (o.s.); R.O., *S.P.* 44/270; Stanhope to Delafaye, 28 June, 11 July 1720 (o.s.). The arrangement about the Tsar is referred to below, ch. xv, p. 427.

can't stand still, but must do something; and to act without orders occasions at least, anxiety'; and to Stanhope he declared with justice: 'Your Lordship is sensible that I have risked very much, I have really done so, which I am not fond of doing, but yet I will never decline it when I see it is necessary.'[1]

According to his Instructions Carteret's main business was to persuade the Swedes to put themselves entirely into the hands of England in order to secure a favourable peace; in other words the Swedes were to gain the support of Germany, Poland and Denmark by concessions of Swedish territory in Germany and so acquire the means of 'recovering their losses towards Finland and Livonia . . . the only thing every true Swede should have at heart', since those 'rich & fertile . . . Dominions . . . situated towards those of the Czar of Muscovy, a powerful & dangerous neighbour', would if he held them give him the means of overrunning Sweden and so becoming 'entire master of the Baltick Sea'. Carteret's arguments were to be supported by the presence of Norris and the Baltic squadron, with orders, not as in former years 'to burn, sink & destroy' Swedish ships, but to give the Swedes every possible help against the Tsar. Within ten days of his arrival at Stockholm Carteret had obtained a decision from the Swedish government which committed it to accept the English policy, the only alternative being complete surrender to the Tsar.

Carteret arrived at Stockholm on 11 July and found things almost desperate. The Tsar's fleet was in the neighbourhood of the capital, prepared to land ravaging parties at any moment if the Russian terms were not accepted: the Danes were attacking Sweden from the side of Norway. A majority of the Senate headed by the Chancellor Cronhielm, 'an eloquent man', Carteret complains, 'which has cost me much labour & time',[2] was in favour of submission to the Tsar, if only to turn their arms against the hated Dane: the Queen, her husband and Marshal Dücker headed the party for resisting the Russians to the last extremity. At first Carteret was denied admission to the Queen, as her full titles had not been inserted in his letters of credence, but,

---

[1] *Add. MSS.* 28156, ff. 23, 102; 22511, f. 88. Whatever may have been the case at that time, Carteret in later life displayed particular fondness for taking risks.
[2] *Add. MSS.* 22511, f. 88.

brushing aside such technicalities, he obtained a private and informal interview. He won her heart by his well-turned 'harangue' to the effect that whereas her late brother Charles, of glorious memory, had displayed all the military virtues, her own accomplishments proved that the Swedish house also possessed the remaining virtues in their highest perfection. Henceforward she and her husband treated Carteret as an intimate friend rather than as the representative of a foreign Power. But there was no time for pretty speeches. Three days after his arrival, when Carteret was writing his first dispatch to Stanhope, Dücker and the Hanoverian envoy came in to tell him that the Russians were on the point of landing: unless the English fleet came up to help them they had no alternative but to submit to the Tsar's terms. Carteret had no authority to order up the fleet, but he reflected that unless Sweden were effectively helped she would either be beaten by the Russians 'and there is an end of Sweden', or she would beat them, when she would be so elated 'that there is an end of the King's business that way', or thirdly, the most likely event, she would make such a peace with Russia that 'all Europe, especially the trading countries, will feel the consequences of the Muscovite power in the Baltic'. So he decided on the spot to send for Norris on condition the Queen would accept the Hanoverian Convention formally surrendering Bremen and Verden, and another with England for a renewal of the defensive treaty of 1700, altered to suit the existing circumstances of Sweden. The Queen and her supporters readily signed these conventions on 22 July, that with Hanover being also ratified, but there was considerable hesitation in the Senate about ratifying the convention with England. Once more as he was writing to Stanhope, on 25 July, 'I was interrupted', says Carteret, this time by emissaries from the Senate requiring a clearer definition of what England would do for Sweden. He had signed a paper stating that the treaty of 1700 would be renewed only so far as it was 'applicable' to existing circumstances: the Senate required the whole treaty, including a guarantee of Sweden's German possessions. Carteret refused to comply with such an impossible condition; Cronhielm and his party were obdurate: there seemed no issue from the impasse after an argument lasting till 3 o'clock in the morning. Carteret said he would give them till 6 o'clock, and, as they did not appear, went off to find Ulrica's husband in his camp six hours' journey distant. At this camp he also found an emissary from the Russian army with the Tsar's proposals for peace; but from the Prince and Marshal Dücker he obtained the letter he required, and, as he drove back late at night, saw the sky already illuminated by the fires of the Russian ravaging parties on the islands. The letter and the imminent danger convinced the Senate; Carteret obtained the ratification in exchange for another explanatory paper stating that by the word 'applicable' nothing was implied to Sweden's disadvantage. 'Our success', Carteret modestly wrote, 'is chiefly owing to the Czar, he at the gates of Stockholm has reasoned best for us'; and his moderation in victory was illustrated later when, after his chief opponent Cronhielm had been severely reprimanded by the Queen and Prince, he observed, 'I now again make court to him and by this incident shall finish the treaty sooner. I am never for pushing a victory too far.' [1] That same night he wrote, as he had promised, to Norris asking him to bring up his fleet forthwith to help Sweden against the Russians.

But Norris did not appear for another month. He had been late in arriving in the Sound this year owing to the calls on the fleet for the Mediterranean, where the Spaniards were still in Sicily, and in the Channel, as a precaution against Ormonde's expedition,[2] and for the same reason his squadron was not up to the usual strength. Four of his ships were not able to join him till the end of August, in spite of Stanhope's urgent appeal to the Lords Justices in England to send them with the utmost dispatch, for 'it would be a great misfortune if for want of some more ships we should lose the opportunity of awing the Czar, saving Sweden, and by giving Peace to the North, of defeating the greatest hope which is now left to Spain, that of forming a strong Allyance in the North'.[3] But even Stanhope, as long as Norris's inferiority in ships and uncertainty about the Danes lasted, enjoined caution,[4] a recommendation which does not seem to have been particularly necessary in Norris's case. Indeed, to judge from his ill-spelt letters to Polwarth, he appears to have cared more for the delights of the bottle and the fair on shore than for active service at sea: 'Demer', he wrote from

[1] Add. MSS. 22511, f. 88.   [2] See above, ch. xii, p. 326.
[3] Quoted in Chance, 337.
[4] H.MSS., Polwarth, ii. 248, Stanhope to Norris, 31 July 1719 (o.s.).

Stockholm, 'has maid me fudeld in drinking your health and
indeed we never faile it when togeather & throw his menes
we have lived all the same bottell life we did under your
Lordship's protection': a certain 'Fruling Wakenig' or 'Vak-
netts' or 'Wackenitzer', as she is indifferently spelt, was much
in his mind; and he waxes almost maudlin on the need of
putting to sea 'so that we had scarce an oppertunity of bowing to the fair before we sett sayle. Thus pour saylors are by
the winds blown from every haven their harts would chuse
to attend the boundless will of Neptune.'[1] But, however
justified in this instance may have been Norris's delay in
responding to Carteret's call, it made it extraordinarily
awkward for Carteret, who had given the Swedes a promise
to summon Norris as the price of the conventions. Before
he knew of this promise Stanhope had written to Carteret
that 'the doings of the Danes puts us under unspeakable
difficulties'. 'If your Lordship is under unspeakable difficulties', Carteret was goaded to retort, 'what must I be in?
The moment a courier arrives my house is full of senators
enquiring about the fleet.'[2]

Still more difficult was Carteret's position when orders
came to him from Stanhope on 26 August that as an additional condition for the appearance of the fleet the Swedes
must agree to a further convention with Prussia for the
formal surrender of Stettin. The excuse given by Stanhope
for this fresh demand was that Carteret's dispatch about the
two conventions already agreed to did not reach Hanover
till after 4 August, the date given to the Prussian treaties,
whereby England and Hanover engaged to procure Stettin
for Prussia as well as Bremen and Verden for Hanover,
whereas in fact the treaties were not signed till a week later.[3]
Carteret naturally found it hard to explain why no previous
mention had been made of Prussia's claim; but the Swedes
had little choice, being now definitely committed to the English
as opposed to the Russian scheme of peace, while a timely
letter from Norris, 'so prudently & discreetly writ that I
could shew it them', announcing that he was at last on
the way to join the Swedish fleet, materially reinforced Carteret's persuasive powers. On 29 August the new convention
between England and Sweden was signed, recapitulating
the cessions of Bremen and Verden to Hanover and of Stettin

---

[1] *H.MSS., Polwarth*, ii. 333, 559. [2] Quoted in Chance, 346.
[3] See above, p. 373.

and the neighbouring district to Prussia, freeing English
commerce from restrictions in the Baltic, promising a subsidy and armed support to Sweden while the war lasted
and George I's good offices in concluding a treaty between
Sweden and either Denmark or the Tsar, preferably the
former; in its final form was included the guarantee of
France to these terms, which had been brought over, largely
by Stanhope's diplomacy with the French court, by the new
French Ambassador Campredon, who also conveyed in his
luggage a large subsidy for Sweden in ingots of gold.[1] On
the conclusion of this, the most important, stage of his
negotiation Carteret wrote this charming letter to his friend
Craggs, with the perhaps too indulgent view of Norris:

'I am glad you are sensible of the scituation I have been in. I
have been in the Avant-Garde—almost an Enfant perdu; but I
have been well sustained by my friends. I have made no retreat,
but maintained my post till the Enemy left me. S^r. John Norris
has done very well. Don't be surprized at his backwardness at
first. Twas for want both of strength and orders. I was uneasy
at it once; but since I have talk'd with him am perfectly satisfied
that his conduct from the beginning has been right. . . . Love
me, Dear Craggs, as I love you. Yours for ever.'[2]

But this was not the end of Carteret's mission. The various
conventions had to be drawn up in the form of treaties, at
which the Swedes were so dilatory that Stanhope had to
remind them that the promised subsidies and support would
not be forthcoming till these treaties were duly completed.[3]
Finally the Hanoverian treaty was signed on 20 November
1719, the English and Prussian treaties on 2 February 1720,
while a convention of 18 January 1720 brought to an end
the disputes between Sweden and Poland.[4] Even then
Sweden had two unreconciled enemies left, Denmark and
Russia. Stanhope was most anxious that peace should first
be made with Denmark, for then Russia would be isolated
in the North and might more easily be made to disgorge
some of her Baltic conquests. Unfortunately the Swedes,
reported Carteret, were so bitter against the Danes that
'they had rather give to the Czar everything than anything
to Denmark';[5] and on their side the Danes were equally

---

[1] Chance, 354–7.   [2] *Add. MSS.* 22511, 27 Sept. 1719.   [3] Chance, 369.
[4] For Stanhope's anxiety to get Poland reconciled to Sweden see R.O., *S.P.*
110/78, Stanhope to Stair, 5/16 Dec. 1719.
[5] Quoted by Chance, 350.

uncompromising. A difficulty also arose between Stanhope and Dubois as to the possession of Rügen and Stralsund: these places had been conquered by the Danes, who, Stanhope thought, should be allowed to retain them: the French were determined that Sweden should recover at least this corner of German territory, so gloriously connected with Gustavus Adolphus's first resistance to Wallenstein's triumphal march through north Germany and Sweden's entry into the Empire. On this point Stanhope gave way and agreed that among the conditions of peace to be proposed should be the recovery by Sweden, for a money-payment, of this last German foothold.[1] England and France, as mediators, having settled the principal conditions of peace, it was left to Carteret and Campredon in Sweden and Polwarth in Copenhagen to bring the principals together. The long course of these negotiations need not be detailed. Carteret secured the acceptance of the preliminaries by the Swedes in June 1720 and then went over to Copenhagen to obtain the assent of Denmark. By the treaty completed on 3 July Denmark returned Wismar, Rügen and Stralsund to Sweden and undertook not to aid the Tsar in any way against her: in return she received a French and English guarantee of ducal Schleswig, rightfully the property of Charles XII's nephew the Duke of Holstein, the surrender of Sweden's share in the Sound tolls, and a money compensation.

Carteret had more than justified Stanhope's choice of so young and inexperienced a man for his difficult tasks at Stockholm and Copenhagen. Imbued with his master's spirit, he had instinctively grasped and acted upon the essential ideas of his policy; and, though he had to fight hard for his ends he had done so with a tact and frankness that increased the respect for himself and his country among all with whom he had dealings. To his friend Craggs he wrote from Stockholm with pardonable pride that 'no ambassador was ever upon a better footing in a country than I am . . . The Court, when I hint at going, are in concern'; and Ulrica's husband said to him, 'Mon ami, ne me regardez pas comme prince mais comme gentilhomme et officier anglais'. At Copenhagen Frederick IV, presenting him with a magnificent jewelled sword, said, 'Milord, comme par votre entreprise j'ai fait la paix, et qu'à cette heure mes armes me sont inutiles, permettez moi que je vous fasse

[1] R.O., *S.P.* 104/220, Stanhope to Stair, 20 Oct. 1719.

présent de mon epée'.[1] Stanhope himself wrote, 'I think you, my Lord Carteret, have done wonders in procuring from Mons. Campredon the Act of Guaranty [for Schleswig] such as it is'.[2] When, after a year and a half's unceasing labour he returned to England in December 1720, he had gone a long way towards securing that peace in the North so ardently desired by Stanhope, by reconciling the Scandinavian Powers, putting an end to the causes of quarrel between Sweden and the Poles and North Germans, and making the Baltic safer for English traders.

But there still remained Russia. Stanhope had hoped in 1719 that Norris with his reinforcements and with the help of the Swedish fleet would be able to drive the Russian fleet off the sea and so reduce the Tsar to the peace he wished in the North.[3] In August Stanhope sent him orders first to try the effect of a letter to the Tsar offering the King's mediation between him and Sweden and requiring a suspension of arms:

'If the answer be to your satisfaction, the King will obtain his end, in the manner he likes best, of saving a brave people, without any loss to his own subjects; but if either an insolent or a captious answer be sent, or none at all, you will then join the Swedes, and act together in the manner you shall judge most effectual to destroy the Czar's fleet, than which a greater service cannot be done to your country. . . . The King . . . judges it a happiness to have at the head of his fleet, at this juncture, a man so able to help out the lameness or imperfection of any orders.'[4]

But Norris accomplished nothing. Although he and the Swedes together could muster some thirty men-of-war, the Russian fleet, composed of ships built chiefly by English artificers, some of them on Norris's own testimony as good as any of the English navy, was almost as strong.[5]   In addition Peter used for ravaging expeditions a swarm of

---

[1] Quoted in A. Ballantyne, *Lord Carteret* (1887), 49, 50, 63. The chief value of this inadequate life of one of the most brilliant and fascinating statesmen of the eighteenth century, consists in the quotations from the *Carteret MSS.* at the British Museum.

[2] R.O., *S.P.* 44/270, Stanhope to Carteret and Polwarth, 8 July 1720. The French had made much difficulty in giving this guarantee, without which Denmark would never have agreed to the treaty.

[3] See above, p. 377.

[4] Mahon, *History*, ii, Appendix, Stanhope to Norris, 17 Aug. 1719 (N.S.).

[5] For the remarkable growth of the Russian fleet in the Baltic between 1711 and 1724 see Michael, ii. 514.

flat galleys, which could take refuge in shoal waters inaccessible to men-of-war, while his main navy prudently retired from the enemy to such well-guarded ports as Reval. But though Norris's difficulties were great, other more adventurous admirals such as his rival Byng would probably have at least taken Stanhope's and Carteret's advice to lie in wait off the Finnish coast and pounce on the Russian fleet as it returned to its harbours of refuge. Norris, however, was possibly too devoted to the 'bottell' and 'the fair' to take excessive risks at sea, and in many quarters had the reputation of being a mere blusterer. Sunderland wrote appealing to Stanhope to send out Jennings or Wager to take his place, for Norris was 'one of those unreasonable, blustering men, that make a great noise and are capable of doing nothing'; and Craggs drily told Newcastle that in spite of 'his personal pique to the Czar and his envy of Byng . . . he truly comes out like all your blusterers a very very wise man'.[1] But Stanhope, always faithful to his old companions-in-arms, seems never to have lost the high opinion he conceived of Norris in Peninsula days.[2] The best that can be said for Norris is that he did not lose the good opinion of Carteret and Stanhope, who were perhaps most qualified to appreciate his difficulties in the Baltic.

Russia indeed still stood out from the Northern settlement; nevertheless Stanhope more than deserved the chorus of approbation that came to him at home and from foreign countries for his masterly conduct of European affairs during 1719 and the first half of the following year. Those eighteen months mark the period of his greatest success as a foreign minister and of the greatest credit he ever enjoyed. In the same year he had made Spain recognize the wisdom of acceding to his Quadruple Alliance, and had put an end to Alberoni's career as the breeder of mischief in Europe. At the same time he had conducted the maze of negotiations which resulted in the Prussian alliance and the reconciliation of all the Northern powers save Russia. In this year for the first time since 1700 he had secured the almost universal peace so sorely needed by Europe. In all his negotiations, while proving himself a good European, he had served his

---

[1] Mahon, *History* ii, Appendix for Sunderland's letter of 4 Aug. 1719, and *Add. MSS.* 32686, f. 137 for Craggs's of 10 Aug. 1719. Stanhop urged Norris on 24 Aug. 1719 to go to the Finnish coast (*Chevening MSS.*).
[2] See above, ch. iv.

country well and raised her reputation to that of the greatest Power in Europe; and except for that one lapse about the Prussian treaty he was straightforward in all his dealings and so regarded in other countries. He had also beaten the Hanoverians in open fight and restored to England complete power over her own foreign policy. To his colleagues his success seemed to have given renewed strength to the ministry and power to carry almost any measure they chose in Parliament. Craggs, Sunderland, Newcastle testified ungrudgingly to their colleague's success and the debt they owed him; the opposition seemed almost silenced; the King's Speech at the opening of Parliament in November 1719 gave expression to the country's just pride in Stanhope's achievement:

'The satisfaction with which I meet you is very much increased at this time, when it has pleased Almighty God so to strengthen the arms of Great Britain and our confederates, and so to prosper our several negotiations, that by his blessing on our endeavours we may promise ourselves to reap very soon the fruits of our successes. I am persuaded it will be accounted, by all my good subjects, a sufficient reward for some extraordinary expense, that all Europe, as well as these kingdoms, is upon the point of being delivered from the calamities of war by the influence of British arms and counsels. One Protestant kingdom has already been relieved by our seasonable interposition; and such a foundation is laid by our late Treaties for an union among other great Protestant powers, as will very much tend to the security of our holy Religion. . . . So far as human prudence can foretell, the unanimity of this session of Parliament must establish, with the peace of all Europe, the glory and trade of these kingdoms on a lasting foundation. I think every man may see the end of our labours. All I have to ask of you is, that you would agree to be a great and flourishing people, since it is the only means by which I desire to become a happy King.' [1]

[1] *P.H.* vii. 602–4.

CHAPTER XIV

CHURCH AND STATE

AFTER resuming the office of Secretary of State in the spring of 1718 Stanhope, though mainly concerned with foreign affairs, still took a leading part in measures designed to establish Whig principles in Church and State. The condition of the Church, bigoted and essentially Tory if not Jacobite at heart, gave cause for anxiety; the Universities, especially Oxford, were the homes of a very restricted learning and of a very abundant disloyalty; the Protestant Dissenters, as a body the most devoted adherents of the new dispensation, were kept in a state of political impotence and restricted in their religious observances by intolerant laws; while the savage code against the Roman Catholics made them almost pariahs in the community and was little short of an incitement to rebellion. Here was ample scope for reform to a man of Stanhope's passionate sense of religious toleration. Hardly less important seemed to him reforms needed in the constitution. He had never forgotten or forgiven Oxford's abuse of the royal prerogative in 1711 when he created twelve peers at once to secure his control of the House of Lords; and was so impressed by the dangers of an early election that he seems to have meditated an indefinite prolongation of the Septennial Parliament. The two reforms he had specially at heart were, first the repeal of the special disabilities of Protestant Dissenters carried by the last Tory government, and second to make it impossible for such action as Oxford's to be repeated. The opportunity of dealing with these questions did not come till the 1718–20 sessions, when Bills were presented to restore privileges of which the Dissenters had been deprived and drastically to limit the King's right of creating peers. The first of these measures was passed, though in less tolerant form than Stanhope had designed; on the second he suffered his most serious defeat.

§ 1. Dissenters' Privileges

The Corporation, Uniformity and Test Acts of Charles II's reign were intended, among other things, to exclude all those not conforming with the Established Church of England

from state or municipal offices and from the teaching profession. After the Revolution, which had been zealously
supported by Protestant Dissenters, the Toleration Act of
1689 had modified in their favour certain provisions of these
and other Acts, so far as the exercise of their religion and their
license to teach was concerned. But the bar to state or
municipal office still remained. The practice, however, had
grown up among Protestant Dissenters of qualifying themselves for office by taking the Sacrament in church once
before election, as the law required, and then relapsing to
the services of their Dissenting chapels. In 1711 this form
of evasion had been stopped by the Occasional Conformity
Act, whereby office holders were forbidden to attend chapel
services on penalty of a heavy fine and loss of office. Many
of the leading Whigs had unfortunately compromised themselves by voting for this measure as a bribe to its chief advocate Nottingham to oppose the preliminaries of Utrecht.
But Stanhope, who in 1711 was a prisoner in Spain, had no
such backsliding on his conscience, and had given ample
proof of his tolerant attitude in the debates on the Schism
Act of 1714, which disabled Dissenters from teaching in
schools.[1] The Schism Act had never been anything but a
dead letter, since the Tories had gone out before they could
put it into operation and the Whigs had never enforced
it: but it still remained on the statute book and might be
revived, while the Occasional Conformity Act was a definite
grievance. The Dissenters naturally felt that, in consideration of their loyal support of the Protestant Succession, the
least the Whigs could do for them was to repeal these two
obnoxious Acts. George I and his ministers were also anxious
to retain their support and early in the reign had employed
a certain J. Barrington Shute to conciliate the Nonconformists
and even to induce them to take commissions on the Irish
establishment in spite of the penalties they thereby incurred.[2]
As early as March 1717 Stanhope, Sunderland, the Lord
Chancellor Cowper and Bernstorff had met to consider
the repeal of the Occasional Conformity Act and also a
Bill for the reform of the Universities, two measures upon
which Stanhope and Sunderland declared the King had

[1] See above, ch. v, pp. 136–7. The various Acts referred to are conveniently
set forth in D. O. Dykes, *Source Book of Constitutional History from 1660* (1930).
[2] Shute's activities are alluded to in *Stowe MSS.* (*Robethon Papers*), 229, ff. 24,
133 (Aug. and Oct. 1716).

set his heart. All seem to have agreed on the repeal, but were not fully decided on the best time for moving in the matter; they also wished to sound the Archbishop as to the views of the Church.[1] In the same month the Dissenters' grievances were referred to in the House of Commons, and a meeting of some 200 members of Parliament was held at the Rose Tavern, near Temple Bar, to discuss the repeal of the two Tory Acts. At this meeting Stanhope himself was present and pronounced in favour of early action, but found many of his supporters doubtful whether the time was opportune.[2]

There were indeed difficulties, which no prudent government could overlook, in reviving ecclesiastical controversy in any new form. Only seven years before the Whigs had burned their fingers badly over the Sacheverell trial and were quite alive to the risks they ran in once more stirring up the ominous cry of 'the Church in danger'. Bolingbroke, then particularly anxious to ingratiate himself with the ministry, wrote to Stair in 1717,

'I am a little apprehensive of the effect which any measures in favour of the dissenters may have among the honestest of the Torys, those who [are not] Jacobites',

and in a later letter he declared that

'if the ministers are driven into the repeal of the Occasional Bill, they will raise a cursed storm. A multitude of Torys who are not for the Pretender, and who may be render'd as affectionate as any men in Brittain to the King's service, will be shock'd att it.'[3]

Recently, too, the religious unrest, chronic for nearly a century, had found new expression in the Bangorian controversy. This controversy was between Hoadly, the former Whig pamphleteer, now Bishop of Bangor, and his more orthodox opponents, who attacked his latitudinarian views on the authority of the Church and the rights of dissent as a direct blow, not only against the Church, but against revealed religion itself. In 1716 Hoadly inaugurated the controversy by his pamphlet with the provocative title, *A Preservative against the Principles of the Non-Jurors*. In March of the following year he expounded his views more fully in a sermon preached before the King and published by authority.

---

[1] *Wake MSS.* iv, Cowper to Wake, 14 Mar. 1716 (o.s.).
[2] Tindal, xxvii. 18.
[3] *Oxenfoord MSS., Bolingbroke Papers*, ff. 37, 43, 17 Dec. 1717, 19 Jan. 1718.

This sermon in its day caused as much of a sensation as the *Essays and Reviews* of a later generation. During the spring and summer of 1717 nearly a hundred pamphlets poured from the press to support or refute the audacious bishop's views; and so heated became the controversy that for two days, it was said, no business could be done in the City. The Non-jurors, too, who refused to recognize bishops or clergy false to their oath of allegiance to the old dynasty, were a body still to be reckoned with. They had many sympathizers in the ranks of the established clergy, especially at Oxford, and even on the bench of bishops, which included the formidable Atterbury, the Jacobite Dean of Westminster and Bishop of Rochester. Thus all the elements were present for a revival of the cry of 'the Church in danger', so powerful an instrument in 1710 in the hands of the Tories against the Whigs and their allies the Dissenters.[1]

One of the chief centres of disturbance in ecclesiastical affairs was Convocation. Since 1664 this body had lost its ancient right of voting its own subsidies to the King, and, for the next twenty-five years, though still formally summoned at the same time as Parliament, did not actually sit. In 1689 William III allowed it to discuss his scheme for a Comprehension of Protestant Dissenters, but was so much disgusted with its intolerance on that occasion that it was not again called together for business till 1700, as a result of the vehement Convocation controversy started by Atterbury in 1697. Since then it had again met regularly to discuss Church discipline and kindred matters, but had proved impracticable and highly troublesome. The upper house, composed of bishops, was fairly amenable to government influence, but the lower house, inspired by men like Atterbury to claim rights in the ecclesiastical sphere parallel with and independent of Parliament, was a constant source of disturbance. In the spring of 1717 it took upon itself to pass motions condemning Hoadly for his heretical opinions and was on the point of sending them up to the bishops for their assent, when, to avoid the scandal and end the envenomed controversy, Convocation was prorogued till the following November.[2] The Pretender took occasion to issue

[1] For the Bangorian controversy see Leslie Stephen, *History of Thought in the Eighteenth Century*, ch. x.
[2] It was stated in a contemporary news-letter that this action was due to Cadogan and that Stanhope and Sunderland denied having a hand in it

a manifesto protesting against the 'Elector's' unconstitutional action and asserting that lasting security for Church and State would never be obtained until he himself was restored: but the manifesto somehow fell flat.[1] Thereafter, though Convocation continued to be formally summoned at the same time as Parliament, letters of business empowering it to meet were issued only once for over a century.[2] This drastic action was surprisingly successful in clearing the air. The bishops of course still had a voice in Parliament, where they could look after the interests of their flocks, if they were so minded: but the bishops of the eighteenth century, when the Whigs' supremacy had been well established, gave little trouble to the dominant power in the state, depending on it as they did for their elevation to the bench or translation to wealthier dioceses. On the other hand, the clergy of the lower house, many of whom were inclined to use Convocation purely for political purposes or for illiberal attacks on dissenting brethren and more enlightened bishops such as Burnet, Hoadly and Gibson, were deprived of one of their most dangerous weapons. However honest may have been this opposition, it was not to be supposed that a statesman of Stanhope's knowledge and breadth of view should suffer it to endanger the Protestant Succession or to cripple the Dissenters, who were among the most valuable and active of English citizens. When Convocation was again allowed to do business in the nineteenth century, the clergy returned to their proper function of considering the moral and spiritual duties of their order and their Church.[3]

It was high time indeed that the leading Protestant state in Europe should make a demonstration in favour of religious toleration. Though more than half a century had passed since the treaties of Westphalia had brought to an end the last so-called religious war and purported to hold the scales even between Protestants and Catholics, religious toleration still played but a small part in European politics. In England there was growing alarm at the recrudescence of religious persecution on the Continent and the tendency of Protestant

(*H.MSS.*, *Portland*, v. 536); but no great importance need be attached to this statement.

[1] *H.MSS.*, *Stuart*, v. 244.

[2] This was in 1741, but even then Convocation was promptly prorogued owing to quarrels between the upper and lower houses.

[3] For the Convocation controversy see Sykes, *Gibson*, ch. ii. For the constitutional points involved see also T. P. Taswell-Langmead, *English Constitutional History* (3rd ed. 1886), 248–51, 429, 695 n. 1, 782–4.

rulers to revert to Catholicism. Huguenots in France were still being sent to the galleys in spite of Louis XIV's assurances to Queen Anne, and even after the Triple Alliance only a few were grudgingly released on Stair's representations to the Regent.[1] In Germany a new Catholic reaction appeared to have set in. In spite of England's protests the clauses of the Treaty of Ryswick which violated the *cujus regio ejus religio* principle of Westphalia had never been repudiated by either France or the Emperor.[2] The Elector of Saxony, still officially the director of the Protestant states in the Diet, had embraced Catholicism as a means of retaining in his family the crown of Catholic Poland: in 1717 his son, the electoral prince, raised a flutter in the Protestant chanceries of Europe by making a pilgrimage to Rome, where, in spite of Sunderland's well-meant endeavours to waylay him with plausible Protestants, he also found salvation.[3] In Poland five Protestant churches were destroyed by Roman Catholic mobs in 1718, and the Roman Catholic clergy were depriving Protestant congregations of their treaty privileges for the exercise of their worship and the education of their children. The Reformed sects were persecuted in the electorate of Mainz and the bishopric of Spires; while in the Palatinate, once a famous stronghold of Calvinism, the Elector's persecuting zeal became so outrageous and his language was so insulting in answer to the protests of the English agent Haldane that Haldane had to be recalled. Complaints were sent to the Emperor and even reprisals made by George as Elector and the King of Prussia against the Catholics in their dominions. In 1720 both Houses of Parliament sent up strong addresses, supported in the Lords by Stanhope, against such treatment of German Protestants.[4] An edict from the Emperor himself in November of that year calling on the Elector Palatine to redress the grievances of his Protestant subjects did not finally dispose of the question.[5] In England, it is

---

[1] *Instructions, France*, i. 110.
[2] See above, ch. vi, pp. 157–8.
[3] R.O., *S.P.* 104/123, Sunderland to Vernon, 22 Oct. 1717. In 1712 the Electoral Prince had made another pilgrimage to Rome, and on that occasion also the English government had sent a series of agents, notably Peterborough, to waylay him. But he was not converted till 1717.
[4] R.O., *S.P.* 104/42, Stanhope to Cadogan, &c., 3 June 1720.
[5] Ib., Stanhope to Vernon, 4 Apr., 16 May, 21 Nov., 19 Dec. 1718; R.O., *S.P.* 104/220, Stanhope to Cadogan, 22 Sept. 1719; R.O., *S.P.* 104/42, Stanhope to Cadogan and St. Saphorin, May–Aug. 1720; see also Chance, 405–10, 415–21, &c.; Droysen, iv. ii. 255 sqq., 285 sqq.; Coxe, *Austria*, 126, 144.

true, the penal laws against Roman Catholics were still exceedingly drastic, but as Carteret said, defending the fines imposed on Roman Catholics after the discovery of the Jacobite plot in 1722, 'there is nothing so alien to the spirit of this nation than persecution for the sake of religion',[1] and there was some excuse for this severity in the country's recent experience of James II, in the dependence of the Pretender on the Pope and Catholic Powers and in the large numbers of Jacobite recruits found in the Roman Catholic community. For the legal exclusion of Protestant Dissenters from official life there was no such excuse. Apart from any question of justice, the elementary motives of political security, as Stanhope wisely saw, made it expedient to remove all sense of grievance from the Protestant Dissenters and make them wholehearted allies of the existing system, especially at a time when Catholic activities on the Continent were causing alarm to all those of the Reformed religion who looked for help from England, the chief Protestant power.

Stanhope himself took charge of the measure for relieving Dissenters of their disabilities. Nursed as he had been on the pure milk of Locke's principles of toleration, he was manifestly well fitted to clear away some of the worst abuses of the penal code; and in this task he had the King for a staunch ally. George I was not usually much interested in the purely internal affairs of his kingdom, but, having stout Lutheran convictions and being deeply concerned in all questions affecting Protestantism, he had already promised the Dissenters that their grievances should be remedied.[2] Such support was all the more welcome, since Stanhope could no longer count on the help of Walpole and his dissatisfied section of the Whigs even for a measure which seemed implicit in the most fundamental Whig doctrines and was to be directed against a policy that Walpole himself had opposed. In the King's speech of November 1717 a promise had been made, in view of the alarming attacks on Protestantism on the Continent, to 'strengthen the Protestant interest' at home, a promise naturally criticized by the Tory Shippen, but almost as coldly received by Walpole in his new zeal for Stanhope's Tory opponents. The bishops, too, were gathering their forces against toleration to Nonconformists. There was indeed a small minority among them, of whom Gibson of Lincoln, Hoadly of Bangor and White Kennett of Peter-

[1] H.MSS., Polwarth, iii. 199.   [2] Michael, ii. 103-4.

borough were the most prominent, prepared for a genuine
policy of toleration.[1] But Wake, the Archbishop of Canterbury, though he had originally voted against the Occasional
Conformity and Schism Acts, was now against their repeal;
and among the most vigorous opponents of a change were
the fiery Bishop Nicolson of Carlisle[2] and Trelawney of
Winchester, both in their younger days counted among the
more liberal Churchmen. Trelawney boasted that of the
twenty-six bishops on the bench twenty were ready to oppose
repeal and was convinced that 'if the phanatigs can get a
bill to their minds, farewell to episcopacy. The corporations
must be kept as they are or the phanatigs by their own money
and the government's will have a parliament which will do
our business at once';[3] while Nicolson exercised all his considerable talents for lobbying against what he called the
'Readmission of Occasional Hypocrisy'.[4] Manningham of
Chichester went so far as to hope for the failure of Stanhope's
Mediterranean policy, as that would depress the Whigs,
'then the poor Church may sleep a little longer with all its
Errors and Defects and Parents may be allowed to teach
yʳ children the Catechism without usurping an authority
over Xt.'[5] Even the Chancellor Cowper, though opposed to
the Occasional Conformity Act, was lukewarm on the question of admitting Dissenters to office.[6] Nor would Sunderland himself go so far as Stanhope, who was for doing away
with the genuine scandal of using the Sacrament simply as
a form of admission to office by boldly repealing the Test
and Corporation Acts in so far as they affected Protestant
Dissenters.[7] At any rate the prospects of obtaining a majority
for the measure in 1717 seemed so doubtful that it was postponed to the following year.

By the winter session of 1718 Stanhope was in a more
favourable position. The lukewarm Chancellor had resigned
in April, the Quadruple Alliance had been signed, the Spanish
fleet had been annihilated by Byng, and the ministry seemed
firmly established. Accordingly on 13 December he introduced into the House of Lords his Bill to which he attached

---

[1] *Wake MSS.*, iv, Gibson to Wake, 22 Nov. 1717.
[2] In 1718 he was translated to the richer bishopric of Derry.
[3] *Wake MSS.*, xv, Trelawney to Wake, 29 Mar. 1717; and iv, 1 Dec. 1717.
[4] Ib. xxi, Nicolson to Wake, 1 Jan. 1718/19.
[5] Ib. xxi, Manningham to Wake, 30 Aug. 1718.
[6] Ib. iv, Cowper to Wake, 14 Mar. 1716/17.
[7] *H.MSS. Portland*, v. 554, 571.

the captivating title 'for strengthening the Protestant interest'. The measure he submitted went beyond Bolingbroke's worst apprehensions, for it not only provided for the repeal of the Occasional Conformity Act as well as the Schism Act, but even proposed to release Protestant Dissenters, in case the incumbent made a difficulty, from the obligation of taking the Sacrament at all in an Established Church on assuming office:[1] in other words, without formally repealing them—a concession to Sunderland's scruples—the measure would have made a breach in the Test and Corporation Acts, then and for over a century longer regarded as the main bulwark of England's happy Establishment. This last provision illustrates Stanhope's practical and enlightened tolerance; it was also the best rejoinder to the Tories' strongest argument in favour of the Occasional Conformity Act, since it proposed to absolve Dissenters from the need of taking the Sacrament in an Established Church, a form meaningless to them and insulting to those who held the beliefs of the Church of England. In his opening speech Stanhope enlarged on the equity and advantage of restoring their natural rights to the Dissenters and of easing them from the stigmatizing and oppressive laws passed in more turbulent times and obtained by indirect methods: their zeal, as he said, for the Revolution and the Protestant Succession deserved no less. Then in a fine peroration he predicted that this relief would make for the union of all true Protestants and strengthen the Church of England itself, for the Church would still remain the head of all Protestant churches and the Archbishop of Canterbury be regarded as the patriarch of the Protestant clergy throughout the world.[2]

After Sunderland had seconded the Bill Devonshire, one of the seceding Whigs, on a point of order complained of the want of notice, but was aptly reminded by Stanhope that Devonshire himself had given no previous notice when he

---

[1] *H.MSS.*, *Portland*, v. 575; *Wake MSS.* iii has the draft of the Bill sent by Sunderland to the archbishop.

[2] This peroration provoked from Nicolson the sarcastic comment addressed to Archbishop Wake: 'I know nobody here that believes one word of the Report, that my Lord of Canterbury will come into the measures now on foot for making His Grace a patriarch of the protestants. To say nothing of their Imperial Reverences (the Arch Superintendents of the Upper and Lower Saxony; &c.) the Moderatour at Edinburgh will no more come into such an alliance than my neighbouring Baptist teacher; who openly bragg'd (the other day in the market) that he'd shortly be as lawful a pastor as the High Priest at Rose.' *Wake MSS.* xxi, Nicolson to Wake, 20 Dec. 1718. (Rose Castle was the residence of the Bishop of Carlisle.)

introduced the far more important Septennial Bill. Lansdowne in a maiden speech made a happy debating point by his reference to the recent Quadruple Alliance:

> 'To whom', he asked, 'do we owe our security in the Protestant establishment, but to the most potent, the most arbitrary, the most famous for persecution of all the Popish powers, the most inveterate and implacable enemies of the Protestant persuasion, France, Savoy and the Emperor? And have not the ministers, one after another, assured us, that these mortal enemies to our souls in another world are our only guarantees for our salvation in this?'

The two archbishops and four bishops, one of whom, as might be expected, was Atterbury, spoke against the Bill, their main line of agreement being that those not in harmony with the religion of the state could not expect to enjoy all its civil benefits; five, including Hoadly and Gibson, were enlightened enough to support it. It is interesting to find that Gibson's chief motive for his action was a conviction that the Tories were a greater danger to the Establishment than the Dissenters. Writing to Bishop Nicolson, then of Derry, he defends his attitude on the Bill on the ground that,

> 'All my political reasonings proceed upon these two positions; that there is no way to preserve the church but by preserving the present establishment in the state; and that there is far greater probability that the tories will be able to destroy our present establishment in the state than that the dissenters will be able to destroy our establishment in the church.'[1]

But Cowper, who had recently resigned the chancellorship, fastened on the vulnerable point of the Bill in attacking the clauses that made a breach in the Test Act. The Bill passed a second reading by 86 to 68; but in committee Stanhope, in deference to Sunderland's fears that those clauses would not get through the Commons, did not insist on them against Cowper's amendment to expunge them. In the House of Commons Walpole, who, it was said, 'bore harder against the Court than any Tory durst attempt to do', once more opposed the relief to Dissenters on the flimsy ground that 'there were people enough to fill all offices without capacitating any more disqualified'. He even went so far in his party rage as to suggest that Stanhope's original clause, 'that would in a scandalous manner have evaded the Test Act',

---

[1] *Bodleian, Add. MSS.*, A269, Gibson to Nicolson, 3 Dec. 1717.

showed the ministry's sinister designs and would be a 'handle
to the disaffected who would inculcate into the minds of
the people that many of the measures which occasioned an
unfortunate prince's abdication were now renewed'. He laid
himself open, however, to a telling attack from Lechmere
for abandoning his former convictions, and did not even
carry all his usual supporters with him into the lobby.
Accordingly the Bill was passed by a majority of 41.[1]

Stanhope, no doubt, could hardly do otherwise than yield
to Sunderland's fears about the Test Act clauses, for the
general feeling of the community was probably not misrepresented by Bolingbroke when he wrote to Stair:

> 'Should the test or the Act of Uniformity be medled with, I
> much apprehend the immediate consequence, and should any
> immediate disorder be prevented the certain seeds of future dis-
> order will be sown.'[2]

Thus all the grace and statesmanlike liberality of his original
proposal to give the Dissenters full civil rights were thrown
away. For after Cowper's amendment had been carried, the
Act for Strengthening the Protestant Interest merely left
them in exactly the same position as they were before 1711,
allowed to evade the spirit of the law if they had once taken
the Sacrament before election. However, this was not quite
the end of the matter. Immediately afterwards the ministry
were able to pass through Parliament an Act for Quieting
and Establishing Corporations (1718), the first of a series of
Indemnity Acts which facilitated the presence of Protestant
Dissenters on corporations for over a century till the repeal
of the Test Act in 1828. By this Act all such members of
corporations as had not complied with the law but whose
tenure of office was not questioned for six months were
confirmed in their offices: thereby no Nonconformists then
holding office could be displaced for the remainder of their

---

[1] The debate in the Lords is fairly well reported in *P.H.* vii. 567 sqq.; little
more than the division list and a list of speakers is given of the Commons proceedings, ib. 584 sqq.; but *H.MSS. Portland*, v. 575–6 has a good account of
Walpole's speech. Among the Whigs Walpole took into the lobby with him
were Stanhope's father- and eldest brother-in-law, Governor Thomas and
Robert Pitt. In the *Wake MSS.* iii is a printed list of the votes cast in the
House of Lords from which it appears that the two Archbishops and thirteen
Bishops voted in person or by proxy against the Bill, and that eleven Bishops,
including Gibson (Lincoln), Hoadly (Bangor), Hough (Worcester), Talbot
(Salisbury), Willis (Gloucester), White Kennett (Peterborough) and Bradford
(Nicolson's successor at Carlisle), voted for it.

[2] *Oxenfoord MSS., Bolingbroke Papers*, f. 58, 28 Dec. 1718.

lives—for in those days corporation offices were normally held
for life—while for the future the limited period for objections
proved in effect a considerable safeguard to Nonconformists
elected to corporations. A further concession was made by
the series of annual Indemnity Acts inaugurated by Walpole
himself in 1727, whereby the qualifying Sacrament could
be taken after, instead of before, election as a bar to possible objections. Thus in effect, though not by such a direct
method as he had originally intended, Stanhope was able to
secure the presence of Nonconformists on corporations, where
there was no local objection; and Walpole, who has hitherto
had the chief merit assigned to him for this sensible evasion
of an intolerant law, merely improved on his method.[1]

Stanhope's tolerant spirit and his comparative freedom
from some of the most deeply rooted prejudices of his contemporaries is still further illustrated by a curious attempt
he made to ease the position of the English Roman Catholics.
He had already in 1714 expressed unusually enlightened
views as to the unwisdom of forcing them by penal legislation
to send their sons abroad to be educated and so filling 'the
tender minds of young men with prejudices against their
own country'.[2] Now that he was in power he showed himself
ready to act in the spirit of his speech, not perhaps from any
special tenderness to Roman Catholics but in the hope of
reconciling them to the dynasty. Their numbers were not
large, some 28,000 in England out of a total population of
over 5,000,000, but they formed a compact and united
community.[3] Their chief legal hardships were that they had
to pay higher taxes than the Protestants, their children could
not be educated in Catholic schools, their priests were liable
to arrest and imprisonment, a Roman Catholic heir might
be dispossessed by the nearest Protestant collateral who chose
to claim the inheritance, and any Justice of the Peace, acting
on mere rumour, might tender to them, on pain of severe
penalties, oaths of supremacy and allegiance which their
conscience forbade them to take. It is true these laws were
often a dead letter, but any common informer might act

[1] The Act for Quieting and Establishing Corporations is 5 George I, c. 6.
Attention was drawn to this law by Mr. T. Bennett in the *Law Quarterly Review*,
xxvi. 400–7 (Oct. 1910), where he points out Hallam's erroneous account, in
ch. xvi of his *Constitutional History*, of Walpole's Indemnity Acts.

[2] See above, ch. v, p. 137.

[3] These figures are taken from a return made in the reign of William and
Mary and quoted in Butler, *Catholics*, iv. 252 sqq.

upon them, and in times of national danger, as in 1715 and 1722, they were put into force. The ferocity of some ardent Protestants against the Roman Catholics is illustrated by a clause in a Bill proposed for submission to the Irish Parliament by the Viceroy's council to render recusant priests liable in certain cases to castration. Stanhope of course advised the King to reject the proposal on account of this 'Clause of Castration which appeared very ridiculous'.[1] But naturally such laws and such ferocious proposals did not tend to encourage loyalty among those subject to them. When, therefore, in the spring of 1718 Stair forwarded a suggestion to Stanhope that some means should be found of reconciling the Roman Catholics to the dynasty by an alleviation of their lot, Stanhope welcomed this idea of 'inducing English Catholics to become by degrees truly and heartily affected to His Majesty's government', adding that the King, whose Roman Catholic subjects were better treated in Hanover than in England, thought well of the proposal, and that he himself 'thought, and had long done so, that it is right in itself'.[2]

It so happened that just then a certain abbé Strickland, an English priest influential at the papal and other courts, was ready with a plan to ease the position of his co-religionaries in England. His idea was to obtain from the Pope permission, hitherto refused, for the English Roman Catholics to take the oath of allegiance to the dynasty, and that for this and certain other concessions on their side the English government would undertake not to put the most obnoxious penal laws into force; for of repeal there could be no question. Strickland had almost won over the Pope when he was checked by the Jacobite faction at Rome, chief of which was the Pretender's agent Cardinal Gualterio, who obtained from the Pope the title 'Protector of England'. Thereupon in 1718 Strickland went to England with a proposal to the English ministers that he should be authorized to obtain the Emperor's support for his negotiation with the Pope. Stanhope himself was then abroad negotiating the Quadruple Alliance, but he had evidently discussed the matter with Craggs, who thenceforward took the chief part in the negotiations, keeping Stanhope fully informed of the course

---

[1] R.O., *S.P.* 104/220, Stanhope to Delafaye, 28 Sept. 1719.

[2] R.O., *S.P.* 104/219 B, Stanhope to Stair, 29 Apr. 1718. See too, the title of *Stowe MSS.* 121 referred to below, p. 398, note.

they took. Craggs sanctioned the scheme and gave Strickland a letter of recommendation to St. Saphorin at Vienna; Bothmer sent another letter to the Hanoverian agent there expressing the King's desire

> 'to give the Roman Catholicks, in his Dominions here, the same Protection and Privileges that he does those in his own Country, their Number being too inconsiderable to give us any great Uneasiness; and even those in Ireland, where they are most numerous, may easily be gained, by granting them some Privileges with relation to their Trade, as well as Religion, which the English, in all Reigns, have refused them; so that we doubt not but their Interest will oblige them to become his Majesty's best subjects.'[1]

The Emperor proved quite willing to help; but he also failed to obtain the desired concession from Rome.

In the last resort Strickland determined to bring pressure on the Pope from the English Catholics themselves. In June 1719 he returned to London, again saw Craggs, Stanhope being then in Hanover with the King, and concerted with him the line to be taken with the English Catholics. The final stages of the negotiation are described in Craggs's reports to Stanhope. A paper was drawn up by Strickland for signature by some of the leading Catholics, approved by Craggs, and submitted to the Duke of Norfolk, Lord Waldegrave and Charles Howard. This paper proposed that English Roman Catholics should depute one of their number to inform the Pope that they could obtain some liberty and security for their religion upon four conditions only:

1. That the Pope should issue his decree already drafted, empowering the Roman Catholics to take the oath of allegiance and make a declaration against the 'abominable doctrine' that the Pope had power to dispense with such allegiance.

2. That the title 'Protector of England' should be taken away from Cardinal Gualterio and conferred on one not obnoxious to the English government.

3. That the indult granted to the Pretender to name Irish bishops should be withdrawn and that the Irish mission should be conducted on lines agreeable to the government.

---

[1] *Historical Account of Advantages to England by the Succession in the Illustrious House of Hanover* (London, 1722), an anti-dynastic and anti-Stanhope pamphlet. He is spoken of in it as 'that Hanoverian tool'. There are several copies of the pamphlet in R.O., *S.P. Dom. Geo. I*, 40, seized by the government messengers at the printer's office as treasonable.

4. That any person sent on the mission to Ireland should be immediately recalled upon any bona-fide complaint that he had given offence to the government.

The paper concludes with the statement that, since none of these demands were contrary to conscience or Catholic doctrine, the government would have no option but to enforce the penal laws if they were not granted at the request of four signatories from the Catholic nobility and four from the Catholic gentry.

Norfolk and Waldegrave at first seemed inclined to sign the paper, but three days later Norfolk told Craggs that he could not do so owing to Charles Howard's opposition, adding that he hoped a more favourable opportunity would soon occur to resume the negotiation. This opportunity never came, in spite of Strickland's advice, followed by Craggs, to arrest Howard and two more leading Roman Catholics under the penal laws, 'with a view to make them squeak' and become more pliable. The real reason, so Craggs reported to Stanhope, for the hesitation of Howard and his friends was due to the advice of Walpole's friend Pulteney, who gave them 'mighty assurances that they would destroy the present Ministry with the King, and so discouraged them from engaging themselves in a falling house'. Once more then Stanhope was foiled by the factious opposition of the Whig dissentients in a beneficent attempt to remove a cause of disunion in the nation. It is the first recorded attempt since the Reformation by a Protestant government in England to arrange a concordat with the Holy See; it was also the first experiment, by an explicit understanding, on the hitherto unexplored path of toleration to Roman Catholics. It was an audacious experiment considering the nearness in time to the Revolution and the ease with which the 'no-popery' cry could be raised. But it is characteristic of Stanhope's courage.[1]

[1] Michael, ii. 121–9, gives an account of Strickland's negotiations in Vienna from St. Saphorin's letters in the Hanover Archives; R.O., *S.P.* 43/57, contains Craggs's full reports to Stanhope of the negotiations with the English Roman Catholics in June-July 1719; copies of Craggs's letters are also to be found in *Stowe MSS.* 121, a little volume entitled *Papers about the Scheme to induce English Catholics to become by degrees truly and heartily affected to H. M. Government*; Butler, *Catholics*, iv. 252–68, also contains Craggs's letters as well as other useful details; *Add. MSS.* 20311 and 20313 (*Gualterio Papers*) contain depreciatory remarks from the Jacobite side on Strickland. Mahon, *History*, ii, Appendix, prints, with a trifling omission, the paper handed to Norfolk, Waldegrave and Howard with a note stating, on the authority of Stanhope's son, the second earl, that it was drawn up by Stanhope himself. This seems unlikely, for Stanhope was

§ 2. *The Universities*

Closely connected with the state of the Church and religion was that of the two English Universities. Cambridge was the more loyal of the two and, in spite of the Oxford gibe about the King finding it necessary to send books to Cambridge when he sent a squadron of horse to Oxford in 1715, seems to have maintained a somewhat higher standard of learning ; but it was also suspect for High Church proclivities and distracted from its proper functions by the resounding quarrels of Bentley with his Fellows at Trinity and by the general want of discipline in other colleges.[1] Oxford, however, was the real thorn to the government. Ormonde had been its Chancellor till he fled to France and was immediately replaced by his Tory brother, Arran. During the Rebellion it had needed a garrison to keep it quiet, and a college Fellow such as Thomas Hearne, who always spoke of George I as the Duke of Brunswick, was typical of its spirit. The King's birthday on 28 May and Restoration Day on the 29th were equally occasions for the riotous display of Jacobite sentiment. Dr. Ayliffe, a Fellow of New College, was deprived of his degrees and expelled for venturing to attack the Toryism and scandals of Oxford common-rooms. Nor is there any exaggeration in the following unvarnished description of University politics sent by one of the rare Oxford Whigs to the nephew of Wake's predecessor Tenison 'at Lamb-Hith'.

'Rev^d S^r.

'You cannot be ignorant of the deplorable condition of the University of Oxford, in which there is an entire Opposition to His Maj^ty and His Government, and that which is most to be lamented, is, This being the Nursery of above one half of the Clergy-men of this Kingdome, The Principles of Rebellion are diffus'd from hence through the whole Nation, and those which should watch over and cure others are infected themselvs. If our Light become Darkness, how great is our Darkness. Perhaps you may say as soon as once the Rebellion is blown over, They will come to themselvs, grow wiser, and return to their

in Hanover at the time and Craggs explicitly states in his letters to Stanhope that it was drawn up by Strickland and submitted to himself for approval. It is tempting to believe that Stanhope did draw it up, but the fact that he probably did not in no way detracts from his merit in countenancing if not initiating the idea of the negotiation.

[1] R.O., *S.P. Dom. Geo. I*, 3 contains reports of 16 June 1715 from the Vice-Chancellor, Sherlock, on Jacobite celebrations at Cambridge.

Duty; But you are utterly mistaken, if these be your Thoughts; for Principles of Opposition have taken deeper Root than you or any Person else can imagine, that is not conversant here upon the Spot.

Rebellion is avowedly own'd and encouraged, and He that do's not run into the same excess, is treated with all the contempt and scorn, that they can pour forth upon him. Some Tutors read Lectures to their Pupils on Hereditary Right etc. And there are several Houses in which there's not so much as One (what they please to call a) Whig. There are but three Houses viz. Wadham, Jesus, & Merton, whose Heads are not violent Tories and Jacobites. Merton stands fairest for a Cure, as having as yet several sound Members left among them. But these will soon be overwhelm'd with a great Majority if there be not some care taken; And whether the Government and His Grace your Uncle ought not a little to look into this Matter I leave you to judge. . . [After setting out the chances for the election of Whig Fellows at Merton and stating that the Warden though a Whig with two votes, is weak, and that, of the existing Fellows, five only are Whigs and the remaining eight Tories, one 'fierce' and another 'violent', he proceeds:] There must be some Persons who are cloth'd both with Power and Interest to bring this about. S^r this is a matter of so much Consequence that it should be worth the Government's while to look after it. The Peace of the Kingdom do's in a great measure depend upon amending the University for one of these things must lose his Crown, or this University must be reform'd. . . . Your humble Servant

'J. R[ussell].

'Novr the 27th 1715.' [1]

So great, indeed, was the scandal that some of the Universities' best friends felt that stringent measures must be taken. At Cambridge the chief points at issue were as to the encroachments at Trinity and Corpus on the rights of the Fellows by their respective Masters, and some uncertainty about the powers of the Bishop of Ely as Visitor; but at Oxford the issue was little short of rank rebellion. Archbishop Wake himself,[2] a loyal son of Christ Church, came to the conclusion that interference by the government was the only effective remedy. Matters came to a head after a serious

[1] *Wake MSS.* xv.

[2] William Wake was translated from Lincoln to Canterbury in 1716, in succession to Archbishop Tenison, but was not as staunch a Whig or as effective an archbishop as his predecessor. Edmund Gibson, who became Walpole's ecclesiastical adviser, succeeded Wake at Lincoln and became Bishop of London in 1723.

riot on the Prince of Wales's birthday in 1717 for which the
townsmen and heads of colleges were censured after inquiry
by the Privy Council and a debate in the House of Lords.
In this debate Atterbury and three other bishops defended
the town and University for not celebrating the Prince's
birthday on three grounds: (a) that the mayor and magistrates did not know that it was the Prince's birthday,
(b) that joy-bells were not rung because of the sixteen
colleges only three had bells to ring, and (c) 'that the
University had a method of expressing their loyalty, more
consistent with the dignity of their founders and the character of their persons, than by illuminations and bonfires',
excuses almost more offensive than the original offence.[1]
This inquiry and the outspoken demands expressed that the
colleges should be deprived of their patronage created great
alarm. The Warden of All Souls and the Vice-Chancellor
wrote to Wake explaining that Oxford was loyal to the core
and had nothing to reproach herself with; to which the
Archbishop drily replied, 'I may truly say y^t you are very
unfortunate in the Reports wh^{ch} are everywhere spread
abroad of y^r Conduct, and the prejudice wh^{ch} I fear those
reports have raised agst you in many who are ye moste
heartily concerned for our public peace and security'.[2] In
the previous year Townshend had already been considering
a scheme for controlling the Universities, in consultation
with Wake, Prideaux the learned Dean of Norwich, the
Chancellor and Chief Justice Parker; Stanhope, Sunderland
and Bernstorff had also been interested in the scheme. As
a result of these discussions a Bill was actually drawn up
in 1717, the effect of which would have been to deprive
for a term of years the Universities and their component
colleges of all rights of appointment and patronage; these
rights during that period were to be vested in royal commissioners with very wide powers of enforcing their decisions;
even the present Chancellors were to be removable at the
King's pleasure and their successors appointed by the Crown.
The reasons given in the preamble for these extreme measures
were that it is

'notorious that many in those Nurseryes dedicated to Religion
Learning Loyalty & Peace have been infected with Principles
of Sedition y^t Riots & Tumults have disturbed the Peace of the

[1] *P.H.* vii. 431–4.
[2] *Wake MSS.* xv, Wake to Warden of All Souls (draft of Mar. 1717).

Universityes & affronted ye Government and the Offenders have
been concealed or at least not detected and duely brought to
Punishment . . . and y^t there can be no reasonable expectation
of enjoying Peace & Tranquility for any long time if the Youth
of the Nobility & Gentry especially such as are designed for
Holy Orders are infected with false Principles utterly inconsistent with our happy Establishment in Church & State.'[1]

The mere rumour of this drastic measure created a flutter
in the Oxford and Cambridge dovecots and in Tory circles
in London. 'The visitation of both universities is very warmly
talked of', writes Edward Harley to Abigail in reference to
an inquiry into the Bentley affair, 'Oxford is to expect but
little favour since her younger sister, the darling, the favourite
is so highly censured'.[2] Trelawney, the bellicose bishop of
Winchester, informed Wake that he would resist to the
uttermost any attempt against the privileges of their common
college Christ Church, where 'I had my breade for more
than twenty yeares; my son Charles hath already had his
neare 8, & my son Edward stands next Easter for ye same
advantages . . . I had rather see Edward a link boy y^n a
Student of Xt Church in such a manner as teares up by y^e
roots y^t constitution.' But even he was forced to agree
'y^t both universitys ought to be scourg'd into perfect duty,
and better manners to ye King & his family', and proceeded
as Visitor to make an example of Tooley, a fellow of Exeter,
for his 'lewdnesse & disloyalty', and argued that all that was
needed could be done by the Visitors, who 'have powr enough
to make a terrifying example of all free talkers . . . so I beg,
I beg, I beseech your Grace to have no hand in ye Bill'.[3]

This measure, if administered for a limited period by
wise commissioners, might possibly have improved the low
political and educational ideas of the Universities, but in the
long run would have proved most pernicious. For, once in
the grip of the State, the Universities would never have
escaped from it and might have become mere forcing-

---

[1] *Wake MSS.* xv contains the proposed Bill *in extenso*; for Townshend's
part in it see Coxe, *Walpole*, ii. 122; C. E. Mallet, *History of the University of Oxford*,
3 vols. 1927, gives some account of the state of Oxford and of this draft Bill in
vol. iii, pp. 40 sqq.; Hallam, *Constitutional History*, in a footnote to ch. xvi quotes
an allusion to this plan in Gutch, *Collectanea Curiosa* (1781), i. 53; but apparently
the full text of the proposed Bill is not to be found elsewhere than in the *Wake
MSS.* Some of its more important clauses are quoted in Appendix D, p. 456.
[2] *H.MSS., Portland*, v. 574, E. Harley, Jr., to Abigail Harley, 7 Dec. 1718.
[3] *Wake MSS.* xv, Trelawney to Wake, 17 Feb., 13 Mar., 1 Apr. 1717.

grounds for supporters of the government. Stanhope himself
appears to have taken no active part in drafting it, but he
welcomed it and adopted it as part of his programme of
reforms intended to establish the Protestant dynasty on a
firmer basis. In 1719, when he had schemes in view affecting
both Lords and Commons, his intention was to combine
these schemes with this Bill to reform the Universities. But
with the failure of the other schemes University reform also
fell to the ground. For over a century the only innovations
at Oxford and Cambridge, due chiefly to Gibson with the political support of Townshend, were the institution of twelve
Whitehall Preachers from each University in 1723 and of the
Regius Professorships in 1724. The preachers were to be
chosen from among the Fellows for their scholarship and gifts
of exposition and were to form a link between the administration and the Universities. Naturally good Whigs were at first
picked out and from their ranks promotions to the Bench
were often made. The main function of the Regius Professors
of History at Oxford and Cambridge was intended to be
the training of young men for the diplomatic or civil service,
not only in history but in foreign languages. These measures
may have done something to bring the Universities into
closer touch with the public life of the country. The alarm
created by the Universities Bill and the redoubled zeal of
such Visitors as Trelawney in suppressing flagrant rebellion
may also have had some temporary effect. But if so, it was
evanescent. Thirty-five years later Pitt, taking up an allusion
to Oxford as a broody hen, remarked:

'I know such a hen, I was bred under such an one, and will tell
the House what she has been doing these twenty years;—raising
a succession of treason—there never was such a seminary; and
we must not be too sure that all she hatched would ever entirely
forget what she had taught them.' [1]

§ 3. *The Peerage Bill*

Stanhope's attempt to deal with the vexed question of
admission to the peerage was no less courageous than his
schemes of toleration for Protestant and Roman Catholic
Dissenters, but certainly not so wise. His chief coadjutor on
the peerage question was no longer the sensible Craggs, but

[1] Williams, *Chatham*, i. 257.

that stormy petrel Sunderland, who was even more bent on the scheme proposed than Stanhope himself. But, whoever was the prime mover, Stanhope cannot escape responsibility for a policy which, it is evident from his speeches and correspondence, he did his utmost to carry. The chief justification for the Peerage Bill of 1719 was found in the simultaneous creation of twelve peers by Lord Oxford in 1711, in order to give his government a majority in the Upper House. At the time, and ever since, the Whigs had protested against what they regarded as an unconstitutional use of the royal prerogative, and Walpole, who was mainly responsible for the indictment against Oxford, had laid special stress on his guilt in advising so wholesale a creation. Even the Tory Swift had admitted that it could be defended only as an unpleasant necessity. Except by severely curtailing the royal prerogative of creating peers, it was argued, further attempts to change the political complexion of the House of Lords, whenever it suited a minister in a minority, could not be prevented. There were also other reasons for limiting the prerogative. Although the Germans at court were precluded by the Act of Settlement from obtaining peerages or profitable offices for themselves, there was nothing to prevent their obtaining money from hungry English suitors for pressing their claims to such advantages on the King; and they made full use of such opportunities. So disturbed was Stanhope at these scandals that, as Craggs wrote to Schaub, 'at the rate we are now going on, Lord Stanhope is on the point of resigning every day . . . It is incredible what prejudice all these sales of Offices and other underhand dealings occasion; . . . nothing is objected to as long as there is money.'[1] By the proposed reform at least one source of profit from such transactions would be dried up. Lastly there was considerable apprehension of what might occur upon the King's death. The Prince of Wales, after his disgrace,[2] had set up a little court of his own composed entirely of Tories and discontented Whigs and, though for the time being powerless, on his accession would probably give the existing system short shrift and secure a favourable House of Lords by raising its adversaries to the peerage. This consideration, which the Duke of Newcastle characteristically blurted out in the House of Lords, was evidently that which weighed most with the King when he

---

[1] Craggs to Schaub, 30 June 1719, quoted in Torrens, i. 230.
[2] See above, ch. x, pp. 266–7.

consented to a curtailment of his own privileges and gave
his enthusiastic approval to the plan: for he hated his son as
cordially as George II in turn hated his heir.

The scheme proposed by the ministry was introduced on
28 February 1719, not in the form of a Bill, but on resolutions
proposed by the Duke of Somerset and seconded by the Duke
of Argyll. The resolutions were:

> 'That the number of English peers should not be enlarged be-
> yond six above the present number, which upon failure of male
> issue might be supplied by new creations; That instead of the
> Sixteen elective peers in Scotland 25 be made hereditary on
> the part of that Kingdom, whose number, upon failure of heirs
> male, should be supplied by some other Scotch peers.'

The choice of mover and seconder was ingenious. Somerset,
though no longer in the ministry, was premier Duke in the
House, since Norfolk, as a Roman Catholic, could not sit:
thus his advocacy gave the proceedings the appearance of
being a spontaneous move of the peerage in defence of its
own rights. Argyll, though sitting as Duke of Greenwich,
was the most prominent Scottish peer and so appeared to
countenance on behalf of his countrymen the proposed
modification of the Act of Union. Somerset based his motion
on the danger to the independence of the House if, as had
occurred in the last reign, it could be swamped by new
creations to serve a temporary political end. After speeches
by Argyll, followed by Carlisle and Sunderland, and by
Oxford in opposition to the motion, the debate was adjourned.
Two days later Stanhope read a message from the King
waiving his prerogative of unrestricted creation of peers.
This message was objected to by some speakers as a breach
of the Lords' privileges in taking notice of a debate in the
House, a topic on which Sunderland and Oxford became so
heated that Stanhope had to interpose to prevent a recourse
to arms. Since then, however, it has become a well-established
constitutional practice, whenever debate arises in Parliament
touching on the royal prerogative, for the King to send a
message waiving his prerogative in the matter under discussion. The Duke of Somerset's resolutions were amplified in
detail on 3 March, after a debate which turned chiefly on
Cowper's criticism of the injustice to the Scottish peers not
included in the hereditary twenty-five; and on 14 March a
Bill founded on these resolutions was introduced and rapidly

passed through the first and second readings and committee stages. To the general principle of the Bill the majority of the existing peers were not unnaturally favourable, since, with no new-comers to swell their number, their power would enormously increase. The Scottish representative peers in Parliament raised no objection, in the expectation, no doubt, that if they voted straight they would be included in the permanent twenty-five; and although most of the other Scottish peers met at Edinburgh and protested against the abrogation of their rights of election, even among them intrigues were set afoot to be included in those twenty-five. Robethon, for example, writes to Polwarth, who had been trying to get his father the Earl of Marchmont's peerage included, that he had been successful in this ambition, 'you owe yours indeed, my Lord, to the good Lord Sunderland, and a little to me'; others were being settled by the private intrigues of Argyll and Roxburgh.[1] Then suddenly on 14 April, the day fixed for the third reading, Stanhope got up in the House of Lords and announced that 'this Bill had made a great noise and raised strange apprehensions; and since the design of it had been so misrepresented, and so misunderstood that it was likely to meet with great opposition in the other House, he thought it advisable to let that matter lie still till a more proper opportunity'. So, for the time being, the Bill was dropped.

Stanhope had not exaggerated the intensity of the feeling already displayed against the Bill. Within a fortnight of Somerset's resolutions a violent pamphlet war, then the usual method of ventilating public opinion on contentious measures, had begun; and certainly the dissentient Whigs had the best of the argument. On 14 March Steele opened the attack with *The Plebeian*, the issues of which for over a month carried on the war against *The Patrician*, another weekly sheet ascribed to Lord Molesworth. Steele also published a *Letter to the Earl of O[xfor]d*—so strange are the whirligigs of politics, for it was partly to Oxford that Steele owed his expulsion from the House of Commons in 1714 for his part in *The Crisis*. In this *Letter* Steele encouraged Oxford in his opposition to the Bill, on the ground that 'the Restraint of the Peers to a certain Number will render the House useless, because it is well known that the great Business is always carried on by Men created first in their own Persons;

[1] *H.MSS. Polwarth*, ii. 75.

and if all such were now to be excluded I need not say what would be the ability of the House': a remark almost as true to-day as then and the most telling argument against any form of hereditary chamber. Addison, as a last effort in politics before his death, brought out *The Old Whig* in support of his former colleagues and as a counterblast to Steele's *Plebeian*; but it was hardly worthy of his ability or even of his good taste. He did not strengthen his quite reasonable point that Oxford's creations had been an abuse of the prerogative by the questionable statement that in ancient times the Crown had no such unlimited right of creating peers; nor was his argument very convincing that the House of Commons would be less liable to corruption if the Crown could no longer dangle peerages before its members, for there were plenty of other means of corruption available. But it is sad to find a writer of Addison's charm and urbanity descending to write of his old friend and coadjutor as 'little Dicky, whose trade it is to write pamphlets'. Steele, in all the heat of this violent political controversy, showed the finer spirit in always speaking of Addison with the respect and affection he never lost for him.[1]

The most damaging onslaught on the Bill, however, came from Walpole himself, who at last found a cause for attack worthy of his steel. In his *Thoughts of a Member of the Lower House* he argued that if the prerogative of creating peers were taken away,

'the House of Lords will be a fixed independent Body, not to be called to account like a Ministry, nor to be dissolved or changed like a House of Commons . . . [The Bill puts] King and Ministry entirely at the mercy of the Lords, and makes the Commons more dependent on the Crown. It takes away from the King the brightest jewel of his Crown, which is the distribution of Honours, and in effect of offices too, which must be at the mercy of that House. It deprives the Commons of England of the Means of attaining those honours which ought to be the Rewards of virtuous Actions, and the Motives of doing them. I presume no one will suggest that all Merit is exhausted by their present Lordships; and therefore what imaginary reason can be give . why any number of Men, who enjoy themselves the highest Dignities and Privileges in a Commonwealth, should shut the Door upon all others who may have equal Birth, Deserts and Fortunes?'

[1] Johnson, *Lives of the Poets*, essay on Addison.

The only advantage of the scheme, as he sarcastically observed in conclusion, was that it had produced a

> 'never-before-known Unanimity amongst our Great Men. It
> has yoked the Lion with the Lamb, the Whigs with the Tories,
> Men in Power with those they have turned out of it: Ministers
> of State are become Patriots, complain of their own Power, and
> join with their profess'd Enemies in lessening that Prerogative
> they have so often Occasion for.'

The incalculable Earl of Peterborough rushed into the fray with some *Remarks* against Walpole's pamphlet, which certainly did not impair its effect; and Walpole drove home his points in another pamphlet entitled *The Moderator*.[1]

But Stanhope and Sunderland had no intention of allowing the victory to rest with their opponents. They had merely dropped the Bill in order to bring it forward again in more favourable circumstances, for which they made careful preparation. In April they held a meeting with 160 of their supporters in the House of Commons to explain the advantages of the Bill.[2] Sunderland was especially active in impressing on office-holders their duty to forward the ministry's proposals, with no uncertain hints of the damage to their personal interests that opposition might entail. He tried to bully Brodrick, brother of the Irish Chancellor Midleton, who had a seat in the English House of Commons, and in an effort to overcome the opposition of Midleton himself became so excited that, like Walpole on another occasion, he had a violent effusion of blood from the nose. Thereafter he was unkindly referred to by Brodrick as 'the gentleman with the bloody nose'.[3] Stanhope, with his scholarly appreciation of classical and historical learning, sought to obtain arguments for his method of dealing with the Lords by inquiring of the abbé Vertot, a learned French writer on Roman history, by what system the Roman senate was recruited. He would have the abbé tell him whether the senatorial dignity once attained could be inherited, and what were the respective powers of dictators, consuls and censors in appointing senators: but it is doubtful if he got much satisfaction from the abbé's erudite answer.[4]

---

[1] *The Retrospective Review*, 2nd series, vol. ii (1828), has an account of this pamphlet war; the writer gives a list of 17 pamphlets for and 11 against the Bill; E. R. Turner, *E.H.R.*, xxviii. 249–54, gives the gist of the most important pamphlets.

[2] Michael, ii. 585, quoting reports in Vienna and Berlin archives.

[3] Coxe, *Walpole*, ii. 170–80, 217; Brodrick also speaks of him as 'the gent. whose nose bled', ib. 191; Torrens, i. 223.

[4] Stanhope's questions and the abbé's reply were published in 1721 in a

The most serious danger to the ministry's plans, however, came from opposition at court, darkly alluded to
by Newcastle as 'underhand insinuations of some and y^e
open opposition of others whom some People would fancy
had, if not ye first, at least a very great share of credit'.[1]
Cadogan was more than ever anxious to supplant Stanhope in the King's favour, since Marlborough's gradual
decay after his stroke in 1716 seemed to promise a speedy
vacancy in the office of Captain-General. He had begun
raising a party of his own within the ministerial ranks and
found some allies among the German courtiers who, according to Craggs, professed to be 'extremely concerned for
the King's prerogative, and, I fancy, do not despair some
day or other to be peers'.[2] So blank indeed seemed the prospect to Stanhope and Sunderland that there was renewed
talk of allowing Bolingbroke to return to England and even
of his bringing to the support of the ministry the Tories
loyal to the Protestant dynasty. But the mere rumour of
such a project seemed to promise greater difficulties than
it would overcome. Walpole, who allowed Bolingbroke to
return a few years later, now tried to lash up the Whigs into
a fury by the mere suggestion that it was intended to pardon
him. Writing of Oxford in his pamphlet on the Peerage Bill,
he alluded to 'his rival in guilt and power [who] even now
presumes to expect an act of the legislature to indemnify
him, and qualify his villainy, and I doubt not but both
expect once more to give laws to the kingdom'. However,
no such heroic remedy proved necessary; a meeting was
arranged by the King's mistress, the Duchess of Munster, between the two chief ministers and Bernstorff, and a working
arrangement was come to whereby the King's favour was
regained and the Peerage Bill was to be again introduced
in the next session; Cadogan himself was conveniently
dispatched on a diplomatic mission.[3]

From May to November 1719 Stanhope was in attendance
on the King in Hanover, responsible for the foreign policy

pamphlet entitled *A Memorial sent from London by the late Earl Stanhope to the Abbé
Vertot at Paris*. I have ventured to assume in the text that Stanhope's questions
had some bearing on the Peerage Bill; otherwise there seems no particular point
in the questions or in their publication.

[1] *Add. MSS.* 32686, f. 151, Newcastle to Stanhope, 14 Oct. 1719.
[2] *Stair Annals*, ii. 104, Craggs to Stair, 10 Mar. 1719. For Cadogan's rivalry
with Stanhope see above, ch. x, pp. 254-5.
[3] Michael, ii. 585-6 throws light on these events from reports of Bonet and
Hoffman in the Berlin and Vienna archives.

of both departments during a particularly anxious period. But by the autumn, when Sunderland joined him, the final success of his policy seemed assured. The French expedition to Spain had met with little resistance, the Spaniards could do nothing more in Sicily, and Alberoni had shot his last bolt. In the North Carteret had been sent to Stockholm and negotiations for bringing about peace between Sweden and all her enemies were in good train; above all, in spite of the Germans, Stanhope had brought to an end the senseless quarrel with Prussia, an object good in itself but also notable as the first decisive blow struck against the German influence on the internal as well as the external affairs of England. Stanhope and Sunderland were therefore able to plan a comprehensive programme for the following session, assured also of support at home, where, instead of the Prince of Wales, still in disgrace, the Regency was composed of officials such as Newcastle and Craggs, all devoted adherents of their absent chiefs.

The programme of legislation was no longer confined to the Peerage Bill, but included a comprehensive scheme for breaking the power of the Jacobites, High Churchmen, and disgusted Whigs, and so giving the existing government an almost unlimited lease of life. The first indications of the scheme appear in letters from Sunderland of October and November, written in the bullying tone characteristic of the writer. To Newcastle he writes in October:

> 'The King is more determined than ever to persist with vigour in the measures you and your friends wish; he is resolv'd to push the Peerage Bill, the University Bill and the Repeal of the Septennial Bill; if this won't unite the Wigs nothing will. The world will be convinced (by what the King will both say and do) that neither Bernstorff nor Cadogan have any Creditt and that he will not suffer any foreigner to meddle in Our affairs. This you may depend on.' [1]

To his supporter Carlisle he wrote more concisely in the following month, insisting on the King's determination to proceed with the Peerage Bill and, 'if the Whigs are reasonable in that, [with a measure] for effectually reforming the Universities, and every other Wig point'. [2] The Peerage Bill is clear enough, the object and form of the University Bill

---

[1] *Add. MSS.* 32686, f. 149, 22 Oct. 1719 (N.S.).
[2] *H. MSS., Carlisle*, 23, 18 Nov. 1719.

have already been described; but what exactly did Sunderland mean by the 'Repeal of the Septennial Bill'?

This measure to repeal the Septennial Act was never passed; it was not even introduced into Parliament; and so well kept was its secret that there is no contemporary explanation of its purport except in a couple of letters exchanged between Newcastle and Stanhope. Even those letters are far from clear. Sometimes a special difficulty occurs in obtaining historical evidence on notorious facts, a difficulty due to their very notoriety, which makes it unnecessary for those familiar with the facts to refer to them except by allusions not always clear to posterity. In this case both Newcastle and Stanhope knew well enough what the other was writing about, so did not trouble to be explicit about what we should much like to know. Was the proposed measure one merely to repeal the Septennial Act of 1715 and so revert to the Triennial Act? This is the view held by Torrens.[1] Or was it one to repeal the Septennial Act without setting any term to the duration of the existing Parliament? This is the view taken by the late Professor Turner[2] and Professor Michael,[3] both, like Torrens, expert judges of historical evidence.

Isolated phrases in Stanhope's letter[4] might be picked out in favour of the view taken by Torrens. It seems, for example, difficult to believe that Stanhope could have been arguing for so unconstitutional a measure as the indefinite prolongation of the existing House of Commons in such sentences as these:

'I will confess to your Grace that I think it for the interest of our countrey to repeal it [Septennial Act] if it stood singly on its merits. . . I am persuaded that it will some time or other force its way through. . . . At the same time give me leave my Dr. Ld. to tell you very freely my thought that if they are against repealing the Septennial I shall have very little hope of succeeding in the peerage.'

Further in support of Torrens's view it may be relevant to point out that if the phrase 'repealing the Septennial Act' be taken in its strictly legal sense, the only effect of such repeal would simply have been that the second section of the Triennial Act dealing with the duration of Parliament, the only section affected by the Septennial Act, would

[1] Torrens, i. 236–8.   [2] *E.H.R.*, xxviii. 255–6.   [3] Michael, ii. 593–5.
[4] Both letters are printed *in extenso* in Appendix E, p. 459.

automatically return into force; and also that the debates of 1734 on a motion to return to triennial parliaments is specifically described in the *Parliamentary History* as relating to the repeal of the Septennial Act. But the expressions of laymen writing to one another privately should not be measured too exactly by the minutiae of legal phraseology. It is hardly possible to doubt, from other phrases in Stanhope's letter—especially when he asks

'whether the most certain way to secure a majority for it [Peerage Bill], be not to secure at the same time in favour of all those, who think the continuance of this Parliament advantageous either to the public or to themselves, the power of continuing it'—

that his intention was to prolong the existence of the Parliament then sitting, not from any special desire to prolong it, but as a bribe to members to pass the Peerage Bill. For evidently that to him was the supreme object.

This view is fully confirmed by the whole trend of Newcastle's argument against Stanhope's proposal, based on the view that

'I cannot apprehend we have any Reason to fear coming to a new Election provided this Parliam^t setts out its time. . . . Should this Parliament be continued it would show a great distrust of ye King's interest in England, and look as if our past conduct wd not be approved of, when on ye contrary we have all ye reason to think yt before this parliam^t ends, ye King's affairs will be upon so glorious a foot it will [be] almost impossible to oppose him;'

and he then characteristically enters into election calculations, ending with the complacent view that,

'by a new Election Mr. Walpole and ye few friends His Party will be able to bring in, will be so incorporated wth ye Jacobites, yt we shall have but little difficulty in dealing with them.'

Stanhope was apparently convinced by Newcastle's arguments, since nothing more was ever heard of this particular Bill, which would assuredly have been introduced at the same time as the Peerage Bill, if, as Stanhope suggests, it was to be used as an inducement to the Commons to pass that measure. In fact, by December Craggs was writing of an alternative scheme for an early election as a means of 'frightening some of our mutinous friends into better manners'.[1] But that Stanhope's and Sunderland's original

---

[1] Mahon, *History*, ii, Appendix, Craggs to Stanhope, 27 Dec. 1719.

idea was to extend the existing Parliament beyond its legal
term is further confirmed by the numerous allusions in
contemporary letters to the possibility of such an extension,
allusions that prove incontestably that such a scheme was
in the air. In May 1720 Governor Pitt writes of 'continuing
the old Parliament' as a possible means of 'eradicating
corruption'; and in the following year a correspondent of
the Molesworths observes that 'the well-disposed do not
know whether to wish for a prolongation of this Parliament
for two or three years or for its conclusion in March next
at the end of its term'.[1] In June of the same year Walpole himself, then in office, was in favour of a prolongation,
'believing he will hardly be able to influence and conduct
another as he has this Parliament'; while Sunderland had
changed round and in his turn was against the experiment.[2]

As originally conceived this triple scheme of Stanhope's
and Sunderland's seems a strange product of Stanhope's
Revolution principles. The House of Lords was to remain
fixed in its existing composition, with a majority favourable
to the government, that could never be impaired by the
Prince of Wales or any other future sovereign; the House
of Commons was to be bribed by a temporary prolongation of its own lease, so as to postpone an election which
might prove unfavourable to ministers; lastly the Universities, the main sources of supply for recruits to politics, the
learned professions and literature, were to be purged of the
taint of opposition principles by government control. Such
a ruthless attempt to overbear all opposition and render the
government unassailable is far less in the style of such Revolution leaders as Somers than of the Rebellion hero Cromwell,
whom in foreign politics Stanhope took as a model. It must,
however, be admitted that in his domestic politics Stanhope
was generally more faithful to the ideas of the Revolution.
The only excuse to be found for such a violent interference
with comparatively free institutions was that of imminent
national danger. To us who can judge after the event there
seems no adequate reason for such panic legislation: but
Stanhope and his friends may well be excused for over-
estimating the danger to the state. Only three years had
passed since the Rebellion, which might have been even more
serious had the Jacobites been more enterprising. This very

---

[1] H.MSS., Dropmore, i. 65; H.MSS., Clements, 313; see also ib. 312, 318.
[2] Coxe, Walpole, ii. 217–19, Brodrick to Middleton, 10 June 1721.

year Ormonde's attempt to rouse the West had failed only
because God's wind had blown once more, while a tiny
force of Spaniards and rebels had been able to land in Scotland and for two months to gather sympathizers without
molestation. When the scheme was being formulated,
Alberoni, unresting in his search for Jacobite and foreign
enemies against England, was still the powerful minister
of Spain. There was as yet no real peace in Europe, and
England's divisions seemed to offer her enemies their
opportunity. Jacobites, Tories, disgusted Whigs, under the
aegis of the heir to the throne himself, carped at every action
of the government even for the defence of the country, the
King's Germans themselves were showing a disposition to
obstruct their King's government, and Atterbury's plot only
three years later showed that the dynasty was not safe even
from members of the legislature.

But whatever the dangers may have been, they could
hardly have been worse than the oligarchic remedy devised
by Sunderland and Stanhope. Fortunate was it that Stanhope was warned in time against one part of his scheme
by his young friend Newcastle, who, whatever his faults,
usually had a fairly acute perception of what the country
would stand. Above all, Newcastle was shrewd in calculating
how far he could carry members of the House of Commons, in
whose choice he took so diligent a part, both of them branches
of political craftsmanship in which Stanhope was singularly
deficient. But on the Peerage Bill the ministers were left to
their fate.

At first all the omens seemed favourable to the measure.
On the very day after Parliament met, 23 November (o.s.),
Alberoni was dismissed, peace had been made with Sweden,
and even the most carping critics had little to say against
Stanhope's triumphant diplomacy; the hated Germans
had been told not to meddle with English affairs and
there was even a prospect of reconciliation in the royal
family. In the House of Lords the Peerage Bill was passed
again within a week. In the House of Commons itself its
passage seemed almost assured up to the very eve of the
session, for at a meeting of dissentient Whigs held at Devonshire House the opinion at first was almost unanimous that
they could not consistently oppose a measure intended to
prevent so scandalous an abuse of the prerogative as Oxford's
simultaneous creation of twelve peers. This argument seemed

all the more irresistible since Townshend and others of the party in the House of Lords had already approved of it in principle. But such timid counsellors had reckoned without Walpole, who was one of the last to speak at this party meeting. Brushing aside all minor considerations, he went to the root of the matter. With a sound appreciation of the principle that it was the business of an opposition to oppose, he refused to give away so glorious an opportunity of harassing a government, against which, so he said, there was a rising spirit of discontent in the country. With all his parliamentary skill and his great financial ability there was much of the rough and ready Squire Western in Walpole, and he knew his country gentlemen to the bone.

'He was sure', he said, 'he could put it in such a light as to fire with indignation at it every independent commoner in England. . . . That the first discovery of this to him was from what he overheard one Mr. —— member for —— say upon it, a plain country gentleman, of about eight hundred pounds a year of a rank equal only to that and with no expectations or views to himself beyond what his condition at that time gave him. But this person talking . . . with heat and some oaths (which was what Mr. Walpole overheard and catched at), "What! shall I consent to the shutting the door upon my family ever coming into the House of Lords?" The same sentiment', concluded Walpole, with his magnificent instinct for a popular electioneering cry, 'the same sentiment might easily be made to run through the whole body of country gentlemen, be their estates then what they would; for my part I am determined that if deserted by my party on this question, I will singly stand forth and oppose it.'

At first there was much confusion and even resentment at Walpole's attitude, but in the end his common sense told, and it was resolved to oppose the Bill with all the strength of the party in the House of Commons.[1]

This decision sealed the fate of the measure in the Commons. When the motion for its commitment was made on 18 December member after member rose to attack it, while its supporters made a very poor figure. Methuen, a former colleague of Stanhope's, spoke against the Bill, and so did Lechmere, an independent member who had only recently attacked Walpole. Stanhope's father-in-law, the 'testy and humoursome' Governor Pitt, taxed the projectors of the Bill with 'mean obsequiousness to foreigners and with

---

[1] *H.MSS.*, *Report XIV*. ix. 459 (*Onslow MSS.*), Speaker Onslow's account.

designs against the liberties of their countrymen'. Sir John
Packington, a much respected country gentleman, reproduced
Walpole's argument at the party meeting, declaring that

> 'the principal design of the ministry was to give one family the
> disposal of all honours and favours. . . . For my own part, I
> never desire to be a lord, but I have a son who may one day
> have that ambition; and I hope to leave to him a better claim
> to it than a certain gentleman (meaning General Stanhope) had,
> when he was made a peer.'

Finally Walpole clinched the matter by stressing the power
it would give the House of Lords and showing how it would
take away all incentive to good service to the state. He
talked of the honours of the peerage as

> 'the constitutional reward of great qualities and actions only in
> the service of the Commonwealth and to be kept open for that
> purpose. The usual path to the Temple of Honour has been
> through the Temple of Virtue; but if this Bill is passed into
> a law, one of the most powerful incentives to virtue would be
> taken away, since there would be no arriving at honour, but
> through the winding sheet of an old decrepit lord, or the grave
> of an extinct noble family. . . . It is a matter of just surprise', he
> continued, 'that a bill of this nature should either have been
> projected or at least promoted by a gentleman [Stanhope], who
> was not long ago seated amongst us, and who having got into
> the House of Peers, is now desirous of shutting the door after
> him. . . . How can the Lords expect the Commons to give their
> concurrence to a bill by which they and their posterity are to
> be for ever excluded from the peerage? . . . That this bill will
> secure the liberty of parliament, I totally deny; it will secure a
> great preponderance to the peers. . . . If gentlemen will not be
> convinced by argument, at least let them not shut their ears
> to the dreadful example of former times; let them recollect that
> the overweening disposition of the great barons, to aggrandize
> their own dignity, occasioned them to exclude the lesser barons,
> and to that circumstance may be fairly attributed the san-
> guinary laws which so long desolated the country.'

This was the parting kick. The division was taken and
the Bill summarily rejected by 269 votes to 177.[1] Nothing
more thereafter was heard in Parliament of any portion
of Stanhope's and Sunderland's great scheme for reforming
the Universities, repealing the Septennial Act, or limiting the
House of Lords by the Peerage Bill.[2]

---

[1] Ib.; *P.H.* vii. 609–27.
[2] Although the provisions relating to the English peerage were definitely

This was a triumph for Walpole and for Walpole alone, without whom the Bill would almost certainly have gone through. And it not only showed Walpole's power, when he chose to exert himself in a worthy cause, but also his statesmanship. For the Bill was thoroughly bad, and, though it was partly directed against an abuse of prerogative, clearly the best way of correcting such abuse was not to create a worse abuse by taking away the prerogative altogether. Had the Peerage Bill become law, the House of Lords would have become firmly entrenched as a narrow oligarchy subject to no restraint from King or Commons—a permanent obstacle to progress. No doubt at some time of strong popular feeling its power would have become so intolerable that it would have been necessary to abolish it or radically to reform it long before our time, perhaps even at the cost of a revolution. But meantime it would have made the House of Commons almost powerless. The main argument, one on which Walpole relied as a means of destroying the measure, may not have been the most inspiring, but at any rate it was a commonsense way of viewing the matter and achieved its object. After this victory Stanhope recognized that such a man could no longer be dispensed with as a support to his own great conception of securing the Protestant system on a sound basis at home and abroad. Soon afterwards he found it possible as well as advisable to reunite the two wings of the Whig party by taking Walpole and his friends into partnership. This was well, because Stanhope was not fitted to be a great leader in domestic politics; nor had he a wise counsellor in the violent and impetuous Sunderland. Unlike Walpole, and unlike his own nephew Chatham, Stanhope had not the inestimable advantage of having been born and bred in England and so understanding almost instinctively the needs and innermost feelings of his countrymen. Had he had this advantage he would never have committed his cardinal mistake of fathering the Peerage Bill; nor perhaps,

dropped after this decisive vote, it appears that Sunderland and Stanhope still had some idea of proceeding with the Scottish provisions. On 13 Jan. 1720/1 Carteret writes to Polwarth, 'I believe before this session is up that a bill will be brought in with relation to the Scots peerage. The English part of the bill will be dropped'; and again on 30 Jan., referring to a talk with Stanhope, 'It is in a manner agreed upon to settle the peerage of Scotland before this session ends by passing if possible that part of the Peerage Bill which relates to that kingdome and to leave out all what related in that bill to England, which has occasioned so warm disputes.' H.MSS., Polwarth, iii. 30, 37, and 33. But after Stanhope's death nothing more was heard even of this part of the project.

on the other hand, would he have yielded to his generous impulse to repeal the Test Act so far as it concerned the Dissenters or to soften the lot of the Roman Catholics, as he might have realized that on those two points Englishmen were not as yet ripe for concession. Fortunately he did realize that with his altogether exceptional knowledge of Europe, far greater than his knowledge of his own country, his real place was as foreign minister, and that an alliance with Walpole was essential for a prudent and sympathetic conduct of home affairs.

CHAPTER XV

THE LAST YEAR—ENGLAND'S DEBT TO STANHOPE

IN contrast to his triumphant achievements of 1719, Stanhope's last year seems one of disillusionment and failure. Abroad a settlement with the Tsar, the one link needed in his chain of treaties and alliances to secure peace in the North, was not attained by him; even his great success in bringing Spain to accept the terms of the Quadruple Alliance was quickly followed by the alienation of the Emperor, no longer in need of England's support, the wrangle with Spain about Gibraltar, and the temporary cooling off of France's ardour for the alliance. At home he had to resist a final effort of the Hanoverians, with the aid of Tories and dissentient Whigs, to recover their ground and upset his policy; then the fair prospect of a reunited Whig party was clouded over by the scandals of the South Sea Bubble, while a venomous attack against his own probity, baseless as it was, embittered even his last moments. But with all these rebuffs Stanhope himself never appears so great as in this last year, meeting his difficulties with all the vigour and serene self-confidence of former years and carrying on the country's business to the end.

§ 1

Before he left for Hanover with the King in the summer of 1720 he was called upon to deal with a plot contrived by Bernstorff and the opposition Whigs to upset the ministry and undo the whole structure of his foreign policy. After his defeat on the Prussian treaty in July 1719, Bernstorff's meddlesome activities were further restricted by a 'resolution the King has taken not to suffer his Germans to meddle in English affairs, he having forbidden them to presume so much as to speak to him about them'.[1] At first Bernstorff, assuming a mask of humility and deference to Stanhope, seemed to accept defeat, but he was really biding his time for revenge. The busy secretary, Robethon, hitherto

---

[1] This decision is reported by Sunderland in a letter to Carlisle of 18 Nov. 1719 (o.s.), *H.MSS.*, *Carlisle*, 23. A rumour of it reached Polwarth, who on 8/19 Dec. 1719 asks Robethon if it was true, *H.MSS.*, *Polwarth*, ii. 403.

Bernstorff's trusted confidant, was the first to suffer, for he was suspected of being too much in the interest of the English ministers, and in August he complained to Polwarth that Bernstorff was quite altered to him and no longer cared for correspondence to go through him; the breach was complete by the following year, when Bernstorff gave Carteret 'very freely... a very disadvantageous account of Mr. Rhobethon... The other ministers excuse Rhobethon . . . but yet they don't love him & say that if he has committed faults, that it is Mr. Bernstorff who has spoiled him.'[1] Very soon too Bernstorff again, so far as he dared, began undermining Stanhope's policy. In December 1719 he was accused of doing 'the utmost of his power to support the Danes & ... the Danes were persuaded of that to such a degree that it made them unreasonable' about restoring Stralsund and Rügen to Sweden.[2] But his master-stroke was not matured till the following year, when the ministry had sustained a serious blow in the rejection of the Peerage Bill and Walpole had once more, during the early discussions on the South Sea scheme, displayed that mastery of finance in which Sunderland and Aislabie were sadly deficient. Taking advantage of this apparent weakness, Bernstorff, in spite of the prohibition against interference with English politics, had engaged in intrigues with some of the 'disgusted' Whigs and with them insinuated to the King that the ministry aimed at reducing him to a cipher and securing autocratic power for themselves.

The plot was first discovered by Sunderland in April 1720, when he was shown a copy of a letter from Bernstorff to the Imperial Vice-Chancellor Sinzendorff containing full details of the intrigue. Bernstorff's choice of a confidant seems curious, but is explained by the fact that Sinzendorff was the most uncompromising opponent at Vienna of Stanhope's efforts to alleviate the persecution of Protestants in the Empire and to draw the Emperor into a coalition against the Tsar; on both points Bernstorff had been his determined if secret ally.[3] In his letter Bernstorff describes the efforts of the 'disgusted Whigs' to convince the King of the evil designs of the 'Cabal' as the ministry is called, who were 'amusing' him with a peace in the South and planning 'to keep the

---

[1] *H.MSS., Polwarth*, ii. 249, iii. 11.
[2] Ib. ii. 388, Carteret to Polwarth, 25 Nov. 1719 (o.s.).
[3] See above, ch. xiii, p. 370.

Czar from a peace in the North' till with the help of Spain
and France they could renew the war in the North and disturb
the peace of the Empire, all as means, not clearly indicated,
of 'running the nation into an Aristocracy as appears by
the frame of the South Sea Bill . . . so as to establish themselves, & be able for the future to give laws to the King &
his son, & even remove them when they shall think proper'.
After this exordium he indicates the scheme concocted to
frustrate the 'Cabal's' evil designs and reverse Stanhope's
foreign policy. Good terms are to be offered to Spain
to secure the South Sea trade and enable the Company to
advance two or three millions to the King as a fund for
bribing the Tsar and other princes of the North to be at
his devotion. Other items in this new programme for
readjusting England's continental relations were to secure
Poland by advancing enough money to Augustus of Saxony
to purchase the hereditary succession to that crown and
so help 'to keep the power of France within bounds' and to
purchase 'some country contiguous . . to the King's German
Dominions, which would enable him to hold the balance
between the Northern powers better than by sending a fleet
yearly to the Baltic, which gives umbrage to the people',
a surprising proposal from those who had objected to
the acquisition of Bremen and Verden by Hanover and the
trouble in which it had involved England. It would be
well, Bernstorff adds, to send an Imperial minister as soon
as possible to London to watch the Cabal and 'find out what
clandestine measures may be carried on with France, which
if not timely discovered, may tend to the prejudice of both
our Masters. You are sensible how dangerous it is to trust
Ministers abandoned to their pleasures, for such have more
than once been corrupted by France.' For the time being
the King should be advised 'to dissemble' so as to give the
Cabal rope to hang themselves and give Bernstorff's friends
'better opportunity to provide ourselves with honest men'
for a new ministry, to be composed of Walpole, Townshend
and other seceding Whigs; there would also 'be roome for
five or six of the leading country Tories to come in for the
rest of the places'. The only existing ministers for whom
offices would be found were Sunderland and Stanhope,
probably thought to be too much in the King's favour to be
entirely displaced, but Sunderland was to be sent over to
Ireland and Stanhope relegated either to the Privy Seal or

to a military command as 'Generall of Horse', where they could do no harm. It is hard to believe, in spite of Bernstorff's assertion, that Walpole and Townshend really countenanced this fantastic scheme; and it bears all the marks of having sprung from Bernstorff's German brain. Even he foresaw some difficulty in carrying it through, for in conclusion he suggests that it might be useful for 'his Imperial Majesty to assist the King with his troops from the Netherlands on any emergent occasion'.[1]

Sunderland was put 'not into a little fright', according to the Harleys' informant, by the contents of this letter, which he at once showed to Craggs and Stanhope. The three ministers evidently thought the letter genuine and took the plot seriously. Within three days they had made their counter plan, it is not known at whose suggestion, but the promptness with which their counter measures were carried out and their devastating effect seem to indicate Stanhope's handiwork. Stanhope was probably not much alarmed at the prospect of any English ministry accepting Bernstorff's ill-digested scheme of foreign policy. But there was a real danger of being supplanted by the Walpole and Townshend section of the Whigs. To avert this danger the plan was to steal the enemy's thunder and divert the lightning that was to blast Bernstorff's enemies by a conductor that would render it innocuous. In principle, Stanhope had no objection to widening the basis of the ministry; for he had always recognized its weakness against the phalanx of Hanover Tories and disgusted Whigs. He had been quite willing to make terms with his friend and rival Bolingbroke after he had left the Pretender's service and seemed disposed to educate the Tories in loyal Hanoverian principles.[2] But the proposal to reverse his attainder had fallen to the ground after Walpole's declaration that he would resist it. Another alternative was to resume relations with those very Whigs who, according to Bernstorff, were trying to supplant the ministry. As long as Walpole's opposition had been merely factious he was neither a serious danger nor worth conciliat-

---

[1] Several English translations (with slight variations) of the original letter written in 'High Dutch' by Bernstorff to Sinzendorff in April 1720 are extant. One is in R.O., S.P. Dom. Geo. I, 21 (43), others are in H.MSS., Portland, v. 594 sqq., with a covering letter of 7 May to one of the Harleys, and H.MSS., Townshend, 104–5. Michael, ii. 613 also mentions a translation of it in French sent to Paris by the French envoy Chammorel on 29 Apr. 1720.

[2] See above, ch. x, pp. 258 sqq.

ing: but recently he had been showing renewed public spirit
and undeniable power. So terms were proposed to Walpole
and his friends.

The negotiations offered but one serious difficulty, that
Walpole insisted on a reconciliation between the King and
the Prince of Wales as a condition of his joining the ministry,
and there the obstacle was not in Stanhope and Sunderland but in the King himself. For three years he had kept
his son as a pariah from the court and almost from society
and still would not hear of forgiving what he deemed his
insolent insubordination. However, Walpole undertook to
obtain from the Prince a complete and unconditional submission to his father; Stanhope, Sunderland and Craggs,
only too glad to put an end to a public scandal and a source
of unpopularity to the dynasty, agreed on their part to persuade the King to accept it. The task was none too easy
in either case; the Prince and Princess were being urged by
the self-opinionated ex-Chancellor, Lord Cowper, to make
conditions for submission which Walpole knew to be in-
admissible, and at last persuaded them to abandon; Stanhope, Sunderland and Craggs found it even harder to
overcome the King's obstinate rancour against his son: 'Can't
the Whigs come back without him?' was all he would say
at first. But at last matters were arranged: on Saturday
23 April (o.s.), 'St. George's Day Patron of England', as Lady
Cowper notes in her diary, the Prince sent a humble letter
to his father and Craggs was sent back with the Prince's
emissary with a message that his son might appear at court.
Up to that point the negotiations had been carried on with
the utmost secrecy, and 'not ten men in all England', wrote
Pulteney to his cousin, had an inkling of what was toward.[1]
Then suddenly on that St. George's Day Stanhope burst in
on the courtiers in the 'outward room' at St. James's, went
up to the two German ministers Bernstorff and Bothmer
and, in the words of Lady Cowper, who witnessed the scene,
said in French to them in his shrill scream,

'Eh bien! Messieurs, la Paix est faite . . . la Paix est faite.
B.—Les Lettres sont-elles arrivées?
S.—Non, non, c'est la Paix ici. Nous allons revoir notre
     Prince.
B.—Notre Prince?

[1] Coxe, *Walpole*, ii. 186, W. to D. Pulteney, 7 May 1720.

S.—Oui, notre Prince, notre Prince; nous l'attendons pour
être reconcilié avec le Roy.

B.—Monsieur, vous avez été bien secret dans vos Affaires.

S.—Oui, oui, nous l'avons été . . . le Secret est toujours nécessaire pour faire les bonnes Choses.

'Bothmar could not bear the Insult, nor the being given up
by his old Master, and burst into tears, which was very faithfully
reported to the Prince and Princess.'

Inside the closet, however, the King was performing his
part with an ill grace. 'Votre conduite, votre conduite', was
all he could find to mutter as the Prince knelt before him
protesting his penitence; and he would hardly speak to him
when they met at the Royal Chapel or at Court in the next
few days. But he was quite affable in a long talk he had with
'cette diablesse Mme la Princesse'; and he allowed his son
to return from the Palace with his guard and the drums
beating, much to the joy of the London mob who huzzaed
and lit bonfires to their hearts' content to celebrate the
family reunion.[1]

Stanhope and Sunderland gained a cheap victory over
Bernstorff and the 'disgusted Whigs'. Of these last only
three, Walpole, Townshend and Methuen, got places in
the ministry and those of little account, Walpole becoming Paymaster, Townshend President of the Council, and
Methuen a Household official—places of a like kind to those
reserved for Stanhope and Sunderland themselves, had Bernstorff's scheme been carried out. Bernstorff himself had
at last to own defeat. He went over to Hanover with the
King in June, but never again returned to England or
ventured to interfere in English politics. The reconciliation
of King and Prince, the price demanded by Walpole for
ceasing opposition, so far from weakening, strengthened the
government, which had suffered in popular estimation from
the royal quarrel, and depressed the hopes of the Jacobites.[2]
Above all Stanhope was freer than ever to pursue his
European policy; and when the catastrophe of the South
Sea Bubble followed a few months later, Walpole, the man
best fitted to deal with the difficulty, was ready to do so
without further bargaining. After the political estrangement

---

[1] Lady Cowper, 128–54, has an account of the negotiations for reconciliation
as viewed by the Prince and Princess of Wales's entourage; Michael, ii. 611 sqq.,
adds some details from reports of foreign ministers in London.

[2] See Atterbury's letter quoted in Mahon, *History*, ii. 3.

had ceased, the old social relations were soon resumed. Sunderland appears as host on two occasions; of the second, in July, when Stanhope was in Hanover, Craggs wrote that the guests at dinner were the Dukes of Devonshire and Newcastle, Lords Carleton, Townshend and Lumley, 'the Speaker and Walpole and I, we got very drunk and others very merry'.[1] Even the ladies on both sides began to exchange civilities, the only exception being Stanhope's sister-in-law Mrs. Robert Pitt, whose husband belonged to the Prince's household. It was foolish of him not to follow his master's example and be reconciled, wrote the wife of Governor Pitt to her daughter-in-law:

'the Duke of Devonshire began, and so it has held on ever since. Nay the ladies too was so inclined to friendship that they did the same. My Lady Townsend and Mrs. Worpoole came to your sister Stanhope the next day to invite her; so that they which stands out now are petty singular, for the Prince and Princes has returned thanks to your brother Stanhope for the great services he has done to the nation and to them. So you see when eyes are opened and malitious storys sett in a true light, what vast alterations it maks in opinions, which I pray God give us all grace and humility to consider as we ought.'[2]

§ 2

Stanhope's spells of duty as minister in attendance on the King at Hanover are the periods in which he appears in his most fertile and expansive mood. More at the centre of the European web at Hanover than in London, he was in closer touch with the Northern problems which preoccupied him so much and he had more personal control of affairs in both the Northern and Southern province. For at Hanover, being alone able to take the King's immediate orders, he corresponded directly with English representatives and foreign ministers in both provinces, leaving little to his colleague in London beyond the duty of keeping the Lords Justices informed of his activities. Not that he ever used his opportunity at Hanover to drive his colleague out of business, as Newcastle and perhaps Carteret tried to do in similar circumstances; but, wherever he happened to be, he was

---

[1] Coxe, *Walpole*, ii. 189, Craggs to Stanhope.
[2] *H.MSS., Dropmore*, i. 64–5, Jane Pitt to Hon. Mrs. Pitt, 7 May 1720. The allusion to humility was no doubt a home-thrust at Mrs. Robert, who being a Villiers probably had no large share of that virtue.

the mainspring of foreign policy and from Hanover could act more promptly and decisively. This, his last sojourn at Hanover, from mid-June to November of 1720, was as full of activity as any of his former visits had been, with work almost as anxious as during the formation of the Quadruple Alliance.

He had too his distractions. There was his own visit to Berlin, and Frederick William's second visit to Hanover, when Stanhope gave a dinner party to him and his own King and waited bare-headed in the street to see their coaches roll away. We also get another pleasant glimpse from Josiah Wilcocks, the chaplain who recorded Frederick William's love of a blue uniform, this time of Stanhope at his devotions. Taking comfort in the thought that 'affairs of religion is likely to take a good turn in the Empire & be amicably accommodated', Wilcocks proceeds: 'My Lord Stanhope's concern for the Protestant interest in general is accompanied with a very exemplary behaviour at Hanover: we have a Chapel in the Court, where his Lordship has never yet failed of coming on Sundays with his family, & my congregation is now pretty considerable.'[1]

In July he received the cheering news from Carteret that the treaty between Sweden and Denmark had been settled:[2] but there was still no treaty between Sweden and Russia, which England was now engaged to secure on the most favourable terms possible for Sweden. To persuade, therefore, or oblige, the Tsar to relinquish some of the Baltic provinces conquered from Sweden as a condition of peace was one of his main preoccupations. Norris had once more been sent to the Baltic in April with Instructions to support Sweden against any Russian attack, but at the same time to forward to the Tsar an offer of the King's mediation for a treaty.[3] However, his errand this year was as bootless as the last. His letters proposing mediation were returned unopened; and his attempts to find and engage the Russian fleet were not only unsuccessful but did not even deter the

[1] Ellis, *Original Letters*, 2nd Series, iv. 320, Wilcocks to Kennett (Bp. of Peterborough). Wilcocks's courtly and pious sentiments were rewarded by the bishopric of Gloucester in the following year. It is tempting to believe that Stanhope's 'family' might refer to his wife and children; but there is no record of their being at Hanover, and *family* often meant the secretary and clerks of a minister. Wives, even the Duchess of Newcastle, seem never to have been asked to accompany their husbands to Hanover.
[2] See above, ch. xiii, p. 380.
[3] *Instructions, Sweden*, i. 142–3.

Russian galleys from perpetrating another raid on the Swedish coast. He looked into Reval, but decided it was impregnable and duly returned home in the autumn.

Early in 1720 it was borne in upon Stanhope that the Tsar could not be brought to terms merely by a naval demonstration in the Baltic. So he set about raising an armed coalition to attack Russia on two sides, through Finland and Livonia. But the circumstances were unpropitious. France, to whom he looked for subsidies, in the early part of the year showed marked coldness to his proposal. The Emperor was too much taken up with religious troubles and with other grievances against George I to take part in distant expeditions; he was even suspected of entertaining the idea of an understanding with the Tsar.[1] The Turks, who might have been inclined to divert Peter's attention, were kept quiet by Bonac, the anti-English French Ambassador at the Porte.[2] Prussia as the price of attacking the Tsar required the cession of Stralsund and Rügen, which had just been returned to Sweden at France's request. The last hope of peace seemed to come from an offer addressed by Admiral Apraksin on behalf of the Tsar to Norris and Finch, the envoy at Stockholm. Stanhope first heard of Apraksin's offer during his visit to Berlin in July, and persuaded Frederick William to write personally to the Tsar offering his joint mediation with England for a peace between Russia and Sweden.[3] But nothing came of this offer. By October Stanhope was relunctantly forced to admit that he could do nothing more to help Sweden. He accordingly wrote to Finch and Norris urging the Swedes to make the best terms they could with Russia, and to do so as soon as possible, lest worse should befall them.[4] By this time relations with the Tsar's government had been definitely broken off. At the beginning of the year an angry correspondence between Stanhope and the Russian ambassador Veselovsky had been published: and in October

---

[1] R.O., *S.P.* 44/270, Stanhope to Cadogan and St. Saphorin, 15/26 July 1720, gives Stanhope's scheme for a coalition against the Tsar; but writing to Finch, 4 Nov. 1720 (N.S.), Stanhope declared the Emperor to be definitely committed to the Tsar.

[2] R.O., *S.P.* 44/270, Stanhope to Sutton, 15/26 July 1720; Stanhope to Stanyan, Cadogan, St. Saphorin and Craggs in June and July on Bonac's intrigues at the Porte.

[3] R.O., *S.P.* 44/270, Letters on the Apraksin offer from Stanhope to Delafaye, Finch and Norris of 11 and 13 July 1720 (O.S.).

[4] *Instructions, Sweden*, i. 146–50.

he had peremptorily ordered Veselovsky's successor Bestuzhef
to leave the country within a week for publishing an abusive
letter against the English government.[1] The fact was that
Peter was in an impregnable position in the Baltic; and he
knew it. When he was told that the Swedes must at least
have Reval restored to them, his answer was: 'Let them
come and take it, if they can.'

Stanhope did not live to see the final defeat of his valiant
efforts to save Sweden from the loss of her former empire
and to prevent Russia becoming the dominant power in the
Baltic. By the Peace of Nystad of September 1721 Sweden
ceded to Russia Livonia, Esthonia, Ingria and part of
Carelia, including the principal ports on the farther side
of the Baltic, Riga, Reval, Narva and Viborg, everything
in fact that Stanhope had tried to recover for Sweden. On
the other hand, Finland was restored to Sweden; and the
Tsar agreed not to interfere in the internal affairs of the
kingdom even on behalf of his protégé the Duke of Holstein.
To the English government the most galling feature was that
whereas George I had claimed to be a party to the treaty,
the only reference to him was a contemptuous admission
by the Tsar that he would discuss mutual grievances in a
friendly spirit. Stanhope's main objection to such a settlement had always been his fear that Russian domination of
the Baltic would seriously endanger English trade, especially
since Peter had steadily refused to consider a favourable
commercial treaty. Stanhope, however, like all other European statesmen of the day, had always underestimated the
lasting power of the 'semi-barbarian upstart', just as he had
always exaggerated the danger to England of his victory.
After Nystad English merchants were not molested to any
serious extent in their Baltic and Russian trade; and within
thirteen years came the first of a series of advantageous commercial treaties with Russia. In fact, till after the middle of
the century, France suffered far more than England from the
new phenomenon of Russian interference in the politics of
western Europe. Stanhope should not, however, be unduly
blamed for his miscalculation about the mysterious power
inherent in the Muscovite dominions and people. Even to-day,
when means of communication are infinitely better than they

---

[1] R.O., *S.P.* 44/271, Stanhope to Delafaye, 1 Oct. 1720 (o.s.); the shrill
Stanhope-Veselovsky correspondence is set forth in Boyer, xix. 154 sqq. and
elsewhere.

were in Stanhope's day, there is still profound ignorance in western Europe of Russian conditions and of the character of the Russian people. Russia is still to a large extent a closed country, partly through the Russians' own fault, as it was under Peter the Great and long afterwards, partly owing to the unwillingness or inability of foreigners to make themselves familiar with the country and its inhabitants. In Stanhope's time Jeffreyes, the accredited agent of the government to Russia, for long sent his reports, often on mere rumour, of events in Russia from the Polish port of Danzig:[1] in our own time for several years since the recent Revolution England had no representative in Russia and even now the chief English newspaper derives its accounts of Russian affairs from a correspondent stationed at Riga, no longer in Russian territory. As we can see more clearly to-day, the Treaty of Nystad was nothing more than a recognition of the inevitable. Sweden had enjoyed her brief period of dominion and European importance during the seventeenth century, but had overshot her bolt, especially after Charles XII had almost sucked dry the life-blood of the country by his unceasing wars. Had it not been Peter, some other ruler would have gathered in Sweden's inheritance; Peter it was, because, contrary to the opinion of the rest of Europe, he had been able by enduring reforms to make Russia for the first time a Power able to hold her own with the greatest Powers in Europe. But this is almost the solitary instance of Stanhope's miscalculation of European forces.

Stanhope's failure to bring about peace with Russia and the Emperor's uncertain attitude were not the only troubles he had during his last sojourn in Hanover. During his flying visits to Paris in January and March 1720 he seemed to have adjusted the difficulties with France about Law and Gibraltar,[2] but new difficulties kept cropping up. In June Stair, since he could not get on with Law, then the most powerful man in France, was finally recalled and succeeded by Sir Robert Sutton. Stair, though his arrogant and suspicious disposition had latterly tended to diminish his utility, had on the whole forwarded Stanhope's policy well and had maintained his country's interests and dignity in

---

[1] See letters of Jeffreyes from Danzig in *H.MSS.*, *Polwarth*, iii, *passim*. He had been ejected from Russia by the Tsar and stayed at Danzig largely in the hope of being readmitted.   [2] See above, ch. xii, pp. 344-5, 348-9.

Paris: but his successor was a disappointment. Craggs complained that, going to the other extreme from Stair, he made himself too cheap with Law, and Stanhope himself came to recognize that Stair had not been so far wrong in his estimate of the Scottish financier.[1] Law's language and threats against England became more outrageous the more settled he became in the saddle. Dubois was for the time being put completely in the shade by the all-powerful Controller-General and his allies the old Huxelles-Torcy camarilla, inveterate foes of the parvenu archbishop and of his English friends. Sabres were rattled and menaces uttered which could no longer be ignored. In July angry dispatches came from Craggs and Stanhope bidding Sutton protest against 'the strange unprovoked language which Mr. Law constantly used against this Nation', the attempts by France to take the mediation of peace with the Tsar entirely out of England's hands, the anti-English activities of Bonac at Constantinople, and, above all, suspicious military preparations made by France, apparently in collusion with Spain and the Jacobites. Craggs went so far as to inform the French ambassador that 'the King had given Orders to arm some ships for the preservation of our Coast, & a squadron is actually fitted out, though under a different pretence & not to alarm the country'.[2] For several months more the alarm continued. Spain's designs on Gibraltar were by no means laid aside, and the help of France to recover that fortress was, with some show of reason, reckoned upon by Philip. As late as October fears of a French diversion in North America obliged Stanhope to authorize reinforcements of four battalions to Nova Scotia, four more to Carolina and a detachment to the West Indies;[3] while the squadron recently equipped was stationed at Port Mahon and the defences of Gibraltar strengthened, all the more owing to the malicious rumour quoted by Delafaye that ministers were so intent on giving up Gibraltar to Spain that they wanted to let Spain appear to conquer it.[4]

[1] Coxe, *Walpole*, ii. 187, Craggs to Stanhope, 8 July 1720; *Stair Annals*, ii. 423, contains an almost apologetic message from Stanhope to Stair on the eve of his departure.

[2] *Instructions, France*, 176–81, Craggs to Sutton, Whitehall, 27 June 1720 (o.s.), Stanhope to Sutton, Pirmont, 15/26 July 1720.

[3] R.O., *S.P.* 44/270, Stanhope to Delafaye, 14 Sept. (o.s.), Stanhope to Craggs, 22 Sept. (o.s.).

[4] See R.O., *Dom. Geo. I*, 23, for orders about Port Mahon and Gibraltar in Sept. 1720.

But before that the collapse of the grandiose Mississippi scheme had much chastened the arrogant Law and his admirers, and, if only for want of funds, the bellicose spirit of the French began to evaporate. When in the summer of 1720 the full gravity of France's financial plight became apparent, Law himself was attacked by the Paris mob and soon deprived of his power and privileges; while Dubois, always faithful to the English alliance, recovered his ground. The danger of hostilities had disappeared within a week of Stanhope's orders for reinforcements to be sent to America; and he was able to return to his more accustomed and congenial task of advising Dubois how to settle France's internal difficulties. The advice he dictated to Destouches, the French envoy at Hanover, coming as it did so soon after his serious causes for annoyance at the proceedings of the French government and especially of Law, is a remarkable testimony to his magnanimity and genuine desire for the well-being of France. His advice briefly was that the Regent should forthwith renounce the Law system and recall the Parlement de Paris, exiled to Pontoise for its opposition to the Mississippi scheme. A plan of financial reconstruction should be devised in consultation with the leading French bankers, not to be put forward as the Regent's own idea but, in order to soothe the Parlement's wounded feelings, suggested to them for presentation as their own idea, 'comme un expédient que la Compagnie [i.e. Parlement] a imaginé pour le soulagement des peuples, et auquel elle supplie S.A.R. de donner son agrément'. Then in promulgating the scheme the Regent should give full credit to the Parlement's co-operation:

'cette conduite . . . non-seulement touchera le Parlement, qui la regardera comme son propre ouvrage, et qui l'enregistrera d'une manière solemnelle, mais charmera les peuples et les raménera à un tel degré de confiance que S.A.R. se trouvera tout d'un coup plus àimée, plus accréditée et plus affermie que jamais.'

As to Law himself, as long as the King was alarmed only at the views Law expressed to the prejudice of England, he had made no attempt to have him removed, trusting entirely to the Regent's good feeling; but now that Law had become dangerous to the well-being of the Regent himself, Stanhope's emphatic advice was that he should be banished from France, 'en lui permettant néanmoins', Stanhope adds with kindly feeling to a fallen enemy, 'd'emporter assez de bien pour jouir d'une retraite agréable'.[1]

With the removal of Law the good correspondence between Stanhope and Dubois was resumed, strengthened as it was by Stanhope's unwearied attempts to induce the Roman Catholic Powers to obtain for him his long-desired cardinal's hat. But the first careless rapture of the Triple Alliance was never quite recovered during Stanhope's lifetime. From the English point of view his efforts to reconcile differences and secure European peace had been almost too successful. France reconciled with Spain, the Emperor with Turkey as well as with Spain, chiefly by his diplomacy, no longer stood in so much need of England as when they were in danger themselves. In a letter to Craggs about plans for the Congress of Cambrai Stanhope has sorrowfully to admit that England would probably still have to face opposition from Spain, France, and the Emperor.[2] Nevertheless he trusted to have removed most of the remaining obstacles to a perfect understanding before the congress met. There he would have been in his element; and had he lived to fulfil his plan of attending it himself with his brilliant young pupil Carteret he would no doubt have moulded it to his will and prevented it from being the fiasco it proved.

But from their very nature foreign relations are in a constant state of flux; the utmost one man or one generation of statesmen can hope to do is to remove some of the complications which render peace more uncertain. In this Stanhope had achieved more success than is given to most statesmen within so short a period. He had removed the essential causes of war in the South, he had all but made a final peace in the North and by his reconciliation of Sweden with Hanover, Prussia, Poland and Denmark had enormously simplified the issues still left to be decided at Nystad.

§ 3

But even Stanhope had little leisure to think of foreign affairs for the remaining months of his life. Hardly had he sent Dubois his advice for repairing the failure of the Missis-

[1] Mahon, *History*, ii, Appendix, Destouches to Archbishop of Cambrai, Hanovre, 8 Septembre 1720. As far as allowing Law to retain means for an agreeable retreat the Regent did not follow Stanhope's kindly advice.

[2] Mahon, *History*, ii, Appendix, Stanhope to Craggs, Hanovre, 1 Octobre 1720.

sippi scheme in France than a letter arrived from the Lords Justices in England announcing that the South Sea Bubble had burst and urging an early meeting of Parliament, 'animated by his Majesty's presence'. This was followed by personal letters from Delafaye to Stanhope imploring that the King should return and summon Parliament without delay and even venturing to suggest, as Townshend had fallen into disgrace for doing in 1715, that if the King himself would not return Parliament might be allowed to meet without him.[1] Stanhope replied that, to quiet the people, Parliament would be summoned earlier; and in fact he and the King returned to England so suddenly that Stanhope had to put off the meeting he had arranged with Carteret at Hanover to receive his reports on the Northern courts, and arrived in London on 11 November (o.s.). Parliament, however, to give ministers time to consider their policy, did not meet till 8 December.[2]

The South Sea Bubble was the unfortunate result of a well-meant attempt to consolidate and reduce the national debts, both capital and interest. In 1717, it will be remembered, Stanhope had carried through Parliament a partial scheme originated for that object by Walpole.[3] By that scheme, with its sinking fund the government's obligations to creditors had already been reduced from 54 to 51 million pounds, but even that amount was regarded as still dangerously high, while the various forms of obligation and the amounts of interest due involved confusion and in some cases excessive burdens on the public. At the end of 1719 the South Sea Company came forward with a proposal to Stanhope to relieve the public burden by incorporating all the national debts in their own stock and accepting a lower rate of interest in the aggregate by putting all the debts 'into one entire duty'. This Company was originally incorporated by Harley in 1711, to take over the then existing floating debt of some 10 million pounds on the security of certain assigned duties and in return to have the monopoly of the South Sea trade with the Spanish colonies, which Harley engaged to secure by the Treaty of Utrecht. The concessions actually obtained by the Treaty, of the Assiento, or slave trade, and of one

---

[1] R.O., *S.P. Dom. Geo. I*, 23, Lords Justices to King, 21 Sept. 1720 (o.s.); Delafaye to Stanhope, 21 Sept. and 11 Oct. (o.s.). See above, ch. ix, p. 238.
[2] R.O., *S.P.* 44/271, Stanhope to Delafaye, 8 Oct. 1720 (o.s.); *H.MSS. Polwarth*, iii. 8, Stanhope to Carteret, 5/16 Nov.
[3] See above, ch. x, pp. 261 sqq.

annual ship loaded with English merchandise for the Spanish fairs in South America, proved a somewhat meagre fulfilment of the hopes entertained of complete free trade with the rich American markets; and, though Stanhope by his treaties of 1715 and 1716 with Alberoni had somewhat improved the terms of the concessions,[1] the returns hitherto had proved disappointing. Nevertheless, with the resumption of more peaceful relations with Spain after the fall of Alberoni, the exaggerated hopes of profit from this monopoly entertained by the South Sea Company and the public remained unabated; and the Company itself rivalled the Bank of England in the reputation of its shares and in political influence.

When the Company's proposal was laid before Stanhope in 1719 he referred it, as being entirely outside his province, to Sunderland as First Lord of the Treasury and Aislabie the Chancellor of the Exchequer, and therefore took no part in the discussions and arrangements made.[2] Some modifications were made by the government in the Company's proposals, which as brought before the House of Commons in January 1720 seemed to offer considerable advantages to the public. The Company agreed to exchange all the public debts held by the Bank of England, the East India Company and private creditors for South Sea shares, and accept from the government a uniform rate of interest of 5 per cent. instead of the varying rates, amounting in some cases to 9 per cent., then being paid by the public; further, from midsummer 1727 this rate was to be reduced to 4 per cent., and as a final consideration for the privilege of thus enlarging their stock the Company offered to pay a sum of 3½ millions to the Exchequer. Thus, if their terms were accepted, from the outset the national debt would be reduced from £51,303,556 to £47,803,556, while the total annual saving in interest would amount to £543,967. On presentation of this proposal the Bank of England, which had hitherto stood aloof from schemes for the consolidation of debts, asked and was allowed to present an alternative proposal, of which the most important difference was the offer of 4½ instead of 3½ millions as an immediate money payment to the Exchequer. The South Sea Company rejoined by overbidding the Bank, which in turn made an advance on its first offer. But the

[1] See above, ch. viii, pp. 207–8.
[2] P.H. vii. 883, Aislabie's second defence before the Lords, 20 July 1721.

government stood for the Company's second offer, which appeared to secure for the public a net gain of £7,567,500, in spite of Walpole's contention that the Bank's offer was the sounder of the two, especially as it specified the terms on which it would buy up the stock of the old creditors, whereas the Company made no such terms, but left itself free to recoup itself by the speculative rise in value of those shares due to the eagerness of creditors to obtain South Sea shares for their government stock. After prolonged discussion the Bill incorporating the Company's proposals was passed by the Commons on 2 April. In the Lords, where it was passed on 7 April, Cowper and the Duke of Wharton were the Bill's chief opponents and it was defended by Sunderland: there is no record of Stanhope taking part in the debates.[1]

Walpole's chief criticism of the scheme was soon amply justified. For their huge outlay on the public the only advantages promised to the South Sea Company were 5 per cent. interest on their enlarged capital for seven years, after which it was to be only 4 per cent., the profits they could obtain from their monopoly of the South Sea trade and the Assiento, and from privileges, promised but not yet granted, in Nova Scotia and St. Kitts. Hence they were almost forced, in order to escape bankruptcy, to rely on the enhancement in value of their own shares. Even before the Bill had passed the shares had risen from 130 to 300 per cent., and by August they were quoted at 1,000; four subscriptions, each for a million pounds' worth of shares, were oversubscribed; and naturally most of the holders of old government stock were glad to exchange them for shares which offered such chances of profits. Criticism of the Company's methods was averted by the issue of shares at par or for no consideration to courtiers and men of influence in Parliament, such as the Duchess of Kendal, Aislabie and Stanhope's cousin Charles in the Treasury, while Craggs and his father the Postmaster-General dabbled in South Sea shares probably with illicit inside knowledge, and Sunderland himself was accused, perhaps unjustly, of accepting similar favours. Then other projectors of schemes for gaining easy money,

[1] *P.H.* vii. 628–912 has an exhaustive account of the whole South Sea business; Sinclair, *History of Public Revenue* (3 vols. 1883), i. 488 sqq. has an admirable short summary of the various schemes proposed to Parliament and of the result of the South Sea plan; see also Macpherson, *Annals of Commerce* (4 vols. 1805), iii. 77 sqq., and Mahon, *History*, ii. 3 sqq. C. B. Realey, *Early Opposition to Sir R. Walpole* (1931) is useful for Walpole's activities.

taking advantage of the fever of speculation engendered by the methods of the South Sea directors, started precarious schemes to catch the money of the excited public. Among the more reputable of these were two Assurance corporations projected by Lords Onslow and Chetwynd, who secured the support of King and Parliament by offering to pay off the Civil List debt of £600,000.[1] Some hundreds of other schemes, vaguer in their objects and with no conceivable chance of earning a profit, were started by almost any rascal who could put pen to paper for the purpose of obtaining subscriptions and as eagerly taken up by the thousands possessed of the new craze for speculation.[2] Hardly anybody escaped the madness. Among others Carteret in Sweden took up shares to the tune of £12,000; the old Duchess of Marlborough invested in South Sea stock but took care to take her profit while she could; and even Walpole had dealings in it and also bought stock for the Princess of Wales. The Prince allowed himself to become governor of a Copper Company which was afterwards declared to be illegal by the Lords Justices. Stanhope, almost alone of all those prominent in the political world or at court, kept himself severely aloof from the orgy of speculation.

The madness continued unabated till August, when the directors of the South Sea Company themselves gave the first impulse to the crash. Finding that the competition of all these bogus companies was interfering with the sale of their own shares, they moved the Lords Justices to issue information against some of the most outrageously irregular. The alarm of speculators in these companies soon spread to those in other companies, including the South Sea itself. During September the Company's stock sank from 1,000 to 300 per cent. and the shares of all the other companies suffered proportionately larger depreciation. A wild panic, increased by the news of the failure of Law's scheme in France, suddenly replaced the exuberant optimism of the previous months. Shares worth hundreds yesterday could now be bought for an old song; thousands of speculators were ruined. The victims' first thought was to find a scapegoat. The Company, the government, the Prince, even the King were assailed with cries of rage and resentment. The government, bereft of its two ablest mem-

---

[1] One of these is the existing Royal Exchange Assurance Company.
[2] A list of some hundred of these Bubbles is given in *P.H.* vii. 655–9, but the list is not exhaustive.

bers, Stanhope and Sunderland, who were both at Hanover, took immediate steps to stop the panic and restore the endangered credit of the nation. Walpole was hurriedly summoned from Norfolk to try to arrange that the Bank of England should come to the assistance of its rival, but, though he drew up a draft agreement, the Bank on consideration refused to accept it. The only course left was to induce the King to return promptly with Stanhope and Sunderland and call an early meeting of Parliament to pass any legislation that might appear necessary to retrieve the disaster.

It was clear, when the King and Stanhope returned from Hanover in November, that the immediate need was to restore the confidence of the public and avoid as far as possible the vindictive and indiscriminate punishments called for by the victims as much of their own folly as of the rascality of some of the projectors. To secure these objects, and especially the first, Walpole had now become indispensable, and he was in a position to make his own terms. For the time being, however, he was content to conduct business in the comparatively humble position of Paymaster-General, though he seems to have received a hint that he would shortly be promoted. Walpole had considerable difficulty, after the opening of Parliament on 8 December, in persuading the House to admit as valid contracts for stock made by the South Sea Company and to allow him to introduce his scheme for restoring public credit before the House had investigated the charges of corruption against the directors. Walpole then unfolded his scheme for restoring public credit by engrafting nine millions of South Sea stock on the capital of the Bank of England and a similar sum on that of the East India Company, a scheme that was accepted because no one had any better one to propose. So far the government had, with some difficulty, effected their main object of saving the wreck of the scheme so far as the general public was concerned. In fact, as it appeared after Stanhope's death, though it was impossible to repair the losses of the countless individuals ruined by the bursting of the bubbles, the government proved to have been right in its estimate of the original scheme's advantage to the public. Even after the concessions which Walpole was compelled to make to the Company to prevent its bankruptcy, by 1727 the various redeemable and irredeemable debts and annuities had been consolidated into one stock at a uniform rate of interest and it was calculated that by the modified scheme the public made an annual profit of £339,631, and a capital saving of £8,490,780.[1]

After Christmas there remained the still more difficult problem to be faced of apportioning blame and retribution where it was due. Walpole and most of the ministry were in favour of letting sleeping dogs lie; but Stanhope, who had not the same reason as some of his colleagues to fear investigation, would not hear of screening the guilty. Refreshed during the short adjournment at Christmas by the opportunity he seized 'to breathe a little at Chevening',[2] he took a leading part in the Lords' proceedings against those guilty of corruption. He moved 'that the Estates of the criminals, whether Directors or not Directors, ought to be confiscated to make good the public losses' and that five of the Directors should be taken into the custody of Black Rod. Then, supported by Cowper and Townshend, he obtained the unanimous vote of the House for his proposal:

> 'That the taking in of stock . . . the giving credit of the same without a valuable consideration actually paid, or sufficiently secured; or the purchasing stock by any Director or Agent of the South Sea Company, for the use or benefit of any persons in the administration, or any member of either House of Parliament, during such time as the late Bill relating to the South Sea Company was depending last year in Parliament, was a notorious and dangerous corruption.'[3]

In this severe attitude he was fully justified, for when almost every courtier or politician of standing was suspected of making the most of his opportunities for illicit profit, 'his reputation', says Speaker Onslow, not in all respects a lenient critic of Stanhope, 'was untouched as to any concern in the South Sea affairs and his interest and authority for that reason much greater with the people than any body's'; and in a later summary of his character Onslow records that 'he died without having acquired any great fortune and without the least suspicion of being touched with the corruption of the preceding year'.[4]

But whether it was from disgust at the corruption he saw

[1] Sinclair, l.c.

[2] This is the reason given by Delafaye for delay in answering a letter from Lord Coningsby, a tiresome and pertinacious correspondent with many grievances; R.O., *Dom. Geo. I*, 25, Delafaye to Coningsby, 3 Jan. 1720.

[3] *P.H.* vii. 697, 702, 9 and 24 Jan.

[4] *H.MSS.*, Clements, 299, A. Onslow to Hon. J. Molesworth, 4 Feb. 1720/1; *H.MSS.*, Onslow, 512.

around him, corruption in which it was whispered that his
chief ally Sunderland and his favourite cousin Charles were
involved, or utter weariness after seven years of almost unremitting labour for the state, or even a hankering once more
for a military career which had been his first choice, it appears
that Stanhope seriously meditated a change of employment
within no long period. Aislabie, already under deep suspicion
of corrupt dealing and soon to be brought up as a culprit
before the House of Lords, resigned his office of Chancellor of
the Exchequer at the end of January. For the time being his
duties were entrusted to Lord Chief Justice Pratt, but this
arrangement was only to last till the end of the session. A
promise had been made to Walpole, who was bearing the
whole brunt of financial business in the Commons, that when
Parliament rose he would be promoted to a position more in
keeping with his responsibilities, not only as Chancellor but
also as First Lord of the Treasury. This would mean finding
another post for Sunderland, and it was proposed that he
should take Stanhope's place as Secretary of State. It is
hardly conceivable that so great a Secretary of State as
Stanhope would have been displaced even by Sunderland,
especially when Craggs might far more easily have been
spared, unless it was at Stanhope's own wish. But he had
always shown an inclination to revert to some high military
appointment, and rumour had several times during the
preceding years connected his name as that of a rival to
Cadogan for the succession to Marlborough's post of Captain-General. One of Mar's correspondents wrote in 1718
that 'Stanhope and Cadogan are competitors for the captain-
generalship on Churchill's decease, who is indeed very crazy
but not crazed'.[1] Now it was apparently decided to appoint
Stanhope as Captain-General, even though Marlborough still
lingered on. Onslow speaks of it as settled and Sir John Vanbrugh announcing the changes at the end of the session takes
this appointment

> 'for granted . . . since the King has written a letter with his own
> hand to the Duke of Marlborough with the greatest expressions
> of kindness and esteem, to let him know it will be much for
> his service in this juncture if he gives up that station. The
> King's writing this letter I have only known as a secret, not
> yet to be spoken of; but that 'tis intended Lord Stanhope
> should be appointed Captain General is talked on everywhere',

[1] *H.MSS.*, *Stuart*, vii. 102, George Flint to Mar, 1 Aug. 1718.

the only difficulty, Vanbrugh must needs maliciously add, coming from the Duchess, who was haggling 'for a pension to support the poor old officer and his wife'.[1]

But Stanhope was to die in harness. On Saturday, 4 February, two days after Vanbrugh was writing of the certainty of his attaining the supreme military command, he seemed in the best of health. Carteret spent a good part of the morning talking with him and later they went to the House of Lords where Stanhope 'spoke several times, as well as he ever did in his life'. The chief business of the sitting was the examination of Sir John Blunt, one of the principal directors of the South Sea Company. At one point of the proceedings Blunt refused to answer a leading question, whereupon he was ordered to withdraw while their Lordships debated 'how to proceed in this unprecedented case'. In the middle of this discussion the young Duke of Wharton, notorious as an abandoned rake and as president of the Hell Fire Club, suddenly interposed with a violent invective aimed at the ministers and most pointedly at Stanhope:

'The government of the best princes', he declared, 'was oftentimes made intolerable to their subjects by ill ministers, which his Grace illustrated by the example of Sejanus, who made a division in the imperial family and made the reign of the Emperor Claudius odious to the Romans.'

Stanhope, overwrought and outraged at the insulting allusion to Sejanus in connexion with the quarrel in the royal family, rose in a white heat of passion. He also could quote the ancient Romans for his purpose and referred to 'the great patriot Brutus, who in order to assert the liberty of Rome, and to free it from tyrants, sacrificed his own degenerate son'.[2] But in the middle of his speech he was so overcome with passion that a blood-vessel burst in his head, and he had to be carried home to bed. A cupping in the night gave him some relief and the next day, Sunday,

'Lord Sunderland and the Duke of Newcastle drank tea with him about noon and he seem'd pretty well; but his illness returned soon after. He went to bed again upon it, sent for Dr.

[1] H.MSS., Onslow, 512; H.MSS., Carlisle, 28, Vanbrugh to Carlisle, 2 Feb. 1720/1; Lord Harley also mentions the report that Stanhope was to have been made 'Generalissimo', H.MSS., Portland, v. 617. Vanbrugh's quarrel with the Marlboroughs about Blenheim is notorious.
[2] Brutus refers to the Duke of Wharton's father the Whig statesman, Marquis of Wharton. Had it been before the reconciliation in the royal family, it might have been an allusion to the relations of George I and his son.

Mead, who make light of his complaints, not apprehending any danger. An apothecary was sent for to give him a clyster, and whilst that was preparing by his bedside, he said "I shall have no occasion for your assistance" and immediately died. His head was open'd to-day', concludes his loving friend and pupil Carteret, '[and] was full of blood; some vessel had burst, and so ended one of the best men we had.'[1]

§ 4

Not mainly for his special gifts as a foreign minister but for his character Stanhope's sudden death, so like in circumstances of time and place to that of his great nephew Chatham, came as an almost irreparable blow to his fellow countrymen.

'I believe', wrote Vanbrugh, worthily interpreting the predominant feeling, 'I believe in the present distracted juncture, the whole Cabinet Council would have been a less loss both to the King and nation, not only for his quite superior knowledge in foreign affairs, but from the great credit he had at present at home, when few others have any at all. He stood quite clear in the eyes of all parties in regard to this devilish South Sea affair, that is like to taint the greatest part of those who were otherwise fit to do business; and has behaved himself with great applause in the House of Lords and with great temper at a time when the passions of others and the differences of the two Houses may lead to disaster.'[2]

Walpole indeed was quite fit to 'do the business', but his cynical and uninspiring outlook introduced at this critical parting of the ways a tone into public life which Stanhope, had he remained in power, might have averted, and which insensibly debased the politics of the next half-century. Those who had worked with him and knew him best felt the loss most deeply. Carteret's tribute, eloquent in its brevity, has been already quoted; Craggs in the formal notifications of his

[1] *H.MSS.*, *Polwarth*, iii. 40, Carteret to Polwarth, 7 Feb. 1720/1. In the following letter of the same date from Robethon to Polwarth a somewhat similar account is given. For the proceedings in the Lords see *P.H.* vii. 705–6. The story referred to by Harley (*H.MSS.*, *Portland*, v. 616, and see above, ch. i, p. 21, note 1), of 'the great debauch' at the Duke of Newcastle's as the cause of Stanhope's death seems improbable, especially in view of the good account Carteret gave of his health on the morning after the supposed debauch and also as Harley attributes Craggs's death to the same cause, for Craggs almost certainly died of smallpox. But it seems to have been current gossip among the ill-intentioned, for the French envoy, Chammorel, also mentions it. A.E., *Angleterre* 335, f. 157.

[2] *H.MSS.*, *Carlisle*, 29, Vanbrugh to Carlisle, 7 Feb. 1721.

death to representatives abroad introduces a touch of feeling
rare in such documents when he announces 'avec un très
sensible déplaisir . . . la mort soudaine du Comte Stanhope
. . . un si zélé et fidèle Serviteur [du Roy] et dont la Réputa-
tion dans les Cours Etrangères ne donnoit pas peu de poids
aux Négotiations comises à ses Soins'.[1]   In another such letter
he picks out 'probity and sincerity' as Stanhope's distinguishing characteristics.   Robethon, also a fellow worker, spoke
of his death as deplorable both for the King and the nation.
Nearly thirty years after his death Pelham says his brother
the Duke of Newcastle 'thinks no minister has made a great
figure but him in the two reigns . . . [and] will imitate him as
far as he can'.[2]   Even the stiff Austrian Pentenriedter, associated with Stanhope during the negotiations for the Quadruple Alliance and afterwards, seemed often to find pleasure
in regaling Polwarth at Cambrai with enthusiastic accounts of
Stanhope's force of character and influence in Europe.[3]

But perhaps of all men his crabbed old master George I
missed him most acutely.   Hearing of his death on that Sunday evening, 'His Majesty was so sensibly touch'd that he
could not eat his supper, and retired for two hours into his
Closet to lament the loss of such an able statesman and Faithful Counsellor and so loyal a subject', and he told Sunderland
and Walpole to let Lady Stanhope know he would do all he
could for her.[4]   At the King's command full military honours
were done to his faithful servant, as his body was borne
through London on 17 February.   The King's and the Prince
of Wales's coaches followed the hearse, behind which came
Stanhope's father-in-law Governor Pitt as chief mourner,
'200 Horse-Grenadiers, 200 Life Guards, 2 battalions of Foot
Guards, all officers being in cypress mourning, scarfs and hat-

---

[1] R.O., *S.P.* 104/42, Craggs to St. Saphorin, 7 Feb. 1720/1.

[2] Yorke, *Hardwicke*, ii. 12, quotes this from a letter of Pelham's of 1748.

[3] *H.MSS.*, *Polwarth*, iii. 41, 102, 162.

[4] *Memoir of Stanhope*. This pamphlet was written by Stanhope's relative, Hugh
Stanhope, who asked Prior to subscribe for it, to which Prior answered that he
had much better write a memoir that would do him more credit.   Hugh retorted
by asking what he could do better than write about 'one who was universally
known for his uncorrupt loyalty and fidelity to his King, his untainted zeal for
the real good and welfare of his country, and his known abhorrence of bribery
and corruption; and that the Earl Stanhope was such is what his very enemies
acknowledge'.   He ended with the spirited observation 'that to reflect on a
person deceased, tho' obliquely, is very unbecoming the character of a gentleman; and they who now cast aspersions on the Earl Stanhope, would not dare
to say half so much to his face, had he been living'.   *H.MSS.*, *Bath*, 501, Hugh
Stanhope to Prior, 6/17 Apr. 1721.

bands, with all other honours due to a great general', accompanied the funeral as far as St. George's, Southwark, where the Guards formed two lines between which the procession went on to Chevening. Here by Stanhope's own home, where he loved 'to breathe a little', was his last resting-place.[1] His monument, designed at his widow's wish by Hunt and fashioned by Rysbrack, was set up in Westminster Abbey ten years later. Nor for the rest of his days was the King unmindful of his promise to care for Stanhope's wife and family. To Lady Stanhope he granted a pension of £2,600, but she survived her lord only two years, leaving a large family of orphaned children. As late as 1726 George was writing to the Duc de Bourbon, then Louis XV's chief minister, to ask that a sum of 143,000 livres, deposited by Stanhope with Cardinal Dubois, 'une grande partie de l'héritage qu'il laissa à ses orphelins', might be recovered and paid over for their benefit.[2]

History has been tardy in recognizing Stanhope as the great man he was. There are some obvious reasons for this neglect. As a soldier he was overshadowed by such giants as Marlborough and Eugene. In domestic politics his spirit, 'too hot and projecting', as Onslow said of him, led him at times to defects of judgement. Even his foreign policy, the branch in which he was supreme, has been neglected by a people only fitfully interested in foreign affairs. His personality has been obscured owing to the dearth of such private letters, letters tossed off without premeditation to friends or loved ones, as are full of the 'great little things' Chatham speaks of as meaning so much in men's lives: and though the state papers revealing his purpose and policy abound, yet such hardly express a man's intimate feelings and real personality, for even Stanhope's blunt directness of speech and rough common sense too rarely emerge from the stilted phrases habitually used in correspondence with ambassadors or kings. His career, crowded as it was with unceasing activity for the public, was cut short before he reached the age of fifty, when he was only just beginning to reveal himself to his countrymen. Not only so, but he left none of his stock

[1] Collins, *Peerage*, iv. 178.
[2] *Treas. Papers, 1714–20*, 64; *H.MSS., Townshend*, 115. From papers at Chevening it appears that the correspondence with the French government about this 143,000 livres was still active in 1771. It has apparently never been returned to Stanhope's heirs.

able to carry on his fame. His widow died too soon; his
children were all of too tender an age to realize what their
father meant to his generation and were left in charge of the
least worthy of their Pitt relations, most of whom had gone
into opposition to Stanhope.

Nevertheless, before he died, his countrymen had begun to
realize Stanhope's 'noble flame', his 'generous end', that
Pope 'long loved nor loved in vain'. To his disinterestedness
his cousin Chesterfield, one not prone to enthusiasm, bore no
exaggerated testimony in recalling to the House of Lords that
he was 'as able and honest a minister as ever served the
Crown, who had the happiness of his country so much at
heart, that he had neglected his own, and left little else to
his son but the honour of having a seat among your Lordships'. But it has been left to later generations to estimate
his work and character as a whole and assign him his place
among our statesmen. During the first critical years of the
Hanoverians, when others among the leaders of the people
wavered in their allegiance or sought from office security for
their own ease and the comfort of their families, Stanhope
remained firm as a rock to the Revolution principles that
were almost a religion to him. To this staunchness, and to his
unquestioned integrity, his rare spirit of toleration, and his
unceasing vigilance were mainly due the defeat of Jacobite
plots and the secure establishment of a Protestant dynasty.
He had his faults, the faults of an impetuous and exuberant
nature: a violent and domineering temper and, especially in
early life, a certain ruthlessness in the pursuit of his ends. But
those ends were never mean or personal, always for what he
believed to be the public weal. Such faults, too, were more
than atoned for by his boyish sincerity and frankness of
utterance which gave him the advantage, both at home and
abroad, over men far cleverer and more subtle than himself. Abroad, indeed, no English statesman ever wielded
such power. This was due largely to his real sympathy with
foreigners, one of the rarest gifts among Englishmen. It was
not merely Dubois and the Regent, but the Emperor and his
stiff Germans, the Prussian drill-sergeant and his ministers,
even at one time Alberoni, that he persuaded and dominated,
not by force, not by flattery, but by his perfect frankness and
by the conviction he inspired that he wished well to them and
their countries.

Stanhope's public spirit, his 'noble flame', and 'generous

end' did indeed inspire two apt pupils in Carteret and the Great Commoner. Carteret, tinged as he was by his master's hot and projecting spirit, a spirit he carried to excess, carried on the Stanhope tradition of looking on Europe as a whole and taking no insular or pettifogging view of England's interests and responsibilities. Chatham, Stanhope's favourite nephew 'the little marshal', improved on Carteret by taking an even more world-wide view; and he combined with his uncle's intense patriotism his deep sense of national duty and of freedom.

But neither of these—not even Chatham—could lay claim to that for which Stanhope should be best remembered—his European spirit. That is his greatest title to fame. 'This general', said Bonet, 'is the only Englishman I know who has a truly comprehensive spirit (einen universalen Geist)'. No worthier expression of this spirit could be found than in a passage of the King's Speech of 11 June 1720, a speech that Stanhope no doubt himself drew up. For this speech proclaims his conception of what should be the aim of our national policy, a conception new then, and even more deserving of remembrance to-day than when it was enunciated and pursued by Stanhope:

'Much the greatest part of Christendom is already freed from the calamities of war. . . . You will see the good effects which our steadiness hath produced: there remains but little on our part to satisfy the world, that more credit, security, and greatness is to be acquired by following the views of peace, and adhering strictly to just engagements, than by depending on the advantages of war, or by pursuing the measures of ambition.'

APPENDIX A

THE STANHOPES IN SPAIN

(Note to Chapter IV, see note 1, p. 114)

[A paper found at Chevening in the handwriting of the historian Lord Stanhope.]

My Father once told me that on the death of my uncle, Charles Stanhope, at the battle of Coruna, Mr. Wilberforce had exclaimed to him, 'How curious a connection has there always been between your family and Spain!'

I have been thinking over the instances of this, they may be stated as follows:

1. Honble Alexander Stanhope for ten years Minister at Madrid.
2. General Stanhope who reduced Minorca, commanded armies on the continent of Spain and was also subsequently as Earl Stanhope special Ambassador to its Court.
3. His brother Lieut^t Alexander Stanhope R.N. died of a fever in Alicant Roads. A.D. 1695.
4. His brother Captn Philip Stanhope R.N. killed at the storming of St. Philip's Castle in Minorca A.D. 1708.
5. His brother Colonel Edward Stanhope killed at the siege of Cardona in Spain A.D. 1711.
6. William Stanhope for many years Minister at Madrid and afterwards Earl of Harrington.
7. Philip, Earl of Chesterfield named Ambassador to Spain for a short period in 1783.[1]
8. Honble Charles Stanhope, Major of the 50th Reg^t who was killed at Coruna A.D. 1809. Thus he was the fourth Stanhope buried on Spanish ground.

Subsequently to Mr. Wilberforce's remark it may be considered as corroborated by the following additions to the list.

9. Honble James H. Stanhope, brother to Charles, who served through the Peninsular campaigns, and received a severe wound at the siege of St. Sebastian's; the not extracted ball leading to his decease in 1825.
10. Honble George Joseph Stanhope attached to the Mission at Madrid from 1824 to 1828.
11. Lord Mahon wrote a 'History of the War of Succession in Spain' published 1832.

[1] Chesterfield's Instructions are dated 17 March 1784, but he never seems to have gone farther than the south of France. He took with him as Secretary another of the family, Arthur Stanhope. [B.W.]

12. Lady Dalmeny illustrated in a folio volume the Ballad of the 'Spanish Lady's Love' published 1846.

Such circumstances though quite uninteresting to the public may be otherwise to the family concerned. It is also perhaps a little remarkable that the Stanhope Crest should be the Lion and Castle—so conspicuous in another form on the historical shield of Leon and Castille.

(signed) Mahon.

1849.

APPENDIX B

THE ACCESSION OF THE DUTCH TO THE QUADRUPLE ALLIANCE

(Note to Chapter XI, p. 290)

It was the general belief of contemporaries[1] that the Dutch had acceded to the Quadruple Alliance, partly perhaps owing to the name given to the Alliance, a belief which persisted down to quite recent times. Weber, *Die Quadrupel Allianz*, was the first writer to show from the documents that the Dutch in fact never became parties to it. There is an even more exhaustive discussion of the question in Michael, ii. 176 sqq. The correspondence in R.O., *S.P.* 104/219 B and 220 illustrates the attempts of the English ministers to bring in the Dutch. The following précis of references in *H.MSS.*, *Polwarth*, i, ii, iii shows what a pother the continued delays of the Dutch caused in English diplomatic circles.

(The dates are given in New Style; all the letters are addressed to Lord Polwarth, ambassador to Denmark, from English representatives in Holland.)

i. 517	1718	25 June.	Hope the province of Holland will agree to come in to the treaty to-day: then the other provinces will, as all waiting to see what that province does.
518		2 July.	Holland [province] resolved to come in yesterday.
ii. 7	1719	7 Jan.	Holland resolved unanimously to come in; copies of resolution sent to other provinces.
20		14 Jan.	States General acceding to Alliance.
45		4 Feb.	States General resolved on 31 Jan. to enter Quadruple Alliance, after waiting for the province of Zealand.
53		11 Feb.	Dutch envoy in London told to sign treaty.
59		18 Feb.	States told Spanish ambassador they had come in.
		22 Mar.	States will accede when their demand for 3 months' extension of time for Spain is granted.
137		6 May.	Hitch because of Emperor's delay in signing Barrier Treaty: but that got over.
141		9 May.	Hope Estates of Holland [province] will soon come to favourable decision on Secret and Separate Articles of the Treaty.
161		27 May.	Estates of Holland [province] agreed to these articles. Hope all will be settled in 7 or 8 days.
162		27 May.	Guelders, Friesland, Overyssel [provinces] have also agreed, hope Groningen will on Monday; Utrecht and Guelders still uncertain.
176		10 June.	It was hoped the States General would have signed last week, but the province of Holland had wanted explanation of some obscure and equivocal passages.
337		14 Oct.	All towns except Amsterdam and Horn, that depend on their contraband trade with Spain, have now consented to the Secret Articles.

---

[1] Lord Hervey (see *Memoirs* (1931 ed.), 51) was an exception.

ii 360		3 Nov.	'Holland [province] has at last acceded to the Quadruple Alliance.'
372		18 Nov.	[But this proves wrong for] Holland will not yet come in because town of Horn still objects.
405		19 Dec.	States General have at last resolved to come into the Separate and Secret Articles without restriction. [But they never did, the last reference to them being in]
iii. 99	1722	31 Mar.	'Beretti Landi said [to Polwarth] it was well the Dutch had not gone into the Quadruple Alliance.'

CORRESPONDENCE ABOUT BYNG'S MESSAGE OF
20 JUNE 1718 (N.S.) TO THE SPANISH COURT

(See chapter XI, pp. 304, 309.)

[From copies in the Chevening MSS.]

BYNG TO WILLIAM STANHOPE

Traduction de l'Anglais.   De la Barfleur sur les Côtes
d'Espagne ce 20me Juin N.S. 1718.

Monsieur,

La Couronne de la Grande Bretagne s'obligea, par les différens Traitez faits à Utrecht le 14me. de Mars 1713, avec l'Empereur et le feu Roy Tres Chretien, de maintenir une exacte observation de Neutralité qui fut alors établie en Italie, et devint guarante de l'Exécution de tout ce qui fut solennellement stipulé au sujet.

Sa Majesté Britannique est aussy engagée par un Traité, fait entre Elle et l'Empereur à Westminster le 25e de May 1716, d'assister, de maintenir et de défendre l'Empereur dans la Possession de tous les Royaumes, Provinces et Droits, dont il jouissoit alors actuellement en Europe.

Et comme Sa Majesté Catholique a ôté à l'Empereur, par la force de ses Armes, le Royaume de Sardaigne et fait encore de grands Préparatifs de Guerre, pour exécuter d'autres desseins sur les États de sa Majesté Impériale en Italie, contraires à la Teneur des dits Traitez.

Le Roy Nôtre Maître a envoyé une Escadre dans la Mediterranée, (du Commandement de laquelle il m'a honoré) et m'a ordonné d'en donner part, à mon Arrivée en ces Mers, à Sa Majesté Catholique, et de luy faire connoître le Propos pour lequel Elle a esté envoyée dans la Mediterranée, lequel est, de porter toutes sortes de Facilités aux Engagements que Le Roy Nôtre Maître a en Vertu des susdits Traitez.

Je vous prie, Monsieur, de me permettre de faire Sçavoir, par votre moyen, à Sa Majesté Catholique mon arrivée avec l'Escadre dans la Mediterranée, et que mes Instructions portent, d'avancer au Nom du Roy Nôtre Maître toutes les Mesures qui pourroient contribuer à un accommodement de tous les Différends arrivez entre Sa Majesté Catholique et l'Empereur.

Et comme une suspension d'Armes et une Cessation de toutes sortes d'Hostilités est nécessaire pour avancer des Négotiations de Paix, J'ay ordre de faire des Instances auprès les deux Partis à présent en Guerre, de cesser de commettre d'autres Hostilités.

S'il plaît à Sa Majesté Catholique d'accepter les bons offices du Roy Nôtre Maître comme d'un Amy commun des deux Partis, pour mettre fin aux Différens et à la Guerre avec l'Empereur, (laquelle si elle continue mettra en Danger la Tranquillité publique de l'Europe) et qu'Elle juge à propos de donner des ordres à Ses Amiraux et Généraux, qu'il y ait immédiatement une Suspension d'Armes, pendant laquelle des Négotiations de Paix pourroient estre entamées, même au Cas que les Troupes de Sa Majesté Catholique, ou une partie d'elles, ayant mis pied-à-terre en Italie avant que j'y puisse arriver, J'ay ordre d'offrir l'assistance de la Flotte du Roy, pour retirer les Troupes du Roy d'Espagne, et de tâcher de mettre fin à toutes Hostilités ultérieures, de part et d'autre, par tous les moyens dont je seray capable.

Mais s'il ne plaît pas à Sa Majesté Catholique d'accepter la Médiation du Roy Nôtre Maître, ni ses bons offices d'Amitié, et qu'Elle persiste dans la Résolution que ses Troupes attacquent les états de l'Empereur en Italie, Je dois vous communiquer, Monsieur, qu'en ce cas J'ay ordre du Roy Nôtre Maître d'emploier tout le Pouvoir de Sa Flotte et de ses forces que j'ay avec Moy, pour maintenir, autant qu'il me sera possible, la Neutralité de Italie, et de défendre les Territoires de l'Empereur, en m'opposant à toute Puissance qui voudra attacquer les États qu'il y possède.

> J'ay l'honneur d'estre, &cᵃ
> (signé) Le Chevalier Byng.

Monsieur Stanhope.

Ce qui est ci dessus est la Traduction et Copie d'une Lettre que le Chevalier Byng, Amiral de la Flotte de Sa Majesté Britannique dans la Méditerranée, m'a écrite, pour communiquer à Sa Majesté Catholique, par mes Mains, le Sujet de Son arrivée dans ces Mers avec la Flotte du Roy Mon Maître et les ordres dont il est chargé. À l'Escurial ce 12me. de Juillet n.s. 1718.

> (signé) W. Stanhope.

Sa Majesté Catholique m'a fait l'honneur de me dire, que Monsieur le Chevalier Byng peut exécuter les ordres qu'il a du Roy Son Maître. À l'Escurial ce 15me. Juillet 1718.

> (signé) Le Cardinal Alberoni.

Mr. William Stanhope's Letter to Sir George Byng

Madrid the 16th July n.s. 1718.

Sir,

Upon Sunday last the 10th instant n.s., Mr. Alex brought me the Honour of your two Letters of the 20th of June o.s., and the same day that I received them, I showed that Letter you desired should be communicated to His Catholick Majesty, to the Cardinal Alberoni, who upon reading it said he could assure me, that the King of Spain would run all hazards, and even be driven out of Spain, before he would recall his Troops or consent to a Suspension of Arms, & that therefore, if your Orders were such as were contained in that Letter, you had Nothing to do but to obey them. He added, that the Spaniards were not to be frighted, and was so well convinced of their Fleets doing their Duty, that tho you should think fit to attack them, he should be in no pain for the Success.

I endeavoured, in the best manner I was able, to represent to him the great attention The King Our Master has always had to the Honour and Intrest of his Cath: Majesty, which it was impossible to give greater Proofs of, than He had done, by his unwearied Endeavours through the whole Course of the present Negociation, to procure the most advantageous Conditions possible for Spain, in which he had succeeded even beyond what any unprejudiced Person could have hoped for; and that altho' by the Treaty of Utrecht for the Neutrality of Italy, which was entered into at the Request of the King of Spain, as also by that at Westminster of the 25th May 1716, His Majesty finds himself obliged to defend the Emperour's Dominions when attacked, He has hitherto acted only as a Mediator, tho ever since the Enterprise against Sardinia, by his Treatys he became a Party in the War, and for this year last past has been strongly called upon by the Emperour to comply with his Engagements for that purpose, & that even now, when it was impossible for him to delay any longer the sending his Fleet into the Mediterranean, it plainly appeared by your Instructions, which you communicated to him (the Cardinal), and by the Orders I had received, that His Majesty has nothing more at heart than that his Fleet may be employed in promoting the Interests of the King of Spain, and hopes his Catholick Majesty will not, by refusing to recall his Troops or to consent to a Cessation of Arms, put it out of his Power to give all the Proofs of the sincere Friendship he always desires to cultivate with His Cath: Majesty.

Upon the whole the Cardinal said, he would lay the Copy of your Letter to me before the King & would acquaint me with his Resolution upon it in two days; Accordingly upon the Tuesday following, I attended him again, who then told me, that the King demanded two Copys of your Letter, and that I should certify their being true ones and that you had received the Orders therein contained, one of which should be returned me again the same Night, with the King's Resolution upon it. I told him I could not certify your having received such Orders, but should make no Scruple as to the Truth of the Copys, which I then signed and delivered to him. He took them again, and promised to return one of them with his Majesty's Resolution upon it, that Night. In this Conference the Cardinal repeated His Cath: Majesty's continuing determined not to recall his Troops or Consent to the Cessation demanded.

Notwithstanding the Cardinal's Promise of giving me the King's Answer that Night, I could not obtain it from him before this day, which delay was evidently intended for the gaining some Days in hopes you would attend the Return of your Courrier, before you put your Orders in Execution.

By what I am able to judge of the Disposition of this Court, I dont find they are in the least inclined to come to any Accomodation; But if any thing shall happen that may give any hopes of their changing their present Sentiments, I wont fail giving you the earliest advice of it, by Express, that is possible.

I have Nothing more to add at present, but most heartily to wish you all possible good success in your Command, both for His Majesty's Service and your own particular honour; being, with all imaginable Esteem and Respect,

Sir, &c.^a

Sʳ George Byng.

The inclosed is a Copy of your Letter with the King of Spain's Answer as the Cardinal return'd it me.

Mr. William Stanhope's Letter to Mr. Secretary Craggs

Madrid the 18th July N.S. 1718.

Sir

.   .   .   .

Upon the 10th I went to the Escurial, where I received a Courrier from Sʳ George Byng, with the Account of his being arrived with the Fleet under his Command at Cape Vincent, upon the 20th June O.S. This Courrier brought me two Letters from the Admiral, one of which he desired I would lay before His Catholick Majesty; setting forth the occasion of His Majesty's sending his Fleet into these Seas, as also the Purport of the Orders he was charged withall. The same day, according to your Orders, I attended the Cardinal Alberoni, and . . . communicated to him Sʳ George Byng's Letter to me, a Coppy of which is herewith inclosed, together with the King of Spain's Resolution upon it, as also a Coppy & a Translation of my Letter to the Admiral, by all which you will be fully informed of every thing that has been done here upon that Affair, and therefore I shall not take up your Time by repeating any part of it to you.

.   .   .   .

I obeyed your Commands, by representing to the Cardinal the King's sincere desire of maintaining the Peace with Spain, by enumerating to him the several notorious Provocations mentioned in your Letter, which His Majesty's thorough Disposition towards it, made him willing to overlook. To all which the Cardinal made some slight Excuses, but concluded with saying, They must judge of His Majesty's Disposition towards them, by his sending his Fleet to assist their Enemy, which was the greatest harm in His Power to do them.

Upon the whole, I think I may Venture to give my Opinion, That a Breach with Spain is at present unavoidable, and therefore hope that the Caution I gave to our Merchants was not unnecessary, tho your taking no Notice of it makes me uneasy, for fear it should not have met with your Approbation.

.   .   .   .

By Letters from Malaga of the 12th instant N.S., I have an Account that Sr. George Byng arrived there with his whole Fleet the day before, where he was taking in fresh Water and designed to pursue his Voyage for Port Mahon upon the 13th.

On Wednesday last the Pope's Nunzio set out from hence, in Consequence of a second Order from the King of Spain, to leave his Dominions in twenty days. The King of Spain has signifyed to all the Bishops and Chapters in his Kingdom, to remitt to him immediatly all the Letters they shall receive from the Nunzio, because he apprehends they may contain Copys of the Pope's Breve, by which he suspends the payment of all the Ecclesiastical Contributions to the King of Spain. This affair is like to cause great Disturbances in the Church. Letters from Genoa of the 9th inst., which came this day by an Express, give an Account of the Spanish Fleets being arrived at the Island of Ischia, five Leagues from Naples.

The inclosed Letter of mine to Sr. George Byng is not yet sent to him, by reason of the Cardinal's refusing to give me an Order for Post Horses, to dispatch the Courrier to the Admiral that came to me from him, notwithstanding I have demanded it every Day; but I hope I shall be able to send him away to-morrow.

I have the Honour to be, with all possible Respect,

Sir, &cᵃ.

(signed) W. Stanhope.

APPENDIX D

THE DRAFT UNIVERSITIES BILL

(Note to Chapter XIV, p. 402)

LORD PARKER TO ARCHBISHOP WAKE[1]

My Lord   Monday.

I take ye Liberty to send yor Grace a Copy of ye enacting part
of ye Bill prepared according to ye last thought when I had y^e
Honor to wait upon y^r Grace and my Ld. Chancell^r. I was in
hopes to have deliver'd it to y^or Grace at ye House today, and to
have had a time fixed for meeting again to deliver myself from
this affair. My Ld Chanc^r has thought of Thursday Evening. . . .

I am &c.

Parker.

Whereas in all well ordered Governments it has been thought
necessary for the Preservation of the Body Politick that Care
should be taken of the Education of Youth not only in Piety
Virtue and good Learning but also in Principles agreeable to the
Constitution under which they live and for that end severall
Colledges in ye two Universityes of Cambridge and Oxford and
likewise the whole Comunityes of the said Universityes have by
the Authority of mãny of his Maties Royall Ancestors been created
and erected into Corporations and Bodies Politick with severall
Priviledges and proper Provisions for the Governm^t of those
respective Bodyes

But it being notorious that many in those Nurseryes dedicated
to Religion Learning Loyalty and Peace have been infected with
Principles of Sedition . . . y^t Riots and tumults have disturbed the
Peace of the Universityes and affronted y^r Governm^t and the
Offenders have been concealed or at least not detected and duely
brought to Punishment

That Party Principles are favour'd to the generall relaxation of
Discipline and to the discouragement of Study and neglect of
sound Learning, wch ceases to be the way to preferment when
Party is more regarded than Merit

And whereas it is evident as well from ye repeated endeavours
to raise insurrections throughout ye Kingdom as from ye wild
attempts of men of turbulent and fanaticall Spirits to make
Schisms and Divisions in the Church and to overthrow the
Supremacy of the Crown (which has allways been so carefully
maintein'd by the Church of England) y^t there can be no reason-

---

[1] This note and the accompanying draft Bill is to be found in the volume
marked *Arch. W. Epist. 15, Universities Charitable and Religious Societies to 1718* in
the *Wake MSS*. at Christ Church, Oxford.

able expectation of enjoying Peace and Tranquility for any long time if the Youth of the Nobility and Gentry and especially such as are designed for holy Orders are infected with false Principles utterly inconsistent with our happy Establishment in Church and State

And there being the highest reason to repose an intire Confidence in his Maties Wisdom and Goodness and y^t he will take all possible care y^t those Seminaryes may answer the proper ends of their Institution

We therefore Your Ma^{tyes} most dutyfull and loyall Subjects ye Lords Spirituall and Temporall and Comõns in the present Parliament assembled do humbly beseech Your Ma^{ty} y^t it may be enacted . . . .

That ye Nomination and Appointm^t of all and every the Chanc^{rs} Vice Chan^{crs} Proctors and other Officers of ye said Universityes and all Heads of Houses Fellows Students Chaplains Scholars and Exhibitioners and all Members of and in all and every the Colledge and Colledges Hall and Halls in the said Universityes or either of them upon all and every Vacancy and Vacancyes of the said Offices Places and Exhibitions which shall become void after the   day of   in the Yeare of our Lord   within the Space of   yeares then next ensueing shall be and is and are wholly rested in the Kings most excellent Ma^{ty}

And be it farther enacted by the Authority aforesaid y^t in order to the more easy filling up and supplying the said Vacancyes of the severall Offices Places and exhibitions it shall and may be lawfull to and for his Most Excellent Ma^{ty} at any time hereafter to nominate and appoint proper Persons to and for the said Offices Places and exhibitions when and as often as the same shall become or be vacant during the Term of   Yeares aforesaid not only by Letters Patents under the Great Seale but likewise when and as often as his Ma^{ty} shall think fitt by any Instrum^t or Instruments under the Privy Seale or Privy Signet or by such Commission and Commissions under the Great Seale of Great Britain as . . . shall be from time to time constituted and appointed for that purpose in both either or each of the said Universityes and in all or any one or more of the Colledges and Halls aforesaid in such manner and form as in such respective Comission and Commissions shall be expressed and directed. . . .

[Particular Counties, Schools, &c., not to lose their scholarship rights.]

[Penalty clause—suspension, fine, or imprisonment—for college or university officials who refuse to admit persons nominated for university or college offices according to this Act, after due conviction before a court of justice.]

[Those outside university and colleges who have right of nomination or appointment still to retain them.]

[Those outside univ^y and colleges who have right of appointing to offices one out of two or more persons nominated by heads or officers of a College shall nominate from a list sent in by Comm^{rs} app^d by this Act.]

And be it farther enacted y^t during the said Term of Yeares ye Chanc^r for ye University of Oxford for the time being shall be removable at the Pleasure of his Ma^{ty} to be determined whenever his Ma^{ty} shall think fitt by any Instrument under the Great Seale or privy Seale or privy Signet   And at the end of the said Yeares the Chanc^r of the s^d University of Oxford for the time being shall hold his sayd Office in such manner as if he had been their newly chosen in ye Ordinary Course of Election and as if this Act had never been made

[Powers of Visitors of Colleges retained.

All Statutes of Univ^y contrary to this Act to be suspended.

Scholarships &c. awarded by Gov^{rs} of Charterhouse, and in all cases where they are not granted by members of Colleges, exempt from this Act.]

CORRESPONDENCE OF STANHOPE AND NEWCASTLE ABOUT THE PEERAGE BILL, ETC.

(*Note to Chapter XIV, p. 411*)

[*Add. MSS.* 32686 ff. 151-3, 155-6]

[*Draft in Newcastle's hand*]

Clarem^t Oct^{or} 14th 1719.

My Dear Lord,

The good news you have sent us of the King's resolution to return soon to us, has putt new life into us all here, and ye great success y^t you have had in every thing you have undertaken abroad, will I hope make every thing easy the next Session, for I believe the most sanguine Man amongst us, could hardly have imagined, y^t so many great and substantial advantages could have been procured for us in so short time, You will give me leave to have a double Pleasure in y^t every one must see to whose Integrity & Ability all our Success is owing. I am very glad to find by my friend Craggs, y^t Ld Sunderland & yourself are entirely of opinion for pushing the Peerage Bill, I must own I can never think our Constitution settled or ye King entirely safe till y^t be passed, The Miscarriage of it ye last year I chiefly attribute to ye under hand insinuations of some, & ye open opposition of others, whom some People w^d fancy had, if not ye first at least a very great share of Credit. This I think will now certainly be removed for I think it appears very plain y^t our Master places His Confidence, where all Honest Men must wish it, wch in my opinion will go a great way towards making every thing easy, and when once People come to see, y^t somebody[1] at present will think himself as ill used if ye Bill does not pass, as any Body hereafter can do if it be, I should hope they would be afraid of acting as y^y did ye last year. I entirely agree y^t every thing ought to be proposed y^t may be an inducem^t to bring about so solid a good as this Bill would be, & therefore I cannot but think ye University Bill very proper to y^t end, as being agreeable to ye Party, & a solid advantage to ye Publick. I must own My Dear Stanhope, I am not of ye same opinion as to ye Repeal of ye Septennial Bill, for I think we shall evidently lose much more by it than we can possibly gett. In ye 1st Place I am farr from thinking it will make ye Peerage Bill go down ye better, some I am sure who are very good friends to ye latter, will strenuously oppose the former, & tho' I own we have but a small chance for any Tories yett y^t un-

[1] i.e. the King.

doubtedly, w^d make 'em ye more determined, & I took ye liberty to tell Ld Sun., when He dropt something of ye kind at Mr Comptroller's y^t I found it had displeased some of our friends. Besides I must own I cannot apprehend we have any Reason to fear coming to a new Election provided this Parliam^t setts out its time, for then ye Party can by no means pretend to be disobliged, should this Parliam^t be continued it would shew a great distrust of ye King's Interest in England, & look as if our past conduct w^d not be approved of, when on ye contrary we have all ye reason to think y^t before this Parliam^t ends, ye King's affairs will be upon so glorious a foot y^t it will [be] almost impossible to oppose him. The Merit of having settled a Universal Peace in Europe, wch by the assistance of His serv^{ts}, He will in all probability have done, will make Him so Popular, y^t I cannot but think He may have w^t Parliam^t He pleases, & His steady adherence to ye Whig interest must & will make y^t unanimous on our side. Towards ye close of ye last Session there was a great many ill Humours stirring, & should this Parliam^t be continued beyond its time nobody knows in w^t shape y^y may appear. Upon ye whole My Dear Lord, I am of opinion & have long been so y^t we shall not fail of a better Parliam^t than this is at present, provided we do not disoblige the party, by parting with this sooner than its time. I think when I have ye happiness & pleasure of seeing you, I can convince you on ye many alterations y^t must be made for ye better, allmost all ye P—— family[1] will be turned out, Most of those y^t had ye cheif hand in choosing ye Parliam^t brought in their own creatures, most of whom I believe we shall be able to deal wth, I will take ye liberty to say y^t I my self will make the difference of 16 votes, many others will & can do ye same, & if ye C^{t2} w^d upon such an occasion, and sure tis worth while, use one proper method, & y^t but very sparinly, I should think we cannot fail. Many private Persons will be at expences for ye Govern^t, & few I fancy will have ye heart to do so against it. I am sure I speak against my own Interest, but I could not forbear giving you my thought upon a Point I thought so essential. Give me leave only to suggest one thing, y^t this Point may be undetermined till we have ye happiness of seeing you on our side ye water, y^t then we may take our lists, & see when we shall mend & where otherwise, & then I dare say ye advantage will appear so great on our side, y^t you will be of my opinion. The great Point I think we ought to aim at is, y^t there should be but two Parties, y^t for & y^t against ye Gov^t, & I cannot but think that by a new Election, Mr Walpole & ye few friends His Party will be able to bring in, will be so incorporated wth ye Jacobites, y^t we shall have but little difficulty in dealing wth them.

[1] i.e. the Prince of Wales's supporters.
[2] i.e. the Court.

My dear Stanhope forgive my long impertinence, I could not forbear troubling you wth my opinion because I was sure you would excuse it, & be assured nothing upon earth can ever alter ye perfect Love & esteem wth wch I am.

Pray my complim^{ts} to Ld Sun. We all here wish Dr B.[1]
may be Bis. of Bristol & D. of Ch. Ch. as being ye best able to stem ye torrent of ye minority.

(Endorsed) His Grace to the E. Stanhope
Octr 14: 1719.[2]

Hanover Oct the 27th o.s. 1719.

My Dr Lord

The King of Prussia will dine here to morrow and stay only two days, this visit will I hope in reality as well as appearance amply make amends for our staying here three days longer than was intended. The King will certainly sett out this day sevennight you will by this messenger receive our convention with Denmark, we have a project on foot for satisfying even the D. of Holstein by engaging him to joyn his interest with the Prince of Hesse in order to gett the Crown settled on the Prince of Hesse for life, and the Duke of Holstein by the same act of the states to be recognized as heir Presumptive after the Queen and Prince if her Ma^{ty} should leave no issue, we shall I believe make some use of Count Fleming, thô not so much as it should seem reasonable to expect from the apparent interest of Poland to curb the Czar. Ld Cadogan is ordered to gett ready to make a tripp to Vienna by his last letters we are made to hope that his negociation at the Hague is concluded in a better way than has been expected of late. Ld Stairs contrary to custome writes in a most sanguine manner from Paris and prepares us to expect speedily the submission of Spain to our terms even the Czar by letters received this day from Berlin is said to putt water in his wine, thus we have a very reasonable prospect of seeing a peace in the south and the north before next spring this good situation of affairs will probably putt our friends in good humour at our opening the Parliament and it seems to us here very adviseable to make the best use and advantage possible of this good humour by getting the Peerage bill, which if dropped or delayed must in my poor opinion be looked upon as lost for ever, it remains therefore I think onely to be considered by those who think this bill necessary, whether the most certain way to secure a majority for it in the House of Commons, be not to secure at the same time in favour

[1] Dr. Boulter, who in fact became Bishop of Bristol and Dean of Christ Church.

[2] *Add. MSS.* 32686, ff. 151-3. Unfortunately this draft of a letter, being written in Newcastle's own hand, is hard to decipher and in one or two places almost illegible.

of all those, who think the continuance of this Parliament advantageous either to the public or to themselves, the power of continuing it. I beg of y^r Grace to think of what has been suggested from hence touching the Septennial bill in this view, if you think we can carry the Peerage bill thro the house of commons without the assistance of so strong an argument ad hominem of the continuing of this house of Commons will be to great numbers there, it will be pretty indifferent to me whither we meddle with the Septennial or not, (thô I will confess to y^r Grace that I think it for the interest of our countrey to repeal it if it stood singly upon its own merits) but whatever my opinion may be of that matter I should very readily submitt my opinion touching it to our friends because I think there is no danger in delaying it, on the contrary I am persuaded that it will at some time or other force its own way through, but the Peerage bill is of a very different nature, I think we must carry it now or never, since it will probably never happen again that a king and ministry will be for it, y^r Grace will easily imagine that nobody can be so mad as to think of proposing any fixed resolution to the King upon matters of this consequence without knowing previously the sense of our friends in England they must govern us and especially our friends of the house of Commons, if what is designed as a service to this house Commons and to the Whigg party be taken otherwise by them it must undoubtedly be dropped but at the same time give me leave My D^r L^d to tell you very freely my thought that if they are against repealing the Septennial I shall have very little hope of succeeding in the peerage. when y^r grace shall see our good master you will learn from himself how much he has heart not to be baffled a second time in this matter, and you will therefore be so good as to turn in y^r thoughts till we doe meet, which is the most likely method to succeed. I am very gladd to find y^r Grace, who can judge as well as anybody, so sanguine upon the choice of a new parliament but the best new parliament will come too late if the Peerage bill be not passed in this, that is my point of view upon which if I lay too great a stress I shall be forgiven by y^r Grace whom I know to be equally zealous for it and if there be any difference of opinion between us it seems only to be which is the best and most certain way to come at it, but as I said before all private opinions must be submitted to what shall appear to be the sense of the bulk of our friends in the house of Commons. it would indeed for this and many other reasons have been happy if we could have been a fortnight sooner in England but we must now make the best use we can of the time we have. I cannot promise that the old man[1] will be left behind but I may safely assure y^r grace that [the] thô he should come the king will doe whatever shall be proposed to him to make every body sensible

[1] i.e. Bernstorff.

that he is not to meddle in English business he is exceedingly piqued and mortified at his declining credit and has taken a very slight occasion to vent his spleen and Resentment against Poor Robethon where he has cruelly affronted without rhyme or reason. Robethon being his immediate subaltern in the German Chancery may be insulted with impunity the rather because whilst we are excluding the Germans avowedly from meddling in English business, we cannot openly support him however we shall I hope disengage him by the assistance of Our Good Dutchess.[1]—Oct: the 28 O.S. at ten in the evening.

The King of Prussia is not yet come but is hourly expected and you may depend upon it that the kings journey will hold for Tuesday next I am ever with the most sincere respect My very good Lord.

Y^r Grace's

Most faithfull & most obedient servant

Stanhope.[2]

[1] i.e. the Duchess of Munster.
[2] *Add. MSS.* 32686, ff. 155–6.

APPENDIX F

MEASURES FOR SUPPORTING THE HANOVER SUCCESSION

(*Note to Chapter V, page 144, note 2*)

[Extract from a letter discovered in an Edinburgh office just as this book was going to press]

Sr You have been often named as one we ought to correspond w^h in a company of honest men here who as they have been of a long time apprized of the danger our sacred and civil liberties and priviledges were in—have made it y^r bufsienefs as far as they were capable to promote a sense of it in others thereby to excite y^m to take proper measures to hinder the enemies of our holy religion, her Maties person & government & the protestant succession in the family of hannover from putting their hellish designs in execution.

Its true we ought certainly to enquire into the causes of the Lords manifasting his just displeasure w^t us in the terrible manner he seems to threaten and to turn away their causes by unfeigned Repentance and reformation looking to the blood of Sprinkling for pardon.

Tho this is the solid and effectual way to remove wrath yet we are to consider ourselves as rational Creatures bound by the most solemn tyes of Duty to God regard to ourselves and love to our posterity to hazard life and fortune in defence. of whats more valueable then both, our religion and liberty wch at present are on the brink of ruine.

That we may be able to make the better stand against the attacks of a bloody cruel enemy wch we every day expect we do not know anything can promote our joint intrest more in the general than one entire confidence in and correspondence among honest men in different corners of the countrey. For this reason our Society have laid it on me to Correspond w^t you, and once aweek to advise you what accompts we have from London, from the different Corners of the Countrey remote from you, what we are doing here and the thoughts of honest men, of matters as they fall out.

They look on you as one zealously concerned for the Support of Religion and liberty and who employs himself w^t the outmost application to get the countrey about you put in a posture of defence, by all prudent lawfull means and they expect youl communicate to us from time to time what advances are made in this work.

[Parliamentary news:—impeachment of Steele, motions about Pretender in Lorraine, Protestant succession in danger &c.]

I have nothing further to add but to intreat in the name of our Society, as our danger is at the door, so no reasonable methods may be left unefsayed for putting yor countrey in a condition to defend themselves and afsist the general intrest y^r providence may require it.

We have made a pretty good progrefs in getting the people here and countrey about provided w^t arms, we are now laying out ourfelves to get y^m instructed how to use them wch goes on suc-cefsfully, both these we recommend to you in a particular, and for y^t end a book of exercise will be sent you by John Martin Book-Seller here to whom please direct your letters, in return to this or what further we shall have occasion to write to you. And y^t the knowledge of handleing arms may be more effectually attained, amongst honest friends in yor bounds, We conceive it might be very usefull to pick up some of the disbanded Souldiers, whither Serjeants, Corporals, or single Sentinells, who may be thought to be weel affected and prudent, and these may be taken care of & encouraged under collour of being imployd in some o^r bufsinefs And a proper place provided, such as a large barn or o^r office house in each paroch or such district, as shall be thought fit, where some of the most tractible may conveen at such times as may be agreed upon, and a—s being lodged in the same place, the exercise may be taught; so y^t these conveening at such a place may be capable to diffuse what they learn as they shall have occasion among y^r Neighbours. . . .

[More news from London:—dismissal of Schültz, Duke of Cambridge not arrived but expected.]

[no signature]

Ed^r May 1 1714

INDEX

[1] The references to James Stanhope can obviously not be exhaustive. His negotiations, foreign policy, and relations with Dubois, Alberoni, &c., must be found generally in the book.

Wintoun, Geo. Seton, 5th Earl of
(*d.* 1749), 187–8, 194–5.
Wogan, Chas. (?1698–?1752), 338.
Wortley-Montagu, Edward (*d.* 1761),
355.
Wortley-Montagu, Lady Mary (1689–
1762), 155 n., 168 n., 355 n.

Wyndham, Sir William (1687–1740),
140 n., 176, 179, 186, 191, 258, 311.

Yorke, Philip (Earl of Hardwicke)
(1690–1764), 245.

Zinzerling, Graf, 62.